Encyclopedia of
American Indian History

Encyclopedia of
American Indian History

VOLUME I

Bruce E. Johansen
Barry M. Pritzker

EDITORS

A B C ⬤ C L I O
Santa Barbara, California • Denver, Colorado • Oxford, England

Copyright 2008 by ABC-CLIO, Inc.

All rights reserved. No part of this publication may be reproduced, stored in a retrieval system, or transmitted, in any form or by any means, electronic, mechanical, photocopying, recording, or otherwise, except for the inclusion of brief quotations in a review, without prior permission in writing from the publishers.

Cataloging-in-Publication Data is on file with the Library of Congress

ISBN: 978-1-85109-817-0   ebook: 978-1-85109-818-7

12   11   10   09   08   1   2   3   4   5   6   7   8

Production Editor: Vicki Moran
Editorial Assistant: Sara Springer
Production Manager: Don Schmidt
Media Editor: John Whithers
Media Resources Coordinator: Ellen Brenna Dougherty
Media Resources Manager: Caroline Price
File Manager: Paula Gerard

ABC-CLIO, Inc.
130 Cremona Drive, P.O. Box 1911
Santa Barbara, California 93116-1911

This book is also available on the World Wide Web as an ebook. Visit http://www.abc-clio.com for details.

This book is printed on acid-free paper. ∞

Manufactured in the United States of America

For our families,
and for future generations

Bruce E. Johansen
Barry M. Pritzker

Contributors

Susan Sánchez-Barnett
Baltimore County Public Schools
Indian Claims Commission
Tee-Hit-Ton v. United States

Carolyn Speros Baughman
University of California, Riverside
Pottery

DeLyssa Begay
Chinle Unified School District
Harjo, Joy

Yale D. Belanger
University of Lethbridge
Aboriginal Peoples Television Network
Alaska Native Brotherhood
Assembly of First Nations
Blackfeet Confederacy
Constitution Act
Cree-Naskapi Act
Department of Indian Affairs and Northern
* Development*
Indian Act
James Bay and Northern Quebec Agreement
James Bay Hydroelectric Project
Métis Nation Accord
Nunavut
Nunavut Land Claims Agreement
Royal Commission on Aboriginal Peoples
Tungavik Federation, Nunavut

Sally Colford Bennett
Johnson County Community College
Captivity Narrative
Factory System
Harrison, William Henry

Jennifer L. Bertolet
George Washington University
Momaday, N. Scott
Relocation
Trail of Tears

Merlene Bishop
Longview Community College
Alcoholism and Substance Abuse

Christine Elisabeth Boston
University of Western Ontario
Hopewell Culture

Daniel L. Boxberger
Western Washington University
Fishing Rights

Stuart Bradfield
Australian Institute of Aboriginal and Torres Strait
    Islander Studies
Domestic Dependent Nation

Arthur Robert Brokop II
Shiprock, NM
Bole-Maru Religion

Charles W. Buckner
University of Memphis
Counting Coup

John M. Bumsted
University of Winnipeg
Bering Strait Theory

Roger M. Carpenter
National Museum of the American Indian
Berdaches
Neolin (Delaware Prophet)
New Agers, "Indian" Ceremonies and
Riel, Louis
Smith, John
Squanto
Uncas

Duane Champagne
UCLA Native Nations Law and Policy Center
Department of Sociology
Termination and Indian Sovereignty (Essay)

Philippe Charland
Université du Québec à Montréal
Canonicus

Ryan Church
Los Angeles, California
Tribal Courts

Ward Churchill
University of Colorado, Boulder
American Indian Movement
Bering Strait Theory
Hawai'i, Legal Status of Native Claims (with Bruce E. Johansen)
Indian Assimilation and Reorganization (Essay)

D. Anthony Tyeeme Clark (Meskwaki)
University of Illinois
Montezuma
Standing Bear, Luther

Richmond Clow
University of Montana
Spotted Tail

Cary C. Collins
Tahoma School District
Sacajawea or Sakakawea (with SuAnn M. Reddick)
Seattle (with SuAnn M. Reddick)

Chip Colwell-Chanthaphonh
Center for Desert Archaeology
Camp Grant Massacre
Eskiminzin

Lysane Cree
Hutchins Grant and Associés
Confederacies
Diabetes
Navajo–Hopi Land Dispute
Longhouse Religion

Steven L. Danver
Journal of the West
All Indian Pueblo Council
Arizona v. California
Land, Identity, and Ownership of, Land Rights
Little Turtle
Mankiller, Wilma
Native American Church of North America
Pyramid Lake Paiute Tribe v. Morton
Russians, in the Arctic/Northwest
Water Rights
Winters v. United States

David H. DeJong
Pima-Maricopa Irrigation Project
Deloria, Vine, Jr.

S. Matthew DeSpain
University of Oklahoma
Black Kettle
North West Company
Oregon Trail

E. James Dixon
University of Colorado, Boulder
Archaeology and the First Americans

Jennifer Nez Denetdale
Manuelito

Alan C. Downs
Georgia Southern University
Aquash, Anna Mae Pictou
Massasoit
Means, Russell
Sand Creek Massacre
Trail of Broken Treaties
Washita Massacre

Jeanne Eder
University of Alaska, Anchorage
General Allotment Act (Dawes Act)
Identity
Termination

C. S. Everett
Cahokia
Indian Civil Rights Act (1968)

Amy S. Fatzinger
University of Arizona
Winnemucca

Kenneth C. Favrholdt
Thompson Rivers University
Dalles Trading Area

Andrew H. Fisher
College of William and Mary
Columbia River Inter-Tribal Fish Commission
Dreamer Cult
Seven Drum Religion
Smoholla
Whitman, Marcus and Narcissa

Sterling Fluharty
University of Oklahoma
EchoHawk, Larry

Mormon Church
National Indian Youth Council
Warrior, Clyde

Hugh W. Foley, Jr.
Rogers State University
Baptist Church
Bearskin, Leaford
Harjo, Chitto
Muskogean Language

Andrew K. Frank
Florida Atlantic University
Creek War
Indian Civilization Fund Act
Mississippian Culture
Osceola
Pueblo Revolt
Seminole Wars

Granville Ganter
St. John's University
Brant, Joseph
Maine Indian Claims Settlement Act
Red Jacket

Daniel R. Gibbs
La Joya Independent School District
Alaska Native Claims Settlement Act
Alaska, United States Purchase of
American Indian Higher Education Consortium
Education
Indian Self-Determination and Education
    Assistance Act
Salmon, Economic and Spiritual Significance of
Tribal Colleges
Yakama War

Matthew T. Sakiestewa Gilbert
University of California, Riverside
Leupp, Francis Ellington

Jason David Gillespie
University of Alberta
Paleo-Indians

Sandy Grande
Connecticut College
Doctrine of Discovery
Marx, Karl, and Native American Societies
Plenary Power

S. Neyooxet Greymorning
University of Montana
Fletcher v. Peck (with Dr. Gregory Campbell)

Michelle A. Hamilton
University of Western Ontario
False Face Society

Karl S. Hele
University of Western Ontario
Catlin, George
Copway, George
Deskaheh
Dumont, Gabriel
Johnson, Emily Pauline
Tenskwatawa

Sherry Hutt
National NAGPRA Program, National Parks Service
Native American Graves Protection and
    Repatriation Act

Robert H. Jackson
Spring, Texas
Demographics, Historical
Spanish Influence

Don Trent Jacobs (Four Arrows)
Northern Arizona University
Education and Social Control
Myth of the Noble Savage
Worldviews and Values

Bruce E. Johansen
University of Nebraska, Omaha
African Americans
Agriculture
Akwesasne Notes
Albany Congress, Native Precedents
American Indian Contributions to the World
American Revolution, Native American
    Participation
Beaver Wars
Black Elk
Boarding Schools, United States and Canada
Bonnin, Gertrude Simmons
Boston Tea Party, Mohawk Images
Buffalo
Campbell, Ben Nighthorse
Canandaigua (Pickering) Treaty
Canassatego
Captain Jack
Cherokee Nation v. Georgia
Cherokee Phoenix and Indian Advocate
Citizenship
Cohen, Felix
Coon Come, Matthew
Cornplanter
Costo, Rupert

Michael Lerma
University of Arizona
    Pan-Indianism

Anne Marie Libério
University of Paris IV, Sorbonne
    Worcester v. Georgia

Fred Lindsey
San Francisco, CA
    National Congress of American Indians
    Totem Poles

Ute Lischke
Wilfred Laurier University
    Canada, Indian Policies of (with David T. McNab)
    Canoes (with David T. McNab)
    Erdrich, Louise (with David T. McNab)
    Hudson's Bay Company (with David T. McNab)

Christopher A. J. L. Little
University of Western Ontario
    Kennewick Man

Brad D. Lookingbill
Columbia College of Missouri
    Sitting Bull

Jean-François Lozier
University of Toronto
    Missionaries, French Jesuit

Barbara Alice Mann
University of Toledo
    Clark, George Rogers
    Cooper, James Fenimore
    Goschocking (Ohio) Massacre of 1782
    Handsome Lake (with Bruce E. Johansen)
    Hiawatha (with Bruce E. Johansen)
    Jingonsaseh
    Mound Cultures of North America
    Mounds, Eastern
    Ohio Valley Mound Culture
    Sullivan, General John and the Haudenosaunee
        Holocaust of 1779
    Women in Native Woodlands Societies

Aliki Marinakis
University of Victoria
    Athapaskan Languages
    Erasmus, Georges Henry
    Indian Shaker Movement
    Na-Dene Peoples
    Peltier, Leonard

    Wakashan Languages

Timothy J. McCollum
Indiana University
    Black Hills (Paha Sapa)
    Great Lakes Intertribal Council
    Humor, as Value

Robert R. McCoy
Washington State University
    Joseph, Younger
    Long March (Nez Percé)

James R. McIntyre
Moraine Valley Community College
    Carlisle Treaty Council
    Scalping in the Colonial Period
    St. Clair, Arthur (with Bruce E. Johansen and
        Robert W. Venables)
    Warfare, Intertribal

David T. McNab
Nipissing University
    Canada, Indian Policies of (with Ute Lischke)
    Canoes (with Ute Lischke)
    Erdrich, Louise (with Ute Lischke)
    Hudson's Bay Company (with Ute Lischke)

Mark Edwin Miller
Southern Utah University
    Banderas, Juan de la Cruz

Samuel Morgan
National Museum of the American Indian
    Oliphant v. Suquamish Indian Tribe

Traci L. Morris-Carlsten
University of Arizona
    Luna, James Alexander
    National Museum of the American Indian

James D. Nason
University of Washington
Native American Museums

Caryn E. Neumann
Ohio State University
    Adena Civilization
    Fallen Timbers, Battle of
    Radiation Exposure Compensation Act

Mark Nuttall
University of Alberta
    Athapaskan Peoples

Nancy J. Parezo
University of Arizona
Ancestral Puebloan Culture
Gorman, R. C.
Mogollon Culture

Vera Parham
University of California, Riverside
Blue Lake, New Mexico
*Bureau of Indian Affairs: Establishing the Existence
    of an Indian Tribe*
Oakes, Richard
United Nations, Indians and

Joy Porter
University of Wales, Swansea
Parker, Arthur C.
Society of American Indians

James Precht
Arizona State University
Gambling
National Indian Gaming Commission

Barry Pritzker
Skidmore College
Pre-contact Indian History (Essay)
Indian Nation Histories, Volume IV

Amy L. Propps
Santa Fe, New Mexico
Boas, Franz
Erickson, Leif
Indian Gaming Regulatory Act
L'Anse Aux Meadows Viking Settlement
Osages, and Oil Rights
United States v. Dann

Michelle H. Raheja
University of California, Riverside
Scholder, Fritz

SuAnn M. Reddick
Salem, Oregon
Sacajawea or Sakakawea (with Cary C. Collins)
Seattle (with Cary C. Collins)

Hugh J. Reilly
University of Nebraska at Omaha
Code Talkers, Navajo
Standing Bear (Ponca): Standing Bear v. Crook
Wounded Knee, South Dakota, Massacre at

Jon Reyhner
Northern Arizona University

Assimilation
Dodge, Henry Chee
Language and Language Renewal
Long Walk (Navajo)
MacDonald, Peter

Kimberly Roppolo
University of Lethbridge
Apess, William
Casas, Bartolome de las
Language, Written, in Americas, Pre-contact
Louis, Adrian
McNickle, D'Arcy
Owens, Louis
Parker, Quanah
Pipes, Sacred
Rose, Wendy
Sun Dance
Sweat Lodges

Natsu Taylor Saito
Georgia State University
Black Seminoles

Gregory Schaaf
Center for Indigenous Arts and Cultures
Banks, Dennis
Basketry
Beadwork
Iroquois Great Law of Peace (Kaianerekowa)
Katsinas
Wampum
Weaving

J. Landon K. Schmidt
University of Tulsa School of Law
*Graham, Mount (Dzil Nchaa Si An), Controversy
    over*
Lone Wolf v. Hitchcock
Sacred Sites

Bradley Shreve
University of New Mexico
Carson, Christopher "Kit"
Praying Villages of Massachusetts
Williams, Roger

Michael W. Simpson
Madison, Wisconsin
Lyng v. Northwest Indian Cemetery Protective
    Association

Wenona T. Singel
Michigan State University
Indian Mineral Leasing Act

Gregory E. Smoak
Colorado State University
  Ghost Dance Religion
  Wovoka

Elizabeth Sneyd
Royal Military College of Canada
  Anishinabe Algonquin National Council

Adam Sowards
  Fur Trade

H. Henrietta Stockel
Sierra Vista, Arizona
  Apache Wars
  Cochise
  Geronimo
  Grant Peace Policy (1870)
  Mission System, Spanish
  Slavery and Native Americans
  Victorio

Steve Talbot
Oregon State University
  California Indians, Genocide of
  Collier, John
  Indian Reorganization Act
  Sohappy, Sr., David

William N. Thompson
University of Nevada, Las Vegas
  Ceremonies, Criminalization of

James Thull
University of Montana
  American Indian Religious Freedom Act

Veronica E. Velarde Tiller
Tiller Research Incorporated
  *Westward Expansion, Indian Wars, and
    Reservations (Essay)*
  *St. Clair, Arthur (with Bruce E. Johansen and James
    R. McIntyre)*

David S. Trask
Guilford Technical Community College, Winston-
    Salem, N.C.
  Anglicans
  Episcopal Church

  Meriam Report
  Welch, James

Christopher Lindsay Turner
National Museum of the American Indian
  Bureau of American Ethnology
  Dams, Fishing Rights, and Hydroelectric Power
  Northwest Ordinance (1787)

Robert W. Venables
Cornell University
  *Indians in the Colonial Era and the American
    Revolution (Essay)*

Sally Roesch Wagner
Matilda Joslyn Gage Foundation
  Feminism, Native American Influences

Amy M. Ware
University of Texas, Austin
  Rogers, Will
  Ross, John
  Sequoyah
  Watie, Stand

Louellyn White
University of Arizona
  Akwesasne Freedom School

John L. Williams
University of Tulsa
  Economic Development
  Trade and Intercourse Acts
  Tribal Sovereignty

Waziyatawin Angela Wilson
Arizona State University
  Forced Marches
  Great Sioux Uprising
  Little Crow

Rosita Worl
Sealaska Corporation
  Alaska Native Claims Settlement Act (1971)

Gayle Yiotis
National Museum of the American Indian
  Cody, William Frederick

Contents

Volume I

Introduction

A BOOK CAN BE A TIME MACHINE, opening a window on the unquestioned judgments and assumptions of authors in other times. Many of these have been delivered with a sense of European-American self-congratulation. Consider John D. Hicks, who, in *The Federal Union: A History of the United States to 1865* (1937) opens a 700-page tome with the words "The civilization that grew up in the United States . . ." implying that nothing worth the name occurred before Columbus planted European seeds here (Hicks, 1937, 1). Paragraph two begins: "America before the time of Columbus had developed no great civilizations of its own" (Hicks, 1937, 1). This text states authoritatively that the Mayas, Aztecs, and Incas could not match "the best that Europe had to offer" (Hicks, 1937, 1), despite the fact that accounts of the Cortez invasion expressed a sense of awe at the Aztecs' capital city Tenochtitlan when they first saw it. In the same paragraph, Hicks develops reasons why he believes that Europeans surpassed America's "primitive civilization": "racial traits may account in part for this failure, but the importance of the environment cannot be overlooked" (Hicks, 1937, 1).

No time and no people speak with a single voice, however. So while Hicks' assumptions of racial superiority remind us of Richard Henry Pratt's advertising slogan for the boarding schools he built ("Kill the Indian, Save the Man") even Pratt's and Hicks' time were informed by other voices that asserted enduring value to Native American peoples and cultures. While Pratt's slogan is sometimes interpreted as an endorsement of genocide in our time, to him it was friendly advice to peoples whom he assumed would die culturally as well as genetically if they held fast to cultures that he considered out of date in a modern world. Multicultural ideas that inform public discourse (as well as census reports) in our time had precedents in Pratt's and Hicks' time. The majority society was just not listening. Consider Walt Whitman, for example, during 1883, as Pratt was fashioning his campaign to save Indians by killing their cultures:

As to our aboriginal or Indian population . . . I know it seems to be agreed that they must gradually dwindle as time rolls on, and in a few generations more leave only a reminiscence, a blank. But I am not at all clear about that. As America . . . develops, adapts, entwines, faithfully identifies its own—are we to see it cheerfully accepting using all the contributions of foreign lands from the whole outside globe—and then rejecting the only ones distinctly its own? (Moquin, 1973, 5–6).

One newspaper, the *Omaha World-Herald,* sent a native woman, Susette LaFlesche (an Omaha), to describe the aftermath of the Wounded Knee massacre. She was married to Thomas Tibbles. Together, a decade earlier, they had roused their city of Omaha in anger over the torturous treatment suffered by the Ponca Standing Bear and his band. Exiled in Indian Territory from their homeland along the Niobrara River (in northernmost Nebraska), the Poncas had escaped and walked home, stopping in the city, their feet bleeding in the snow, so hungry that they had chewed on their moccasins. General George Crook volunteered to be the defendant in a legal case that established the Poncas' right to return home.

History is full of surprises. The same year that Hicks' book was published, Matthew W. Stirling, chief and later director of the American Bureau of Ethnology for thirty years (1928–1958), stated in *National Geographic* that the Albany Plan of Union (1754) was fundamentally shaped by the Iroquois Confederacy through Benjamin Franklin (Stirling, 1937). Such an idea is hardly universally accepted, even in our time. For one, Steven Pinker, in *The Blank Slate,* asserted that the same idea was flimsy enough to dismiss without explanation in two words: "1960s granola" (Pinker, 2002, 298).

Historically, we stand with Whitman and Stirling. *The Encyclopedia of American Indian History* attempts to redress assumptions that any single culture is superior to any other. American Indian voices were available to historians in the 1930s; it was, after

all, a time of major Native rights assertion under the Indian Reorganization Act, but many non-Native historians seemed not to be listening. The writings of Dr. Charles A. Eastman (or, to use his Dakota name, Ohiyesa) and Luther Standing Bear were widely published, among many others. Major nineteenth-century feminists (Elizabeth Cady Stanton and Matilda Joslyn Gage, to name two) had acknowledged their debt to Native matriarchal societies. Still, one can hardly imagine Hicks having any use for an encyclopedia entry titled "American Indian Contributions to the World."

We start with six essays, written by our co-editors and members of our editorial board, which focus on the themes that dominate particular eras in American Indian history. So, for example, if a reader wants to find out why the Trail of Tears migration happened when it did, s/he would find that context covered in the essay dealing with the period from 1800 to 1850. The late Vine Deloria, Jr. once advised non-Indian scholars to study the history of topics of contemporary importance to Native peoples, and a section of the encyclopedia addresses those issues that are prominent both in the history of Native peoples and in Native societies today. These entries range from archaeology and pre-contact Native history to topics like gaming and water rights, which are still so relevant. Subsequent sections deal with the most important events of American Indian history, aspects of Native cultures that have had ramifications in history, Native interactions with non-Indian governments, and the roles of both individuals and groups in American Indian history. One of the most important sections of the encyclopedia, the histories of particular Native nations, is absolutely vital to the stories we're seeking to have told and deserves to be highlighted. Also, primary sources from throughout American Indian history are presented so that readers can get a flavor of how different people viewed these events as they happened.

The occupancy of most of North America by Europeans on a sustained basis is less than 200 years old—four consecutive human lives then, less than three now. Thus, the importance of American Indian history to the recent history of all peoples on this continent is clear. The history is written in what we call our homeland—many of our cities, half the constituent states in the federal union that calls itself the United States, bear names that have Native roots.

If there is one thing we've learned from trying to organize and do justice to such a vast and important subject, it is that there is no way to present this material that is perfect for everyone. Different people learn best in different ways. However, we've endeavored to be as clear as possible, making the large number of materials and resources as easy to locate and use as possible. An encyclopedia is not a cast-iron product, but a collection of many contributors' work. In our case, this is a mixture of Native and non-Native voices. Selection of subject matter is subject to judgment, and interpretation, and will be reviewed—something or someone is included, someone or something else is ignored, or given short shrift. We can say only that we have done our best.

Bruce E. Johansen and Barry M. Pritzker, Editors
Steven L. Danver, Project Editor

References and Further Reading
Hicks, John D. *The Federal Union: A History of the United States to 1865.* 1937. Boston: Houghton-Mifflin.
Moquin, Wayne. *Great Documents in American Indian History.* 1973. New York: Praeger.
Pinker, Steven. *The Blank Slate: The Modern Denial of Human Nature.* 2002. New York: Viking (Penguin Putnam).
Pritzker, Barry M. *Native America Today: A Guide to Community Politics and Culture.* 1999. Santa Barbara, CA: ABC-CLIO.
Stirling, Matthew W. "America's First Settlers, the Indians." *National Geographic* 72:5 (1937), cited in Bruce E. Johansen, comp. *Native America and the Evolution of Democracy: A Supplementary Bibliography.* 1999, 140. Westport, CT: Greenwood.

Encyclopedia of
American Indian History

Chronological Essays

Pre-contact Indian History
(ca. 20,000 BCE to ca. 1500 CE)

The histories of the Native people of North America are ones of adaptation and diversity. This is true for the long "precontact" period as well as for today. The cultures most commonly cited as "prehistoric" (a misnomer, since the term implies both that writing was absent and that only natural events out of people's control, not political and cultural ones, shaped the development of Indian societies) are presented as snapshot descriptions of cultural fluidity. Far from being stopped in time, these cultures had antecedents and evolutions that depended for their direction on a multiplicity of factors, including climate, geography, and cultural influences and traditions. Most likely, over 100 million inhabitants who spoke at least 1,000 languages inhabited the Americas before New World diseases wiped out up to 98 percent of them, beginning in the late fifteenth century. In North America, a region of roughly 9 million square miles, population estimates range from 2 million or so to upward of 16 million.

Who were the first people, and how did they arrive? The most popular migration theory has northeast Asians—Siberians—following big game into North America over a land bridge called Beringia, made possible by the decline of the sea level due to glaciations, across what is now the Bering Strait between Siberia and Alaska. According to this theory, increasing numbers of people made their way into the interior of Alaska, the Bering Refugium, and moved south along the ice-free corridor of the MacKenzie River Valley. In an alternative version of the theory, people migrated southward through interior British Columbia, perhaps during an interglacial period.

In the early twentieth century, near Folsom, New Mexico, the first indisputable proof of human antiquity in the Americas was found in the form of a spear point stuck between the ribs of an extinct species of bison (buffalo). In the tradition of naming Paleo-Indian cultural or historical periods after point types, which themselves are named by the site at which they are first found, this bilaterally flaked, or fluted, stone point was named the Folsom point. A few years later, near Clovis, New Mexico, similar (if somewhat larger) points were found. The development of radiocarbon dating techniques in 1948 made it possible to ascertain the date of material

containing carbon 14 (that is, formerly living matter) with a high degree of accuracy. Using this technique—by dating bones found alongside the stone artifacts—scientists dated the Folsom site to about 8,500 BCE and the Clovis site to about 9,500 BCE. Later archaeological finds revealed the extremely wide geographical distribution of the Clovis point throughout much of North America and even south to Central America.

Based on a number of factors, including the extinction of Pleistocene big game (presumably caused at least in part by an explosion of Clovis point–driven hunting as well as climate changes) and the lack of any older site in North America, the date for the first appearance of people in North America was widely thought for some time to have coincided with the appearance of the Clovis points. However, beginning in the mid-1970s, this theory began to unravel. Early human sites were discovered in present-day southwestern Pennsylvania and even in South America (Chile and Peru) dating from at least 12,000 BCE. The Topper site in South Carolina may date to roughly 13,000 BCE, and sites in Mexico have yielded artifacts that may date to 21,000 BCE. Moreover, no Clovis sites have been discovered in Alaska, the ice-free corridor, or along the Pacific Coast.

Other important evidence that casts doubt on the traditional explanations of original immigration includes the demonstrated antiquity of water travel. Boat travel may be as old as 800,000 years in parts of Southeast Asia. Certainly people traveled to Australia on boats roughly 40,000 years ago. With the likelihood that the first northeastern Asians had access to boats came the necessity of including sea travel in the mix of theories regarding the peopling of the Americas. Artifacts found on Santa Rosa Island, off the Southern California coast, and dating to roughly 11,000 BCE suggest that boats were in use at that time. Indeed, some scientists believe that the Siberian migration proceeded not along an interior ice-free corridor but along the coast.

Two other theories involve migration from the east. One posits a migration from northern Europe and along the northern ice shelf that presaged the Norse migration around 1000, perhaps using umiak-like boats. Supporters of this theory point to the similarities between the Clovis point and the

bifacial projectile points made by northern European Solutreans between 16,000 and 19,000 years ago. (They do not, however, explain the 5,000-year gap.) Artifacts found near Cactus Hill, Virginia, suggest, but do not confirm, a Solutrean connection. This theory also accords more closely with some Native narratives involving very early east-west migrations. The second theory regarding coastal migration from the east has people arriving by boat directly across the Atlantic from southwestern Europe.

At this time, evidence for migration theories remains circumstantial. None of the earliest known archaeological sites are located near the Bering Strait or within the Bering Refugium. Nor is there proof of coastal migration routes. Even during the peak of the Ice Age, some areas of Beringia were always open to game and to humans; so no period of time for human entry into North America can be ruled out completely. Most scientists now conclude that humans inhabited North America well before 10,000 BCE, perhaps as early as 35,000 years ago and perhaps considerably earlier than that. The earliest humans likely entered North America from northern or northeastern Asia in a series of incursions over tens of thousands of years along a number of different routes, including land and, at the southern margins, sea. Further movement southward could have occurred through the ice-free corridor and/or along the Pacific Coast. Clovis, once considered the ancestor of all North American human culture, is now generally regarded as one of several ancient human cultural complexes.

With the one possible exception previously mentioned, none of these theories take any note of traditional Native American explanations of how people came to live in North America. Some Indian cultures date their population of this world from an emergence from worlds beneath it. Long migrations, generally involving east-west rather than north-south travel, figure prominently in the earliest histories of some groups. Many societies account for their origins with creation stories, often involving magical or tricky beings, such as Coyote or Raven. Such trickster characters often figure prominently in the creation of human ills such as death and suffering, while a benevolent Great Spirit is given credit for creation as well as for religion and even social and political organization. The Great Spirit is not generally considered to be responsible for ills that befall individuals, which are often said to result from improper action associated with immorality or violations of that which is sacred. Because of the association of the Great Spirit with creation and everything connected to it, most native North Americans lived in a highly sacred world, whose boundaries, locations, rules, and traditions most people took very seriously.

However or whenever the first humans arrived, by about 9,500 BCE, North America was populated by nomadic bands of Paleo-Indian hunter-gatherers. Depending on location, most food consisted of now extinct animals such as horses (today's horses are not descended from those of this era), camels, wooly mammoths, large bison, musk ox, mastodon, lions, and giant beavers, as well as deer, elk, caribou, and fish, berries and roots. People hunted using spears with stone points, made more effective in some areas by the *atlatl*, or spear-throwing stick. People continued the fluted-point technological tradition that earlier produced Clovis and Folsom points until roughly 5,000 BCE. Workmanship (flint knapping) of the stone blades (spear points, knives, scrapers, engravers, etc.), some of which were utilitarian and others apparently ceremonial, was often of extraordinary quality.

A new era (Archaic, or early Holocene) began about 10,000 years ago, as the glaciers continued to recede and the climate warmed. New areas to the north became available for habitation. The land features began to assume their present form, and many of the large grazing animals became extinct. Human populations grew from perhaps a few hundred thousand to many millions, and with the rise in population came increased cultural diversity and technological innovation. Techniques developed by early Holocene peoples for exploiting a variety of local resources proved to be so successful that they lasted, in many cases and with the subsequent addition in some areas of agriculture, until the period of Afro-European settlement. To a significant extent, population growth, along with the formation of multiethnic population centers in several "culture areas," was the result of complex historical events such as trade, warfare, diplomacy, and religious movements, as well as of climatic and other natural changes. Indeed, we must take care when using traditional conceptions of culture areas not to ignore the agency of Native people in giving rise to a multiplicity of rich, fluid histories. With that caveat, it can be helpful to think broadly about Native settlement in North America in terms of culture areas, or regions, because, while environment is not determinative of culture, the two have meaningful correlations.

Southwest

Four native culture traditions—the Pueblos, the Uto-Aztecan O'odham, the Yuman, and the far more recent Na-Dene, or Dene (Apache and Navajo)—flourished in the Greater Southwest, located from southern Colorado/Utah and southeast California west across Arizona and New Mexico. The Southwest is a rugged land of extraordinary diversity: baking low deserts; towering, snow-capped mountains; deep canyons; mesas; and high plains. Rainfall is relatively low, especially in the southern deserts, although snowfall in the higher elevations can be plentiful. The region is drained mainly by the Colorado River and its tributaries and by the Rio Grande. Indigenous foods include agave, piñon nuts, cactus fruits, wild onions and potatoes, and a variety of berries, nuts, and seeds. Early people wove baskets, sandals, and cloth from wild fibers. Around 1500 BCE, people living in southern New Mexico began planting maize (corn) and squash, a skill they probably learned from their neighbors to the south. Beans, making up a third of the American staple crops, probably arrived around 500 BCE. (Beans contain high levels of the essential amino acid lycene, which corn lacks and which aids in the digestion of the protein found in corn. Moreover, while corn depletes nitrogen from the soil, beans, being legumes, return it to the ground; the two crops complement each other.) The people continued to harvest other plant and animal resources, however, and did not establish permanent settlement, or begin making pottery until roughly 300 BCE.

At about that time, a community located in the Gila River Valley constructed an irrigation canal about 5 kilometers (3 miles) long. This community, and others with a similar culture, became known as Hohokam. The modern Pima and Tohono O'odham (Papago) people are generally believed to have descended from the Hohokam, which may usually be seen as the frontier of Mexican civilization at that time. The Hohokam people constructed a village near present-day Snaketown that, enlarged and further developed, lasted until roughly 1450. During those 1,700 years or so, people planted fields watered by extensive irrigation systems, using stone manos and metates to grind their maize. They manufactured pottery (for storage, cooking, and ornamentation) and made ornaments from shell, turquoise, copper, macaw feathers, and other material acquired from extensive trade networks extending west to the Pacific Ocean, south deep into Mex-

ico, and east to New Mexico and beyond. Their rectangular, single-unit homes and ball courts indicated population centers that were relatively self-sufficient. As is often the case with thriving agricultural communities, Hohokam religious and artistic development was rich and complex.

The Ancestral Puebloans represent another Southwestern cultural tradition. Located in the north and east of the region, the Ancestral Puebloans are the predecessors of the modern Pueblo Indians and are culturally descended from earlier so-called Basket Maker people (400–700). The Ancestral Puebloans also created extensive trade networks, acquiring goods, and some cultural traditions as well, from as far away as Mexico, California, and the Great Plains. Ancestral Puebloan people made and used bows and arrows, grew cotton, and stored their food surpluses in pits. The accumulation of significant food surpluses led directly, in some areas, to the replacement, around 700, of early adobe or masonry houses by expanded apartment-style buildings (pueblos), some with hundreds of rooms. These people also developed a highly complex religious/ceremonial life involving underground spaces, called kivas, and various supernatural beings. Major population centers flourished at Mesa Verde and Chaco Canyon (as many as 6,000 to 10,000 people lived there around 1100, with complex and highly developed systems of trade, transportation, and ceremonialism), as well as in the upper Rio Grande Valley.

The two other major Southwestern cultural traditions are the Mogollon and the Patayan. The Mogollon, characterized by outstanding red-on-brown and black-and-white ceramics, centered in the mountainous regions of southeastern Arizona and southwestern New Mexico. Classic Mogollon Mimbres pottery reveals images of many kinds of fish found in the Gulf of California. The Mogollon people lived in partially excavated houses, which were well insulated and appropriate for the higher altitudes. The descriptor "Patayan" imperfectly describes a great diversity of Yuman-speaking cultures west and north of the Hohokam. The Yumans, too, cultivated crops after about 2,000 years ago, although mainly by taking advantage of annual floods, as opposed to the Hohokam method of constructing vast irrigation channels.

Southwestern agricultural societies all underwent a major transformation from roughly 1250 to 1400. During this period, the great Hohokam and Ancestral Puebloan population centers all but disappeared. The reasons for this disappearance remain

somewhat unclear. Prolonged drought is the most likely factor, but intercommunity warfare and soil exhaustion also may have played a role. Also, what now appears as wholesale abandonments may at the time have been more gradual population shifts. In any case, while populations unquestionably become dispersed during this period, the region remained marked by a great deal of cultural continuity.

California

California encompasses unique cultural elements as well as those of regions including the Southwest (in the extreme southeast), the Great Basin (in Death Valley and the extreme west), the Northwest Coast (in the extreme northwest), and the Plateau (in the extreme northeast). The region includes deserts, high mountains, an enormous central valley, and over a thousand miles of coast. Not surprisingly, ancient lifestyles differed widely throughout this extremely diverse region. As mentioned, people first entered California no later than 11,000 BCE and possibly as early as 19,000 years ago or even earlier. About 9000 BCE, people in some parts of the region, particularly along the south coast, began supplementing reliance on (and generally extensive) hunting, gathering, and fishing by collecting seeds and grinding them with milling stones.

By about 3000 BCE, people had evolved distinct local cultural and subsistence patterns. The most common language groups were Hokan, Penutian, and Uto-Aztecan, although some people spoke languages from groups including Athapaskan, Yukian, and Algonquian. The Windmiller culture of central California was characterized by a relatively rich tradition of arts and crafts. The primary materials were stone, bone, wood, and shale, which was acquired in trade from coastal groups. Windmiller people also made pottery, twined baskets, and finely crafted charmstones. They buried their dead face down and oriented toward the west. Along the central coast, people used fast, highly maneuverable boats to reach offshore islands. They also set out on these boats to kill dolphins, porpoises, whales, and other marine life.

By about 3000–2000 BCE, as sea levels stabilized, coastal populations became among the densest in North America. By at least 1,500 years ago, the basic patterns of many "historic" California groups had been established. Coastal people had been eating marine life for millennia. Many inland people depended on acorns and buckeyes as important food staples. People collected acorns in the fall. After removing the kernels from the acorns, women sundried them, pounded them into flour, and then leached out the bitter tannic acid using a variety of methods. The only crop people actually cultivated was tobacco, although some groups modified the natural environment through techniques such as irrigation, transplantation, and burning to create favorable environments for certain wild plants and even animals.

Many groups also created rock art, by painting and/or by carving or pecking, from as early as 1000 BCE. Trade, mainly with close neighbors but not uncommonly with distant groups, was very well developed. People either bartered for goods (including salt, acorns, fish, beads, baskets, hides, pelts, obsidian, and bows) or purchased them with items such as dentalium shells, clamshell disk beads, and magnesite beads. Basketry, in particular, was extremely well developed in California, especially in the central regions. Although groups were fairly territorial, intercourse between them generally did not include organized warfare, and such conflicts as existed were generally settled quickly and with compensation for any loss incurred.

Most California Indians employed shamans (doctors) to mediate between the physical and the spiritual worlds. Shamans served both as religious leaders and healers. Some groups had secret religious societies, such as those associated with Kuksu rituals (a type of world renewal ceremony) and various spirit visitors or ghosts. Northern peoples also celebrated first salmon rituals, which provided an opportunity to gather in larger groups, to relate histories and mythologies, and to display wealth. In the south, mourning ceremonies were the most important, while across the region other ceremonies revolved around life cycle events such as puberty, astronomical occasions, and other natural phenomena. Perhaps not completely unlike a more contemporary period in California's history, some ceremonies required spiritual leaders to ingest psychotropic drugs, such as datura. Tobacco was also an important part of many rituals. Many California groups, especially in the north, observed a fairly rigid caste system, and some groups kept slaves.

Northwest Coast

The tendencies toward rigid caste systems and ostentatious displays of wealth were most pro-

nounced in the rugged Northwest Coast, a region extending from Northern California to southern Alaska. This region, roughly 1,500 miles long but only about 100 miles deep, is defined by water: sounds, inlets, fjords, bays, and rivers. A cool, wet climate is fairly uniform throughout the region. Several cultural developments preceded the relatively stable subsistence patterns that lasted until contact with non-Native groups. This stability generally dates back to the time when sea levels stabilized, between 4,000 and 5,000 years ago, although the timetable varied across the region, and other cultural practices, such as sedentary villages, social ranking, extensive woodworking, and distinctive regional art styles, emerged later, in some cases much later. Native people spoke at least forty dialects of languages in the Athapaskan, Haida, Tsimshian, Wakashan, Chimakuan, Salishan, and Penutian language families.

Two natural resources above all—fish, especially salmon, and cedar—played an enormous role in Northwest Coast life for millennia. Five types of salmon predominated: pink, coho, chum (dog), Chinook, and sockeye. Rituals celebrating the annual return of the salmon were common. Depending on location, people used a variety of methods to catch salmon, including nets, spears, and traps. People ate a wide variety of other fish, of course, such as halibut, eulachon, and herring, as well as shellfish, land mammals, plants, and roots such as camas and wapato. Red cedar formed the core of Northwest Coast technology. From it, people made clothing, baskets, plank houses, bowls, steam-bent boxes, and canoes, as well as a variety of artistic and ceremonial items. Other raw materials included obsidian, jade, jasper, amber, shells, whalebone, and stone. In general, the level of craftsmanship of tools and other objects was extremely high. Although most men could craft objects of wood, canoe making was a particularly specialized profession.

With the gradual accumulation of wealth, hierarchical social ranking became a key feature of most Northwest Coast societies. Status was quite rigid and tended to be inherited, although some movement was possible. Typically, four groups existed: nobility, upper-class free, lower-class free, and slaves (who were technically not members of society at all). Kin groups, which owned various rights and privileges, including subsistence areas, songs, and rituals, were identified by crests. Everything inheritable was said to originate from a supernatural spirit through an ancestor. Particularly in more recent times, the

whole system of ranking and kin groups was confirmed and advanced by the potlatch, a complex ritual that featured feasting, singing, dancing, history recitation, and ostentatious gift giving. Potlatches also served to distribute surpluses, confirm alliances, and reinforce cooperation among kin groups.

Guardian spirits formed the basis of most Northwest Coast religion. Spirits could inhere in both animate and inanimate objects. Like most things they could be inherited, but individuals could acquire them as well through the vision quest, a rigorous process begun around the onset of adolescence and completed whenever the spirit became manifest. Spirits were generally associated with particular songs, dances, and skills. Most Northwest Coast art was heraldic in nature, announcing power and identity, and deriving in part from the spirit world. The well-known totem poles, carved and painted with heraldic or crest designs, were just one example of this ubiquitous type of art. People traded with each other and with inland groups, but the fact that the Northwest Coast is a relatively isolated region containing abundant natural resources militated against extensive trade.

Plateau

Unlike the Northwest Coast, the Plateau region, defined loosely as the drainage basins of the Columbia and Fraser Rivers, is a land of extremes. The northern region is heavily forested and moderately wet, bitter cold in winter, and baking hot in summer, while the south tends toward sagebrush desert. To a significant extent and notwithstanding technological developments, such as specialized grinding tools (ca. 3000 BCE) and the bow and arrow and woodworking tools (ca. 500 BCE), the Plateau lifestyle changed relatively little from the first occupation of the region (well before the time of the so-called Kennewick man in eastern Washington, about 9,200 years ago) until the seventeenth century. The most important language families of the region were Sahaptin (Penutian) and Interior Salish. Most Plateau groups depended for food on fish, especially salmon, which were speared, netted, or, especially in the north, caught with hook and line. Other food staples included berries and roots (actually bulbs and tubers such as camas and bitterroot), which women gathered with special sticks and cooked in earth ovens. Some areas contained both large and small game.

Extended families tended to live in semisubterranean earth houses with conical roofs, entry to

which was gained through the roof. Perhaps after about 1700 BCE, people also utilized summer houses made of tule mats. Some villages were occupied all year long, but generally people followed the food supply. Like their California neighbors, some groups manipulated their natural environment through regular burning to increase the yield of certain plant and animal foods. People using twined Indian hemp tule, and spruce and cedar root made a great variety of products, such as hats, bedding, nets, mats, and fine baskets. Canoes, both dugout and bark, served for water transportation.

With relatively easy access to neighboring regions of North America, Plateau people traded widely and extensively. Indeed, The Dalles, located at the head of the Columbia gorge, was one of the most important trade centers in North America. At the same time, valuing autonomy, relative equality, and cooperation, Plateau people tended to avoid warfare, both among themselves or with outsiders. Kin networks often extended over great distances. Specialized leaders arose only for special occasions, and political leadership, which might be exercised by either sex, depended on an ability to persuade rather than to overpower or to enforce decisions.

In general, Plateau ceremonialism was based on individual relationships with guardian spirits, which might be associated with either animate or inanimate objects. Boys and girls entering puberty generally undertook spirit quests, which consisted of travel to remote places where they encountered their spirit helper as manifested in special songs and powers. In turn, sacred spirits required certain forms of respect, a mutual process that helped to ensure harmony between people and their environment.

Great Basin

Similar in many ways to the Plateau, and occupying roughly 400,000 square miles of land between the Rocky Mountains and the Sierra Nevada, is an area commonly referred to as the Great Basin. The main differences between the Plateau and the Great Basin are the absence (except for neighboring peoples) in the Basin of salmon and the existence, where water existed at all, of more closed-water fisheries. This arid region consists generally of high deserts and valleys as well as freshwater and saltwater lakes.

With the exception of the Hokan-speaking Washoe, all Great Basin inhabitants spoke dialects of Numic (Shoshonean) languages. Perhaps to a greater extent than in any other region, and notwithstanding

several significant environmental changes, much of the Great Basin was characterized by a remarkable cultural continuity from about 7000 BCE until late in the nineteenth century.

In part reflecting the relative paucity of food in the region, people of the Great Basin were peaceful and highly nomadic, with small, fluid, extended-family camps located mainly around such water as existed in the region, although semipermanent villages eventually developed in some of the more productive areas. People hunted game, such as birds, rabbits, deer, and antelope; they fished in the few freshwater lakes; and they gathered a variety of grasses, seeds (piñon), nuts (acorn), and other plants, as well as some insects (grasshoppers, crickets, some caterpillars, and fly larvae). Successful rabbit or mountain sheep drives were generally followed by a festival that included gambling, singing, dancing, and courtship. Some border groups experimented with agriculture, the Southern Paiute growing maize, beans, and squash, and the Owens Valley Shoshone building extensive irrigation canals to increase the amount of wild foods. The basic raw materials for baskets and containers were willow, grasses, and roots, as well as (depending upon location) stone, bone, obsidian, and wood. People fished using nets, weirs, basket traps, spears, and hook and line. Like their neighbors to the north and west, some groups practiced environmental management by selective burning and pruning.

Housing in the Great Basin typically consisted of brush windbreaks in summer and conical pole (pine and/or juniper) frame structures supporting a covering of brush, bark, grass, and/or tule. Some northern groups used skins to cover the frames. Doorways generally faced east. People wore little clothing except in the coldest weather, when they might wear fur or twined-bark breechclouts as well as blankets of sewn rabbit- or buffalo-skin. As long as 7,000 years ago, people living in the Great Basin were part of extensive trade networks reaching across the region west to the Pacific Ocean. Traditional spirituality centered on various beings that were capable of influencing human existence. People practiced both individual (spirit dreams or visions) and communal (round dance) ceremonies, some of which were associated with life cycle events. Part of maintaining a harmonious relationship with their environment was the respect that people accorded to food and medicinal items, both plants (over three hundred of which were used medicinally) and animals.

Beginning about 500, people of a highly diverse culture, now known as Fremont, inhabited the eastern edge of the Great Basin. One feature of the Fremont culture was farming: People in this area, probably under the influence of their Pueblo neighbors to the south, began supplementing their regular diet with maize, beans, and squash as early as several hundred years BCE. Several hundred years later, people added the bow and arrow to their tool kit of atlatls and darts, and they began settling down in relatively stable communities. Fremont culture was characterized by these developments as well as by the existence of moccasins, clay figurines and containers, distinctive rock art, and other traits. By around 1400, the Fremont culture became dispersed to the point of disappearance.

Great Plains and Prairie

To the east of the Great Basin, the Plateau, and the Southwest lay the huge Great Plains and Prairie, a grassy region of roughly 1.5 million square miles located between the Rocky Mountains and the Mississippi River, and from west-central Canada to Texas. The Plains are characterized by their altitude, wind, and aridity, while in lower, more humid regions the prairie grasslands extend east to the forests of the Midwest. The Plains' greatest river is the Missouri and its tributaries. The flat topology allows frigid polar air in the winter and scorching heat in the summer; these contrasts often give rise to dramatic weather events, such as blizzards and tornadoes. People exhibiting Clovis cultural attributes were present in the Great Plains 12,000 years ago; human habitation may well have extended back considerably farther than that. These early hunters stalked ancient species of big game and then their successors, the bison. As the region warmed and the big game moved north and died out, the Plains became depopulated to the point where no evidence of human habitation has been found from about 5000 BCE to 3000 BCE. From around 2500 BCE, as the bison population recovered, to 500 BCE, people living in small camps hunted bison, elk, deer, antelope, and other creatures; used grinding stones to process seeds; and gathered pine seeds, wild onions, juniper bark, and yucca (in the west).

Beginning around 2,500 years ago, people living in the Plains began to be influenced by the Adena and Hopewell cultures to the east (see "Southeast"). Villages appeared in some of the river valleys, inhabited by people living in oval pole wigwams. People

began growing maize in an area from about Kansas City to the Dakotas. They buried their dead in mounds (although, unlike true Hopewell culture, the tombs revealed no status differentiation). Items indicating the presence of vast trade networks, eastward and westward perhaps even to the Pacific Coast, included conch, olivella and dentalium shells, and copper beads. Bows and arrows appeared throughout the Plains early in the first millennium CE. Around 850, as contact increased with neighboring peoples, agricultural settlements became more pronounced throughout the Missouri Valley, although these farmers continued to rely extensively on bison for their food. In the central Plains, people built rectangular wooden homes framed by posts and partially insulated with earth, often located on a bluff above a river flood plain.

In present-day south-central Wisconsin, a town later known as Aztalan appears to have been an outpost of the great Mississippian capital Cahokia (see "Southeast"). People living here and in similar towns cultivated corn, squash, sunflowers, probably chenopods, and tobacco. The societies of the upper midwestern Mississippi, known as Oneota, were characterized by the almost exclusive use of agriculture as well as by extensive trade and the use of pottery. Strangely, tuberculosis seems to have appeared among the Oneota people, perhaps brought over to the Americas by the Norse, who were attempting to colonize the Gulf of Saint Lawrence region at about this time. In the western Great Lakes region, people improved the soil by adding ash and charcoal, although they also hunted and fished to ensure a stable, nutritious diet. In general, the farther west people lived, the less they practiced agriculture and the more they hunted bison. People's possessions and gear were carried in bundles lashed between poles by specially trained dogs.

By the fifteenth century, or roughly 250 years before the introduction of the horse changed life on the Plains dramatically and forever, populations were increasing all across the region, but especially in the northern parklands. New arrivals included Caddoan groups from east Texas, such as the Pawnee, and Apacheans from western Canada. Toward the east and Missouri River Valley regions, farming towns grew to contain as many as a hundred houses, and, in a sign of increased competition for land, the towns were increasingly defended with stockades and ditches. Rectangular houses gave way to a more rounded style along the Missouri, while hunting camp dwellings were usually hide

tipis. All across the region, but especially in the west, bison remained plentiful, as did elk, beaver, and numerous other game (High Plains people did not eat fish as a rule). People tended to follow the game out onto the open areas in summer and back into the wooded areas in winter. The favored way to take bison was by driving them over cliffs or to the head of a ravine or by stalking them individually or surrounding them in groups and then shooting them with arrows. In the southern High Plains, Apachean groups became heavily influenced by the Pueblo people to their west, becoming small-scale farmers as well as bison hunters. Conversely, some of the region's nomadic hunters, such as the Kiowa, may once have been Pueblo dwellers who moved east to follow the bison during the droughts of the fourteenth century.

People ate bison meat fresh or cut into strips and then dried and stored. Mixed with fat and berries, the meat, called pemmican, could last for several months, generally throughout the winter. Clothing, which in some areas was decorated with porcupine-quill embroidery, was derived mainly from bison and/or deer. Bison parts also provided containers (hides and stomach), tools (bones), rattles (hoof), bowstrings and thread (sinew), ropes and belts (hair), spoons and cups (horn), and other items. Authority was highly transient and was earned by traits such as bravery, spiritual attainment, generosity, and a sense of humor. For many Plains people, the circle was a sacred shape, symbolic of the interconnectedness of the universe. As a circular object, the pipe bowl was also associated with the sacred, and agreements concluded over a pipe of tobacco were not broken in theory or practice. The Great Mystery, *Wakan Tanka*, presided over an array of sacred natural beings and phenomena. Like some Native Americans in other regions, Plains people entering adolescence tended to hold vision quests in which, through the benefit of purification and self-deprivation, they received power or "medicine" that could be used for certain specific purposes. Such medicine was often accompanied by songs and dances, and it had a physical manifestation as well (the sacred bundle). Another way to communicate with the sacred realm was through visions, generally obtained either through dreaming or as part of ceremonies.

Southeast

Settlement patterns differed considerably in the Southeast, a region generally described as bounded by the eastern Great Plains and a line running east-west from about Delaware to Iowa. It is fairly flat, except for the Appalachian Mountains, and generally warm to hot, and wet, except less so in the northern and northwestern regions. The area was heavily forested with some grassy prairies, except along the Gulf Coast, where semitropical vegetation and swampland prevailed. The Southwest was dominated by Muskogean speakers, but Algonquians and Siouans were also present.

Due to the relative wetness of the Southeast, the regular flooding of major river systems, and rising sea levels as a result of melting glaciations, evidence of early human history is particularly scarce. People were in the region no later than about 12,000 BCE. By roughly 5000 BCE, people lived in some small settlements; ate deer and other large animals, fowl, shellfish, fish, nuts, berries, and seeds; and made various tools (including canoes), baskets, and ornaments. People from different settlements probably engaged with each other at popular fishing or trapping sites, leading to trade and other forms of human interaction. Along the coast, people may have traded with people as far away as Central and South America. Early cultivation, including squash and sunflower, dates from at least 1400 BCE, with maize appearing almost 1,000 years later. Inconclusive evidence suggests that one early town—Poverty Point, near Vicksburg—may have been founded by Olmec (Mexican) traders. The town, which was more than 7 miles across, contained mounds over 75 feet high. Artisans made fine beadwork, stone tools, and clay balls designed to serve as heating elements.

Beginning in about 500 BCE, the Adena culture formed along the Ohio River in present-day Ohio, West Virginia, Kentucky, and Indiana. Most Adena people ate food that they hunted or gathered, supplemented with domesticated plant foods (squash, sunflower, amaranth, chenopod, and marsh elder). Population density was relatively low; camps were characterized by hot-rock cooking ovens and areas of specialized activity (perhaps tool making or weaving). In addition, Adena culture was characterized by relatively complex communal burial rituals. Burial mounds grew by successive burials and cremations, with various ornaments (made of copper, mica, and other material), tools (points, axes, atlatls), and other items (such as sacred pipes) being buried with the body or ashes. Adena trade networks stretched throughout much of the Southeast. The Adena people also often constructed circular earthworks more than 300 feet in diameter with interior

ditches and exterior banks. Unlike at Poverty Point, Adena people tended to live in scattered dwellings rather than in towns.

The Adena probably evolved to some extent into the later, and even more complex, Hopewell culture, also based in the central Mississippi and lower Ohio Valleys, which flourished between about 100 BCE and 450. The Hopewell differed from the Adena primarily in the cultivation of maize and in the loose integration of a huge region by political/trade leaders who legitimated their power with status symbols of rare, exotic material such as gold, obsidian, and silver in the form of hawks, stags, bears, and snakes. After the Hopewell declined, due in part to the onset of a cooler climate, people living farther south continued to enjoy a relatively high standard of living.

With the warm-up of the Midwest around 750, and the introduction of a new variety of maize, a new period, the Mississippian, developed. The fortified city of Cahokia, located near present-day St. Louis, was the center of Mississippian culture, which appears to have formed from flourishing Gulf Coast and lower Mississippi Valley societies. Cahokia began around 950 and lasted until roughly 1450. At its peak around 1100, Greater Cahokia was probably home to as many as 50,000 people, of whom up to 15,000 lived in the capital itself. This was North America's largest settlement until Philadelphia took over the distinction shortly after 1800. Other major Mississippian cities included Moundville, Etowah, and Spiro.

In addition to its sheer size, a distinguishing feature of Cahokia was its earthen platform mounds. The largest was originally more than a hundred feet high and with more area than a football field. People built wooden platforms on some of the mounds to serve as palaces or mausoleums. They also erected huge (30-inch-diameter) posts on the mounds and in the plazas adjacent to the mounds. These posts may have had ritual and/or astronomical significance. Cahokia's trade networks were huge, stretching north to the Great Lakes, east to the Atlantic Ocean, south to the Gulf of Mexico, and west to Texas. They may even have extended to Mexico. Food, largely including corn, beans, and squash, was abundant, and people built wattle-and-daub houses beside their fields on the outskirts of the city. Characterized by a focus on rank and power, Mississippian ceremonialism was, along with art, cosmology, and other aspects of the culture, sophisticated and rich.

Northeast

The region characterized as Northeast encompasses close to a million square miles. It extends from the Atlantic Ocean westward to where the woodlands shade into prairie, and from the mid-Atlantic area north to the boreal forest. Geologically, the Appalachian Mountains and the Great Lakes dominate the region, which is well watered and drained by major rivers such as the Saint Lawrence, Hudson, Ohio, and Susquehanna. Almost all Northeastern Indians spoke Algonquian or, to a lesser extent, Iroquoian languages. The first people probably arrived from the southwest at least 12,000 years ago, moving north with the big game and the receding glaciers. Food staples by about 4500 BCE included deer, caribou, and sea mammals. Most people may have congregated along the coast, but, owing to the raised sea levels since that period, any sites of early human coastal habitation would be well underwater. With a general warming from about 3000 BCE, the variety of foods in the Northeast increased to include hickory trees, abundant and reliable river fish runs, and many smaller mammals and fowl as well. Technological innovation grew as well to include fishhooks and nets, woodworking tools, dugout canoes (birchbark in the north), and soapstone bowls.

People in the region began using pottery around 1000 BCE. Evidence suggests that the custom did not arrive from the south, as might be expected. Local residents may have either invented it independently or learned it from contacts in the far northwest or even from the far northeast—Scandinavia and northern Europe. Around this time, people began smoking and cultivating tobacco. By roughly 2,000 years ago, small, nomadic hunter-gatherer-fisher communities lived in rectangular houses generally made of poles covered with slabs of bark. Corpses were sprinkled with red ochre powder and buried with a variety of ornaments and tools and with tobacco and pipes. Adena artifacts and mounds appear as far east as the eastern Great Lakes and western New York; however, in general the Northeast was not heavily influenced by Mississippian cultural traditions.

It was not until about 1000 that Northeast Indians—notably, the Iroquois (Haudenosaunee) of New York—began to cultivate maize, beans, squash, and sunflowers using slash-and-burn agricultural techniques. With this development, populations increased and became somewhat more sedentary. Competition for arable land, combined with the Iro-

quoian desire to dominate the region economically, was a major factor in two developments: (1) the dramatic expansion of warfare, along with ritualistic forms of war-related activities, including, in some areas, cannibalism, and (2) the formation of the Haudenosaunee Confederacy, or Iroquois League, by Hiawatha (Aionwantha) and Deganawidah (The Peacemaker), probably in the twelfth century.

The Iroquois League was a remarkable peace treaty among five nations: Cayuga, Mohawk, Oneida, Onondaga, and Seneca. Freed from internecine warfare, the League's member nations were free to turn their attentions without, which they did with astonishing effectiveness, ultimately dominating an area from the Hudson to the Ohio River Valley and the Saint Lawrence to the Susquehanna. Iroquoians generally lived in heavily fortified towns surrounded by fields of crops. Descent within families and clans, as well as political leadership, was matrilineal. Some clans had their own wooden houses, which could be up to 400 feet long. Among their ceremonies was the False Face Society, whose members lured curing forest spirits into homes through the use of grotesque carved masks.

Although some Algonquian people south of the Saint Lawrence region grew crops, in general they relied less on agriculture and more on hunting, gathering, and fishing (fish, shellfish, and sea mammals). Instead of longhouses, Algonquians tended to live in dome-shaped wigwams covered with sheets of birch bark, slabs of elm or conifer bark, mats, or hides. People transported their goods on sleds, pulled by men, or in canoes. A seasonal routine prevailed in which people availed themselves of the richness of the sea in summer, of running fish near rapids in spring and fall, and of interior hunting grounds in winter. Their fishing and trapping technology was highly sophisticated, and the ratio of labor to comfort was, in general, quite favorable. People used shell beads, called wampum, to maintain tribal records and during some ceremonies.

Subarctic

The harsh Subarctic was another region in which life changed relatively little in several thousand years. The Subarctic is characterized by the well-watered boreal forest. Long, cold winters, followed by springs filled with biting insects, limited the aboriginal population considerably. The two main language groups were Athapaskan (Dene), mainly in the west, and Algonquian, mainly in the east.

Despite the challenging climate, trade networks, which became quite extensive, began at least 10,000 years ago. The Laurel culture of Manitoba and northern Ontario (ca. 1000 BCE–800 CE) was characterized by coiled, impressed, incised, and fired pottery. Warfare tended to be small-scale and local, especially in the east. Religious traditions varied through the vast region of the Subarctic. If there was a common theme, it was respect for all of nature and the existence of natural powers, which might be acquired or accessed by means of fasting or spirit quests.

Depending on locations, people hunted caribou and moose, the big game, with stone blades and snares. They moved around using snowshoes and canoes, living in bark- or hide-covered, pole-frame houses or tents. After they acquired the bow and arrow, between 1,000 and 2,000 years ago, they began driving moose and caribou into corrals or lakes, where they were shot. Fowl and smaller animals also were snared or shot. Among the many tools, clothing and other items made from animal parts included the ubiquitous *babiche,* or semisoftened rawhide, that was used for everything from snares to netting and bowstrings. People tended to travel overland, although canoes made of bark or moose hide were not uncommon in some areas.

Arctic

The Arctic, 12,000 miles across from the western Aleutian Islands to Greenland, is, in its way, a land of great contrasts. During most of the year it is covered by ice and snow. In the short summer, under a sun that never sets, the tundra blooms, and water returns to its liquid form. The coastal people in the Arctic are the Inuit, while people living in the interior are considered Indians. Roughly 10,000 years ago, people in the Aleutian Islands were building oval, semisubterranean whalebone and driftwood houses covered with sod, which they entered through the roof. As the sea level stabilized, around 5,000 years ago, coastal villages became more established. Much of the interior west at that time was grassland—the perfect environment for bison—which early Indians burned to ward off forest encroachment. In other parts of the Arctic, people ate sea mammals (such as seal and walrus), polar bear, birds, and, where available, fish. By about 2000 BCE, people in northern Alaska were living in protoigloos (houses entered through a sloping passageway); these people heated and cooked with driftwood- or

bone-fed fires. To the east, people lived mainly in hide tents.

People now known as Dorset lived in the far northeast from about 500 BCE until about 900 (1500 in northern Quebec and Labrador). These people depended mainly on sea mammals for meat, hides, and cooking oil. They dressed in fur parkas; made bone, ivory, and wood carvings; and lived in igloos, or domed shelters of snow blocks. They apparently pulled their sleds themselves without the aid of dogs. They hunted seals with spears, but not with the bow and arrow, at blowholes and on the ice's edge. In the west, people of the so-called Norton culture began using pottery and building permanent settlements. In the far north and west, people began the tradition of wearing highly polished plugs of stone or bone (labrets) in their lower lips or cheeks about 2,500 years ago. Coastal residents along the Bering Strait began using highly maneuverable kayaks and, for whaling, more substantial umiaks, as well as special knives and harpoons. With a more stable food supply, people were able to build large villages of up to several hundred homes. Their society grew wealthy and stratified. They also developed sophisticated artistic traditions, which were influenced by their contact with people in northeast Asia, along with technological innovations that included iron blades of hammered iron and copper and dogsleds. This pre-Inuit, or so-called Thule, culture was well established in Alaska and far northwestern Canada by 1000 CE and throughout most of the rest of the Arctic shortly thereafter. At about this time, the Thule encountered another group of intrepid explorers, the Norse.

By about 1500, then, between 2 million to as many as 18 million people lived in North America. The highest population densities were in the salmon-rich communities of the Northwest Coast and in parts of California, as well as among some villages in the Northeast, Midwest, and Southeast. As might be expected across such a vast land, cultural traditions were extremely diverse. Some groups barely survived in the harshest climates of the Great Basin and the Subarctic, while others enjoyed plenty of food year-round. Some groups had changed relatively little for thousands of years, while others had developed numerous complex, sophisticated forms of social organization, religious practice, and artistic traditions. In all cases, however, the appearance of large and permanent groups of non-Natives, begin-

ning about 1500, introduced an element of change that was to have the most profound effects on native societies over the following several hundred years.

Barry M. Pritzker

See also Adena Civilization; Agriculture; Ancestral Puebloan Culture; Archaeology and the First Americans; Athapaskan Peoples; Basketry; Bering Strait Theory; Buffalo; Cahokia; Dalles Trading Area; Demographics, Historical; False Face Society; Haudenosaunee Confederacy, Political System; Hiawatha; Hohokom Culture; Hopewell Culture; Kennewick Man; Mississippian Culture; Mogollon Culture; Mound Cultures of North America; Na-Dene Peoples; Natchez Culture; Paleo-Indians; Potlatch; Pottery; Totem Poles; Trade; Wampum.

References and Further Reading
Campbell, Lyle, and Marianne Mithun, eds. 1979. *The Languages of Native America.* Austin: University of Texas Press.
Carlson, Roy L., ed. 1982. *Indian Art Traditions of the Northwest Coast.* Burnaby, B.C.: Archaeology Press, Simon Fraser University.
Champagne, Duane, ed. 1994. *Chronology of Native North American History.* Detroit, MI: Gale Research.
Collins, June McCormick. 1974. *Valley of the Spirits.* Seattle: University of Washington Press.
Cordell, Linda S. 1984. *Prehistory of the Southwest.* Boston: Academic Press.
Dickason, Olive P. 1992. *Canada's First Nations: A History of Founding Peoples.* Norman: University of Oklahoma Press.
Dobyns, Henry F. 1983. *Their Number Became Thinned.* Knoxville: University of Tennessee Press.
Dumond, D. E. 1977. *The Eskimos and Aleuts.* London: Thames and Huston.
Fagan, Brian M. 1995. *Ancient North America.* London and New York: Thames and Hudson.
Galloway, Patricia, ed. 1989. *The Southeastern Ceremonial Complex: Artifacts and Analysis.* Lincoln: University of Nebraska Press.
Gibbon, Gary, ed. 1998. *Archaeology of Prehistoric Native America.* New York: Garland Publishing.
Ives, John W. 1990. *A Theory of Northern Athapaskan Prehistory.* Boulder, CO: Westview Press.
Jennings, Jesse D. 1983. *Ancient North Americans.* San Francisco: W. H. Freeman.
Jennings, Francis. 1984. *The Ambiguous Iroquois Empire.* New York: W.W. Norton.
Johansen, Bruce E. 2005. *Native Peoples of North America.* Westport, CT: Praeger.
Kehoe, Alice Beck. 1992. *North American Indians,* 2nd ed. Upper Saddle River, NJ: Prentice Hall.

Kroeber, A. 1939. *Cultural and Natural Areas of Native North America*. Berkeley: University of California Press.

Laughlin, William, and Albert B. Harper, eds. 1979. *The First Americans: Origins, Affinities, and Adaptations*. New York: Gustav Fischer.

Mason, Ronald J. 1981. *Great Lakes Archaeology*. New York: Academic Press.

Maxwell, Moreau S. 1985. *Prehistory of the Eastern Arctic*. Orlando and London, FL: Academic Press.

Nichols, George P., ed. 1988. *Holocene Human Ecology in Northeastern North America*. New York: Plenum Press.

Paterek, Josephine. 1994. *Encyclopedia of American Indian Costume*. Santa Barbara, CA: ABC-CLIO.

Pauketat, Timothy, and Diana DiPaulo Loren, eds. 2005. *North American Archaeology*. Malden, MA: Blackwell Publishing.

Pritzker, Barry M. 1998. *Native Americans: An Encyclopedia of History, Culture and Peoples*. 2 vols. Santa Barbara, CA: ABC-CLIO.

Ross, Thomas E., and Tyrel G. Moore, eds. 1987. *A Cultural Geography of North American Indians*. Boulder, CO: Westview Press.

Sturtevant, William, ed. 1978. *Handbook of North American Indians*. Washington, DC: Smithsonian Institution.

Swanton, John R. 1946, reprinted 1979. *The Indians of the Southeastern United States*. Bureau of American Ethnology Bulletin 137. Washington, DC: Smithsonian Institution. Bureau of American Ethnology Bulletin 137.

Tanner, Helen Hornbeck, ed. 1987. *Atlas of Great Lakes Indian History*. Norman: University of Oklahoma Press.

Wedel, Waldo R. 1961. *Prehistoric Man on the Great Plains*. Norman: University of Oklahoma Press.

Wright, Gary A. 1984. *People of the High Country*. New York: Peter Lang.

Wright, J. Leitch, Jr. 1981. *The Only Land They Knew*. New York: The Free Press.

Indians in the Colonial Era and the American Revolution
(1500 to 1800)

You who are wise must know,
that different Nations
have different conceptions.

　　—Canassatego, an Onondaga
　　　　Haudenosaunee addressing
　　　　English colonial officials in 1744

This essay focuses primarily on the Indian nations who lived in what is now the United States between 1492 and 1800. Within its limited length, many Indian nations and many significant themes cannot be addressed. But the inquisitive reader is invited to explore the rest of this encyclopedia and the many other volumes that have been written about the First Nations of the Americas.

For the First Nations and for Europeans and non-Indian Americans, the year 1492 is indeed a major turning point in history, but is also part of a continuum. Far less than 5 percent of the human history of the Americas has occurred since 1492 because far more than ten thousand years of Indian history had already shaped the Western Hemisphere. Both the First Nations and the Europeans brought into 1492 all the ideas and trends that their respective cultures had developed during the previous centuries.

Thus the actions of both the First Nations and the Europeans were shaped by their prior experiences. For example, the First Nations in the Southwest had experienced a collapse of some of their major societies due to setbacks such as droughts (especially 1276–1299), as well as wars with other Indian nations. The Pueblo and other peoples in the Southwest, who had survived droughts and the other challenges, confronted the Spanish invasion of the early 1500s as yet another challenge in a sequence of challenges, not simply as "the" challenge. A comparable series of crises prior to 1492 occurred to the east: from areas such as eastern Oklahoma and eastern Iowa, eastward throughout the Mississippi and Ohio Valleys, and all the way to the Southeastern Atlantic coast. Many of the various cultures known collectively today as the Mound Builders collapsed at different times during the centuries prior to 1492. Thus the Creeks in the Southeast, one of the surviving cultures of the pre-1492 Mound Builders, perceived Spanish invasions in the

early 1500s as another in a series of challenges. In the Northeast, as early as 1142, a leader known as The Peacemaker inspired the establishment of a new confederacy among five previously warring nations: the Mohawks, Oneidas, Onondagas, Cayugas, and Senecas. The Iroquois Confederacy—the Haudenosaunee, or People of the Longhouse—survived despite the collapse of several trading partners and sometime rivals living to the west of them—several of the Mound Builders societies. The long-lived experience of the Haudenosaunee living on the eastern periphery of the Mound Builders carried over after 1492 when new trading partners and sometime rivals—the French, Dutch, and English colonists—placed the Haudenosaunee on the periphery again. This time, instead of turning their philosophical, diplomatic, and trading skills westward toward the Mound Builders, they turned eastward to deal with the Europeans.

Of course, the Europeans were also products of their recent past. While Indian nations were still slowly regrouping after droughts and cultural collapses, the Europeans were still striving to cope with the trauma of the Black Death (bubonic plague). The severe traumas caused declines in populations on both sides of the Atlantic and raised a common question: had people lost the approval of their respective gods and spiritual pantheons? Another common factor on both sides of the Atlantic before 1492 caused continual upheaval: warfare. In Indian America before 1492, the presence of warfare as a factor of human life was manifested in the stockaded towns in the East and the fortified towns in the Southwest. Across the Atlantic, virtually all of Europe was at war, either nation to nation or with the Muslims. Spain brought to the Americas all the methods and legal constructs of their wars against the Muslims in the Iberian Peninsula, ongoing since 711 and only recently ended with their 1492 victory at Granada. In the 1580s the English transferred the methods of their imperial war against Ireland directly to the Roanoke colony in North Carolina. By fighting Muslims in Eastern Europe, Captain John Smith gained the military experience he then brought to Virginia. In 1624, he noted frankly that the current war between the

English at Jamestown and the Powhatan Indians was but an episode in human history:

> What growing state was there ever in the world which had not the like? Rome grew by oppression. . . .

The Significance of the Pre-1492 Worldviews of Indian America

American Indians and invading Europeans possessed very different worldviews. The specific details of the worldview held by each American Indian nation and each European nation were varied and complex, but one of the basic differences in overall philosophies related to the nature of creation itself. The spiritual foundation of most American Indian nations was that the world was made up of interdependent and equal beings: Humans and all other beings had separate mortal functions but equal spiritual identities (what might be termed equal "souls"). In contrast, Europeans believed that only humans had souls. For Europeans, the world was a divinely ordained hierarchy—what might be termed "the Genesis Pyramid." Humans, the only beings possessing souls, were atop this ecological pyramid. Beneath the humans were mortal beings that lacked souls and were thus objects or things intended for use by the superior humans.

These differences in worldviews clashed in many ways, but for the First Nations one of the most significant conflicts was when furbearing animals in the north and deerskins in the south became commodities in trade with the Europeans. Taking pelts and skins, along with the meat, for local use was part of the interdependent worldview that Indian hunters followed in the past. Now the demand for animals was part of a larger and vicious cycle: If Indians did not hunt enough, they could not buy enough guns from their local European ally to defend their nations against their European and local Indian enemies. They were compelled to kill more animals or face national defeat. Many religious and political leaders during the centuries after 1492 called for a rejection of the European trade goods and a return to traditional ways, but the appeals did not square with the realities of national life and death. Given the circumstances, it is not surprising that so many of the Indian nations involved in European trade had whole segments of their people accept one form or another of Christianity, many trying to layer the new religion onto traditional beliefs: After all, if you were a Christian, you were comfortably on top of the Genesis Pyramid. Animals were no longer equal souls; they were now objects ordained by the European god to serve the needs of humans. And, although human slavery had been a part of some Indian cultures prior to 1492, the enslavement of other Indians became another major source of wealth in the race to make an Indian nation strong enough to survive the new realities. Further, the example of all the Europeans, even the English Quakers, showed that the enslavement of Indians and then Africans was an integrated part of the European economy and Christianity. Despite the appeal of alternatives, most Indian individuals resisted conversion to Christianity, but they struggled to survive economically while trying to maintain their traditional religions. The final choice was apathy. The paradox of all these choices continued after 1800 and remains a dilemma for Indian people in the twenty-first century.

Differing worldviews often emerged during diplomatic encounters. For example, in 1734, the Creek leader Tomochichi set sail for England as an emissary to demonstrate the Creeks' support of the new colony of Georgia. When he met George II, Tomochichi was carrying eagle feathers that had been passed throughout the Creek Confederacy to signify unity of purpose. King George was referred to by his own people by what was also the symbol of his power: "the Crown." The eagle feathers represented a consensus of the Creek people, while the Crown represented a hierarchy over "subjects." Each nation pledged friendship to the other (the king did not stress the point that England, by the "right of discovery," considered the Creeks to be subjects). After the meeting, Tomochichi was asked by the Earl of Egmont, a trustee of the Georgia colony, if he was impressed by the king's palace and England in general. Tomochichi replied that, while the English had more material goods than the Creeks, the English were probably not any happier than Indians and that "the English lived worse than the Creeks who were a more innocent people." Before he returned to his homeland, Tomochichi also explained that he was uncomfortable around only one man: the archbishop of Canterbury, who appeared to him to be a formidable conjurer.

The roles of women reflect the spiritual teachings of balance that most Indian nations followed,

as women balanced men both politically and economically. A Creek leader known only as the Woman of Cofitachique encountered Hernando de Soto in 1539 but was unable to persuade him to enter her country peacefully. Instead, he took her hostage and enslaved many of her people to bear the supplies of his expedition. Among the Cherokees, the duties of Gigau (Beloved Woman) demonstrate the significance that women brought to the Cherokee nation, just as the Clan Mothers among the Haudenosaunee balanced the male leaders. During the era of the American Revolution, Nancy Ward, the Cherokees' Beloved Woman, chose to support the Cherokee majority who sought neutrality during the war, while among the Haudenosaunee during the same era, the Mohawk leader Mary (Molly) Brant encouraged Haudenosaunee alliances with the British. While their decisions may in retrospect be criticized, the fact is that no white woman during the American Revolution, including Abigail Adams or Martha Washington, had a small fraction of these Indian women's authority or status. In fact, it was the status of Indian women within the First Nations that caused some white women, captured by Indians during colonial wars, to refuse to return to white settlements after the wars. Other women fled to Indian communities voluntarily. The security and happiness that these women found are illustrated by a servant woman, possibly black, who had fled to live among a Haudenosaunee nation, probably the Oneidas, shortly before or during the American Revolution. In 1784 at Fort Stanwix, New York, she talked with François Barbé-Marbois, a French colleague of the Marquis de Lafayette. Barbé-Marbois decided to draw her out because

> her color and bearing did not seem quite savage. I asked her in English who she was. She pretended at first not to understand. Pressed with my questions she told me that she had formerly served at the home of a planter in the State of New York, but that she had tired of the position of a servant and had fled, and that the Indians had welcomed her, and that she lived very happily among them. 'The whites,' she told me, 'treated me harshly. I saw them take rest while they made me work without a break. I ran the risk of being beaten, or of dying of hunger, if through fatigue or laziness I refused to do what I was told. Here I have no master, I am the equal of all the women in the tribe, I do what I please without anyone's

saying anything about it, I work only for myself,—I shall marry if I wish and be unmarried again when I wish. Is there a single woman as independent as I in your cities?'

For Indian people after 1492, perhaps the greatest loss, the greatest trauma, was not the steep drop in population due to war and disease, although that was traumatic enough—on average, only 10 percent of any particular Indian nation survived. It may not have even been the political, geographic, or personal family losses. Perhaps the greatest loss with the greatest effect over the centuries was spiritual. Why did the spiritual forces with whom Indians had communicated for centuries, even thousands of years, not intervene when the Europeans turned to conquest, as all Europeans eventually did? This concern not only raised a philosophical issue, it caused some to doubt the religious leaders who were trying to continue the Indian religions of the past. In turn, their concern was another factor that made the various Christian faiths of the newly arrived Europeans more attractive. One of the most eloquent and poignant philosophical responses was by an Aztec poet in Mexico. This anonymous poet wrote the following lines about the year 1523, two years after the Spaniards and their Indian allies overran the Aztec capital at Tenochtitlan and the sister city state of Tlatelolco:

> Nothing but flowers and songs of sorrow
> are left in Mexico and Tlatelolco
> where once we saw warriors and wise
> men.
> We know it is true
> that we must perish
> for we are mortal men.
> You, the Giver of Life,
> you have ordained it.
> We wander here and there
> in our desolate poverty.
> We are mortal men.
> We have seen bloodshed and pain
> where once we saw beauty and valor.
> We are crushed to the ground;
> we lie in ruins.
> There is nothing but grief and suffering
> in Mexico and Tlatelolco
> where once we saw beauty and valor.
> Have you grown weary of your servants?
> Are you angry with your servants,
> O Giver of Life?

Columbus and the Right of Discovery: Rapacious Fiction Turned into Legal Fact

The voyage of Columbus in 1492 set in motion traumatic changes in the histories of the First Nations and the Europeans, but it also has a direct relevance to the laws and legal issues of the twenty-first century. The United States still claims that the so-called right of discovery makes the U.S. government sovereign over Indian people and all the lands they once occupied or continue to occupy. The United States is not alone in this position, for the doctrine of the right of discovery provides the initial legal foundation for Canada and for all the other internationally recognized nations whose boundaries lie within the Western Hemisphere. The convoluted history of the right of discovery begins in 1492 when Columbus set sail from Spain carrying a document from the Spanish monarchs proclaiming that any land and peoples Columbus might "discover" would automatically become, respectively, the property and the subjects of the sovereign rulers of Spain. In 1493 and again in 1494, Pope Alexander VI sanctioned the right of discovery through the sacred intervention of the Catholic Church, thereby making the right of discovery a religious as well as a political principle. The pope also sanctioned the division of the entire Western Hemisphere between Spain and Portugal. Not surprisingly, the Catholic monarchs of other nations including England and France resented this, and they subsequently sent out their own ships, declaring their own nations' rights of discovery (England asserted the right of discovery following the 1497 voyage of John Cabot, while France claimed the right of discovery after the 1524 voyage of Giovanni de Verrazano). After the American Revolution, the new United States claimed that its new nation had inherited England's right of discovery.

On March 29, 2005, the United States Supreme Court case delivered its decision in *City of Sherrill, New York v. Oneida Indian Nation of New York et al.* Justice Ruth Bader Ginsburg wrote the majority opinion that ruled against the Oneidas. Only one of nine Justices dissented: Justice John P. Stevens. In *Sherill*, Justice Ginsburg and the Supreme Court blithely reaffirmed the doctrine of discovery:

> Under the 'doctrine of discovery,' *County of Oneida v. Oneida Indian Nation of N.Y.*, 470 U.S. 226, 234 (1985) (*Oneida II*), 'fee title to the lands occupied by Indians when the colonists arrived became vested in the sovereign—first the

discovering European nation and later the original States and the United States.'

The doctrine of discovery has legal precedents in United States law, especially since 1823 when the Supreme Court asserted the right of discovery in *Johnson and Graham's Lessee v. William M'Intosh*. But the institution of slavery had precedents too, and the Supreme Court has ceased affirming that abomination.

The United States as a Transformed "Wilderness"

In the *Sherill* case, Justice Ginsburg also contended that, with the arrival of the whites, the land was "converted from wilderness." In fact, the land was the domain of the Haudenosaunee—the Iroquois Confederacy, which in spite of all the odds survives to the present day. When the Europeans first encountered the Haudenosaunee, they lived in towns and grew extensive crops of corn and other foods. Their extensive trade routes crisscrossed New York and, linking with the trade routes of other First Nations, reached the Atlantic Coast, the Gulf of Mexico, and the western Great Lakes. Thus Ginsburg's contention that New York State was a wilderness is a lie, but it is an old lie. It is a thinly veiled restatement of *vacuum domicilium*, another legal term inherited from the era of Columbus. The Latin term *vacuum domicilium* means "lacking habitation"—empty land that is not used. By defining Indian homelands in this manner, Europeans asserted that the lands were wild and open to settlement. The concept of *vacuum domicilium* was so widely accepted that the English philosopher Sir Thomas More incorporated the idea in his famous *Utopia*, published in 1516. In part, More's *Utopia* is a summary of the rights of the European conquerors in the Western Hemisphere (those who use "utopian" to mean "ideal" need to reread the book!). In More's view, these conquerors, these Utopians, are of course idealistic and never venal, but they also understand that a just war can be carried out if land is not used:

> If the natives won't do what they're told, they're expelled from the area marked out for annexation. If they try to resist, the Utopians declare war—for they [the Utopians] consider war perfectly justifiable, when one country denies another its natural right to derive nourishment from any soil which the original owners are not using themselves.

Discovery and the Rights of Indians

The right of discovery doctrine was a magic wand that the Europeans claimed gave them absolute sovereignty over the Indian peoples they encountered. Under the doctrine, Indian nations ceased to be sovereign and were defined as protectorates at best and at worst entirely subordinate. The right of discovery also automatically made every individual Indian a "subject" of a European government. Thus, if Indians rose up against a European colonial power, they were legally regarded as "rebels" who were resisting a legitimate sovereign government; they were committing treason. Under European law at the time, rebels had no human rights. This was extended specifically to Indians in 1512 by the Spanish: The "Requirement" warned Indians that rebellions would not be perceived as wars between equal states, but rather as wars by the Spanish against "vassals who do not obey and refuse to receive their lord and resist and contradict him." Legally, then, the warriors and their families had no rights. In battle, all could be slaughtered. If any were captured, they had no rights as prisoners of war: They could be enslaved or killed, and their property could be confiscated.

If Indians were treated humanely—despite their "treason"—such treatment was regarded by the Europeans as an act of mercy, not of justice. Efforts to mitigate this harsh legal reality were occasionally made by European political leaders and religious reformers, such as the sixteenth-century Spanish priest-philosopher Bartolomé de Las Casas, but they have always been in the minority. Furthermore, even white reformers like Las Casas believed that the white occupation of most Indian lands and the triumph of Western civilization were inevitable, but that the process of assimilating the Indians into this inevitable future should be carried out through the highest concepts of white ethics and justice. This "Las Casas attitude" is exemplified by prominent white philosophers such as Roger Williams (seventeenth century), Benjamin Franklin (eighteenth century), Helen Hunt Jackson (nineteenth century), and John Collier (twentieth century).

The Impact of European Trade Goods

The impact of European trade goods caused Indian nations to adapt in ways that would alter their pre-1492 cultures. An example of this phenomenon after 1492 was observed in 1634 by Harmen Meyndertsz van den Bogaert. He ventured westward into the Mohawk Valley from Fort Orange, a Dutch trading post established in 1619 at what is now Albany, New York. He was one of the first Dutch traders to enter Mohawk territory, part of the Haudenosaunee (Iroquois Confederacy). But he discovered that trade goods had preceded him, perhaps brought in along Indian trading routes such as those that linked the Mohawks to New England, to French Canada, or to English Virginia. On December 13, 1634, van den Bogaert arrived at the Mohawk town of Onakahoncka:

> We came to their first castle that stood on a high hill. There were only 36 houses, row on row in the manner of streets, so that we easily could pass through. These houses are constructed and covered with the bark of trees, and are mostly flat above. Some are 100, 90, or 80 steps long; 22 or 23 feet high. There were also some interior doors made of split planks furnished with iron hinges. In some houses we also saw ironwork: iron chains, bolts, harrow teeth, iron hoops, spikes, which they steal when they are away from here.

Van den Bogaert's assumption that the iron goods were stolen is an indication of a European attitude all too typical of early contact. But what is most remarkable in his account is his description of the traditional longhouses that the Mohawks had already fitted with plank doors swinging on iron hinges. Did these doors with iron hinges affect the interior, communal nature of the longhouses, each of which was the home of several matrilineal families under the guidance of one of the oldest women? Subtle changes brought by the installation of iron hinges were more than matched at this Mohawk town by a far less subtle change: Smallpox had already broken out in the town. Sadly, both iron hinges and smallpox were the result of trade. Gradually, the Mohawks and their neighbors moved out of longhouses and into smaller homes to lessen the impact of the infectious smallpox virus.

One of the major items of trade was the horse. For example, by the end of the 1600s in the Southeast, the Creeks traded deerskins, furs, and corn to the Apalachees in Florida for Apalachee horses. The Creeks then traded most of the horses to the English. But this trade was constantly interrupted by wars between the two peoples—a warfare often encouraged by the rival European powers in the region: the Spanish, the English, and the French. In 1701, the

Spanish persuaded the Apalachees to raise the prices of horses, and the Creeks went to war as a result. In the Southwest, horses became important trade items, especially after 1680 when the Pueblo leader Popé and his allies at least temporarily liberated the Pueblos and other Indian nations in the Southwest from Spanish rule. Plains Indians soon traded, and occasionally raided, for horses raised by the Pueblos or Spaniards. After the Spanish reconquered the Pueblo nations, the Pueblos stayed on their horses and even served as mercenary cavalry for the Spanish. For example, in 1720 on the Platte River in Nebraska, forty-five Spanish troops supported by sixty Pueblos fought Pawnee and Oto warriors, who fought on foot. The battle went against the Spanish troops, but a courageous charge from some of their mounted Pueblo allies saved the Spaniards from annihilation.

Trade with Europeans was important everywhere, including Alaska. In 1740, a young Russian scholar, Stephan Petrovich Krasheninnikov, accompanied Captain Vitus Bering on a voyage that led to Russia's claim to northwestern North America, including Alaska. Both the Russians and the Inupiats sought peaceful relations and trade, but Krasheninnikov noted that the Inupiats were already using iron knives. Thus by 1740, European trade goods had reached the Inupiats either through other First Nations or directly from Europeans.

What kinds of European goods were traded? In 1761, Sir William Johnson, Superintendent for Indian Affairs in the Northern Colonies, prepared a list. Johnson's list exemplifies how pervasive trade goods had become in the daily life of Indian peoples. Entitled "A List of Such Merchandise as is Usually sold to the Indians," Johnson included coarse woolen blankets of various colors (called strouds); "French Blankets in great Demand being better than ours" (even though the war with the French was ongoing!); English blankets; Welsh cottons; "Flowered Serges"; "Calicoes"; "Linnens & ready made Shirts, of all Sizes"; needles; awls; knives; "Jews Harps small & large"; "Stone & plain rings"; "Hawks bells'; horn combs; "Brass Wire different Sizes"; "Scizars & Razors"; "Looking Glasse"; Brass & tinn Kettles large & Small"; "Women & Childrens Worsted and Yarn Hose with [an ornamental pattern called] Clocks"; "Roll of Paper Tobacco. Also Leaf D[itt]o"; "[tobacco] Pipes long & Short"; "Red Leather trunks in Nests" (chests or suitcases in which ever smaller ones nested within a larger one); black and white wampum; "Silver Works . . . which the Indians wear"; "Tomahawks or small hatchets well made";

"Pipe Hatchets"; "Tobacco, & Snuff boxes"; "Pewter Spoons"; "Gilt Gill [four-ounce] Cups"; gunpowder; flints; "Small bar lead of l 1/2 lb each"; "Goose, Duck, & Pidgeon Shot"; fowling muskets; beaver and fox traps; iron spears for fishing and killing beavers; and "New England, or [New] York rum."

Captured by White People

"Captured by Indians" is a phrase that frequently appears in history books and has been a theme of novels and Hollywood movies. The records show that, after a European-Indian war, captured whites, from the north to the south, were returned to their European colonies. We have abundant accounts of this in what are termed "captivity narratives." But where are the accounts about the return of Indians "captured by white people"? The simple fact is that, after every war, which the whites eventually always won, Indian prisoners were typically sold into outright slavery or extended periods of servitude. For example, in 1599 Acoma, a pueblo atop a 350-foot mesa in what is now New Mexico, rose against Spanish invaders led by Juan de Oñate, but Oñate's troops successfully stormed the pueblo. Of Acoma's approximately 1500 inhabitants, 600 were killed, chose suicide by jumping off the mesa, or were murdered by the Spaniards after they had surrendered. Hundreds of others escaped. About 500 women and children and seventy or eighty men who had surrendered were taken prisoner. Prisoners were treated mercilessly by Oñate, who regarded them as rebels against a legitimate sovereign and hence without rights. Oñate sentenced twenty-four warriors who were over twenty-five years of age to slavery for life—after the Spaniards chopped a foot off each of the warriors, as a reminder of the danger of resistance to Spanish will. Two Hopis, seized along with the Acoma warriors, had their right hands cut off and sent back to their mesa-top towns as a warning to the Hopi people not to entertain any plans of war. Other men and women were sentenced to twenty years of slavery. Oñate dealt with the children of Acoma as follows:

> All of the children under twelve years of age I declare free and innocent of the grave offenses for which I punish their parents . . . . I place the girls under the care of the father commissary, Fray Alonso Martinez, in order that he, as a Christian and qualified person, may distribute them in the kingdom and elsewhere in

monasteries or other places where he thinks that they may attain the knowledge of God and the salvation of their souls.

The boys under twelve years of age I entrust to Vicente de Zaldivar Mendoza, my sargento mayor, in order that they may attain the same goal.

Also under this sentence, seventy girls—a considerable proportion of Acoma's future mothers—were taken to Mexico and distributed among various Catholic convents. As for the mesa-top town itself, Oñate ordered Acoma to be completely leveled, and it was not reoccupied until the people sentenced to twenty years of servitude could finally return and rebuild it.

After New England's King Philip's War (named after the Wampanoag leader King Philip, Metacomet), the Pilgrims and the Puritans believed that the surviving Indian prisoners had forfeited all rights and could be sentenced to work for whites in New England for specific lengths of time and that many could even be sold into slavery in the West Indies or elsewhere. Hundreds of Indian men, women, and children, including Philip's wife and son, were sold into slavery and shipped to Virginia, Spain, Portugal, the Azores, the Spanish West Indies, Bermuda, and the Mediterranean coasts, including Tangier.

Ultimately, all colonists, whether they were Catholic, Protestant, or Jewish, sold Indian slaves. Furthermore, some of the most enthusiastic suppliers of Indian slaves were other Indians. Indian slave traders captured other Indians from rival nations and sold them as slaves to European colonists, who shipped them out of ports such as Charleston, New York City, Montreal, and Quebec. By the late 1600s, for example, the Creeks in the Southeast constantly raided the Choctaws and brought columns of Choctaw prisoners to Charleston's slave market. In exchange, the Creeks obtained manufactured items such as kettles, guns, knives, woolen goods, calico dresses, shirts, brass earrings, and silver gorgets. By the mid-1700s, the Comanches and other Plains Indian nations were selling Indian captives as slaves to the Pueblos and Spaniards.

In addition, trade agreements and treaties between Indian nations and Europeans, in both the North and the South, often had the provision that the European trade was in part dependent on Indian willingness to capture and return any black slaves who escaped into Indian country. For example, in 1768, General Thomas Gage reported on the slave hunting of the Creeks:

> [T]he Creeks have restored such of the Negroe Slaves, as could be taken; they were also in pursuit of others, who made their escape from the Indian Towns, when they found they were to be delivered up. The Scalp of one of those Fugitives was brought in and delivered to the Commissary, which Circumstance will break that Intercourse between the Indians and Negroes, so much to be dreaded by all the Southern Provinces.

The value of Indians as deterrents to fugitive slaves was a constant in colonial history. The English names given to a few prominent eighteenth-century Cherokees speak for themselves: Slave Catcher of Chota, Slave Catcher of Kitruwa, Slave Catcher of Conutory, Slave Catcher of Tomatly, and Slave Catcher of Conasatchee.

The North was no different. For example, on October 4, 1774, the Oneida Haudenosaunee in what is now New York State, with the approval of the entire Iroquois Confederacy, agreed to provide New England Indians—including Narragansetts, Mohegans, Montauks, Pequots, and Niantics—with a portion of Oneida lands. In this treaty, the Oneidas and the British addressed the fact that blacks had intermarried or were living among these nations. This was regarded by the British as encouraging a potential refuge for the other blacks or mixed-race people who might later use the area as a base to stimulate a slave revolt. Thus the Oneidas agreed to a treaty provision that carefully defined how the land

> shall not be possessed by any persons, deemed of the said Tribes, who are descended from, or have intermixed with Negroes, or Mulattoes.

This policy also suggests one reason why the remnants of eastern Indians who did not remove from their homelands had, and continue to have, a mixed-race heritage.

African American history, Indian history, and colonial white history, as exemplified by the preceding evidence, are intertwined. The myth persists that the first black slaves were introduced into the English colonies in Virginia in 1619, when in fact no less a figure than Sir Francis Drake brought black slaves to the Roanoke Colony in 1586 (they were undoubtedly slaughtered when Drake agreed that the

colonists should leave Roanoke and return to England). Furtheremore, these were not the first enslaved Africans to arrive in what is now the United States. In 1526, the Spanish established a short-lived colony in the borderland of Georgia/Florida, bringing with them African slaves. These Africans managed to join with local Indians in driving out the Spanish, marking the first successful black slave revolt within the present borders of the United States. But interracial unity became the exception, not the rule. Both in the North and in the South, European powers promised to continue trading with the Peoples of the First Nations, with one of the conditions being that any escaped black slave encountered by a First Nation would be returned.

Epidemic Diseases

The First Nations had no immunities to diseases accidentally introduced by the Europeans. Diseases such as smallpox and the bubonic plague, combined with conquest and enslavement, wiped out 90 percent of Native populations. But direct contact with the invaders was not the only way diseases spread. At least one wave of epidemics was accidentally introduced by the Spanish into the Indian nations along the Florida coast between 1513 and 1521. The disease was unintentionally carried by Indian traders along the commercial network among Indian nations that had existed long before 1492. Along these trade routes, the epidemic reached the Seneca Nation in what is now western New York by 1525. Only one instance of intentional biological warfare is documented: in 1763 at Fort Pitt during the war organized by the Indian leader Pontiac. But whites took advantage of the diseases by expanding the settlements during epidemics and by using the coincidence of epidemics to attack Indian nations already weakened, as in 1622 when the Puritans attacked the Massachusetts nation. Epidemic diseases were also intensified whenever Europeans forced Indians into resettlements, such as California's Catholic missions, where Indians labored and died for the benefit of cross and empire. They lived in crowded conditions that made them more susceptible to epidemic diseases. The actual conditions at the missions contrast dramatically with the romance and beauty associated with the flowering grounds of today's tourist attractions.

The 1763 Treaty of Paris marked the end of the Seven Years' War, known in North America as the French and Indian War. No Indian diplomats were present. This treaty and the second Treaty of Paris in 1783 that ended the American Revolution are the most significant treaties in Indian history east of the Mississippi. The most significant impact of the 1763 Treaty on the First Nations was the transfer of Canada by France to Great Britain (a transfer based on France's right of discovery, which Britain now claimed to inherit). This clause forced all the Indian nations north of the Ohio River into a trade dependence on the British. Previously, while the French were in Canada, Indian nations could stand neutral, side with the French, or side with the British. After the treaty, they could no longer play one off against the other in trade agreements. Furthermore, the British decided to pay for the war at the same time it consolidated its new power. While this decision resulted in new taxes, which many of the white colonists opposed, it also meant that the British could charge the First Nations higher prices for trade goods because there was no competition from France. Even before the Treaty of Paris was signed, the Indian allies of the defeated French (Quebec had fallen in 1759) joined with a few of the Indian nations usually allied with the British to rally behind the Ottawa leader Pontiac.

Under the 1763 Treaty of Paris, Britain returned Cuba to Spain in exchange for Spanish-held Florida. When Spain abandoned Florida, however, she did not abandon her converted Catholic Indian populations. The Spanish feared that their Calusa and other Indian allies on the west coast of Florida would not fare well under British rule. Furthermore, about eighty Calusa families were devout converts to Catholicism. Interestingly, under the Spanish, the Calusas had also carried on their pre-1492 tradition by sailing back and forth to Cuba in seagoing canoes, trading. Spain decided to give refuge to the eighty Calusa families, and in 1763 the families made their way to Cuba, where they took up permanent residence. Ironically, these mission Indians reestablished an Indian presence on Cuba that the Spanish had annihilated two centuries earlier.

California Indians were also affected by the 1763 Treaty of Paris. After vacating Florida and turning it over to the British in exchange for Spain's right to reoccupy Cuba, Spain moved to secure the far western frontier by moving up the California coast. In addition to expanding Spanish holdings in North America, this effort was also intended to secure the area against possible pressures from both Russia and Britain. Spain established missions as stepping-stones in its occupation of coastal California, with

the first of twenty-one missions, San Diego de Alcalá, founded in 1769. California Indians were crowded into the missions to work for crown and cross, to be converted to Catholicism, to die of epidemics, and to be buried in mass graves.

The Era of the American Revolution (1763–1783)

The so-called era of the American Revolution (1763–1783) was actually an era of two parallel revolutions. The better-known one is that of the colonists who went to war against each other in their "war for independence." Paralleling that conflict were the revolutions and civil wars among American Indian nations, such as the revolution from 1763 to 1766 by the Ottawas and other Great Lakes Indians under Pontiac and the civil wars among the Cherokees and the Haudenosaunee during the American Revolution. By the 1760s, the dilemma among both Natives and colonists was how to effectively coordinate society after Britain no longer faced its French rival in Canada. While the stakes were as different as the cultures were, the dilemmas for the First Nations and for the whites (in both London and the colonies) were remarkably similar: How much change could the establishment safely concede, and how much change could the revolutionary thinkers push upon the old system before open warfare broke the societies apart? Like their colonial neighbors, the American Indian nations finally divided into factions. The differences and the similarities soon became a stew, called the American Revolution, a single continental cauldron.

The Treaty of Paris of 1783 ended that revolution, but, like its 1763 counterpart, no Indian representatives were present. Yet the British used the right of discovery to transfer to the United States jurisdiction over the Indian lands east of the Mississippi. Thereafter, the United States claimed, through the transfer, both the right of discovery and absolute sovereignty over Indian people. During the negotiations that led to the treaty, the original intent of the United States, at least as it was conveyed to their Spanish ally, was to establish a right of sovereignty over the land with regard to other non-Indian nations (such as Britain, Spain, and France). However, regarding Indian nations, the United States intended to claim only the right of preemption—the right of the United States to obtain Indian lands to the exclusion of other non-Indian powers. In Paris, in August 1782, the Spanish negotiator Conde de

Aranda (Pedro Pablo Abarca de Bolea) recorded, in his diary, a discussion he had with U.S. negotiator John Jay of New York. Regarding the lands that lay west of the English colonies, Aranda asserted:

"That territory belongs to free and independent nations of Indians, and you have no right to it."

John Jay replied:

"These are points to be discussed and settled between the Indians and ourselves. With respect to the Indians we claim the right of preemption; with respect to all other nations, we claim the sovereignty over the territory."

Once the treaty was signed, however, the bolder assertions of the United States to complete sovereignty, through the British transfer of the right of discovery, became clear to the British and to their Indian allies. This assertion was immediately challenged by the First Nations (and it has been challenged in court proceedings down to the present day). For example, during a May 1783 meeting with the commander at Niagara, a Mohawk chief, Aaron Hill (Kanonraron), expressed anger and amazement that the British could even think of breaking their honor and their treaties by granting the Patriots jurisdiction over the lands of the Haudenosaunee and other Indians. As reported on May 18, 1783, by the British commander Allan Maclean "exactly as translated":

[T]hey told me they never could believe that our King could pretend to Cede to America What was not his own to give, or that the Americans would accept from Him, What he had no right to grant. . . . That the Indians were a free People Subject to no Power upon Earth, that they were faithful Allies of the King of England, but not his Subjects . . . it was impossible . . . to imagine, that the King of England Should pretend to grant to the Americans, all the Whole Country of the Indians Lying between the Lakes and the fixed Boundaries, as settled in 1768 between the Colonies and the Indians. . . . That if it was really true that the English had basely betrayed them by pretending to give up their Country to the Americans Without their Consent, or Consulting them, it was an act of Cruelty and injustice that Christians *only* were capable of doing, that the

Indians were incapable of acting So . . . to friends & Allies, but that they did believe We had Sold & betrayed them.

Indian Treaties

The word "treaty" today has a specific legal definition in the United States: a formal agreement between nations ratified by the U.S. Senate. But the history of treaty making on both sides of the Atlantic is actually the history of diplomacy, because a treaty, broadly, is any formal agreement between nations. Before 1492, competing Indian nations throughout the Western Hemisphere conducted both war and formal diplomacy that led to agreements and treaties among themselves. Many First Nations, such as the Creeks and the Cherokees in the South and the Haudenosaunee in the North, were able to fight wars and negotiate treaties from positions of relative strength, factors enhanced by the European-American colonists' need for Indian allies in their own colonial wars with rival colonial powers. After the American Revolution, however, wars and treaties became increasingly one-sided in direct proportion to the United States' ever increasing population and economic power.

Thus while treaties in the 1790s still reflected at least some semblance of the balances of power evident before the American Revolution, after the War of 1812 treaty terms were decidedly weighted in favor of the United States, especially with regard to how much the United States could intrude in the affairs of Indian nations. The difference between earlier and later treaties is demonstrated by a comparison of the 1794 Treaty of Canandaigua made between the Haudenosaunee and United States with the 1868 Treaty of Fort Laramie made by the United States with the Lakotas and the Arapahos. Articles Two and Four of the 1794 treaty assert a clear separation of each signatory's jurisdiction. Article Two states: "The United States acknowledge [plural] the lands reserved to the Oneida, Onondaga, and Cayuga Nations to be their property; and the United States will never claim the same." Article Four declares that "the Six Nations, and of them, hereby engage that they will never claim any other lands within the boundaries of the United States; nor ever disturb the people of the United States." Article Two of the 1794 treaty also notes that the Six Nations has the clear right to determine whether any other Indian "friends" can live among them, noting that

"the United States will never . . . disturb them or either of the Six Nations, nor their Indian friends residing thereon and united with them, in the free use and enjoyment thereof: but the said reservations shall remain theirs, until they choose to sell the same to the people of the United States who have right to purchase." Future issues will be resolved through mutual negotiation "by the Six Nations or any of them, to the President of the United States, or the superintendent by him appointed."

Contrast this clear separation of jurisdiction with the 1868 treaty, which states in Article Two that the United States has the right to exert control—"the consent of the United States"—over which Indians can reside on the lands. The treaty also grants the United States a right to intrude into the affairs of the Indian nations: "The President may, at any time, order a survey of the reservation" and that "the United States may pass such laws on the subject of alienation and descent of property as between Indians and their descendants as may be thought proper." Thus, future issues would be resolved not through the mutual negotiation called for in the 1794 Treaty of Canandaigua, but by unilateral decisions by the United States government.

The Shawnee Quest for Pan-Indian Unity (1745–1813)

In 1745, the Shawnee Indians living along the Ohio River realized that it was time to halt the English colonial expansion to the east of them. The next year, 1746, the Shawnees began to promote new alliances among Indian nations east of the Mississippi. Such a pan-Indian movement was not yet necessary among Indian nations on the Pacific Coast, the Rockies, the Great Basin, or the Plains—they were still politically independent, although the Plains nations were increasingly dependent on trade either with the French to the east of them in the Mississippi Valley or with the Spanish in the Southwest. And in the Southwest, pan-Indian movements, such as that of Popé among the Pueblos, Apaches, and Navajos in the 1680s, had been overwhelmed by 1700. The Shawnees' vision of a pan-Indian movement intended to create a new Indian unity from the north to the south. This unity would be stronger than the regional alliances and confederacies that already existed, such as the networks of the Creek Confederacy and the Haudenosaunee (Iroquois Confederacy). The Shawnees had a unique perspective on the situation on the frontier because some of their nation

lived in the South, near and even among the Creeks, while others lived in the North. Neither the northern nor the southern Shawnees had the power of larger nations such as the Creeks, and so the Shawnees more readily realized Indian vulnerability.

In February 1746, the Shawnees sent emissaries throughout the Mississippi Valley and the Southeast trying to convince Indians to give up their old rivalries and unite against the Europeans. The Indians' dependence on white trade goods, however, constantly worked against the Shawnees' proposal, for the Europeans and then the United States could use trade agreements as diplomatic maneuvers to divide Indian nations. During the French and Indian War, the Shawnees at first sided with the British, but English immigrants forced the Shawnees to defend their homelands until peace was made by 1758. The Shawnees now attempted to mediate peaceful solutions, but in 1774 this effort collapsed when white frontiersmen again forced them into what became known as Lord Dunmore's War, named for the governor of Virginia. This spilled over into the American Revolution, where the Shawnees tried to stop the expansion of white frontiersmen who were allied with the Patriot cause. The Shawnees provided major leadership after the American War in battles against the expanding United States, helping to defeat Governor Arthur St. Clair in 1791 but suffering defeat in 1794 along with other Indian nations at the Battle of Fallen Timbers. Thereafter, the Shawnee vision continued to inspire many Indian people and would reach its culmination under the Shawnee leader Tecumseh. In 1813, Tecumseh was killed on a northern battlefield during the War of 1812 and his southern allies were also defeated. The Shawnee vision, ongoing since 1745–1746, died with Tecumseh.

The Flow of North American History after 1750

Events after 1750 forever altered the pulse of Indian history north of Mexico. For more than a thousand years before Columbus, and for two centuries after Columbus, American Indian history had been shaped from south to north. The great Indian civilizations of Mesoamerica had exerted their influence northward and eastward, creating wave after wave of cultural frontiers north of Mexico. Then Spanish conquistadors moving northward from occupied Mexico or from the Caribbean invaded the Southwest and the Southeast. By the middle of the eigh-

teenth century, however, the momentum had been altered. The Southern frontiers remained both important and dynamic, but, during the late 1600s and the early 1700s, events to the Northeast increasingly became the most important influences on all of American Indian history north of Mexico. By 1750, the primary locations of the events defining the destiny of the continent shifted. From 1750 until 1800, the vast continent north of Mexico was shaped primarily by events and decisions coming from the Northeast and, after 1800, from all areas east of the Mississippi.

In the centuries after 1800, as in the previous three centuries, there were at least four basic choices that Indian nations followed to survive as intact nations:

1. Spiritual reformations
2. Continued nonviolent resistance, both through negotiations such as treaties and in appeals to white laws and courts
3. Continued military resistance
4. Adaptation of white manufactured goods and technology

As for the United States, after 1800 it broke every colonial treaty it had inherited from the British and all of the more than 395 treaties that the United States made with Native nations.

The Triumph of the Arts and the Human Spirit

An encouraging conclusion to this survey is the fact that American Indians continued to produce a wide range of stunning art. This is evident in painting, wooden and stone sculpture, rock art, pottery, quillwork, and beadwork. Music and dance never ceased to be important, as both old and new music and dance sought to link the First Nations with continued spiritual inspiration or a reaffirmation of social bonds. Both before and after 1800, the First Nations never ceased to express the highest aesthetics and creative beauty of the human spirit.

Robert W. Venables

See also American Revolution, Native American Participation; Canandaigua, Treaty of; Canassatego; Doctrine of Discovery; Franklin, Benjamin; Haudenosaunee Confederacy, Political System; Mission System, Spanish; Mound Cultures of North America; Spanish Influence; Slavery; Tecumseh; Treaty

Diplomacy, with Summary of Selected Treaties; Tribal Sovereignty; Williams, Roger; Women in Native Woodland Societies.

References and Further Reading

Allen, Robert S. 1992. *His Majesty's Indian Allies: British Indian Policy in the Defence of Canada, 1774–1815*. Toronto, ON: Dundurn Press.

American State Papers, Class II, Indian Affairs. 1832. Vol. 4 of *American State Papers. Documents, Legislative and Executive, of the Congress of the United States*. Washington, DC: Gales and Seaton.

Anderson, Fred. 2000. *Crucible of War: The Seven Years' War and the Fate of Empire in British North America, 1754–1766*. New York: Alfred A. Knopf.

Anonymous. 1846. "The Early Records of Charleston." In *Chronicles of the First Planters of the Colony of Massachusetts Bay, from 1623 to 1636*. Edited by Alexander Young. Boston: Charles C. Little and James Brown.

Atkin, Edmond. [1755] 1967. *The Appalachian Frontier: The Edmond Atkin Report and Plan of 1755*. Edited by Wilbur R. Jacobs. Lincoln: University of Nebraska Press.

Barlowe, Arthur. 1955. "Discourse of the First Voyage." In *The Roanoke Voyages, 1584–1590*, Vol. 1. Edited by David Beers Quinn, 91–116. London: Hakluyt Society.

Beauchamp, William M. 1921. *The Founders of the New York Iroquois League and Its Probable Date: Researches and Transactions of the New York State Archaeological Association*. Vol. 3, No. 1. Rochester, NY: Lewis H. Morgan Chapter, New York State Archaeological Association.

Bemis, Samuel Flagg. 1962. *Jay's Treaty: A Study in Commerce and Diplomacy*, rev. ed. New Haven, CN: Yale University Press.

Berkhofer, Robert F., Jr. 1979. *The White Man's Indian*. New York: Random House Vintage Books.

Berlo, Janet C., and Ruth B. Phillips. 1998. *Native North American Art*. Oxford and New York: Oxford University Press.

Biggar, H. P., ed. 1924. *The Voyages of Jacques Cartier*. No. 11. Ottawa, ON: Publications of the Public Archives of Canada.

Billington, Ray Allen. 1974. *Westward Expansion: A History of the American Frontier*, 4th ed. New York: Macmillan.

Bolton, Herbert E. 1921. *The Spanish Borderlands*. New Haven, CN: Yale University Press.

Bond, Richmond P. 1952. *Queen Anne's American Kings*. Oxford: Oxford University Press.

Boyd, Julian P., ed. 1938. *Indian Treaties Printed by Benjamin Franklin, 1736–1762*. Philadelphia, PA: Historical Society of Pennsylvania.

Bradford, William. 1952. *Of Plymouth Plantation*. Edited by Samuel Eliot Morison. New York: Random House.

Bradford, William, and Edward Winslow. [1622] 1966. *Journall of the English Plantation at Plimoth*. Ann Arbor, MI: Readex Microprint.

Bradford, William, and Edward Winslow. [1622] 1865. *Mourt's Relation or Journal of the Plantation at Plimouth*. Boston: John Kimball Wiggin.

Calloway, Colin G. 1994. *The World Turned Upside Down: Indian Voices from Early America*. Boston: Bedford/St. Martin's.

Calloway, Colin G. 1995. *The American Revolution in Indian Country: Crisis and Diversity in Native American Communities*. Cambridge, UK, and New York: Cambridge University Press.

Calloway, Colin G. 1997. *New Worlds for All: Indians, Europeans, and the Remaking of Early America*. Baltimore, MD: Johns Hopkins University Press.

Campisi, Jack. 1988. "The Oneida Treaty Period, 1783–1838." In *The Oneida Indian Experience: Two Perspectives*. Edited by Jack Campisi and Laurence M. Hauptman. Syracuse, NY: Syracuse University Press.

Cappon, Lester J., et al. 1976. *Atlas of Early American History: The Revolutionary Era, 1760–1790*. Princeton, NJ: Princeton University Press.

Caughey, John. 1938. *McGillivray of the Creeks*. Norman: University of Oklahoma Press.

Cave, Alfred A. 1996. *The Pequot War*. Amherst: University of Massachusetts Press.

Champlain, Samuel de. 1907. *Voyages of Samuel de Champlain, 1604–1618*. Edited by W. L. Grant. New York: Charles Scribner's Sons.

Coe, Michael, Dean Snow, and Elizabeth Benson. 1986. *Atlas of Ancient America*. New York: Facts on File.

Cohen, Felix. [1942] 1972. *Handbook of Federal Indian Law*. With a foreword and other material by Robert L. Bennett and Frederick M. Hart. Albuquerque: University of New Mexico Press.

Colden, Cadwallader. [1747] 1958. *The History of the Five Indian Nations Depending on the Province of New-York in America*. Ithaca, NY: Cornell University Press.

Commager, Henry Steele, ed. 1973. *Documents of American History*, 9th ed. Upper Saddle River, NJ: Prentice-Hall.

Cook, Frederick, ed. 1887. *Journals of the Military Expedition of Major General John Sullivan Against the Six Nations of Indians*. Auburn, NY: Knapp, Peck & Thomson.

Cook, Sherburne F. [1940, 1943] 1976. *The Conflict Between the California Indian and White Civilization*. Berkeley: University of California Press.

Corkran, David H. 1962. *The Cherokee Frontier: Conflict and Survival, 1740–1762*. Norman: University of Oklahoma Press.

Corkran, David H. 1967. *The Creek Frontier, 1540–1783*. Norman: University of Oklahoma Press.

Cotterill, R. S. 1954. *The Southern Indians: The Story of the Civilized Tribes Before Removal.* Norman: University of Oklahoma Press.

Crane, Verner W. [1929] 1964. *The Southern Frontier, 1670–1732.* Ann Arbor: University of Michigan Press.

Deloria, Vine, Jr., and Clifford M. Lytle. 1998. *The Nations Within: The Past and Future of American Indian Sovereignty,* 2d ed. Austin: University of Texas Press.

Deloria, Vine, Jr., and Raymond J. DeMallie. 1999. *Documents of American Indian Diplomacy.* Vol. 1. Norman: University of Oklahoma Press.

Deloria, Vine, Jr., and David E. Wilkins. 1999. *Tribes, Treaties, and Constitutional Tribulations.* Austin: University of Texas Press, 1999.

Dobyns, Henry F. 1983. *Their Numbers Become Thinned: Native American Population Dynamics in Eastern North America.* Knoxville: University of Tennessee Press.

Douglas, Frederick H., and René d'Harnoncourt. 1941. *Indian Art of the United States.* New York: Museum of Modern Art.

Downes, Randolph C. 1940. *Council Fires on the Upper Ohio.* Pittsburgh, PA: University of Pittsburgh Press.

Edmunds, R. David. 1983. *The Shawnee Prophet.* Lincoln: University of Nebraska Press.

Edmunds, R. David. 1984. *Tecumseh and the Quest for Indian Leadership.* Boston: Little, Brown and Company.

Emerson, Thomas E. 1997. *Cahokia and the Archaeology of Power.* Tuscaloosa: University of Alabama Press.

Erhard, Thomas Erhard. 1970. *Lynn Riggs: Southwest Playwright.* Southwest Writers Series. No. 29. Edited by James W. Lee. Austin, TX: Steck-Vaughn.

Every, Dale Van. 1964a. *Ark of Empire: The American Frontier, 1784–1803.* New York: Mentor Books.

Every, Dale Van. 1964b. *The Final Challenge: The American Frontier, 1804–1845.* New York: Mentor Books.

Fenton, William N. [1972] 1998. *The Great Law and The Longhouse.* Norman: University of Oklahoma Press.

Fitzhugh, William W., and Aron Cowell, eds., curators. 1988. *Crossroads of Continents: Cultures of Siberia and Alaska.* Washington, DC: Smithsonian Institution.

François, Marquis de Barbé-Marbois. 1929. *Our Revolutionary Forefathers: The Letters of François, Marquis de Barbé-Marbois.* Edited by Eugene Parker Chase. New York: Duffield & Co.

Franklin, Benjamin. 1987. *Writings.* Edited by J. A. Leo Lemay. New York: Library of America.

Garratt, John G. 1985. *The Four Indian Kings.* Ottawa, ON: Publications of the Public Archives of Canada.

George-Kanentiio, Doug. 2000. *Iroquois Culture & Commentary.* Santa Fe, NM: Clear Light Publishers.

Gibson, Charles. 1966. *Spain in America.* New York: Harper & Row.

Gibson, Charles, ed. 1968. *The Spanish Tradition in America.* New York: Harper & Row.

Gray, Robert. 1609. *A Good Speed to Virginia.* London: Felix Kyngston for William Welbie.

Hackett, Charles Wilson, ed. 1942. *Revolt of the Pueblo Indians of New Mexico and Otermín's Attempted Reconquest, 1680–1682.* Translated by Charmion Clair Shelby. Vol. 1. Albuquerque: University of New Mexico Press.

Hakluyt, Richard. 1609. *Virginia Richly Valued, By the Description of the Maine Land of Florida, Her Next Neighbor.* London: Felix Kyngston for Matthew Lownes.

Hakluyt, Richard. [1582] 1850. *Divers Voyages Touching the Discovery of America and the Islands Adjacent.* Edited by John Winter Jones. London: Hakluyt Society.

Hamilton, Edward P., trans. and ed. 1964. *Adventure in the Wilderness: The American Journals of Louis Antoine de Bougainville, 1756–1760.* Norman: University of Oklahoma Press.

Hammond, George P., and Agapito Rey, eds. 1953. *Don Juan de Oñate: Colonizer of New Mexico, 1595–1628.* 2 vols. Albuquerque: University of New Mexico Press.

Hanke, Lewis. 1951. *Bartolomé de Las Casas: An Interpretation of His Life and Writings.* The Hague: Martinus Nijhoff.

Hanke, Lewis. 1959. *Aristotle and the Indians.* Bloomington: Indiana University Press.

Hanke, Lewis. 1974. *All Mankind Is One.* DeKalb: Northern Illinois University Press.

Hariot, Thomas. [1588] 1955. "A Briefe and True Report." In *The Roanoke Voyages, 1584–1590.* Vol. 1. Edited by David Beers Quinn, 317–387. London: Hakluyt Society.

Harris, William. [1676] 1963. *A Rhode Islander Reports on King Philip's War: The Second William Harris Letter of August, 1676.* Edited by Douglas E. Leach. Providence: Rhode Island Historical Society.

Henry, Alexander. [1809] 1971. *Attack at Michilimackinac.* Edited by David A. Armour. Mackinac Island, MI: Mackinac Island State Park Commission.

Hodge, Frederick W., and Theodore Lewis, eds. 1907. *Spanish Explorers in the Southern United States, 1528–1543.* New York: Charles Scribner's Sons.

Hodge, Frederick Webb, ed. [1907] 1969. *Handbook of American Indians North of Mexico.* Vol. 2. Westport, CN: Greenwood Press.

Honour, Hugh. 1975. *The New Golden Land: European Images of America from the Discoveries to the Present Time.* New York: Pantheon.

Horigan, Michael. 2002. *Elmira: Death Camp of the North.* Mechanicsburg, PA: Stackpole Books.

Horsman, Reginald. [1967] 1992. *Expansion and American Indian Policy, 1783–1812.* Norman: University of Oklahoma Press.

Hotz, Gottfried. 1970. *Indian Skin Paintings from the American Southwest: Two Representations of Border Conflicts Between Mexico and the Missouri in the Early Eighteenth Century.* Translated by Johannes Malthaner. Norman: University of Oklahoma Press.

Hudson, Charles. 1997. *Knights of Spain, Warriors of the Sun: Hernando de Soto and the South's Ancient Chiefdoms.* Athens: University of Georgia Press.

Huey, Lois M., and Bonnie Pulis. 1997. *Molly Brant: A Legacy of Her Own.* Youngstown, NY: Old Fort Niagara Association.

Hunt, George T. 1940. *The Wars of the Iroquois.* Madison: University of Wisconsin Press.

Hurt, R. Douglas. 1987. *Indian Agriculture in America: Prehistory to the Present.* Lawrence: University Press of Kansas.

Hurtado, Albert L. 1988. *Indian Survival on the California Frontier.* New Haven, CN: Yale University Press.

Jackson, Helen Hunt. [1881] 1995. *A Century of Dishonor: A Sketch of the United States Government's Dealings with Some of the Indian Tribes.* Norman: University of Oklahoma Press.

Jacobs, Wilbur R. 1966. *Wilderness Politics and Indian Gifts.* Lincoln: University of Nebraska Press.

Jacobs, Wilbur R., ed. 1967. *The Appalachian Indian Frontier: The Edmond Atkin Report and Plan of 1755.* Lincoln: University of Nebraska Press.

Jacobs, Wilbur R. 1972. *Dispossessing the American Indian.* New York: Charles Scribner's Sons.

Jemison, G. Peter, and Anna M. Schein, eds. 2000. *Treaty of Canandaigua 1794.* Santa Fe, NM: Clear Light Publishers.

Jennings, Francis. 1975. *The Invasion of America: Indians, Colonialism, and the Cant of Conquest.* Chapel Hill: University of North Carolina Press.

Josephy, Alvin M., Jr. 1961. *The Patriot Chiefs: A Chronicle of American Indian Leadership.* New York: Viking.

Kappler, Charles J., ed. [1904] 1972. *Indian Treaties, 1778–1883.* New York: Interland Publishing.

Kenner, Charles L. 1969. *A History of New Mexican–Plains Indian Relations.* Norman: University of Oklahoma Press.

Kessell, John L. 1987. *Kiva, Cross, and Crown: The Pecos Indians and New Mexico, 1540–1840.* Albuquerque: University of New Mexico Press.

Klinck, Carl F., ed. 1961. *Tecumseh: Fact and Fiction in Early Records.* Upper Saddle River, N.J.: Prentice-Hall.

Labaree, Leonard W., ed. 1961. *The Papers of Benjamin Franklin.* Vol. 4. New Haven, CN: Yale University Press.

Lanning, John Tate. 1935. *The Spanish Missions of Georgia.* Chapel Hill: University of North Carolina Press.

Lauber, Almon Wheeler. 1913. *Indian Slavery in Colonial Times Within the Present Limits of the United States.* Studies in History, Economics and Public Law No. 134. New York: Columbia University Press.

Laws of the Colonial and State Governments, Relating to Indians and Indian Affairs, from 1633 to 1831, Inclusive. [1832] 1979. Stanfordville, NY: E. M. Coleman.

Leach, Douglas E. [1958] 1966. *Flintlock and Tomahawk: New England in King Philip's War.* New York: W. W. Norton.

Leder, Lawrence H., ed. 1956. *The Livingston Indian Records, 1666–1723.* Gettysburg: Pennsylvania Historical Association.

Leon-Portilla, Miguel, ed. 1962. *The Broken Spears: The Aztec Account of the Conquest of Mexico.* Boston: Beacon Press.

Lepore, Jill. 1998. *The Name of War: King Philip's War and the Origins of American Identity.* New York: Alfred A. Knopf.

Lincoln, Charles H., ed. 1913. *Narratives of the Indian Wars, 1675–1699.* New York: Charles Scribner's Sons.

Lyons, Oren, and John Mohawk, eds. 1992. *Exiled in the Land of the Free.* Santa Fe, NM: Clear Light Publishers.

Martin, Joel W. 1991. *Sacred Revolt: The Muskogees' Struggle for a New World.* Boston: Beacon Press.

McCool, Daniel. 1994. *Command of the Waters: Iron Triangles, Federal Water Development, and Indian Water.* Tucson: University of Arizona Press.

McLoughlin, William G. 1993. *After the Trail of Tears: The Cherokees' Struggle for Sovereignty, 1839–1880.* Chapel Hill: University of North Carolina Press.

McKenney, Thomas L. [1846] 1973. *Memoirs, Official and Personal.* Lincoln: University of Nebraska Press.

McNeill, William H. 1976. *Plagues and Peoples.* New York: Doubleday.

Melvoin, Richard I. 1989. *New England Outpost: War and Society in Colonial Deerfield.* New York: W. W. Norton.

Minge, Ward Alan. 1991. *Ácoma: Pueblo in the Sky*, rev. ed. Albuquerque: University of New Mexico Press.

Montaigne, Michel de. 1958. *Essays.* Translated by J. M. Cohen. Harmondsworth, UK: Penguin.

Morgan, William N. 1980. *Prehistoric Architecture in the Eastern United States.* Cambridge, MA: MIT Press.

O'Callaghan, E. B., and B. Fernow, eds. 1855. *Documents Relative to the Colonial History of the State of New York.* 15 vols. Albany, NY: Weed, Parsons and Company.

Parkman, Francis. [1870] 1991. *The Oregon Trail and The Conspiracy of Pontiac.* New York: The Library of America.

Parkman, Francis. 1877. *Count Frontenac and New France Under Louis XIV.* Boston: Little, Brown & Company.

Parkman, Francis. [1884] 1983. *France and England in North America.* Vol. 2. New York: Library of America.

Parkman, Francis. 1892. *A Half Century of Conflict.* Vol. 1. Boston: Little, Brown, and Company.

Peckham, Howard H. 1947. *Pontiac and the Indian Uprising.* Princeton, NJ: Princeton University Press.

Peckham, Howard H. 1964. *The Colonial Wars, 1689–1762.* Chicago: University of Chicago Press.

Penney, David W., and George C. Longfish. 1994. *Native American Art.* Detroit, MI: Hugh Lauter Levin Associates.

Phillips, Ruth B. 1998. *Trading Identities: The Souvenir in Native North American Art from the Northeast, 1700–1900.* Seattle: University of Washington Press.

Pierce, Richard A. 1972. "Alaska's Russian Governors: Ivan Kupreianov." *Alaska Journal* 2, no. 1: 21–24.

Ramenofsky, Ann F. 1987. *Vectors of Death: The Archaeology of European Contact.* Albuquerque: University of New Mexico Press.

Rowlandson, Mary. 1913. *Narrative of the Captivity of Mrs. Mary Rowlandson.* In *Narratives of the Indian Wars.* Edited by Charles H. Lincoln. New York: Charles Scribner's Sons.

Royce, Charles C. [1900] 1971. *Indian Land Cessions in the United States . . . Extract from the Eighteenth Annual Report of the Bureau of American Ethnology.* New York: Arno Press.

Sauer, Carl Ortwin. 1971. *Sixteenth Century North America: The Land and the People as Seen by the Europeans.* Berkeley: University of California Press.

Schoolcraft, Henry R. [1846] 1975. *Notes on the Iroquois: Or, Contributions to the Statistics, Aboriginal History, Antiquities and General Ethnology of Western New York.* Millwood, NY: Kraus Reprint.

Seaver, James E. [1824] 1963. *A Narrative of the Life of Mrs. Mary Jemison.* New York: American Scenic and Historic Preservation Society.

Smith, Buckingham, trans. 1866. *Narratives of the Career of Hernando De Soto in the Conquest of Florida As Told By A Knight of Elvas and In A Relation by Luys Hernandez de Biedma Factor of the Expedition.* New York: Bradford Club.

Smith, John. [1612] 1910. *Travels and Works of Captain John Smith.* Edited by Edward Arber. 2 vols. Edinburgh, UK: John Grant.

Smith, William. [1765] 1966. *An Historical Account of the Expedition Against the Ohio Indians, in the Year 1764.* Ann Arbor, MI: Readex Microprint.

Spicer, Edward H. 1962. *Cycles of Conquest: The Impact of Spain, Mexico, and the United States on the Indians of the Southwest, 1533–1960.* Tucson: University of Arizona Press.

Stone, William Leete. 1838. *The Life of Joseph Brant—Thayendanegea: Including the Border Wars of the American Revolution.* Vol. 2. New York: Alexander V. Blake.

Strachey, William. [1618] 1849. *The Historie of Travaile into Virginia Britannia.* Edited by R. H. Major. London: Hakluyt Society.

Stuart, Paul. 1987. *Nations Within a Nation: Historical Statistics of American Indians.* Westport, CN: Greenwood Press.

Sugden, John. 1985. *Tecumseh's Last Stand.* Norman: University of Oklahoma Press.

Sugden, John. 1997. *Tecumseh: A Life.* New York: Henry Holt.

Sugden, John. 2000. *Blue Jacket: Warrior of the Shawnees.* Lincoln: University of Nebraska Press.

Sullivan, James, et al., eds. 1921–1965. *The Papers of Sir William Johnson.* 14 vols. Albany, NY: State University of New York Press.

Swanton, John Reed. 1911. *Indian Tribes of the Lower Mississippi Valley and Adjacent Coast of the Gulf of Mexico.* Bureau of American Ethnology Bulletin 43. Washington, DC: Smithsonian Institution.

Swanton, John Reed. 1922. *Early History of the Creek Indians and Their Neighbors.* Smithsonian Institution Bureau of American Ethnology Bulletin 73. Washington, DC: Smithsonian Institution.

Sword, Wiley. 1985. *President Washington's Indian War: The Struggle for the Old Northwest, 1790–1795.* Norman: University of Oklahoma Press.

Thompson Kelsay, Isabel. 1984. *Joseph Brant, 1743–1807: Man of Two Worlds.* Syracuse, NY: Syracuse University Press.

Thornton, Russell. 1987. *American Indian Holocaust and Survival: A Population History Since 1492.* Norman: University of Oklahoma Press.

Thwaites, Reuben G., ed. 1899. *The Jesuit Relations and Allied Documents.* Vol. 41. Cleveland, OH: Burrows Brothers.

Tucker, Glenn. 1956. *Tecumseh: Vision of Glory.* Indianapolis, IN: Bobbs-Merrill Company.

Underhill, John. [1638] n.d. *Newes From America; Or, A New and Experimentall Discoverie of New England; Containing, A True Relation of Their War-like proceedings these two years last past, with a Figure of the Indian Fort, or Palizado.* New York: Underhill Society of America.

Usner, Daniel H., Jr. 1992. *Indians, Settlers, & Slaves in a Frontier Exchange Economy: The Lower Mississippi Valley Before 1783.* Chapel Hill: University of North Carolina Press.

Vanderwerth, W. C., ed. 1971. *Indian Oratory: Famous Speeches by Noted Indian Chieftains.* Norman: University of Oklahoma Press.

Vaughan, Alden T. 1965. *New England Frontier: Puritans and Indians, 1620–1675.* Boston: Little, Brown and Company.

Vecsey, Christopher. 1996. *On the Padres Trail.* Notre Dame, IN: University of Notre Dame Press.

Velarde Tiller, Veronica E., ed. 1996. *American Indian Reservations and Trust Areas.* Washington, DC: U.S. Department of Commerce.

Venables, Robert W. 1980. "Iroquois Environments and 'We the People of the United States.'" In *American Indian Environments: Ecological Issues in Native American History.* Edited by Christopher Vecsey and Robert W. Venables. Syracuse, NY: Syracuse University Press.

Venables, Robert W. 2005. *American Indian History: Five Centuries of Conflict & Coexistence.* 2 vols. Santa Fe, NM: Clear Light Publishers.

Verano, John W., and Douglas H. Ubelaker, eds. 1992. *Disease and Demography in the Americas.* Washington, DC: Smithsonian Institution.

Villagrá, Gaspar Pérez de. [1610] 1933. *History of New Mexico.* Translated by Gilberto Espinosa. Los Angeles, CA: Quivira Society.

Vries, David de. [1655] 1909. "Short Historical and Journal-Notes." In *Narratives of New Netherland, 1609–1664.* Edited by J. Franklin Jameson, 186–234. New York: Charles Scribner's Sons.

Washburn, Wilcomb E., ed. 1964. *The Indian and the White Man.* Garden City, NY: Doubleday Anchor Books.

Washburn, Wilcomb E. 1971. *Red Man's Land/White Man's Law: A Study of the Past and Present Status of the American Indian.* New York: Charles Scribner's Sons.

Washburn, Wilcomb E., ed. 1973. *The American Indian and the United States: A Documentary History.* 4 vols. Westport, CN: Greenwood Press.

Washburn, Wilcomb E. 1975. *The Indian in America.* New York: Harper & Row.

Whiting Young, Biloine, and Melvin L. Fowler. 2000. *Cahokia: The Great Native American Metropolis.* Urbana: University of Illinois Press.

Williams, T. Harry. 1985. *The History of American Wars from Colonial Times to World War I.* New York: Alfred A. Knopf.

Wilson, Edmund. 1960. *Apologies to the Iroquois.* With a Study of the Mohawks in High Steel by Joseph Mitchell. New York: Vintage.

Winthrop Papers. 1938. *Winthrop Papers.* Vol. 2. Boston: Massachusetts Historical Society.

Winthrop Papers. 1943. *Winthrop Papers.* Vol. 3. Boston: Massachusetts Historical Society.

Indian Immigrants and Removals
(1800 to 1850)

By 1800, more than three centuries after Columbus's first landfall in North America, many Native American peoples across the continent had yet to be touched significantly by the physical presence of European-American migration, although non-Native diseases had already swept much of the continent. While some Indians had adopted Euro-American animals (such as the horse), guns, and other trade goods, many in the interior of North America still swore no allegiance either to any European power or to the United States of America. Within the space of one century, however, the U.S. frontier would leap from the East Coast to the West Coast. By 1890, very few of North America's surviving Native people would be able to say that they lived independently, as had their great-grandparents.

In 1800, America north of the Rio Grande was under claim by the new United States, Britain, France, and Spain, but most of the same area still was primarily occupied by Native American peoples. The edicts of European treaty making held that the United States extended westward to the east bank of the Mississippi River. In another decade, the United States' European-issued title would extend, via the Louisiana Purchase, to the Rocky Mountains.

Only the Eastern Seaboard was thickly settled by non-Natives and their descendents in 1800, although they exerted significant influence in other parts of the continent. The territory to the west was home to a few mountain men, some traders, and a few soldiers in a few small forts, as well as missions, both Catholic and Protestant. The United States' main day-to-day diplomatic activity in 1800 was aimed at maintaining relationships with the many Native nations occupying territory that European nations claimed on paper. A thin ribbon of French influence had followed the Saint Lawrence River to the Great Lakes, then southward along the Mississippi River to New Orleans. Most of the present-day western United States south of the Oregon and Wyoming borders was claimed by a disintegrating Spanish empire, which was no longer able to sustain its far-flung missions, military outposts, and mining areas. Mexico assumed much of this structure after 1822.

Following the turn of the century, a tide of Anglo-American humanity spilled across the Appalachian Mountains, into the rich bottomlands of the Mississippi, the fertile valley of the Ohio, and westward. From 1830 to 1890, three human generations, the Anglo-American frontier advanced from the woods of Georgia, with the passage of the Indian Removal Act of 1830, to California, with the gold rush of 1849, and inland again to the prairies of South Dakota. In 1890, the U.S. census declared the frontier closed. During this time, some Native peoples resisted removal and remained on their homelands. One example was the Six Nations of the Iroquois Confederacy.

Benjamin Franklin once had conjectured that North America would not fill with the offspring of Europe for at least a thousand years, a risky prediction because he didn't even know the exact size of the continent. He missed the date the continent would fill with the progeny of the Old World by roughly 900 years. How very wrong he was.

Between 1790 and 1840, roughly 4.5 million non-Indians surged across the Appalachians, more than the total population of the United States in 1790 (3.9 million, as recorded in the first national census). In 1790, two-thirds of those 3.9 million people lived within fifty miles of the Atlantic Ocean or watercourses leading to it; by 1850, the borders of the United States had reached the Pacific Ocean.

The Louisiana Purchase (1803) nearly doubled the country's size, at least on paper. A few months after the deal was signed, President Jefferson sent Meriwether Lewis and William Clark to survey the area and to reach the Pacific Ocean. They were led much of the way by Sacajawea (Lemhi Shoshone). For nineteen months, Sacajawea guided Lewis and Clark over the Rocky Mountains toward the Pacific Coast near present-day Astoria, Oregon. Without her, the expedition probably would have halted for lack of direction. She also negotiated friendly relations with Native peoples along the way.

In one century, sped by a massive increase in immigration from Europe, economic development, and technological change (most notably, for example, the arrival of the transcontinental railroads), as well as the ravages of imported diseases, Native American free space in the contemporary United States (south of Alaska) shrank to nearly nothing. By the time of the massacre at Wounded Knee, at the end of 1890, North America's Native peoples would

be living mainly on reservations controlled by the U.S. government or in its rapidly growing cities. North America in 1800 was about to witness the most rapid surge of humanity in the history of the human race. In that year, the non-Indian population of the U.S. portions of the Mississippi Valley had risen to 377,000. By 1830, the non-Indian population of the same area was roughly 900,000.

The explosion westward required political accommodation. Mention the name "Andrew Jackson" to most Americans, and the phrase "Jacksonian Democracy" may spring to mind. The folklore of today's Democratic party has it that its trademark donkey came from a time when Jackson's opponents called him an "ass," upon which Jackson adopted the animal as his own symbol. To the descendents of Native Americans who survived the period, however, the mention of Jackson's name may bring to mind the Bataan Death March of World War II and even comparisons with Hitler and Stalin, because the coercion their ancestors endured resembled the forced collectivization of Soviet agriculture and the assignment of many people to prison camps in Siberia. There was very little that was democratic for Native peoples about Jackson's handling of relations with them.

As non-Native immigration began to explode across the Appalachians into the Ohio Valley and Great Lakes shortly after 1790, Native resistance expressed itself in attempts at new confederations along lines of mutual interest. Native resistance surged shortly after the turn of the century. The Shawnee Tecumseh, a major military leader and alliance builder, sought to stop Euro-American expansion into the Ohio Valley area early in the nineteenth century, after alliances led by Pontiac, Brant, and Little Turtle had failed. As the number of non-Indian immigrants grew, Tecumseh began to assemble the Shawnees, Delawares, Ottawas, Ojibwas, Kickapoos, and Wyandots into an alliance with the aim of establishing a permanent Native American confederation that would act as a buffer zone between the United States to the east and English Canada to the north. Tecumseh urged all Indians in the area to unite as brothers, as sons of one Mother Earth. He scoffed at the idea of selling the land. "Why not sell the air?" he asked. Sale of land, to Tecumseh, was contrary to the ways of nature.

Territorial Governor (and Army General) William Henry Harrison (who later popularized his battle with Tecumseh at Tippecanoe in his successful campaign for the presidency with the campaign slo-

gan "Tippecanoe and Tyler Too") tried to undermine the growing strength of Tecumseh's Native alliance by negotiating treaties with individual Native nations. Because only a portion of each tribe or nation's warriors elected to follow Tecumseh, Harrison found it easy enough to find "treaty Indians" among those who did not elect to fight. By 1811, Harrison had negotiated at least fifteen treaties, all of which Tecumseh repudiated.

Harrison's wariness of Tecumseh's power sprang from a deep respect for him. "The implicit obedience and respect which the followers of Tecumseh pay to him is really astonishing and more than any other circumstance bespeaks him [as] one of those uncommon geniuses, which spring up occasionally to produce revolutions and to overturn the established order of things," said Harrison. He continued: "If it were not for the vicinity of the United States, he would, perhaps, be the founder of an Empire that would rival in glory Mexico or Peru. No difficulties deter him" (Hamilton, 1972, 159).

Tecumseh was particularly galled by Harrison's choice as his territorial capital the village of Chillicothe, the same site (with the same name) as the Shawnees' former principal settlement. The name itself is anglicized Shawnee for "principal town." At one treaty council, Tecumseh found himself seated next to Harrison on a bench. Tecumseh slowly but aggressively pushed Harrison off the edge of the bench, then told him that this was what the immigrants were doing to his people. They were being slowly squeezed off their lands. During his last conference with Tecumseh, Harrison bid the chief to take a chair. "Your father requests you take a chair," an interpreter told Tecumseh, to which he replied, defiantly: "My father! The sun is my father and the Earth is my mother. I will repose upon her bosom" (Johansen, 2000, 65). Tecumseh then sat, cross-legged, on the ground.

Tecumseh also was angry over Harrison's treaty of September 30, 1809, with the Delawares, Potawatomies, Miamis, Kickapoos, Wea, and Eel River peoples. For $8,200 in cash and $2,350 in annuities, Harrison had laid claim for the United States to roughly 3 million acres of rich hunting land along the Wabash River in the heart of the area in which Tecumseh wished to build his Native confederacy. When Tecumseh and his brother, also a Shawnee war chief, complained to Harrison that the treaty terms were unfair, Harrison at first rebuked Tecumseh by saying that the Shawnees had not even been part of the treaty. The implicit refusal to recognize

Tecumseh's alliance angered the Indians even more. At a meeting August 12, 1810, each side drew up several hundred battle-ready warriors and soldiers. Harrison agreed to relay Tecumseh's complaints to the president, and Tecumseh said that his warriors would join the Americans against the British if Harrison would annul the treaty.

Nothing came of Harrison's promises, and in 1811 bands of warriors, allied with Tecumseh, began ranging out of the settlement of Tippecanoe to terrorize nearby farmsteads and small backwoods settlements. Harrison said he would wipe out Tippecanoe if the raids did not stop; Tecumseh said they would stop when the land signed away under the 1810 treaty was returned.

Tecumseh then journeyed southward in an unsuccessful effort to bring the Creeks, Chickasaws, and Choctaws into his alliance. While Tecumseh was traveling, the command of the existing alliance fell to Tecumseh's brother, Tenskwatawa, who was called The Prophet. On September 26, 1811, Harrison decamped at Vincennes with more than nine hundred men, two-thirds of them Indian allies. He built a fort and named it after himself on the present-day site of Terre Haute, Indiana. Harrison then sent two Miamis to The Prophet to demand the return of property Harrison alleged had been stolen in the raids, along with the surrender of Indians he accused of murder. The Miamis did not return to Harrison's camp. The governor's army marched to within sight of Tippecanoe and met with Tenskwatawa, who invited them to make camp, relax, and negotiate. Harrison's forces did stop but set up in battle configurations, as The Prophet's warriors readied an attack. Within two hours of pitched battle, Harrison's forces routed the Indians, then burned the village of Tippecanoe as Tenskwatawa's forces scattered into the woods. Tecumseh fled to British Canada, where he was appointed a brigadier general. Tecumseh met Harrison's forces in battle at the Battle of the Thames, where he was killed October 13, 1813.

While Tecumseh's allies were routed from the old Northwest by force, the government sought to remove the "civilized tribes" of the Southeast by legal edict. President Jackson, Supreme Court Chief Justice John Marshall, and Cherokee Chief John Ross became the three most influential leaders in the debate over the removal of the Cherokees from their homeland in present-day Georgia, Alabama, the Carolinas, and Tennessee. The removal of the Cherokees and several other Native nations during the 1830s allowed the expansion of non-Native populations southward and westward through parts of Georgia, Alabama, Mississippi, and neighboring states. At roughly the same time, the industrial application of Eli Whitney's cotton gin created a mass market in moderately priced cotton clothing. Within a decade after the Trail of Tears (in Cherokee, *nuna-daa-ut-sun'y*, "the trail where they cried"), some southern Native nations' homelands had been replaced by cotton fields tended and harvested by slaves.

President Jackson, having retired from his Army career of Indian fighting, avidly supported the Removal Act of 1830, which led to the Cherokees' Trail of Tears. Ross was the Cherokees' foremost advocate against removal (aided by Major Ridge and others) and the man most responsible for taking two major cases to the Supreme Court. Marshall worked the facts of the conflict into legal doctrine that has shaped law regarding Native Americans for almost two centuries. During the debate over removal, which continued through most of Jackson's presidency, the entire United States debated assertions of "states' rights" vis-à-vis the federal government and the Cherokees, in a prelude to the coming dissolution of the union during the Civil War less than three decades later.

The removal of the "civilized tribes" from their homelands is one of the most notable chapters in the history of American land relations. Jackson's repudiation of Chief Justice Marshall's rulings, which supported the Cherokees' rights to their homelands, demonstrated contempt of the Supreme Court, an impeachable offense under the Constitution. The subject of impeachment was not seriously raised, however. During the incendiary years before the Civil War, the removals became intertwined with the issue of states' rights. Had Jackson accepted the rulings of Justice Marshall, who was doing his constitutional duty, the Civil War might have started during the 1830s.

The explosion of westward migration after roughly 1800 also generated enormous profits in land speculation. Fortunes were made in early America not usually by working the land, but by buying early and holding large parcels for sale after demand increased dramatically because of non-Indian immigration. As a frontier lawyer in Tennessee, Jackson often took his fees in land rather than money, which was as scarce along the frontier as land was plentiful. He thus acquired immense holdings with which he began a mercantile establishment and bought a plantation. Jackson quickly

acquired more than a hundred slaves, making him one of frontier Tennessee's largest owners of human capital. He traded actively in slaves and occasionally wagered them on horse races in a display of expendable wealth. Andrew Jackson's slaves and plantation placed him squarely within the interests of the races and classes whose members benefited most from Indian removal.

Before 1800, non-Native immigration in the South had been limited mainly to the pine barrens of coastal Georgia, on land that was practically useless for farming before the advent of modern commercial fertilizers. The immigrants, seeing the value of the developing cotton culture, cast a covetous eye on the fertile inland valleys that were occupied by the Five Civilized Tribes, who had utilized them for hundreds of years. As waves of land speculators and other immigrants moved in to evict them, the Creeks, Cherokees, Choctaws, Chickasaws, and others were doing exactly what the Jeffersonians thought they should: building farms and towns in the European manner. The "civilized tribes" were well on their way to becoming some of the most prosperous farmers in the South.

Andrew Jackson thought that Indian treaties were anachronisms. "An absurdity," he called them, "Not to be reconciled with the principles of our government" (Johansen, 2000, 88). As Jackson elaborated in a letter to President James Monroe (another advocate of Indian removal) in 1817:

> The Indians are the subjects of the United States, inhabiting its territory and acknowledging its sovereignty. Then is it not absurd for the sovereign to negotiate by treaty with the subject? I have always thought, that Congress had as much right to regulate by acts of legislation, all Indian concerns as they had of territories, are citizens of the United States and entitled to all the rights thereof, the Indians are subjects and entitled to their protection and fostering care (McNickle, 1949, 193).

The confused and convoluted grammar aside, it is not easy to decipher what General Jackson is saying. Is he declaring the Indians to be citizens? Legally, that was not the case until a century later. Is he personally annulling the treaties, which had been signed by parties who regarded each other as diplomatic peers barely two generations earlier? Whatever the nature of his rhetoric, the ensuing decades made clear, especially for the native peoples of the

South, just what Jackson meant by "protection and fostering care."

Whether in purposeful contravention of the treaties or because he thought he had the right to annul them personally, within a decade Jackson cooperated with the land industry to move tens of thousands of Native peoples from their homelands. Jackson, who as a general told his troops to root out Indians from their "dens" and to kill Indian women and their "whelps," struck only a slightly more erudite tone as president. In his second annual message to Congress, he reflected on the fact that some non-Natives were growing "melancholy" over the fact that the Indians were being driven to their "tomb." These critics must understand, Jackson said, that "true philanthropy reconciles the mind to these vicissitudes as it does to the extinction of one generation to make way for another" (Stannard, 1992, 240).

Jackson did not seek the removal of the Cherokees and other "civilized tribes"—the Cherokee, Choctaw, Chickasaw, Creek, and Seminole—because they didn't know how to make productive use of the land. On the contrary, four of the five (the exception being the Seminoles, who had escaped to Florida) were called "civilized tribes" by the immigrants precisely because they were making exactly the kind of progress the Great White Father desired of them: becoming farmers, educating their children, constituting governments modeled on the United States. Immigrants, many of them Scots and Irish, had married into Native families. Some Indians, including their foremost leader against removal, John Ross, himself seven-eights Scots-Irish, owned plantations and slaves.

The removals began in 1831, with four thousand Choctaws bound for western Arkansas. The winter was harsh, but during the next few years it often was even worse. The cruelty of the removals was compounded by governmental mismanagement and by Indian agents who kept for themselves much of the money that the government had appropriated to feed people while they were being moved. That summer, cholera spread through areas of the South, returning each summer until 1836. Only the Chickasaws managed to transport much of what they owned westward (agents complained about the bulk of their livestock and baggage). The rest of the people suffered cruelly, complaining that they had been driven off their own lands like wild wolves, the shoeless feet of their women and children bleeding from the long marches over rough terrain. Indian agents, infamous for their penny-pinching, sometimes hired rotten

boats to transport Indians across rivers. Many of the boats sank, with the loss of uncounted lives. Dead Indians didn't cost anything to feed, so the agents pocketed their per-capita allowance.

During the Creek War, people led by Chitto Harjo and others were driven into the forests and swamps by white squatters. Their homes were taken, and many starved. A newspaper of the time described their destitution: "To see a whole people destitute of food—the incessant cry of the emaciated creatures being *bread! bread!* is beyond description distressing. The existence of many of the Indians is prolonged by eating roots and the bark of trees. Nothing that can afford nourishment is rejected, however offensive it may be. They beg their food from door to door. It is really painful to see the wretched creatures wandering about the streets, haggard and naked" (Brandon, 1964, 227).

Having subdued the Creeks, General Jackson next received orders to quell what the War Department politely called "troubles" in Georgia, principally among the Seminoles, who had escaped to Florida and begun to shelter exslaves (who, with their offspring, became known as Black Seminoles). By 1818, Jackson's troops were chasing them into Florida, which was still under Spanish jurisdiction (the area would be ceded to the United States in 1821). Having seized several Spanish forts along the way, Jackson withdrew. He then endured a debate in Congress over his extranational expedition. Jackson also reaped popular acclaim from expansion-minded Americans, which swelled his ambitions for the presidency.

The Seminoles, most of whom were descended from Creeks, had elected to ally with the Spanish rather than with the United States, an act of virtual treason to General Jackson. Furthermore, Seminoles were giving shelter to runaway slaves. In some cases, the Seminoles and the escaped slaves had intermarried over generations. The pretext of Jackson's raid was the recovery of "stolen property," runaway slaves. After the United States purchased Florida from Spain, slave-hunting vigilantes invaded the area en masse, killing Seminoles as well as blacks. In the 1830s, President Jackson's proposal to remove the Seminoles from Florida to Indian Territory was met with widespread Indian refusal.

Moving deep into the swamps of southern Florida (an area that, ironically, was being used as a removal *destination* for other native peoples), the Seminoles fought fifteen hundred U.S. Army troops to a bloody stalemate during seven years of warfare.

They were never defeated, and they never moved from their new homeland. Osceola, whose name was derived from *asi-yahola*, meaning Black Drink Crier, was the best-known leader of the Seminoles during their pursuit by the U.S. Army. He was opposed by some of his own people, one of the better-known of whom was Emathla.

Jackson's policy—"move the Indians out"—became the national standard after his election as president in 1828. Alabama had already been created in 1819 from Creek and Cherokee territory; Mississippi was created in 1817 from Choctaw and Chickasaw country. These two states, along with Georgia, passed laws outlawing tribal governments and making Indians subject to state jurisdiction, after which open season was declared on remaining Native lands.

All of this violated treaties that had been concluded between Indian nations and the federal government. Confronted with this fact, President Jackson told the Indians that he was unable to stand by the treaties because they raised nettlesome issues of states' rights, an emerging issue in the decades before the Civil War. Instead, Jackson proposed that the Indians be moved westward. At first, the moving of whole tribes was proposed as a voluntary act. In the meantime, land speculators and squatters closed a deadly vise on lands that had been home to the newly "civilized" tribes for thousands of years. On December 19, 1829, the Georgia legislature passed a statute declaring the laws and Constitution of the Cherokee nation null and void. One U.S. marshal said that land speculators in Georgia were "some of the most lawless and uncouth men I have ever seen." A federal agent wrote to President Jackson: "A greater mass of corruption, perhaps, has never been congregated in any part of the world" (Brandon, 1964, 227).

As he refused all concessions, Jackson himself wrote to his wife describing the poverty to which they had been reduced: "Could you only see the misery and the wretchedness of those creatures, perishing from want of food and picking up the grains of corn scattered from the mouths of horses" (Tebbel and Jennison, 1960, 181).

Alexis de Tocqueville, author of *Democracy in America,* witnessed portions of the early removals:

> At the end of the year 1831, whilst I was on the left bank of the Mississippi, at a place named by the Europeans Memphis, there arrived a numerous band of Choctaws. These savages

had left their country, and were endeavoring to gain the right bank of the Mississippi, where they hoped to find an asylum which had been promised them by the American government. It was in the middle of the winter, and the cold was unusually severe; the snow had frozen hard upon the ground, and the river was drifting huge masses of ice. The Indians had their families with them; and they brought in their train the wounded and the sick, with children newly born, and old men upon the verge of death. They possessed neither tents nor wagons, but only their arms and some provisions. I saw them embark to pass the mighty river, and never will that solemn spectacle fade from my remembrance. No cry, no sob was heard amongst the assembled crowd; all were silent. The Indians had all stepped into the bark which was to carry them across, but their dogs remained upon the bank. As soon as these animals perceived that their masters were finally leaving the shore, they set up a dismal howl, and plunging all together into the icy waters of the Mississippi, swam after the boat (Reeves, 435, 436, 448.).

As the State of Georgia and the Removal Act sought to destroy it, the Cherokee Nation was the scene of remarkable economic progress. By the time the Removal Act was passed in 1830, the Cherokees had 22,000 cattle, 7,600 horses, 46,000 swine, 2,500 sheep, 762 looms, 2,488 spinning wheels, 172 wagons, 2,943 plows, 10 saw mills, 21 grist mills, 61 blacksmitheries, 18 schools, 8 cotton gins, and 1,300 slaves. All of these things indicated that they led prosperous lives very much like those of the European-American settlers who sought their land.

The preremoval Cherokee Nation also was the birthplace of the only written language in human history to have been developed by a single person. That person was Sequoyah (from *sikwaji,* meaning "sparrow" or "principal bird" in Cherokee). Sequoyah is one of the most remarkable figures in American history. With a quick mind and active imagination, Sequoyah became intrigued by the "talking leaves," the written language of the whites. By 1809, Sequoyah had started work on a written version of the Cherokee language using pictorial symbols, but he abandoned the method as untenable after he had created more than a thousand symbols. Next, Sequoyah reduced the Cherokee language to two hundred and then finally to eighty-six charac-

ters that represented all of its syllables or sounds. He derived the resulting syllabary in part from English, Greek, and Hebrew characters in mission school books. At first he was thought by some to be engaging in witchcraft. Sequoyah's home was razed on one occasion, destroying his notes.

Sequoyah came to believe that their ability to communicate in writing gave the European immigrants great power. He looked at writing as a measure of equity with Europeans. Sequoyah completed his writing system during 1821. The same year, before an assembly of Cherokee leaders, he proved the viability of his system by writing messages to his six-year-old daughter that she understood and answered independently.

The Cherokee tribal council formally adopted Sequoyah's syllabary soon after this demonstration. By the mid-1820s, the written language had been taught in eighteen schools to thousands of people. The language invented by Sequoyah (after whom the giant redwoods in California were later named) had neither silent letters nor ambiguous sounds. Many Cherokees learned its system of writing in three or four days. In recognition of his accomplishments, a bust of Sequoyah was placed in the Statuary Hall of the United States Capitol. By 1824, white missionaries had translated parts of the *Bible* into Cherokee. In 1828, the Cherokee Tribal Council in north Georgia started a weekly newspaper called the *Cherokee Phoenix and Indian Advocate.* The newspaper, printing bilingual editions in Cherokee and English, enjoyed great success until it was suppressed in 1835 by the State of Georgia for advocating Cherokee rights to their lands in that state.

President Jackson's adamant support of Indian removal placed him on a direct constitutional collision course with Chief Justice John Marshall, who was in the process of evolving legal doctrines vis-à-vis Native American land rights on which he had been working before Jackson was elected. Marshall was Chief Justice in 1810, when *Fletcher v. Peck,* the first case directly related to American Indians, came before the Supreme Court. The "Cherokee cases" that came before Marshall's court between 1823 and 1832 would display, in broad and emphatic relief, how closely much of early nineteenth-century American life was connected to the dynamics of land speculation that propelled westward movement.

Marshall's legal opinions outlining Native Americans' status in the United States legal system took shape as he defined the Supreme Court's place in United States political society as a whole. When

Marshall became Chief Justice in 1801, the Supreme Court was little more than a clause in the Constitution. For thirty-five years as Chief Justice, Marshall played a major role in defining the Court as an institution. By the time he wrote the Supreme Court's opinion in *Worcester v. Georgia* (1832), Marshall was seventy-seven years of age and increasingly frail. Despite difficulties with his voice, he read the entire twenty-eight-page decision before the court.

In legal analysis, the term "Marshall Trilogy" is used to describe as a group Chief Justice John Marshall's rulings in *Johnson v. M'Intosh, Cherokee Nation v. Georgia,* and *Worcester v. Georgia.* In these three cases, Marshall developed legal doctrines that defined the relationship of the United States, the individual states, and Native American nations. In these opinions, according to legal scholar Charles F. Wilkinson, "Marshall conceived a model that can be described broadly as calling for largely autonomous tribal governments subject to an overriding federal authority but essentially free of state control" (Wilkinson, 1987, 24).

The Marshall Trilogy is so important in American Indian law because the key precepts of Marshall's three opinions have been interpreted by lawyers, judges, legal scholars, and government officials in many different ways. The Bureau of Indian Affairs (BIA), for example, used Marshall's words "dependent," "pupilage," and "ward" to construct a cradle-to-grave social and political control system in which Indians have been regarded legally as incompetents or children would be in other social and legal contexts. Ironically, because of Marshall's rulings, Native peoples were removed from their homelands under a legal rubric that gave birth to a "trust" doctrine, under which the same federal government that executed the removal was charged with safeguarding their lands and rights.

If President Jackson did not actually *say* "John Marshall has made his decision, now let him enforce it," his failure to protect Cherokee sovereignty with military force showed that "he certainly meant it," according to Leonard Baker, a biographer of Marshall (Baker, 1974, 746). By ignoring Chief Justice Marshall's opinion in *Worcester v. Georgia,* he showed his frontier constituencies that he supported a belief popular among states' rights advocates of the time: that the Supreme Court should be stripped of its power to review the rulings of state courts. Marshall repudiated the states' rights advocates' belief that Section 25 of the Judiciary Act prohibited the Supreme

Court from hearing the case. A bill that would have repealed Section 25 of the Judiciary Act of 1789 (which gives the U.S. Supreme Court power to rule on appeals from state courts) was debated on the floor of the House of Representatives, voted on, and defeated on January 29, 1831.

Even though ignored by President Jackson, Marshall's opinions shaped the relationship of the United States to Native American nations within its borders. The 1934 Indian Reorganization Act and legislative efforts promoting self-determination after the 1960s were based in part on Marshall's opinion that the rights of "discovery" did not extinguish the original inhabitants' legal as well as just claim to retain possession of their lands and to use it according to their own jurisdiction.

Although John Ross continued to protest removal for several more years, the state of Georgia coerced Cherokees to sell lands for a fraction of their value. Marauding immigrants plundered Cherokee homes and possessions. The U.S. Army forced Cherokee families into internment camps to prepare for the arduous trek westward. As a result of unhealthy and crowded conditions in these hastily constructed stockades, many Cherokees died even before their Trail of Tears began.

In preparation for the Cherokees' removal, Ross was evicted from his mansion and was living in a dirt-floored cabin. When John Howard Payne, author of the song "Home Sweet Home," came to visit him at the cabin, just across the Georgia state line in Tennessee, the Georgia State Guard crossed the state line and kidnapped both men. Realizing that the federal government did not intend to protect the Cherokees, Ross and others reluctantly signed the Treaty of New Echota in 1835 and prepared, with heavy hearts, to leave their homes.

James Mooney described how the Cherokees were forced from their homes: "Squads of troops were sent to search out with rifle and bayonet every small cabin hidden away in the coves or by the sides of mountain streams. . . . Families at dinner were startled by the sudden gleam of bayonets in the doorway and rose up to be driven with blows and oaths along the trail that led to the stockade. Men were seized in their fields or going along the road, women were taken from their wheels, and children from their play" (Van Every, 1966, 242). A U.S. Army private who witnessed the Cherokee removal wrote: "I saw the helpless Cherokee arrested and dragged from their homes, and driven by bayonet into the stockades. And in the chill of a

drizzling rain on an October morning I saw them loaded like cattle or sheep into wagons and started toward the west. . . . Chief Ross led in prayer, and when the bugle sounded and wagons started rolling many of the children . . . waved their little hands goodbye to their mountain homes" (Worcester, 1975, 67).

By 1838, the Cherokees had exhausted all their appeals. As they were being forced to leave their homes, the Cherokees passed a "memorial," which expressed the manifest injustice of their forced relocation in these words:

The title of the Cherokee people to their lands is the most ancient, pure, and absolute known to man; its date is beyond the reach of human record; its validity confirmed by possession and enjoyment antecedent to all pretense of claim by any portion of the human race. . . . The free consent of the Cherokee people is indispensable to a valid transfer of the Cherokee title. The Cherokee people have neither by themselves nor their representatives given such consent. It follows that the original title and ownership of lands still rests with the Cherokee Nation, unimpaired and absolute. The Cherokee people have existed as a distinct national community for a period extending into antiquity beyond the dates and records and memory of man. These attributes have never been relinquished by the Cherokee people, and cannot be dissolved by the expulsion of the Nation from its territory by the power of the United States Government (O'Brien, 1989, 57).

More than four thousand Cherokees died of exposure, disease, and starvation, about a quarter of the total Cherokee population. Quatie, Ross's wife, was among the victims of this forced emigration. After removal, the miserable conditions continued. Many Cherokees died after they arrived in Indian Territory as epidemics and food shortages plagued the new settlements.

Ralph Waldo Emerson weighed in solidly with John Ross. Emerson wrote to President Martin Van Buren April 23, 1838, calling the impending Trail of Tears "a crime." "You, sir," Emerson wrote to the president, "will bring down that renowned chair in which you sit into infamy if your seal is set to this instrument of perfidy; and the name of this nation, hitherto the sweet omen of religion and liberty, will stink to the world" (Moquin, 1973, 105).

In our time, the forced marches of the removed Native nations have been called "genocide." However, despite the cruelty of the marches they were forced to undertake, and the death and disease that dogged their every step, the surviving members of the peoples who were removed to Indian Territory quickly set about rebuilding their communities. Much as they had in the Southeast, the Creeks, Cherokees, and others built prosperous farms and towns, passed laws, and set about organizing themselves once again. Within three generations, however, the land that in the 1830s had been set aside as Indian Territory was being sought by non-Indians because it contained oil and because the frontier had closed everywhere else.

Bruce E. Johansen

See also *Cherokee Nation v. Georgia;* Disease, Historic and Contemporary; *Fletcher v. Peck;* Harrison, William Henry; Horse, Economic Impact; Indian Removal Act; Jackson, Andrew; Land Rights, Identity and Ownership of; Osceola; Ross, John; Seminole Wars; Sequoyah; Tecumseh; Trail of Tears; Treaty Diplomacy, with Summary of Selected Treaties; Tribal Sovereignty; *Worcester v. Georgia.*

References and Further Reading
Baker, Leonard. 1974. *John Marshall: A Life in Law.* New York: Macmillan.
Beckhard, Arthur J. 1957. *Black Hawk.* New York: Julian Messner.
Black, Nancy B., and Bette S. Weidman. 1976. *White on Red: Images of the American Indian.* Port Washington, NY: Kennilkat Press.
Brandon, William. 1964. *The American Heritage Book of Indians.* New York: Dell.
Bryant, Martha F. 1989. *Sacajawea: A Native American Heroine.* New York: Council for Indian Education.
Cherokee Nation v. Georgia (5 Peters 1, 1831).
Cole, Donald B. 1993. *Presidency of Andrew Jackson.* Lawrence: University Press of Kansas.
Collier, John. 1947. *Indians of the Americas.* New York: New American Library.
Deardorff, Merle H. 1951. *The Religion of Handsome Lake: Its Origins and Development.* American Bureau of Ethnology Bulletin No. 149. Washington, DC: B.A.E.
Eckert, Allan W. 1992. *A Sorrow in Our Heart: The Life of Tecumseh.* New York: Bantam.
Edmunds, R. David. 1983. *The Shawnee Prophet.* Lincoln: University of Nebraska Press.
Edmunds, R. David. 1984. *Tecumseh and the Quest for Indian Leadership.* Boston: Little, Brown & Company.

Edmonds, Della and Margot. 1979. *Sacajawea of the Lewis and Clark Expedition*. Berkeley: University of California Press.

Eggleston, Edward, and Lillie Eggleston-Seelye. 1878. *Tecumseh and the Shawnee Prophet*. New York.

Frazier, Neta L. 1967. *Sacajawea: The Girl Nobody Knows*. New York: McKay Co.

Griffith, Benjamin W., Jr. 1988. *McIntosh and Weatherford: Creek Indian Leaders*. Tuscaloosa: University of Alabama Press.

Hamilton, Charles, ed. 1972. *Cry of the Thunderbird*. Norman: University of Oklahoma Press.

Harold, Howard. 1971. *Sacajawea*. Norman: University of Oklahoma Press.

Hobson, Charles F. 1996. *The Great Chief Justice: John Marshall and the Rule of Law*. Lawrence: University Press of Kansas.

Jackson, Donald, ed. 1964. *Black Hawk: An Autobiography*. Urbana: University of Illinois Press.

Johansen, Bruce E. 2000. *Shapers of the Great Debate on Native Americans: Land, Spirit, and Power*. Westport, CT: Greenwood Press.

Johansen, Bruce E., and Donald A. Grinde, Jr. 1997. *The Encyclopedia of Native American Biography*. New York: Henry Holt.

Johnson v. M'Intosh (8 Wheaton 543, 1823).

Josephy, Alvin, Jr. 1961. *The Patriot Chiefs*. New York: Viking.

Mann, Barbara A. 1997. "The Last of the Mohicans" and "'The Indian-haters.'" In *Forbidden Ground: Racial Politics and Hidden Identity in James Fenimore Cooper's Leather-Stocking Tales*, Ph.D. Dissertation, University of Toledo, 168–182, 219–229.

McNickle, D'Arcy. 1949. *They Came Here First: The Epic of the American Indian*. Philadelphia, PA: J. B. Lippincott Co.

Moquin, Wayne. 1973. *Great Documents in American Indian History*. Westport, CT: Praeger.

Moulton, Gary. 1978. *John Ross: Cherokee Chief*. Athens: University of Georgia Press.

Moulton, Gary, ed. 2001. *The Journals of the Lewis and Clark Expedition*. 11 vols. Lincoln: University of Nebraska Press.

Nabokov, Peter. 1991. *Native Testimony*. New York: Viking.

Nebard, Grace R. 1932. *Sacajawea*. Glendale, CA: Arthur H. Clark.

O'Brien, Sharon. 1989. *American Indian Tribal Governments*. Norman: University of Oklahoma Press.

Oskinson, John M. 1838. *Tecumseh and His Times*. New York.

Parker, Arthur. 1913. *The Code of Handsome Lake, the Seneca Prophet*. New York State Museum Bulletin No. 163. Albany.

Porter, C. Fayne. 1964. *Our Indian Heritage: Profiles of Twelve Great Leaders*. Clifton Park, NY: Chilton.

Rogin, Michael Paul. 1975. *Fathers and Children: Andrew Jackson and the Subjugation of the American Indian*. New York: Alfred A. Knopf.

Satz, Ronald N. 1975. *American Indian Policy in the Jacksonian Era*. Lincoln: University of Nebraska Press.

Seymour, Flora W. 1991. *Sacajawea: American Pathfinder*. New York: Macmillan.

Smith, Jean Edward. 1996. *John Marshall: Definer of a Nation*. New York: Henry Holt.

Stannard, David. 1992. *American Holocaust: Columbus and the Conquest of the New World*. New York: Oxford University Press.

Tebbel, John, and Keith Jennison. 1960. *The American Indian Wars*. New York: Bonanza Books.

Thwaites, Reuben Gold. 1904–1905. *The Original Journals of Lewis and Clark*. New York.

Tocqueville, Alexis de. 1898. *Democracy in America*. Translated by Henry Reeve. New York: Century Co.

Tucker, Glenn. 1956. *Tecumseh: Vision of Glory*. Indianapolis, IN: Bobbs-Merrill Company.

Vanderworth, W. C. 1971. *Indian Oratory*. Norman: University of Oklahoma Press.

Van Every, Dale. 1966. *Disinherited: The Lost Birthright of the American Indian*. New York: William Morrow & Co.

Wallace, Anthony F. C. 1970. *The Death and Rebirth of the Seneca*. New York: Alfred A. Knopf.

Wallace, Paul A. W., ed. 1958. "Captivity and Murder." In *Thirty Thousand Miles with John Heckewelder*, 170–207. Pittsburgh, PA: University of Pittsburgh Press.

Washburn, Wilcomb E., ed. 1973. *The American Indian and the United States: A Documentary History*. New York: Random House.

Waters, Frank. 1993. *Brave Are My People: Indian Heroes Not Forgotten*. Santa Fe, NM: Clear Light Publishers.

Weeks, Philip. 1990. *Farewell, My Nation: The American Indian and the United States, 1820–1890*. Wheeling, IL: Harlan Davidson.

Wheaton, Henry. 1866. *Elements of International Law*. Boston: Dana.

Wilkinson, Charles F. 1987. *American Indians, Time, and the Law: Native Societies in a Modern Constitutional Democracy*. New Haven, CT: Yale University Press.

Worcester, Donald, ed. 1975. *Forked Tongues and Broken Treaties*. Caldwell, ID: Caxton.

Westward Expansion, Indian Wars, and Reservations
(1850 to 1900)

Indians west of the Mississippi River began the second half of the nineteenth century largely independent. By 1875, most Indians were confined to reservations. By 1900, any Indians still in existence were totally dependent on the goodwill of the U.S. government, were systematically being deprived of their unique cultures, and had no control over their lives or their futures. In 1850, a decreasing Indian population estimated at 388,000 (Royce, 1899, 537), with Late Stone Age technology and largely unaware of the threat, faced a United States of America with a population of 23 million people, growing at 21 to 26 percent per decade (Meinig, 1998, 265), with Industrial Age technology and largely unconcerned with those already using the land of the West. Each of the hundreds of Indian nations dealt with the European-American invasion on its own. To varying degrees, each nation was alien in language, culture, and interest to every other. To the Indians of the West in 1850, the White Man was just another strange tribe. By the time the Indians learned just *how* strange, it was too late. Not until the end of the century did there arise a sense of common Indian interest transcending tribal cultural boundaries. By then, any hope of resisting Euro-American control was gone.

At the midpoint of the nineteenth century, the Indians of the West were adjusting to such significant cultural changes as introduction of the horse and firearms, which spread northward and westward, respectively, increasing intertribal contact. Among the many Indian nations, particularly on the Great Plains, the horse revolutionized the cultures of many nations, including the Cheyenne, and in the Great Basin and the Southwest, where the Utes and the Apaches, respectively, had taken to horseback. Several nations had been forced west from the Great Lakes area in a "bow wave" effect, as Euro-Americans settled the Old Northwest in larger and larger numbers. However, most western Indians had little reason to believe that life for their grandchildren would be much different than their own.

At the same time, the United States was growing in population, wealth, and power. The second half of the nineteenth century was a time of profound change for Euro-Americans too. The railroad made it possible to travel vast distances in days. The telegraph moved information thousands of miles in an eyeblink. The Civil War destroyed the Old South. The machine took over from animal and human power. The discovery of gold gave the illusion of easy wealth. All these developments pushed Euro-Americans into the lands of the West.

Indian contact with Euro-Americans came in waves. One pattern of expansion was common, although not every contact happened in the same order. First on the scene were "mountain men" and traders. The mountain men were tolerated because there were so few of them. The traders were welcomed because they provided access to the White Man's goods. These forerunners were risk takers, gambling their lives to trade inexpensive goods for precious furs and information. Traders like George Bent were very careful to understand the cultures and personalities of the Indians with whom they traded, frequently marrying Indians, and often provided the communications link between the Indians and the Whites who followed.

The next wave consisted of the land exploiters—miners, ranchers, speculators, and road and railroad builders. Unlike the traders, they had no interest in understanding the Indians. Usually they wanted the Indians kept away from their projects. The gold rushes in California, Colorado, Montana, and Dakota Territory, in particular, attracted large numbers of such men very quickly, changing the racial complexion of these areas in a year or less. Once the land exploiters had enough clout to demand protection from Indians, the Army was dispatched to provide security. With the soldiers came their families, civilian contractors, and camp followers.

From the Indians' perspective, the last wave consisted of the farmers and townspeople. Sometimes, the farmers came first and towns grew up to support them. Alternatively, the town grew up around an Army fort, a railroad facility, or a trading post, providing the goods and services that farmers found attractive. The two might arrive together, in the same wagon train. A real estate developer might lay out an entire community, town, and farms, and advertise the development to potential immigrants. Because farming requires the exclusive use of land,

the arrival of farmers indicated the final occupation of the land by Euro-Americans.

Given their incompatible goals, cultures, and perceptions, the collision between Euro-Americans and Indians was inevitable. Both wanted the same land. The Indians wanted to live their own lives, and Euro-Americans wanted to change the Indian way of life. Each saw the other as alien, inferior, and frightening. But the Euro-Americans not only survived the collision, but prospered for a number of reasons.

The first reason for the Euro-American success in the West was a simple preponderance of numbers. The Old World diseases had created pandemics in the Americas, killing much of the Indian population, and they would continue to do so. Mortality from disease, injury, and starvation remained high, limiting Indian population growth. On the other hand, not only were Euro-Americans having large families, but immigration from overseas was increasing. In the 1850 census, the population of the United States was 23 million (U.S. Census, 2002, Table 1). It grew to 75 million by 1900 (U.S. Census, 2002, Table 1). The consensus is that the Indian population in 1850 in what are now the Lower 48 was estimated at 350,000 to 400,000. It *decreased* over the next five decades to 237,000 (U.S. Census, 2002, Table 1). As Euro-American settlers moved into Indian country, they soon outnumbered the Indians by large margins. For each Euro-American in the West, there were fifty to three hundred or more back East. An Indian tribe had only its own people.

The second reason for Euro-American success was the wide disparity in technology. Indian tribes were Late Stone Age cultures. (The Five Civilized Tribes were an exception. They had access to most rural Euro-American technologies of the time.) Otherwise, Indians did not have the skills to mine ores or to work hard metals, and they were dependent on imports for metal tools and weapons. Indian implements for living were handmade by tribal members from natural materials and were supplemented by imports. Euro-American settlers imported steel tools, manufactured clothing, and other factory goods from the East, where they could be made by machine cheaply and in great quantities.

Most tribes that practiced agriculture did not grow enough food to have surpluses to export and often required imports of grain to survive even before contact with Euro-Americans. For example, the Apaches brought meat and skins to the Pueblo Indians to trade for corn and Mexican trade goods. For Euro-Americans, the invention of the heavy iron plow, the cotton gin, and other agricultural machinery led to a large-scale monoculture that produced large surpluses, so that one American farmer could support many others beyond his own family. The wide use of the tin can for food storage and transportation provided dietary variety far from growing areas. Having enough to eat was rarely a problem for a Euro-American in the West, whereas an Indian band was fortunate if people did not starve to death during the winter, droughts, or other catastrophes.

Indians moved on foot or, if of high enough status, on horseback, and freight moved by pack animal—horse or human. For Euro-Americans, by 1850 there were already 8,000 miles of railroad in the United States east of the Mississippi (Hine, 1973, 111). It was the preferred means of moving both people and cargo overland for long distances. The steamship enabled reasonably fast up- and downstream movement along waterways, along coastlines, and between the East and West Coasts. Even away from the waterways and rails, west of the Mississippi, the animal-drawn wagon was the primary passenger and freight hauler with a far greater capacity than the travois, which dragged loads behind horses (and, before they were utilized, humans or dogs). Coupled with their ability to form large, complex organizations, their means of transportation gave the Euro-Americans a major advantage in both speed of movement and quantities moved.

For the Indians in the West, and more often than not for Euro-Americans as well, information traveled at the speed of a horse. However, as telegraph lines were installed across the West, Euro-Americans could send and receive information instantaneously from thousands of miles away. This permitted the rapid coordination of large-scale commercial and military actions, and the Euro-American population back East would learn about an event in Indian Country before other Indian tribes could learn of it.

Finally, the Euro-American advantage in weapons technology was decisive. The primary weapons of the western Indians were the war club, knife, hatchet, spear/lance, and bow. Imported firearms, steel knives, hatchets, spearheads, and arrowheads were preferred but expensive. In the West, almost every Euro-American adult male and many women and children had firearms and steel knives. The shoulder-fired weapon evolved from the muzzle-loading smoothbore musket, with an effective range of about a hundred yards in the hands of a well-trained marksman and heavy stopping power

out to that distance, to the lever- or bolt-action breech-loading rifle capable of killing at a thousand yards. The five- or six-shot revolver was the sidearm of choice, with an effective range of ten or fifteen yards. The U.S. Army also had artillery.

As the Nez Percés demonstrated in 1877, the Indians could make excellent use of rifles and pistols, but the Euro-Americans had one further advantage. With their industrial base and transportation networks, the United States could easily equip large numbers of soldiers and civilians with high-quality firearms and large quantities of ammunition and put them in the field almost anywhere. As with people, numbers mattered.

Third, Euro-Americans succeeded in driving the Indians out of most of the West by their willingness to deceive both the Indians and their own people, make promises that could not be kept, break other promises, rationalize immoral actions, ignore illegal acts, tolerate incompetence, and condone greed to accomplish their objective of the moment. The most common and most important promise made by government representatives to Indians was that whites would not enter their reservations without permission. Even if it had the political will to keep miners, settlers, and others from trespassing, the distances were too vast and the terrain too difficult for enforcement as a practical matter. The Army could never have been large enough to cover all the ground. However, as in the Black Hills in 1875 when an expedition led by Lieutenant Colonel George Custer reported finding gold, the Army was sometimes actively involved in encouraging trespassing. White occupation of Indian land was ignored, as was the sale of alcohol, even though both acts were against U.S. law.

Euro-Americans tolerated incompetence and graft in Indian Affairs that they would never have accepted in other areas of government. Government positions and contracts to provide food and other goods were considered political patronage. Incompetent and venal Indian agents aggravated tensions by callous disregard for the Indian perspective on events.

Greed was tolerated when it supported national objectives. The gold rushes in California, Colorado, and Dakota Territory devastated subsistence ranges, despoiled sacred sites, and led to the enslavement and extermination of whole tribes, but they added large amounts to the national wealth and attracted foreign investment. Therefore, Euro-Americans generally and the federal government in particular tolerated and even encouraged prospecting. Similarly, railroads were seen as constituting a strategic connection between East and West. Because the government was unable or unwilling to build them, private companies were subsidized by grants of land, leading to the partition and destruction of the buffalo herds on the Great Plains. These moral lapses facilitated a wide variety of activities that had the effect of opening up Indian land to white settlement and ultimately destroying the Indian will to resist. They were frequently the cause of Indian resistance that led to Army suppression. Combined with the disparities in technological levels and in the numbers of people, this willingness to abandon honor in favor of results created a force that was impossible for the Indians to stop.

Examples of this behavior include the treatment of the Indians in California, where commissioners negotiated treaties with Indians who had no understanding of what they were signing away. Most of the treaties were never ratified, neither reservation boundaries nor the removal of whites from reservations was enforced, and other promises were ignored. By 1870 only four reservations existed, and only about 30,000 Indians remained, mostly in Southern California (Meinig, 1998, 49). In 1854, Texas provided two small reservations along the Red River for the remnants of the native Indian tribes, but in 1859 Texas settlers demanded that land and 2,000 Indians were removed to Indian Territory (Gibson, 1980, 348). The failure to prevent encroachment on reservations in Washington led to the Yakama War (1855), the flight of the Nez Percés (1877), the Bannock War (1878), and the Sheepeater War (1879). In each case, the underlying cause of Indian dissatisfaction was Euro-American encroachment on Indian subsistence areas, and the flash point was the Indian belief that an entire band or tribe would be held responsible for the violent acts of one or a few warriors. A similar pattern of events led to the Ute War of 1878–1879, which followed a vicious propaganda campaign by the state government to turn sentiment back East against the tribe.

An important process in the relationship between Indians and Euro-Americans consisted of the negotiation, execution, ratification, and enforcement of treaties between Indian nations and the U.S. government. The Constitution of the United States gives Congress authority over Indian affairs and the federal government the authority to make treaties with foreign governments. Indian treaties typically provided that the parties would stay at peace with

each other and that the United States would give the Indians future compensation—money, goods, and services, often called *annuities*—and secure territory—a reservation—in exchange for large tracts of land being used by the Indians for subsistence. They also might provide for the removal of the Indian tribe to a reservation away from their present homes. However, treaties were interpreted differently by Indians and the U.S. government.

Indians were experienced in negotiating peace agreements with other Indian nations. They tended to see such agreements as bargaining between equals in status (if not in power), binding on those at the signing and on their followers. The U.S. government usually chose to interpret treaties as binding the entire tribe of each Indian leader signing. The government was not concerned with the Indians' interpretation. Government officials thought that they were dealing with inferior, uncivilized people who should appreciate the respect they were being shown in the treaty-making process. Indian treaties had less moral significance than treaties with "civilized" European countries.

Indians incorporated oral representations and the spirit of the negotiations into the meaning of a treaty, and they expected substantial compliance until the circumstances that drove the negotiations changed, if ever. The intent of the treaty was to be observed. Indians knew that leaders could not absolutely control the activities of every warrior and that some violations would almost certainly occur. However, such violations were treated as personal matters, to be dealt with by the individuals concerned, not as matters concerning the entire nation. For Euro-Americans applying the principles of the Anglo-American legal system, the written treaty document was the entire agreement. Oral representations were overruled by the written treaty, and the government expected the Indians to comply precisely with every promise they made. It did not apply this standard to its own compliance.

The Indians participating in the negotiation process were almost without exception illiterate and could put no faith in a written document. For the Indian leaders, a treaty was the exchange of promises between the U.S. leaders and themselves. Symbols of respect presented to Indian leaders often had a positive effect on reaching agreement on treaties. While the government representatives may have thought it was childish, Indians truly valued medals, military uniforms and insignia, U.S. flags, and other gifts that to them symbolized their social

acceptance as equals and friends by the United States.

An Indian leader's authority to negotiate was his moral authority as a successful war leader, a charismatic leader, and an elder. If he traded away too much for too little in return, his authority would decrease and perhaps vanish altogether. For the U.S. government, negotiating was done by a peace commission appointed by the president. Orally, commissioners tended to overstate their authority, but the written treaties included provisions that made the government's performance of its obligations dependent on the actions of Congress in ratifying the treaty and appropriating funds. Indians were expected to act immediately on their obligations under a treaty, and they felt betrayed if the treaty was not ratified by the Congress, if ratification was delayed, or if the treaty was changed before it was ratified—all common results when treaties arrived at Congress's door. Indians were even angrier when a ratified treaty with which they had already complied was changed or abrogated by subsequent U.S. government actions. The courts did not have the authority to deal with the consequences of that kind of breach of a treaty. That was the responsibility of the president and Congress.

Indians facing the inevitable breach of their treaties had four options. First, they could sue the government in federal court. In the second half of the nineteenth century, the Five Civilized Tribes were the only Indians with the sophistication and resources to attempt this. Second, they could petition the Great White Father to help them. This was naive and rarely accomplished anything. The Indians generally did not understand the Constitutional and political limits on the president's authority or the president's inability as a practical matter to push the federal bureaucracy into action. Third, they could try to enforce the treaty with their own power, resisting and retaliating for the transgression by force. This choice consistently caused the U.S. government to send the Army after them and often led to the termination of the treaty they were trying to enforce. Fourth, they could do nothing and just tolerate the breach. After the end of Apache resistance in 1886, this was the only option left. With the fluid nature of tribal leadership, more than one of these options might be chosen by different tribal factions. Young and warlike warriors might retaliate with raids on settlements or infrastructure, irrespective of the wishes of tribal elders. The Euro-Americans interpreted the raids by a few

hotheads as the entire tribe going to war, and, typically, the entire tribe suffered.

The Constitution of the United States says that ratified treaties with sovereign states are the law of the land. However, treaties, like statutes, may be amended or repealed by subsequent congressional and presidential action. There were five limitations on the U.S. government's flexibility. First, title to land granted by a treaty could not be disturbed without compensation. For this reason, any further attempt to reduce Indian land after a treaty required another treaty, or agreement. Second, Indian treaties and many statutes created a trust relationship, imposing on the U.S. government as the trustee obligations to act in good faith toward the Indians and in the Indians' best interests. Third, the courts repeatedly stated that the government owed the Indians a moral obligation to observe the terms of treaties due to the unequal negotiating positions of the parties. Fourth, the government was limited by internal Euro-American politics, including public opinion. Fifth, the government was limited by the practical limits of power on the ground. Of the five limitations, only the first two could be enforced in the courts.

The terms of treaties from 1850 until Congress ended the practice in 1871 were remarkably consistent. The Indian parties promised to withdraw to a more or less specific reservation and give up any rights to the balance of the lands they claimed. They promised to be faithful to the United States and follow no other "civilized" power (meaning Great Britain or Mexico). They promised to keep the peace with the United States and its people. The United States promised that the Indian parties would have their reservation forever, subject to federal laws on land ownership. Usually a cash payment was to be made each year for several decades, although the treaties were vague as to how this payment was to be made and to whom. The government would provide the Indians with food, particularly for the winter. Finally, the government would supply an itemized list of goods and services. The nature of these goods, in treaty after treaty, demonstrates one of the government objectives in the treaty process—changing the traditional Indian culture from that of nomadic hunting and gathering to that of settled, "civilized" agriculture. In addition to farming equipment, goods included Euro-American-style clothing.

While the treaties were uniformly one-sided, worse for the Indians was the U.S. government's general failure to perform its obligations. Leaders like Ouray of the Utes, who understood that the terms of the treaties were unequal, also understood that circumstances had changed and accepted the treaty terms as the best hope for tribal survival. They believed that, with a protected territory, annual monetary payments, and enough food to balance the loss of subsistence areas, they could survive the flood of whites moving into their lands. Often they believed they had no choice and simply hoped for the best. Had these obligations been met, many of the saddest events in the collisions between Indians and Euro-Americans would not have happened.

With some important exceptions, the U.S. government delegated the performance of its obligations under these treaties to un- or self-interested bureaucrats and contractors. The positions were filled on the basis of the personal decisions of senior officials, inviting corruption and favoritism. The government agencies involved demonstrated both incompetence and corruption in fulfilling their material obligations. Contracts for goods and services were awarded in the same way and rarely audited. Sometimes malfeasance was due to greed. Others failed to perform their duties out of racist malice toward the Indians. Some were stupid, insensitive, or lazy. Others manipulated the performance of obligations for what they thought were positive objectives, such as assimilation, religious salvation, or maintaining peace.

The delivery of material compensation—annuities, food, and other goods and services—failed at several levels. First, Congress had to appropriate the funds, and sometimes did not do so for political reasons that had nothing to do with treaty obligations to the Indians. Compensation might be delayed, diverted, or embezzled by agency employees. Sometimes it was paid to the wrong person, even to the wrong tribe. Food frequently arrived spoiled and insufficient in quantity to support a tribe deprived of its familiar form of sustenance. The food might be so alien to the recipients that they got sick on it or refused to eat it. A tribe of hunters might be given plows and seed, but no training on how to farm successfully.

Much of this incompetence and malice might have been tolerated by the Indians had the U.S. government fulfilled its promise to secure their remaining lands from Euro-American infiltration. However, in many instances when a tribe's large tracts of land were desirable or were found to contain gold, the government failed to prevent Euro-American occupation and settlement. Similarly, railroads were seen

in the United States as critical to the nation's economy, growth, and security. Therefore, obstacles to the extension of rail lines throughout the West were not tolerable. Furthermore, Euro-American land hunger showed little respect for unmarked reservation boundaries. The attitude that "unoccupied" land was there to be taken for "productive" uses—agriculture, ranching, mining, commerce—continued to motivate speculators, developers, and migrants to occupy reservation lands.

The government lacked both the resources and the interest to protect Indian lands from Euro-American occupation. U.S. civil law enforcement and territorial militias did not enforce such restrictions on their own people—on themselves. That left the Army, which was stretched thin, controlled by civilians in Washington ignorant of western conditions, and all too often bigoted against Indians as a race.

In the midst of this misfeasance and malfeasance, many soldiers, government officials, contractors, and other Euro-Americans were both competent and dedicated to what they perceived as the best interests of the Indians. Traders often earned the respect of the Indian nations with which they dealt and served loyally as interpreters for the Indians in treaty negotiations. Agents, commissioners, and soldiers often sent honest and objective reports to Washington, even though their observations were filtered through their cultural biases. Idealists campaigned for the government to fulfill its obligations. However, even the most supportive of Euro-Americans pressed for actions like allotment and residential schools, which would lead to the destruction of the Indians as independent nations and unique cultures.

In 1871, Congress stopped making treaties with Indian nations, deciding that they were not "sovereign" foreign states. From that point, relations between Indian tribes and the U.S. government took the form of agreements, statutes enacted by the normal process, or by executive orders from the president. The terms of agreements were similar to those of treaties, but agreements raised none of the peculiar legal issues of treaties, such as tribal sovereignty.

Other than "vested" rights, meaning that Indians had a property interest such that they could not be taken away without due process of law and just compensation, by 1900 the rights of Indians were whatever the U.S. government chose to grant them. By means of treaties and agreements, Euro-Americans controlled all but a few small patches of the United States.

Euro-Americans, including the elected and appointed officials in the U.S. government, believed that fallow land was unoccupied and therefore freely available for agriculture, ranching, forestry, mining, and other uses. This belief came from a variety of sources, in particular the Anglo-American legal tradition. Such concepts as adverse possession and best use confirmed European traditions of land use and the more recent Euro-American tradition of homesteading. Also reinforcing this belief were the Euro-American beliefs in Manifest Destiny and the superiority of their civilization—racism. Euro-Americans still believed that agriculture was the foundation of society and that the farmer was the epitome of manhood. Given internal U.S. politics and economic incentives, the Euro-American migration west is not a surprise. For all these reasons, the government actively encouraged migration to western lands by farmers through homestead acts and cheap land sales.

North-South politics were important in the years before and during the Civil War. The balance of power between Slave States and Free States was swinging away from the South as the population of the North grew at a much faster rate than that of the South. Both North and South encouraged the colonization of the West to influence the political makeup of potential new states. After the Civil War, the largest motivating factor for migration was financial opportunity. Speculators and real estate developers sought land that they could buy and sell at a profit. Settlers were looking for better and more farmland, broader pastures for cattle, and new markets for services and trade. The desire for land suitable for cotton plantations led Southerners to migrate to eastern Texas and Indian Territory before and after the Civil War.

Infiltration by mining interests and miners was no less disruptive. In California, the massive influx of miners led to the near destruction of the Indians of California. Those who resisted were chased down and destroyed. Cross-country travel to California, followed by the construction of the Transcontinental Railroad and other permanent transportation routes, disrupted other Indians' subsistence and migration patterns. The Forty-Niners in California wanted to push the local Indians out of the gold fields, leading to the 1850–1851 Mariposa War. Prospecting in southern Oregon led to the Rogue River War of 1855–1856. Abusive behavior by miners in southwestern Idaho led the Northern Paiutes to take up arms in 1860. Prospectors crossing the Great Plains

and squatting in prime winter quarters led to the 1864–1865 Cheyenne-Arapaho War. Miners trespassing on the Sioux reservation to get to Montana triggered the Bozeman Trail War in 1866–1867. The gold rush in the Black Hills of Dakota Territory, long a holy place for Sioux and other Plains tribes, led to the Lakota War of 1875–1877.

The Colorado gold rush led to confrontations between miners and Indians in Kansas and Nebraska. The actual mining area was not important to any Indian nations, but the strike attracted more than twice as many immigrants as did the California gold rush. In 1858–1859, more than 100,000 people crossed Kansas and Nebraska to reach the Rockies (West, 1998, xv). The Cheyennes, who dominated the central Plains at this time, had already deforested the area's river valleys, but Euro-American immigrants used the same routes for moving people and freight. Many of them settled in the river valleys when Indians were elsewhere on the Plains, and the Army chose some of the most fertile wooded areas remaining for fortifications. This shut the Cheyennes out of the best horse pastures. Also, the miners occupied critical Cheyenne and Arapaho winter quarters in the eastern Rocky Mountains. Buffalo herds drifted east and refused to migrate across the settled river valleys, splitting them into northern and southern herds and intensifying competition between the Western Plains tribes and the Pawnee and other Eastern Plains tribes.

In 1866 the northern Plains Indians recognized the disruption caused by Euro-Americans traveling on the Bozeman Trail to the Montana gold strike. This was land reserved to the Sioux, in particular, in the First Treaty of Fort Laramie in 1851. The Sioux and their allies attacked parties of miners and especially prospectors, until the Army was ordered to protect travelers on the trail. Many Sioux resisted, while the Crows attempted to play the United States against the Sioux while remaining neutral. The Army troops deployed and the forts built were insufficient to provide real security, and the Sioux and their allies were successful in stopping the Army. With the completion of the Transcontinental Railroad into Colorado, another route to the Montana gold fields developed that did not trespass on Plains Indian lands, and the Army withdrew under the terms of the Second Treaty of Fort Laramie in 1868.

The initial prospectors who responded to the lure of gold tended to move on when the claims were played out or all the good claims taken. How-

ever, the Euro-Americans and others who came to support and exploit the miners often stayed and started commercial, industrial, or agricultural communities. Sometimes, as in Nevada and Montana, mining continued as an industrial rather than individual enterprise, and extraction from more difficult ores and other minerals such as copper or coal required capital-intensive operations. However, time after time, when mining reached this stage, there were no longer any Indians in the area.

While gold rushes repeatedly triggered confrontations between Indians and Euro-Americans, it was *land* that attracted most settlers to the subsistence areas of the Indians. Land was a speculative investment, a desirable transportation corridor, or just a bigger ranch or farm. Indians learned to be more afraid of surveyors than of prospectors.

The U.S. government granted over 131 million acres of western land to railroads between 1850 and 1875 (Hine, 2000, 282). As they were built, the railroads provided corridors along which Euro-Americans settled. The railroad was the dominant means of long-distance transportation to markets back east. Towns sprung up where the railroads set up roundhouses and maintenance facilities. Finally, the railroads were major real estate developers in their own right, exploiting their broad land grants. The railroads and their associated influx of settlers divided the buffalo herds, making hunting buffalo much harder for the Plains Indians. By providing easy access for commercial hunters, the railroads facilitated the final destruction of the buffalo herds in the 1870s.

In the winter of 1858–1859, bands of southern Cheyenne returned to their usual winter quarters along the Front Range of the Rocky Mountains to find thousands of Euro-American miners and others, with entire cities (including what would become the city of Denver) laid out in lots on some of the best living sites. At noon on April 22, 1889, about 50,000 people galloped or ran into what had been some of the choicest land on the Indian reservations in what is now Oklahoma. These are two dramatic examples of the speculative fever attached to "unoccupied" western land. Land long used for subsistence by Indians was variously granted by the government to individuals and organizations (such as the railroads), purchased from the government, homesteaded, or simply squatted on. Speculators moved into an area early, locating and acquiring (legally or otherwise) prime land for agriculture and commerce. They would lay out entire towns in lots on

the ground, organize entire counties, and sell the lots back east to prospective settlers. It was a process repeated over and over.

Ranchers saw the Great Plains, western Texas, and the valleys of the Great Basin as perfect for large-scale cattle ranching. Soon after the Civil War, Texas ranchers began driving herds north to the Plains, establishing large ranches that exploited the open grasslands. With the railroads reaching across the Plains, ranchers had easy access to eastern markets. Cattle competed with the buffalo and provided a nearly irresistible target for hungry Plains Indians.

Farming expanded rapidly in Oregon, Washington, and the central valley of California. Homesteaders occupied more and more of the most productive land as the century passed, forcing out the subsistence plants and animals on which the Indians of California and the Northwest lived and pushing the Indians themselves into less fertile country. In the Great Plains, farmers moved west along the east-west rivers, staying near water. This blocked the north-south migration of buffalo and occupied most of the Plains Indians' watering areas. The trees left by the Indians were soon chopped down by the white settlers for construction and fuel, leaving nomadic Indians without fuel or shelter. Irrigation extended the breadth of farming from the river valleys, and the development of dry farming techniques late in the nineteenth century made the western Plains attractive to farmers. The young farmer who was crowded out of Ohio, Pennsylvania, or Kentucky could afford to set up a much larger farm in Kansas or Iowa.

In the early nineteenth century, many Euro-Americans believed that "civilized" whites and "savage" Indians could not live side by side. With a whole continent to the west, it became U.S. government policy to remove Indians beyond what was then thought to be the potential limits of Euro-American settlement. Many tribes in the Southeast, the Ohio Valley, and the Great Lakes area were bribed, coerced, or forced to move to reserved lands—reservations—west of the Mississippi River, leading to such incidents as the Cherokee Trail of Tears in 1838–1839. By 1850, Euro-Americans were settling in large numbers in the eastern Plains and across the Mississippi and Missouri Rivers. Removal again became government policy.

The stated purposes for removal and reservations were to move perceived Indian security threats farther away from settled areas, to protect Indians from Euro-American speculators and criminals, to concentrate Indians in more easily supervised areas, and to lead them to take up a settled, "civilized" way of life. Other purposes were to open up land for Euro-American exploitation and to make Indians dependent on the U.S. government for security, food, and essential services. Some tribes were removed more than once. When the tribes along the Mississippi and Missouri Rivers in Nebraska and Kansas were removed to Indian Territory, included were tribes such as the Sac and Fox that had been removed from the Ohio Valley and the Great Lakes area a generation earlier.

Reservations were always significantly smaller than the lands left behind and almost always too small to permit the extensive hunting and gathering that had previously been the tribes' mode of subsistence. Furthermore, they were often far away from the lands they knew how to use. The reservation was a new place, with different terrain, plants, and animals. One exception was the original Sioux reservation in the northern Plains, the result of the Second Treaty of Fort Laramie. This covered much of what is now western Nebraska, South Dakota, and North Dakota, as well as large parts of eastern Montana, Wyoming, and Colorado. While smaller than the area controlled by the Sioux tribes previously, it was large enough for the Sioux to continue their existing lifestyle. In 1851 and 1858, the Sioux in Minnesota were concentrated on a small reservation. When their 1862 revolt was suppressed, the survivors were removed to this reservation.

The government was generally unable to prevent Indians from leaving their reservations for hunting, religious gatherings, or war. For example, while the Quakers supervised the Indian Territory reservations in the 1870s, warriors from the southern Plains Indians, who had been removed to reservations there, came to the Indian Territory reservations to draw rations, went raiding into Texas and Mexico, then returned to their reservations and boasted of their exploits. The Army could not intervene on the reservations except at the request of the Indian agents, and, as pacifists, the Quaker agents refused to make the requests. Thus the Army and the Texas Rangers were forced to track raiders across hundreds of thousands of square miles of western Texas, usually without success. In other areas the situation was less extreme. The Indian agent might withhold food or other annuity payments until missing warriors returned, and the Army had more freedom to take action on the reservation. Still, there were very few soldiers to patrol a vast territory. If small parties

of off-reservation Indians were doing no harm to Euro-American settlers, they were usually ignored. As buffalo and other prey disappeared, this became less of an issue.

Many reservations were reduced in land area as the nineteenth century proceeded. For example, in the 1850s, the reservations of the Five Civilized Tribes covered most of the eastern and southern parts of what is now Oklahoma. In a generation they had adapted to their new homes and prospered. However, the Civil War divided the people of the Tribes, as it did the border states of Missouri and Kentucky. The Choctaws, the Chickasaws, the followers of those who had supported removal, the planters and slave owners, and those who already mistrusted the federal government supported the Confederacy, while those who had opposed removal, most full-bloods, and traditionalists supported the Union. Internal fighting left the reservations devastated. Many members of the Five Civilized Tribes fought for each side. However, their participation on the Confederate side was used as a pretext to shrink their prewar reservations by half, which provided territory for the relocation of southern Plains tribes to Indian Territory.

Within the United States throughout the nineteenth century, the Euro-Americans who worked the hardest on behalf of Indians were people of faith (usually Protestant Christians) and others with similar philosophical positions who sincerely believed that the future of the Indians depended on teaching them Euro-American culture and integrating them as citizens of the United States—assimilation. These Euro-Americans had no doubt that their religion and their culture, what they termed "civilization," were superior in every way to the native culture of the Indians. The best method of ensuring the survival of the Indians was to civilize them.

The Roman Catholic church had long served this function in the Southwest under the Spanish and Mexicans. The Army encouraged Protestant missionaries, protecting them when possible. In 1865, the Army awarded contracts for the operation of reservation schools to Protestant missionary societies. When the operation of the Indian agencies was moved from the Army to the Department of the Interior in 1870, contracts for the agencies were awarded to twelve Christian denominations. Consistent with the assimilation strategy were the annuity terms of the Indian treaties. The explicit goal was to transform nomadic hunter-gatherers into stable, static farmers. As the Indians learned the skills of agriculture and the life of the farmer, they would automatically become "civilized."

In the nineteenth century, nobody in the United States expressed any interest in preserving living Indian cultures. Even those who most fervently wanted to help the Indians and those who believed in the image of the noble savage also believed that the Indian culture was a thing of the past, something to be swept away by modern civilization. Museums and other institutions were created to collect artifacts of the material culture of the Indians, but this was done to remember the past, not to preserve the present or to facilitate the future of Indian cultures.

Another assimilationist theory for preserving the Indians arose from Euro-American ideas about private property and the significance of the individual over the group. In addition to the widely held idealistic view of the farmer as the bedrock of democracy, social theorists of the times associated collectivism with primitive savagery. Civilization required that individuals become the key unit of economic and political life. Collective—tribal—control of land was therefore in the way of bringing the Indians to a civilized state. Allotment was the process of taking land under common tribal control and granting title to specific tracts of it to individual Indians. The explicit rationale behind allotment was that Indians would assimilate into mainstream Euro-American culture if they became individual farm owners and their tribal institutions no longer had any authority over them. Those who supported the Indians believed that allotment would allow them to survive by further integrating them into the Euro-American culture. Others saw allotment as a way of destroying tribal institutions and loyalties and a further incentive to permanent settlement, making Indians less dangerous and easier to control than in the past. There were also less idealistic reasons for allotment. Indians were to be allotted small tracts that added up to substantially less land than in the existing reservations and that left large tracts available for the government to sell to others.

In 1887, Congress passed the General Allotment Act, usually called the Dawes Act after its sponsor, Senator Henry Dawes. The Dawes Act provided that the allotments were to be held in trust by the government for twenty years, so that they could not be sold. However, an exception provided that an Indian who was declared competent to handle his own affairs by the local Indian agency could sell his land. Such declarations were quickly abused. Indians

received private allotments without either the skills or resources to farm them profitably, motivating them to sell even without fraud. Some Indian communities resembled checkerboards, with allotments interspersed with land owned by non-Indians. Other tribes learned how to manipulate the system to preserve contiguous land. However, more than half of all reservation land was lost to Indian control.

Some tribes, including the Five Civilized Tribes, were exempt from the Dawes Act at first, although many of them were subsequently brought under its terms. The allotment process took time. Tribes with valuable farmland or other resources tended to be allotted sooner. Many reservations took on the checkerboard pattern, with Indian-owned land interspersed with non-Indian–owned land. Several tribes studied the allotment system carefully and exploited it to keep control of important resources, sacred places, and contiguous land holdings. Some even asked for allotment, sensing that Anglo-American style land titles were more secure than vague treaty promises.

Tribal governments and extended family and clan units did not fade away, as Indians found ways around the allotment system. However, as Indians were coerced into selling their allotments to pay taxes or tricked into selling, they lost more and more land. Indian farming decreased, as allotment owners found they could lease their property to whites. The utter failure of the Dawes Act to accomplish its goals would not be dealt with until well into the twentieth century.

Tribal governments became powerless and remained so until the Indian Reorganization Act of 1934. Tribes were crowded onto less and less land, causing increased poverty and disease. Mobility for hunting and gathering, already severely limited by the reservation system, was almost destroyed altogether. Extended families were broken up, and other long-standing collective institutions were destroyed or crippled.

A person born in 1830—Indian or Euro-American—was twenty years old in 1850 and seventy years old in 1900. The changes described in this article happened within that person's adult lifetime. What the person saw in 1900 could not have been imagined in 1850.

For many Euro-Americans, 1900 concluded in a general mood of incredible optimism. The useful areas of the West had been colonized successfully. Survival in the face of nature was rarely a major concern. Technology in every field of human endeavor was advancing rapidly, allowing people to live longer, live better, and do more. The United States of America was a world power, with a seat at the table with the ancient empires of Europe. At home, the countryside was generally peaceful.

The Indians of 1900 saw their world occupied by Euro-Americans, their own people confined to a small part of the land they used to roam. They saw their people disappearing. They saw the proliferation of *things* in the Euro-American community, things that enabled people to do more and live more comfortably. Their grandchildren coveted such things but could have them only at the price of giving up the remnants of their own culture, if then. Indians could see two futures for their people. Some would assimilate into the White Man's world, becoming white in every way but skin color. Others would stifle and stagnate on the reservation, perhaps preserving parts of a culture that was under continuous assault. Those who tried to bridge the gap and have both cultures would too often lose both and fall into alcoholism or worse.

There was hope. Young Indians from different nations attending residential schools learned a common language and found that they had many other things in common. A sense of common *Indian* interests, beyond the family, clan, and tribe, was developing. Indians who went off to the Spanish-American War with Teddy Roosevelt's Rough Riders found themselves earning the respect and admiration of their comrades of other races. These were small rays of sunlight in an otherwise bleak, cloudy future.

And the Indians were still here. Outnumbered, outproduced, outgunned, run off their land, cheated, robbed, and slaughtered, they were still here. In spite of the best efforts of good people to turn them into white Americans, they were still here. On a road paved with intentions both good and bad, *they were still here.* The Indians who survived the second half of the nineteenth century, saving most of their culture and some of their land, would be the seeds from which the Indian renaissance of the twentieth and twenty-first centuries would grow.

Veronica E. Velarde Tiller

See also Apache Wars; Boarding Schools, United
    States and Canada; Buffalo; Bureau of Indian
    Affairs: Establishing the Existence of an Indian
    Tribe; California Indians, Genocide of; Canada,
    Indian Policies of; Ceremonies, Criminalization
    of; Education and Social Control; Forced
    Marches; Fort Laramie Treaty of 1868; General

Allotment Act (Dawes Act); Genocide; Ghost Dance Religion; Horse, Economic Impact; Reservation Economic and Social Conditions; Tribal Sovereignty; Trust, Doctrine of.

References and Further Reading

Barrington, Linda, ed. 1999. *The Other Side of the Frontier: Economic Explorations into Native American History.* Boulder, CO: Westview Press.

Calloway, Colin G., ed. 1996. *Our Hearts Fell to the Ground: Plains Indian Views of How the West Was Lost.* Boston: Bedford/St. Martin's.

Cohen, Felix S. 1942 [1971 reprint]. *Handbook of Federal Indian law.* Albuquerque: University of New Mexico Press.

Davis, Mary B., ed. 1994. *Native America in the Twentieth Century: An Encyclopedia.* New York: Garland Publishing.

Doyle, Susan Badger. 1991. "Intercultural Dynamics of the Bozeman Trail Era: Red, White, and Army Blue on the Northern Plains, 1863–1868." Ph.D. dissertation, University of New Mexico Press.

Ellis, Richard N. 1972. *The Western American Indian: Case Studies in Tribal History.* Lincoln: University of Nebraska Press.

French, Laurence Armand. 2000. *Addictions and Native Americans.* Westport, CT: Praeger.

Gibson, Arrell Morgan. 1980. *The American Indian: Prehistory to the Present.* Lexington, MA: D. C. Heath and Company.

Greenwald, Emily. 2002. *Reconfiguring the Reservation: The Nez Perces, Jicarilla Apaches, and the Dawes Act.* Albuquerque: University of New Mexico Press.

Hine, Robert V. 1973. *The American West: An Interpretive History.* Boston: Little, Brown and Company.

Hine, Robert V., and John Mack Faragher. 2000. *The American West: A New Interpretive History.* New Haven, CT: Yale University Press.

Hirschfelder, Arlene, and Martha Kreipe de Montaño. *The Native American Almanac: A Portrait of Native America Today.* New York: Prentice Hall General Reference.

Keegan, John. 1993. *A History of Warfare.* New York: Alfred A. Knopf.

Meinig, D. W. 1998. *Transcontinental America.* Vol. 3: *The Shaping of America: A Geographical Perspective on 500 Years of History.* New Haven, CT: Yale University Press.

Neshoba, compiler. Available at: newhistoryheadlines. http://nativenewsonline.org/history/. Accessed April 27, 2005.

Prucha, Francis Paul. 1977. *A Bibliographical Guide to the History of Indian-White Relations in the United States.* Chicago: University of Chicago Press.

Prucha, Francis Paul. 1994. *American Indian Treaties: The History of a Political Anomaly.* Berkeley: University of California Press.

Royce, Charles C., comp. 1899. *Indian Land Cessions in the United States.* In *H.R. Doc. No. 736*, 56th Cong., 1st Sess.

U.S. Census. 2002. "United States—Race and Hispanic Origin: 1790 to 1990." Available at: http://www.census.gov/population/ documentation/twps0056/tab01.pdf. Accessed 2002.

Utley, Robert M. 1973. *Frontier Regulars: The United States Army and the Indian 1866–1891.* Bloomington: Indiana University Press.

Vogel, Virgil J. 1972. *This Country Was Ours: A Documentary History of the American Indians.* New York: Harper & Row.

West, Elliot. 1998. *The Contested Plains: Indians, Goldseekers, & the Rush to Colorado.* Lawrence: University Press of Kansas.

Worcester v. Georgia 31 U.S. (6 Pet.) 515(1832).

Wright, Ronald. 1992. *Stolen Continents: The Americas Through Indian Eyes Since 1492.* Boston: Houghton-Mifflin.

Indian Assimilation and Reorganization
(1900 to 1945)

The dawn of the twentieth century found Native North Americans on the verge of extinction, the population reduced to less than a quarter of a million in the U.S. portion of the continent. What remained of the Natives' land base was rapidly dwindling under the impact of the General Allotment Act, their jurisdiction was usurped by the Major Crimes Act, their spiritual practices largely prohibited by federal regulations, and their children increasingly removed from their families, communities, and societies, for placement in government-run residential schools. There they were systematically stripped of their cultural identity and indoctrinated to view the world—and themselves—in terms preferred by the Euro-Americans who had subjugated their peoples.

All of this occurred as part of an officially proclaimed policy of "assimilation," taking as its goal the elimination of all American Indians, culturally recognizable as such, by some point in the late 1930s. In his first annual message (1901), President Theodore Roosevelt, to the enthusiastic applause of his Indian Commissioner, Francis Leupp, touted assimilationist initiatives, allotment, and compulsory "education" in particular, as "a mighty pulverizing engine to break up the tribal mass" (Dippie, 1982, 244; Leupp, 1910, 79–95). Small wonder that the literature of the period was suffused with references to American Indians as a "vanishing race."

Two years after Roosevelt's message, the U.S. Supreme Court, by declaring federal authority over Indians to be "plenary in nature"—i.e., full, complete, and judicially unchallengeable—in its 1903 *Lone Wolf v. Hitchcock* opinion, affirmed the government's prerogative to "pulverize" native cultures in virtually any manner it saw fit. At a stroke, the *Lone Wolf* opinion formalized the status of indigenous peoples in the United States as essentially interchangeable with that imposed on the populations of Hawaii, Puerto Rico, Guam, the Philippines, and other newly acquired U.S. colonies abroad.

Thus licensed by the high court, both Congress and the officials charged with implementing whatever legislation it enacted, displayed less concern than ever for Indian rights. On the reservations, the already "near-dictatorial powers" delegated by the secretary of interior to his agents in the field (Deloria and Lytle, 1983, 10) were substantially reinforced. Under such conditions, the crushing weight previously placed on Native cultures increased dramatically. While there are any number of additional lenses through which effects can be assessed, the following focal points seem especially useful.

Loss of Land through the "Alchemy of Race"

Between 1887, when the General Allotment Act (25 U.S.C.A. § 331) was implemented, and 1934, when it was finally rescinded, the aggregate landholdings of American Indians were diminished from some 138 million acres to barely 52 million (McDonnell, 1991, 121). Of the residue, "nearly 20 million [acres] were desert or semiarid and virtually useless for any kind of . . . farming ventures" (Deloria and Lytle, 1983, 10). Of the 86 million acres lost, 60 million had been declared "surplus" under a provision of the Act by which the government had empowered itself to take such action, once every Indian on any given reservation had received his or her individual parcel of land (McDonnell, 1991, 2, 121; Washburn, 1986, 68–69). Originally, the parcels allotted averaged 160 acres apiece, but the size was reduced to 80 acres in some locales by amendatory legislation passed by Congress in 1891 (26 Stat. 794), each of them to be held in trust by the government for twenty-five years after allotment.

A key question with regard to the whole process is how the government determined who qualified as an "Indian" for purposes of allotment, thereby becoming "eligible" to receive a land parcel. On this, the Act itself is mute, stating only that the policy would be carried out by "special agents appointed by the President for such purpose, and the agents in charge of the respective reservations on which the allotments are directed to be made, under such rules and regulations as the Secretary of Interior may from time to time prescribe" (Washburn, 1986, 69–70). Nor, to date, has any analyst addressed the issue, either leaving it unmentioned or declaiming that "[w]hat it means to be an 'Indian,' legally and culturally, is and has always been a complicated question, but is a question I do not address here" (Banner, 1981, 8).

Plainly, the matter *must* be addressed, since it has a direct bearing on the number of parcels allotted and therefore on the quantity of "surplus" acreage remaining for non-Indian acquisition once the allotment process was declared to be complete on each reservation. In this regard, the fewer Indians there were, the better; such, unquestionably, was the perspective of many—perhaps most—of those, in government and out, who supported the Act in 1887. Indeed, a systematic reduction of the Native land base appealed to settlers, railroad magnates, merchants, populists, southerners, apostles of western expansion, and even the Indians' new "friends." More pointedly:

> The most powerful business interests in the West were becoming convinced that they had a direct interest in the expansion of agricultural production. As a result they were increasingly interested in both gaining entry to and reducing the size of tribal holdings (Hoxie, 1984, 46).

Such desires coincided quite neatly with the fact that the sponsor of the Allotment Act, Massachusetts Senator Henry L. Dawes, was heavily influenced in his views on Indians by John Wesley Powell, founding director of the U.S. Bureau of Ethnology, as well as the ethnologist Alice Fletcher. Dawes, together with most of his "loyalists" in the Senate, also belonged to the so-called Friends of the Indian, a Christian reform group subscribing to the social evolutionary theories set forth by the anthropologist Lewis Henry Morgan and embraced by both Powell and Fletcher, as well as such prominent ethnographers as James Mooney and George Bird Grinnell.

Although it has been argued that, as a social evolutionist, Morgan "explicitly rejected racial classifications" (Hoxie, 1984, 116), quite the opposite is true. An "emphasis on blood and its use as a vehicle of inheritance of [cultural] traits . . . continued to be an important theme in Morgan's . . . writings," even in such late works as *Systems of Consanguinity and Affinity of the Human Family* (1871) and *Ancient Society, or the Researches in the Lines of Human Progress from Savagery through Barbarism to Civilization* (1871). In substance, "Morgan believed that culture was hereditary" and therefore that the best—or at least most humane—"solution to the Indian problem" would be to simply "breed" the

race out of existence (Bieder, 1986, 223, 226, 233; Hilden, 1995, 149–150).

> Through selective breeding, Morgan thought, Indians could be absorbed into the white population with little or no negative effect [upon the latter]. Morgan concluded from his observations that the half blood was inferior to the pureblood Indian both physically and mentally, "but the second cross, giving three-quarters Indian, is an advance upon the native; and giving three fourths white is a still greater advance" resulting in near equality with the white ancestor. "With the white carried still further, full equality is reached, tending to show that Indian blood can be taken up without physical or intellectual detriment" (Bieder, 1986, 231; Morgan, 1871, 207).

Indeed, Morgan held that a dash of Indian "blood" would be of benefit to those he described as "Anglo-Saxons," serving to "improve and toughen our race" (Morgan, 1959, 55). The commonality of such thinking with that marking the eugenics movement, which was then gathering momentum in the United States and reaching its ugly culmination in Nazi Germany during the 1930s and 1940s, is obvious. Although Powell refined Morgan's theory by adding a heavy dose of environmental conditioning, it is instructive that he "considered *Ancient Society* so valuable that, as director of the American Bureau of Ethnology, he made it required reading for field-workers of the bureau" (Bieder, 1986, 243).

While it may be that "the impact of anthropologists on Indian policy making was cumulative" rather than direct, they nonetheless "set the terms for informed discussions of Indian affairs in the 1880s" (Dippie, 1982, 167; Hoxie, 1984, 28, 23).

What is most important in the connection at hand is that Morgan, Powell, and their colleagues advocated an Indian policy "built on the science of ethnology" (Bieder, 1986, 241). It follows that they adhered to an ethnological understanding of who should be classified as Indians and that their views were shared both by the legislators who formulated federal Indian policy and, in some ways more importantly, by the bureaucrats who implemented it.

The implications are obvious. As Felix Cohen observed in his magisterial *Handbook on Federal Indian Law,* "If a person is three-fourths Caucasian and one-fourth Indian [by 'blood'], that person would not

ordinarily be considered an Indian for ethnological purposes" (Cohen, 1942, 19). Although Cohen goes on to explain that "[r]acial composition is not always dispositive in determining who are Indians for purposes of Indian law" and that a number of nonethnological legal definitions of "Indianness" have in fact been effected over the years, it will be recalled that no such definition was advanced in the Dawes Act, as the General Allotment Act is often called.

It is well-established that traditional Native North American methods of determining group membership were usually kinship-based and quite inclusive; "naturalization" by marriage, adoption, and other such means was rather common, irrespective of racial pedigree. In fact, as the noted Santee author and activist Charles Eastman observed in 1919, since no concept of "race" was present in any American Indian tradition, Indians were traditionally "color blind," exhibiting "no racial prejudices" at all (Hertzberg, 1971, 186). It follows, quite apart from a considerable "cross-pollination" between indigenous peoples themselves over untold generations, that both whites and African Americans had been steadily incorporated into many Native societies for two centuries or more by the time allotment became an issue.

Put bluntly, Indians were given to understand that "Congress could make or unmake an Indian, regardless of genealogy, ethnological data, Treaty commitments, or tribal preference. So could an employee of the Indian Bureau, acting under interpretation of federal law or the directive of an administrative superior" (Unrau, 1989, 3). It was abundantly obvious, however, that both Congress and the federal executive would rely on ethnological concepts for this purpose, as they had since the 1817 Treaty with the Wyandots (9 Stat. 904), the eighth article of which specified that persons "connected with said Indians, by blood" would be treated differently than "the Indians" themselves. Variations on the theme had been reiterated in fifty-three treaties before treaty making with Indians was ended

through an 1871 initiative spearheaded by Dawes (Churchill, 2003, 212; Hoxie, 1984, 32).

The Curtis and Burke Acts

Ultimately, it was not until passage of the Curtis Act (30 Stat. 495–519) in 1898 that the entitlement of "mixed-bloods"—as opposed to "half-breeds"—to receive allotments was legally acknowledged. Here, the focus was on the "Cherokees, Creeks, Choctaws, Chickasaws, Seminoles, and Osage, Miamies [sic] and Peorias, and Sacs and Foxes, in the Indian Territory" of Oklahoma (Washburn, 1986, 72), peoples who had been specifically exempted from the Dawes Act itself because they consisted in large part of persons of less than one-half degree of Indian blood and there was an at least tacit understanding that they would be subject to subsequent legislation (Hoxie, 1984, 154; Unrau, 1989, 22).

Allotment of mixed-bloods under the Curtis Act was, however, attended by a quid pro quo amounting to the dissolution of the so-called Indian Territory, as well as the indigenous nations situated therein. Hence it was strenuously resisted by traditionalist "full-bloods," especially the Keetoowah NightHawks led by RedBird Smith among the Cherokees and Chitto Harjo's Crazy Snakes among the Creeks, exacerbating divisions within the native polities affected that continue to this day. Nonetheless, the job was completed by 1907, at which point the supposedly "permanent" Indian Territory became the state of Oklahoma.

> Though Federal jurisdiction over the Indians and their [individually-allotted] lands was reserved, the destruction of tribal governments and the aggressive actions of white Oklahomans resulted in the passage of an act of May 27, 1908 [35 Stat. 312–316], repealing the restrictions on the sale of classes of land hitherto protected by the Federal Indian

---

* Although Euro-American racial vernacular was widely adopted by American Indians during the late nineteenth century, it is important to note that they generally employed it in a very different manner. The terms "full-blood" and "mixed-blood," for example, have tended to be used much more as cultural than as biological signifiers. Thus, a person of racially mixed ancestry is often referred to as a "full-blood" if she or he holds to a traditional outlook, while a person embracing Euro-American values is referred to as a "mixed-blood," even if of "pure" Indian lineage. Such usage continues at present, although more conventional—i.e., explicitly racial—definitions have attained a steadily increasing traction in native discourse since the 1930s, with the result that both sets of connotations are simultaneously at play when such terms are used by Indians (Fowler, 311–352; Harmon, 12–13; Meyer, 1994, 118–122; Pickering, 82–83; Sturm, 56–57, 72).

relationship, and imposing taxes on such lands (Washburn, 1971, 136).

This proved such a boon to white homesteaders and more especially to a range of corporate interests that in May 1906, even before Oklahoma statehood was effected, the Dawes Act itself was amended in such a way as to remove federal trust protection from many of the allotments already made on reservations outside Indian Territory. Championed by South Dakota Representative Charles Burke, the amendment (34 Stat. 182)—usually referred to as the Burke Act, in honor of its sponsor—"authorized the Secretary of Interior to issue a fee patent to an allottee at any time, upon determination that the individual was 'competent and capable of managing his or her affairs.' Upon issuance of one of these premature patents, the land was [removed from trust and thereby rendered] expressly subject to alienation, encumbrance, and taxation," while U.S. citizenship was conferred by the same transaction upon the Indian involved (Deloria and Lytle, 1983, 10).

A year later, Congress went further still, amending the Burke Act with a statute (34 Stat. 1018) granting Indian Commissioner Leupp the power to sell allotments belonging to "noncompetent" Indians, and in 1908 he was authorized through another pair of amendatory statutes (34 Stat. 1015–34; 35 Stat. 70) to begin the long-term leasing of such allotments as might still be nominally "owned" by allottees. In any event, of 2,744 premature fee patents issued between 1907 and 1910, some two-thirds had passed from Indian ownership; by 1917, the number of such patents had climbed to more than 8,000 with a loss rate of roughly 90 percent (McDonnell, 1991, 89–90, 100, 110).

Despite these devastating statistics, newly installed Indian Commissioner Cato Sells announced in 1917 that federal policy would be "liberalized" by issuing fee patents to "all able-bodied adult Indians of less than one-half Indian blood," while relaxing still further the manner in which fee-patented land could be acquired by non-Indians, even though it was situated within ostensible reservation boundaries (Commissioner of Indian Affairs, 1975, 214). In March 1919, Sells "liberalized" the rules still further, including "half-breeds" themselves among those subject to receiving "forced-fee" patents to their allotments (McDonnell, 1991, 107). The racial bar was thus raised: While land parcels were typically allotted only to those of at least "one-half degree of Indian

blood" under provision of the 1887 Act, by 1920 a blood quantum of *more than* one-half was required for an Indian to stand a reasonable prospect of retaining his or her property (Hoxie, 1984, 182).

Although the latter group as a whole was legally defined as being "incompetent" to manage its own affairs, individuals within it could nonetheless be declared competent by the Indian Commissioner for purposes of receiving a fee patent. Commissioner Sells therefore "liberalized" the procedures employed by the so-called competency commissions created by his predecessor, Robert G. Valentine, to make case-by-case assessments (McDonnell, 1991, 90, 94, 98–102). Using Sells' tidy race-based formula, the commissions issued 17,176 fee patents from early 1917—about 10,000 of them on a forced-fee basis, over the objections of the Indian owners—through the end of 1920, more than twice the number issued over the preceding decade (Hoxie, 1984, 182; McDonnell, 1991, 110, 116).

More than a million acres were involved, and everywhere the results were the same (Hoxie, 1984, 183). On the Crow Reservation in Montana, as many as 95 percent of all patentees lost or mortgaged their land at rates running as high as 12 percent by the end of the decade (McDonnell, 1991, 106–107). At Fort Peck, the figure was 90 percent; at Flathead, 75 percent; at Winnebago and Blackfeet, much the same. And on the Sioux Complex of reservations in the Dakotas, at Cheyenne River, 75 percent of the land subject to fee patents was lost, on Standing Rock and Rosebud even more (McDonnell, 1991, 106–107, 114).

> [On the] Pine Ridge reservation . . . most of the Natives were full bloods, unable to read, write, or speak English, who could in no way be classified as competent. Yet they received fee patents and soon sold their land. The proceeds often went for provisions and "worthless trinkets." Many patentees got a loan or mortgage on their land, and without any business experience or understanding of the need to pay taxes and interest on loans, they were often swindled out of it when white lenders foreclosed (McDonnell, 1991, 106).

While Pine Ridge may in many respects be emblematic of the whole, undoubtedly the most egregiously racist of all the various competency pro-

ceedings occurred on the White Earth Reservation in Minnesota, following a 1914 Supreme Court holding that the issuance of fee patents and consequent sale of land parcels allotted to "full bloods" had been fraudulent and that land thus lost to allottees would have to be restored (*U.S. v. Nichols-Chisolm Lumber*).* This raised the questions of who the full-bloods were and whether/how persons claiming such status could "prove" their status. The quandary was "resolved" when assistance was offered by "Dr. Ales Hrdlicka, director of anthropology at the Smithsonian Institution, and Dr. Albert E. Jenks, an anthropologist at the University of Minnesota, [who, together] claimed to have devised certain scientific tests capable of distinguishing between mixed-bloods and full-bloods" (Meyer, 1994, 168).

"Pioneer[s in] the field of eugenics" and believing they could make a "determination of blood status on distinguishing physical characteristics," Hrdlicka and Jenks, assisted by Hal Downey of the University of Minnesota's Department of Animal Biology, set to work on the "White Earth Case" in 1916 (Meyer, 1994, 168–169). In short order, they commenced to examine their subjects' physiognomies using methods virtually interchangeable with those employed by German "racial hygienists" only a few years later. Diameters of hairs were measured—ten per person were required to establish a "scientific standard"—as were foot sizes, nose and cranial proportions. Skin was scratched, blood was typed, ear wax texture was assessed, urine was analyzed, and skin tone and amounts of body hair were catalogued.

All told, Hrdlicka and his colleagues examined 696 of about 800 Indians claiming to be full-bloods, verifying the "pedigree" of only 126. Although subsequent analysis revealed that the experts' application of the latest techniques in "racial science" had led them to attribute "full-blood" children to "mixed-blood" parents and to identify siblings born of exactly the same parents as being of different "racial compositions," the results were employed not only in "settling" the land fraud issue but in

compiling White Earth's so-called Blood Roll, approved by a federal district court in 1920 (Meyer, 1994, 170–171). By the latter year, roughly 90 percent of all White Earth patentees had been dispossessed (Banner, 1981, 284; McDonnell, 1991, 106).

Transition

Somewhat ironically, Charles Burke, who was appointed Indian Commissioner in 1921, finally put a stop to Sells' wholesale rush to separate American Indians from what little remained of their 1887 estate, in no small part because those rendered landless, destitute, and for the most part unemployable had been applying for welfare assistance at a dramatically increasing rate. The toll taken on Indian land was by then staggering, however. In all, the issuance of fee patents under the provisions of the Curtis and Burke Acts had resulted in the loss of some 23 million acres of the land remaining to Native people *after* the reservation "surpluses" had been stripped away (Banner, 1981, 282–283; McDonnell, 1991, 121). Additionally, Commissioners Leupp and Sells in particular had forced the sale of some 3.4 million acres of allotted land to "noncompetent" Indians. In all, some 100,000 native people had been left landless by the time Burke took office (McDonnell, 1991, 121).

The competency commissions were abolished, along with the policy of issuing forced-fee patents to all allottees evidencing "one-half or less Indian blood," and Burke "became the first commissioner to cancel a fee patent" (McDonnell, 1991, 111, 112). In 1927, after he had facilitated a judicial finding that fee patents "issued during the trust period without the application or consent of the allottee" were illegal (*U.S. v. Benewah County*), he was instrumental in convincing Congress to enact a statute (U.S. Statutes at Large, Vol. 45 at 1247) authorizing cancellation of all forced-fee patents, "provided the Indian owner had not sold or mortgaged any part of the patent" (McDonnell, 1991, 117).

Such gestures were mainly for show, of course: Under the 1927 statute, in combination with a 1931

---

* The situation resulted not from the Burke Act, but from the so-called Clapp Act (U.S. Statutes at Large, Vol. 34 at 353, 1034), thus named for its sponsor, Minnesota Senator Moses Clapp, passed as a rider to the 1906 Indian Appropriations Act and applicable only to White Earth. Clapp's initiative prefigured Indian Commissioner Sells' 1917 racial definition of "competency" by declaring that all "mixed-bloods" on the reservation would henceforth be considered legally competent and therefore issued fee patents to their allotments, whether they wanted them or not. The only problem was that he neglected to explain what was meant by the term "mixed-blood." On judicial challenge, the federal district court ruled, rather arbitrarily, that "at least one-eighth degree white blood" was required. The ruling was appealed and overruled by the circuit court, which held that any admixture of white "blood" was sufficient. The latter view was upheld by the Supreme Court on June 8, 1914 (Meyer, 1994, 153, 167).

follow-up (U.S. Statutes at Large, Vol. 46 at 1205), passed after Burke left office and authorizing the cancellation of patents "on *any portion* of an Indian's land that had not been sold and was not presently encumbered by mortgage [emphasis added]," only about 470 forced-fee patents were ever actually cancelled (McDonnell, 1991, 117–118). The main effect of Burke's posture was thus not to restore land to Indians from whom it had been wrongfully taken, but rather to radically scale back the rate of loss. By 1930, when Charles Rhoads replaced Burke as commissioner of Indian Affairs, the number of fee patents issued for the year had dropped to 113, and in 1933 Rhoades' successor, John Collier, effectively halted their issuance altogether (McDonnell, 1991, 120).

Of the allottees who retained their property by that point—a total of 246,579 people, holding 40,848,172 acres on a hundred reservations (Kickingbird and Ducheneaux, 1973, 23; McDonnell, 1991, 121), very few enjoyed the benefit thereof. "World War I [had afforded] the Indian Office an excellent excuse to expand its leasing policy" established by Commissioner Leupp under the earlier mentioned 1908 amendments to the Burke Act, in the name of the war effort (McDonnell, 1991, 47).

> During the war the Indian Office leased huge tracts of land to individuals and corporations . . . without the consent of the Indians and then closed its eyes as lessors violated the terms of those leases. . . . The push for leasing was an important part of the general push by whites for control of Indian land during the war. In the name of wartime emergency the Indian Office approved leases to large cattle companies and sugar beet companies that violated Indian rights. Moreover, the leases, often forced on Indians as essential war measures, were left in place after the war ended (McDonnell, 1991, 62, 47).

Actually, the policy was expanded considerably after the war, largely on the basis of a 1919 statute (U.S. Statutes at Large, Vol. 39 at 128) allowing both allotted and unallotted irrigable reservation lands to be leased, essentially at the discretion of the Indian commissioner, for as long as ten years. Thus empowered, in 1920 Commissioner Sells approved approximately 40,000 leases, covering some 4.5 million acres of the best remaining reservation land (McDonnell, 1991, 47–48). This enforced a situation, created in large part by chronic undercapitalization, wherein

fewer than 20 percent of the Indians still owning allotments on most reservations were able to use their land for agricultural or grazing purposes (Berthrong, 35; McDonnell, 1991, 46, 64–65, 123). Further, since the leases were steeply discounted—annual rates were as low as 8 cents per acre—and, since the Bureau of Indian Affairs (BIA) made little effort to collect even that pittance, many leaseholders never bothered to pay even that; few, if any, allottees could live on their "rental income." Hence, many of them ended up working as hired hands on their own property simply to survive (McDonnell, 1991, 60–70; Moore, 1996, 131–136).

Commissioner Burke not only did nothing to halt Sells' leasing policy—of which he heartily approved—he streamlined it in 1921 by authorizing the superintendent on each reservation to approve farming and grazing leases without approval from Washington. By 1925, the fourth year of Burke's tenure, the number of such leases was slightly higher than the benchmark set by Sells in 1920, although total allotment acreage involved had declined to "only" 4 million (McDonnell, 1991, 48–50). As the extent of mineral deposits on many reservations became increasingly apparent over the course of the decade, moreover, the leasing of huge tracts for "resource development activities"—i.e., mineral extraction—became increasingly frequent (Ambler, 1990, 44–46; Hoxie, 1984, 186–187).

> Indian-owned mineral lands were developed without the Indians' permission and with little economic benefit to them. . . . The formal policy of leasing mineral lands began in 1891 when Congress authorized mining leases on treaty reservations for up to ten years [26 Stat. 794 § 3]. As the demand for oil and other resources grew in the early twentieth century and as new mineral deposits were uncovered in the Southwest, the call for more liberal leasing legislation grew louder, [resulting in passage of] a law on June 30, 1919 [41 Stat. 3] authorizing the secretary of interior to lease reservation land in Arizona, California, Idaho, Montana, Nevada, New Mexico, Oregon, Washington, and Wyoming for the mining of metalliferous minerals [on a *twenty*-year timebase] (Ambler, 1990, 40; Hoxie, 1984, 186; McDonnell, 1991, 50–51).

Commissioner Burke's leasing policy was further reinforced by passage of the General Mineral

Lands Leasing Act of 1920 (41 Stat. 437), the Indian Oil and Gas Leasing Act of 1924 (43 Stat. 244), and a 1927 statute (44 Stat. 1347) specifying that reservations or portions of reservations established by executive order rather than by treaty should be handled like any other "public lands" for purposes of resource development (Ambler, 1990, 39–41). Plainly, there was a campaign afoot to "integrate native resources into the American economy" (Hoxie, 1984, 187) and to do so in a manner both conceptually and structurally indistinguishable from the forms of internal colonialism imposed on indigenous peoples by European immigrant states the world over (Nietschmann, 1994, passim; Thomas, 1966–1967, passim). Just as plainly, this implied a fundamental change in federal Indian policy.

For the mineral wealth of Native North America to be exploited in the most efficient manner, so the thinking went, it had to be administered in trust, subject to the centralized authority of federal economic planners. Since what remained of reservation lands already occupied the necessary trust status—a matter confirmed in the *Lone Wolf* opinion as deriving from the government's "plenary power" over Indians (Ambler, 1990, 44–48; Clark, 1999, 97; Coulter and Tullberg, 1984, 198–203)—it was suddenly imperative that they *not* be dissolved, at least not until the extent of their mineral assets could be fully assessed.

From this standpoint, Commissioner Burke's policy of abruptly curtailing his predecessors' enthusiastic liquidation of Indian landholdings, while placing a steadily increasing emphasis on large-scale mineral leasing, makes perfect sense. By 1928, the government's longstanding goal of forcing Indians and their reservations to "vanish" had been quietly abandoned in favor of "reorganizing" them for a sustained existence as little more than "domestic" resource feeders contributing to the profitability of U.S. state and corporate enterprise.

Ongoing Effects

While it is true that the vast erosion of the American Indian estate precipitated by allotment was effectively halted by 1930 and was to some extent reversed over the next several decades, this in itself did not imply a corresponding restoration of use and benefit of the remainder to Native people. To the contrary, one of the legacies of the allotment era is that the massive sell-off of forced-fee patents left many reservations so checkerboarded—honeycombed, really—with non-Indian property holdings

that it has proven all but impossible to consolidate the land necessary to attain anything resembling economic self-sufficiency. The problem is compounded by the fact that, on some reservations, *all* irrigable land was acquired by whites before the process was halted.

> It is exceedingly difficult to create . . . grazing or farming units on allotted reservations because quite often there are not enough allotments contiguous to one another to make up an economically feasible block of land for [such] use [and the] tribe has to overcome previous allocations by the courts in order to begin new development using their [reserved] water rights (Deloria and Lytle, 1983, 255).

Serious jurisdictional problems also attend non-Indian ownership of alienated fee patent allotments within reservation boundaries.

> Civil and criminal jurisdiction depends upon the existence of trust lands. Whenever an allotment goes out of trust, the tribe loses jurisdiction over that area and must rely on negotiated agreements with state and county governments in order [to regain it]. Zoning for economic development and housing and enforcement of hunting and fishing codes is exceedingly difficult when the area under consideration is not wholly trust land (Deloria and Lytle, 1983, 255–256).

Even where allotments remain in trust status, the checkerboard effect has been exacerbated by the increasingly fractionated ownership of individual parcels, otherwise known as the heirship problem. The name derives from the fact that the whole thrust of allotment was, from the outset, to strip away as much reservation land as possible, as rapidly as possible, under the premise that Indians, as such, would soon be "extinct." With no consideration of the prospect that the native population might eventually rebound, no land was reserved to accommodate future increases in the number of Indians. Hence, the descendents of the original allottees were consigned to receive "equitable shares" in their ancestors' land parcels, a practice conforming to the requirements of Anglo-American rather than indigenous law (Kickingbird and Ducheneaux, 1973, 24).

The upshot is that it has become necessary to employ "complicated computations involving com-

mon denominators as large as 54 trillion" to decipher the individual interests in a given allotment. With hundreds of heirs now holding interest in a single piece of property, it is all but impossible to obtain agreement among the owners concerning its use or disposition. By 1970, nearly six million of the roughly 10 million remaining acres of allotted lands were tied up in this fashion, with at least one-half of a million acres standing idle, and another 1.5 million leased to whites (Deloria and Lytle, 1983, 255–256; Kickingbird and Ducheneaux, 1973, 24–30; Washburn, 1971, 150–152).

Overall, consolidation of land on the reservations—that is, a reversal of the effects of allotment—remains "the major unsolved economic problem of Indian tribes" in the first years of the twenty-first century, just as it was at the beginning of the twentieth. "Until tribes are able to own their lands in one solid block," Vine Deloria, Jr., observed during the early 1980s, "they cannot reasonably make plans for use or development of their resources." Since then, however, "the Indian land situation [has grown] increasingly more serious, with no prospect of relief" (Deloria and Lytle, 1983, 255–256).

Both the magnitude and the urgency of this allotment-induced circumstance are readily apparent in the sheer depth of the poverty afflicting Indian Country today. The data are more reflective of conditions customarily associated with the Third World than areas in a country boasting "the world's most developed economy." At the end of the twentieth century, American Indians comprised by far the poorest population category recorded in the U.S. Census, with per-capita income on some reservations averaging about $3,000 per year, unemployment running into the 80th percentile range, approximately the same percentage of houses classed as "substandard" or "uninhabitable" (Strickland, 1997, 52–53; Wilkins, 2002, 158–159; Wilkinson, 2005, 22, 348–349).

> The Indian health level is [also] the lowest and the disease rate the highest of all population groups in the United States. The incidence of tuberculosis is over 400 percent higher than the national average. Similar statistics show that the incidence of strep infections is 1,000 percent higher, meningitis is 2,000 percent higher, and dysentery is 10,000 percent higher. Death rates from disease are shocking when Indian and non-Indian populations are compared. Influenza and pneumonia are 300 percent greater killers among Indians. Diseases such as hepatitis are at epidemic proportions. Diabetes is almost a plague. And the suicide rate for Indian youths ranges from 1,000 to 10,000 [percent] higher than for non-Indian youths; Indian suicide is epidemic (Strickland, 1997, 53).

Indians also suffer infant mortality and die of malnutrition, exposure, and "accidents" at rates far beyond those evidenced by non-Indians. Reservation Indians have a life expectancy of barely fifty years, a noticeable increase from the forty-two years an Indian could expect to live during the early 1960s, perhaps, but still a lifespan one-third shorter on average than that enjoyed by the general population (Steiner, 1968, 197–200; Strickland, 1997, 53; Wilkinson, 2005, 22).

It must be borne in mind that these conditions prevail despite the fact that, by 1990, the unavailability of land, in combination with the extremity of their peoples' destitution, had displaced 56 percent of all federally recognized Indians from their reservation homelands (Indian Health Service, 2006). Were they to have asserted their right to stay, things would be *far* worse. Such data lend substance to Sartre's contention that colonialism is inherently genocidal (Sartre, 1968, 63; Sartre, 1964, 30–47).

Creation of the Internal Colonial System

Notwithstanding the foregoing realities, it is currently the official position of the U.S. government that American Indians exercise a form of "internal self-determination," established under the 1934 Indian Reorganization Act (or IRA, ch. 576, 48 Stat. 934) and subsequently reinforced through legislation such as the Indian Self-Determination and Educational Assistance Act of 1975 (88 Stat. 2203), which not only fulfills their rights under international law but presents a model appropriate for emulation on a global basis (National Security Council, 430). Such claims bear scrutiny.

As stated in the United Nations' 1960 Declaration on the Granting of Independence to Colonial Countries and Peoples (U.N.G.A. Res. 1514 [X]), and elsewhere, "All peoples have the right to self-determination; by virtue of that right, they freely determine their political status and freely pursue their economic, social, and cultural development." The 1966 International Covenant on Economic,

Social and Cultural Rights (U.N.G.A. Res. 2200 [XXI]), as well as the International Covenant on Civil and Political Rights (U.N.G.A. Res. 2200 [XXI]), also set forth in 1966, not only reiterate the 1960 Declaration's legal definition, but offer further clarification.

> All peoples may, for their own ends, freely dispose of their natural wealth and resources without prejudice to any obligations arising out of international economic co-operation, based upon mutual benefit, and international law. In no case may a people be deprived of its own means of subsistence.

Both of the 1966 covenants go on to require that "All States Parties to the Present Covenant, including those with responsibility for the administration of Non-Self-Governing and Trust Territories, shall promote the right of self-determination, and shall respect that right [as defined above], in conformity with the provisions of the Charter of the United Nation." The 1960 Declaration adds that the "pretext" of purported concern over the "inadequacy of political, economic, social and cultural development" is legally invalid as a basis for denying, delaying, or qualifying any people's right to self-determination (Weston, Falk, and D'Amato, 1990, 344, 371, 376).

The Indian Reorganization Act

The template on which the IRA appears to have been constructed was the Interior Department's creation of what it called the Navajo Grand Council in 1923. This was done after the previous council, organic to the Navajos themselves, declined to approve an exploratory lease of a 4,000-acre tract on the reservation by a subsidiary of the Standard Oil Corporation. Having unilaterally devised "a new form of government" for the Navajos, chartered it, vetted its members, and required that representatives of the Indian Bureau be present at all meetings, Commissioner Burke was able to pronounce the problem solved: The Grand Council simply delegated authority to sign oil leases on its behalf to a federal commissioner.

Also during 1923, Interior Secretary Hubert Work commissioned a National Advisory Committee, usually called the Committee of One Hundred because of the number of prominent business and church leaders involved, to reexamine the "Indian Question" and make policy recommendations. The committee's report, delivered in January 1924, urged that a high priority be placed on conferring U.S. citizenship on all Indians who had not been previously made citizens by other means, including those who had refused to accept it. The Indian Citizenship Act (8 U.S.C.A. § 1401 [a] [2]) was effected shortly thereafter, consummating a tension over the question of national allegiance among many native people that has persisted into the present.

Other items on the committee's agenda, overlapping as they did with those advanced in several ambitious studies completed by the Bureau of Indian Affairs itself over the next several years would figure significantly in the formulation of the IRA. The best-known of the latter efforts, *The Problem of Indian Administration*—published in 1928 and usually referred to as The Meriam Report after its principal author, Lewis B. Meriam—catalogued the ugly panorama of material degradation to which Indians were being subjected and called for a range of policy reforms, especially with regard to the manner and environments in which native children were being "educated."

Many of the recommendations made by Meriam and his colleagues were ultimately included in the IRA. However, future Indian Commissioner John Collier, who would be the legislation's moving force, seems to have been influenced most powerfully by a proposal advanced before a Senate committee during hearings conducted in 1930. This involved a scheme to convert the Klamath Reservation in southern Oregon into a federally chartered Klamath Indian Corporation, in which tribal members would be "stockholders." The resulting enterprise, devoted mostly to timber harvesting, would be "governed" under federal supervision by what amounted to a corporate board elected by—and from among—the stockholders (Deloria and Lytle, 1983, 49–50, 144).

Although he helped scuttle the plan for technical reasons, it is instructive that Collier described the underlying idea as "the most important new step in Indian affairs since the general allotment act" and asked the senators gathered in consideration of it to "imagine the Menominees, and again the Chippewas of Minnesota, and again the Navajos [as] incorporated tribes." In Collier's view, the major difficulty with the concept—apart from "qualifying . . . tribal members to vote in corporate elections"—was deciding how "some Federal agency"—by which he obvi-

ously meant the BIA—might be restructured in such a way as to assure efficient "supervision" of as many as two hundred and fifty disparate entities of the sort proposed (Deloria and Lytle, 1983, 50–51; Taylor, 1980, 63–91).

While the IRA is routinely touted as having been a New Deal for Indians, ushering in a renewal of indigenous sovereignty, self-governance, and economic revitalization, even the brief summary of "ongoing effects" of the federal allotment policy suggests that precisely the opposite has proven true. Examining certain of the Act's provisions in more detail will reveal why (Taylor, ix–xiii, 92–118, passim).

Illusions of Democracy

A standard myth is that, rather than being forced, the Native peoples who underwent federal reorganization did so voluntarily. As an "exercise in the transplantation of democracy," however, the IRA was in its very conception a travesty. Indeed, its first presumption was that the governments of *every* American Indian people would be reorganized on a common model involving the adoption of a constitution, bylaws, and electoral procedures, other than those explicitly refusing to do so. The law allowed refusal (and some Native nations exercised this right). This, of course, placed the burden of action on those who sought to preserve or restore their own forms of governance, a polar reversal of standard democratic procedure (Deloria and Lytle, 1983, 141, 171).

Since the only form of refusal accepted as valid by federal authorities was a "majority vote" of "eligible voters," moreover, opponents of reorganization were placed in a contradictory and degrading Catch-22 position, having no viable means of expressing their opposition other than by participating in the very process they opposed— i.e., voting against it—an act many of the peoples considered antithetical to the traditionally consensus-based modes of governance they were seeking to preserve.

This was so because Collier, although he was certainly aware that this was the typically polite way of saying "no" in many native societies, opted for the most part to simply ignore the implications attending mass abstentions. A classic illustration is the referendum conducted at Hopi in 1936, when roughly 85 percent of the eligible voters, deeply committed to

maintaining their time-honored Kikmongwe form of government, actively boycotted the referendum, only to have Collier falsify the tribal census as a means of casting the impression that reorganization had been decisively approved (Tullberg, 35–37). More egregious still was Collier's practice of counting abstentions as affirmative votes to foster such illusions.

> For seventeen tribes, comprising a total population of 5,334, this [practice] reversed an otherwise negative vote. That is, in each instance the actual vote cast indicated that the majority of those Indians who participated in the [referendum] had opted to reject the act, but when the votes of the Indians who did not participate were added in favor of adoption, the act was construed as having been accepted. On the Santa Ysabel Reservation in California, for instance, 43 Indians voted against the Indian Reorganization Act and only 9 voted to accept it. Still, the Santa Ysabel tribe came under the act because 62 eligible tribal members who did not vote were counted as being in favor of adoption. Hence, the final tabulation was viewed as 71 in favor of adoption, 43 opposed (Deloria and Lytle, 1983, 172).

Topping it all off was the fact that those deemed eligible to vote in the referenda were the persons and/or descendents of persons inscribed on tribal "base rolls" by federal authorities as a concomitant to determining allotment eligibility. With the parameters of the native polity thus preestablished in accordance with their own rather than native criteria, officials were able to utilize other techniques— imposing or removing residency requirements, for example—to manipulate the outcomes of various tribal referenda (Barsh, 1982, 45; Deloria and Lytle, 1983, 141, 164–165). The deck was thus stacked in every possible manner to ensure that Indians "voluntarily" reorganized. Under such circumstances, the mystery is not why 181 peoples ended up doing so, but that 77 managed to make their rejections stick (Deloria and Lytle, 1983, 172).

On the Matter of "Self-Governance"

Claims that the IRA imbued native peoples with a genuine form of "democratic self-governance" usually begin with the argument that the governing

bodies created under the Act were and are "constitutionally-based." Such notions are readily dispelled by the nature of the constitutions themselves, however. While the Act set forth the principle that each people was entitled to write its own constitution, each such document was subject to approval by the secretary of interior (although, as always, secretarial authority was delegated to the commissioner of Indian Affairs). Those, like the Yankton Sioux who tried to exercise their prerogatives in this respect, found themselves checkmated by an inability to secure approval.

This led to a series of "tribal constitutions," which were remarkably similar to one another and in many ways interchangeable for the simple reason that they were not written by the people to be governed under them, but instead "by attorneys within the Department of Interior" (Deloria and Lytle, 1983, 173). Quite predictably, the resulting boilerplate "foundational documents" empowered the governments based on them to do very little without approval of the Indian Commissioner (O'Brien, 1989, 83).

The question thus becomes, as Vine Deloria, Jr., once posed it, "If these powers could be delegated or withheld from tribal governments completely at the discretion of the secretary, what true authority was left to the tribe?" (Deloria and Lytle, 1983, 143). The answer, of course, is virtually none. Clear indication that the tribal governments created under the IRA were never really conceived as exercising actual *governing* authority will be found in Section 16 of the Act, which requires that each people adopting a constitution simultaneously adopt a set of bylaws. The phrase "constitution and bylaws" is associated more with corporate than with sovereign governmental entities (one will search in vain for the governmental bylaws of any United Nations member state).

Given this, it is unsurprising that the tribal governance provisions found in Section 16 of the IRA are followed in the very next section by provisions for chartering each native people adopting a constitution as "a defined class of Federal corporations, to wit, incorporated Indian tribes or communities" (Deloria and Lytle, 1983, 156). In at least one instance, the Interior Department held that a corporate charter might be considered "equivalent" to a tribal constitution, a tribal business committee the equivalent of a tribal government. In effect, then, the intended function of IRA "governments" was to serve essentially as corporate boards, the authority of which was directly subordinated to that of the Interior Department.

Bluntly put, the main purpose of the "reorganized" governments was to sign off on leases and other contracts, thereby signifying "tribal consent" to various "economic development" ventures established "in their behalf" by the federal government (Robbins, 132, 1979; Ortiz, 1979, 70).

A Question of Trust

As an enticement to convince Native peoples to reorganize themselves on the federally preferred corporate footing, the IRA provided that those who did would be able to draw on a revolving credit fund to underwrite the start-up of enterprises designed to revitalize tribal economies. An initial sum of $10 million was allocated to this purpose in the Act's Section 10, while a further $2 million per year was promised in Section 5 to assist reorganized peoples to reacquire the acreage necessary to consolidate their landholdings and to establish reservations for several peoples left landless by allotment, and yet another half million per year was designated to subsidize educational vocational training and the like. Congress never delivered on these commitments, however.

> The House Subcommittee on Interior Appropriations, led by Congressman Jed Johnson of Oklahoma, provided only about one-quarter of the $12.5 million authorized by the IRA. In the following years, Johnson was instrumental in cutting the revolving credit fund to $2.5 million, the annual land purchase fund to $1 million, the funds allocated for tribal organization to $150,000, and education loans to $175,000 (Deloria and Lytle, 1983, 174).

By 1945, a full decade after the Act was implemented, only $5,245,000, just over half the promised *up-front* capitalization, had been paid into the credit fund (Kelly, 1976, 311). Thus starved for liquidity, most of the eagerly anticipated tribal enterprises foundered or never really got off the ground, and the Indians were left with little alternative but to watch as huge swaths of land they'd hoped to use for other purposes were leased to mining corporations and the like as a means of generating at least *some* income, thereby establishing certain of the more mineral-rich areas as veritable "resource colonies."

This drift toward enforced dependency was sometimes augmented by large-scale federal im-

poundments of Indian livestock, devastating what remained of many indigenous subsistence economies. While such programs were ostensibly carried out as a means of curtailing environmental damage caused by overgrazing, the alternate use to which the land was put by authorities turned out in some cases—on the Navajo Reservation, for example—to be the vastly more destructive practice of strip-mining coal and other minerals.

The terms of the leases negotiated by federal officials to allow the extraction of reservation minerals by major U.S. corporations are telling. Pursuant to the acts of 1920, 1924, and 1927, as well as an Omnibus Tribal Lands Leasing Act passed in 1938 (52 Stat. 347), such contracts "ensured that [tribal] revenues generated from these nonrenewable resources [were] only a fraction of what it should have been," with royalty rates often pegged at less than 20 percent—sometimes as low as 2 percent—of market norms.

The already inordinate profitability of non-Indian mining operations in Indian Country accruing from such steeply discounted rates was, by the end of the 1960s, enhanced dramatically by the federal practice of releasing the corporations involved from meeting the occupational safety and environmental protection standards applicable in other locales, permitting often huge savings in overhead expenses.

As it turns out, Indians were *never* allowed to use their own money to better their circumstances. Instead, recent litigation has revealed that somewhere "between 300,000 and 500,000 Indians have been deprived of between ten and forty *billion* dollars as a result of over one hundred years of trust fund mismanagement by the federal government" [emphasis added] (Bowman, 2004, 543–544). Among other things, it has been shown that, beginning at least as early as 1887, the government has consistently "lost, dissipated, or *converted to the United States' own use* the money of [Indian] trust beneficiaries" and has "destroyed records bearing upon [its] breaches of trust" [emphasis added] (Bowman, 2004, n10; *Cobell v. Babbitt*, 1999; *Cobell v. Norton*, 2004; *Cobell v. Kempthorne*, 2006).

This concerns only the trust accounts assigned to individual Indians. If the accounts of the peoples ostensibly "compensated" for land losses since the early nineteenth century were subjected to the same scrutiny, along with lease and royalty payments accruing from the 1890s onward—and especially since passage of the IRA—the total would likely be

far greater, well over $100 billion by some estimates (Heilprin, 2006; Schneider, passim).

The Continuation of Racial Alchemy

Perhaps the most insidious of all the IRA's lingering effects has been its entrenchment of the racial definition(s) of Indianness, first applied in a comprehensive fashion under provision of the General Allotment Act in 1887 and thereafter solidified under the Curtis and Burke Acts. While the 1934 Act provides that all persons appearing on the federally created base roll of each Native people, as well as their descendents, "regardless of [their] degree of blood," could be entered on the membership roll of each people as it reorganized, the reality was that blood quantum criteria had been employed in establishing the base rolls themselves (Deloria and Lytle, 1983, 150–151).

The Interior Department attorneys who wrote the boilerplate constitutions, through which the ground rules of reorganization were spelled out to Native peoples, were, moreover, advised by a team of anthropologists steeped in ethnological methods. It is thus not especially mysterious how many of the peoples on whom a constitution was bestowed discovered—often to their surprise—that their own traditions required that members meet Indian Commissioner Collier's preferred standard of at least one-quarter-degree Indian blood. Any change to this baseline racial requirement for tribal enrollment could be made only if approved by the Secretary of Interior.

Thus, a survey of enrollment criteria pertaining to 162 of 306 federally recognized tribes conducted during the late 1980s revealed that 131 required a blood quantum of one-quarter or more. Of these, one required that enrollees be of at least "three-eighths Indian blood," while seventeen would enroll no one of less than half-blood, including the children of a duly enrolled parent (Snipp, 1989, 362–365). A survey of 302 tribes, conducted during the mid-1990s, recorded 204 as asserting such requirements (Thornton, 1997, 37). In many cases, it was also required that the applicant's quantum accrue from the specific people with whom she or he sought to enroll (Snipp, 1989, 312; Thornton, 1987, 190–191), a stipulation known to produce bizarre results.

[Consider the situation of a child] who is one-eighth Lower Brule Sioux, one-eighth Cheyenne-Arapaho, one-eighth Blackfoot, and

one-eighth Turtle Mountain Chippewa. She is . . . one-half Indian. But each tribe of her ancestry requires its citizens to document a one-quarter blood degree *from that tribe only*. From the perspective of each of her tribes, therefore, this child is ineligible for citizenship; she is simply a non-Indian. . . . Indeed, even children of exclusively Indian ancestry can find themselves denied tribal citizenship due to similar circumstances (Garroute, 2003, 19–20).

Were the situation not vexing enough, the racial definition of Indians advanced in the IRA has since multiplied into at least thirty-three, and perhaps as many as *eighty*, different—and often conflicting—definitions of Indianness in U.S. law, all of them formulated for the convenience of federal authorities rather than Indians (O'Brien, 1991, 1481).

Since this welter of statutory definitions affects everything from eligibility for federal health and education services to the exercise of rights under statutes such as the Indian Child Welfare Act (92 Stat. 3069) and the Indian Religious Freedom Act (92 Stat. 469), the matter is hardly insignificant. While tribes have for some time been technically free to abandon blood quantum requirements—and a minority of them have—the government's ongoing imposition of a "quarter-blood minimum" as the normative requirement for receipt of federal services presents an all but insurmountable barrier to their doing so. Since funding is allocated on the basis of a per-capita computation wherein only those meeting the quarter-blood standard are included, provision of medical and other services to tribal citizens failing to meet federal requirements can only be underwritten at the expense of those which do.

Ultimately, the present drift toward redefining Native identity exclusively in terms of enrollment in a federally sanctioned tribe, reduces to little more than a reassertion—or continuation—of the allotment era agenda wherein the smallest possible number of Indians would be recognized. In this regard, we would do well to recall that the goal of federal policy during that era was to make Indians, as such, ultimately "vanish" altogether. Here, the implications of the normative "quarter-blood standard" of Indianness now enforced by federal and tribal officials alike must be considered.

By the year 2080, should long-standing trends continue, "persons with [half] or more Indian blood quantums" are projected to comprise only 8 percent of the identified Native population—as compared to 87 percent in 1980—while one-third will fall somewhere between quarter- and half-blood. The remaining 59 percent will be of less than one-quarter Indian blood, while full-bloods will have all but disappeared (Snipp, 1989, 166–167; Thornton, 1987, 237).

Arguably, then, should appreciable sectors of Native North Americans continue to embrace the "alchemy of race and rights" concocted by federal authorities during the nineteenth century, they will have engaged, however unwittingly, in a form of "autogenocide." As Cherokee demographer Russell Thornton explained nearly twenty years ago, given the ever-increasing proportion of the Native population displaced from the reservations to urban locales:

> Intermarriage will further reduce the relative numbers of American Indians by reducing the blood quantum of further generations. This [will] likely increase intermarriage rates, since there will be fewer potential American Indian mates. It may [thus] be that the demographic effects of less natural increase, more intermarriage, and less tribalism will ultimately eliminate American Indians as a distinct population, whereas 400 years of population decimation after European contact did not (Thornton, 1987, 239).

In effect, such trends project "a scenario in which tribes will find themselves redefined as technically 'extinct,' even when they continue to exist as functioning social, cultural, political, linguistic or residential groupings" (Garroute, 2003, 58). Put another way, insistence on tribal enrollment as the *sine qua non* of Indianness, along with quarter-blood quantum as the normative requirement for a place on the rolls, leads unerringly to the prospect that "American Indians as Indians may eventually end, in the words of T. S. Elliot, 'not with a bang but a whimper' " (Thornton, 1987, 239).

Ward Churchill

See also Assimilation; Boarding Schools, United States and Canada; Bureau of Indian Affairs: Establishing the Existence of an Indian Tribe; Canada, Indian Policies of; Ceremonies, Criminalization of; Citizenship; Collier, John; Disease, Historic and Contemporary; Economic Development; General Allotment Act (Dawes Act); Identity; Indian Reorganization Act; Meriam Report; Reservation Economic and Social Conditions; Society of American Indians; Tribal Sovereignty; Trust, Doctrine of; *Winters v. United States*.

References and Further Reading

Adams, David Wallace. 1995. *Education for Extinction: American Indians and the Boarding School Experience, 1875–1928.* Lawrence: University Press of Kansas.

Ambler, Marjane. 1990. *Breaking the Iron Bonds: Indian Control of Energy Development.* Lawrence: University Press of Kansas.

Banner, Stuart. 1981. *How the Indians Lost Their Land: Law and Power on the Frontier.* Cambridge, MA: Belknap/Harvard University Press.

Barsh, Russel. 1982. "When Will Tribes Have a Choice?" In *Rethinking Indian Law.* National Lawyers Guild, Committee on Native American Struggles, 43–47. New Haven, CT: Advocate Press.

Bieder, Robert E. 1986. *Science Encounters the Indian, 1820–1880: The Early Years of American Ethnology.* Norman: University of Oklahoma Press.

Bowman, Christopher Barrett. 2004. "Indian Trust Fund: Resolution and Proposed Reformation to the Mismanagement Problems Associated with the Individual Indian Money Accounts in Light of *Cobell v. Norton.*" *Catholic University Law Review* 53 (Winter): 543–576.

Churchill, Ward. 2003. "The Crucible of American Indian Identity: Native Tradition Versus Colonial Imposition in Postconquest North America." In *Perversions of Justice: Indigenous Peoples and Angloamerican Law.* Edited by Ward Churchill, 201–246. San Francisco: City Lights.

Clark, Blue. 1999. *Lone Wolf v. Hitchcock: Treaty Rights and Indian Law at the End of the Nineteenth Century.* Lincoln: University of Nebraska Press.

Cobell v. Babbitt, 91 F.Supp. 2d 1 (1999).

Cobell v. Norton, 391 F.3d 251 (D.C. Cir. 2004).

Cobell v. Kempthorne, ___ F.3d ___ (D.C. Cir., July 11, 2006).

Cohen, Felix. 1942 [1982 reprint]. *Handbook on Federal Indian Law.* Charlotte, VA: Michie Co.

Commissioner of Indian Affairs. 1975. *1917 Annual Report.* In *Documents in United States Indian Policy.* Edited by Francis Paul Prucha, 213–214. Lincoln: University of Nebraska Press.

Coulter, Robert T., and Steven Tullberg. 1984. "Indian Land Rights." In *The Aggressions of Civilization: Federal Indian Policy since the 1880s.* Edited by Sandra L. Cadwalader and Vine Deloria, Jr., 185–213. Philadelphia: Temple University Press.

Deloria, Vine, Jr., and Clifford M. Lytle. 1983. *American Indians, American Justice.* Austin: University of Texas Press.

Dippie, Brian W. 1982. *The Vanishing American: White Attitudes and U.S. Indian Policy.* Middletown, CT: Wesleyan University Press.

Garroute, Eva Marie. 2003. *Real Indians: Identity and the Survival of Native America.* Berkeley: University of California Press.

Gedicks, Al. 1993. *The New Resource Wars: Native American and Environmental Struggles Against Multinational Corporations.* Boston: South End Press.

Heilprin, John (Associated Press). "Congress Must Pick Figure in Indian Suit." *Indian Trust: Cobell v. Kempthorne.* Available at: http://www .Indiantrust.com/index.cfm?FuseAction= Articles.ViewDetail&Article_id=346& Month=3&Year=2006). (accessed March 1, 2006)

Hertzberg, Hazel L. 1971. *The Search for an American Indian Identity: Modern Pan-Indian Movements.* Syracuse, NY: Syracuse University Press.

Hilden, Patricia Penn. 1995. *When Nickels Were Indians: A Mixed-Blood Urban Story.* Washington, DC: Smithsonian Institution.

Hill, Patricia, 1992. *The Alchemy of Race and Rights: The Diary of a Law Professor.* Cambridge, MA: Harvard University Press.

Hoxie, Frederick E. 1984. *A Final Promise: The Campaign to Assimilate the Indians, 1880–1920.* Cambridge, UK: Cambridge University Press.

Indian Health Service. 2006. *Indian Population.* Available at: http://info.ihs.gov/Files/ IndianPopTrends-Jan2006.pdf.

Kelly, Lawrence. 1976. "The Indian Reorganization Act: Dream or Reality?" *Pacific Historical Review,* 44 (1976): 291–312.

Kickingbird, Kirke, and Karen Ducheneaux. 1973. *One Hundred Million Acres.* New York: Macmillan.

Leupp, Francis E. 1910. *The Indian and His Problem.* New York: Scribner's.

McDonnell, Janet A. 1991. *The Dispossession of the American Indian, 1887–1934* Bloomington: Indiana University Press.

Meriam, Lewis B., et al. 1928. *The Problem of Indian Administration.* Baltimore, MD: Johns Hopkins University Press.

Meyer, Melissa L. 1994. *The White Earth Tragedy: Ethnicity and Dispossession at a Minnesota Anishnaabe Reservation, 1889–1920.* Lincoln: University of Nebraska Press.

Moore, John H. 1996. "Cheyenne Work in the History of U.S. Capitalism." In *Native Americans and Wage Labor.* Edited by Alice Littlefield and Martha C. Knack, 122–143. Norman: University of Oklahoma Press.

Morgan, Lewis Henry. 1871. *Systems of Consanguinity and Affinity of the Human Family.* Contributions to Knowledge No. 17. Washington, DC: Smithsonian Institution.

Morgan, Lewis Henry. 1877. *Ancient Society or Researches in the Lines of Human Progress from Savagery through Barbarism to Civilization.* Chicago: Charles H. Kerr.

Morgan, Lewis Henry. 1959. *The Indian Journals, 1859–62.* Ann Arbor: University of Michigan Press.

Nietschmann, Bernard. 1994. "The Fourth World: Nations Versus States." In *Reordering the World: Geopolitical Perspectives for the Twenty-First Century*. Edited by George J. Demko and William B. Woods, 225–242. Boulder, CO: Westview Press.

O'Brien, Sharon. 1989. *American Indian Tribal Governments*. Norman: University of Oklahoma Press.

O'Brien, Sharon. 1991. "Tribes and Indians: With Whom Does the United States Maintain a Relationship?" *Notre Dame Law Review,* 66: 1461–1502.

Ortiz, Roxanne Dunbar. 1979. "Sources of Underdevelopment." In *Economic Development in American Indian Reservations*. Native American Studies Development Series No. 1. Edited by Roxanne Dunbar Ortiz, 61–75. Albuquerque: University of New Mexico.

Robbins, Lynn A. 1979. "Structural Changes in Navajo Government Related to Development." In *Economic Development in American Indian Reservations*. Native American Studies Development Series. Edited by Roxanne Dunbar Ortiz, 129–134. Albuquerque: University of New Mexico.

Sartre, Jean-Paul. 1964, 2004. *Colonialism and Neocolonialism*. New York: Routledge.

Sartre, Jean-Paul. 1968. *On Genocide*. Boston: Beacon Press.

Schneider, Craig. "Lawsuit Seeks Billions for Land Leasing: The Interior Department Has Spent over $100 Million to Reconcile Accounts of American Indians; More Than $100 Billion May Be Lost." *CFO.com*. August 31, 2005. Available at: http://www.cfo.com/printable/article.cfm/4342517?f=options.

Snipp, C. Matthew. 1989. *American Indians: The First of This Land*. New York: Russell Sage Foundation.

Steiner, Stan. 1968. *The New Indians*. New York: Harper & Row.

Strickland, Rennard. 1997. *Tonto's Revenge: Reflections on American Indian Culture and Policy*. Albuquerque: University of New Mexico Press.

Taylor, Graham D. 1980. *The New Deal and American Indian Tribalism: The Administration of the Indian Reorganization Act, 1934–45*. Lincoln: University of Nebraska Press.

Thomas, Robert K. 1966–1967. "Colonialism: Classic and Internal," *New University Thought*, 4, no. 4: 39–43.

Thornton, Russell. 1987. *American Indian Holocaust and Survival: A Population History Since 1492*. Norman: University of Oklahoma Press.

Thornton, Russell. 1997. "Tribal Membership Requirements and the Demography of 'Old' and 'New' Native Americans." *Population Research and Policy Review*, 16, no.: 33–42.

Unrau, William E. 1989. *Mixed Bloods and Tribal Dissolution: Charles Curtis and the Quest for Indian Identity*. Lawrence: University Press of Kansas.

Washburn, Wilcomb E. 1971. *Red Man's Land, White Man's Law: A Study of the Past and Present Status of the American Indian*. New York: Scribner's.

Washburn, Wilcomb E. 1986. *The Assault on Indian Tribalism: The General Allotment (Dawes Act) of 1887*. Malibar, FL: Krieger.

Weston, Burns H., Richard A. Falk, and Anthony D'Amato, eds. 1990. *Basic Documents in International Law and World Order*, 2nd ed. St. Paul, MN: West.

Wilkins, David E. 2002. *American Indian Politics and the American Political System*. Lanham, MD: Rowman & Littlefield.

Wilkinson, Charles. 2005. *Blood Struggle: The Rise of Modern Indian Nations*. New York: W. W. Norton.

Young, Calvin. M. 1956. *Little Turtle*. Fort Wayne, IN: Public Library of Fort Wayne and Allen County.

Termination and Indian Sovereignty
(1945 to 2000)

Changes in U.S. policy have occurred throughout Indian history, and Indian leaders and communities have struggled to preserve self-government in the context of each with varying degrees of success. Since 1950, American Indian nations have continued to preserve land, political autonomy, community, and cultures. U.S. government policies for American Indians during the 1950–2006 period waver and change: The termination policy of the 1950s was followed by the self-determination policies in the late 1960s and 1970s, with a trend toward less favorable legal and political environments and policies since the 1980s and with an increasingly conservative U.S. political, legal, and cultural environment during the early 2000s.

Through all these changes, American Indians have steadily sought new ways to accommodate U.S. policy and institutions, and they have increasingly formed national organizations; strengthened tribal governments; and sought to recover cultures, languages, community, and land, and to regain control over everyday life on Indian reservations. Many Indians have migrated to urban areas, sought work, and, in recent years, increased their ownership of private businesses.

The present period is marked by U.S. policies that foster American Indian assimilation and integration into the mainstream. In many ways, the American public and policy makers see American Indians as an historical ethnic group, not unlike many ethnic groups and identities in American history and culture. Yet ethnic groups have homelands on other continents and often come to the United States seeking economic livelihood or religious or political freedom. Most immigrant ethnic groups seek to assimilate, become U.S. citizens, and adopt much of the U.S. culture. Not broadly understood or recognized by U.S. policy makers and the general public, however, is the viewpoint of indigenous U.S. Indians who have lived on the land and practiced self-government from time immemorial. Indian nations derive their claims to self-government and land from their creation teachings and from their long-time political, national, and cultural presence that preceded the formation of the U.S. Constitution and nation. Indigenous peoples seek to preserve their land, their government, and their culture, and they have not actively sought integration or total

assimilation into American life and culture. American Indian communities resist the general patterns of assimilation and integration into American culture and society. Consequently, American Indians are not well understood, and often U.S. government policies reflect strong trends toward the assimilation and integration of American Indians into U.S. society, which Indian communities and organizations often actively oppose.

Since the 1960s, legal and policy changes have allowed American Indian communities to seek self-government, economic development, and cultural maintenance or reclamation in ways more open than at any time since before 1871, when the U.S. ended treaty making with Indian nations. Between 1871 and the middle 1960s, the U.S. government extended direct administrative control over many Indian communities, governments, and cultures. Even the Indian New Deal of the 1930s did little to empower tribal communities. In a significant way, contemporary policy unravels some, although not all, legal and political constraints that were imposed on Indian nations and governments during the period of nearly total control established after 1871. Through internal dynamics and change in American society, U.S. government policy changed after the termination policy of the 1950s and sought ways to economically include Indian communities in American society. The changes in policy resulted in the strengthening of tribal governments, and the tribal government organizations we know today are to a large extent a result of government policies implemented between 1965 and 1980. Although the legal and legislative opportunities created during the 1965–1980 period are formative for the current period, they were short-lived, as the bureaucratic, juridical, and legislative practices and policies of the U.S. government have became increasingly less favorable toward tribal governments and communities after 1980.

While government policies from the 1960s to about 1980 created new government capabilities and legal opportunities, a second trend better characterizes present-day Indian policy. While Indian communities have often fought vigorously to maintain their rights to land, and self-government in the post-1871 period, these days Indian communities and organizations have become more self-aware about

indigenous rights, tribal self-government, and pre-serving community and culture. American Indian political and cultural consciousness has become national, pan-Indian, and international. Before 1871, most tribal communities were still well taught within their own traditions and cultures and sought to assert their governments and cultures from within their traditions. After a century of U.S. administrative control over tribal institutions and government policies of assimilation and integration, many Indian communities were deprived of significant aspects of their languages, their religions, their community organizations, and their control over justice, land, and self-government.

At the same time, most Indian people speak English, many have high school or college educations, and have learned to work within the U.S. market and political systems. Given the legal and bureaucratic opportunities of the 1960s and 1970s, Indian communities, students, and leaders—becoming increasingly aware of their history—sought to restore their values, cultures, and political and legal rights. A general understanding of Indian legal and political history became more common among leaders and students, as well as among community members, as tribal communities actively sought to reclaim land, self-government, culture, and language, at the same time starting to engage and participate in markets and U.S. political institutions on their own cultural terms.

The broad national consensus about tribal political identity and tribal relations with the U.S. government and nation has characterized the most recent U.S.–Indian policy period, even after the post-1980 emergence of relatively less favorable federal legal, legislative, and bureaucratic support. American Indian tribal communities are mobilized to pursue many of their political and cultural goals and values in new ways and in the new contemporary circumstances of U.S. policy, amid the increasing globalization of markets, information, technology, and culture. The story of recent Indian–U.S. relations is one of tribal cultural mobilization and opportunity, although within the constraints of U.S. political, legal, and cultural institutions. An overview of contemporary U.S. government policy and the rise of American Indian cultural and political mobilization follows.

Termination Policy

The termination policy sought to dismantle Indian reservations, divide or sell the land, distribute the proceeds to tribal members, and incorporate Indians as full citizens of the United States. Congress passed acts to introduce the termination policy in the early 1950s and instructed the Bureau of Indian Affairs (BIA) to make lists of the tribal communities most ready to enter permanently into U.S. society. The termination policy emphasized the assimilation and integration of Indians into U.S. life. On its face, the termination policy appears to break Indian treaties—agreements between Indian tribes and the United States that often guarantee ownership of Indian lands (the reservation) in exchange for compensation or other diplomatic considerations. The courts, however, as in *Lone Wolf v. Hitchcock* (1903), deem treaties with Indians breakable if such action is in the collective interests of the United States and the Indian tribes. Congress, by the early 1900s, assumed primary policy-making authority in Indian affairs, because the U.S. Constitution says in the commerce clause that Congress will manage trade and relations with Indian tribes.

With the application of the Indian New Deal policy under Franklin Roosevelt starting in the middle 1930s, Indian policy was generated from the U.S. Congress, which began to pass legislation aimed at the assimilation of Indian communities. World War II intervened, but, after the end of the war, Congress revisited older efforts to pass resolutions and legislation opening the way to dismantle Indian reservations economically and politically and to move Indian people into full participation in U.S. society. Congressional supporters of termination believed that Indian people should be released from tribal governments and reservations so that they could enjoy full rights and participation in the United States.

Indian people were relocated from Indian reservations to urban areas, where they were assisted in seeking employment. Because the economies of most Indian reservations could not support Indian populations, many tribal members had migrated during the 1920s and World War II to urban areas in search of employment. The BIA's relocation program, however, was designed to move whole Indian families and people off the reservation and into the cities. In the early 1950s, Congress enacted PL83-280, usually known as Public Law 280, or PL280, the 280th law passed by the 83rd Congress. PL280 transferred the administration of criminal justice from federal administration to some state governments. With passage of the act, Indian reservations in six states saw their jurisdiction transferred and several other states

followed, requiring the use of state courts for criminal offenses. Tribal members in PL280 states were served by state and county police, especially if there were no tribal police or courts. BIA funded and generally managed the courts, and police served non-PL280 communities during the 1950s. The initial intent of PL280 was to assist termination procedures by delegating police and court authorities to states and counties withdrawing services that had been generally provided by the federal government to non-PL280 reservation communities. However, Congress did not provide additional funding to states and counties, which caused some financial and service difficulties.

Between the early 1950s and the early 1970s, one hundred and ten Indian reservations were terminated. A few reservations targeted for termination, such as the Turtle Mountain Reservation in North Dakota, mobilized political support from their congressional delegations and avoided termination. Several reservations, including the Turtle Mountain Reservation, Klamath Reservation in Oregon, and Menominee Reservation in Wisconsin, were targeted early in the termination process because they were deemed more economically capable and therefore ready for termination. More than forty tribal reservations in California were terminated, mostly small rancherias. Many communities in California were willing to adopt termination because they were greatly underserved by the BIA and saw few prospects for their communities under continued BIA administration. Some tribal communities, including the Lakota and Dakota reservations in South Dakota and the Warm Springs Reservation in Oregon, mobilized state political initiatives or their congressional delegations and lobbied successfully to avoid PL280 implementation on their reservations. Other tribes in Nevada were allowed to adopt PL280 in the early 1960s, but the Nevada tribes opted to withdraw or "retrocede" from PL280 and return to BIA-funded police and courts in the 1970s. States like California, Oregon, Nebraska, and Minnesota had most of their tribal communities assigned to PL280 law and police services.

The results of termination soon became apparent, and the outcomes for many communities, including the large Klamath and Menominee Reservations, were bleak. The tribal communities lost significant tribal assets and were subject to new taxes and market competition. Poverty increased, many businesses failed, additional lands were lost, and communities were broken up.

Other tribal communities observed the events among the terminated tribes and started to organize state, congressional, and national tribal organizations to prevent additional terminations of reservation communities. Congressional and state support was often forthcoming because states saw the termination policy as an unfunded mandate. (As reservation communities were dismantled, any new costs were borne by local county and state institutions.) Tribal communities rallied around the National Congress of American Indians (NCAI), a national organization created by BIA employees in 1944, although there were similar earlier lobbying organizations proposed and developed during the 1930s. The NCAI developed into a national lobbying organization, and many tribal communities joined. Each tribe, a sovereign nation, has one vote in NCAI decision making. Each tribal community is respected as a member of the NCAI. The threat of more terminations across Indian country mobilized considerable resistance to the policy. By the end of the 1950s, NCAI and Indian leaders, with the help of Congress members and state and local support, were able to prevent new terminations. By 1960, the termination policy was defeated, although some terminations that were initiated before 1960 continued sporadically into the 1970s. The defeat of the termination policy was an early victory for NCAI and a national coalition of Indian leaders. NCAI became a national lobbying organization for tribal legislative issues and interests in Congress. Indian tribes had stopped termination, and many Indian groups were interested in influencing the government to develop policies that included Indian interests and values.

In the early 1960s, tribal leaders, students, community leaders, and scholars met in Chicago and other places to discuss the future of Indian policy. Tribal leaders and advocates looked to develop new policies that supported tribal governments; increased self-determination; secured Indian lands; encouraged Indian language, culture, and religion; and addressed issues of poverty and health. Indian people wanted a voice in their affairs, and they wanted the government to introduce policies that supported tribal community and economic development and that honored and upheld treaties. Government policy did not have a clear direction in the early 1960s, although some efforts at supporting economic development had minor impact. Nevertheless, direct response by the U.S. government to the increasingly mobilized Indian leadership was minimal and, while perhaps sympathetic, was without

direct motivation or capability to respond to the demands in some segments of the Indian community for major reform in Indian policy. Most tribal governments, however, remained within the administrative and financial influence of the BIA, where policies were not yet significantly affected by the new proposals for reform. Those governments and reservation leaders depended on BIA administration and funding, and most reservation tribal leaders were not in strong positions to challenge longstanding BIA control over reservation institutions. Tribal communities and leaders were constrained by BIA-imposed and -controlled tribal government forms, such as IRA (Indian Reorganization Act) constitutional governments or business councils, which did not encourage tribal government autonomy, functionality, or self-sufficiency.

The Rise of Self-Determination Policy (1965–1980)

Self-determination policies eventually emerged from the efforts of a wide variety of Native American communities, activists, tribal leaders, Indian national organizations, and U.S. government policy makers during the 1960s. Inasmuch as U.S. government policy in Indian Country is often greatly influenced by changing cultures and political philosophies in mainstream U.S. politics, the 1960s were greatly influenced by the civil-rights movement, poor peoples' movements, and the changing cultural and political orientations surrounding debates and activism growing out of the Vietnam War. Minority groups and poor peoples began to seek recognition, aid, and redress from the federal government. The political campaigns of John F. Kennedy and his vice presidential partner, Lyndon B. Johnson, formed a democratic coalition of minority groups, bringing poor peoples together regarding civil rights issues. With this winning political coalition in 1960 and in 1964, Lyndon Johnson carried the Democratic party coalition with an overwhelming majority. Federal policies turned toward redistributing federal taxes and wealth, with policies encouraging civil rights, greater opportunity, education programs, environmental concerns, and new programs to alleviate poverty. President Johnson's administration formulated the Great Society programs, designed to assist poor people, minority groups, and others to gain better access and opportunity in American society. Congress passed many of the administration's legislative proposals in the early and middle 1960s, and soon substantial numbers of programs and significant funds flowed to many formerly disenfranchised groups and communities.

While engaged in national politics and in developing Indian policy and issues, tribal leaders generally were not active in the democratic movement or the policy development of the Great Society programs. During the early 1960s, federal administration in Indian Country was managed by the BIA. In the middle 1960s, the Office of Economic Opportunity (OEO) started to allocate community action program (CAP) grants directly to local communities. This plan was based on requests from many programs, especially urban poor peoples' movements that wanted to avoid top-down federal bureaucratic administration and actively participate in the decision making and administration of projects designed to assist local communities. Bypassing federal bureaucracies, federal funds were allocated directly to the community action boards, which received, administered, and distributed the allocations for local projects.

A question arose among federal officials and policy makers about whether Indian communities and tribal governments were eligible for CAP funds. The BIA wanted to administer all federal funds to Indians, but the OEO was suspicious of the track record and control that BIA administration maintained over tribal communities. OEO decided to send CAP grants directly to tribal governments. This was a major change in policy. Under the BIA few federal program funds went directly to tribal government administrations; instead, they generally were allocated to the BIA, which administered many programs and initiatives on behalf of the tribal governments. The OEO CAP grants were allocated directly to tribal governments, who were in a position to form community action boards and to administer and allocate funds according to local needs. The CAP grants bypassed the BIA administration, and many tribal governments for the first time gained access to and control over substantial grant funds. Following the OEO example, other federal agencies began to establish direct relations with tribal governments and determined tribal eligibility for grant programs. By the late 1960s and 1970s, tribal governments received funds from a variety of federal agencies for housing, education, drug control, police, tribal court administration, antipoverty programs and other purposes. The BIA, while still a central administrative feature of reservation administration, began to reform its programs to assist the delivery of

social and administrative services to tribal governments and Indian reservation communities.

The new attention from federal agencies in the middle and late 1960s revitalized tribal government organizations and administrations. Many tribal governments gained access to federal funds, along with control over the administration and distribution of significant funding. Previously, most tribal governments had few staff, little political power, and very little discretionary financing, and they were often subject to strict control by BIA administration. The new influx of grants and relations with many federal agencies enabled tribal governments to obtain more resources and to work with a variety of funding sources. Tribal governments, often still based on relatively weak government constitutions, bylaws, or business councils, soon became more capable organizations that began to interact and gain influence with federal agencies, like other local and state governments. Many tribal governments gathered considerable numbers of federal grants, increased administrative staffs, and established greater control over the distribution of program resources in local communities. Political leadership became more competitive as the stakes for tribal government leadership became more serious.

The tribal governments we know today were largely forged during the 1965–1980 period. During this time, many federal agencies allocated significant funds to the administration of tribal governments, which became recognized governmental entities in the federal-state-local system. The official self-determination policy was kicked off by President Richard Nixon in the late 1960s. The president took the new policy orientation from the then current trends in Indian Country, as tribal governments sought more direct federal funding and worked to strengthen tribal government resources, employees, and program capabilities.

During the 1960s, the Zuni Pueblos sought to decrease federal and BIA control over their communities by contracting all federal programs through the Zuni tribal government. Using a little known and until then rarely used law, the Zuni strengthened control over their own institutions and government by contracting all federal services whenever possible, thereby gaining considerable administrative control of federal programs on their reservation. The Zuni model was mentioned by President Nixon as a new template for Indian self-determination. The new plan for the local administration of federal programs by the tribal government was eventually passed by Congress as the Self-Determination and Education Act of 1975 (Public Law 93-638). The Self-Determination Act created mechanisms for tribal governments and Indian-owned organizations to contract for the delivery of federal service to reservation communities. Tribal governments could now contract for BIA services on reservations, and many slowly began to work toward that end. Tribal communities in the 1970s began to contract for education programs, gaining greater participation and administration of education in reservation communities. More complicated programs, such as health clinics, tended to be avoided by many tribal governments, which generally pursued contracting according to their administrative and management capabilities. The Navajo tribal government became a major contractor of BIA and federal programs, but the contracting of federal services was varied across Indian Country. The contracts became known generally and informally as "638" contracts, named after the Congressional Public Law 93-638 (PL93-638, the 638th public law passed by the 93rd Congress).

The Self-Determination and Education Act of 1975 created a contracting mechanism for tribal governments to administer locally programs intended for tribal communities. The effect of the Act was to increase tribal government administration of federal programs, and it helped to extend and strengthen the powers of tribal governments, as well as taking away additional program autonomy from BIA administration. However, while contemporary tribal governments use 638 contracting extensively they do not possess the infrastructure to contract all BIA programs. The Self-Determination Act strengthened tribal organizations and increased local delivery and management of programs for reservation members. Nevertheless, the contracts were governed by BIA or federal rules and regulations, and funding came from Congress and was funneled through federal or BIA agencies that monitored the contracting processes. Tribal governments gained standing for funding and administrative purposes similar to local and state governments, but most tribal governments lack independent sources of income and had few discretionary resources to implement plans, programs, and economic development that represented tribal values, interests, and goals. Most tribal governments have acquired greater bureaucratic and program capacities since the 1960s, but most remain dependent on federal funding and administrative rules for most of its programmatic operational activities.

As time passed, many tribal governments provided program assistance and jobs to tribal communities, but the new arrangements maintained considerable dependency on federal funding, and federal rules and regulations dominated most program implementation. Most tribal governments did not have significant alternative sources of income. Although tribal governments have the right to tax, such measures generally are contrary to Indian cultures, and taxes do not meet with acceptance in most tribal communities. Consequently, tribal government leaders began to look toward reservation economic development for discretionary funds. Some leaders began to say that tribal governments needed to move away from federal dependency and engage market economies to help relieve tribal communities from poverty and dependence. Some federal programs offered business loans to aid investment in tourism and hotels in Indian Country. From the 1960s to the 1990s, however, there were few economic successes in Indian Country that did not depend on the sale of raw materials or gambling enterprises. The Mississippi Choctaws developed some manufacturing industries and provided work for community members and local non-Indians, but in general most reservation economies were far from providing their communities with American levels of economic well-being.

Tribal communities and governments increasingly are looking to establish more productive reservation economies as a means of generating autonomous revenues that they can use to pursue the goals of restoring tribal cultures and communities, as well as reclaiming land and strengthening tribal government capabilities and self-government. Toward these ends, some communities have sought to discuss reorganizing tribal governments to make them more effective and more responsible to tribal cultures and communities. Many tribal governments have looked to markets and businesses to create jobs, income, and tribal government revenues. The trend in Indian Country, however, has not been toward fostering individual entrepreneurship, as in American society, but rather most tribal communities, at least in their early steps, have favored a form of tribal capitalism, where tribal governments manage and own tribal assets and produce income for the tribal government that is available to support collective tribal programs and needs. The organization of the successful Mississippi Choctaw businesses are a main case in point. As time has passed, however, many tribal governments have sought creative legal and market mechanisms to preserve tribal communities, norms, and values, at the same time creating tribal corporations or enterprises that are profitable in market competition.

Multiple Pathways to Self-Determination

The development of the U.S. government self-determination policy is only one movement that characterizes the present period of government policy, tribal government, and American Indian community relations. Also helping to characterize the revival and development of contemporary Indian identity, communities, and tribal governments are Red Power activism; the tribal community college movement; cultural, religious, and language reclamation; federal and tribal legal developments; the international indigenous rights movement; and Indian market capitalism. The multidimensional roots along with the broad international recognition of Indian rights, cultural aspirations, and search for greater cultural and political autonomy, are part of the indigenous movement and the self-determination movement among American Indian communities.

Indian communities have been active throughout history in defense of their lands, territories, cultures, and governments. Historically, tribal leaders and communities mostly were raised within their cultures and traditions and, while having some contact with the United States, generally were well socialized within their own cultures and values. After 1871, active assimilation and Christianization programs began to change and introduce alternative forms of knowledge, worldviews, education, science, and ways of life. Tribal communities became multicultural, and tribal members held varying degrees of traditional knowledge as well as American or modern knowledge and understandings. Furthermore, their world has changed considerably over time. Most contemporary tribal leaders do not think that it is possible to return to the traditional societies and cultures of several hundred years ago. The emphasis is on upholding traditions and norms when they maintain identity and community, but tribal communities and leaders also are looking for pathways to the future. They want to uphold community and culture, at the same time engaging the globalized political, economic, informational, and cultural challenges of the twenty-first century. Tribal cultures and values will be preserved and used as tools to help formulate ways by which Indian peo-

ple and future generations will live in the contemporary and future world. Indian people, like all human groups, confront change, but they want to do so from the point of view of their communities, values, and ways of living.

Between 1871 and 1965, many Indian people and communities were discouraged from speaking their languages, practicing Indian ceremonies and religions, or otherwise living in ways informed by tribal values. Indian students were taught in government and state schools how to live in U.S. society, and they were encouraged to abandon Indian identities, cultures, and tribal membership and to join U.S. society as economically independent citizens. The U.S. government assimilation and Christianization programs had varying success. During the 1920s and after the 1950s, many Indian reservation people migrated to urban areas in search of education and employment. Many individuals and whole tribes by the 1960s had lost many aspects of their communities, identities, cultures, and values. In the contemporary period, many Indian people retain social and political identities as American Indian, but often many do not have strong or nurturing relations with their communities and cultures. Several generations of Indian people have been living in urban areas, and most have had only occasional contact with their tribal communities. There are over 4 million people on the 2000 U.S. Census who say they are at least part Indian, while only about 600,000 Indians live on reservations. About two-thirds of self-identified Indians live in urban areas. The urbanization and government assimilation programs have greatly changed and diversified the cultural makeup of Indian people. Many Indian communities and individuals have been separated from their communities, cultures, land, or tribal governments. Tribal communities are not composed of Indian people steeped in their tribal cultures and traditions, and many tribal members have had little shared contact with their cultures. The contemporary movement toward recovering tribal community and values involves recovering and reclaiming tribal culture, values, and identity.

The Red Power movement of the 1960s and 1970s had many characteristics of a cultural reclamation movement. The heyday of the Red Power Movement took place between the takeover of Alcatraz Island in late 1969 and the Longest Walk of 1977. During this period, Indian activists took over at least seventy-five locations, which were used as platforms to articulate Indian issues and rights and often to

express land claims. Many of the members of the Alcatraz takeover in 1969–1971 were urban Indians or students, many of whom did not have strong cultural ties to their communities. Many visitors to Alcatraz Island during the takeover period learned from discussions about tribal history, policy, and issues and conditions on Indian reservations. Many were then motivated to carry on activism to support Indian rights and issues and to pass information on to others. Soon there followed other takeovers, of which the most well-known was the BIA headquarters in Washington, DC (in 1972) and the Wounded Knee standoff on Pine Ridge Reservation in South Dakota the next year. The takeovers attracted international attention and highlighted Indian history, grievances, and rights in the mass media. Many Indians who were living American urban lives became inspired to recover their identities, to reclaim tribal histories and cultures, and to support strengthened tribal governments and communities. One reason that American Indian Movement (AIM) members returned to Pine Ridge in the early 1970s was that they believed they did not have sufficient grounding in traditional knowledge and wanted to learn from elders and spiritual leaders who retained an understanding of Lakota religion and ceremonies. Lakota elders at the Pine Ridge and Rosebud Reservations were surprised at how boldly the activists came to seek traditional understanding and knowledge. The elders were emboldened by the activists, and many more openly started to perform ceremonies, such as the Ghost Dances and Sun Dances, that had long been practiced away from the eyes of government agents. Many activists and spiritual elders began to practice traditional religions and ceremonies more openly and more often, and many younger members apprenticed themselves to learn more about traditional religion, ceremonies, and languages. Many communities are now seeking ways to recover, reclaim, and use traditional knowledge and language in their communities.

Many elders soon started teaching language and culture in newly formed tribally controlled community colleges on Indian reservations. The founders of the colleges were primarily local tribal people dedicated to improving educational opportunities in their communities. In the late 1960s, the Navajo Community College was formed, and several others soon followed. The new Indian community colleges sought federal legislation and financial aid to support student scholarships. The Tribally Controlled Community College Assistance Act

(PL95-471) was enacted by Congress in 1978. The tribal colleges formed a national organization, American Indian Higher Education Consortium (AIHEC), and soon admitted more colleges. By 2006 there were thirty-five tribally controlled community colleges in AIHEC.

Along with the contracting of reservation day schools by the tribal governments, these colleges reflect a concern for education that is informed by community culture and participation. Many Native students finish high school but do not want to leave the reservation community to enter college, but the tribally controlled community colleges have given many reservation Indian students the opportunity to remain in their community, while gaining the knowledge and skills useful for employment and for building stronger Indian communities, nations, and governments.

Many tribal communities continued to pursue primary rights and issues, often with the support of lawyers funded through legal aid or through the Native American Rights Fund (NARF). Tribal communities asserted land claims and made challenges to open discussion and legal disposition from broken treaties or forgotten laws and rights. Before the 1960s, Indian communities were less able to pursue legal claims in U.S. courts, and U.S. courts were often unsympathetic. For decades, the Indian tribes in Washington State pursued fishing rights from treaties signed during the 1850s providing that Indians could fish in their ancient fishing places and that they were entitled to take fish "in common" with immigrating Anglo-Americans each season. In 1974, a legal decision by Judge George Boldt, often called the Boldt decision, upheld the fishing treaty rights of many Washington tribal communities. Boldt interpreted the treaty phrase "in common with" to mean that Indians had a right to as much as half the salmon harvest. His decision was upheld on appeal.

Treaty rights, including fishing rights, also were contested in Wisconsin and Michigan, where tribal communities gained less favorable rulings, but ones that partially upheld treaty rights. The Alaska Natives during the 1960s, after Alaska was established as a state, claimed most of the territory of Alaska, and eventually a negotiated settlement in Congress resulted in the Alaska Native Claims Act of 1971. The Alaska Natives land claims were negotiated with Congress, setting the stage for the settlement of other major claims. Lawyers working with the northern Maine Indians made an argument that land had been illegally treated from Maine Indians,

such as the Passamaquoddy and Penobscot, in violation of the federal Non-Intercourse Acts, passed as early as 1790, that prohibit states from treating for land with Indians without federal approval. The Passamaquoddy land-claim settlement in Maine (1980) led to negotiated land settlements, and other tribes in the original thirteen colonies began to seek federal recognition and land from the U.S. government. In the early 1980s, the Pequots, their reservation under Connecticut state administration from the 1650s, sought and gained congressional approval for federal recognition. The Narragansetts of Rhode Island did the same, and more recently the Mohicans of Connecticut also received federal recognition.

Many of the terminated tribes also pursued reclamation of tribal government and community through legal action. During the early 1970s, a group of Menominees worked through Congress to obtain an act that restored federal recognition. A difficult lobbying process ended successfully, and the Menominees recovered part of their former reservation. Soon many other terminated communities sought congressional acts for restoration to federally recognized tribal status. In California, either by court cases or legislation, more than forty terminated tribes were restored to federal recognition. California Indian Legal Services, at one time a federally funded organization, helped many tribes with developing courts cases and working through the restoration procedures. The large majority of the hundred and ten terminated tribes have been restored, and those communities have reclaimed land and renewed tribal governments.

A related contemporary community movement is composed of Indian communities that have not been federally recognized and that are seeking recognition. To date, more than five hundred and sixty Indian communities are federally recognized as Indian tribes by the U.S. government, most of them through treaty relations or Congressional acts. Federal recognition allows a community to enjoy federal trust relations with the United States, especially protections for Indian reservation lands, so that they cannot be taken from or sold by the tribe without permission and oversight from the BIA or Secretary of the Interior. More than two hundred communities have petitioned for federal recognition and more nonrecognized Indian communities may be eligible.

Currently, tribal communities seeking recognition apply to the Office of Federal Acknowledgment. The situation of nonrecognized Indian communities was documented in a congressional report on Indian

issues produced by the Senate Committee on Indian Affairs during the middle 1970s. Legislation enabling the BIA to solicit, analyze, and make recommendations for recognition was passed into law in the late 1970s. The process for tribal communities to secure federal recognition is difficult, expensive, and time-consuming, and relatively few have been recognized through the formal BIA procedures. Perhaps only several cases are considered each year, but the entire process may take decades. Recent reorganizations in the Office of Federal Acknowledgment are designed to speed up the process. Tribal communities seeking federal recognition often do not have enough resources to fulfill the requirements proving continuous political community throughout their history to the present. Many tribal communities, often ignored and marginalized throughout their recent history, are in difficult positions to comply with federal recognition requirements. Nevertheless, many communities continue to seek federal recognition, acquire land, and form tribal governments.

Not only are tribal communities mobilized at the national and local levels, but many tribal leaders and nations, particularly groups of Iroquois, Lakota, and Hopi, have approached the United Nations (U.N.) and other international institutions seeking the recognition of indigenous rights and the preservation of cultural and political autonomy. International conferences have been held on indigenous issues, and indigenous leaders and communities have spent years working on a document called the Draft Declaration on the Rights of Indigenous Peoples, which has not received broad support and recognition within the United Nations, even though indigenous peoples from around the world participate in drafting it. Some American Indian leaders and organizations seek international alliances and international bodies to induce nation-states such as the United States to recognize indigenous rights. During the 1970s, many indigenous groups protested outside the United Nations building to gain a voice and recognition. The protests led to a series of international conferences on indigenous issues and, more recently, to the establishment of NGO (non-government organization) status for indigenous peoples in the U.N. There are some differences of opinion about the value of indigenous peoples working within the U.N. One argument is that the U.N. is a club of nation-states that fears potentially politically destabilizing effects on less established democracies or nation-states. Therefore the assertions of indigenous rights for greater cul-

tural and political autonomy will not find significant support in the U.N. Others argue that the participation and presence of indigenous peoples in the U.N. and in other international venues, as well as international recognition of indigenous rights, will create a moral standard providing protections to indigenous peoples that would otherwise not be available to them.

American Indians and indigenous peoples around the world have increasingly mobilized to pursue greater political and cultural autonomy and protections that will enable them to live and work more in accord with their cultural and political traditions. Recent decades have been characterized by greater cultural, political, and economic mobilization among American Indians at the local, national, and international levels. Many Indian groups and organizations have emerged at national levels, pursuing professional, artistic, media, sport, cultural, economic, and political goals. The mobilization of American Indian communities, not only at local community levels, but also at national and political levels, is a significant marker for present-day Indian policy. More than ever before, American Indian individuals are participating in U.S. national organizations and institutions, often pursuing tribal cultural and political goals within the framework of U.S. and international organizations. In many ways, American Indian communities, leaders, and organizations have come to actively participate in U.S. national political and cultural organizations and generally play by U.S. rules.

Most American Indians have strong loyalties of citizenship to the United States, but at the same time many believe that the United States should recognized the history, legal, and international relations of Indians with the United States. Since the granting of U.S. citizenship to American Indians in 1924, many have retained two citizenships, one as a member of a tribal community and the other as a citizen of the United States. While most American Indian individuals and communities are loyal to the United States and fight honorably in U.S. wars, American Indians seek recognition of their rights to tribal governments, culture, and land from time immemorial, which predate the adoption of the U.S. Constitution and the formation of the United States.

On a variety of fronts over the past fifty years, American Indians have mobilized to realize their claims to cultural and political autonomy and have done so as active participants within U.S. institutions and political relations. In a certain sense, Indian

groups and political activities are incorporated into U.S. political and institutional culture, but they continue to pursue unique goals of cultural and political autonomy that are often contrary to U.S. legal and political culture. No other ethnic or political group advocates for the preservation and enhancement of self-government, for the recovery and continuity of non-Western culture, and for institutional and political forms. The unusual goals and interests of American Indian nations make interaction with core American institutions, cultural groups, and political interests very difficult, and hence Indian issues are often not easily solved or well understood.

The Most Recent Policy Period (1980–2006)

Since 1980, the U.S. political environment for American Indian goals and values has become less forthcoming overall. The trend in U.S. policy is toward fiscal conservatism, and, while there is more emphasis on local government autonomy, there is also more emphasis on local governments finding their own ways to support their needs. While the trends toward greater local self-sufficiency is congruent with many Indian government goals, many reservation communities still do not have local economies that can support their populations, and cutbacks in federal funding have created less support for tribal governments and programs. Many tribal governments have retained many of the gains in bureaucratic and government organization created during the 1960s and 1970s. While tribal governments and communities have become better organized and mobilized since 1980, the decline in federal resources, as well as in legal and administrative support, has led to fewer new opportunities for assertion or for the accomplishment of tribal political and cultural goals. The BIA's administration slowly is moving toward management of trust responsibility, with less emphasis and funds for the delivery of services to Indian communities.

While funding from the federal government has declined, so have legal and court opportunities as a result of more conservative supreme and district courts. During the 1960–1980 period, tribal communities won several significant cases upholding the powers of tribal governments as long as they had not been explicitly withdrawn by an act of Congress or violated the U.S. Constitution. During the 1980s and 1990s, however, court cases brought before the federal courts began to chip away at earlier legal

gains. While much of the legal action of the 1960s to 1980s helped to reaffirm Indian rights to self-government under U.S. law, recent cases have eroded the internal powers of tribal governments. The conservative courts have been less willing to recognize long-standing land claims, the powers of tribal courts over non-Indians, the trust land for Alaska Natives, and the rights of Indians to keep sacred places free from non-Indian interference. A string of legal losses has discouraged Indian lawyers and governments from pursuing remedies in U.S. federal and state courts.

A major exception to the trend has been the affirmation of tribal government sovereignty in the *California v. Cabazon Band of Mission Indians* in 1987. The *Cabazon* case provided significant legal support for Indian gaming in California and elsewhere and quickly led to a resolution of state and Indian interests surrounding gaming in the Indian Gaming Regulation Act of 1988 (IGRA). Congress sought to regulate Indian gaming and invite negotiated compacts between states and tribal governments on how gaming would be managed on Indian reservations. The gaming scenario illustrates the dynamics of the latest policy period. While the support of Indian issues and goals from U.S. government executive, legislative, and judicial institutions is less than in the past, Indian communities are more mobilized and willing to take advantage of any new opportunities they see in their economic, political, or cultural interests. The IGRA enabled many Indian communities eventually to work out with states ways in which to foster gaming establishments on Indian reservations.

Most Indian communities as late as the 1990s were relatively impoverished. Gaming was not a government program advocated by federal policy makers, and most government-formulated economic development projects in Indian Country have been short-lived and generally limited in success. Gaming emerged from tribal groups, like the Cabazon, who actively sought ways to develop market economies on reservations, often with extremely limited assets and possibilities. Tribal communities fought hard in state and federal legislatures, through referenda, and in negotiations with state governments, as well as in courts, to establish tribal rights to manage gaming establishments on reservations. While many Indian communities may have second thoughts about gaming on moral grounds, for many tribal communities gaming is one of few options available to them. The IGRA includes rules requiring that at least 70 percent of tribal gaming profits be redistributed for pro-

grams, infrastructure, and support of tribal members or tribal government. Gaming revenues are shared within the community; they support tribal communities and can be used for the diversification of the reservation economy and for future investment. Well over two hundred Indian communities are managing gaming establishments, but probably less than thirty make large profits. Isolated rural communities are not well located to draw significant gaming revenues, and, although tribal gaming is grossing in excess of $12 billion annually, the funds are not evenly distributed throughout Indian Country.

Indian Policy Now and in the Future

Indian communities have entered a policy era in which U.S. political institutions are less favorable to tribal interests and goals. At the same time, tribal communities never before have been so willing and able to participate in American national political and cultural institutions, but on their own terms. Most American Indians want and are willing to participate in American society, but they also want to uphold Native identity and tribal rights, including territory, self-government, and traditional cultural orientations. American Indians are more capable and better equipped than ever to participate in American society, but they want to do so with reference to their own histories, cultures, and political rights. Tribal communities will continue to mobilize themselves and become more capable in expressing their views and interests. Most likely, tribal communities and Indian individuals will become part of American society and institutions, not fully assimilated, but as

dual citizens. If U.S. policies remain austere, then tribal communities will be encouraged to seek market-based solutions to their economic and government problems. While tribal communities will become more capable of participating beneficially in U.S. society and the economy on their own cultural and political terms, most likely those capabilities and opportunities will be spread unevenly around Indian Country.

Duane Champagne

See also American Indian Movement; Assembly of First Nations; Canada, Indian Policies of; Economic Development; Education; Hazardous Waste; Identity; Indian Self-Determination and Education Assistance Act; Individual Indian Monies; Land, Identity and Ownership of, Land Rights; Language and Language Renewal; Language, Written in America, Pre-contact; National Congress of American Indians; National Indian Youth Council; Native American Museums; New Agers, "Indian" Ceremonies and; Pan-Indianism; Red Power Movement; Reservation Economic and Social Conditions; Royal Commission on Aboriginal Peoples; Termination; Tribal Sovereignty; United Nations, Indians and.

References and Further Reading

Light, Steven Andrew, and Kathryn R. L. Rand. 2005. *Indian Gaming and Tribal Sovereignty: The Casino Compromise*. Lawrence: University Press of Kansas.

Nagel, Joane. 1996. *American Indian Ethnic Renewal: Red Power and the Resurgence of Identity and Culture*. New York: Oxford University Press.

Treat, James. 2003. *Around the Sacred Fire: Native Religious Activism in the Red Power Era*. New York: Macmillan.

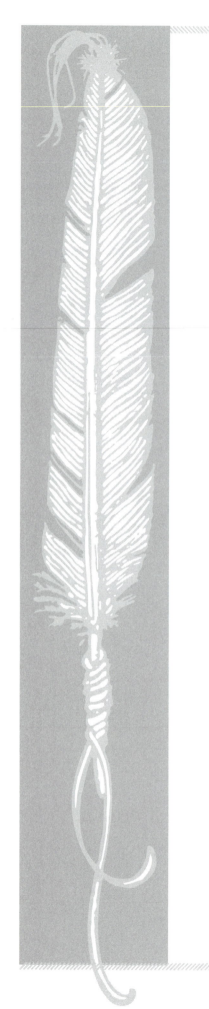

Issues in American Indian History

Alcoholism and Substance Abuse

"Drink no firewater of the white man. It makes you mice for the white men who are cats. Many a meal they have eaten of you."

—Skenando, Oneida chief, ca. 1800

Substance abuse has been at the core of many Native social problems since the initial contact with European invaders and the British colonizers in the seventeenth century. Native American substance abuse must be considered in the context of cultural relativity. The cycle began with cultural trauma and loss, and stereotyping and discrimination perpetuated it through the generations. All of these factors combined to create a cultural form of post-traumatic stress disorder that continues to affect both reservation and urban Natives. Profound disruptions of Native lifeways that began in 1492 and continue to the present time have formed the foundation for Indian drinking patterns, substance abuse, and substance dependency problems (Mancall, 1995).

Professional research from such sources as the federal Substance Abuse and Mental Health Services Administration, the Center for Addiction and Substance Abuse at the University of New Mexico (CASAA), as well as other pertinent research reports, indicate that Native American addiction and substance abuse stems from culturally based phenomena. The research prior to the mid-1980s focused primarily on males and on Southwestern tribes and indicated binge drinking as the most prevalent pattern in alcohol abuse and addiction. Research done since that time indicates that anxiety, dependency, conflict, and feelings of powerlessness and hopelessness associated with poverty and cultural isolation are at the heart of the pattern. Ironically, powerlessness and hopelessness are also two dominant emotional states associated with children of addictive families; hence the two factors reinforce the conditions that have bred substance abuse among Native peoples (Arbogast, 1996).

A survey conducted among the Navajo in the 1980s by the Center on Alcoholism, Substance Abuse, and Addictions (CASAA) indicated that 80

percent of respondents believed that Native American alcoholism was a racially genetic problem and that they were biologically predisposed to alcoholism as a race. Biological predisposition to addiction is a valid phenomenon, but it exists in the context of *family* genetics, rather than racial genetics. Familial addiction predisposes those in any particular genetic lineage in which it occurs. Considering the number of Native families impacted by intergenerational trauma, cultural loss, and grief for the past four hundred years, the widespread effect of the disease of addiction is staggering (May, 1988).

History and Origins of Use and Abuse: Seventeenth–Nineteenth Centuries

Alcohol was first introduced to North American Indians in the 1600s by the British for trade purposes. The British government's goal was the assimilation of Indian people into colonial culture, and trade was an essential component of this goal. The British Empire needed to import furs and skins acquired in trade with Indians, who had to be participants in the commerce market if they were to become "civilized." Alcohol brought to the colonies was made available in the seventeenth century to the Eastern Woodlands and Southeastern Indian nations, and it was transported to the Great Lakes region and to the Ohio and Mississippi Valleys by the mideighteenth century. Indians living near colonial settlements had greater access than those living farther away.

The colonists' assimilation goals backfired. Indians treated alcohol as a powerful medicine that had to be taken in large quantities to benefit from the effects. Drinking all the alcohol at once reflected a conscious choice, not behavior learned from colonists (Mancall, 1995). Native Americans had no prior history of social drinking, although some fermented beverages were used among Native nations in spiritual ceremony before the arrival of Europeans (Mancall, 1995).

Indians were viewed by most Europeans as savages and heathens, unable to "hold their liquor"; hence the myth of the "drunken Indian" began under these circumstances. Increasingly concerned about the behavior of intoxicated Indians, many colonial cities enacted laws making it illegal to sell or trade alcohol to Native people. Peter Chester, governor of West Florida in 1774, was quoted in a local newspaper regarding Indian alcohol use: "It is often

bad enough with White people when they are drunk, therefore what can be expected from Indians who are void of sense and reason, born in savage ignorance and brought up in the same way, but the most barbarous and inhuman murders and cruelties?" (Mancall, 1995).

Colonial laws against liquor sales to Indians went largely unenforced, however, allowing the liquor trade to continue and creating a negative reaction cycle between stereotypical attitudes about Indian alcohol use and continued consumption by Native people (Mancall, 1995). Beginning in the early 1800s, alcohol was also used as a tool by the U.S. government to dupe Indian people out of their lands. Many government agents and high-ranking military men "facilitated" the treaty-signing process by exploiting Indians with alcohol (Maracle, 1994).

As Native people began to incur increasing cultural losses in the next two hundred years, drinking became a method of escape from the pain of intergenerational cultural loss, trauma, and grief. Tragically, the stereotypes were thus perpetuated, and the foundation of Native American alcoholism was well-established by the 1800s, the time of forced removal from their land onto reservations. Alcohol was supplied to them by government-appointed Indian agents and used in part as a means of keeping Indians subdued. The U.S. government continued the practices begun by the early colonial governments, aiding in the perpetuation of drinking patterns established in the early 1600s (Arbogast, 1996).

Twentieth-Century Problems

By the early twentieth century, the drunken Indian stereotype was inseparable from other stereotypical and discriminatory attitudes. By that time, most tribes had been forced from ancestral lands onto reservations. They had lost their means of livelihood and were forbidden to practice cultural traditions and spiritual practices. Christian missionaries exacerbated the situation, lobbying Congress to outlaw Native spiritual practices they considered "barbaric." Without the practice of spiritual ceremonies that formed the basis of their well-being, Indian people became dangerously deprived from a mental-health perspective, enabling addiction. The United States established Indian Boarding Schools in the early 1800s as a last-resort effort at cultural annihilation. Children as young as six years old were taken forcibly from their parents and transported

hundreds and sometimes thousands of miles to boarding schools. These schools had policies forbidding children to speak their languages or to dress in traditional fashion. Students were assaulted by brainwashing techniques that told them being Indian was shameful and dirty. Their daily routines were managed by militaristic practices with bells and whistles signaling when they were to walk, stand, sit, and eat. These alienating practices were deliberately designed to "Kill the Indian and save the man." Many Indian children died of tuberculosis and pneumonia in poorly heated dormitories. Many died of what seemed to be broken hearts or what might be medically termed depression today. They simply wasted away from the pain and sadness of grief (Lomawaima, 1994).

Additionally, boarding schools forced children to attend Christian services and to recite biblical scripture with the intention of squelching their Native spiritual beliefs. Children were forbidden any type of contact with their families. Placed in dormitory sleeping arrangements that were supervised by adult school employees, those who were caught whispering among themselves in their Native languages were punished. Sexual and physical abuse by boarding school staff was rampant. The Carlisle boarding school in Pennsylvania was notorious for the punishment of solitary confinement, where children were placed in small, dark, unheated rooms for days with only bread and water to eat. Many died of malnutrition or pneumonia.

Young adults graduated from the boarding schools cut off from their cultural and familial foundations, unable to speak their languages, and untrained for occupations other than labor and domestic work. In rare instances, a few boarding schools trained young girls in nursing, although these girls were allowed to work only as nurses' aides. Indian graduates were thrust unprepared onto the fringes of white society where they faced poverty, chronic unemployment, and discrimination. This additional cultural attack by U.S. government policies exacerbated the pain of cultural loss, familial disintegration, and poor self-esteem stemming from a negative cultural identity. Many turned to suicide as an escape and to alcohol as a means of medicating the pain and grief (Lomawaima, 1994).

The termination of the sovereign status of certain Native tribes, a congressional policy of the early 1950s, was another attempt at assimilation that resulted in forced relocation for many Native peo-

ple. The tribal members affected by the policy moved from reservations into urban areas with little to no adequate preparation. Federal policy connected with the program failed to provide Native people with the financial and occupational preparation they were promised. Many were given small amounts of cash, one-way bus tickets to urban areas, and promises of good jobs and job training that never materialized. Additionally, they were culturally unprepared for urban life. They were given substandard housing, which was often in ghetto areas dominated by other minorities, making it difficult for Native people to maintain cultural traditions (Carr, 1996).

Poverty and cultural isolation exacerbated preexisting unresolved cultural grief and trauma, and successive Native descendents suffered from continued cultural isolation and further identity loss. This reaction cycle, combined with poor cultural identity, was negatively reinforced by continued substance abuse, effectively expanding it to urban areas. Inordinately high rates of substance abuse among Native American adolescents has resulted in higher rates of suicide per capita than those among other minorities, fueled as it has been by unresolved cultural grief and poor cultural identity.

In many Indian communities, alcoholism and other substance abuse are closely linked with involvement in the justice system. Alcohol is not sold on reservations, and liquor stores in cities located nearby draw many Indian customers, who drink and then drive back home under the influence. The sad toll of alcohol-related fatalities touches many reservation families, as do arrest and conviction for vehicular homicide. For the individuals convicted of that offense, incarceration generally means confinement in federal prisons hundreds of miles away from home and family, further exacerbating the pain of cultural loss and grief created by the initial problems of substance abuse and addiction.

The Methamphetamine Epidemic

In the years since 2000, methamphetamine (meth) use has been wreaking havoc on Native nations. According to a report by the National Survey on Drug Use and Health (2005), the prevalence of meth use by American Indians and Alaska Natives was the second highest among all demographic groups surveyed, which included Pacific Islanders, Hispanics, African Americans, and Caucasians.

Meth is a stimulant that can cause extreme paranoia, psychosis, dementia, and amnesia. A meth high involves prolonged periods of time without food and sleep. Additionally, it can cause high blood pressure, stroke, and heart attack as a result of the rapid heart rate that occurs for extended periods of time. Meth has been easier to buy on some reservations than marijuana, although, ironically, federal "war on drugs" policies focus mainly on marijuana. Meth use among Natives in the northern Plains area may have begun when Indian cowboys traveling the rodeo circuit used it to cope with long-distance driving and subsequently to stay alert after traveling when competing in rodeo events (Farquhar, 2005).

The Navajo Nation in Arizona has been hit especially hard by methamphetamine use. Their governing council voted in early 2005 to outlaw the drug, making its possession and sale punishable by a fine of up to $5,000 and a year in tribal jail. The Chippewa-Cree Business Committee on the Rocky Boy Reservation in Montana adopted a "get tough" plan to curtail drug use that would result in the creation of a tribal drug court, workshops, and community forums to educate tribal members. Additional plans call for a centralized drug registry to track meth offenders and dealers from one reservation to the next, which they believe will play a major role in eliminating traffickers who exploit existing alcohol addicts among Native people, because polysubstance dependency is more difficult to treat and to recover from.

Similar efforts have developed on the Wind River Reservation, home to the Arapaho and Eastern Shoshone, where an extensive drug ring was broken up in 2005. The perpetrators attempted to circumvent state law enforcement jurisdictions by developing an elaborate business plan for distributing meth on reservations, where it was not yet illegal. Rosebud, Pine Ridge, Yankton, and Santee Sioux Reservations, as well as Wind River, were targeted by the elaborate scheme. The plan was carried out by dealers establishing residency on the reservations, developing relationships with Indian women, and giving away free samples of meth. The Indian recipients of this "business plan" eventually became methamphetamine addicts and distributors themselves in an effort to fund their own addiction. Through the combined law enforcement efforts of the Wind River Reservation Police and the state of Wyoming, the original distributors were arrested, tried, and convicted (Farquhar, 2005).

Multijurisdictional drug task forces have developed between reservation and state law enforcement for tracking and arresting meth users since 2005. The sprawling land base of Native nations has been an easy target for dealers establishing distribution operations because tribes have lagged behind states in developing meth legislation (www.Indianz.com/News). There is an especially grave concern about meth addiction among Native Americans. Many have survived alcoholism extending back several generations, but the current generation's survival is dubious, because the drug's damaging effects are far more serious than those of alcohol (Farquhar, 2005). The new tribal laws against meth will make it easier for Indian and non-Indian law enforcement organizations to work together in putting more pressure on reservation dealers.

Peyote and the Native American Church

Peyote use by members of the Native American Church has often been confused with substance abuse by mainstream America. Peyote is considered to be a sacred substance by American and Mexican Indians and has a rich history extending back as far as 200 CE in Mexico (Smith, 1996). The Native American Church plays a role for many Indian people in recovery from substance abuse that cannot be overstated. The peyote ceremony prohibits alcohol and drug use for a designated time before and after, and peyote ingestion itself reduces the craving for alcohol. Peyote use is legalized for ceremonial uses only by the Native American Church, which has become a pan-Indian spiritual practice in twenty-three states. Ceremonies are conducted by Road Men who are legally authorized to use, transport, and possess peyote for ceremonial purposes. In 2005, the Navajo Nation created a law limiting peyote use to Native American Church members with the hope of preventing its use by "New Age" spiritual seekers who come onto the reservation seeking peyote experiences.

Addiction Treatment and Recovery

The subject of substance abuse among Native Americans must include information about treatment and recovery efforts to avoid the impression that Native substance abuse is a hopeless illness. In the past ten years, the most successful treatments

have been culturally specific and holistic (Bordewich, 1996). Prior to the development of culturally specific treatment, the dropout and relapse rates among Indians were much higher because conventional mainstream addiction recovery approaches were antagonistic to Native values. Most contemporary treatment programs include the core beliefs of the Medicine Wheel, the Circle of Life encompassing the physical, mental, emotional, and spiritual aspects of human life. Successful Native treatment programs include a transcendental worldview and an emphasis on wellness rather than on the disease model of health.

Non-Native treatment counselors must learn to understand Native values and have a working knowledge of historical influences as the root causes and perpetuators of substance abuse (J. T. Garrett and M. W. Garrett, 1994). In a research project conducted by the Minnesota Department of Human Services Chemical Dependency Division in 1995, Indian women were participants in a culturally specific substance abuse treatment program. The project's objective was to gather information used to develop a treatment approach that was successful in developing a healthy recovery model for Native people. Each of the women participants was surveyed to determine what she valued as most effective in recovery. The results overwhelmingly pointed to successful cultural involvement, including Native community social events, participation in spiritual ceremonies such as Sun Dance, Sweat Lodge, Native American Church, Talking Circle, and tribally specific healing ceremonies such as the Navajo Sing.

The participants also viewed recovery as a community issue rather than as an individual issue, suggesting a focus on wellness; avoiding labels of "sick," "powerlessness," and "victim"; and an emphasis on strength and resilience. These women considered regaining the loss of cultural identity to be the key factor in treatment and recovery. The ability to regain and maintain healthy cultural values in conjunction with a community-focused approach is echoed in other culturally specific treatment programs, such as White Bison and Eagle Lodge in Colorado.

Since community is a vital core value among Native people, other culturally specific programs that have been developed for prevention as well as treatment are community oriented in their approach. Relapse prevention is also considered to be a culturally specific approach since the basis of maintaining sobriety for Indian people also requires cultural and social activities. For Native Americans, the Circle of Life was broken centuries ago in the initial causes of substance abuse, and healing must focus on restoration of the Hoop.

Merlene Bishop

References and Further Reading
Arbogast, Doyle. 1995. *Wounded Warriors*. Omaha, NE: Little Turtle Publications.
Bordewich, Fergus. 1996. *Killing the White Man's Indian*. New York: Doubleday.
Carr, Gwen. 1996. "Urban Indians, the Invisible Minority." In *News from Indian Country*, V.X., N.8, Vol. X, No. 8 (April 30, 1996).
Farquhar, Brodie. 2005. "Meth Wreaks Havoc on Reservations," *Jackson Hole Star-Tribune*, August 11, 2005.
Garrett, J. T., and Michael Walkingstick Garrett. 1994. "The Path of Good Medicine: Understanding and Counseling Native American Indians." *Journal of Multicultural Counseling and Development* 22 (July): 134–144.
Herring, Roger T. 1992. "Seeking a New Paradigm: Counseling Native Americans." *Journal of Multicultural Counseling and Development* 20 (January): 35–43.
Indianz.com. Web site containing information relating to Indian issues. Available at: www.Indianz.com. Accessed December 28, 2006.
LaFramboise, Teresa, Ph.D., Joseph E. Trimble, Ph.D., and Gerald D. Mohatt, Ph.D. 1990. "Counseling Intervention and American Indian Tradition: An Integrative Approach." *The Counseling Psychologist* 18 (4): 628–654.
Lomawaima, K. Tsianina. 1995. *They Called It Prairie Light*. Lincoln: University of Nebraska Press.
Mancall, Peter A. 1995. *Deadly Medicine*. Ithaca, NY: Cornell University Press.
Maracle, Brian. 1994. *Crazywater: Native Voices on Addiction and Recovery*. New York: Penguin.
National Survey on Drug Use and Health. 2005. *National Survey on Drug Use and Health: National Findings*. Rockville, MD: Office of Applied Studies, SAMSHA. Available at: www.Indianz.com.
Schultes, Richard Evans, and Albert Hoffman. 1992. *Plants of the Gods — Their Sacred Healing and Hallucinogenic Powers*. Rochester, VT: Healing Arts Press.
Smith, Husten. 1998. *One Nation Under God: The Triumph of the Native American Church*. Santa Fe, NM: Clear Light Publishers.
State of Minnesota. 1995. *It's A New Day*. St. Paul: Minnesota Department of Human Services, Chemical Dependency Division.

Archaeology and the First Americans

Introduction

It is unclear when or how people first came to the Americas. Native American oral histories on the subject vary, and different groups have different histories. Some describe journeys by land through different worlds and environments, while others describe coming by water, and others believe that the first people originated of the American continents. The first Europeans to come to the Americas in historic times believed that Native Americans originated in the Old World (Europe, Africa, and Asia), based on their biblical beliefs that the genesis of all people occurred in the Garden of Eden. In addition to oral and biblical histories, archaeological research provides science-based evidence addressing the question of human origins in the Americas by dating geological events and artifacts in the context of environmental change. Most archaeological sites are dated by the radiocarbon method, and radiocarbon years can be different than calendar (solar) years. The dates used in this presentation are calibrated to calendar years.

Migration Routes and Colonization

Scientific evidence indicates that humans originated and evolved in the Old World, first in Africa, then colonizing Asia, Europe and, later, Australia. There are many early (200,000- to 20,000-year-old) sites throughout the Americas that some researchers suggest were occupied prior to the last Ice Age, but the dating or integrity of all these sites has been questioned by subsequent research. The fossil remains of early humans, such as *Homo erectus* and Neanderthals, found in Africa, Europe, and Asia are hundreds of thousands years old. However, the fossil remains of humans found in North and South America are not that old. In fact, the earliest reliably dated human remains from the Americas are only about 13,350 years old. This and other evidence suggests people first arrived in the Americas no more than about 18,000 years ago, near the end of the last Ice Age. The limited extent of ice-free migration routes during that time limited possible migration routes available to the first people to colonize the Americas.

The idea that humans may have first entered the Americas via a land route in the high northern lati-

Clovis spear points, similar to ones eventually discovered throughout the North American continent, have a distinctive design with six-inch long, two-inch wide, fluted points. (Warren Morgan/Corbis)

tudes was first suggested by a Spanish priest, Fray de Acosta, more than 400 years ago. Over time, this concept became deeply embedded in scientific thought. Archaeological evidence indicated that people living in central Asia hunted large Ice Age animals, like the extinct wooly mammoth, as well as other animals that did not become extinct during the last Ice Age, such as bison. According to this theory, early people, hunting large Ice Age animals, crossed the land bridge into Alaska and then moved south into central-western Canada. From there they were able to colonize the more southern areas of North America and eventually South America. This theory seemed plausible because some of the oldest archaeological sites in the Americas contained the bones of Ice Age animals similar to those people had hunted in Asia. Research conducted in the 1980s and 1990s questioned the viability of this theory and led to a reconsideration of other routes.

The climate was much colder during the last Ice Age, and massive glaciers formed a huge ice sheet covering most of Canada. The ice blocked access

between what is today Alaska and the continental United States. Polar sea ice extended south into the Atlantic, covering Greenland, Iceland, and all but the most southern areas of Ireland and England. Because much of the earth's water was trapped in glacial ice, the sea level was lower than it is today. The continental shelves and the floor of the Bering and Chukchi Seas were exposed as dry land, creating the Bering Land Bridge. The geography of the Ice Age limited migration routes into the Americas to four possibilities: (1) the Beringian Mid-Continental, (2) the Northwest Coastal, (3) the Pacific, and (4) the Atlantic (see Figure 1). By analyzing the environmental conditions that existed during the last Ice Age, it is possible to evaluate each of these possible routes.

The Beringian Mid-Continental route presumes that hunters and gatherers first entered North America from Asia across the Bering Land Bridge. They then moved south into central-western Canada through a hypothetical ice-free corridor. Geologists working in Canada have demonstrated that such a corridor did not exist during most of the Ice Age and that connections between eastern Beringia and areas south of the continental glaciers were not established until about 13,000 years ago. Supporting this conclusion, no animal bones dating between 25,000 to 13,000 years ago have been found in the region formerly believed to have been ice-free. This evidence indicates that the ice-free corridor did not exist during the last Ice Age. It precludes a midcontinental route for human entry between about 21,000 and 13,000 years ago, possibly even later.

However, glacial melting (a process known as deglaciation) along the Northwest Coast of North America had begun by 16,800 years ago and was sufficiently advanced to enable people using watercraft to colonize coastal areas by 15,350 years ago. The remains of land and sea mammals, birds, and fish dating to this time have been discovered along the Northwest Coast, demonstrating sufficient resources for people to survive. Because earlier geologic misinterpretations indicated that the region had been ice covered until about 11,350 years ago, very little archaeological work has been undertaken to explore this region as a possible migration route.

Whereas the Bering Land Bridge–ice-free corridor model for human colonization requires an economy based on hunting terrestrial mammals, freshwater fishing, and pedestrian travel, the coastal hypothesis suggests an economy based on marine mammal hunting, saltwater fishing/shellfish gathering, and the use of watercraft. Each would have

required different types of adaptations to the New World. If the coastal colonization hypothesis is to be fully evaluated, the late Pleistocene coastal archaeology of western North America will require additional and sustained research efforts equivalent to those that have traditionally focused on midcontinental North America.

Some researchers believe humans may have crossed the vast expanse of the Pacific, colonizing South America and later moving into North America. Support for this theory is based on sites such as Monte Verde in southern Chile and Tiama-Tiama in northern Venezuela, which may be older than any site in North America. Biological evidence suggests that some of the earliest skeletons found in South America share similarities with examples from Polynesia and Australia.

A North Atlantic migration has been proposed by some who recognize similarities in tool-making technology between the Clovis complex of North America, dating to between 13,300 and 12,850 years ago, and the Solutrean tradition of Europe. This has led some archaeologists to suggest that, with the use of watercraft, Solutrean people (maritime hunters and fishing people) may have been able to reach North America from Europe by moving westward along the sea ice edge of the North Atlantic during the last Ice Age. Although the Solutrean tradition ended about 19,000 years ago in Portugal and Spain, the theory suggests that several pre-Clovis sites in North America, possibly including Meadowcroft Rock Shelter and the Cactus Hill site (Figure 2), may indicate continuity between the two cultural traditions.

While all these migration theories are possible, the preponderance of linguistic and biological evidence indicates that Native Americans most likely originated somewhere in northeastern Asia. The Northwest Coast, midcontinental, and Pacific routes lead from there to the Americas. Because the midcontinental route was not open until 11,000 to 11,500 years ago and transoceanic travel is so dangerous, the most plausible route for the first colonization of the Americas seems to be along the southern coast of the Bering Land Bridge and then southward along the Northwest Coast of North America.

These potential migration routes were not mutually exclusive. The colonization of the Americas may have involved many groups of people, possibly originating from different places in the Old World at different times. Migration was probably a complex process that spanned a long period of time. There are

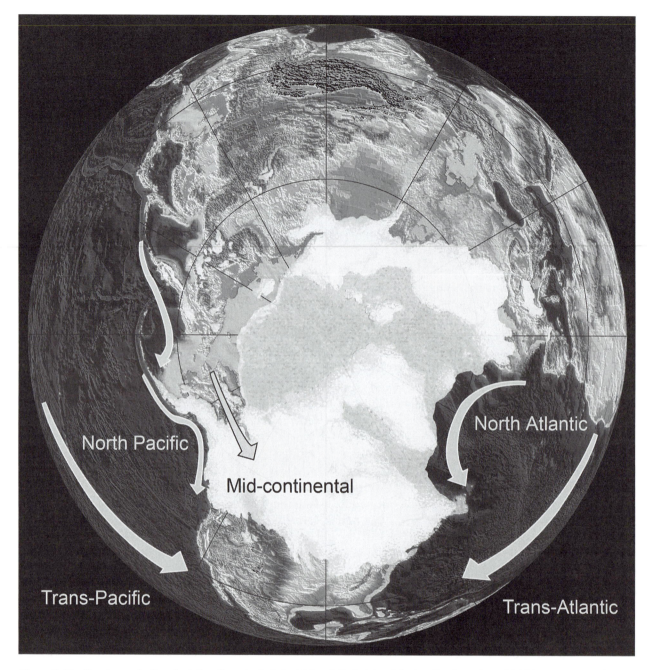

Figure 1. North polar projection depicting the extent of glacial ice at the height of the last Ice Age, about 21,000 years ago, with possible colonization routes.

tantalizing biological and technological clues that suggest that, prior to the arrival of Europeans in the fifteenth century, there was possible contact, and possibly even colonization, between the Americas and Australia, Polynesia, Europe, and even Africa.

Many sites in the Americas that appear to be reliably dated and interpreted are older than 13,000 years. Some of the better-known sites in North America include Meadowcroft Rock Shelter in Penn-sylvania (19,000 years old), Cactus Hill in Virginia (18,000 years old), the Schaefer and Hebior sites in Wisconsin (14,200 years old), Swan Point in Alaska (13,900), Little Salt Springs in Florida (13,800 years old), and Manis Mastodon site in Washington State (13,700 years old) (Figure 2). Archaeological sites dating to this time period are rare and appear to have been occupied by few people for short periods of time. The little data available suggest that the

1. Swan Point
2. Manis Mastodon
3. Schaefer/Hebior
4. Meadowcroft Rock Shelter
5. Cactus Hill
6. Little Salt Springs

Figure 2. The locations of select archaeological sites possibly older than 13,000 years in North America.

population was small and that people made their living by hunting, gathering, and foraging. It is possible that many sites dating to this time period are currently underwater because they were located along the coast and were flooded by the rising sea level at the end of the Ice Age.

Regional Development (13,500–10,000 years ago)

Archaeologists generally separate the archaeology of North America into time periods that are subdivided into traditions and complexes. The term "Paleo-Indian tradition" was introduced during the 1940s and is widely used to characterize sites older than about 9,000 years. These sites contain stone projectile points that generally have a characteristic "flute"

extending from the base toward the tip, along with a wide variety of other artifacts and later "lanceolate" types of projectile points (Figure 3). The people who made and used these tools subsisted by hunting, fishing, and foraging; they often hunted large animals such as bison. The Paleo-Indian tradition is recognized throughout most of North America. This is the earliest evidence, based on artifacts found at diverse archaeological sites throughout North and South America, documenting the widespread settlement of the New World.

In the area east of the Mississippi River, there appears to have been a gradual transition from Paleo-Indian tradition to artifact assemblages characteristic of later archaeological cultures. In the central part of the North American continent (the Great Plains region), the Paleo-Indian tradition includes

are believed to be about the same age as the Clovis and Folsom complexes because they are stylistically similar to the examples from the Great Plains. They are commonly referred to as the Western Fluted Point tradition. However, another group of artifacts found throughout the Far West includes stone projectile points with "stemmed" bases rather than flutes. Although they have not been firmly dated, some archaeologists believe they are as old as Clovis artifacts, possibly even older. The remains of plants, animals, birds, and fish indicate that the economy of the people of the Western Stemmed and Fluted Point traditions and those living on the Great Plains practiced a generalized economy, occasionally hunting large mammals such as mammoth and bison, but more typically harvesting a wide array of resources, including birds, fish, and plant foods whenever and wherever they were available.

In the Far North, in an area known as eastern Beringia (Alaska and areas of extreme northwestern Canada that were not covered by glacial ice during the last Ice Age [Figure 1]), the oldest archaeological remains are very different. They are called the Denali complex. The earliest radiocarbon dates for the Denali complex are about 13,900 calendar years ago, and the complex appears to have persisted until at least 8,000 years ago. The artifacts are very similar to those characteristic of the Upper Paleolithic (the latter period of the Old Stone Age) in Europe and Asia, and they clearly have their origins there. Along with a variety of other types of tools, these people used tiny slivers of stone, called microblades, inset in slots carved in antler or bone projectile points. These types of artifacts are very different from those of the Paleo-Indian and Western Stemmed and Fluted Point traditions, suggesting that these artifacts were made by different groups of people with different cultural backgrounds.

Summary

When the continental glaciers started to melt about 17,000 years ago, the sea level rose rapidly. Land that previously had been covered by glaciers was exposed for the first time since the beginning of the last Ice Age and was rapidly colonized by plants and animals. People living along the coasts of North America retreated inland in response to rising sea levels. In other areas, people also began to occupy new environments created by deglaciation.

Scientific evidence suggests that North and South America were the last continents on Earth to

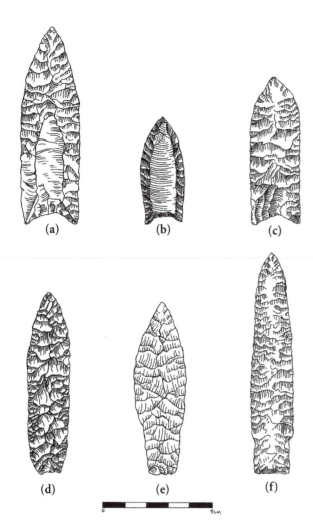

Figure 3. Early North American stone projectile point types: (a) Clovis, (b) Folsom, (c–f) later point forms (Dixon, 1999, 214).

the Clovis complex dating from 13,300 to 12,900 years ago and the Folsom complex, which lasted from 12,900 until 11,800 years ago. Clovis sites are the only ones associated with mammoth hunting in North America. (Folsom sites are most commonly associated with bison hunting.) Mammoths (Ice Age animals related to elephants) became extinct at this time. This and other evidence has led some scientists to suggest that the first people to colonize the Americas may have caused the extinction of these and other large mammals as a result of overhunting or possibly the introduction of new diseases. However, other theories suggest that their extinction was due to environmental change.

Fluted points have been found in the far west of North America, the region extending from the continental divide of the Rocky Mountains west to the Pacific Ocean. In the Far West these types of artifacts

be occupied by people. Colonization took place during a time of dramatic climate change when the sea level was rising rapidly, many Ice Age animals were becoming extinct, the land was rebounding (rising upward) as the great weight of the glaciers disappeared, and terrestrial ecosystems were undergoing massive reorganization. Understanding the timing, origins, culture, and technology of the first people to occupy the Americas is important because these adaptations established the foundation for the subsequent cultural development in the Americas and for the rich and diverse cultures that followed.

E. James Dixon

See also Bering Strait Theory; Kennewick Man; Paleo-Indians.

References and Further Reading

Adovasio, J. M., J. D. Gunn, J. Donahue, and R. Stuckenrath. 1978. "Meadowcroft Rockshelter, 1977: An Overview." *American Antiquity* 43: 632–651.

Akazawa, T., and E.J.E. Szathmary, eds. 1996. *Prehistoric Mongoloid Dispersals.* New York: Oxford University Press.

Bradley, B., and D. Stanford. 2004. "The North Atlantic Ice-Edge Corridor: A Possible Palaeolithic Route to the New World." *World Archaeology* 36, no. 1: 469–478.

Burns, J. A. 1996. "Vertebrate Paleontology and the Alleged Ice-Free Corridor: The Meat of the Matter." *Quaternary International* 32: 107–112.

Dillehay, T. D. 2000. *The Settlement of the Americas: A New Prehistory.* New York: Basic Books.

Dixon, E. James. 1999. *Boats, Bones, and Bison: Archaeology and the First Colonization of Western North America.* Albuquerque: University of New Mexico Press.

Fagan, B. M. 1987. *The Great Journey: The Peopling of Ancient America.* London: Thames and Hudson.

Fladmark, K. R. 1979 "Routes: Alternative Migration Corridors for Early Man in North America." *American Antiquity* 44: 55–69.

Frison, G. C. 1991. *Prehistoric Hunters of the High Plains.* New York: Academic Press.

Gustafson, C. E., D. Gilbow, and R. D. Daugherty. 1979. "The Manis Mastodon Site: Early Man on the Olympic Peninsula." *Canadian Journal of Archaeology* 3: 157–164.

Jablonski, N. G., ed. 2001. *The First Americans.* San Francisco: California Academy of Sciences Scientific Publications.

Koppel, T. 2003. *Lost World: Rewriting Prehistory— How New Science Is Tracing America's Ice Age Mariners.* New York: Atria Books.

Madsen, D. B., ed. 2004. *Entering America: Northeast Asia and Beringia Before the Last Glacial Maximum.* Salt Lake City: University of Utah Press.

Parfit, M. 2000. "Hunt for the First Americans." *National Geographic.* (December), 40–67.

West, F. H., ed. 1996. *American Beginnings.* Chicago: University of Chicago Press.

Assimilation

Assimilation is the process of losing one culture and taking on another. Members of any given culture are naturally ethnocentric in that they tend to believe that the culture they are born into is the right and natural way for people to live and those who live differently are not "normal." Two logical conclusions can arise from ethnocentric thinking. At worst, one can consider other groups inferior and subject to genocide or compelled to exist in second-class citizenship or even slavery. On the other hand, groups lower down on a supposed social-evolutionary scale could be helped to progress and become like the members of the dominant culture, in other words to assimilate and become "civilized."

It is not normal to give up one's mother culture. However, in colonial and immigrant situations at least partial assimilation is common because either the colonial power introduces an educational system based on its language and culture or immigrants try to adjust to living in a new country. For American Indians, after what sometimes was an initial period of equality, European colonists soon got the upper hand militarily and sought to impose their culture on Indians through missionary activity and schooling.

Because of a drive in Christianity to convert nonbelievers, European colonists sought to make Christians of American Indians. Indians saw Christianity as more than the acceptance of a specific religious theology; they saw it as a way of life that involved living like the colonists, speaking their language, dressing like them, and becoming farmers. Catholic Jesuits and Franciscans were especially active in Canada and in Central and South America, working to Christianize and assimilate Indians, while Protestants made similar efforts in the British colonies. Protestant missionary John Eliot, for example, helped set up fourteen "Praying Towns" of converted Indians near Boston between 1651 and 1674.

Male Native American students in physical education class, Carlisle Indian Industrial School, Carlisle, Pennsylvania, ca. 1902.
(Library of Congress)

After the American Revolution, Thomas J. McKenney, the United States Superintendent of Indian Trade from 1816 to 1822, lobbied the U.S. Congress for a national system of Indian schools run by missionaries and supported by the government. In 1818 a House committee declared:

> In the present state of our country, one of two things seems to be necessary: either that these sons of the forest should be moralized or exterminated. Humanity would rejoice at the former, but shrink with horror from the latter. Put into the hands of their children the primer and the hoe, and they will naturally, in time, take hold of the plough; and, as their minds become enlightened and expand, the Bible will be their book, and they will grow up in habits of morality and industry, leave the chase to those whose minds are less cultivated, and

become useful members of society (Prucha, 1984, 150).

Christian missionary work in Asia and Africa was used as an example of what could be done for Indians.

In 1819 Congress passed the Indian Civilization Act authorizing spending up to $10,000 a year to pay missionaries and other interested individuals to teach Indians "for the purpose of providing against the further decline and final extinction of the Indian tribes, adjoining the frontier settlements of the United States, and for introducing among them the habits and arts of civilization." Funding under this act continued until its repeal in 1873. While $10,000 had a lot more purchasing power than it does today, even combined with Indian treaty funds, relatively few Indian children actually received any kind of schooling under this Act.

Despite the fact that the Five Civilized Tribes of the Southeast, including the Cherokee, showed considerable progress toward assimilation in the early years of the nineteenth century, some starting small plantations and owning slaves, the U.S. government, especially under President Andrew Jackson, chose to emphasize a policy in the 1820s and 1830s of what is now called ethnic cleansing to make Indian lands available to white settlers. Most of the eastern tribes were forcibly exiled to lands in the West. Living in Indian Territory (now the state of Oklahoma) and on Indian reservations elsewhere in the west (including small reserves in Canada), Indians were able to keep some of their tribal culture alive. However, increasing demands by immigrants for land and assimilationist pressures led to a whittling away of the U.S. Indian reservations.

After the Civil War, in 1868, President Ulysses S. Grant's Peace Commissioners reported that, "In the difference of language to-day lies two-thirds of our trouble . . . Schools should be established, which children should be required to attend; their barbarous dialect should be blotted out and the English language substituted." Speaking English was a sign of assimilation. In the 1870s, as railroads reached across the United States, the U.S. government put more money into assimilating Indians through schools. A leader in this effort was Army Lieutenant Richard Henry Pratt, who founded the Carlisle Indian Industrial School in Pennsylvania in 1879. Pratt's idea of starting a boarding school for Indians in the eastern United States was to get Indian children as far away from their parents as possible so that they would totally assimilate. Pratt believed there was nothing of value in Indian cultures and his goal was total assimilation, to "[k]ill the Indian and save the man," an advertising slogan he coined to promote the boarding schools. To reinforce the assimilationist English-only classroom education at Carlisle, Pratt also placed Indian students into white households for months or more in what he called the Outing System. He wanted Indian students to become Christians, stay in the East after they left Carlisle, become U.S. citizens, and even to intermarry with whites. Twenty-four more boarding schools patterned after Carlisle were started in the next quarter century, but these schools were all built in the West, closer to Indian reservations. The Canadians duplicated the U.S. system with their residential schools but continued to fund mostly Anglican and Catholic efforts up to the 1960s rather than having the government directly operate the schools, as increasingly became the case in the United States. Three of the U.S. boarding schools remained open in 2005 as Indian high schools overseen by Indian school boards.

In the 1880s an unrealistic optimism prevailed in regard to assimilation, as exemplified by the government's Indian School Superintendent who declared in 1885 that, "if there were a sufficient number of reservation boarding-school-buildings to accommodate all the Indian children of school age . . . the Indian problem would be solved within the school age of the Indian child now six years old" (Reyhner and Eder, 2004, 75). In conjunction with the expansion of government schooling for Indians on and off reservations, under the Dawes Allotment Act of 1887, "surplus land" on many reservations was thrown open to white settlement. At the same time, Indians were pressured to take small allotments to farm, which they eventually could sell, and to move toward U.S. citizenship.

When Darwin's theory of evolution became well-known in the late nineteenth century, a corollary theory of Social Darwinism became popular that put forth the idea that cultures evolved and that Euro-American culture was the highest level of evolution, with other cultures being lower down on the evolutionary scale. Although there was no scientific basis for this theory, it fed the egotism and ethnocentrism of white Americans and Europeans and provided renewed justification for assimilating American Indians into Euro-American white culture.

Albert Kneale, who started teaching Indians in 1899, noted in his autobiography that the U.S. government's Indian Bureau "at that time, always went on the assumption that any Indian custom was, per se, objectionable, whereas the customs of whites were the ways of civilization" (Reyhner and Eder, 2004, 163). However, this ethnocentrism was not unique to dominant colonizing powers such as the Canadian and U.S. governments. Kneale, who worked thirty-six years as a teacher, principal, and Indian agent, also noted:

> Every tribe with which I have associated is imbued with the idea that it is superior to all other peoples. Its members are thoroughly convinced of their superiority not alone over members of all other tribes but over the whites as well. . . . I have never known an Indian who would consent to being changed into a white man even were he convinced that such a change could readily be accomplished (Reyhner and Eder, 2004, 162–163).

Because of this Indian ethnocentrism, Kneale concluded that many Indians remained unassimilated even though in boarding schools they "were taught to despise every custom of their forefathers, including religion, language, songs, dress, ideas, methods of living" (Reyhner and Eder, 2004, 195). Under these conditions, some Indians developed what John Ogbu (1995) has termed an "oppositional identity," rejecting schools as a place for becoming "white."

Assimilation became a national political issue in the late nineteenth century as first Irish Catholics and then Eastern Europeans increasingly flooded into the United States, threatening the dominance of the mostly Protestant earlier immigrants from northwestern Europe. The fact that the Catholics were more successful than the Protestants in setting up schools for Indians using government funding led to the government's ending funding for missionary schools in the 1890s and operating their own schools, which tended to teach a nondenominational Protestant-oriented Christianity.

The U.S. government repeatedly demanded in the 1880s that all instruction in missionary and government schools be in the English language. The government also banned traditional Indian religious ceremonies, including the Sun Dance of the Plains Indians. Similar policies in Canada were not reversed until 1960. In the United States, tribal police under the control of Indian agents enforced the suppression of Indian traditional religious activities, and parents who would not send their children to school risked having rations cut off and even being jailed. In 1894, nineteen Hopi men were sent to the military prison on Alcatraz Island in San Francisco Bay. Such harsh measures led to some assimilation, but also to resistance. Hopi artist Fred Kabotie, who was born in 1900 and who attended boarding school, recalled, "I've found the more outside education I receive, the more I appreciate the true Hopi way. When the missionaries would come into the village and try to convert us, I used to wonder why anyone would want to be a Christian if it meant becoming like those people" (Reyhner and Eder, 2004, 201). Students entering Indian schools received white clothes, haircuts, and names. Corporal punishment and school "jails" were used to enforce the assimilationist English-only school rules.

In the 1890s, as students began to return to their homes after attending boarding school, it became apparent that many had not assimilated in the way Pratt and others had hoped. In addition, a growing group of people began to see Indian cultures as a valuable part of the American heritage and something worth preserving. Voices raised against total assimilation included those of the founding director of the U.S. Bureau of Ethnology John Wesley Powell, Clark University President G. Stanley Hall, and anthropologist Franz Boas. Powell and Hall emphasized the need for understanding the values of Indian cultures, while Boas put forward the idea of "cultural relativism," where white cultures were not better than Indian cultures—just different.

The Great Depression that started with the stock market crash of 1929 made many Americans question the superiority of their capitalistic society. Some had doubted that superiority even earlier as they worked in settlement houses in the slums of New York and Chicago. One such doubter was John Collier, who became Commissioner of Indian Affairs after the election of Franklin D. Roosevelt. In 1920 Collier had seen something in American Indian cultures that he found missing in mainstream American culture and that he found to be "manipulative, exploitive, and imposed." As a result, he concluded, "*Assimilation*, not into our culture but into modern life, and *preservation and intensification of heritage* are not hostile choices, excluding one another, but are interdependent through and through. . . . It is the ancient tribal, village, communal organization which must conquer the modern world" (1963, 203, 234, emphasis in original). As commissioner from 1933 to 1945, Collier hired anthropologists to work in the Indian Office, including students of Franz Boas such as Dr. Ruth Underhill, who became Supervisor of Indian Education.

In the twentieth century, Indian students increasingly attended public schools, where it was felt they would assimilate faster sitting side by side with white students. In Canada this trend accelerated in the 1950s. However, it was not unusual to find the white students sitting in the front, the mixed-blood students in the middle, and the full-blood students sitting in the back of "integrated" classrooms. In larger schools, Indian students could be relegated to special education "opportunity rooms."

A major factor in breaking down the isolation of Indian reservations and promoting assimilation was the experiences of the many American Indians who served in the armed forces, especially during both world wars. Serving alongside white Americans, unlike blacks who served in segregated units, Indians improved their English and learned about

the outside world. Indians' service in World War II promoted a conservative call "to set Indians free" from their reservations. After the war, Indians were encouraged to leave their reservations and relocate to cities where it was hoped they would find jobs, and the Republican administration under Dwight Eisenhower sought to complete the assimilation of American Indians by terminating their reservations. However, Indian groups like the National Congress of American Indians founded in 1944 fought these efforts and only a few tribes were actually terminated.

Despite some culturally sensitive efforts, such as under Collier's leadership, Indian education in the United States stayed essentially assimilationist into the 1960s. Then the civil rights movement began to create a climate for more culturally appropriate education. The Bilingual Education Act was passed in 1968, which, although intended at first for Mexican-Americans, was soon expanded to include American Indians. However, its main purpose was to teach English and often Indian languages were taught only for a few minutes a day by teachers without language training, too often resulting in students' learning only a few words of their tribal language and a superficial knowledge of their traditional culture.

Canadian Minister of Indian and Northern Affairs Jean Chrétien stated in 1972 that Indian education continued to be "a whitewash, . . . a process to equip him with white values, goals, language, skills needed to succeed in the dominant society" that served "no purpose in the child's world. . . . Rather it alienates him from his own people" (Milloy 1999, 199). In the United States an Indian Education Act was passed in 1972 to provide culturally relevant supplemental programs for Indian students in public schools, and in 1975 Congress passed the Indian Self-Determination and Education Assistance Act, allowing tribes to contract with the Bureau of Indian Affairs to run their own schools. In 1978 an Indian Religious Freedoms Act was passed, making it "the policy of the United States to protect and preserve for American Indians their inherent right of freedom to believe, express, and exercise the traditional religions of the American Indian, Eskimo, Aleut, and Native Hawaiians." The 1978 Act reversed the suppression of traditional Indian religions and an Indian Child Welfare Act that stated "that an alarmingly high percentage of Indian families are broken up by the removal, often unwarranted, of their children from them by nontribal public and private agencies

and that an alarmingly high percentage of such children are placed in non-Indian foster and adoptive homes and institutions." The 1990 Native American Languages Act supported the continued use of American Indian languages.

From 1998 to 2002, votes on antibilingual education English for the Children propositions were spearheaded and financed in California, Arizona, Massachusetts, and Colorado by Ron Unz, a computer millionaire. Unz portrayed himself as "a strong believer in American assimilationism," and he wrote of the "social decay and violence" in the new multiethnic California and how the passage of Proposition 227 would save America from ethnic divisiveness (1999). While a flood of immigrants, especially from Mexico, brought on by the loosening of immigration regulations in 1965 were Unz's targets, American Indians were not exempted from the provisions of the initiatives he backed. Indian tribes in Arizona saw its English for the Children proposition as a direct attack at their attempts to revitalize their languages and strongly opposed it. In a September 2000 press release, Navajo Nation President Kelsey Begaye declared that the "preservation of Navajo culture, tradition, and language" was the number one guiding principle of the Navajo Nation. Unfortunately, in democracies the rights of minorities can become subject to the tyranny of the majority, and the English for the Children laws were passed by voters in three of the four states where they were introduced, including Arizona.

In the twenty-first century, globalization is impacting indigenous peoples worldwide with assimilationist pressures. Assimilation, which was greatly aided by the breakdown of isolation as roads were paved and Indians switched from horses to cars so that they could easily visit border towns, has vastly accelerated with the spread of movies, television, and video games, even into isolated reservation homes. The positive effects of assimilation and globalization are often touted, but this is not always the case. Omaha doctor Susan La Flesche found over a century ago that "voting and citizenship marked the beginning of alcohol abuse on the reservation. Local politicians with whiskey to dispense came to solicit the Omahas' votes, explaining to them that since they had the same rights as white men they could drink all they wanted" (Reyhner and Eder, 2004, 82). Too often assimilation is into a popular culture that is materialistic, hedonistic, and individualistic. In 1999 Northern Cheyenne educator Richard Littlebear found that the breakdown of tribal culture by

assimilationist pressures led Indian youth to look to urban gangs for a sense of identity, importance, and belongingness, whereas he saw a return to their own tribal culture could offer the same needed sense of identity in a much healthier way. In 2005 when an Ojibwe high school student on the Red Lake Reservation in Minnesota shot and killed a teacher and seven students, Navajo Nation President Joe Shirley issued a statement that the breakdown of traditional tribal culture and poverty were responsible for creating the conditions on Indian reservations that made such a horrendous act possible.

Jon Reyhner

See also Anglicans; Baptist Church; Boarding Schools, United States and Canada; Boas, Franz; Bureau of Indian Affairs: Establishing the Existence of an Indian Tribe; Canada, Indian Policies of; Ceremonies, Criminalization of; Collier, John; Constitution Act; Department of Indian Affairs and Northern Development; Education; Episcopal Church; General Allotment (Dawes Act); Genocide; Identity; Indian Act; Indian Civilization Fund Act; Indian Removal Act; Indian Self-Determination and Education Assistance Act; Language and Language Renewal; *Lone Wolf v. Hitchcock*; Meriam Report; Mission System, Spanish; Missionaries, French Jesuit; Mormon Church; Praying Villages of Massachusetts; Red Power Movement; Ross, John; Royal Commission on Aboriginal Peoples; Termination; *Worcester v. Georgia.*

References and Further Reading

Adams, David Wallace. 1995. *Education for Extinction: American Indians and the Boarding School Experience 1875–1928.* Lawrence: University Press of Kansas.

Chalcraft, Edwin L. 2004. *Assimilation's Agent: My Life as a Superintendent in the Indian Boarding School System.* Lincoln: University of Nebraska Press.

Collier, John. 1963. *From Every Zenith: A Memoir.* Denver, CO: Sage Books.

Crawford, James, ed. 1992. *Language Loyalties: A Source Book on the Official English Controversy.* Chicago: University of Chicago Press.

Mankiller, Wilma Pearl. 2004. *Every Day Is a Good Day: Reflections of Contemporary Indigenous Women.* Golden, CO: Fulcrum.

Milloy, John S. 1999. *A National Crime: The Canadian Government and the Residential School System, 1879 to 1986.* Winnipeg: University of Manitoba Press.

Niezen, Ronald. 2003. *The Origins of Indigenism: Human Rights and the Politics of Identity.* Berkeley: University of California Press.

Ogbu, John U. 1995. "Understanding Cultural Diversity and Learning." In *Handbook of Research on Multicultural Education.* Edited by J. A. Banks and C.A.M. Banks, 582–593. New York: Macmillan.

Pratt, Richard Henry. 2004. *Battlefield and Classroom: An Autobiography.* Norman: University of Oklahoma Press.

Prucha, Francis Paul. 1984. *The Great Father: The United States Government and the American Indians.* Lincoln: University of Nebraska Press.

Reyhner, Jon, and Jeanne Eder. 2004. *American Indian Education: A History.* Norman: University of Oklahoma Press.

Reyhner, Jon. 2001. "Cultural Survival vs. Forced Assimilation." *Cultural Survival Quarterly* 25, no. 2: 22–25.

Unz, Ron. 1999. "California and the End of White America." *Commentary* (November). 17–28.

Bering Strait Theory

According to the Bering Strait migration theory, the people now known as American Indians originated in Asia and wandered into the western hemisphere by way of a land bridge that once joined the eastern reaches of Siberia to western Alaska. This belief is now anthropological orthodoxy, taught as "fact" to schoolchildren and assumed virtually as self-evident "truth" in popular consciousness. The accepted timing of this presumed migration has shifted over time. During the first half of the twentieth century, it was widely believed to have begun no more than 4,000 years ago, although "reputable" scholars preferred the range of two to three millennia. Beginning in the late 1940s, it was declared that the crossing might have commenced as many as 15,000 years earlier. By the early 1990s reports noted that research in genetics and linguistics revealed a need to consider a number of other possible migration routes and a longer time line (some researchers have suggested as many as 30,000 years).

With the exception of a few marginalized academic "mavericks," the only significant resistance to the land bridge migration hypothesis comes from the Native North Americans who continue to embrace the origin stories of their own peoples' traditional understandings. They are regularly dismissed as adhering to a primitive mythic/religious worldview, long since displaced by the presumptively superior methods of Western science. However, the migration theory itself has not been supported by scientific evidence, but instead is

consistently tailored to meet the religious and/or political needs of Euro-American society.

Columbus's "discovery" of the western hemisphere and its large human population was difficult to reconcile with the Christian origin story of human descent from Adam and Eve. While some attempted to avoid the problem by classifying American Indians as nonhuman, most Western theologians preferred to believe that Indians were the progeny of the lost tribes of Israel. In 1650, rabbinical scholar Israel ben Mannasseh argued that Tartar migrants, with Jewish tribes among them, crossed an ancient land bridge now covered by what he termed the Strait of Anian sometime after the Assyrian conquest of 721 BCE. The "lost tribe" theory was embraced by American religious leaders from the Puritan Cotton Mather and the Quaker William Penn to Joseph Smith, founder of the Mormon Church.

Others, such as Thomas Jefferson, abandoned the theory of Judaic origins for the more "scientific" notion, also embedded in ben Mannasseh's thesis, that the earliest migrations across the land bridge were composed primarily of "Mongoloid stock." This, according to Jefferson, explained the resemblance between American Indians and the peoples of eastern Asia. Jefferson's motives were secular rather than religious; he hoped to reinforce the still-prevalent argument that Indians were no more genuinely indigenous to this land than the later arriving European settlers. A fervent advocate of human liberty who owned hundreds of slaves, Jefferson is not easy to read as an archaeologist. As a student of indigenous languages, he sometimes maintained that their number and complexity indicated a great antiquity for Native American cultures.

The immigrants came up with all manner of explanations for the human presence in the Americas. Constantine Samuel Rafinesque claimed to have discovered and deciphered what he called the *Walam Odum,* wooden tablets said to contain hieroglyphs depicting the settlement of North America by Lenape (Delaware) Indians, who crossed the frozen Bering Strait from Asia approximately 3,600 years ago. Since exposed as a crude hoax, it was defended by eminent archaeologists, ethnologists, linguists, and historians as recently as 1987.

In fact, the Bering Strait migration theory is not only unsupported but *countered* by available scientific evidence. One major problem is chronology, for until recently Western science insisted—and the belief is still prevalent—that modern humans did not appear in Europe until some

40,000 years ago. If so, it was unlikely that they could have spread across Asia to the far reaches of Siberia and then into North America until, at the earliest, some 20,000 years ago. In keeping with this theory, as late as the 1940s, scientists such as Ales Hrdlicka, curator of the Smithsonian Institution's National Museum, insisted that humans had inhabited the Americas for no more than 2,000 or 3,000 years.

The theory disregarded several important finds: the 1926 discovery near Folsom, New Mexico, of projectiles embedded in the bones of bison that had been extinct for some 10,000 years; the 1932 discovery of projectile points near Clovis, Texas, beneath a layer of earth containing Folsom points and lodged in the skeletons of wooly mammoths and camels extinct for twelve millennia; and the 1931 recovery of human skeletal remains in deposits from the last Ice Age.

Subsequently, however, geologists realized that the land bridge over which the migration supposedly took place would have been exposed only during an Ice Age, the most recent of which ended 10,000 years ago. In 1948 University of California anthropologist Alfred Louis Kroeber, who had replaced Hrdlicka as the "dean of the profession," was forced to revise anthropological orthodoxy, but he conceded a maximal date of human occupancy of only 12,000—then 15,000—years. Well before then, however, another eminent anthropologist and geologist had concluded that the "San Diego" skulls, discovered in 1926, were well over 40,000 years old. As radiocarbon and other dating techniques have evolved, human remains and artifacts found near Sunnyvale, California, and El Bosque, Nicaragua, have been dated to 70,000 years, and stone tools were found in San Diego's Mission Valley in a geological stratum more than 100,000 years old. By the mid-1960s, Louis Leakey, discoverer of *Australopithecines,* the oldest known protohuman remains, was convinced that evidence of even older sites, perhaps even the oldest of those occupied by fully modern humans (*Homo sapiens sapiens),* might be found in North America.

According to geologists, the most recent time when the whole of Beringia was above water lasted from approximately 35,000 to 10,000 years ago, but the conditions permitting human transit, if they existed at all, were limited to the period of maximum glaciation, approximately 25,000 to 15,000 years before the present. This renders problematic not only the evidence of human habitation that

significantly predates the 15,000-year maximum conceded by anthropologists, but also the locations and nature of these findings. How did people who first entered Alaska perhaps 15,000 years ago manage to establish themselves as far south as New Mexico or as far east as Pennsylvania at approximately the same time? How could they reach sites in present-day Venezuela, Brazil, and Chile more than 14,000 years ago? Evidence indicates that Fells Cave near Tierra del Fuego, at the very tip of South America, was inhabited about 8,500 years ago, and Monte Verde in Chile was occupied at least 13,000 years ago. In fact, several sites in South America predate Clovis in North America.

A related difficulty is raised by the Koster site in Illinois. While only approximately 8,000 years old, it clearly hosted a sizable and long-settled agrarian culture. How did the descendents of the primitive hunter-gatherers who are supposed to have crossed the Bering land bridge accomplish this in just a few thousand years, when it is generally accepted that it took the sedentary cultures of Mesopotamia about thirty millennia to do the same?

The Bering Strait thesis also presumes dispersal from the far northwest toward the south and east, yet many sites along the southern Atlantic seacoast substantially predate those in New England and eastern Canada. As a rule, coastal sites tend to be older than those in the interior. Even in Beringia, the oldest recorded site of human occupancy in eastern Siberia, is located at Lake Baikal, about 2,500 miles from the Strait. It appears to be an isolated and anomalous settlement, reliably dated at a little less than 20,000 years. On the American side, the most proximate site is the Old Crow/Bluefish Cave complex in the western Yukon, where there is evidence of numerous settlements. By some estimates, that area was occupied at least 24,800 years ago. If one applies the scientific method of proceeding from facts to conclusions, the available evidence indicates that, if anyone walked across an Ice Age Beringian land bridge, it was indigenous Americans moving into Asia rather than vice versa.

Another major difficulty with the land bridge theory relates to environmental conditions. Unless the migrants walked across 2,500 miles of open ice that was up to two miles thick, they would have followed an ice-free corridor approximately along the course of the McKenzie River today. If such a corridor existed, it would have opened up at the end of the last Ice Age, too late to account for most of the sites mentioned. Moreover, climatic evidence indi-

cates that in such a passage the air temperature would have been about 20 degrees *colder* than the surface of the glacial plateau.

And then there is the question of geography. As Vine Deloria, Jr., has pointed out, to even reach Beringia from the most proximate sites of habitation in Siberia, people would have had to cross two significant mountain ranges to arrive at the thousand or so miles of barren marshlands constituting the strait, after which they would have encountered the numerous mountain ranges that cut across present-day Alaska, both above and below the Arctic circle. The question becomes not so much whether this could have been done, but why anyone would have bothered. The standard response is that the "paleoliths" endured such hardships eventually to feed on the "megafauna" flourishing in the more temperate regions of Ice Age North America. Just how would Stone Age residents of the Asian steppes have known that an abundance of large game animals flourished 5,000 miles away, over a dozen mountain ranges, across a swampy land bridge, and through a frigid corridor? The anthropological establishment responds that the megafauna were already using the Beringian land bridge to migrate from North America into Asia, traversing that same daunting geography in the opposite direction. In other words, "science" tells us that humans could have gone in only one direction, but the mammoths could have, and apparently wanted to, move in the other.

Some scholars have pointed out the implausibility of these scenarios. One anthropologist proposes that people crossed the Bering Strait from Asia, then dispersed along both the western and the eastern seaboards. This is more consistent with the datings in coastal regions but does not explain why anyone would have traversed 3,000 miles across the North American Arctic before turning south. Others have speculated that people migrated along the southernmost edge of the land bridge, then moved south along the Pacific coastline before turning east. This avoids reliance on the theory of an ice-free corridor and allows dating back to perhaps 35,000 years.

The perceived need to restrict the inhabitation of the Americas to a very recent period also has been eased by the recently emerging consensus that *Homo sapiens sapiens* may have lived in the Middle East and southern Africa for at least seventy, rather than merely forty millennia. We may be on the verge of yet another revision of Western scientific orthodoxy that accounts for some—although by no means all—

of the inconsistencies in the data but maintains the political utility of the Bering Strait migration theory.

Unlike these constantly shifting and generally unsupported "scientific" theories, indigenous people have always had explanations of their origins in the Americas that exhibit both internal integrity and consistency. Because anthropologists always begin with the presumption that people could not possibly have been in this hemisphere for so long, they have dismissed the many vibrant accounts shared by native wisdom keepers of their ancestors' interactions with giant beavers, stiff-legged bears, and hairy elephants as myths and legends. However, as evidence from other disciplines has accumulated to support a much longer occupancy, these legends been slowly accepted as more literal accounts.

The Hopi Four Worlds chronicle, for example, depicts the Hopi as having lived through ages of fire, water, and ice before the beginning of the present era. Slowly, western science has acknowledged that they may have been here during the last Ice Age, perhaps even during the extensive flooding that ended some 25,000 years ago. Nonetheless, accounts of the Hopi experience of a world of fire are still dismissed as preposterous. Other peoples, including the Klamaths, Nisquallys, and Wishrams in the Northwest, have oral histories with detailed accounts of volcanic activity in the region, including the formation of Crater Lake and the last eruption of Mount Hood. These accounts were uniformly dismissed until recent geological studies revealed that the antiquity of such volcanic events have in some cases been significantly overestimated. The traditional understanding of the Lakota that they originated in the Black Hills, the Cherokee accounts of emerging from water, and the Tohono O'odham descriptions of mysterious dinosaurlike creatures have invariably been disparaged or ignored, while "scientific" findings are never subject to corroboration by way of their consistency with the knowledge of indigenous people.

There is much that we do not know about the origins of humanity. What is clear, however, is that rigid adherence to the latest catechisms of purported scientific "truth" only prevents us from being able to understand why, for example, ancient petroglyphs in Arizona's Havasupai Canyon depict the African ibex or the oldest recorded sample of corn pollen, estimated to be 80,000 years old, was discovered 200 feet below Mexico City. Accepting the growing weight of evidence that Native Americans did not necessarily come from somewhere else—not to mention the evidence that American Indians had domesticated dogs 30,000 years ago— might help explain why agriculture appears to have originated in this hemisphere. In light of the dramatic gaps in contemporary theories of human evolution, the questions raised by the notion of an American genesis based on some sort of "multiregional evolution" are no more daunting than those created by the Bering Strait migration theory.

Ward Churchill

See also Archaeology and the First Americans; Paleo-Indians.

References and Further Reading

Biolsi, Thomas, and Larry J. Zimmerman, eds. 1997. *Indians and Anthropologists: Vine Deloria, Jr., and the Critique of Anthropology.* Tucson: University of Arizona Press.

Carter, George F. 1980. *Earlier Than You Think: A Personal View of Man in America.* College Station: Texas A&M University Press.

Ceram, C. W. 1972. *First American: A Story of North American Archaeology.* New York: Mentor Books.

Churchill, Ward. 2005. "About That Bering Strait Land Bridge . . . A Study in the Falsity of 'Scientific Truth.'" In J. Lehmann, ed., "Social Theory as Politics in Knowledge," *Current Perspectives in Social Theory* 23: 368.

Deloria, Vine, Jr. 1995. *Red Earth, White Lies: Native Americans and the Myth of Scientific Fact.* New York: Scribner's.

Durham, Jimmie. 1993. *A Certain Lack of Coherence: Writings on Art and Cultural Politics.* London: Kala Press.

Friend, Tim. 1993. "Genetic Detectives Trace the Origin of First Americans." *USA Today* (September 3).

Goodman, Jeffrey. 1981. *American Genesis: The American Indian and the Origins of Modern Man.* New York: Summit Books.

Hopkins, David M., ed. 1967. *The Bering Land Bridge.* Stanford, CA: Stanford University Press.

Kuhn, Thomas. 1967. *The Structure of Scientific Revolutions.* Chicago: University of Chicago Press.

MacGowen, Kenneth, and Joseph A. Hester, Jr. 1962. *Early Man in the New World,* 2nd ed. Garden City, NY: Doubleday.

Oestreicher, David M. 1996. "Unraveling the *Walam Odum.*" *Natural History* 14 (October): 14–21.

Sanders, Ronald. 1992. *Lost Tribes and Promised Lands: The Origins of American Racism,* 2nd ed. New York: HarperPerennial.

West, Frederick Hadleigh, ed. 1996. *American Beginnings: The Prehistory and Paleontology of Beringia.* Chicago: University of Chicago Press.

Boarding Schools, United States and Canada

Richard Henry Pratt (1840–1924), a U.S. Army officer who founded the boarding school system as an assimilationist device, was a reformer who coined the slogan "[k]ill the Indian and save the man" to describe their educational goal. The phrase was designed initially as an advertising slogan to be used in Congress to request appropriations for a nationwide system of Indian schools around 1900.

Pratt's Indian schools were run with Army style boot camp discipline, the idea being to remake Indian children in the image of small farmers and urban workers with the rudiments of Anglo-American cultural heritage. The Carlisle Indian Industrial School, Pratt's first, was run on an Army model. Students were strictly regimented and forced to divest themselves of all vestiges of Indian identity. They wore uniforms, and their hair was cut. Mis-

sionaries also were brought in to teach them Christianity. Runaways were punished severely. Discipline was sometimes personal and petty.

Pratt described his philosophy in a book, *Battlefield and Classroom: Four Decades with the American Indian, 1867–1904.* His educational experiment began in the 1870s with seventy-two Native men, most of them Cheyenne, who were imprisoned in an old Spanish fort at Saint Augustine, Florida. In 1878, this "class" "graduated," and Pratt approached Congress for an appropriation to begin an Indian industrial school on an abandoned army post at Carlisle, Pennsylvania. To recruit students for his new school, Pratt visited the Sioux of the High Plains. One hundred and sixty-nine students traveled eastward in 1879 to form Carlisle's first class. Included was Luther Standing Bear, who later became a well-known author. Standing Bear later recalled his days at Carlisle in *My Indian Boyhood.*

Native American students participate in a mathematics class at the Carlisle Industrial Indian School in Carlisle, Pennsylvania, ca. 1903. The use of textbooks and a structured academic routine added to the rigid atmosphere at the boarding school. (Library of Congress)

The schools were established at a time when industrial enterprises were expanding rapidly in the United States. At the same time, the European-American settlement frontier was crossing the western half of the present continental United States. The curriculum of the schools was intensely vocational. "This is to be an industrial school to teach young Indians how to make a living among civilized people by practicing agricultural and mechanical pursuits and the usual industries of civilized life," Pratt wrote (1987, 235). He approached Congress for money to buy a long list of items to further Indians' induction into what he regarded as civilized industrial society: carpenters' tools, blacksmiths' forges and anvils, sewing machines, paint brushes, tools for making shoes and harnessing horses, printing presses and type.

Pratt ran the boarding schools on a model that was appropriate for training a factory workforce during the late nineteenth century. Thus, the communal lifeways of many American Indians were to be replaced by an emphasis on individual labor, which was regarded as a commodity in the capitalistic marketplace. Pratt continuously stressed the value of boarding school education and the Anglo-American world of work as two stops on the same avenue of assimilation for Native Americans.

By the 1880s, as the non-Native settlement frontier closed in the middle of the continent, government policy toward Indian education was marked by debate. One faction wanted to remove Native children from their homes under governmental or religious sponsorship and, person by person, remake the Indians into English-speaking, God-fearing participants in an agricultural and industrial economy, all within one generation. The other faction advocated extermination of surviving Indians. There was no room on this range of ideas for Indians' practice of their own cultures, what today we call "self-determination."

Even as many boarding school students were stunted by physical and psychological abuse, and as hundreds died in influenza and tuberculosis epidemics, a few overcame all obstacles to become well-known in Anglo-American culture. The Associated Press named Jim Thorpe, a graduate of the Carlisle Indian School, the greatest American athlete in America during the first half of the twentieth century. Luther Standing Bear, a Lakota author, is another prominent example. Thus, mixed with memories of pain, isolation, and despair, the boarding schools produced occasional testaments to their value as havens from an aggressive non-Native world that could be very hostile to the few hundred thousand Native American people who survived the Indian wars.

Boarding schools usually were purposefully located far from children's homes to break down ties to their families and cultures. During their scholastic careers, many Native children were "outed" (i.e., lent) to European-American families for as many as three years. Students who were outed often performed domestic labor (for women) and farm or urban wage labor (for men). Young men were trained in agriculture, carpentry, blacksmithing, harness and shoemaking, printing, tailoring, and baking. Young women were trained in cooking, sewing, and laundry.

The outing policy was based on an assumption that Native American children were less intelligent than European-Americans. During the 1940s, the Bureau of Indian Affairs and University of Chicago researchers set out to test this assumption. They compared Indian children's intelligence with that of non-Indians in a rural Midwestern area. They used performance tests in which comprehension of English was not the main factor in defining intelligence, testing Hopi, Navajo, Sioux, Papago, and Zuni children. A group of Hopis averaged a score of 111 to 117 on a battery of tests. A comparison group of European-American children scored 101 to 103 on the same tests. Pine Ridge children averaged 101 to 114 on the tests, and the other Indian groups scored in similar ranges (Havighurst and Hilkevitch, 1944).

Native people displayed an unexpectedly (to many non-Natives) intense attachment to their traditions. This attachment, combined with boarding school curricula that profoundly rejected Native values and self-worth, often resulted in fostering self-defeat, suicide, and/or alcoholism (also eventually a form of suicide). Some students rebelled outright at the contradictions they were being taught compared to the lives they knew and the traditions they were taught at home. At the same time, the boarding school system had a curious effect on some of its best students of a more activist era. It turned some of them into the Indian militants of the 1960s. That such a transformation is not totally unique to the twentieth century may be seen in the case of Wovoka, the man who initiated the Ghost Dance and was raised in a Christian, settler family during the early years of the boarding schools.

The boarding school system was based on an assumption that making students accept the degradation of their traditions as an objective fact would cause them to accept acculturation. The Carlisle

School published one essay that its teachers regarded as "excellent":

Question: To what race do you belong?
Answer: The human race.

Question: How many classes belong to this race?
Answer: There are five classes belonging to the human race.

Question: Which was the first?
Answer: The white people are the strongest.

Question: Which are the next?
Answer: The Mongolian or yellows.

Question: The next?
Answer: The Ethiopians or blacks.

Question: Next?
Answer: The American or reds.

Question: Tell me something of the white people.
Answer: The Caucasian is way ahead of all the other races. He thought more than any other race, he thought that somebody must [have] made the earth, and if the white people did not find that out, nobody would ever know it—it is God who made the world (Weeks, 1990, 224–225).

When the Bureau of Indian Affairs (BIA) forbade traditional ceremonies such as the Sun Dance and the rituals of the kiva, Native people took them underground. The same was true of shamanistic practices, which survived stringent attacks by those who regarded them as acts of "paganism." The off-reservation boarding schools were designed to immerse Native students in Anglicized culture and to strip them of their own, beginning with language. English was taught and enforced as the *lingua franca*. Speaking Native languages often earned the offender punishment, which was often of a violent nature. Even under such pressure, however, many Native languages, the vessels of many hundreds of cultures, survived.

As allotment reduced the Native land base, enrollment in BIA-sponsored schools increased. Between 1895 and 1905, the number of off-reservation boarding schools designed on the Carlisle model rose from nineteen to twenty-five, and their enrollment doubled to 9,736. The number of boarding schools on reservations increased from seventy-five to ninety-three, with enrollment rising from 8,068 to 11,402 (Olson and Wilson, 1984, 90–100).

Reliving the Boarding School Experience in Canada

The paternalistic assumptions of Pratt's schools also influenced Canadian educational policies. In 1908, Canadian Minister of Indian affairs Frank Oliver forecast that the residential school system would "elevate the Indian from his condition of savagery" and "make him a self-supporting member of the state, and eventually a citizen in good standing" (Johansen, 2000, 12). Canadian officials sent delegations south of the border to study boarding schools in the United States before establishing their own system. By the early twenty-first century, hundreds of Native people in Canada were suing churches and the federal government there because of maltreatment at these schools.

Even after decades, the memories of Native Americans who were forced to attend Canadian boarding schools have a searing quality. "It was like jail," Warner Scout, who was fifty-four years old in 1999, told the *Calgary Herald*. "The scar will be there for the rest of our lives" (Lowey, 1999, A-1). Scout, who is one of two thousand Canadian natives seeking legal redress for boarding school abuse, recalled regular beatings and taunts that he was "an ugly savage" (Lowey, 1999, A-1).

Scout was taken from his adopted family to attend the Saint Paul residential school, operated by the Anglican Church of Canada on the Blood Reserve near Lethbridge, in southern Alberta. There, he said, "Teaching . . . was beaten into us" (Lowey, 1999, A-1). Scout watched as one Indian student was forced to eat his own vomit after he threw up into a bowl of porridge. Students who wet their beds had urine rubbed in their faces, and those who spoke the Blackfoot language had their heads shaven.

Jackie Blackface, who was fifty-two in 1999, recalled being beaten with a tractor's fan belt at an Anglican school on the Siksika First Nation Reserve east of Calgary. Federal Canadian law at the time gave the Indian agent on each Native reserve authority to invade homes and order children aged seven or older into residential schools. Parents who did not cooperate were threatened with time in jail.

More than a hundred thousand Native American students attended residential schools across

Canada until the 1980s. Most of these schools were funded by the Canadian federal government and operated by employees of the Catholic, Anglican, Presbyterian, and other churches. During early years of the twenty-first century, hundreds of men and women filed lawsuits outlining the physical and sexual abuse they said they were forced to endure as children in these schools. Eventually, settlements could reach billions of Canadian dollars, possibly devastating the financial resources of the churches that had maintained the schools.

Why has a drive to apologize and compensate for the abuses of boarding schools developed in Canada while the issue has been virtually untouched in the United States? The seeds were sown in the summer of 1990 at Oka, Quebec, on and near the Kanesatake Mohawk Reserve. At that time, a confrontation over a long-ignored land claim reverberated across Canada, causing intense soul-searching by many non-Native Canadians. This wave of questioning expressed itself in the appointment of the Royal Commission on Aboriginal Peoples, which, in 1996, published a massive, multivolume study of the many ways in which Native Americans had had their land stolen and their rights abused throughout Canadian history.

Part of this report (Volume 1, Chapter 10) documented the abuses of the boarding schools, providing a basis for the establishment of a $350 million "healing fund" by Canada's federal government. It also prompted a tidal wave of lawsuits because the healing fund is reserved for community projects, not for individual compensation. Individual compensation must be sought through the Canadian court system or by negotiation with agencies of the federal government.

The graphic sexual nature of boarding school abuses shocked many Canadians. Their sense of disgust was hardly alleviated by the fact that many of the abuses took place at the hands of priests, nuns, and other clerics. The Royal Commission found that abuse was systemic, not occasional or accidental. Thousands of Native young people are said to have died in the schools, and thousands more were scarred for life by physical and sexual abuse.

Aboriginal people often realized the purpose of the schools to begin with, according to the report of the Royal Commission: "The Aboriginal leader George Manuel, a residential school graduate, was more blunt. The schools, he wrote, were the laboratory and production line of the colonial system . . . the colonial system that was designed to make room

for European expansion into a vast empty wilderness needed an Indian population that it could describe as lazy and shiftless . . . the colonial system required such an Indian for casual labor" (Royal Commission, n.d.).

The Royal Commission on Aboriginal Peoples found that the effects of the residential schools' concerted campaign to obliterate Aboriginal habits and associations, languages, traditions, and beliefs, in concert with its vision of radical resocialization, were compounded by mismanagement and underfunding, by the provision of inferior educational services, and by the woeful mistreatment, neglect, and abuse of many children—facts that were known to the department and the churches throughout the history of the school system. In the words of the Royal Commission's report, the purpose of the schools was to

> release [the children] from the shackles that tied them to their parents, communities and cultures. The civilizers in the churches and the department understood this and, moreover, that it would not be accomplished simply by bringing the children into the school. Rather it required a concerted attack on the ontology, on the basic cultural patterning of the children and on their world view. They had to be taught to see and understand the world as a European place within which only European values and beliefs had meaning; thus the wisdom of their cultures would seem to them only savage superstition (Royal Commission, n.d.).

The main enforcement mechanism in this transformation from "permissive" aboriginal life to white Canadian discipline was punishment, much of it violent. In 1943, the principal of St. George's School (located on the Fraser River, just north of Lyttons, British Columbia) disclosed that a set of shackles had been used routinely "to chain runaways to the bed." Furthermore, "At the heart of the vision of residential education—of the school as home and sanctuary of motherly care—there was a stark contradiction, an inherent element of savagery in the mechanics of civilizing the children. The very language in which the vision was couched revealed what would have to be the essentially violent nature of the school system in its assault on child and culture. The basic premise of resocialization, of the great transformation from 'savage' to 'civilized', was violent" (Royal Commission, n.d.). In 1936, G. Barry, district inspector of schools in

British Columbia, described the Alberni Indian Residential School on Vancouver Island, "where every member of staff carried a strap" and where "children have never learned to work without punishment" (Royal Commission, n.d.). In 1896, according to the Royal Commission's report, Agent D. L. Clink refused to return a child to Red Deer School because he feared "he would be abused." Without reprimand from the principal, a teacher had beaten children severely on several occasions, and one of them had had to be hospitalized. "Such brutality," Clink concluded, "should not be tolerated for a moment" and "would not be tolerated in a white school for a single day in any part of Canada" (Royal Commission, n.d.).

The Royal Commission also included a report by a senior official in western Canada, David Laird, on Norway House in 1907. The report detailing "frequent whippings" over an eight-year period of a young boy, Charlie Clines, for bed-wetting. The severity of his punishment was not, Laird asserted, "in accordance with Christian methods." Clines hated the new Anglo world that was being thrust on him so much that he ran away from the school and slept in weather so severe that he lost several toes to frostbite.

In 1902, Johnny Sticks found his son, Duncan, dead of exposure, after he fled from the Williams Lake, British Columbia, industrial school. Nearly four decades later, in 1937 at the Lejac school, four boys ran away and were found frozen to death on the lake within sight of their community. They were wearing only summer clothes. In both cases, investigations uncovered a history of neglect and violence in evidence given by staff, children, and some graduates. Some students complained that they were given rotten, worm-ridden meat and punished if they didn't eat it. In 1921, a visiting nurse at Crowstand School discovered nine children "chained to the benches" in the dining room, one of them "marked badly by a strap" (Royal Commission, n.d.). Children were frequently beaten severely with whips, rods, and fists, chained and shackled, bound hand and foot and locked in closets, basements, and bathrooms.

The Royal Commission reported that in 1919, a runaway student from the Anglican Old Sun's school was captured, shackled to a bed, and, with his hands tied, "most brutally and unmercifully beaten with a horse quirt until his back was bleeding." The accused, P. H. Gentlemen, admitted to having used a whip and shackles. Canon S. Gould, the general secretary of the Missionary Society, mounted a curious defense: that such a beating was the norm "more or less, in every boarding school in the country." Gentlemen remained at the school.

Writing in 1991 of her experience in both Anglican and Catholic schools, Mary Carpenter told an all-too-familiar story: After a lifetime of beatings, going hungry, standing in a corridor on one leg, and walking in the snow with no shoes for speaking Inuvialuktun, and after having a heavy, stinging paste rubbed on her face (to stop her from expressing her Inuit custom of raising eyebrows for "yes" and wrinkling noses for "no"), she lost the ability to speak her native language.

The Aboriginal Commission found that:

By the mid-1980s, it was widely and publicly recognized that the residential school experience . . . like smallpox and tuberculosis in earlier decades, had devastated and continued to devastate communities. The schools were, with the agents and instruments of economic and political marginalization, part of the contagion of colonization. In their direct attack on language, beliefs and spirituality, the schools had been a particularly virulent strain of that epidemic of empire, sapping the children's bodies and beings. In later life, many adult survivors, and the families and communities to which they returned, all manifested a tragic range of symptoms emblematic of "the silent tortures that continue in our communities" (Royal Commission, n.d.).

While school supervisors acknowledged and sometimes even took pride in stern discipline, including corporal punishment, they said very little about the deepest secret of the system: sexual abuse of the children. The official files ignore the issue almost completely. Any references were encoded in the language of repression that marked the Canadian discourse on sexual matters. One report at Red Deer School commented that "the moral aspect of affairs is deplorable." Others wrote of "questions of immorality" of "the breaking of the Seventh Commandment" (Royal Commission, n.d.).

In 1990, the Toronto *Globe and Mail* reported that Rix Rogers, special advisor to the minister of national health and welfare on child sexual abuse, had commented at a meeting of the Canadian Psychological Association that the abuse revealed to date was "just the tip of the iceberg" and that closer

scrutiny of the treatment of children at residential schools would show that all children at some schools were sexually abused. A 1989 study sponsored by the Native Women's Association of the Northwest Territories found that eight out of ten girls under the age of eight had been victims of sexual abuse, and 50 percent of boys the same age had been sexually molested as well.

On January 7, 1998, Minister of Indian Affairs Jane Stewart read a Statement of Reconciliation into the record of Canada's federal Parliament at Ottawa that acknowledged the damage done to the Native population, including the hanging of Louis Riel after he led a rebellion of Indian and mixed-race people in western Canada in 1885. The government apology stopped short of pardoning Riel, a step that aboriginal leaders have demanded for decades. Stewart did, however, apologize for the government's assimilation policies, including the abuses of boarding schools.

"Attitudes of racial and cultural superiority led to a suppression of aboriginal culture and values," Stewart said. She continued:

> As a country, we are burdened by past actions that resulted in weakening the identity of aboriginal peoples, suppressing their languages and cultures, and outlawing spiritual practices. We must recognize the impact of these actions on the once self-sustaining nations that were disaggregated, disrupted, limited or even destroyed by the dispossession of traditional territory, by the relocation of aboriginal people, and by some provisions of the Indian Act. The time has come to state formally that the days of paternalism and disrespect are behind us and we are committed to changing the nature of the relationship between aboriginal and non-aboriginal people in Canada (Bourrie, 1998).

Phil Fontaine, leader of the Assembly of First Nations, a coalition of nationwide aboriginal groups, said that the apology paves the way for lasting peace between Native peoples and the Canadian government. "This celebrates the beginning of a new era," Fontaine told Interpress Service. "It is a major step forward in our quest to be recognized as a distinct order of government in Canada" (Bourrie, 1998).

Some aboriginal leaders were not happy with the reconciliation statement. Representatives of the Inuit, Native women's groups, and Metis said they did not believe the apology was strong enough. They were critical because the statement did not refer in more detail to the wrongs done to their communities. The same groups also maintained that the money involved in recompense was too little and too late. Inuit and Metis leaders, who are not included in the Assembly of First Nations, also complained that Stewart's later statements did not mention specific programs for them.

Other non-Indian Canadians complained that the surge of lawsuits for residential school abuse would clog the court system, bankrupt some religious denominations, and strain the Canadian federal budget, requiring new taxes. By the end of the year 2002, according to the Canadian government, more than 19,000 Native persons had entered some form of claim, a number equal to roughly 15 to 20 percent of the boarding schools' living alumni. This legal backlog included four class action suits. Indian plaintiffs won all five boarding school abuse trials held during the late 1990s, two in Saskatchewan and three in British Columbia. By 2006, the Canadian federal government had paid out at least $50 million worth of individual compensation.

In late October 1998, the United Church of Canada, the country's largest Protestant body (including three million Presbyterians, Congregationalists, and Methodists) issued an apology for physical and sexual abuse meted out to Native students at boarding schools it had operated. The apology was made shortly after the disclosure of evidence indicating that church officials knew of the abuse as early as 1960 and did nothing to stop it. Peter Grant, an attorney for former students at a British Columbia boarding school, had presented evidence indicating that the vice principal at the Port Alberni residential school was convicted of indecently assaulting male students between 1948 and 1968. Arthur Plint, who supervised the school's dormitories, pleaded guilty in 1995 to "dozens of sexual assaults," according to the Associated Press. He was sentenced to eleven years in prison. British Columbia Court Justice William Brenner ruled that both the federal government and the church were "vicariously responsible" for Plint's assaults on Native young people.

"I apologize for the pain and suffering that our church's involvement in the Indian residential school system has caused," the Reverend Bill Phipps, the church's chief executive (or "moderator"), told a news conference on October 27 (Associated Press, 1998). "We are aware of some of the damage that some of this cruel and ill-conceived system

of assimilation has perpetuated on Canada's first nations," Phipps said. "We are truly and humbly sorry" (McIlroy, 1998, 5).

One of Grant's clients, Willy Blackwater, said that the church should be prepared to compensate abuse victims with money as well as with words. Harry Daniels, president of the Congress of Aboriginal Peoples, said, "These things are nice to hear, but talk is cheap" (Associated Press, 1998). The Anglican and Roman Catholic churches of Canada expressed repentance for their role in boarding school abuses, but, as of 2002, they had not apologized, in part because they fear legal liability. The United Church seems to have decided that it will settle with litigants out of court.

The Royal Commission concluded that:

The terrible facts of the residential school system must be made a part of a new sense of what Canada has been and will continue to be for as long as that record is not officially recognized and repudiated. Only by such an act of recognition and repudiation can a start be made on a very different future. Canada and Canadians must realize that they need to consider changing their society so that they can discover ways of living in harmony with the original people of the land (Royal Commission, n.d.).

The Royal Commission called for a full investigation into Canada's residential school system, "to bring to light and begin to heal the grievous harms suffered by countless Aboriginal children, families and communities as a result of the residential school system" (Royal Commission, n.d.). Although not the forum the Royal Commission may have intended, such a public inquiry has begun to unfold, case by specific case, in many Canadian courtrooms. The economic stakes of boarding school compensation in Canada were reflected by the fact that, by late 2002, the Canadian federal government had reserved $1.7 billion to settle up to 18,000 native residential school lawsuits brought for physical and sexual abuse. The government was planning to require plaintiffs to waive rights to future litigation, including claims based on loss of language and culture.

Bruce E. Johansen

See also Assimilation; Canada, Indian Policies of; Education; Genocide; Indian Self-Determination and Educational Assistance Act; Royal Commission on Aboriginal Peoples.

References and Further Reading
Associated Press. 1998. "Canada's United Church Apologizes for Abuse at Indian Schools." Associated Press Canada (October 28).
Bourrie, Mark. 1998. "Canada Apologizes for Abuse of Native Peoples." Interpress Service (January 8). Available at: http://www.oneworld.org/ips2/jan98/canada2.html.
Havighurst, Robert J., and Thea R. Hilkevitch. 1944. "The Intelligence of Indian Children as Measured by a Performance Scale." *Journal of Abnormal and Social Psychology* 39: 419–433.
Johansen, Bruce E. 2000. "Education—The Nightmare and the Dream: A Shared National Tragedy, a Shared National Disgrace." *Native Americas* 12, no. 4 (Winter): 10–19.
Lowey, Mark. 1999. "Alberta Natives Sue over Residential Schools." *Calgary Herald* (1999): A-1.
McIlroy, Anne. 1998. "Canadians Apologize for Abuse." *Manchester Guardian Weekly* (November 8): 5.
Olson, James S., and Raymond Wilson. 1984. *Native Americans in the Twentieth Century.* Urbana: University of Illinois Press.
Pratt, William Henry. [1964] 1987. *Battlefield and Classroom: Four Decades with the American Indian, 1867–1904.* Edited by Robert M. Utley. Lincoln: University of Nebraska Press.
Royal Commission on Aboriginal Peoples. 1996. Vol. 1, Chapter 10. Available at: http://www.prsp.bc.ca/vol1ch10_files/Vol1%20Ch10.rtf. Accessed February 25, 2003.
Weeks, Philip. 1990. *Farewell My Nation: The American Indian and the United States, 1820–1890.* Wheeling, IL: Harlan Davidson.

Citizenship

Even though citizenship in the United States was not extended to American Indians as a whole by federal statute until the Citizenship Act of 1924, members of many Native tribes and nations had become citizens before that, usually after they accepted the legal terms of assimilation. Citizenship sometimes was part of treaty negotiations, as well as allotment legislation. Some individual American Indians were offered citizenship for service in the U.S. armed forces, even as others were denied the right to vote by some federal courts. An American Indian woman could become a citizen by marrying a man who held citizenship status (but not vice versa). Despite the existence of some open doors, the opportunity of acquiring citizenship via naturalization, as provided

An allotment official and his interpreter grant U.S. citizenship to Oglala Sioux Chief American Horse in 1907. The Indian Citizenship Act of 1924 granted the right of U.S. citizenship to Native Americans who were not already citizens. (Library of Congress)

to immigrants from abroad, was denied to Indians living in the United States.

An offer of citizenship to members of Native nations usually included destruction of their collective government and land base. Treaties in 1855 and 1862 involving the Wyandots (Hurons) and Ottawas, for example, required the Indians to relinquish their collective identity in return for U.S. citizenship and individual land ownership. A series of treaties in the 1860s gave the president and the courts the power to determine when adult male allottees had become sufficiently "intelligent and prudent" to conduct their affairs and interests. The treaty of 1867 with the Potawatomies permitted women who were heads of families or single adult women to become citizens in the same manner as males, and authorized the Tribal Business Committee and the agent to determine the competency of Indians to manage their own affairs (ORACLE, n. d.)

Citizenship "was a move by the federal government to absorb Indians into the mainstream of American life. No doubt Indian participation in World War I accelerated the granting of citizenship to all Indians, but it seems more likely to have been the logical extension and culmination of the assimilation policy" (Nebraska Studies, n.d.). To this day, some Native Americans reject the rights of U.S. citizenship (such as voting) as a sign of colonialism. A few have refused to pay taxes and have found themselves prosecuted for this action by the Internal Revenue Service.

Some Native Americans have contended that citizenship would erode their peoples' distinct status as sovereign nations. In the words of one observer, "United States citizenship was just another way of absorbing us and destroying our customs and our government. How could these Europeans come over and tell us we were citizens in our country? We had

our own citizenship. By its [the Citizenship Act of 1924] provisions all Indians were automatically made United States citizens whether they wanted to be so or not. This was a violation of our sovereignty" (Nebraska Studies, n.d.).

Charles Curtis (1860–1936), of Kansa and Osage heritage, was one of the most prominent advocates of citizenship as a method of assimilation. The first American Indian to do so, Curtis served as a Republican member of the U.S. Senate from 1907 to 1913 and again from 1915 to 1929. Curtis rose to majority leader (1924–1929) and served as Herbert Hoover's vice president (1929–1933). As chairman of the Senate Committee on Indian Affairs in 1924, Curtis sponsored the Indian Citizenship Act.

As allotment and its provisions for citizenship were being legislated, the Supreme Court denied citizenship to Indians who wished to take the policy to its logical conclusion. In 1884, in *Elk v. Wilkins*, Indians were denied the right to vote despite the wording of the recently passed Fourteenth Amendment to the U.S. Constitution. The U.S. Supreme Court held in *Elk v. Wilkins* that an Indian is not made a citizen by the Fourteenth Amendment. This position held even if the Indian is living apart from his nation or band. The court also ruled that acts of Congress do not generally apply to Indians unless they are specifically mentioned.

At issue was the constitutional status of American Indians for purposes of citizenship and voting. The Fourteenth Amendment granted citizenship to "all persons born or naturalized in the United States, and subject to the jurisdiction of the United States." Did American Indians fall under this definition? A federal district court ruled that it did not apply to Indians who had not been "born subject to its jurisdiction—that is, in its power and obedience" (*McKay v. Campbell* 16 Fed. Cas. 161 [1871] [No. 8840]).

For instance, John Elk had been born outside U.S. jurisdiction, but moved to Omaha as an adult and lived what the court described as a "civilized" life. He sought to become a citizen and exercise the right to vote in Omaha elections during 1880. The Supreme Court ruled that the Fifteenth Amendment (which grants the right to vote to all persons regardless of race) did not apply in Elk's case, because he was not born in an area under U.S. jurisdiction. Therefore, Elk was not a citizen within the meaning of the Fourteenth Amendment. The fact that Elk had abandoned his Indian relatives and lifeways did not matter to the court. Elk's citizenship and voting rights were denied because the court held that an affirmative act was required of the United States before an Indian could become a citizen. The Supreme Court's opinion cited a dozen treaties, four court rulings, four laws, and eight opinions of the U.S. attorney general requiring "proof of fitness for civilization" as a precondition of granting Indians citizenship and voting rights.

Six years after John Elk's desire for citizenship was denied, Congress passed the Indian Territory Naturalization Act (26 Stat. 81, 99–100), which allowed any Indian living in Indian Territory to apply for citizenship through the federal courts. The aim of this Act was to break down communal loyalties among Native Americans in Indian Territory as it moved toward statehood as Oklahoma.

Vine Deloria, Jr., commented on *Elk v. Wilkins:* "Thus, while federal courts were busy maintaining the plenary power of Congress over Indians, and classifying Indian tribes as wards of the federal government, and denying an international dimension to Indian political existence, the individual Indians seeking to exercise their constitutional rights were being told that they were, in effect, no more than the children of [foreign] subjects" (Deloria, 1985, 146–147).

Bruce E. Johansen

See also Assimilation; Domestic Dependent Nation; *Elk v. Wilkins;* Indian Civilization Fund Act; Plenary Power; *Standing Bear v. Crook;* Tribal Sovereignty; Trust, Doctrine of.

References and Further Reading
Deloria, Vine, Jr. [1974] 1985. *Behind the Trail of Broken Treaties: An Indian Declaration of Independence.* Austin: University of Texas Press.
Elk v. Wilkins 112 U. S. 94 (1884).
Nebraska Studies. 1900–1924. 1924 Citizenship Act. Available at: http://www.nebraskastudies.org/ 0700/ frameset_reset.[html? http://www .nebraskastudies.org/0700/stories/ 0701_0146.html. Accessed May 16, 2006.
ORACLE. "Strangers in Their Own Land: American Indian Citizenship in the United States. Available at: http://www2.univ-reunion.fr/~ageof/text/74c21e88–344.html. Accessed May 16, 2006.

Demographics, Historical

Historical demography entails the study of fertility and mortality patterns, along with changes in historic populations. Several themes dominate the dis-

cussion of Native American historical demography. These include the demographic collapse of many populations over several centuries following 1492, the establishment of sustained contact between the Old and New Worlds, and the survival and recovery of some Native populations. A number of factors contributed to demographic collapse, including war, slavery, and the introduction of highly contagious diseases, such as smallpox and measles.

Smallpox created such chaos in the Inca Empire that Francisco Pizarro was able to seize an empire as large and populous as Spain and Italy combined with a force of only 168 men (Mann, 2002, 43). By the time imported diseases were done with Native Americans, according to Dobyns, 95 percent of them had died, the worst demographic collapse in recorded human history (Mann, 2002, 43). All across America, "Languages, prayers, hopes, habits, and dreams, entire ways of life hissed away like steam" (Mann, 2002, 46).

Henry Dobyns has estimated that the population of Mexico declined from between 30 and 37.5 million people in 1520 to 1.5 million in 1650, a holocaust of a severity unknown in the Old World (Dobyns, 1966, 395–449). Even if one argues that Dobyns' figures are too high, cutting them almost in half, to 20 million in 1520, would produce a mortality rate in 130 years of 92.5 percent (Driver, 1969, 457).

A second theme in Native American historical demography is cultural and biological mixing, called in Spanish *mestizaje* and in French *mestissage*. This entailed not only biological mixing with peoples from Europe and Africa, but also sociocultural mixing.

A comprehensive overview of Native American historical demography is not possible in this article, but it can introduce the major topics that scholars have discussed and debated in recent years, including research focused on the Native Peoples of the American Southwest, northern Mexico, and the Andean and Rio de la Plata regions of South America, as well as studies of the demography of peoples drawn into missions established by the Franciscans, Jesuits, and Dominicans on the fringes of Spanish America. The sources available for the study of Native American population trends include early conquest accounts, censuses, baptismal and burial registers, government reports, and other types of documents. This entry also examines epidemiology through a discussion of epidemics as well as how demographic patterns among Native Peoples com-

pared to contemporary European populations. It also considers the topic of miscegenation or biological and cultural mixing and passing.

Today a general consensus exists that the Americas sustained large populations when Europeans first established sustained contact after 1492 and that the Native populations experienced drastic declines in numbers after 1492. Instead of engaging in a numbers game, trying to make educated guesstimates of contact population sizes, this entry explores the dynamics of population decline. There is one fundamental assumption made in the model of "virgin soil epidemics" that Native populations in the Americas were more susceptible to epidemics of highly contagious crowd diseases such as smallpox introduced after 1492. This may be an overly simplistic assumption that does not take into consideration other factors related to mortality during epidemics and patterns of morbidity and mortality. An examination of contemporary European demographic patterns calls into question the assumption of high susceptibility and the buildup of immunities to disease. A host of maladies routinely killed as many as 10 to 20 percent of children in Europe, and the individuals lucky enough to survive built up some immunity from their exposure as well as from antibodies acquired from their mothers. However, surviving childhood disease did not mean that adults could not become ill from the same diseases a second time.

Until the acceptance by doctors of the germ theory in the late nineteenth century, there were few effective treatments for the maladies introduced into the New World from the Old World. Medical knowledge had a basis in the ancient Greek humoral theory that posited disease to be caused by an imbalance in the four basic elements: earth, air, water, and fire. According to the humoral theory, a fever is caused by an excess of fire, and the proper treatment is to reduce the fire. This gave rise to bloodletting as a common treatment, which, of course, only weakened the patient by depleting the immunological system. The other prevailing theory for the cause of disease was miasma, which held that clouds of noxious gas floating in the air caused disease. The gas originated from rotting vegetation, rotting corpses, and garbage, among other things. Practical responses to the belief in miasma included the clearing of garbage and drainage of standing water, which could be beneficial. Garbage, for example, attracted rats that could carry fleas. Mosquitoes breed in standing water and carry a variety

of diseases, including yellow fever and malaria. Doctors also made use of what most accurately could be called folk remedies. A 1797 document distributed throughout Spanish California suggested, among other things, to clean the eyes of smallpox victims with water made from rose petals. This treatment first appeared in a fifteenth-century Spanish medical text.

Smallpox was one of the great killers of Native Americans, and two treatments reached the Americas in the eighteenth century. The first was called inoculation by variolation, and it entailed injecting a healthy person with pus from a ripe pustule from a smallpox victim. The expectation was that the individual inoculated would develop a milder infection, and evidence from the period suggests that mortality rates were lower among those inoculated when compared to people naturally infected. At the same time there was considerable resistance to the use of inoculation when introduced in the eighteenth century, primarily because of the fear that inoculation would help spread the contagion. Doctors in Mexico first used inoculation by variolation during a smallpox outbreak in Mexico City in 1779, and Dominican missionaries successfully inoculated Native residents of several missions in Baja California in 1781.

The second smallpox prophylaxis introduced in the eighteenth century was the cowpox vaccine, first described in the late 1790s by English doctor Edward Jenner. Jenner was a country doctor, and he noted that milkmaids did not contract smallpox, which was still a problem in England. Milkmaids inhaled dry cowpox pustules and became infected with cowpox, which is related to smallpox but not fatal to humans. The milkmaids developed antibodies that protected them from smallpox. In 1803, the Spanish government sent a medical team to the Americas to disseminate the cowpox vaccine. The team transported the vaccine on the arms of infected children and maintained the chain of infection from child to child.

How did epidemics spread among Native peoples? Extensive trade networks existed in the Americas prior to the arrival of Europeans, and diseases may have been conducted along them. For example, archaeologists have encountered evidence of trade, including copper bells produced in central Mexico and bird plumes in sites in northern Mexico such as Casas Grandes in Chihuahua, and the native communities of New Mexico. Conversely, turquoise from New Mexico has been discovered in pre-Hispanic sites in central Mexico. When Europeans arrived in

different parts of North America and came into contact with Native populations, disease spread to the Natives as a result of the contacts. Contagion spread from one Native community to another, carried in the bodies of merchants or other travelers. Early accounts of European exploration and colonization report the spread of epidemics in advance of Europeans.

It cannot be assumed that disease spread uniformly among Native populations or that rates of morbidity and mortality were uniform from population to population. A number of factors limited the rates of morbidity and mortality. Maladies such as smallpox and measles spread through contact between people sneezing or in other ways of exchanging body fluids. Contagion spreads in dense populations, but not as easily among dispersed populations, particularly among small bands of hunter-gatherers that migrated in search of food within a clearly defined but often extensive territory. In the sixteenth and early seventeenth centuries, for example, Spaniards explored and conquered the populations living in western Mexico in Sinaloa and Sonora, and up into what today is the southwestern United States, including Arizona and New Mexico. The first Spanish descriptions of the region described sophisticated tribal states based on compact nucleated communities. In some areas, such as northern Sonora and southern Arizona, this settlement pattern gave way to a more dispersed *ranchería* settlement pattern characterized by homesteads dispersed over a large area, usually in a river flood plain. Scholars speculate that the more dispersed settlement pattern was an adaptation resulting from the spread of lethal epidemics in the sixteenth and seventeenth centuries.

Several other factors influenced the impact of epidemics on Native populations. The frequency of epidemics is important, and it is possible to construct tentative epidemic chronologies in some regions of European settlement. For an epidemic to spread among and between populations, there must be enough susceptible individuals not previously exposed to the contagion to maintain the chain of infection. Moreover, pathogens such as smallpox are inefficient in the sense that either they kill the host or the host survives. The pathogen then dies out and the epidemic ends until the next outbreak, which will occur when once again there are enough susceptible hosts to maintain the chain of infection. Generally, a given pathogen finds enough susceptible hosts about once a generation, after a population has

recovered and grown following the previous epidemics. However, if a series of epidemics spread through a population with a greater frequency, the possibility of recovery following the outbreak is diminished.

Useful parallels can be drawn between demographic trends among the Native populations in the Americas and contemporary European populations. Two aspects of demographic patterns in Europe are relevant to a discussion of Native American population trends. The first is the culling of the population by lethal epidemics, such as the Black Death in the fourteenth century that killed perhaps a third of Europe's population and its subsequent outbreaks. The epidemics slowed or temporarily stopped population growth, but, following the epidemic episodes, the population recovered. Early modern Europe was a patriarchic society, and the father generally controlled the lives of his children until such time as he decided to let them marry. Moreover, in rural communities, a son generally could not start a family until he had his own land and could establish economic independence. Mortality crises (mortality at three times the normal rate) often caused a redistribution of wealth and enabled sons to marry at a younger age. European populations rebounded or recovered following epidemics as a result of increased birth rates. Discussions of epidemics in the Americas in the sixteenth and seventeenth centuries focus on reports of horrific mortality, but rarely do they examine whether the Native populations rebounded or recovered following the epidemics.

The second consists of patterns of mortality in nonepidemic years in European populations when maladies such as smallpox and measles became established as endemic maladies that killed as many as 10 to 20 percent of the children every year. Contagion spread and reached epidemic proportions when a large pool of susceptible people had been born since the previous epidemic outbreak. To understand the recovery of larger Native populations, it is necessary to document the patterns of mortality among Native populations in nonepidemic years, when maladies such as smallpox became chronic childhood diseases. Furthermore, it is essential to examine birth rates and the age and gender structure of a population, to show whether sufficient numbers of women of childbearing age survived epidemics to reproduce.

At the same time, other factors also contributed to Native population losses, although all causes for depopulation were interrelated and should not be discussed in isolation. These include war; famine resulting from food shortages and crop losses due to drought, excessive rainfall, frost, locust infestation, and other causes; enslavement; and migration. People died in war, but in the early modern period more casualties resulted from the spread of disease and famine than from actual battlefield losses. Armies on campaign in contemporary Europe lived in filthy conditions and bred disease. The armies then spread disease when they moved from place to place. The same occurred in the Americas. Moreover, armies lived off the land and took food supplies that civilian populations needed to survive. Additionally, armies deliberately destroyed crops to weaken the enemy. This took place, for example, during the Sullivan-Clinton campaign against the Iroquois during the American Revolution. The army systematically destroyed growing crops, and many Iroquois died from starvation during the ensuing winter.

Famine also contributed to mortality, and epidemics frequently occurred in conjunction with it. Some scholars believe that food shortages led to the weakening of the immunological system that then resulted in epidemic outbreaks. However, recent studies have suggested that the relationship between famine and epidemics was the movement of large numbers of people in search of food, who spread disease as they moved from place to place. Studies of historical famines have identified one common phenomenon: the movement of people from the countryside into towns and cities and the discovery of abandoned bodies of famine and disease victims. Priests recorded in burial registers the discovery of the dead on the steps of churches or near cemeteries.

Migration, forced or voluntary, contributed to mortality and population losses as well. The Trail of Tears (the forced relocation of thousands of Cherokee in the late 1830s) is a good example of how mortality contributed to population losses. Causes for mortality during the forced relocation to Oklahoma included accidents, food shortages, and the less than ideal hygienic conditions on the trail. But again the movement of peoples also contributed to the spread of epidemics. The enslavement of Native peoples was common and also contributed to population losses. Slavery removed adults from the population, and the enslavement of women of childbearing age had the greatest consequence. Moreover, the forced movement of people also contributed to the spread of disease.

Did the native populations acquire immunities to smallpox and the other maladies brought to the Americas after 1492? No convincing evidence exists to support this assumption. New insights on this subject come from recent research on historic epidemics in Spanish America that are documented in detail in burial registers and censuses and that recorded the number of deaths or in some instances the actual numbers of victims of contagion during an outbreak. Burial registers exist for Spanish-Americans from the seventeenth century, but records are more complete for the eighteenth century, some two centuries after the Spanish arrived in the Americas. As suggested, the frequency of epidemic outbreaks and the initial size of a population are critical factors in determining epidemic mortality and the short- and long-term consequences of epidemics.

Consider two case studies of eighteenth-century epidemics: one from the Baja California missions established after 1697 in northwestern Mexico and the other from the Jesuit missions of Paraguay. The second example is a bit far afield, but information on patterns of mortality and epidemic mortality is rich and can be applied to understand demographic collapse of Native populations in North America.

Hernan Cortes attempted to colonize Baja California in the mid-1530s, and Spanish colonists and foreign pirates visited the peninsula sporadically over the next 160 years. In 1697, the Jesuits negotiated permission to establish missions at their own expense and in 1697 established the first mission, named Loreto. The Jesuits and later the Franciscans and Dominicans operated missions for about 140 years, and during this period most of the native peoples declined in numbers to virtual biological and cultural extinction. Burial registers and other contemporary sources identify twenty-five epidemics in the missions between 1697 and 1808, a span of 111 years. This works out to an average of an epidemic every 4.4 years. During nonepidemic years there was heavy infant and child mortality in the missions, and generally during epidemics both children and adults died. It was the combination of high infant and child mortality (some 90 percent of children died before reaching age ten) and the frequently recurring lethal epidemics that decimated the Native peoples of Baja California (Jackson, 1981, 347).

A discussion of two of the Baja California missions for which there are complete records from the date of foundation gives a sense of the rapid decline of the native population. For Santa Gertrudis, established in 1751, a 1755 census recorded the population of the mission as 1,586 and as 1,730 seven years later in 1762. This last figure was the highest recorded population for the mission. Over the next four decades the surviving population dropped rapidly. For example, smallpox killed 296 in 1781, and in the following year only 317 survived. In two decades the mission experienced a net decline of some 1,400 people. The numbers continued to drop, and only 137 remained in 1808. A second example is San Fernando, established in 1769 by Franciscan missionary Junipero Serra. In 1775, the population of the mission totaled 1,406, but only 19 remained in 1829 (Jackson, 1981, 370–372).

The Native peoples of Baja California were hunters and gatherers living in small bands. They were fragile populations that could not recover following epidemics because of the frequency and severity of the outbreaks and because of the high mortality among small children. The pool of potential mothers of childbearing age shrank, and each succeeding generation was much smaller than the previous. By the beginning of the twentieth century only two small populations survived in the mountainous north of the peninsula.

The Jesuits established missions among the Guarani in Paraguay and the surrounding areas of Argentina and Brazil after 1610. Unlike the Native peoples of Baja California, the Guarani were sedentary agriculturalists living in clan-based villages, and they moved to the Jesuit missions by the thousands. In 1732, some 141,000 lived on thirty missions, or an average of 4,700 per mission. This was a much larger number than in the Baja California missions. Lethal epidemics spread through the missions, but enough women of childbearing age survived to ensure the reproduction of the population. An analysis of the gender structure shows that the mission populations were generally balanced, with slightly more girls and women than boys and men.

In nonepidemic years the heaviest mortality was among young children, as was the case in contemporary Europe. In 1724, for example, a typical nonepidemic year, 173 young children and 63 adults died at San Lorenzo Martir mission. In 1739, smallpox broke out at the mission, killing 1,026 young children and 1,655 adults in a total population of 4,814. In other words, 55.7 percent of the population died in one year. In 1764, smallpox killed 1,596 Guarani living on the Santa Rosa mission out of a population of 3,292, and during the same epidemic in 1765 1,833 died at the Loreto mission, which had a population of 4,937 prior to the outbreak. These were

extreme examples of mortality during the epidemics; smaller numbers of Guarani died at other missions in the region (Jackson, 2005, 350–359).

In some cases, epidemics continued to ravage Native communities for centuries after first contact with Europeans. The Spanish first colonized Paraguay in 1537, and the Guarani had been exposed to smallpox and other diseases for several hundred years. Yet lethal epidemics continued to kill as many as half of the population of a community. The contagion may have mutated, but the evidence strongly suggests a different pattern. Smallpox struck the missions about once a generation, or approximately every twenty years. Epidemics of smallpox have been documented in 1718, 1738–1740, and 1764–1765. In nonepidemic years, as already noted, more children than adults died, but still large numbers of children survived childhood between the major epidemics. The contagion proved to be lethal among the children born after the previous outbreak, who had not been previously exposed. There is one final point to be made regarding the smallpox epidemics of 1738–1740 and 1764–1765: The mobilization and movement of large numbers of soldiers contributed to the spread of smallpox in both instances (Jackson, 2003, 55–56).

Biological mixing and sociocultural passing, known as miscegenation, also contributed to demographic change following the arrival in the Americas of peoples from the Old World. Recent studies of *mestizaje* and the creation of race/caste categories in Spanish America provide insights that can also be applied to other parts of the Americas. One recent study (Jackson, 1999) compared the race and caste categories on the colonial north Mexican frontier with those in a rural zone in Bolivia dominated by haciendas and corporate indigenous communities. The Spanish caste system created categories that ostensibly delineated degrees of mixture based on the documentation of bloodlines and skin color, but also on the application of sociocultural and economic criteria that shifted over time. Under the caste system the Spanish collapsed all Native American ethnic groups into a single fiscal category of "Indian," based on an obligation to pay tribute and provide labor services. The stereotypical sociocultural and economic criteria used to define Indian status shifted over time and were idiosyncratic. In the Cochabamba region of Bolivia, for example, the Spanish and later the Bolivian government categorized Indians as residents of corporate native communities legally recognized by the Crown. At the same time, residents of those communities could move to the Spanish towns, adopt a European style of dress, learn a little Spanish, and pass as people categorized as being of mixed European and Native ancestry. They also passed from the ranks of tribute payers.

During the nineteenth century, following Bolivian independence, the economy of the Cochabamba region shifted, and in the 1870s the government passed legislation that abolished the corporate Native communities and attempted to force the community residents to take private title to their lands. There was also a growth in the number of smallholders identified by government officials as not being Natives, since the definition of Indian status was linked to residence on corporate Native communities with communal land tenure. As this sociocultural and economic shift occurred, the population defined as being Indian came to be people of mixed ancestry. This change did not include a distinction based on language, since even today Quechua is still the dominant language spoken in the countryside (Jackson, 1999).

A similar creation of a caste system did not occur on the north Mexican frontier, primarily because rigid distinctions between Native and non-Native were not as important. Sacramental registers and censuses did not record or did not consistently record race/caste terms. At the same time the Spanish engaged in the practice of creating new "ethnicities" in an attempt to make order out of the many Native polities and communities that existed in northern Mexico and in what today is the American Southwest. One example is the creation of Apache to identify different bands of Native peoples spread across Arizona, New Mexico, Texas, and neighboring regions. A second example is the creation of an ethnic group called the Nijoras, Natives who in reality were slaves brought into Sonora by the Spaniards from the Colorado River area, ostensibly as war captives who had been ransomed.

Many Native communities, bands, and polities disappeared in the centuries following the arrival of the Europeans, whereas other groups survived, recovered, and experienced population growth after about 1900. A variety of factors help explain survival and later population growth. A key one was improvement in health care and in the development of medicines to combat disease in the late nineteenth and twentieth centuries, as well as the mass inoculation of the non-Native populations in the Americas that brought pathogens such as smallpox

under control. The control of smallpox in the cities in the Americas meant that there were fewer epidemic outbreaks that could spread to the Native populations. Moreover, in the United States and Canada the creation of reservations managed, and mismanaged, by bureaucracies such as the Bureau of Indian Affairs led to public health measures for Native populations. At the same time, the relocation of Native groups to reservations with the sociocultural changes that the bureaucrats attempted to impose created new problems, such as sociocultural disintegration, poverty and marginalization, alcoholism and fetal alcohol syndrome, and high rates of suicide.

Some Native groups survived by incorporating new members to replace those killed in recurring epidemics. This was the practice among the Iroquois, for example. The Iroquois engaged in wars with neighboring groups and incorporated captives into their communities. The introduction of the horse revolutionized the society and culture of Native peoples who previously had lived on the fringes of the Great Plains. The horse made it possible to live full-time on the Great Plains, following the huge buffalo herds; living in a more dispersed and shifting settlement pattern buffered somewhat the spread of epidemics. Larger Native populations suffered declines resulting from disease and the other factors already discussed, but the degree of decline did not reach a threshold at which the drop in the number of women of childbearing age precluded recovery.

In the twentieth century, Native populations grew in the Americas, as did the number of wannabes. As occurred in the United States in 1970 and 1980, changes in the definitions of census categories could greatly expand the number of people categorized as Indian. The 1990 Census reported that 1.8 million people classified themselves as Native American, more than three times as many as the 523,600 reported thirty years earlier. The 1890 U.S. Census reported 228,000 American Indians. The trend continued in the 2000 Census, in which more than 4.1 million people said they were at least partially Native American, an increase of more than 100 percent in ten years, and thirteen times the official figure of about 300,000 a century earlier. Part of the increase was due to an excess of births over deaths among Native Americans. The census figures must be qualified because they rely on self-identification.

Robert H. Jackson

See also Disease, Historic and Contemporary; Spanish Influence.

References and Further Reading

Alchon, Suzanne. 1992. *Native Society and Disease in Colonial Ecuador.* Cambridge, UK, and New York: Cambridge University Press.

Alchon, Suzanne. 2003. *A Pest in the Land: New World Epidemics in a Global Perspective.* Albuquerque: University of New Mexico Press.

Brandao, Jose. 2000. *Your Fyre Shall Burn No More: Iroquois Policy Toward New France and Its Native Allies to 1701 (The Iroquoians and Their World).* Lincoln: University of Nebraska Press.

Cook, Nobel David. 1998. *Born to Die: Disease and New World Conquest, 1492–1650.* Cambridge, UK, and New York: Cambridge University Press.

Cook, Nobel David. 2001. *Secret Judgements of God: Old World Disease in Colonial Spanish America.* Norman: University of Oklahoma Press.

Cook, Sherburne, and Woodrow Borah. 1971–1979. *Essays in Population History.* 3 volumes. Berkeley and Los Angeles: University of California Press.

Denevan, William. 1976. *The Native Population of the Americas in 1492.* Madison: University of Wisconsin Press.

Dobyns, Henry F. 1966. "Estimating Aboriginal American Population." *Current Anthropology* 7: 395–449.

Dobyns, Henry. 1976. *Spanish Colonial Tucson: A Demographic History.* Tucson: University of Arizona Press.

Dobyns, Henry. 1983. *Their Numbers Become Thinned: Native American Population Dynamics in Eastern North America.* Knoxville: University of Tennessee Press.

Driver, Harold E. 1969. *Indians of North America,* 2nd ed. Chicago: University of Chicago Press.

Flinn, Michael. 1981. *The European Demographic System, 1520–1820.* Baltimore, MD: Johns Hopkins University Press.

Jackson, Robert H. 1981. "Epidemic Disease and Indian Depopulation in the Baja California Missions, 1697–1834." *Southern California Quarterly* 63: 308–346.

Jackson, Robert H. 1994. *Indian Demographic Decline: The Missions of Northwestern New Spain, 1687–1840.* Albuquerque: University of New Mexico Press.

Jackson, Robert H. 1999. *Race, Caste, and Status: Indians in Colonial Spanish America.* Albuquerque: University of New Mexico Press.

Jackson, Robert H. 2001. "Una frustrada evangelización: las limitaciones del cambio social, cultural y religioso en los 'Pueblos Errantes' de las misiones del Desierto Central de Baja California y la región de la costa del Golfo de Texas (A Frustrated Evangelization: The Limitations to Social, Cultural and

Religious Change Among the 'Wandering Peoples' of the Missions of the Central Desert of Baja California and the Texas Gulf Coast)." *Fronteras de la Historia* 6: 7–40.

Jackson, Robert H. 2003. "Missoes nas fronteiras da America Espanhola: analise comparativa." *Estudos Ibero-Americanos* 24: 51–78.

Jackson, Robert H. 2004. "Mortality Crises in the Jesuit Missions of Paraguay, 1730–1740." *World History Review* 1: 2–23.

Jackson, Robert H. 2004. "Congregation and Depopulation: Demographic Patterns in the Texas Missions." *Journal of South Texas* 17: 6–38.

Jackson, Robert H. 2005. *Missions and Frontiers of Spanish America: A Comparative Study of the Impact of Environmental, Economic, Political, and Socio-Cultural Variations on the Missions in the Rio de la Plata Region and on the Northern Frontier of New Spain.* Scottsdale, AZ: Pentacle Press.

Jackson, Robert H., with Anne Gardzina. 1999. "Agriculture, Drought, and Chumash Congregation in the California Missions (1782–1834)." *Estudios de Historia Novohispana* 19: 69–90.

Mann, Charles C. 2002. "1491: America Before Columbus Was More Sophisticated and More Populous Than We Have Ever Thought—and a More Livable Place Than Europe." *The Atlantic Monthly* (March): 41–53.

McCaa, Robert. 1995. "Spanish and Nahuatl Views on Smallpox and Demographic Catastrophe in Mexico." *Journal of Interdisciplinary History* 25: 397–431.

Newson, Linda. 1995. *Life and Death in Early Colonial Ecuador.* Norman: University of Oklahoma Press.

Reff, Daniel. 1991. *Disease, Depopulation, and Culture Change in Northwestern New Spain, 1518–1764.* Salt Lake City: University of Utah Press.

Shoemaker, Nancy. 2000. *American Indian Population Recovery in the Twentieth Century.* Albuquerque: University of New Mexico Press.

Stannard, David. 1992. *American Holocaust: The Conquest of the New World.* Oxford and New York: Oxford University Press.

Thornton, Russell. 1990. *American Indian Holocaust and Survival: A Population History Since 1492.* Norman: University of Oklahoma Press.

Trigger, Bruce. 1987 [reprint]. *The Children of Aataentsic: A History of the Huron People to 1660.* Toronto, ON: McGill-Queen's University Press.

White, Richard. 1991. *The Middle Ground: Indians, Empires, and Republics in the Great Lakes Region, 1650–1815.* Cambridge, UK, and New York: Cambridge University Press.

Disease, Historic and Contemporary

When English explorer George Vancouver sailed into Puget Sound in 1793, he met Indian people with pockmarked faces and found human bones and skulls scattered along the beach, the grim reminders of an earlier epidemic. Such scenes were echoed coast to coast in North America during the surge of non-Native exploration and settlement.

Epidemics of smallpox, measles, bubonic plague, influenza, typhus, scarlet fever, and many other European diseases sharply diminished Native American populations and curtailed economic productivity, generating hunger and famine, even before the non-Natives' physical arrival in the New World, often from visiting fishing vessels. As birth rates fell, many survivors allayed their losses with alcoholic beverages, further reducing Native societies' vibrancy and economic productivity. Societies that had been constructed on kinship ties dissolved as large parts of many families were wiped out. Survivors faced the world without family elders' help. The ravages of disease undermined the traditional authority of Native American healers, who found their practices useless against imported pathogens.

Historian Colin Calloway described the widespread impact of epidemics on Native American political, economic, and social institutions:

> The devastating impact of disease cannot be measured only in numerical losses. Epidemics left social and economic chaos in their wake and caused immeasurable spiritual and psychological damage. Killer diseases tore holes in the fabric of Indian societies held together by extensive networks of kinship and reciprocity, disrupted time-honored cycles of hunting, planting, and fishing, discouraged social and ceremonial gatherings, and drained confidence in the old certainties of life and the shamans who mediated with the spirit world (Calloway, 1990, 39).

The arrival of imported pathogens affected Native groups differently, depending on the economic conduct of their lives. Sedentary groups were hit the hardest, while migratory groups (such as the Cheyennes after about 1800), who left their wastes (which drew disease-carrying flies and other insects) behind, suffered less intensely, at least at first. Migratory peoples also left behind water that they may

have contaminated, usually exchanging it for fresh supplies. The Cheyennes were quite conscious of water contamination and always set up camp so that their horses drank and defecated downstream from human occupants. The Cheyennes consciously fought the spread of disease by breaking camp often and scattering into small family groups, so that one infected family would not bring disease to an entire band.

A major epidemic hit present-day Massachusetts in 1616, four years before the landing of the Mayflower at Plymouth Rock. The disease may have been brought ashore by visiting European fishermen, who had been exploiting the rich coastal banks for many years. While the worst of the bubonic plague killed one in three people in Europe, continuing waves of epidemics of other imported diseases all but destroyed many Native societies and economies within a few years of non-Natives' first landfall in a given area. Plagues of various pathogens—smallpox, influenza, measles, and others—took nearly all of the Western Abenakis and at least half the Mohawks. A disease frontier spread across North America about a generation, generally, before non-Native settlers, traders, and miners reached a given area.

The plagues brought to the Americas by contact with the Old World have not ended, even today. The heritage of suffering brought by imported diseases left their mark on Native America well into the twentieth century. For example, between 1988 and 1990, 15 percent of the Yanomami of Brazil, who had only limited contact with people of European descent until this time, died of malaria, influenza, and even the common cold. As late as 1955, the annual Native American death rate from gastrointestinal illnesses was 15.4 per 100,000 among Native Americans, compared to 3.6 in the United States as a whole. The death rate from tuberculosis was 57.9 per 100,000 in 1955, compared to a nationwide average of 8.4. From alcoholism, the rate was at least 60 per 100,000, compared to a national average of 8.1.

During the last half of the twentieth century, some diseases declined dramatically among Native Americans. The death rate from gastrointestinal diseases fell from 15.4 per 100,000 in 1955 to 4.2 in 1983; the national average in 1983 was 2.8. For tuberculosis, the 1983 rate was 3.3 per annual deaths per 100,000, down from 57.9 in 1955; the national rate fell from 8.4 per 100,000 in 1955 to 0.5 in 1983. For alcoholism, the Native American rate of at least 60 per 100,000 in 1955 declined to about 28 in 1983.

Disease and Demography

The question of the number of people who lived in the Americas prior to permanent contact with Europeans has become the subject of a lively debate during the last third of the twentieth century. The debate involves two very different ways of looking at historical and archaeological evidence. One side in the population debate restricts itself to a strict interpretation of the written evidence at hand. Another point of view accepts the probability that observers (usually of European ancestry) recorded only a fraction of the events that actually occurred in the Americas.

The fact that disease was the major cause of Native depopulation is not at issue. Both sides agree on the importance of disease in the depopulation of the Americas to the point at which many European immigrants thought they had come to an empty land that was theirs for the taking. The debate is over the *number* of Native people who died, the size of the economic decline caused by disease, and the magnitude of suffering endured by Native Americans.

Henry F. Dobyns estimates that about 16 million Native Americans lived in North America north of Mesoamerica, the area populated by the Aztecs and other Central American native nations, at the time of Columbus's first voyage (Dobyns, 1983, 42). Since population densities were much greater in Central America and along the spine of the Andes, an estimate of 16 million north of Mesoamerica indicates to Dobyns that 90 to 112 million native people lived in the Americas before the year 1500, making some parts of the New World as densely populated at the time as many fertile areas of Europe and Asia.

One measure of the demographic (and therefore economic) destruction Native Americans have faced during the last five centuries may be gained by comparing Dobyns' estimate of 90 to 112 million in 1492 to contemporary environmental activist Winona LaDuke's calculation of the number of indigenous people alive in 1992—28,264,000, 25 to 30 percent of the precontact total (LaDuke, 1992, 55). Given the magnitude of population loss, one can only begin to imagine the economic consequences on societies in which 80 to 90 percent of the people died within periods ranging from a few years to a century.

Dobyns' estimates of indigenous population at contact represent a radical departure from earlier tallies. The first "systematic" count was compiled during the early twentieth century by James Mooney, who maintained that 1,153,000 people lived in the land area now occupied by the continental United

States at first contact. Mooney calculated the 1907 Native population in the same area at 406,000. Dividing the country into regions, he calculated the percentage loss ranging from 61 percent (in the North Atlantic states) to 93 percent in California.

Defending his precontact population estimates, Dobyns argues that the absence of evidence does not mean the absence of phenomenon, especially where written records are scanty, as in America before or just after permanent European contact. Dobyns maintains that European epidemic diseases invaded a relatively disease-free environment in the Americas with amazing rapidity, first in Mesoamerica (with the Spanish), arriving in Eastern North America along native trade routes long before English and French settlers arrived. The fact that Cartier observed the deaths of fifty natives in the village of Stadacona in 1535 indicates to Dobyns that many more may have died in other villages that Cartier never saw. Because of the lack of evidence, conclusions must be drawn from what little remains, according to Dobyns, who extends his ideas to other continents as well: "Lack of Chinese records of influenza does not necessarily mean that the Chinese did not suffer from influenza; an epidemic could have gone unrecorded, or records of it may not have survived" (Dobyns, 1989, 296).

Critics of Dobyns assert that "there is still little certain knowledge about pre-1500 population levels" and that " . . . Dobyns has been accused of misusing a few scraps of documentary evidence we have in an effort to sustain his argument for widespread 16th-century epidemics" (Snow and Lanphear, 1988, 16). To critics of Dobyns, the fact that fifty natives were recorded as dying at Stadacona means just that: Fifty natives died, no more, no fewer. To Dobyns, however, such arguments "align themselves with the Bandelier-Rosenblatt-Kroeber-Steward group, which minimizes Native American population magnitude and social structural complexity" (Dobyns, 1989, 289).

While Snow and Lanphear maintain that "there were often buffer zones between population concentrations or isolates that would have impeded the spread of diseases" (Snow and Lanphear, 1988, p. 16), Dobyns has replied that the practice of trade, war, diplomacy, and other demographic movements obliterated such "buffer zones" and aided the spread of disease. Snow and Lanphear also assert that the sparseness of Native populations in North America above the Rio Grande impeded the spread of disease, a point of view that does not account for the speed with which smallpox and other infections spread once they reached a particular area.

Dobyns not only denies that buffer zones existed, but maintains that smallpox was only the most virulent of several diseases to devastate New World populations. The others included measles, influenza, bubonic plague, diphtheria, typhus, cholera, and scarlet fever. According to Dobyns, "The frontier of European/Euroamerican settlement in North America was not a zone of interaction between people of European background and vacant land, nor was it a region where initial farm colonization achieved any 'higher' use of the land as measured in human population density. It was actually an interethnic frontier of biological, social, and economic interchange between Native Americans and Europeans and/or Euroamericans" (Dobyns, 1983, 43). The most important point to Snow and Lanphear, however, is "where one puts the burden of proof in this argument, or, for that matter, in any argument of this kind . . . We cannot allow ourselves to be tricked into assuming the burden of disproving assertions for which there is no evidence" (Snow and Lanphear, 1989, 299–300).

Given the evidence, however, even Snow and Lanphear acknowledge that between two-thirds and 98 percent of the Native peoples inhabiting areas of the northeastern United States died in epidemics between roughly 1600 and 1650. The Western Abenakis, for example, declined from 12,000 to 250 (98 percent), the Massachusett (including the Narragansetts) from 44,000 to 6,400 (86 percent), the Mohawk from 8,100 to 2,000 (75 percent), and the Eastern Abenakis from 13,800 to 3,000 (78 percent) (Snow and Lanphear, 1988, 21).

David Henige of the University of Wisconsin/Madison also criticizes Dobyns for "remorseless attention to disease to the exclusion of all else," as the major cause of depopulation among Native peoples. "We might well ask why he does not consider the possible role of such factors as warfare, land exhaustion, climatic pressure, or cultural changes" (Henige, 1989, 306).

Bruce E. Johansen

See also Demographics, Historical.
References and Further Reading:
Ashburn, Percy M. 1947. *The Ranks of Death: A Medical History of the Conquest of America*. New York: Coward-McCann.
Calloway, Colin. 1990. *The Western Abenakis of Vermont, 1600–1800: War, Migration, and the Survival of an Indian People*. Norman: University of Oklahoma Press.

Calloway, Colin. 1997. *New Worlds for All: Indians, Europeans, and the Remaking of Early America.* Baltimore, MD: Johns Hopkins University Press.

Cook, Sherburne F., and Leslie B. Simpson. 1948. "The Population of Central Mexico in the Sixteenth Century." In *Ibero-Americana*, No. 31. Berkeley and Los Angeles: University of California Press.

Denevan, William M., ed. 1976. *The Native American Population of the Americas in 1492.* Madison: University of Wisconsin Press.

Dobyns, Henry. 1976. *Native American Historical Demography: A Critical Bibliography.* Bloomington: Indiana University Press.

Dobyns, Henry F. 1983. *Their Numbers Became Thinned.* 1983. Knoxville: University of Tennessee Press.

Dobyns, Henry F. 1989. "More Methodological Perspectives on Historical Demography." *Ethnohistory* 36, no. 3 (Summer): 285–298.

Henige, David. 1989. "On the Current Devaluation of the Notion of Evidence: A Rejoinder to Dobyns." *Ethnohistory* 36, no. 3 (Summer): 304–307.

LaDuke, Winona. Summer, 1992. "Indigenous Environmental Perspectives: A North American Primer." In *Indigenous Economics: Toward a Natural World Order.* Edited by José Barreiro. *Akwe:kon Journal* 9, no. 2 (Summer): 52–71.

Mooney, James. 1928. *The Aboriginal Population of North America North of Mexico.* Smithsonian Misc. Collections 80(7). Edited by J. R. Swanton. Washington, DC: Smithsonian Institution.

Ramenofsky, Ann F. 1987. *Vectors of Death: The Archeology of European Contact.* Albuquerque: University of New Mexico Press.

Snow, Dean R., and Kim M. Lanphear. 1988. "European Contact and Indian Depopulation in the Northeast: The Timing of the First Epidemics." *Ethnohistory* 35, no. 1 (Winter): 15–33.

Snow, Dean R., and Kim M. Lanphear. 1989. "'More Methodological Perspectives: A Rejoinder to Dobyns." *Ethnohistory* 36, no. 3 (Summer): 299–303.

Stannard, David E. 1992. *American Holocaust: The Conquest of the New World.* New York: Oxford University Press.

Wright, Ronald. 1992. *Stolen Continents: The Americas Through Indian Eyes Since 1492.* Boston: Houghton-Mifflin.

Economic Development

The future of tribal governments and cultural survival relies heavily on economic development. For more than two hundred years, the U.S. federal government has exercised control over Indian economies and resources. This control damaged tribal economies and thwarted efforts at redevelopment. Only since the 1970s has the federal government recognized that the continuing cycle of poverty and social issues in Indian Country can be addressed best by tribal governments.

However, due to past federal land policy, tribal governments lack the traditional tax base on which state and local governments rely. Therefore, tribal governments must rely on economic development for the revenues required to provide strong and effective governments for their citizens. This circumstance obliges the tribal government to act as a business participant more than other governments that possess traditional tax bases such as state and local governments.

Additionally, Native American governments face several obstacles in economic development such as federal involvement, reservation politics, and the perceptions of potential investors on issues such as sovereign immunity. To date, for the majority of Native governments, economic development has mainly consisted of the exploitation of natural resources and gaming (since the passage of the Indian Gaming Regulatory Act). However, many tribes and nations are working on strategies to diversify their economies. These tribes realize that the lack of economic diversity leaves any government extremely vulnerable to the loss of governmental revenues.

A Brief History of Tribal Economies

A brief review of the history of tribal economies leads to an excellent understanding of the origins of the challenges facing tribal economic development. When Europeans first arrived in the area later to be the United States, the Native peoples' social organization and trade rivaled that of Europe. The area contained an estimated 4 to 10 million people. At least 2 million Native Americans lived east of the Mississippi River. The tribal governments of these people exercised all internal and external aspects of sovereignty, including shaping their own economies and taxation.

In the first hundred years following the Europeans' arrival, Native American societies and governments underwent dramatic changes. To a limited extent, European illnesses made their entry into the

John Collier, Indian Affairs Commissioner, with Blackfoot chiefs. (Library of Congress)

continent and began affecting the indigenous population. Access to European trade goods became a key component in war, alliances, and population movements.

The next fifty years brought extreme changes to tribal economies, cultures, and governments. As the European-descended population in North America increased, intercultural commerce flourished between the Europeans and the Native Americans. During this time, Indians became fully integrated into the world economy by trading with European counterparties. Unfortunately for Native Americans, as economic relations increased, their contact with Europeans and the associated European diseases likewise increased. By 1750, the Native American population east of the Mississippi River dropped to approximately 250,000, whereas the European and African population east of the Mississippi River increased from approximately 250,000 in 1700 to 1.25 million in 1750.

In less than fifty years, the forces of new economies, of their impact on the environment, and of new diseases completely reordered the Native American world. The survivors consolidated into the historically known tribes. The massive death toll strained social and governmental institutions. However, regardless of the enormous changes and their weakened status, Native American governments maintained their autonomy and sovereign authority to determine economic and trading policy.

As Native American dependence on European goods increased, the tribes' ability to maintain relations with more than one European power became increasingly imperative. By maintaining their independence and carefully navigating the competing interests of the major European powers, Native Americans often secured better access to European trade goods than their Euro-American neighbors.

Unfortunately for the tribes, their ability to maintain multiple foreign trading relationships was

severely compromised by Britain's defeat of France in the Seven Years War. As the French withdrew from the continent, the British obtained nearly absolute power over European relationships with the tribes. With no other European counterbalance, the British attempted to tightly control trade with the Indians. This trade behavior, combined with several instances of land encroachment, ignited Indian wars against British settlements. To avoid the expense of war, the British Crown issued the Royal Proclamation of October 1763, reserving the lands not duly ceded or purchased from the Indians to the Indians. Although the declaration also asserts a protectorate concept of the British over the Indian tribes, the tribal nations maintained control over their resources and economies. However, on the eve of the American Revolution, the supremacy of one European power had severely eroded tribal control of external economic factors.

After the American Revolution, British control of the external relations of the tribes east of the Mississippi passed to the new American republic. To some extent, the entry of this new power helped restore trading options to Native American tribes. In addition to the new American republic, Britain remained active on the continent and Spain returned to Florida.

Fresh from its victory over the world's greatest power of the time, the American republic made the same mistake as the British approximately twenty years earlier. In the first three years after the treaty ending the American Revolutionary War, the United States executed a series of treaties with Native Americans claiming nearly all of present-day western New York and Pennsylvania and eastern Ohio. Even before the adoption of the U.S. Constitution, the Confederation Congress arranged for the area's development through the Land Ordinance of 1785 and the Northwest Ordinance of 1787.

In July of 1790, the U.S. Congress asserted complete control over all trade with American Indian tribes by passing the Indian Trade and Intercourse Act of 1790. Based on the constitutional authority to regulate commerce with the Indian tribes (known as the Indian Commerce Clause), the act recognized tribal sovereignty and centralized control of relations between the tribes and the states. This centralized control extended to tribal land resources and prohibited land sales to any party other than the U.S. federal government.

Contemporaneous with asserting control over all trade with the Indian tribes, the new American republic launched a military offensive against the Ohio River Valley tribes. After experiencing two crushing defeats, the United States chose diplomacy and treaties over open warfare with the tribes. The new strategy involved an economic component, known as the "civilization" program. The program assumed that shifting Indian economies from a mix of hunting, gathering, and agriculture to the Euro-American small farm economy model would require a much smaller tribal land base and would therefore open more lands to Euro-American settlement.

To implement the program, the U.S. Congress enacted a series of laws between 1790 and 1820, known collectively as the Trade and Intercourse Acts. These laws vested exclusive control of the external relations of tribal economies in the federal government. Federal policy evolved to one of economically leveraging land cessions from the tribes. The United States used the Natives' debt owed to federally licensed traders to leverage land cessions throughout the western frontier. President Thomas Jefferson illustrated this economic policy by explaining to Indiana's territorial governor that the debt of influential Indians beyond their means could ease the way to increased land cessions.

The 1803 Louisiana Purchase ended France's presence in North America and added to the United States a vast area west of the Mississippi River. Thus, the tribes found themselves even further isolated within an ever growing sphere of exclusive American influence. Only Britain and a continually weakening Spain remained to counter American influence.

The American victory in the War of 1812 even further isolated the Native nations and tribes. Britain withdrew to Canada and played only a small part in future North American affairs. In 1820, the Spanish ceded Florida to the United States. With this cession, the last of the Native Americans' potential European allies withdrew from the region. The tribes found themselves surrounded and highly outnumbered by Euro-Americans. Exploiting its newly powerful position, the United States under the leadership of Andrew Jackson imposed a series of treaties (often illegally) that transferred millions of acres by 1820 from a variety of tribes to the United States.

Between 1821 and 1832, the U.S. Supreme Court decided three cases (known as the Marshall Trilogy) that had huge implications for tribal sovereignty, land, and economies. In the 1823 case of *Johnson v. M'Intosh*, the Court addressed the legiti-

macy of Indian land ownership and a tribe's restriction against transferring lands only to the centralized federal government. The Court decided this case attempting to establish consistency in land titles and to create a basis for the national public domain.

Chief Justice John Marshall used the medieval doctrine of discovery to accomplish this goal. Under this doctrine, the "discovering" European nations held ultimate ownership rights to the land, subject to the Indians' "right of occupancy." A discovering power could extinguish this right of occupancy by purchase or conquest. In this instance, Marshall reasoned that the United States was the successor to Great Britain's rights as a discovering nation.

The decision limited the disposition of tribal land only to the federal government. Thus, the alienation of the main tribal economic resources, its land base, was placed completely under federal control. Marshall did, however, recognize an Indian sovereign's control of its land resources while the land remained in tribal possession.

By 1831, in an environment promoting the forced removal of all tribes to areas west of the Mississippi River, the U.S. Supreme Court was forced to define the status of Indian tribes within the U.S. constitutional scheme. In *Cherokee Nation v. Georgia,* the Court recognized tribal sovereignty by finding that, although the Cherokee Nation is a "state" (meaning a government), it was not a "foreign nation." Instead, Chief Justice Marshall created the new concept of "domestic dependent nations." The decision was politically expedient because it allowed the Court to avoid the question of the validity of the Georgia laws over Cherokee territory by ruling that the Cherokee Nation did not have standing under the court rules then in place.

A year later, in *Worcester v. Georgia,* two men used their status as American citizens to bring the issue of Georgia versus Cherokee sovereignty back to the U.S. Supreme Court. The Chief Justice identified only three specific references to tribes in the constitution: (1) war powers, (2) treaty powers, and (3) the regulation of commerce with foreign nations, among the states, and with the Indian tribes. The Court found that the Indian tribes possessed exclusive authority within their territorial boundaries. Concurrently, the Court also found that Cherokee tribal sovereignty existed under the exclusive control of the federal government.

Even victory in the U.S. Supreme Court could not save the Cherokee Nation and most of the other Eastern tribes from forced removal to lands west of the Mississippi. The forced relocations, known as the many Trails of Tears, brought great hardship and the loss of many lives to most American Indian tribes. The Cherokee cases did, however, establish the guiding principles of tribal sovereignty that, although diluted, continue in Indian law today. Further, Indian perseverance and tenacity sustained their sovereign governments against great odds, although tribal economies languished in the face of such chaos.

Within one hundred years of U.S. independence, the organized Indian battle against the American government ended. Relocation and reservation programs added to the increasing isolation and challenges of maintaining and developing tribal economies. Although Indians existed on reservations surrounded by a Euro-American world, they managed to maintain their unique cultures and governments. Disruption in tribal economies and food sources forced many tribes to rely heavily on federal subsidies or payments. This situation left the tribal economy open to interference and control from Washington.

Although the doctrines set forth in the Marshall Trilogy established inherent tribal sovereignty, the Supreme Court also recognized Congress's absolute (or plenary) power in determining the survival of all or a portion of the tribes' sovereignty. Thus, the tribes were subjected to the political whims of a body in which they had no representation.

In 1871, Congress passed an act ending the practice of negotiating treaties with the Indian tribes. By the 1880s, federal policy became one of forced assimilation. In 1885, Congress placed Indians under federal jurisdiction for certain crimes. Beginning with the General Allotment Act of 1887, Congress exercised its plenary power over the next twenty years to break up the large tribal communal landholdings by allotting specified acreage to tribal members and selling "surplus" lands to non-Indians.

By the late 1920s, the American government recognized the assimilation programs as a huge economic and human rights disaster. The allotment program had resulted in the transfer of over two-thirds of Indian lands into non-Indian hands within twenty years. In 1928, 96 percent of Indians earned less than $200 per year. By 1933, 49 percent of Indians living on reservations were landless. With the typical allotment being too small for productive use.

Only 7 percent of Indian land was being used by Indians by 1935. Deprived of their land base and governmental systems, economic conditions remained dismal for Indians. Further, misguided policy and an arrogant, misdirected, inefficient, and inconsistent administration of federal Indian programs exacerbated the problems.

The 1930s brought New Deal reformers led by John Collier. At their urging, Congress passed the Indian Reorganization Act (IRA). The Act was designed to assist tribes in organizing their governments and in developing their economies. The Act intended economic development to reflect the values of the traditional tribal society. It also secured the remnants of the tribal land base by immediately repealing the allotment laws and restoring "surplus" reservation lands to tribal ownership. To strengthen the tribal governmental structure, the IRA (and other associated acts) funded the organization of governments and tribal corporations for select tribes.

By 1940, however, critics of Indian reorganization took control of Congress. Indian appropriations took a nosedive, as critics of the program sought to strangle the reorganization work and as World War II drew away financial and human resources. (Many Indian leaders left to participate in the war.) Collier eventually resigned as critics mounted new and more effective assaults on his person and his administration. Upon his departure, Congress pressured the new bureau leaders to revive assimilation, this time through the termination of the tribal-federal relationship.

By 1953, Congress initiated the termination of tribal governments through a series of laws designed to end the relationship between the federal government and Indian governments and people. In 1954, Congress began the termination of more than a hundred bands and tribes.

Ironically, the termination policy helped reinvigorate the various interests that had begun organizing during the reforms of the 1940s. Protests, combined with the states' reluctance to bear the costs associated with assuming authority over Indian Country, eventually killed the momentum of the termination policy. With the Civil Rights Movement underway, federal policy concerning Indian Country began to shift again in the 1960s. By the early 1970s, congressional reports determined that the termination policies had resulted in yet another round of economic and cultural disaster in Indian Country.

President Lyndon B. Johnson announced the modern federal Indian policy in 1968 in a special address to Congress entitled the "Forgotten Americans." This was the first time a president had devoted a special address to Congress exclusively to Indian affairs. Two years later, President Richard M. Nixon announced the official policy of "self-determination" for tribes. Basically, the president's recommendations to Congress were to (1) reject termination, (2) grant the right to control and operate federal programs to the tribes, (3) restore specific sacred lands, (4) grant the right to control federal education funds and Indian schools to the tribes, and (5) pass legislation to encourage economic development.

In a series of acts passed in the 1970s, Congress began reversing the termination process and instituting the policy of self-determination. The trend has continued with Congress allowing for the expansion of tribal land bases, for greater control of natural resources, for recognition of "inherent sovereign powers," and even for amending the major environmental statutes to recognize "tribes as states."

As the legislative and executive branches embraced self-determination, the U.S. Supreme Court moved from the traditional protector of sovereignty into a role of limiting tribal sovereignty through judicial determination. In 1978, the Court initiated the modern trend of judicial termination of inherent sovereign powers. Since then, a series of cases have slowly chipped away at tribal sovereignty. Specifically, the Court has determined that tribal sovereignty is limited by treaties or statutes and has also lost the powers that are *inconsistent with their status* as domestic dependent nations.

Even in the Supreme Court's latest decision concerning tribal sovereign powers, *United States v. Lara*, the majority preserves its past analysis and restrictions on tribal authority. The case, however, recognizes congressional authority to "relax" the restrictions. The Court notes that such congressional authority may face constitutional challenges if relaxing the restriction interferes with a state's authority or creates due process or equal protection issues.

Inconsistency and rapid changes in federal Indian policy (e.g., from the Indian Reorganization Act in the 1930s to federal termination of tribes in the 1950s) left Indian Country and its economies in chaos. Congress's use of its plenary power to forcibly assimilate tribal members damaged self-

government and often fractionated or destroyed the Native resource base. Administrative policies and inefficiencies squandered Indians' capital and resources. All combined to destroy almost completely tribal economies that had been deteriorating since the Trade and Intercourse Acts first installed federal monopolies on trade with the Indians and promoted indebtedness. Poverty ran rampant in Indian Country. The lack of predictability and stability destroyed the incentive for tribal or nontribal investment in tribal economies.

Since the 1970s, both the executive and administrative branches have embraced a policy of tribal self-determination. Congress has enacted several statutes aimed at reversing the disastrous federal intervention of the last hundred years. Support of these programs appears to be continuing in both the executive and legislative branches.

In contrast to executive and legislative efforts to renew tribal governments, the modern judiciary has turned from the traditional protectors of inherent Indian sovereignty, with absolute deference to Congress's plenary power, to self-appointed arbiters of the survival of inherent tribal sovereignty. The latest Court trend appears to limit all remaining sovereign power to only the members of the tribe, regardless of whether those powers were being exercised within Indian Country. Unfortunately, the Court appears to lack the ability to see the practical application on Indian Country. As a tribe or nation loses its ability to enforce tribal regulations on nonmembers on tribal land, it loses control of its territory. This situation severely compromises the territorial integrity of the tribe. A tribe must increasingly rely on state control over nonmembers to maintain order in its territory. Therefore, the current judicial trend erodes elements of self-government that are important to sustained economic development.

The Economic Situation in Indian Country Today

Indian Country still suffers from widespread poverty. Despite federal programs and philanthropic contributions, sustained economic development has yet to occur. Without sustained economic development, Indian Country will continue to suffer high unemployment, dependence on welfare and other government programs, and social problems including drug and alcohol abuse.

With a huge list of obstacles against them, such as the lack of capital and a well-educated or trained populace/workforce, tribal governments struggle for sustained economic development. Even with these obstacles, most tribal governments remain determined to increase opportunities for the tribe's youth while working to preserve culture. After decades of federal programs designed to demean and destroy the traditional way of life, tribal elders want to restore pride, self-worth, and belonging to the young people. Achieving such goals requires sustained economic success.

To achieve sustained economic growth, Indian tribes must attract investment into Indian Country. When deciding where to place their money, investors compare investment opportunities with opportunities elsewhere in the United States or, to some extent, around the world. Generally, any business considers the risks involved in three fundamental factors when investing in Indian Country (or anywhere): efficiency, predictability, and enforceability. Efficiency is the ability to complete the project effectively in a timely manner. Predictability means that the investment parameters remain constant enough to allow for a return on investment over the life of the project. Enforceability means that the pertinent project contracts can be enforced.

American Indian self-government allows the tribes and nations to best accomplish economic development, whereas decisions made by the federal bureaucracy often do not result in sustained economic development. Tribal control returns the decision-making process to those most affected by the decision's consequences. Thus, tribal sovereignty and self-determination are inextricably linked to sustained economic development and prolonging poverty in Indian Country.

To effectively achieve sustained economic development, tribes must create governmental structures that carefully balance tribal and business needs and that reflect the tribes' cultural foundations. Without such a foundation, the formal tribal government is likely to lack legitimacy and fail to gain respect in the tribal community. A government that lacks legitimacy also lacks the ability to create an environment for economic development.

Even with legitimate government structures, Native tribes and nations must still create attractive business environments. Tribal governments (as with any governments) should establish the appropriate rules for economic development within the tribes'

sphere of influence. The tribal government should set general strategic goals and direction. However, often Native governments become entangled in the day-to-day business decisions to which they are not well suited. Most economically successful tribes have insulated the day-to-day operations from politics. Investors look for protections, such as that of an independent judiciary, that protect them against tribal politicians turning their power into personal gain. The tribal government (like any government) must carefully monitor its position in the business environment.

To attract investment and to create sustained economic development, tribes must have formalized rules and procedures in place. This helps outside investors determine the business environment and increases their comfort level when investing in Indian Country. These formal institutions should include good financial controls and monitoring, record systems, professional personnel standards, and grievance procedures. Further, the tribes need to maintain a good business reputation for their tribal governments, as well as for any of their divisions or corporations.

If done correctly, these formal institutions will create an environment that brings investment into Indian Country. The tribes must create an environment with predictability and continuity, especially in tax and regulatory matters. To attract capital, investors must achieve risk and return profiles similar to (if not better than) non-Indian opportunities. Tribes must also confront the suspicions of business owners who fear that sovereign immunity may be used unfairly in business dealings by tribal governments and entities to gain competitive advantage.

Tribal Economic Development Entities

To achieve sustained economic development and to attract business partners and investors to Indian Country, tribes need a coherent strategy. Tribes must choose a strategy that includes a tribal economic development structure, and they should be able to clearly explain the reasons behind the structure. Randomly choosing, mixing, or changing structures defeats the underlying goals of bringing predictability and consistency for sustained economic development. The potential entities or structures can take two approaches: (1) economic development through the direct participation of the tribal government and (2) economic development through a tribally affiliated corporation.

When a tribe or nation decides to directly participate, it usually creates a division or agency of government under which to pursue economic development. Using this approach, the tribal government directly participates in the day-to-day business decisions.

This type of structure offers the advantage of simplicity. It involves only actions by the tribal government. It is a completely internal process; it requires neither federal bureaucratic involvement nor the development of a tribal corporate code. As an integral part of the tribal government, an economic development division of the tribe also falls within the tribe's sovereign immunity.

A tribe or nation that is directly involved in economic development must also acknowledge the disadvantages. As discussed, the tribes most successful in economic development have insulated economic development from tribal politics. In a direct participation strategy, all staffing, structure, and business decisions are subject to the whims of tribal politics. This situation greatly affects the prospects of predictability and consistency for potential investors, thereby injuring the tribe's chances of sustained economic development.

A Native tribe or nation is well served to make the business environment familiar and comfortable for potential investors. Contracting with a governmental entity is unfamiliar and thus uncomfortable for investors, and many potential investors will be unfamiliar with doing business in Indian Country. Additionally, tribal governments vary widely so that past dealings with a division of another tribe may provide little guidance for investors. Further, though useful to the tribes, a potential business partner is going to be very wary of the tribe's sovereign immunity. The inability of a business partner to enforce contractual obligations greatly detracts from the predictability, consistency, and enforceability required to foster sustained economic development.

However, from a tribal government's perspective, it would be unwise for a Native government to completely waive its sovereign immunity, potentially opening the way for state judicial interference in its governmental business activities. Therefore, every transaction between a tribal economic development division or agency and a business partner would require a limited waiver of sovereign immunity. A long list of limited tribal waivers, however, may slowly erode sovereign immunity, and requir-

ing a continuous use of waivers in each document creates a lingering issue in long-term relationships.

To add consistency, predictability, and familiarity to tribal dealings with potential business partners and investors, tribes have borrowed the concept of corporations from European-American law. The underlying premise of corporate law requires a specific legislative act or constitutional provision granting sovereign authority to create a corporation. Under these basics of corporate law, the tribe may use (a) its inherent sovereign powers to create a corporation within tribal territory, (b) federal sovereign powers in the Constitution's Indian Commerce Clause, or (c) a state's sovereign powers.

Since a corporation requires a statutory or constitutional basis, a tribe must either adopt its own corporate statutes or amend its constitution. Either tribal action constitutes an exercise of inherent tribal authority. Once a tribal statutory or constitutional basis for incorporation exists, the tribe may then charter a corporation pursuant to its sovereign authority.

Using a tribal corporate code to incorporate a tribal development entity, the tribe incurs both advantages and disadvantages. Depending on the tribe's relationship with the Bureau of Indian Affairs, incorporation under a tribal corporate code may be a completely internal process that avoids major federal bureaucratic involvement. The tribal corporation has some degree of separation from the tribal government and associated politics, and an independent board is possible. However, as a creation of tribal statute or resolution, the tribal corporation can still be affected by radical changes in tribal corporate law.

Using a constitutional process to create a tribally chartered corporation can require the approval of the federal bureaucracy. Although time-consuming, any hurdles for constitutional changes place another layer of insulation between the tribal corporation and the tribal government. Any radical changes in the provision authorizing the corporation would also require clearing the same hurdles. In contrast, an easily changed tribal constitution provides little protection against tribal politics that may detrimentally affect predictability and consistency.

Using the federally charted tribal corporation (also known as a Section 17 corporation) also has certain advantages. The tribes are not required to pass any statutes. They simply vote to avail themselves of the provisions of the federal law. The authority for these actions is inherent in the federal government, and congressional statute creates the opportunity. Further, once issued, the termination of the charter requires an act of Congress.

However, using this option requires involving the federal bureaucratic process. The Department of the Interior must approve and issue the corporate charter. In enacting the IRA, Congress recognized that sovereign immunity could put the tribes at a competitive disadvantage. Therefore, it provided for the ability of the secretary of the Interior to waive sovereign immunity for Section 17 corporations. As originally conceived, the federal charter for Section 17 corporations often includes a "sue and be sued" provision.

Using a state-charted corporation may also provide some advantages. Potential business partners and investors find this vehicle the most familiar, and an independent board is possible. However, incorporation under state authority creates tax and sovereign immunity questions.

In any situation, a tribally chartered corporation still falls within the tribe's sovereign immunity, which causes the same concerns among potential business partners as previously discussed. However, in this situation, the tribal government itself never faces waiving sovereign immunity. The corporation can make broad waivers without directly affecting its parent, the tribal government. To avoid confusion and any impact on tribal governments, the tribes should take special care during incorporation to explicitly divest the tribal corporation from the tribal government's authority to waive sovereign immunity. Further, tribes must carefully avoid mixing the authority of the tribal government with that of the tribal corporation.

From an investor's perspective, contracting with a tribal corporate entity is more familiar. Companies are used to contracting with other companies. Also, a board at least somewhat insulated from politics adds consistency and predictability to the relationship.

Conclusion

Native Americans have shown a great deal of tenacity in maintaining their inherent right to self-government. Even in the aftermath of great destruction and upheaval, tribes have managed to re-form inherently sovereign governments from the remnants of scattered peoples in a relatively short period of time. After almost 200 years of federal intervention, these sovereigns survive and at long last are getting the opportunity to determine their own course under the federal government's

program of self-determination. Tribal economic development is crucial to tribes' ability to realize their true potential as sovereigns. Sustained economic development by tribes requires the ability to exercise sovereign rights.

John L. Williams

See also Bureau of Indian Affairs: Establishing the Existence of an Indian Tribe; Columbia River Inter-Tribal Fish Commission; Council of Energy Resource Tribes; Department of Indian Affairs and Northern Development; Domestic Dependent Nation; General Allotment Act (Dawes Act); Indian Gaming Regulatory Act; Indian Reorganization Act; Indian Self-Determination and Education Assistance Act; Land, Identity and Ownership of, Land Rights; National Indian Gaming Commission; Plenary Power; Reservation Economic and Social Conditions; Trade and Intercourse Acts; Tribal Sovereignty.

References and Further Reading

Axtell, James. 1985. *The Invasion Within: The Contest of Cultures in Colonial North America.* New York: Oxford University Press.

Calloway, Colin. 1997. *New Worlds for All: Indians, Europeans, and the Remaking of Early America.* Baltimore, MD: Johns Hopkins University Press.

Center for Educational Technology in Indian America. *American Indian Contents Standards: History.* Available at: www.ldoe.org/cetia/history.htm. Accessed January 29, 2004.

Cherokee Nation v. Georgia 30 U.S. 1 (1831).

Cornell, Stephen. 1988. *Return of the Native: American Indian Political Resurgence.* New York: Oxford University Press.

Hecht, Robert. 1989. *Continents in Collison: The Impact of Europe on North American Indian Societies.* Lanham, MD: University Press of America.

Johnson v. M'Intosh 21 U.S. 543 (1923).

Richter, Daniel. 2001. *Facing East from Indian Country: A Native History of Early America.* Cambridge, MA: Harvard University Press.

Worcester v. Georgia 31 U.S. 515 (1832).

Education

Native American education is not a new idea or even a Euro-American idea. Indians were educated prior to their first contact with Europeans. Just as they had their own cultures, their own governments, and their own histories, Native peoples taught their own young as well. Indian education *by* Indians has always had goals similar to "all societies, to perpetuating family values, language, religion, politics, economies, skills, sciences, and technologies" (Lomawaima, 2002, 422). On the other hand, these features of Native culture were targeted for eradication by European colonizers and form the key element in the acculturative educational initiative imposed on Indians by outsiders.

Indian education has for centuries put the federal government at odds with Native governments, as mainstream values have come into conflict with traditional values. Federal control has been imposed on Indian tribes and nations, as well as on individuals, in an attempt to subjugate and exploit them rather than provide them with a practical, desirable education. In response to this treatment, "students devised strategies to assert independence, express individuality, develop leadership, use Native languages, and undermine federal goals of homogenization and assimilation" (Lomawaima, 2002, 423). Finally, Indians have asserted individual tribal and pan-Indian sovereignty, winning their right to educational self-determination.

Since colonial times, Indian education has involved struggles for educational autonomy where the education of Indian children is concerned. The goal was local control and the implementation of tribal sovereignty in the development of curriculum and in deciding who will govern school boards. Most contemporary Indian education goals concentrate on "effective local control, and locally relevant curriculum, language materials, and pedagogical methods" (Lomawaima, 2002, 424). Since the civil rights movements of the 1960s, there have been many victories in realizing this goal of self-determination and self-empowerment.

Lomawaima explains that, traditionally, Indian education generally "utilize[s] structured and age-or-ability-graded curricula developed by social and ceremonial groups such as kivas (Pueblo), houses (Northwest Coast), kin-defined clans (nearly everywhere), social classes (such as the Yurok Talth) and/or, women's or men's societies" (Lomawaima, 2002, 425). Using specialists, Native educational systems built successive layers of skill and knowledge in various subjects important to the group. Students are often separated or divided into *programs* of "selected groups" and guided in the learning of "selected knowledge." In other words, "higher education is not necessarily open to, or sought out by, everyone" (Lomawaima, 2002, 425).

From the late 1800s through the 1920s, there was little agreement about the goals and methods of Indian education. "Policymakers, professional edu-

A group of Navajo children study English at a public school in 1948. (Bettmann/Corbis)

cators, federal bureaucrats, and interested citizens argued over Indian abilities as they proposed radically different visions of the Indian 'place' in America" (Lomawaima, 2002, 427). Indians were the only interested parties not consulted in this discourse (Lomawaima, 2002, 427). During this era, industrial (vocational) schooling for Indians was intended to coincide with Congress's passing the General Allotment Act of 1887. This act stripped many Indian tribes and nations of their lands, thus forcing them to give up their traditional lifestyles and assimilate. At the same time the Act provided access to this land to the constituents of those who had voted for it. Federal educational initiatives were geared to condition Indians to work individual plots of land while simultaneously eroding the idea of common, tribal property (Lomawaima, 2002, 430).

Brenda Child explains that, while the General Allotment Act (1887) fragmented Indian communities by breaking up tribal landholdings, the boarding schools—especially the schools located off-reservation—destroyed Indian family structure. One can only imagine the profound despair of having lost home, family, livelihood, and important elements of culture. These hardships were compounded by high rates of death and disease suffered by Indians, especially during the height of the era of allotment and the boarding school period. The land remaining in the hands of Indians was not sufficient to sustain their traditional ways of securing their sustenance such as hunting, fishing, and harvesting fruits and wild rice and the maple sap, used for making sugar (Child, 1998, 361). The high death rate created many orphans. Child emphasizes the effects of

the additional pressures of allotment on these orphans. Traditionally, these children would have been adopted within the tribal community—often by extended families—where they were "treated with kindness, and little distinction was made between 'natural' children and those adopted." Due to the unraveling of the community fabric, these children were taken by the federal government to be adopted outside the community (Child, 1998, 366).

While the boarding school policy may have been intended to assimilate Indians into mainstream society, it sometimes had the opposite effect. Many Indian children saw the "boarding school experience" as a means to come into contact with other Indians—building the first foundations of a pan-Indian viewpoint—away from European-American society (Lomawaima, 2002, 436).

Generally, Indian people have been absent from discussions concerning Indian education, which has historically been applied by non-Indians. The results have been devastating to Indian peoples, fragmenting entire cultures. Now, through self-determination initiatives such as tribally controlled community colleges (TCCC), Indians regained control of their own destinies to aid in the reconstruction of their cultures.

Margaret Connell Szasz thoroughly chronicled Indian education from the 1980s through the 1990s. She explains that the Bureau of Indian Affairs (BIA) was given the responsibility for educating Indian children in the late nineteenth century (1977, 1). This responsibility was executed in a variety of venues, including boarding schools and day schools, both off and on the reservations. Conditions at most of these schools were harsh. Boarding schools were overcrowded, and children had insufficient food. Sick children were not cared for properly, resulting in epidemics. Preadolescent students worked "long hours in the shops, the gardens, and the kitchens" (Szasz, 1977, 2) as a means of reducing operating expenses. Discipline was strict, and life was regimented by stern superintendents and their staff. Academics were too basic, coursework was not applicable to reservation life, and the vocational training left most students who have been unable to succeed in an urban environment (Szasz, 1977, 2).

In 1928, the Brookings Institute, an independent group of experts, published the Meriam Report, which included an analysis of the BIA's Education Division's methods and success in educating Indian young people. The report found many problems and provided a myriad of suggested reforms (Szasz, 1977, 1–3). Among the suggestions were to build more day schools on the reservations that would also serve as community centers, to integrate Indian culture into the curriculum of the boarding schools, while making instruction more pertinent to the life needs of students, and to provide salaries for professional educators. Many of the suggestions were implemented during John Collier's tenure as the commissioner of Indian Affairs between 1933 and 1945, but then an era of stagnation ensued for about fifteen years (Szasz, 1977, 3).

The National Congress of American Indians, founded in 1944, saw education as a major priority during the war years, but its priorities turned to fighting termination shortly afterward. Termination was a direct assault on Indian communities in an attempt to dissolve the relationship that had long been established between the Indians and the federal government. Although the fight against termination had been a great distraction from educational issues, it gave many Indians the experience of dealing with federal bureaucracies that later proved necessary in the broader battles for sovereignty in the 1960s (Iverson, 1998, 7). In 1969 the Kennedy Report was released by the U.S. Senate Special Subcommittee on Indian Education, providing new hope for Indian education (Iverson, 1998, 160). The report exposed misappropriations of funds by state public schools that served Indian students and opened the door for a change in policy (Iverson, 1998, 5–6).

In 1961 approximately 800 American Indians met in Chicago for the American Indian Chicago Conference (AICC) in a pan-Indian attempt to address the problems of Native Americans and find solutions by working with the federal government to better help themselves. They produced a forty-nine-page document called the Declaration of Indian Purpose. They proposed to avert the crisis that Indians faced in America at the time, which was mainly the result of abject poverty. Much of this Indian poverty was a direct result of the termination policy of the federal government (Lomawaima, 2002, 131–132).

In recent decades, Native American communities considered some common issues. They want to undo the effects of urban migration's draining of population in Indian communities, as well as the loss of tribal unity and values, by economic rejuvenation and social improvements such as educational advancements. At the same time, the BIA wants to discontinue the use of boarding schools and the old system of day schools by placing Indian children in public schools. According to Peter Iverson, "by 1980

about 80 percent of all Native children attended public schools" (Iverson, 1998, 159). In the mid-1960s through 1970s, off-reservation schools, such as Chiloco in Oklahoma and Phoenix Indian School in Arizona, were in decline as public schools on reservations took their place (Iverson, 1998, 159–160). Into the 1980s these "off-reservation schools attracted a steadily higher percentage of students who had serious problems" (Iverson, 1998, 160).

While Indians fought for control of their education during the 1960s and 1970s, they began to realize significant victories along the way. These victories included increased funding for public schools located on many reservations, "the development of community or contract schools," the founding of tribally controlled community colleges, and a higher enrollment and graduation rate by Indian students in mainstream institutions of higher education (Iverson, 1998, 160).

Another indication of the victories during this period was a shift in government policy, as "from the mid 1960s through the 1970s Congress passed more legislation relating to Indian education [than] it had approved during the prior two centuries" (Iverson, 1998, 160). This new legislation included the Elementary and Secondary Education Act of 1965, which encouraged "community involvement" and also assisted low-income families; the Indian Education Act of 1972; and the Indian Self-Determination and Education Assistance Act of 1975. With this new legislation also came provisions for more control by the United States Office of Education, to reach those Indian students overlooked by the BIA (Iverson, 1998, 160).

The new legislation had been ushered in by the Kennedy Report. The report described the national Indian education policy as "a failure of major proportions," yet it provided no viable solutions to the problems that it pointed out. This lack of solutions on the part of the federal government provided opportunities for Indians to take control of the issue in the form of contract schools (Iverson, 1998, 160). Rough Rock Demonstration School, opened in 1966 on the Navajo reservation in Arizona and was the first contract school, followed by Ramah Navajo High School, also in Arizona, and Busby School on the Northern Cheyenne reservation on Montana (Iverson, 1998, 161).

Another factor that helped to determine the direction of many aspects of Indian education was a large number of newly registered Indian voters. These voters began to influence the composition of public school boards in areas with large Indian student enrollments. By the early 1970s, seventy-eight public school district boards had a majority of Indian board members (Iverson, 1998, 161). Thanks to these initial changes in Indian self-determination, Indian children can now study their own language in the same venue as English, rather than having to "[scrub] toilets with a toothbrush" for speaking their Native languages (Iverson, 1998, 162).

The first Native-controlled community college was the Navajo Community College (NCC), founded in 1968. It shared the facilities with a BIA boarding school at Many Farms, Arizona, while awaiting the completion of its own facilities at Tsaile, Arizona, in 1973. Funding to continue the operation of the school was guaranteed by the Navajo Community College Act of 1971, along with financial support from the Navajo Nation and privately sponsored foundations. In 1997, the school's name was changed from NCC to Diné College, to utilize the Navajos' name for themselves (Iverson, 1998, 162). Also founded in the late 1960s through early 1970s, were the Oglala Lakota College on the Pine Ridge (Sioux) Reservation and Sinte Gleska College on the Rosebud (Sioux) Reservation, both in South Dakota (Iverson, 1998, 162–163). These first institutions provided a basic template for the rest to follow.

One important development that coincided with the founding of many of the TCCCs was a new commitment of non-Indian institutions to the success of Indian students in higher education (Iverson, 1998, 164). Another advantage to Indian (and non-Indian) students that developed during these years was the offering of new Indian studies programs in institutions of higher learning throughout the United States. The programs provided scholarship relevant to the enhancement of Native community colleges and their missions, and stimulated the formation of their teaching cadres as well (Iverson, 1998, 164). With more urban Indians finding a forum for discussions of Native American issues, they saw a need for a national Native-controlled university that would serve the needs of nonreservation Indians.

Deganawidah-Quetzalcoatl University (D-Q U) was cofounded in 1970 by Jack Forbes and other Indian and Chicano scholars (Iverson, 1998, 163). Forbes had advocated such an institution to teach Indians to control their own futures since 1961. The new university was housed in an abandoned military communications facility near Davis, California, under reclamation procedures for "surplus land,"

similar to those invoked unsuccessfully at Alcatraz Island. Department of Health, Education and Welfare officials wanted D-Q moved to the campus of the University of California at Davis, but D-Q refused (Iverson, 1998, 163).

When the Tribally Controlled Community College Act was passed in 1978, D-Q's board members saw an opportunity to gain support and stability, and hopefully end many of the school's financial problems, by becoming an urban TCCC. The decision was made to make the transition and the Chicano board members stepped down, leaving an all-Indian board of trustees. D-Q had already joined the American Indian Higher Education Consortium in 1972 (Iverson, 1998, 163–164).

TCCCs had not yet become the standard for tribal higher education initiatives when Northwest Indian College (NWIC) began as the Lummi Aquatic Training Program in 1969. "[W]ith 18 trainees under the Manpower Development and Training Act (MDTA) and the Economic Development Administration (EDA) funding for the purpose of providing skilled technicians for the new Lummi Aquatic Project [LAP]" (Lummi Archives, 2002, 1). After the first eighteen students completed the program, eight became assistant instructors, eight went on to colleges or universities, and two became full-time employees of the LAP. Sixty-four Lummis enrolled in the second session of the program, of whom forty continued to an advanced program at the LAP (Lummi Archives, 2002, 1).

As the Lummi Nation received requests to train members of other tribes, an intertribal approach became one of the core principles of the program. In 1972, the school—Lummi Indian School of Aquaculture (LISA)—was officially formed. In the first two years of operations, students from twenty-five Native nations and tribes, from across the United States, received certificates of graduation from LISA. These students learned the necessary skills to return to their tribes to help solve "similar water resource development problems" (Lummi Archives, 2002, 2).

The federal funding that made the aquaculture program possible in the beginning was due to "[t]he Democratic sweep of 1960 [which] initiated yet another switch in federal Indian policy" (Boxberger, 1989, 131). In 1961, the Kennedy administration halted the termination process, a policy of the 1950s aimed at relocating Indians into urban centers in an attempt to "terminate" tribalism and reliance on the federal government, by assimilation into mainstream society; the policy had had limited success

and had proved extremely detrimental to most Indian communities and to the individuals who participated. While relocation continued, it was restructured into a program that provided financial aid and vocational training. Until this time, "[g]enerally the relocatees were unskilled and undereducated" (Boxberger, 1989, 130).

Many Lummis who left their reservation during the 1950s and 1960s returned in the 1970s. Their arrival was the result of changes in the commercial fishing opportunities ushered in by court decisions. The Boldt decision of 1974, for example, upheld Indian fishing rights as provided by the Treaty of Point Elliot in 1855 (Boxberger, 1989, 154). This return of tribal members, along with the favorable court decision, did not, however, put an end to the Lummis' legal or economic troubles.

By this time, more than half of the Lummis' reservation land had passed into non-Indian ownership. The Indian gillnet (salmon fishing) fleet was dilapidated, and seasonal unemployment was soaring as high as 80 percent in the Lummi Nation (Boxberger, 1989, 131, 147, 149). By the 1970s, the primary means of subsistence on the Lummis Reservation was welfare (Boxberger, 1989, 150). The state of Washington relentlessly pursued court battles against Indian fishing rights in the Puget Sound area, and state regulators harassed Indian fishermen. With yet another change in federal Indian policy, the Indian Self-Determination and Education Act (1975), signed into law by the Nixon administration, the Lummis found themselves able to receive federal funding for educational and economic development. The Lummi Indian School of Aquaculture was the direct result of this act. These new laws also provided for more Indian control of the salmon resource (Boxberger, 1989, 132).

LISA has been of great importance to the Lummis and other tribes throughout the United States, by providing an opportunity to develop or enhance water use and fisheries. However, the school has never been the commercial success that is so desperately needed on a reservation with few economic resources. There seem to be three reasons for the failure of LISA: First, the bulk of government funding dried up; second, management turnover was so high that the project was mismanaged; third, all of this occurred during a time when the Boldt decision turned the Lummis' attention to catching fish, rather than raising fish. However, it did form the basis for the development of an institution of higher learning by the Lummis and for carrying the concept out as

an intertribal endeavor. Coming out of the turbulence of the court battles, Washington State's application of its interpretation of fishing laws, and the Indians' fish-ins as a means of protesting this application of the law, the founders of LISA/NWIC and its students have traditions steeped in nonconformity and protest, as does D-Q. This student body has become, by all indications, a solid foundation for Native American higher education in the region (Boxberger, 1989, 152–153).

When examining the history of Indian education, one can easily recognize the importance and interdependence of the foundations of activism and the civil rights movements; the creation of new legislation regarding Indian education and self-determination; and the social change that came about as a result of this legislation. This is what created the atmosphere in which the tribally controlled community colleges were born.

As in most social movements, government support, indigenous leadership, public sympathy, and effective mobilization strategies advanced the cause. The effort and reform came at the right historical moment to benefit from the larger reform efforts. Higher education expanded for many Native Americans due to the sociopolitical changes that took place during the 1960s and 1970s. These changes, in turn, had an effect on Native American higher education. They provided more educators and administrators—Indian and non-Indian—who where more aware of Indian issues and the needs of Native Americans. These individuals created the foundations of Native American education—the specialized Native curriculum.

Daniel R. Gibbs

See also American Indian Higher Education Consortium; Assimilation; Boarding Schools, United States and Canada; Bureau of Indian Affairs: Establishing the Existence of an Indian Tribe; Canada, Indian Policies of; Education and Social Control; Indian Reorganization Act; Indian Self-Determination and Education Assistance Act; Language and Language Renewal; National Congress of American Indians; Pan-Indianism; Reservation Economic and Social Conditions; Royal Commission on Aboriginal Peoples; Tribal Colleges; Tribal Sovereignty.

References and Further Reading

Boxberger, Daniel L. 1989. *To Fish in Common: The Ethnohistory of Lummi Indian Salmon Fishing*. Lincoln: University of Nebraska Press.

Boyer, P. 1997. *Tribal Colleges: Shaping the Future of Native America*. Princeton, NJ: Carnegie Foundation for the Advancement of Teaching.

Child, Brenda. 1998. *Boarding School Seasons: American Indian Families, 1900–1940*. Lincoln: University of Nebraska Press.

Iverson, Peter. 1998. *We Are Still Here: American Indians in the Twentieth Century*. Wheeling, IL: Harlan Davidson.

Lomawaima, Tsianina. 2002. "American Indian Education: *By* Indians versus *for* Indians." In *A Companion to American Indian History*. Edited by Philip J. Deloria and Neal Salisbury. Malden, MA: Blackwell Publishing.

Lummi Indian School of Aquaculture. Lummi archives. Available at: http://www.nwic.edu/archive/aquaculture%20project.htm 8/3/2002, 1. Accessed December 26, 2006.

McClanahan, Alexander J., and Hallie L. Bissett. 2002. *Na'eda: Our Friends: A Guide to Alaska Native Corporations, Tribes, Cultures, ANCSA and More*. Anchorage, AK: CIRI Foundation.

Reyhner, Jon. 1988. *Teaching American Indian Students*. Norman: University of Oklahoma Press.

Szasz, Margaret Connell. 1977. *Education and the American Indian: The Road to Self-Determination Since 1928*. Albuquerque: University of New Mexico Press.

Education and Social Control

Federal control of Indian education in the United States began as, and largely has continued to be, a way for the dominant social interests of the U.S. government to control American Indian cultures and prevent their various unique philosophical perspectives from being sustained. Beginning with the earliest treaties in the late 1700s up until the last ones in 1871, the government agreed to provide vocational training in return for land and peace settlements. In truth, the educational provisions were designed to assimilate Indians. In fact, for the most part such education was contracted out to religious groups whose main purpose was to convert Indian people.

After ongoing conflict throughout the 1800s between U.S. troops and American Indians, specifically the nations that did not want to sign treaties or by those reacting to broken treaties, Congress established boarding schools in 1879 as an alternative to shooting Indians. Army officer Richard H. Pratt convinced legislators that it would cost less money to "[k]ill the Indian and save the man" than to use bullets. Children were forced into boarding schools

where all aspects of Indian culture were forbidden. Indian families who would not send their children to the schools were sometimes imprisoned and those on reservations were denied rations.

Federal treaties continued to guide the U.S. inclination to provide education for American Indians, but beginning in 1917 more and more responsibility was transferred to state public schools. In 1928, the Meriam Report, which harshly criticized the boarding schools, enhanced this transfer to the states, although the federal government continued to finance the programs. Education was henceforth administered largely through the newly established Bureau of Indian Affairs, but public schools receiving funds for Indian Education still did not involve Native peoples in the education process and assimilation remained the goal.

The 1965 Elementary and Secondary Education Act, the 1972 Indian Education Act, the 1975 Indian Self-Determination and Education Assistance Act, the 1978 Tribally Controlled Community College Assistance Act, and the 1990 Native American Language Act attempted to reduce school problems, illiteracy and dropout rates in Indian schools, enhance educational opportunities for Indian students, and replace U.S. control of Indian education with more Native-controlled policy and curriculum decisions. Problems continued, however, and in 1998 an executive order entitled, "American Indian and Alaska Native Education" stated a commitment to improve academic performance and reduce dropout rates of the half million or so elementary and secondary Native students who attend state public schools.

Funding for the 1965 Elementary and Secondary Education Act was reauthorized in 1994 as Title IX, and in 2001 funding for the 1972 Indian Education Act was reauthorized as Title VII, Part A, in the No Child Left Behind Act. Both reauthorizations specifically recognize that American Indians have unique educational and culturally relative academic needs, as well as distinct language and cultural needs. Title VII (Indian, Native Hawaiian, and Alaska Native Education) allows for grants to school districts that focus on culturally related activities and Native-specific curriculum content. A stipulation requires that such activities and curriculum must be "consistent with state standards." As a result, the forced assimilation of boarding school approaches to Indian education has, in significant ways, merely been replaced by another, more subtle approach to assimilation goals in that state standards and the process identified by NCLB for implementing compliance to them often contradict the very goals of cultural relevance intended by Title VII.

This more subtle hegemony in modern education may be the most effective method of social control of all those employed against American Indians under the guise of education policy. Indian education systems are still shaped by non-Indian social, cultural, and economic purposes that differ from those of traditional Indian people.

A majority of teachers in Indian schools are non-Indian and those who are Indian have been certified in teaching through teacher education programs that emphasize dominant cultural values. Not only the curriculum, but the form of most education programs for Indian children, ignores the values of various First Nations. For example, learning goals more in line with traditional American Indian philosophies relate to specific roles for men and women in society; to a strong experience of democratic ideals and freedom at an early age; to a concept of authority that does not recognize position but instead honors wisdom or ability; to a teaching style that is indirect; and to learning styles that are about the observation, imitation, and acceptance of responsibility. Aspects of American education that violate indigenous approaches to education are punishment, the concept of a delinquent child, the social stigma emphasizing incompetence, materialism, competition, irrelevant and fragmented curriculum, a deemphasis on creative expression, the absence of spirituality, and alienation from Nature.

A number of American Indian scholars are claiming that "anti-Indianism" is a major challenge to education in America and that it is rampant and largely unrecognized in television programming, in Hollywood films, in popular and academic literature, and in textbooks, radio talk shows, magazines, and newspapers. As the purpose of education for all Americans moves more and more toward the goals of global competition and less and less toward creating good people and a healthy world, the loss of and continual suppression of American Indian cultural assumptions for education continue to be a major concern.

Four Arrows–Don Trent Jacobs

See also Assimilation; Boarding Schools, United States and Canada; Bureau of Indian Affairs: Establishing the Existence of an Indian Tribe; Education; Indian Self-Determination and Educational Assistance Act; Meriam Report.

Reference and Further Reading
Jacobs, Don Trent (Four Arrows). 2006. *Unlearning the Language of Conquest: Scholars Expose the Deceptions of Anti-Indianism in America.* Austin: University of Texas Press.

Environment and Pollution

When most American Indians were assigned reservations late in the nineteenth century, many of the lands given them were assumed to be relatively worthless for economic activities deemed valuable to Anglo-American settlers, whose main interest was agriculture. The reservations were assigned at the dawn of fossil-fueled industrialism, decades before the atomic age—ironically, as it turned out, because areas that appeared so barren to the untrained eye held, underground, a wealth of mineral and metal resources. In particular, Indian reservations in the United States possess a substantial proportion of the uranium and coal within U.S. borders. During the ensuing century and a quarter, the circumstances of industrialization and technical change have made many of these treaty-guaranteed lands very valuable.

According to a Federal Trade Commission (FTC) report distributed in October 1975, an estimated 16 percent of the U.S. uranium reserves that were recoverable at market prices were on reservation lands; this was about two-thirds of the uranium on land under the legal jurisdiction of the U.S. government. There were, at that time, almost four hundred uranium leases on these lands, according to the FTC, and between one million and two million tons of uranium ore a year—about 20 percent of the national total—were being mined from reservation land.

American Indians living within the borders of the United States have therefore developed an intimate relationship over the years with exploiters of resources. Products affecting reservation environments in the United States range from atom bombs to kitty litter. Even a brief summary of environmental issues facing indigenous peoples in the United States reveals a range of problems equal to those of any Third World nation. Native lands repeatedly have become targets for proposals whose sponsors seem to ignore the fact that these lands have human inhabitants. Witness the Inuit (Eskimos) of Point Hope, Alaska, whose land had once been proposed as the site of a new harbor to be created with

Aerial view of the Hanford Nuclear Reservation in Washington, on the banks of the Columbia River. (Roger Ressmeyer/Corbis)

nuclear weapons. The harbor was never created, but the Point Hope Eskimos still found themselves hosting uninvited nuclear waste. Other Alaskan Eskimos have found their reindeer rendered inedible, polluted with a number of heavy metals. Similar problems afflicted the Yakamas, who found themselves unwilling neighbors of the Hanford Nuclear Reservation in Eastern Washington. Residents of geographically diverse communities, from the Akwesasne Mohawk in northern New York State to the Yaquis near the U.S.–Mexico border, suffer from the devastation wrought by dioxin, PCBs, and other pollutants.

Akwesasne:
The Land of Toxic Turtles

Within the living memory of a middle-aged person in the early twenty-first century, Akwesasne (the

Mohawk name for the St. Regis Mohawk reservation that straddles the U.S.–Canadian border in New York State) has become a toxic dumping ground riskier to human health than many urban areas. These environmental circumstances have, in two generations, descended on a people whose whole way of life once was enmeshed with the natural world, a place where the Iroquois origin story says the world took shape on a gigantic turtle's back. In our time, environmental pathologists have found turtles at Akwesasne that qualify as toxic waste.

The Akwesasne reservation was abruptly introduced to industrialism with the coming of the Saint Lawrence Seaway during the middle 1950s. Shortly thereafter, industry began to proliferate around the Mohawks' homeland. A General Motors foundry opened, followed by aluminum plants and steel mills that provided raw materials and parts for the foundry. When Ward Stone, a wildlife pathologist for the New York State Department of Environmental Conservation, began examining animals at Akwesasne in the 1980s, he found that the PCBs, insecticides, and other toxins were escaping from designated dumps. After years of use, the dump sites had leaked, and the toxins had spread into the food chain of human beings and nearly every other species of animal in the area. The Mohawks' traditional economy, based on hunting, fishing, and agriculture, had been literally poisoned out of existence.

While no federal standards exist for PCBs in turtles, the federal standard for edible poultry is three parts per million. The federal standard for edible fish is two parts per million. During the fall of 1987, Stone found a male snapping turtle that contained 3,067 parts per million in its body fat—a thousand times the concentration allowed in a domestic chicken and sixty times the minimum standard for hazardous waste. Contamination was lower in female turtles because they shed some of their own contamination by laying eggs, whereas the males store more of what they ingest. Two years earlier, working in close cooperation with the Mohawks, Stone had found a masked shrew that somehow had managed to survive in spite of a PCB level of 11,522 parts per million in its body, the highest concentration that Stone had ever seen in a living creature, and 250 times the minimum standard to qualify as hazardous waste. Based on these and other samples, Stone declared Akwesasne to be one of the worst PCB-polluted sites in North America. In 1986, pregnant women were advised not to eat fish from the Saint Lawrence, historically the

Mohawks' main source of protein. Until the 1950s, Akwesasne had been home to more than 100 commercial fishermen, and about 120 farmers. By 1990, fewer than ten commercial fishermen and twenty farmers remained.

In March 1990, the Environmental Protection Agency (EPA) released its Superfund cleanup plan for the General Motors foundry. The cleanup was estimated to cost $138 million, making the General Motors dumps near Akwesasne number one on the EPA's "most-wanted" list and also the costliest Superfund cleanup job in the United States. In 1991 the cost was scaled down to $78 million, but the General Motors dumps were still ranked as the country's most expensive toxic cleanup.

"We can't try to meet the challenges with the meager resources we have," said Henry Lickers, a Seneca employed by the Mohawk Council at Akwesasne. Lickers has been a mentor to today's younger environmentalists at Akwesasne. He also has been a leader in the fight against fluoride emissions from the Reynolds plant. "The next ten years will be a cleanup time for us, even without the money," said Lickers (Johansen, 1993, 19).

The destruction of Akwesasne's environment is credited by Lickers with being the catalyst that spawned the Mohawks' deadly battle over high-stakes gambling and smuggling. "A desperation sets in when, year after year, you see the decimation of the philosophical center of your society," he said (Johansen, 1993, 19).

The Mohawks are not alone. Increasingly, restrictive environmental regulations enacted by states and cities are bringing polluters to Native reservations. "Indian tribes across America are grappling with some of the worst of its pollution: uranium tailings, chemical lagoons and illegal dumps. Nowhere has it been more troublesome than at . . . Akwesasne," wrote Rupert Tomsho, a reporter for the *Wall Street Journal* (Tomsho, 1990, 1).

Some attempt has been made to replace contaminated soils in parts of Akwesasne and to dredge some of the Saint Lawrence River. Given the large area that has been polluted and the persistence of the pollutants in the food chain, in 2005 large areas of soil and water remained toxic enough to cause people to refrain from growing food or eating fish caught in local waters. Despite the cleanup efforts, pollution at Akwesasne remains a major health problem. Katsi Cook, a Mohawk midwife who has studied the degree to which mothers' breast milk has been laced with PCBs at Akweswasne, said,

"This means that there may be potential exposure to our future generations. The analysis of Mohawk mother's milk shows that our bodies are, in effect, part of the [General Motors] landfill" (LaDuke, 1994, 45).

The Yaquis and Pesticide Contamination

The Yaquis are an indigenous, farming people who live and work in the environs of the Yaqui Valley in Sonora, Mexico, spanning the border between the United States and Mexico. Beginning after World War II, due to a lack of available water and financing, many Yaquis became unable to support their own farms. Faced with the prospect of starvation, these people were forced to lease their lands to outsiders, mainly corporate farmers, who were heavy users of pesticides, herbicides, and fungicides. The use of these chemicals, usually applied by aerial spraying, by tractor, and by hand, brought widespread contamination of the land, water, and people. As valley farm operations, including irrigation and transport systems, became mechanized, the resulting Green Revolution hastened the further consolidation and corporatization of farming in the region. Farmers in the valley reported planting two crops a year, with pesticides applied as many as forty-five times per crop. Pesticide compounds included multiple organophosphate and organochlorine mixtures, as well as pyrethroids. Between 1959 and 1990, thirty-three different compounds—including DDT, dieldrin, endosulfan, endrin, heptachlor, and parathion-methyl—were used for the control of cotton pests alone. As recently as 1986, 163 different pesticide formulations were sold in the southern region of the state of Sonora. Substances banned in the United States, such as lindane and endrin, were and are readily available to farmers living in the Mexican parts of the valley.

Moreover, pesticide use is widespread and continues throughout the year with little governmental control. Contamination of the resident human population has been documented, with women's breast milk containing concentrations of lindane, heptachlor, benzene hexachloride, aldrin, and endrin all above limits set by the Food and Agricultural Organization of the United Nations for women after one month of lactation (Guillette, Meza, Aquilar, Soto, and Garcia, 1998). During 1990, high levels of multiple pesticides were found in the cord blood of newborns and in the breast milk of valley residents.

(Local children are usually breast-fed, then weaned onto household foods.)

Angel Valencia, a spiritual leader of the Yaqui tribe in the village of Potam, described the effects of these chemicals among valley residents. Valencia spoke as a representative of the Arizona-based Yoemem Tekia Foundation, an affiliate of the International Indian Treaty Council. "I have seen with my own eyes the effects of daily contact with these pesticides—it burns their skin, they lose their fingernails, develop rashes and in some cases they have died as a result of exposure to these poisons. . . . The tragedy of this situation makes me both sad and angry—to think of what has been done to the innocent children who are the future of the Yaqui people. They will not be able to grow and develop, as they deserve to" (Johansen, 2004, 369).

During the 1990s, Elizabeth Guillette, an anthropologist and research scientist at the University of Arizona, studied the impacts of pesticide exposure on Yaqui children. Guillette's studies confirmed the observations of Valencia. In her study, children of the agrarian region were compared to children living in the foothills, where pesticide use is generally avoided. The study selected two groups of four- and five-year-old Yaqui children who resided in the Yaqui Valley of northwestern Mexico. These children shared similar genetic backgrounds, diets, water-mineral contents, cultural patterns, and social behaviors. The major difference was the level of their exposure to pesticides. Guillette adapted a series of motor and cognitive tests into simple games the children could play, including hopping, ball catching, and picture drawing. The study was constructed in this manner to minimize variables that can affect the outcome of a pesticide study on child growth and development. The population had to meet the requirements of similar genetic origin, living conditions, and related cultural and social values and behaviors, all of which are necessary for comparable study and reference groups.

Guillette had assumed that any differences between the two groups would be subtle. Instead, she recalled, "I was shocked. I couldn't believe what was happening" (Luoma, 1999). According to an account by Jon R. Luoma in *Mother Jones,* "The lowland children had much greater difficulty catching a ball or dropping a raisin into a bottle cap—both tests of hand-eye coordination. They showed less physical stamina, too. But the most striking difference came when they were asked to draw pictures of a person. . . . Most of the pictures from the foothill chil-

dren looked like recognizable versions of a person. The pictures from most of the lowland children, on the other hand, were merely random lines, the kind of unintelligible scribbles a toddler might compose. . . . It appeared likely they had suffered some kind of brain damage" (Luoma, 1999).

During a follow-up trip in 1998, two years after her initial visit, Guillette found that both groups of children (who at that time were in primary school) had improved their drawing ability. While the lowland children's drawings looked more like people than before, the foothill children were drawing far more detailed images. The lowland youngsters were still evidencing some motor problems, particularly with balance. "Some of these changes might seem minute, but at the very least we're seeing reduced potential," Guillette said. "And I can't help wondering how much these kinds of chemicals are affecting us all" (Luoma, 1999).

No differences were found in the physical growth patterns of the two groups of children. Functionally, however, Guillette and her colleagues wrote, "The exposed children demonstrated decreases in stamina, gross and fine eye-hand coordination, 30-minute memory, and the ability to draw a person" (1998). Guillette gave children red balloons for the successful completion of tasks. "Well over half of the lesser-exposed children could remember the color in the object, and all remembered they were getting a balloon. Close to 18 percent of the exposed children could not remember anything," and only half could remember they were getting a balloon. "It was quite a contrast," she said (Mann, 2000, C-9).

"Valley children appeared less creative in their play. They roamed the area aimlessly or swam in irrigation canals with minimal group interaction. Some valley children were observed hitting their siblings when they passed by, and they became easily upset or angry with a minor corrective comment by a parent." These aggressive behaviors were not noted in the foothills. "Some valley mothers stressed their own frustration in trying to teach their child how to draw," said Guillette and colleagues (1998).

Guillette said she noticed that exposed Yaqui children would walk by other persons and strike them without apparent provocation. Otherwise, they tended to sit in groups and do nothing. Foothill children, by contrast, were always busy, engaged in group play. "I'd throw the ball to a group of kids. In the valley, one child would get the ball and just play

with it himself," she says. The foothills children played with the ball as a group (Mann, 2000, C-9). Yaqui mothers from the valley also reported more problems getting pregnant and higher rates of miscarriages, stillbirths, neonatal deaths, and premature births.

Concluding her study, Guillette raised a question that summarized the concerns of parents in the lowlands of the pesticide-ridden valley: "Environmental change has placed the children of the agricultural area of the Yaqui valley at a disadvantage for participating in normal childhood activities. Will they remain at risk for functioning as healthy adults?" (Guillette et al., 1998). As if in answer to this question, neurotoxicologist David O. Carpenter of the State University of New York at Albany has said, "I know of no other study that has looked at neurobehavioral impacts—cognition, memory, motor ability—in children exposed to pesticides. The implications here are quite horrendous," he said, "because the magnitude of observed changes is incredible—and may prove irreversible" (Raloff, 1998).

The Point Hope Eskimos: An Atomic Harbor and a Nuclear Dump

On the far northwest coast of Alaska, Inuit (Eskimo) people have, since the 1950s, been resisting plans of the U.S. Atomic Energy Commission (AEC) to demonstrate the "peaceful" uses of atomic energy by blowing open a new harbor at Point Hope with a series of underground atomic blasts. The government shelved the plan, which was called Operation Chariot, in 1962. After that, without telling the Inuit, the federal government turned parts of their homeland into a nuclear dump.

Unknown to local residents, the U.S. government conducted a nuclear experiment in their backyard. It stored forty-three pounds of radioactive soil near Point Hope that came from within a mile of ground zero of a nuclear blast in Nevada. The soil contained strontium 85 and cesium 137 (Badger, 1992, B-5). The strontium typically would have lost all its radioactivity years before its deposit at Point Hope, and the cesium would still have had about half its radioactivity after thirty years, according to government officials. The purpose of the experiment, according to the AEC, was to test the toxicity of radiation in an arctic environment. The dump experiment was carried out by the U.S. Geological Survey under license from the AEC.

The fact that the area was occupied by Native people seemed not to matter to the government. Point Hope, the closest settlement to the dump, is an Inuit village of about 700 people, most of whom make a living as whalers. It is one of the oldest continuously occupied town sites in North America. The Inuit did not learn of the nuclear dump until Dan O'Neill, a researcher at the University of Alaska, made public documents he had found as he researched a book on the aborted plan to create a harbor in the Alaskan coast with nuclear weapons. O'Neill, using the Freedom of Information Act, learned that the nuclear waste had been stored in the area as part of Project Chariot, which was declassified in 1981. According to O'Neill, the nuclear dump was clearly illegal and contained "a thousand times . . . the allowable standard for this kind of nuclear burial" (Grinde and Johansen, 1995, 238–239). The nuclear waste that was buried near Point Hope remained unmarked for thirty years, during which time hunters crossed it to pursue game and caribou migrated through it. Not until September 1992 did the U.S. government admit that it had buried 15,000 tons of radioactive soil at Cape Thompson, twenty-five miles from Point Hope, on the Chukchi Sea in northwestern Alaska. For many years, the Inuit in the area have suffered cancer rates that far exceeded national averages. The government acknowledged that soil in the area contained "trace amounts" of radiation, but denied that its experimental nuclear dump had caused the Inuits' elevated cancer rate. Until the dumps were disclosed during the late 1990s, the Inuit in Port Hope had no clue as to why the incidence of cancer in their village had jumped to 578 per 100,000 within two generations. Some doctors blamed the rise in cancer rates on smoking by the Inuit. In 1997, Dr. Bowerman, chief medical officer of the Borough of Barrow, Alaska, published findings linking the increase in cancer incidence to the burial of nuclear waste near Port Hope (Colomeda, 1998).

"I can't tell you how angry I am that they considered our home to be nothing but a big wasteland," said Jeslie Kaleak, mayor of the North Slope Borough, which governs eight Arctic villages, including Point Hope. "They didn't give a damn about the people who live up here." When Senator Frank Murkowski, Republican of Alaska, visited the village, an elderly woman threw herself at him and shouted, "You have poisoned our land!" (Egan, 1992, A-26). Energy Department spokesman Tom Gerusky acknowledged that the Geological Survey erred in burying the waste but said a person standing on the mound for a year would be exposed to only a small fraction of radiation received in a single cross-country jet flight (Badger, 1992, B-5).

Radiation afflicting the Inuit of this area also may stem from dumping by the former Soviet Union. It is unclear how much radioactivity from above-ground nuclear blasts by the Soviet Union may have drifted into the Arctic, but some U.S. officials have said the amount could be considerable. There is also concern that the Bering and Chukchi Seas are contaminated by radioactivity: Russia has acknowledged that over the last three decades the Soviets dumped old submarines with damaged nuclear reactors and more than 10,000 containers of nuclear waste in the waters of the Far North (Egan, 1992, A-26).

The environmental devastation of remote areas in the Arctic is only one part of social disintegration that is afflicting the Inuit of the far north. In 1960, before widespread energy development on Alaska's North Slope, the suicide rate among Native people there was 13 per 100,000, comparable to averages in the United States as a whole. By 1970, the rate had risen to 25 per 100,000; by 1986, the rate had risen to 67.6 per 100,000. Homicide rates by the middle 1980s were three times the average in the United States as a whole, either 22.9 or 26.6 per 100,000 people, depending on which study was used. Death rates from homicide and suicide reflected rising rates of alcoholism. In the mid-1980s, 79 percent of Native suicide victims had some alcohol in their blood at the time of death. Slightly more than half (54 percent) of the people who committed suicide were legally intoxicated (Grinde and Johansen, 1995, 238–239).

The Yakamas: Hanford's Radioactive Legacy

The Hanford Nuclear Reservation, in eastern Washington State, released very large amounts of irradiated water 30 miles upstream from the Yakama reservation between 1945 and 1989. Due to this decades-long bath of radiation dumped directly into the river system, seafood around the mouth of the Columbia River became poisoned. In the early 1960s, one Hanford employee ate local oysters and set off the plant's radiation alarm when he returned to work the following day (Weaver, 1996, 49). An investigation revealed that the day before he had eaten a

can of oyster stew contaminated with radioactive zinc. The oysters had been harvested in Willapa Bay, along the Pacific Coast in Washington State, 25 miles north of Astoria (Schneider, 1990, A-9).

The 560-square-mile Hanford Nuclear Reservation was established during 1943 on lands traditionally used for hunting, fishing, and gathering by the Yakamas and Umatillas. The same area is adjacent to the homeland of the Nez Percé. The Hanford facility produced the plutonium used in the atomic bombs dropped on Hiroshima and Nagasaki. Thus, releases of radioactive materials have been contaminating these peoples, as well as the Coeur d'Alene, Spokane, Colville, Kootenai, and Warm Springs Tribes for many years. Unaware of the contamination for years, indigenous people collected berries near the Columbia, hunted for eels in its tributaries, and took salmon from its waters. In 1986, after disclosure that radiation was secretly released into the air and water from 1944 until January 1971 (when the last of the eight reactors was closed), Yakama leaders were among the first to call for a thorough study of the danger.

For nearly thirty years, ending in 1971, eight of the nine nuclear reactors at the Hanford complex were cooled by water from the Columbia River. Millions of gallons of water, pumped directly through the reactor cores, picked up large amounts of nuclear material, making the Columbia downstream the most radioactive river in the world, according to state and federal authorities (Schneider, 1990, A-9). In July 1990, a federal panel said some infants and children in the 1940s absorbed enough radioactive iodine in their thyroid glands to destroy the gland and cause an array of thyroid-related diseases. Although Hanford has stopped producing plutonium, recently released documents indicate that radioactive materials leaking from storage tanks there have continued to contaminate groundwater in the area. *New York Times* reporter Keith Schneider described the Columbia below the Hanford Reservation: "Dammed in the 1950's below Hanford and developed by industrial companies, the river's water is green and gray now. Salmon runs are much smaller than they were before World War II, and Johnny Jackson, a 59-year-old fisherman . . . , said some fish he catches were marred by deep, infected welts and growths. . . . Documents declassified beginning in 1986 noted that 'radiation spread to the river's bacteria, algae, mussels, fish, birds and the water used for both irrigation and drinking'" (Schneider, 1990, A-9).

In 1954, the radiation situation at Hanford was reviewed in secret meetings held at the Washington, DC headquarters of the Atomic Energy Commission, which operated the plant. Lewis L. Strauss, the commission's chairman, flew to Hanford that summer and was told that "levels of radioactivity in some fish in the Columbia River, particularly whitefish, were so high that officials were considering closing sport fishing downstream" (Schneider, 1990, A-9). Ducks, geese, and crops irrigated with Columbia River water also were said to pose a potential health threat.

The public was never alerted. In a memorandum prepared on August 19, 1954, Dr. Parker urged the government to keep the problem secret because the radiation levels were still within safety guidelines and closing sport fishing would compel the plant to discuss the issue publicly and compromise secrecy. "The public relations impact would be severe," he wrote (Schneider, 1990, A-9).

An effort to compensate victims of Hanford's radioactivity has largely stalled in the courts, as government committees debate the definition of toxicity and whether residents in the area were exposed to enough radioactivity (absent other factors) to provoke a large spectrum of debilitating ailments (including thyroid disease, cancers, miscarriages and other reproductive disorders) that many local people associate with releases of radioactivity from the Hanford Reservation. One study, the Hanford Environmental Dose Reconstruction (HEDR), produced results that were inconclusive enough to prevent any significant movement toward compensation for the Yakamas and other "downwinders." Many of the victims have complained that the study required them to remember after roughly fifty years the food they ate, its sources, and a variety of other detailed lifestyle factors. In the meantime, the Department of Energy under the George W. Bush administration has drastically cut cleanup funds for the Hanford site, slowing decontamination in the area.

Bruce E. Johansen

See also Disease, Historic and Contemporary; Hazardous Waste; Uranium Mining; Ward Valley, Hazardous Waste Controversy.

References and Further Reading
Badger, T. A. 1992. "Villagers Learning a Frightening Secret: U.S. Reveals That It Has Buried Radioactive Soil Near Alaska Town 30 Years Ago. Residents Fear That Atomic Testing May Have Damaged the Food Chain." *Los Angeles Times* (December 20): B-5.

Churchill, Ward, and Winona LaDuke. 1986. "Native America: The Political Economy of Radioactive Colonialism." *The Insurgent Sociologist* 13, no. 3 (Spring): 51–84.

Colomeda, Lori A. (Salish Kootenai College, Pablo Montana) 1998. "Indigenous Health." Speech delivered in Brisbane [Australia] on September 9. Available at: http://www.ldb .org/vl/ai /lori_b98.htm. Accessed December 30, 2006.

Egan, Timothy. 1992. "Eskimos Learn They've Been Living Amid Secret Pits of Radioactive Soil." *New York Times* (December 6): A-26.

Eichstaedt, Peter. 1995. *If You Poison Us: Uranium and American Indians.* Santa Fe, NM: Red Crane Books.

Gedicks, Al. 1993. *The New Resource Wars: Native and Environmental Struggles Against Multinational Corporations.* Boston: South End Press.

Grinde, Donald A., Jr., and Bruce E. Johansen. 1995. *Ecocide of Native America: Environmental Destruction of Indian Lands and Peoples.* Santa Fe, NM: Clear Light Publishers.

Guillette, Elizabeth A., Maria Mercedes Meza, Maria Guadalupe Aquilar, Alma Delia Soto, and Idalia Enedina Garcia. 1998. "An Anthropological Approach to the Evaluation of Preschool Children Exposed to Pesticides in Mexico." *Environmental Health Perspectives* 106 (June): 6. Available at: http://www.anarac.com /elizabeth_guillette.htm.

Johansen, Bruce E. 1993. *Life and Death in Mohawk Country.* Golden, CO: North American Press/Fulcrum.

Johansen, Bruce E. 2004. *Indigenous Peoples and Environmental Issues: An Encyclopedia.* Westport, CT: Greenwood Press.

Johansen, Bruce E., and Roberto Maestas. 1979. *Wasi'chu: The Continuing Indian Wars.* New York: Monthly Review Press.

LaDuke, Winona. 1994. "Breastmilk, P.C.B.s, and Motherhood: An Interview with Katsi Cook, Mohawk." *Cultural Survival Quarterly* 17, no. 4 (Winter): 43–45.

Lickers, Henry. 1995. "Guest Essay: The Message Returns." *Akwesasne Notes* New Series 1, no. 1 (Spring): 10–11.

Luoma, Jon R. 1999. "System Failure: The Chemical Revolution Has Ushered in a World of Changes. Many of Them, It's Becoming Clear, Are in Our Bodies." *Mother Jones.* Available at: http://www.motherjones.com/mother_jones /JA99/endocrine/html.

Mann, Judy. 2000. "A Cautionary Tale About Pesticides." *Washington Post* (June 2): C-9.

Schneider, Keith. 1990. "Washington Nuclear Plant Poses Risk for Indians." *New York Times* (September 3): A-9.

Tomsho, Rupert. 1990. "Reservations Bear the Brunt of New Pollution." *Wall Street Journal* (November 29): 1.

"Uranium/Nuclear Issues and Native Communities." 2001. Indigenous Environmental Network. Available at: http://www.ienearth.org/nuciss.html. Accessed December 30, 2006.

Weaver, Jace, ed. 1996. *Defending Mother Earth: Native American Perspectives on Environmental Justice.* Maryknoll, NY: Maryknoll.

Gambling

Since Congress enacted the Indian Gaming Regulatory Act (IGRA) in 1988, Indian gaming has grown tremendously. By 2003, casinos and bingo halls owned by federally recognized Indian communities amassed $17 billion in revenue (Light and Rand, 2005, 7). Indian communities with successful operations have used gaming revenues to fund community services such as police and fire protection, education, health and elder care, and even language revitalization programs as well as direct payments to community members. Gaming has offered sorely needed job opportunities to both Indians and non-Indians, and some communities have gained political leverage on the local, state, and even national levels.

However, not all Indian communities own casinos, and many gaming communities earn little or no profit from their operations. The relative success of Indian casinos depends heavily on location, and the population of a given community greatly affects the actual or potential impact of gaming revenue. Despite this reality, many Americans perceive Indian gaming as a windfall for all American Indians, and despite the fact that Indian gaming accounts for only less than one-quarter of national revenues from gambling (Light and Rand, 2005, 7), some Americans view Indian gaming as an unfair economic advantage given to Indians.

These misperceptions stem partially from a popular focus on a few very successful Indian casinos. In particular, the Mashantucket Pequots of Connecticut have garnered a great deal of negative attention. The Pequots, who earned federal recognition in 1983, own Foxwoods Resort Casino, the largest casino in the world. This unprecedented success by a newly recognized community has attracted vehement critics. Law student Jeff Benedict attacks the Mashantucket Pequot tribe in his book *Without Reservation,*

The Foxwoods Resort Casino in Connecticut is the largest gaming facility in the world. Since Congress approved gaming on Indian grounds, casinos and bingo halls owned by federally recognized Indian communities earned $17 billion in revenue by 2003. (Dave G. Houser/Corbis)

contending that tribal members are imposters claiming Pequot identity only to take advantage of Indian gaming. Kim Isaac Eisler's *Revenge of the Pequots* makes similar claims. Although even though Pequot leaders and scholars do not take these accusations seriously, the books have sold well and have resonated with non-Indians who view Indian identity racially.

The media has often reinforced these negative perceptions. Popular television shows such as *Family Guy, King of the Hill, Malcolm in the Middle, The Simpsons, Sopranos,* and *South Park* all have broadcast episodes about Indian gaming, and many of these sitcoms have suggested that anyone claiming to be an American Indian can open a casino. Popular national newspapers and magazines, such as the *New York Times* and *Time,* have also featured articles about Indian gaming. *Time* featured a two-part exposé in 2002 that attacked Indian gaming in part for not providing economic uplift to all Indians, a common criticism. However, only federally recognized communities are eligible to open gaming facil-

ities, and profits from casinos go to the individual communities, which are separate and sovereign entities. This sovereignty forms the legal basis for Indian gaming.

Because Indian nations existed before the United States of America or even European colonization, they have inherent sovereignty that was reinforced by early treaties, which recognized them as foreign powers, but the courts began to redefine and limit this sovereignty in the nineteenth century. Three decisions decided by the Supreme Court under Chief Justice John Marshall, known as the Marshall Trilogy, set the boundaries between federal, state, and tribal government authority. First, in *Johnson v. McIntosh,* the court limited tribal sovereignty by deciding that the federal government owned tribal lands by virtue of discovery and that tribes themselves enjoyed only the rights of occupancy, meaning Indian communities could sell land only with the permission of the federal government. Second, in *Cherokee Nation v. Georgia,* the court defined Indian nations as domestic dependent nations,

rather than foreign powers, and described Indian communities as wards of the federal government. Finally, in 1832, the court ruled in *Worcester v. Georgia* that states had no jurisdiction on reservations unless expressly granted by Congress. This decision effectively limited the role of states in the affairs of federally recognized Indian communities but also endorsed the supremacy of Congressional power in Indian Country.

Using this power, Congress delegated some power over reservations to states in 1953. During the 1950s, federal Indian policy returned to an emphasis on assimilation. This new emphasis, combined with deepened concern for fiscal responsibility under the Eisenhower administration, led Congress to work toward ending the federal government's responsibility to American Indians and abolishing the Bureau of Indian Affairs. This effort, known as termination, sought to bring Indian communities under state jurisdiction and make them subject to the same laws and entitled to the same privileges as other citizens. As part of this effort to end the trust relationship between Indian communities and the federal government, Congress passed Public Law 83–280, which allowed individual states to accept criminal jurisdiction over Indians within their borders without Indian consent. Although federal officials repudiated termination in the 1970s, the states that accepted criminal jurisdiction over Indians through PL280 retained this power even after the termination era ended. These states would play a key role in the evolution of Indian gaming.

Paralleling state efforts to use legalized gambling to raise revenues through state lotteries, a number of Indian communities turned to gaming to raise much-needed revenue in the 1970s. The federal government under Ronald Reagan further encouraged this development in the 1980s as it reduced funding for Indian programs and asked Indian leaders to focus on economic development on reservations. Indian gaming emerged as an issue when a number of communities opened bingo halls with payouts that exceeded the limits established by the states in which they were located.

In response, local officials threatened to raid these establishments, resulting in federal court cases to determine jurisdiction on the reservations. The most important decisions resulting from these cases originated in states with criminal jurisdiction on tribal lands granted by Congress through PL280. The Seminole tribe of Florida began offering high-stakes bingo in the 1970s, resulting in threats by the Broward County Sheriff's Department to make arrests. The Seminoles received a court injunction, and a federal court case ensued. In *Seminole v. Butterfield*, the federal district court decided the Seminole operation was legal despite the state of Florida's criminal jurisdiction on the reservation. The court concluded that Florida law limited only gambling and was therefore regulatory rather than criminal. Consequently, even a PL280 state such as Florida could not interfere with an Indian gaming operation within its borders.

Despite this victory, state and county officials continued to challenge the legality of Indian gaming. In California, another PL280 state, several communities opened bingo parlors and card rooms with pots exceeding state limits in the early 1980s. The Barona Group of the Capitan Grande Band of Mission Indians opened their own bingo parlor on their reservation in San Diego County, encountering the same local reaction as the Seminoles. In the resulting *Barona* [*Barona v. Duffy*, 694 F. 2d 1185 (1982)] decision, the federal court upheld the earlier *Seminole* decision, reinforcing the legality of Indian gaming. In 1980, the Cabazon Band of Mission Indians opened a casino, and the city of Indio raided the establishment just three days after its opening. After a legal victory in 1981, the Cabazon opened the Bingo Palace in 1983, and, despite numerous court decisions allowing Indian gaming, the Riverside County Sheriff's Department raided the facility soon after the opening. In 1987, Cabazon litigation resulted in a Supreme Court decision upholding the right of federally recognized communities to offer gambling if state law allowed any form of gambling. Since only Utah and Hawaii allowed no form of legal gambling, the *Cabazon* decision effectively opened the door to gambling for most federally recognized Indian communities.

The decision also forced Congress to pass legislation to regulate Indian gaming. In response to earlier court decisions, Congressman Morris Udall proposed legislation to regulate Indian gaming in the early 1980s, but, until the *Cabazon* decision, the legislation had insufficient support. After the decision, Congress passed the IGRA. The law created a new federal agency, the National Indian Gaming Commission (NIGC), to regulate Indian gaming. It also established three categories of Indian gaming, each regulated differently. Congress defined traditional social gambling as Class I gaming and allowed Indian communities to regulate it. They labeled bingo, lotto, pull tabs, punch boards, tip jars, instant

bingo, and nonbanked card games as Class II gaming and tasked the newly created NIGC with its regulation. Finally, Congress designated all other games Class III. Class III gaming required a compact between the American Indian community and the state approved by the Department of Interior.

The compact process became the most contentious part of the IGRA because it extended state jurisdiction over all Indian communities with Class III gaming. Senator Harry Reid of Nevada, the architect of the compact provision, had opposed legislation to regulate Indian gaming before the *Cabazon* decision made the growth of these businesses inevitable, and, even after passage of the IGRA, Reid still opposed gambling as a means of economic development for indigenous people. Despite this opposition, Reid insisted that the compact provision for casino gambling balanced the interests of gaming communities and the states and honored tribal sovereignty. However, many critics of the IGRA viewed the compact requirement as an assault on tribal sovereignty since it extended the role of the states in Indian affairs even in states that had no previous role, effectively extending PL280 in the area of gambling.

Critics also have pointed to a number of problematic omissions in the IGRA. For example, the IGRA did not designate which state officials were responsible for negotiating compacts with Indian communities, contributing to confusion on the part of communities forced to deal with multiple branches of state government. Congress also failed to adequately address the possibility of off-reservation casinos. In 1987, the Bureau of Indian Affairs pursued a prohibition on Indian communities acquiring off-reservation land for gaming but retreated when faced with indigenous opposition; however, the IGRA did limit gaming on land acquired after October 17, 1988, providing for seven circumstances that would allow gaming on newly acquired trust lands. Of the seven circumstances, the provision allowing gaming on new trust lands with the governor of the state's consent proved the most controversial. Many Indian communities opposed this provision because it eroded tribal sovereignty, while state legislatures opposed it because it allowed the governor to act unilaterally. The Siletz tribe of Oregon challenged this provision, but it was upheld. However, the Louisiana legislature successfully blocked a compact for the Jena Band of Choctaw on newly acquired land unilaterally approved by the state's governor.

While these omissions in the IGRA proved problematic, one portion of the law ultimately proved unconstitutional. The provisions for tribal–state compacts required states to negotiate in good faith and granted Indian communities the right to sue states when they did not. Critics of the law argued immediately that this solution to stalled negotiations violated the states' Eleventh Amendment immunity from lawsuits. These critics proved correct when the Supreme Court heard arguments concerning this provision in 1996. In 1991, the Seminole tribe sued the state of Florida and its governor, alleging that the state refused to negotiate a compact for Class III gaming. The state called for a dismissal of the case based on their sovereign immunity. In *Seminole Tribe of Florida v. Florida,* the court broadly defined Eleventh Amendment sovereign immunity for states, deciding that Indian communities could bring federal suits against the states only if the state consented to being sued. This decision gave states an unfair advantage in compact negotiations not intended by Congress, further straining the notion that the required negotiations with the state were between two equal sovereigns.

Despite this decision limiting Indian gaming, many non-Indians believed it was growing uncontrollably, and some states have sought to limit this growth. In Connecticut, the state legislature proposed a number of bills aimed at curtailing casino gambling. One proposal suggested that all Indian communities without federal recognition be stripped of state recognition thereby destroying any hope for receiving federal recognition with its accompanying right to offer gaming. In Arkansas, a bill to grant state recognition to the Northern Cherokee included a few caveats. The recognition would only apply to arts and crafts and scholarships, not to smoke shops or gaming of any kind, and the recognition would grant no rights not enumerated in the state constitution. Certainly, the merit of claims for recognition was not the primary concern in these states. These specific measures reflect a new concern of both state governments and many non-Indians that potential gaming profits motivate many attempts to gain federal recognition. Unfortunately, this concern affects the way many people view all efforts to gain federal recognition, even when the community began seeking recognition before the IGRA.

Other states made even greater efforts to resist the expansion of Indian gaming. In Arizona, both United States Attorney Steve McNamee and State

Attorney General Bob Corbin initially voiced hopes that the IGRA could be used to stop the Fort McDowell tribe and other Arizona tribes from expanding multimillion-dollar gambling operations, and Arizona Governor Rose Mofford failed to reply to requests from six Indian communities to begin compact negotiations, leaving these communities in legal limbo. This refusal to negotiate led to a suit by the Yavapai-Prescott Indian tribe in 1991, but, before a decision in favor of American Indian interests the next year, U.S. marshals and agents of the FBI raided gaming operations in five separate Indian communities to end the use of gambling machines the federal government deemed illegal without a tribal–state compact. Agents executed all but one of these raids without resistance, but at Fort McDowell's Bája Entertainment Center, community members created a human chain and roadblock, preventing FBI agents from leaving with seized gambling machines. The standoff at Fort McDowell led Arizona Governor Fife Symington to go to the reservation and negotiate with community president Clinton Pattea. The two men agreed to a ten-day cooling-off period, and compact negotiations soon followed. Four communities negotiated compacts, but the White Mountain Apache, Tohono O'odham, and Pascua Yaqui demanded 2,500 gaming devices and twenty tables for banked card games, considerably more than the state offered.

Failure to reach an agreement forced negotiations into mediation, which former Chief Justice of the Arizona Supreme Court Frank Gordon decided in favor of the tribes. Governor Symington responded by calling for a special legislative session on gaming a week after Gordon's decision, hoping to outlaw all casino gambling in the state, thereby freeing the state to shut down similar operations on Indian reservations. Trying to resolve this impasse without direct federal intervention, Secretary of the Interior Bruce Babbitt proposed a compromise, and eight Indian communities signed compacts with the state based on Babbitt's proposal.

Despite successful resolution of this issue, Governor Symington tried to block the expansion of Indian gaming again in 1995 when the Salt River Pima-Maricopa Indian Community sought a compact for Class III gaming. Encouraged by *Rumsey v. Wilson,* a Ninth Circuit Court of Appeals case that decided states need not negotiate with Indian communities for any form of gambling not legal in the state, Symington refused to negotiate a compact, resulting in a suit by the Salt River Community against the state.

Ultimately, the court dismissed the Salt River claim when the Supreme Court ruled in *Seminole Tribe of Florida v. Florida* that Indian communities could not sue states without the state's consent. However, the Salt River Community simultaneously pushed a fairness initiative that compelled the governor to sign a standard compact with any federally recognized tribe requesting an agreement. Through community efforts, the initiative became Proposition 201, which Arizona voters approved in 1996, leading to a compact for the Salt River Community in 1998.

After 1998, compact negotiations ceased to be an issue in Arizona, but the Department of Gaming, the state agency charged with the regulation of Indian gaming, continued state hostility toward gaming communities. In 1996, Director Gary Husk reversed earlier decisions by ruling that the department would no longer count multistation gaming machines as one unit. The same year, Husk filed a suit to close the Tohono O'odham Desert Diamond Casino, and finally, despite IGRA restrictions against state regulation of nonbanked card games, Husk announced in 1997 that poker games run by compacted communities violated state law.

An arbitration panel decided the poker question in favor of Indian communities in 1999, and state and Indian leaders successfully negotiated compromises on all the other issues. With these issues behind them by the end of the century, both the state and Indian communities looked to renegotiate gaming compacts before the deadline of 2003. The Arizona Indian Gaming Association (AIGA), a seventeen-tribe organization, began television and direct-mail advertising as early as November 2001. These efforts paved the way for a successful initiative, which placed Proposition 202, the AIGA compact proposal, on the ballot for November 2002. This proposition defeated two competing proposals and became the model for the renegotiated compacts. This proposal allowed Indian communities to expand their casinos but also required larger payments to the state.

California followed a pattern similar to that of Arizona. In 1998, California Indian communities used the initiative process to force Governor Pete Wilson to allow slot machines at Indian casinos with Proposition 5. After a decision by the California Supreme Court invalidating the proposition because it violated the state's constitution, gaming

communities again used the initiative process. This time, they proposed an initiative amending the California constitution to allow Las Vegas–style casinos. Proposition 1A passed in 2000. By 2002, California faced a large budget shortfall, and Governor Gray Davis, who had supported earlier Indian initiatives, now pushed for larger contributions to the state from Indian communities in exchange for expanded casinos. Before achieving this goal, Davis faced a recall election in 2003. During the recall election, Republican candidate Arnold Schwarzenegger made Indian gaming a campaign issue, insisting that Indian communities needed to pay their fair share to reduce California's deficit. Schwarzenegger won the election.

The frustrations expressed by many state officials and average citizens are based on the misperception that Indian gaming does not benefit non-Indians, but Indian casinos and bingo halls created 460,000 jobs and generated $5 billion in tax revenue for federal, state, and local governments in 2003 (Light and Rand, 2005, 85). Indian casinos, which are often in economically underdeveloped areas, help decrease unemployment, increase per capita income, and lessen local dependence on welfare programs in surrounding non-Indian communities. Furthermore, Indian communities often make annual payments to state and local governments based on compact agreements, create additional jobs as they expand their operations, invest in local businesses as they diversify their economies, and donate generously to local charities. Gaming also allows Indian communities more self-determination as their ability to fund tribal programs increases, and the money from successful casinos gives some communities increased access to local, state, and federal government officials. As some reservation economies improve through gaming, community members often return to the reservation to live and work, reversing earlier population trends.

However, not all of the results of Indian gaming are positive. The financial success of Indian gaming enterprises varies greatly. In 2003, the top 10 percent of Indian casinos earned two-thirds of gaming revenue, while 25 percent of gaming operations earned only enough revenue to maintain the facility and fund a few modest tribal programs (Light and Rand, 2005, 13). In communities with successful casinos, financial success has sometimes magnified internal divisions, even leading to challenges to the legitimacy of tribal leaders, and increased access to government officials has led to Indian entanglement in the lobbying scandal involving Republican Jack Abramoff. Despite these negatives, Indian gaming continues to grow and will remain a part of American reality for the foreseeable future. As Indian casino owners face an increasingly saturated market, many communities are improving their facilities, adding hotels, restaurants, golf courses, and other businesses to complement their casinos. At the same time, they are diversifying their holdings by investing in unrelated businesses to protect them should the casino business ever become unfeasible or unprofitable.

James Precht

See also Economic Development; Indian Gaming Regulatory Act; Indian Self-Determination and Education Assistance Act; National Indian Gaming Commission; Reservation Economic and Social Conditions; Tribal Sovereignty.

References and Further Reading

Bays, Brad A., and Erin Hogan Fouberg, eds. 2002. *The Tribes and the States: Geographies of Intergovernmental Interaction.* Lanham, MD: Rowman & Littlefield.

Bodinger de Uriarte, John J. 2003. "Imagining the Nation with House Odds: Representing American Indian Identity at Mashantucket." *Ethnohistory* 50, no. 3: 549–565.

Cramer, Renée Ann. 2005. *Cash, Color, and Colonialism: The Politics of Tribal Acknowledgement.* Norman: University of Oklahoma Press.

Darian-Smith, Eve. 2004. *New Capitalists: Law, Politics, and Identity Surrounding Casino Gaming on Native American Land.* Belmont, CA: Wadsworth.

Eadington, William. 1999. "The Economics of Casino Gambling." *The Journal of Economic Perspectives* 13, no. 3: 173–192.

Eadington, William, ed. 2002. *Indian Gaming and the Law.* Reno, NV: Institute for the Study of Gambling and Commercial Gaming.

Gabriel, Kathryn. 1996. *Gambler Way: Indian Gaming in Mythology, History, and Archaeology in North America.* Boulder, CO: Johnson Books.

Hosmer, Brian C., and Colleen M. O'Neill, eds. 2004. *Native Pathways: American Indian Culture and Economic Development in the Twentieth Century.* Boulder: University Press of Colorado.

Jorgensen, Joseph G. 1998. "Gaming and Recent American Indian Economic Development." *American Indian Culture and Research Journal* 22, no. 3: 157–172.

Kallen, Stuart, ed. 2006. *Indian Gaming.* Farmington, MI: Greenhaven Press.

Lane, Ambrose I., Sr. 1995. *Return of the Buffalo: The Story Behind America's Indian Gaming Explosion.* Westport, CT: Bergin & Garvey.

Light, Steven Andrew, and Kathryn R. L. Rand. 2005. *Indian Gaming and Tribal Sovereignty: The Casino Compromise.* Case Studies on Contemporary Social Issues. Series edited by John A. Young. Lawrence: University Press of Kansas.

Mason, W. Dale. 1998. "Tribes and States: A New Era in Intergovernmental Affairs." *Publius* 28, no. 1: 111–130.

Mason, W. Dale. 2000. *Indian Gaming: Tribal Sovereignty and American Politics.* Norman: University of Oklahoma Press.

McCulloch, Anne Merline. 1994. "The Politics of Indian Gaming: Tribe/State Relations and American Federalism." *Publius* 24, no. 3: 99–112.

Mezey, Naomi. 1996. "The Distribution of Wealth, Sovereignty, and Culture Through Indian Gaming." *Stanford Law Review* 48, no. 3: 711–737.

Mullins, Angela, and David Kamper, eds. 2000. *Indian Gaming: Who Wins?* Contemporary American Indian Issues Series. Los Angeles, CA: UCLA American Indian Studies Center.

National Indian Gaming Commission. Available at: http://www.nigc.gov. Accessed May 29, 2006.

Peroff, Nicholas C. 2001. "Indian Gaming, Tribal Sovereignty, and American Indian Tribes as Complex Adaptive Systems." *American Indian Culture and Research Journal* 25, no. 3: 143–159.

Twetten, Daniel. 2000. "Public Law 280 and the Indian Gaming Regulatory Act: Could Two Wrongs Ever Be Made into a Right?" *The Journal of Criminal Law and Criminology* 90, no. 4: 1317–1352.

Genocide

The Native nations of North America have endured relentless campaigns intent on destroying them and all aspects of their cultures for more than 500 years. Indeed, with varying intensity, government policies, corporate enterprises, and religious missions directed against American Indians can be best described as implements of genocide.

Definition

Although states have long sought to eradicate identifiably different groups, tribes, and peoples for thousands of years, the notion of genocide has a relatively recent origin, combining ancient root words, *genos* (people) and *cide* (killing). The term, coined by Raphael Lemkin, came into common usage only after the Second World War, largely in response to the systematic destruction of Jews, Gypsies, homosexuals, and others deemed subhuman by the Nazi regime. In 1946, the United Nations codified the concept in the Convention on the Prevention and Punishment of Genocide. Article II defined it as acts "intent to destroy, in whole or in part, a national, ethnical, racial or religious group," including inflicting physical and/or psychological harm, fostering living conditions likely to lead to death and destruction, killing, the removal of children, and curtailing reproduction. Although not drafted to include the American Indian experience, activists and advocates began to reference genocide following the rise of Red Power amid the Vietnam War. More recently, the Columbian Quincentenary in 1992 sparked a wave of analytic inquiries and political applications of genocide to Native American history.

Distinctiveness

In contrast to many genocides, which have been characterized by a single, systematic, state-sponsored program directed at annihilation during a specific period of time, the Native nations of North America have endured a more diffuse, extended, plural, and unrelenting onslaught. The number of tribes and nations, their geographic locations, and their unique histories of interaction with European-Americans make the discussion of genocide much more complicated, as does the range of colonial powers (principally Spain, France, and Great Britain), newly established states (specifically the United States and Canada), and nongovernmental actors (especially corporate entities and Christian missionaries). As a consequence, one might be tempted to speak of multiple genocides or overlapping genocidal impulses, rather than a single destructive policy or event. Particularity and diversity, however, should not distract from the shared experience of destruction and dispossession.

Depopulation and Devastation

American Indian tribes experienced massive depopulation following (and in some cases in advance of) their exchanges with Europeans and European-Americans. Indigenous communities routinely lost at least 90 percent of their members, resulting in an overall drop from more (and perhaps much more)

than 5 million in the present-day United States to a low of 250,000 in 1890. To be sure, many (arguably most) of these deaths resulted from epidemic diseases; however, many others were caused by state violence, policies directed at removal, and efforts to assimilate Native Americans. In fact, guided by explicitly racist ideologies that rendered them as primitives, animals, hostiles, predators, and impediments to progress, the genocidal projects directed at American Indians exhibit two equally destructive features (biological and cultural) at once. On one hand, an array of policies and programs sought to eradicate individuals and their cultural, spiritual, and traditional beliefs and behaviors. On the other hand, more "enlightened" policies and programs intended to create new, non-Indian people through the replacement of native languages, institutions, and practice with the supposedly superior elements of Western civilization.

Destruction

Ever since the arrival of Christopher Columbus, American Indians have endured the effects of ideologies and actions aimed at their destruction. Importantly, these effects meet the United Nations definition of genocide.

Organized violence is perhaps the clearest expression of efforts to exterminate American Indians. For more than five centuries, military campaigns and vigilante actions proved pivotal to strategies to address the "Indian problem." George Washington compared indigenous peoples with wolves, deserving the same treatment, and Colonel John M. Chivington declared in 1864, "Kill them all boys, nits make lice" (Stannard, 1993, 131). The governor of California officially urged the extermination of all American Indians in his state during 1851; General William Sheridan affirmed nearly two decades later, "The only good Indians I ever saw were dead" (Drinnon, 1990, 539). The press also sometimes endorsed murderous actions, offering news coverage and editorials inciting settlers to take up arms against Native communities. Killing, often on a massive scale, followed from these provocations.

The soldiers with Columbus delighted in the torture and mutilation of men, women, and children. Author Barry Lopez, summarizing a report by the Spanish priest Bartolome de las Casas, wrote: " 'Such inhumanities and barbarisms were committed in my sight,' he says, 'as no age can parallel. . . .' The Span-

ish cut off the legs of children who ran from them. They poured people full of boiling soap. They made bets as to who, with one sweep of his sword, could cut a person in half. They loosed dogs that 'devoured an Indian like a hog, at first sight, in less than a moment.' They used nursing infants for dog food" (Mass Crimes, 2003). Lopez writes, "One day, in front of Las Casas, the Spanish dismembered, beheaded or raped three thousand people." Las Casas referred to the Spanish incursion as "a continuous recreational slaughter" (Lopez, 1990, 6–7).

Similarly, British colonists engaged in scorched-earth campaigns against indigenous peoples, burning villages and slaughtering their occupants, perhaps most notably during the Pequot War and King Philip's War. American forces waged an unrelenting series of wars in the nineteenth century, each punctuated by massacres such as those at Sand Creek in 1864 and Wounded Knee in 1890. Moreover, during much of the eighteenth and nineteenth centuries, bounties were awarded for American Indian scalps.

Organized violence was expressed in another form of destruction as well, namely removal, which resulted in many deaths and the loss of indigenous traditions. Eager to claim natural resources, secure labor, and seize land, the dispossession and displacement marked British colonial efforts in the seventeenth and eighteenth centuries as well as federal and state government programs in the nineteenth century. The Trail of Tears clearly illustrates these undertakings and their implications. The Cherokee, Chickasaw, Choctaw, Creek, and Seminole all faced involuntary removal, the usurpation of national sovereignty, internment in concentration camps, forced marches from areas in the southeastern United States to what is now Oklahoma, violence, and intimidation. Combined, these traumas resulted in mortality rates ranging between 25 and 50 percent. The Cherokee Nation, for instance, lost between 4,000 and 8,000 citizens during its trek westward. This pattern of ethnic cleansing would repeat itself for the next half century, as tribal groups were pushed out of their homelands and onto reservations.

Internment of formerly free indigenous peoples on reservations dramatically altered their lives and living conditions. Conventional means of dwelling and subsistence were irrevocably altered following relocation, and, with such alterations, entire ways of knowing, being, and relating to the world suffered

relentless assault. Corruption and government assistance programs brought with them malnourishment, worsening public health, and diminished life expectancy. At the same time, the traditional sources of physical and spiritual power were systematically eradicated. On one hand, white entrepreneurs and policy makers targeted the buffalo, for instance, hunting it to near extinction and with it the horse cultures of the plains dependent on it. On the other hand, lawmakers and missionaries undermined and in many cases outlawed indigenous cultural practices and traditions. Spiritual traditions, including the Sundance and the Potlatch, became criminal offenses.

Seemingly more benevolent programs like boarding schools, which were designed to educate and uplift Native Americans, often had equally disastrous intentions and consequences. In reality, such undertakings sought to transform American Indians, erasing them as they made them more "American." The boarding school system stressed assimilation. American Indian children were removed from their home communities, often taken against their parents' wishes, if not by outright force, and taken to distant residential schools. Here, their hair was cut, and they were made to dress in alien and awkward attire. Living a life of structure and discipline, they were forced to speak English exclusively and taught European-American history, customs, and rituals. Stripped of their cultures and isolated, children often experienced homesickness. They became vulnerable as well to physical and mental abuse and disease— which sometimes resulted in death. Boarding schools aimed, in the words of Colonel Richard Henry Pratt, founder of Carlisle Industrial School, to "[k]ill the Indian and save the man," contributed in a very real way mightily to the genocide of Native Americans.

More recently, American Indian communities have suffered from a more subtle form of genocide: population control. For many decades, until at least the late 1970s, the Indian Health Service subjected Native American women to involuntary sterilization, medical interventions with no other intent than to reduce reproduction. Some estimates suggest that upward of one-third of American Indian women of childbearing age underwent the procedure during the short period of its execution.

Past genocidal policies and practices continue to reverberate in Indian Country today, manifesting themselves in a range of social problems, including alcoholism and drug abuse, suicide and interpersonal violence, and the high number of high-school dropouts. Significantly, as they have done for more than five centuries, American Indians survive against the odds, fighting efforts to destroy Native cultures and communities, while struggling to defend the validity and vitality of indigenous traditions, languages, and rights.

C. Richard King

See also Boarding Schools, United States and Canada; Buffalo; Bureau of Indian Affairs: Establishing the Existence of an Indian Tribe; California Indians, Genocide of; Camp Grant Massacre; Canada, Indian Policies of; Disease, Historic and Contemporary; Forced Marches; Goschochking (Ohio) Massacre of 1782; Hazardous Waste; Jackson, Helen Hunt; Long March; Long Walk; Metacom, and King Philip's War; Mission System, Spanish; Pequot War; Reservation Economic and Social Conditions; Sand Creek Massacre; Trail of Tears; Wounded Knee, South Dakota, Massacre at.

References and Further Reading

Drinnon, Richard. 1990. *Facing West: The Metaphysics of Indian Hating and Empire Building.* New York: Schoken Books.

Lopez, Barry. 1990. *The Rediscovery of North America.* Lexington: University Press of Kentucky.

"Mass Crimes Against Humanity and Genocides: Past Genocide of Natives in North America." 2003. Religious Tolerance.org citing Barry Lopez. Available at: http://www.religioustolerance.org/genocide5.htm. Accessed May 30, 2006.

Niezen, Ronald. 2000. *Spirit Wars: Native North American Religions in the Age of Nation Building.* Berkeley: University of California Press.

Stannard, David E. 1993. *American Holocaust: The Conquest of the New World.* New York: Oxford University Press.

Thorton, Russell. 1990. *American Indian Holocaust and Survival: A Population History Since 1492.* Norman: University of Oklahoma Press.

Trafzer, Clifford E., and Joel R. Hyer, eds. 1999. "Exterminate Them." In *Written Accounts of the Murder, Rape, and Slavery of Native Americans During the California Gold Rush, 1848–1868.* East Lansing: Michigan State University Press.

Wallace, David. 1997. *Education for Extinction: American Indians and the Boarding School Experience 1875–1928.* Lawrence: University Press of Kansas.

Hazardous Waste

Introduction

Hazardous waste problems are pervasive in Indian Country. The following examples, selected from a range of locations, are only a few of many that could be discussed. In Alaska, toxic residues are imperiling the integrity of reindeer meat on the Seward Peninsula, and, on the Aleutian Islands, Native people have had to deal with wastes left behind by the U.S. military. The Penobscots in Maine have been contaminated by dioxins created as a by-product of the chlorine bleaching process in making paper in the mills that surround their homeland. In New Mexico, the Isleta Pueblo's water supply, downstream from Albuquerque along the Rio Grande, has been contaminated as well.

The Seward Peninsula of Alaska: Don't Eat the Reindeer

The Seward Peninsula of Alaska has been extensively mined during the last hundred years for cadmium and various lead-bearing ores. These ores are easily absorbed by plants that provide the food eaten by ungulates; the ores then concentrate in the liver, kidney, and muscle tissues. In some cases, health officials have warned local Native peoples to avoid eating reindeer, once a dietary staple. In addition, contamination from weapons testing, accidental pollution, or illegal dumping may have found its way into the lichens of northwestern Alaska, thereby accumulating in reindeer and caribou tissue (University of Alaska at Fairbanks, 2000).

The Native people on the Seward Peninsula live a subsistence lifestyle in which a high percentage of their diet comes from local plants and animals. The incidence of cancer and other diseases appears to be rising among the indigenous people in this region who subsist on contaminated reindeer and other "country food." The people in local villages are particularly concerned that contamination from air pollution, mining operations, and dump sites are concentrating in the tissue of subsistence animals, posing a health risk (University of Alaska at Fairbanks, 2000). The University of Alaska's Reindeer Research Program has detected high levels of cadmium and lead in several species. If similar concentrations were to be found in meat, consumption of 40 to 60 grams of meat per week would exceed the recommended intake rate (University of Alaska at Fairbanks, 2000).

Bombs Away in the Aleutian Islands

Almost six decades after a military base was established to fend off possible Japanese attacks on the United States during World War II, the U.S. Navy in 2001 joined with the Environmental Protection Agency (EPA) to remove unexploded bombs near an indigenous Aleut community on Adak Island, in the Aleutians, 1,200 miles west of Anchorage, Alaska. The removal of unexploded ordnance will allow the Aleuts to develop industry on the site. During World War II, the U.S. Army established a military presence on the island to counter Japanese forces that briefly occupied Attu and Kiska islands in the Aleutians.

The abandoned Army base was designated as a Superfund site in 1994 and closed in 1997. The cleanup is a combined effort by the Navy, the EPA, the U.S. Fish and Wildlife Service, the Aleutian/

Unexploded ordnance sign on Adak Island, Alaska, in 1965. (Jack Fields/Corbis)

Pribilof Island Association, the Aleut Native Corporation, and the Adak community. It was a part of a 47,000-acre land exchange between the federal government and the Aleut Corporation that will allow the local Aleut community to develop a fish-processing industry, a fueling facility, and a regional hub for air cargo traffic.

"Addressing unexploded ordnance contamination has stymied cleanups at other sites in the U.S.," said Aleut Corporation commissioner Michele Brown. "We needed to put Adak back to good use, so endless delay was not an option. The project team devoted long hours and ingenuity to identify and remediate risks, resulting in a responsible, effective, environmentally protective decision that allows the Aleut Corporation to move a step closer to creating good jobs for [indigenous] Alaskans" (Navy, 2001).

Organochlorine Contamination and the Penobscots

Rebecca Sockbeson, a Penobscot, described "the devastating impact of dioxins in my community," to international negotiators of a treaty to eliminate or ban the most widespread persistent organic pollutants (Sockbeson, 1999). She said that her nation of nearly 500 people live on an island in the river, close to seven pulp and paper mills.

Dioxins are created as a by-product of the chlorine bleaching process in making paper and are discharged from all seven of these mills. Dioxins, highly potent toxic chemicals that may cause cancer and other health problems, were being poured daily into an adjacent river. Sockbeson said that her people once survived on the fish from this river, but "now we are dying from it." She continued:

> Neither dioxin nor cancer is indigenous to the Penobscot people, however they are both pervasive in my tribal community. My people face up to three times the state and national cancer rate, moreover, those that are dying of cancer are dying at younger and younger ages, our reproductive generation. This means that unless you take action to eliminate dioxin and other persistent organic pollutants, there will be no Penobscots living on the island by the end of the next century (Sockbeson, 1999).

The health and survival of Sockbeson's Penobscot band are also threatened by a choice mothers must make: Should they breast-feed their children (imparting superior nutrition) and thus pass on to them their body burdens of PCBs and dioxins? "With this," she concluded, "I humbly, respectfully and desperately urge you to draft a treaty that insures the existence of the Penobscot and other indigenous peoples who are so disproportionately impacted by dioxin." Such a treaty is required, she said, so "that the breast and spoon we feed our babies with is not filled with cancer, diabetes, learning disabilities, and attention deficit [disorder]" (Sockbeson, 1999).

The Isleta Pueblo Tastes Albuquerque's Effluent

By the late 1980s, people of the Isleta Pueblo, six miles downstream on the Rio Grande River from the Albuquerque metropolitan area, began to experience problems that were outside their historical experience. Their corn and bean crops were stunted and five grandmothers, all from the same neighborhood (and all about the same age) were diagnosed with stomach cancers that killed all of them within a few months.

Political authorities on the reservation pressured the state's Department of Environmental Quality for a toxicological evaluation. The results indicated that Isleta Pueblo's water supply was being contaminated by a number of sources upstream, including a slaughterhouse that was dumping ground-up animal carcasses into the river. The leakage of petroleum waste products also was detected from a wrecking yard, and the city of Albuquerque was found to be dumping raw sewage into the Rio Grande.

Soil tests at Isleta indicated dangerous levels of benzine (a lethal solvent) and nitrates. They soon discovered the cause: As the people of Isleta Pueblo had blessed the ground for spring planting in their annual Winter Dance, Albuquerque's main sewer line had ruptured. According to a report by Paul Vandevelder in *Native Americas,* "Millions of gallons of raw effluent poured into the river and flowed downstream to Isleta. City officials called to warn the tribe but said there was nothing they could do; it was too late . . . the Rio Grande was percolating with putrid green foam" (Vandevelder, 2001, 43).

The city of Albuquerque later told the U.S. Environmental Protection Agency that correcting the problems that were ruining Isleta's water would cost $300 million and entail $15 million a year annually in additional operating costs. Isleta's right to enforce water quality standards

through the Environmental Protection Agency was upheld by federal courts, a major legal victory for Native American peoples faced with the toll of off-reservation pollution. The case was presented in the context of religious freedom, with sacred ceremonies requiring clean water. In December 1997, the U.S. Supreme Court reviewed the Tenth Circuit's decision in favor of the Isleta Pueblo, requiring water cleanup by the city of Albuquerque.

Bruce E. Johansen

See also Environment and Pollution; Genocide; James Bay and Northern Quebec Agreement; Mining and Contemporary Environmental Problems; Radiation Exposure Compensation Act; Reservation Economic and Social Conditions; Uranium Mining; Ward Valley, Hazardous Waste Controversy.

References and Further Reading

"Navy, Environmental Protection Agency to Clean Unexploded Ordinance off Adak Island." 2001. Environment News Service. December 14. Available at: http://ens-news.com. [Accessed December 15, 2001]

Sockbeson, Rebecca. 1999. "Statement by Rebecca Sockbeson for IRATE (Indigenous Resistance Against Tribal Extinction), and IEN (Indigenous Environmental Network)." International POPs Elimination Network (IPEN) PCB Working Group. September 8. Available at: http://www.ipen.org. Accessed 2003.

University of Alaska at Fairbanks. "Heavy Metal Levels in Reindeer, Caribou, and Plants of the Seward Peninsula." 2000. Current Research Programs, Reindeer Research Program. April. Available at: http://reindeer.salrm.uaf.edu/html/research.html. Accessed January 2, 2007.

Vandevelder, Paul. Spring, 2001. "A Native Sense of Earth." *Native Americas* 18, no. 1: 42–49.

Land, Identity and Ownership of, Land Rights

Basic American Indian land law and limited tribal sovereignty were established very early in American history, through the Supreme Court decisions of Chief Justice John Marshall. The decisions of the Marshall court during the 1830s affecting the Cherokee and other southeastern tribes laid the foundation for tribal sovereignty over land. In *Cherokee Nation v. Georgia* (1831), the court declared that the Cherokees constituted a "domestic dependent nation" whose members were to be considered wards of the United States and whose rights were to be protected by the federal government.

The next year, in *Worcester v. Georgia*, the Marshall court explained the idea of tribal sovereignty in greater detail when it declared that "Indian nations had always been considered as distinct, independent political communities, retaining their original natural rights, as the undisputed possessors of the soil." Even though President Andrew Jackson ignored the Supreme Court's decision confirming Cherokee land rights and moved them over the Trail of Tears to Indian Territory in Oklahoma, the Marshall Court's opinions in these cases have been cited throughout American judicial history in a multitude of other suits as setting the precedent for confirming tribal land rights.

Land tenure rights for Native Americans were severely tested later in the nineteenth century through various federal actions aimed at forcing the assimilation of American Indian peoples. Federal policy, as set out in the General Allotment Act of 1887 (more popularly known as the Dawes Severalty Act), attempted to do away with Native peoples' land bases through the distribution of 80- or 160-acre parcels of reservation land to individual tribal members. Not only did this act break up tribal reservation land, challenging the widely held American Indian idea of communal land ownership and making even more land available for non-Indian settlement, but it also made the Indians who received their allotments U.S. citizens, causing them to be subject to the laws and taxes of the states.

The U.S. Supreme Court confirmed this change in American Indian land policy in *Lone Wolf v. Hitchcock* (1903). In this decision, the Supreme Court informed Native tribes and nations that the courts themselves were no longer the final recourse for Native attempts to protect their land rights against intrusion by the federal government through claims to sovereignty. Congress alone was deemed responsible for American Indian policy, and its decisions in these matters were held not to be open to judicial review.

The situation for the Pueblo nations was even more desperate during the opening decades of the twentieth century. Because their land holdings had been conferred by the Treaty of Guadalupe Hidalgo and not by an act of Congress reserving the land for them, the Pueblos were excluded from the provisions that set out federal relationships with American Indians as outlined in the Trade and Intercourse Act of

1834. This status granted the Pueblos citizenship as landowners and thereby subjected them to taxation and to the laws of the state of New Mexico. Regarding land law, this made the Pueblo nations subject to the same statutes that governed all land holdings in the state. Any recourse taken to dispute non-Indians who squatted on Indian lands would have to be taken up with the New Mexico state courts, which, like many other state court systems, had a well-earned reputation of hostility toward the claims of Indian tribes, and not with the federal government or the Bureau of Indian Affairs (BIA).

The breakup of lands, the diminution of sovereignty, and the assimilation of Indian peoples formed the basis of American Indian policy until the 1930s. This negative view of Indian land rights and tribal sovereignty in general would not be challenged in any meaningful way until the rise to prominence of Red Progressive reformer John Collier during the 1920s, the publication of the 1928 Meriam Report, which outlined the deficiencies of the American Indian policy centered around the General Allotment Act, and, with Collier's appointment as Commissioner of Indian Affairs after Franklin D. Roosevelt's election in 1932, the passage of the Wheeler-Howard Act of 1934 (popularly known as the Indian Reorganization Act). Upon his confirmation, Collier immediately began to dismantle the prior system of Indian management and create a new system that included more protection and self-determination for the tribes. Although he faced stiff opposition from assimilated Indians and local BIA officials who feared they might lose their jobs, Collier had his Indian Reorganization Act (IRA) introduced in Congress in 1934.

The centerpiece of Collier's efforts to reform Indian policy, the act stated that "hereafter no land of any Indian reservation, created or set apart by treaty or agreement with the Indians, Act of Congress, Executive order, purchase, or otherwise, shall be allotted in severalty to any Indian." Collier's plan envisioned each Indian nation submitting a charter that included its territorial limits and membership, but that reflected its own traditional governmental forms. Collier's bill also established its own charters as superseding former forms of government, a move that was sure to antagonize traditional elements and place the government in the hands of more assimilated elements. The commissioner was authorized to arrange and classify the functions and services the BIA administered, allowing tribes to choose which services they would like to assume.

Most importantly, the IRA reversed the policy of land allotment, authorizing the Secretary of the Interior to withdraw the remaining "surplus" lands after allotment. No more Indian land was to be sold away. The IRA specified powers that tribal councils could exercise without seeking the permission of the federal government, reversing the tendency of the federal government until that point to place more and more restrictions on Indians' self-determination. Debates regarding the efficacy of Collier's reforms and the extent of his commitment to Indian cultural forms have continued ever since he took office. Some Indians, especially those who had been educated in white institutions, who adopted Christianity, or who otherwise assimilated, did not support Collier's call for an end to individual land allotments. Moreover, many agents and other BIA officials disagreed wholeheartedly with his program of cultural preservation, tribal government, and land consolidation, and they refused to implement much of his program on the local level. However, there can be no doubt that the dim view of Indian tribal sovereignty and American Indian land rights that characterized federal Indian policy before had changed radically.

However, not long after Collier's resignation in 1945, Congress asked for a list of tribes that would be "ready to succeed on their own," initiating the policy of termination. In 1953, Public Law 83-280 (PL280) placed Indians in five western states under state law enforcement jurisdiction and allowed states wishing to assume jurisdiction to amend their state constitutions to make it possible. Senator Arthur Watkins became the leading advocate of termination, using some of the same tactics (counting silence as assent, mischaracterizing the tone of meetings) that Collier had used to claim that he spoke for Indian desires and interests.

The Klamaths, Menominees, and Utes found themselves trading one trustee (the federal government) for another (private banks that had no knowledge of or sympathy for their needs). In 1954, the National Congress of American Indians (NCAI) met to discuss how to fight termination, exerting pressure on Congress to vote against it. During the 1960s, the Democrats waffled on termination, not implementing it but not decrying it. The NCAI tried to keep its distance from the Civil Rights Movement in the late 1950s, but the poor conditions created by PL280 resulted in the need for the group to approach Congress for redress.

All of these acts, laws, and decisions have had varying degrees of influence on the self-determination over land that Indian tribes have been able to exercise. Although cuts in federal funding during the Reagan administration damaged the ability of the tribes to exercise their sovereignty, in sum, the amount of sovereignty has increased greatly over the course of the twentieth century. These changes in federal views toward Indian tribal sovereignty and land rights demonstrate that, during the 1920s and 1930s, a shift occurred in both government and public perception of Indian tribes. Those changes have only haltingly been implemented and have many times been reversed when the federal government found them inconvenient, but the early twentieth century did signal a fundamental change in how the government addressed the problem of Indian land rights.

Steven L. Danver

See also Cherokee Nation v. Georgia; Collier, John; General Allotment Act (Dawes Act); *Lone Wolf v. Hitchcock;* Meriam Report; *Worcester v. Georgia.*
References and Further Reading
Deloria, Vine, Jr., and Clifford M. Lytle. 1983. *American Indians, American Justice.* Austin: University of Texas Press.
Deloria, Vine, Jr., and Clifford M. Lytle. 1984. *The Nations Within: The Past and Future of American Indian Sovereignty.* Austin: University of Texas Press.
Prucha, Francis Paul. 1984. *The Great Father: The United States Government and the American Indians.* Lincoln: University of Nebraska Press.
Prucha, Francis Paul. [1984], ed. *Documents of United States Indian Policy,* 2nd. ed. Lincoln: University of Nebraska Press

Mining and Contemporary Environmental Problems

Mining, most notably of gold, has been one of the primary motors of invasion of the New World. Columbus had gold on his mind, as did Cortes and many other Spanish conquistadors. The discovery of gold deposits played a major role in the Cherokees' Trail of Tears, the invasion of the Black Hills, and the dispossession of Native peoples in California. The Lakota holy man Black Elk called gold the yellow metal that drives white men crazy.

Native peoples' problems with mining continue today. With the coming of an economy based on fossil fuels and other forms of industrial energy, coal and uranium have joined gold as targets of opportunity (and sources of pollution) on many Indian reservations. What follows is a small but indicative sample of this issue as it plays out in Native America; more complete descriptions of mining pollution afflicting Native nations in the United States fill many books and articles.

The Hopis and Navajos: Turning Black Mesa to Coal Slurry

Coal burning generates more than half of the electricity consumed in the United States, and a sizable percentage of that coal comes from strip-mines on American Indian reservations. One example is the large electricity-generating complex on the Navajo nation at the Four Corners, the conjunction of Arizona, New Mexico, Colorado, and Utah. Since 1974, the Mojave Generating Station and the Navajo Generating Station have been polluting the world's air. The Mojave Generating Station alone uses 18,240 tons of coal per day at full load. Combined, the two plants require 12 million tons of coal a year and are the largest polluters in the country. Astronauts saw the pollution cloud from these coal-fired plants from the moon (Giuliano, 2001). The six Four Corners coal-fired power plants, completed in the 1970s, emit pollution that on some days fills the local atmosphere with higher levels of sulfur and nitrogen oxides than the air of New York City or Los Angeles (Schneider, n.d.).

A significant proportion of the coal that powers the Four Corners power plants is strip-mined from Black Mesa, Arizona, home of the Hopi Indian Reservation (which is also home to several thousand Navajo) and the site of a Peabody coal mine. On Black Mesa, Peabody Western Coal Company (a subsidiary of the Peabody Group) uses more than 3 million gallons a day (1.4 billion gallons a year) of once pristine, potable groundwater that leaves the aquifer as coal slurry, a coal-and-water mixture.

The aquifers that once provided 60,000 people on Black Mesa with water were by the year 2000 being depleted much faster than nature could replenish them. Computer models run by hydrologist Ron Morgan indicate that by 2050, not even allowing for Peabody's coal-slurry needs, "virtually every spring on the Hopi homelands will be bone dry" (Vandeveldger, 2000, 14). Morgan also estimates that by 2050 the aquifer will have been drawn down at ten times the rate that it is being recharged. "All

the computer models tell us that these depletions are right around the corner," according to Morgan (Vandevelder, 2000, 14).

The slurry pipeline, which was owned by Enron Corp. before its bankruptcy, transports its coal-water mix 273 miles to the Mojave Generating Station in Laughlin, Nevada, where it is converted into electricity for the use of consumers in Nevada, California, and parts of Utah and central Arizona. In the meantime, many of the Dine (traditional Navajo) who live at Black Mesa and in most other areas of the reservation have no electricity.

In the late 1990s, the Hopi Nation complained that Peabody Coal was underpaying for its coal. The resulting renegotiation increased the company's payments by 10 percent, or about $1 million per year. The deal was sweetened by a $1 million bonus paid at the signing of the agreement. By 1998, coal revenues accounted for nearly 40 percent of the Navajo Nation's governmental budget and 80 percent of the Hopi Nation's budget (Four Corners Clamor, 1998). One critic asked, "Will this increase help the 50 per cent unemployed Navajo out on the Rez, and will it raise the yearly average income of $750? Since the wells under the Rez are almost dry, from whence will come the water needed to move this coal to Albuquerque and Nevada?" (Four Corners Clamor, 1998).

Many Navajo and Hopi moved from the path of the growing Peabody mine, accepting the company's offer of new homes with plumbing and solar power. Others, however, have decided to remain in their traditional homes. Maxine Kescoli is one of a number of elders who have refused to move to make way for expansion of the coal mine. Peabody has mining rights to the land under her traditional Navajo hogan, which is one mile from the Kayenta Mine. "My umbilical cord is buried here," Kescoli said (Four Corners Clamor, 1998).

To illustrate why she prefers to remain in her traditional home, Kescoli called on *hozho*, the Navajo foundation of belief, "To walk in beauty." This belief runs counter to the exploitation of coal and other resources. This clash is evident not only at Black Mesa, but in many areas of the Navajo Nation where coal is mined. Emma Yazzie, another elder, herded sheep and goats in the shadow of the Four Corners' strip mine draglines until she died, even as pollution fouled her home. She walked to the bottom of strip mines near her home and impeded the draglines—a one-woman, antimining protest movement (Johansen and Maestas, 1979, 143–146).

The clash of cultures is very sharp:

During the past 30 years, 10,000 Navajo sheepherders have been removed from land near Black Mesa, some at gunpoint. Four thousand graves and sacred places have been desecrated. Charges are that the Peabody Coal Company, U.S. agents, and Hopi police have impounded livestock illegally. . . . All of the wells may be dry within four years. Peabody Coal plants trees as "restoration." All of the trees are dead. This is not "walking in beauty" (Four Corners Clamor, 1998).

Before the mid-1970s, Black Mesa was home to several thousand Navajo and Hopi sheepherders, weavers, silversmiths, and farmers whose families had lived there for several hundred years. Over the years, many of these people were forced off Black Mesa by the encroaching strip mine. During the late 1980s, a United Nations report described the case of the forced relocation as one of the most flagrant violations of indigenous peoples' human rights in the western hemisphere (Black Mesa Indigenous Support, n.d.-a).

Coal-fired power plants emit more toxic pollution than any other form of electricity production. For every megawatt hour of electricity produced, coal, depending on its composition, generates an average of 2,000 pounds of carbon dioxide, 13.8 pounds of sulfur oxides, 4.8 pounds of nitrogen oxides, and 3.2 pounds of particulate matter. By comparison, natural gas emits an average of 1,205 pounds of carbon dioxide per megawatt hour, 0.008 pound of sulfur oxides, 4.3 pounds of nitrogen oxides, and negligible particulate matter (Giuliano, 2001).

The scope of Peabody's operation at Black Mesa can be sketched using statistics: During 1998, for example, Peabody Western Coal Company removed just under 11.8 million tons of coal from its Arizona mines. Since mining began on Black Mesa three decades ago, close to 40 billion gallons of groundwater have been pumped to feed Peabody's coal-slurry pipeline. With the pipeline conveying as much as 43,000 tons of slurried coal per day, the company pumps as much as 120,000 gallons of water per hour (Black Mesa Indigenous Support, n.d.-b). The coal slurry competes with local residents for the only source of water for the Hopi and Western Navajo. By the late 1990s, Peabody's strip mine at Black Mesa had expanded to 100 square miles, "the largest privately-owned coal mine in the world" (Black Mesa

Indigenous Support, n.d.-a). Into this pit have fallen burial and sacred sites, religious structures, and ancestral Puebloan ruins.

The U.S. government has relocated 9,000 Navajos to Sanders, Arizona, on land contaminated by the largest radioactive waste spill in North America, in and near the Rio Puerco. According to one source, "Some people living there have died from cancer or are dying from it now. The birth defect rate is outstanding. . . . The suicide rate is outstanding as well" (Black Mesa Indigenous Support, n.d.-a). A radiation meter outside a school on the relocation lands registers 700 rads. The relocation agents have resisted complaints that the "new lands" are contaminated, by saying that people will be unaffected if they do not drink the water (Schneider, n.d.). There is, however, no other water source in the area. People live in trailers, their traditional economy and way of life destroyed.

Other families of Navajo refugees from Black Mesa have drifted from place to place for many years. Some live in shacks, others live in vehicles, while the lucky ones squeeze in with other family members (Black Mesa Indigenous Support, n.d.-a).

> Others [have] found themselves having to pay for water, heat, food, electricity, [and] taxes, things they never had to deal with before. Many of the elders speak little or no English— people who had no experience with a cash economy have been moved to border towns. These Navajos were warehoused in substandard housing. . . . While the relocation law required the federal government to provide community facilities and services and to minimize the adverse social, cultural, and economic effects of relocation, that promise remains unfulfilled almost two decades later. Many find it impossible to get jobs, and they are forced into homelessness. The genocide is complete (Black Mesa Indigenous Support, n.d.-a).

Iyawata Britten Schneider wrote in *Country Road News:* "In Arizona, the Department of Interior and the Bureau of Indian Affairs created a land dispute between the Hopi and Dine people by acquiring land and paying the Dine large sums and the Hopi next to nothing. This land dispute was then used to support the passage of the Relocation Act of 1974 that forced the move of 10,000 Dine to 'new lands.' This relocation brought with it increased health

risks, high suicide rates, and severe depression among the Dine. The movement of the Dine allowed for the leasing of more land for the coal mines" (Schneider, n.d.).

Coal mining is antithetical to traditional herding and agriculture in the region. According to Schneider:

> Because the southwest is arid and has high winds, coal dust can be seen on the sheep herds, on the land, in the water supply and the air. Residents of the coal mining areas suffer from chronic lung disease and high cancer rates. Livestock drinking water from nearby ponds die within a few hours and traditional crops fail. In its reparation [sic] of land, Peabody does not separate the topsoil from the bottom, leaving the soil with high saline content. Vegetation has not survived in this soil (Schneider, n.d.).

The Black Mesa coal-slurry pipeline is also prone to occasional spills, such as one that occurred over two-and-a-half years between 1999 and 2001. Black Mesa Pipeline, Inc. agreed to pay penalties of $128,000 for discharging almost 485,000 gallons of coal slurry in northern Arizona. The Arizona Department of Environmental Quality discovered the violations during a series of inspections of Black Mesa's facilities. "Had the pipeline been properly maintained, these spills would not have occurred," said Alexis Strauss, water division director for the U.S. Environmental Protection Agency's Pacific Southwest Office. "Desert ecosystems are quite fragile, and filling arroyos with crushed coal is unnecessary and unacceptable" (Arizona Water Resource, 2001).

Increasing numbers of Hopis and Navajos have been protesting the fact that Peabody's use of local water is destroying their way of life. Former Hopi Chairman Ferrell Secakuku joined Navajos from Big Mountain in 2001 to protest the use of aquifer water for the Black Mesa coal slurry and to urge the creation of new, sustainable forms of energy. "We found out the water table is being depleted," Secakuku said, denying reports by the federal government and Peabody Western Coal Co. that have claimed otherwise (Norrell, 2001). Secakuku spoke to a crowd of American Indians and other environmentalists that included longtime opponents of Navajo relocation at Big Mountain. Secakuku and other protesters entered the offices of Black Mesa Pipeline, Inc. to urge officials to halt the slurry pipeline that annually depletes

1.3 billion gallons from the Navajo aquifer. He said using water to transport coal threatens to leave the Hopi village of Moenkopi without water by the year 2011. "Every time you breathe, Peabody is pumping 50 gallons," Secakuku told the crowd (Norrell, 2001). During the protest, Roberta Blackgoat held a sign proclaiming, "The Creator is the Only One who is Going to Relocate Me" (Norrell, 2001).

In defense of the mine, Peabody Coal's John Wasik, executive for southwestern operations, said: "Continued operation of the Black Mesa Mine is in the public interest and will provide long-term economic benefits to the Hopi Tribe and the Navajo Nation. It also provides an essential and secure energy supply for more than 1 million Southwest families who rely on [it for] electricity." Peabody further maintains that the mine "will inject about $1.5 billion in direct economic benefits into reservation economies in royalties, taxes, wages, and vendor contracts over the proposed extension [of mine operations]" for fifteen years, from 2005 to 2020 (Wanamaker, 2001, C-1). The mine employed about 250 people in 2002; 96 percent of the mine's work force and 82 percent of its supervisory staff were Native American, according to the Peabody company (Wanamaker, 2002, C-1).

Having lost much of their precious water to coal mining and power generation, the Hopis by 2005 faced a new and paradoxical mine-related threat: unemployment. The mine is shutting down because the sole power plant it supplies, the Mohave Generating Station, is closing under a legal agreement with environmental groups that sued because of repeated pollution violations. The closures could force the layoff of at least 150 of the Hopi Tribe's five hundred employees. In addition, 13 percent of the Navajo Nation government's nonmine labor force would lose jobs, along with 300 mine workers (Helms, 2005).

Having had trouble living with the mine, Hopi Tribal Chairman Wayne Taylor, Jr. said that they might face economic ruin without it. "I carry within me a very real fear that our way of life the Hopi Way will soon become a way of the past," he said. "Our culture, one of the oldest in North America, is dying. Our crisis is both immediate and long-term" (Helms, 2005). Taylor said coal royalties paid to the Hopi tribe by Peabody Energy, operators of the mine, generate more than one-third of Hopi tribal government revenue. "Try to imagine, if you will, a municipality, a county or a state losing one-third of its government revenues," Taylor said (Helms, 2005). More than half

of Hopi adults are already unemployed. "There is a desperate need for housing. Many of the traditional sandstone homes are crumbling and in disrepair. Forty percent of the houses lack adequate plumbing and kitchen facilities," Taylor said (Helms, 2005). "For the Navajo, the situation may be even worse," he said. "We understand that 13 percent of Navajo government's non-mine labor force would lose their jobs." Additionally, the 300 Navajos who work at Black Mesa would lose their average wages of $60,000 to $70,000, according to Taylor (Helms, 2005).

The closure of the mine and generating station were slated for December 31, 2005. Although the closing was "a certainty," according to Navajo Nation Attorney General Louis Denetsosie, negotiations continued in 2006, and Denetsosie said he still hopes the plant will reopen after being equipped with pollution-control equipment (Edwards, 2005, 1-D).

The Gros Ventres and Assiniboines: Gold Mining and Cyanide Poisoning in Montana

The Little Rocky Mountains of Montana, which long have been regarded as sacred by the Assiniboine and Gros Ventre people, are now laced with the effluent of open-pit gold mines that have produced toxic acid mine drainage. Andrew Schneider of the Seattle *Post-Intelligencer* described Gus Helgeson, the president of Island Mountain Protectors, a Native American environmental and cultural organization, standing atop Spirit Mountain as he scanned "the gashes, pits and piles of rock that once was his tribe's most sacred land. . . . The strong man weeps" (Schneider, 2001). Spirit Mountain is part of the Little Rockies, an island of mountains in the nearly flat prairie. To Native Americans, the mountains were valued for their deer, bighorn sheep, herbs, natural medicines, and pure water. Gold mining has destroyed all of that.

In 1884, Pike Landusky and Pete Zortman discovered gold on land traditionally held by the Assiniboine and Gros Ventre. The following year, these tribes were moved to the Fort Belknap Reservation, which was named for a U.S. Secretary of War. The Assiniboine and Gros Ventre gave up 40,000 acres of land in exchange for a government promise to feed, clothe, and care for them. At the time, federal Indian agents said nothing about the gold that was buried in Spirit Mountain, but they made it clear the tribes could either agree to their terms or starve. The

agreement called for the two tribes to sell portions of their gold-laced land to the federal government for livestock and other goods. Under the terms of the General Mining Law of 1872, however, the government turned around and sold the land to individuals and private companies for $10 an acre.

Over several decades, according to Schneider's account, "scores of shafts were driven into the Little Rockies, and an estimated $1 billion in gold and silver was taken out of the ground—more than $300 million by the last owner of the mine, Pegasus Gold Corp. of Canada" (Schneider, 2001). Underground mining continued until the 1950s, after which open-pit strip-mining was initiated. In 1979, with gold prices rising rapidly, the Pegasus Gold Corp. and a subsidiary, Zortman Mining Inc., built mines that extracted gold from heaps of low-grade ore with cyanide solutions.

The Pegasus Gold Company, which owned several mines in the Little Rocky Mountains of Montana, went bankrupt when gold prices fell sharply after 1980, "leaving the state of Montana with a $100 million cleanup liability and the tribes with the prospect of perpetually polluted water" (Huff, 2000). Cyanide-assisted gold mining continued until 1990, during which time the mine was expanded nine times without any substantial environmental review, despite cyanide spills into the water table used by the Indians (Abel, 1997).

By 1990, the Assiniboines and Gros Ventres began to challenge the environmental side-effects of cyanide-heap gold mining, forming a Native environmental advocacy group, Red Thunder, which joined with non-Indian environmental groups to resist federal permits for the Zortman-Landusky's mine's next requested expansion. The group's appeal was denied. In December 1992, Pegasus applied for another expansion of the mine, as Red Thunder joined with another Native environmental group, Island Mountain Protectors. Both prepared plans to challenge the expansion under the federal Clean Water Act, maintaining that the cyanide-leach method used in the mine was poisoning the reservation's water supply.

During July 1993, an intense thunderstorm brought a flood of acidified mine wastewater into the town of Zortman, after which the Bureau of Land Management (BLM) required the mine's owners to develop a new reclamation plan. At about the same time, an Environmental Protection Agency study found that the mine had been "leaking acids, cyanide, arsenic and lead from each of its seven

drainages" (Abel, 1997). The state of Montana soon joined the EPA in a suit based on the Clean Water Act, which was settled out of court in July 1996, with Pegasus and Zortman Mining pledging to pay $4.7 million in fines to the tribes, the federal government, and the state. The mine's owners also pledged to follow a detailed pollution control plan in the future.

Shortly thereafter, a request to triple the mine's size (from 400 to 1,192 acres) was approved by the Montana Department of Environmental Quality and the BLM (Abel, 1997). In January 1997, The Fort Belknap Community Council, National Wildlife Information Center sued the Montana Department of Environmental Quality, alleging that the agency's decision to allow an expanded mine violated state law.

During September 1997, federal and state environmental agencies fined Pegasus and Zortman Mining $25,300 for violating the clean water settlement by polluting a stream in the Little Rockies the previous summer. John Pearson, director of investor relations for Pegasus, asserted that discharges were the result of "acts of God" during "extraordinarily heavy rains" (Abel, 1997). By late 1997, with gold prices (and Pegasus's share price) declining rapidly, the company warned that its mine would close by January 1, 1998, if the expansion plan was not accepted. The state of Montana and local Native environmental activists wondered whether Pegasus would survive long enough as a corporate entity to complete promised reclamation of existing mines. In January 1998, Pegasus filed for Chapter 11 bankruptcy protection.

In the meantime, Pegasus left behind open pits that were described by Schneider:

> Pegasus dug pits the size of football fields and lined them with plastic or clay. Crushed ore was dumped in mounds as high as 15 feet and soaked with a mist of cyanide. It was the largest cyanide heap–leach operation in the world. . . . The heavily contaminated water trickled and flowed through fissures in the mountain, into the surface streams and underground aquifers that supply drinking water for 1,000 people who live in and around Lodge Pole and Hays, reservation towns north of the mountains (Schneider, 2001).

Streams flowing off the mountain, smelling of rotten eggs (the chemical signature of sulfide), were

cloudy and lifeless. "This is death," said John Allen, a tribal spiritual leader, as he filled his hands with putrid muck. "The mines take millions in gold from our land and leave us poisoned water. The miners and the government experts have argued for years about whether the water is bad. All they have to do is look, but they choose not to see" (Schneider, 2001). Allen, who was forty-six years of age in 2001, has thyroid problems, as do three of his siblings. His father has lymphatic cancer. Doctors who specialize in environmental medicine have told the Assiniboines and Gros Ventres that the diseases they suffer stem from contaminated water. Environmental advocates among the two tribes also report a high rate of stillbirths.

Bruce E. Johansen

See also Black Elk; Navajo-Hopi Land Dispute; Trail of Tears; Uranium Mining.

References and Further Reading
Abel, Heather. 1997. "The Rise and Fall of a Gold Mining Company." *High Country News* 29, December 22: 24. Available at: http://www.hcn .org/servlets/hcn.Article?article_id=3860. Accessed January 2, 2007.

Arizona Water Resource. 2001. "Black Mesa Spill Nets $128,000 Fine." *News Briefs* 9, no. 6 (May/June). Available at: http://ag.arizona .edu/AZWATER/awr/mayjune01/news.html. Accessed January 2, 2007.

Black Mesa Indigenous Support. No date-a. "A Brief History of relocation on Black Mesa." Available at: http://www.blackmesais.org/ cultural_sen_history.html. Accessed January 7, 2007.

Black Mesa Indigenous Support. No date-b. "Clean Coal's Dirty Facts." Available at: http://www .blackmesais.org/clean_coals_dirty_facts.html. Accessed January 7, 2007.

Edwards, John G. 2005. "Mohave Plant's Closure Coming." *Las Vegas Review-Journal* (December 24): 1-D.

Four Corners Clamor. 1998. "Figure This One!" VI, no. 1: 6. Available at: http://www.ausbcomp .com/redman/clamor6.htm#newdeal. Accessed January 2, 2007.

Giuliano, Jackie Alan. 2001. "Killing Tomorrow for a Few Megawatts Today." *Environment News Service* (March). Available at: http://ens.com] Accessed March 31, 2001. /ens/mar2001/ 2001L-03–30g.html.

Helms, Kathy. 2005. "Hopis Face Uncertain Future; Chairman Taylor Laments Lack of Water, Jobs and Mine Closures." *Gallup Independent*, February 4. Available at: http://www .gallupindependent.com/2005/feb/ 020405hopis.html. Accessed January 2, 2007.

Huff, Andrew. 2000. "Gold Mining Threatens Communities." *The Progressive* Media Project, July 11. Available at: http://www .progressive.org. Accessed July 31, 2000.

Johansen, Bruce, and Roberto Maestas. 1979. *Wasi'chu: The Continuing Indian Wars.* New York: Monthly Review Press.

LaDuke, Winona. 1992. "Indigenous Environmental Perspectives: A North American Primer." *Native Americas* 9, no. 2 (Summer): 52–71.

Norrell, Brenda. 2001. "Hopi and Navajo Protest Pipeline." *Asheville* [North Carolina] *Global Report* 129 (July 5–11). Available at: http:// www.agrnews.org/issues/129/nationalnews .html. Accessed January 2, 2007.

Schneider, Andrew. 2001. " 'A Wounded Mountain Spewing Poison:' *Seattle Post-Intelligencer* Special Report, June 12. Available at: http://seattlep-i.nwsource.com/specials/ mining/27076_lodgepole12.shtml. Accessed January 2, 2007.

Schneider, Iyawata Britten. No date. "Environmental and Human Rights Devastation in the Southwest." *Country Road News*. Available at: http://www.countryroadchronicles.com/ Articles/CountryRoadNews/]

Vandevelder, Paul. 2000. "Between a Rock and a Dry Place." *Native Americas* 17, no. 2 (Summer): 10–15.

Wanamaker, Tom. 2002. "Hopi Tribe Opposes Lease Extension on Water-Thirsty Black Mesa Mine." *Indian Country Today*, February 13: C-1.

Pan-Indianism

Pan-Indianism has historically been a reaction to European arrival and westward expansion. In general, pan-Indianism may be defined as a conglomeration of intertribal Native American people who organize in an effort to accomplish a set of specific goals. Pan-Indian movements have had proponents and critics from all segments of modern-day society. It is simultaneously evidence of the adversity of Native American culture and proof that European cultural imperialism has successfully erased many tribes from existence.

The earliest examples of pan-Indianism are typically linked to Native American revolts. Native Americans pooled their intertribal resources to resist colonization, as exemplified by the several revolts between 1680 and 1700 including the Pueblo Revolt, the Great Southwest Revolt, and King Philip's War. Pan-Indian resistance continued in the United States with leaders such as Pontiac, Neolin the Prophet,

and Tecumseh creating pan-Indian alliances that crossed tribal lines. Their collective goal involved preserving Native autonomy over land by preventing European settlers from spreading westward.

The late 1800s saw the emergence of at least three pan-Indian movements. First came the movement to make modern-day Oklahoma an intertribal Indian state to be governed by a pan-Indian set of laws and cultural practices based in the traditions of several tribes. Second was the Ghost Dance movement that spread across the Great Plains, promising to return the land to its condition prior to European arrival. U.S. agents interpreted Ghost Dance activities as a revolt and killed Sitting Bull, leading up to the massacre at Wounded Knee. The Ghost Dance movement was stopped, and many former ghost dancers became active in the so-called peyote cult, forming the third pan-Indian movement. Peyote use is most commonly linked to the Native American Church, which merges intertribal groups with Christian and Native American spiritual practices.

As European colonial activity evolved, so did the reaction that Native Americans embarked on in terms of pan-Indian activity. Perhaps a product of European efforts to assimilate Native Americans via boarding schools, many graduates went on to form pan-Indian organizations based on the notion of a shared national Indian identity. The process of assimilation allowed for the emergence of middle-class, educated Natives who attempted to utilize U.S. laws to make improvements in the lives of reservation and urban Native Americans. These organizations tended to take practical approaches to promoting the needs of impoverished Native Americans by advancing integration into mainstream U.S. political and economic institutions.

An early example of a pan-Indian integration organization was the Society of American Indians (SAI) formed in 1911 to monitor U.S. policy and its effect on Native American communities. Although the SAI was concerned with improving the education and integration of Native Americans, the group could not agree on how best to accomplish these goals. Its drive for U.S. citizenship for all Native Americans was realized in 1924, the same year the SAI disbanded.

Another successful pan-Indian organization is the National Congress of American Indians (NCAI). The NCAI initially focused on Native American education and legislation, much like the SAI, but expanded its efforts to job training and legal aid for Native people. Today the NCAI serves as a beacon for federal policy and legislation impacting tribal government and individual Native Americans. Since its origin, the NCAI has expanded its focus to include environmental resource management, elder and youth health care, and the promotion of religious freedom for Native Americans.

Amid the tide of ethnic movements during the 1950s and 1960s for increased integration and self-determination, a pan-Indian civil rights movement emerged. These civil rights organizations followed a pattern similar to other ethnic groups. As the sixties went on, newer civil rights organizations emerged with more extreme ideologies and actions than the previous organizations.

In 1961 the National Indian Youth Council (NIYC) emerged as a predominantly college student–based organization tasked with ensuring political visibility for Native American youth. The NIYC resorted to civil disobedience as a way of garnering exposure for the issues they deemed important. In 1967, a California-based group called the United Native Americans followed the path of NIYC but focused on reservation and urban pockets of Native populations. A year later, the most famous pan-Indian organization, the American Indian Movement (AIM), began patrolling the streets of Minneapolis and St. Paul to monitor the abuses police forces exerted in Native communities. AIM would emerge on the national scene because of their tactics and their involvement with many acts of disobedience against U.S. authority.

AIM is credited with bringing many issues to national visibility and, in the process, lost some members to prison and death. AIM worked with many other pan-Indian organizations to reclaim Alcatraz Island, the former site of an island prison in San Francisco Bay, on November 9, 1969. The resulting media attention was utilized to bring forward a long existing pan-Indian consciousness that rejected many of the principles of U.S. legitimacy. For the first time in U.S. history, notions of manifest destiny, U.S. nationalism, and the American Indian as conquered people were being challenged in front of a national mainstream audience.

Members of AIM took controversial stands on issues in Indian Country as well. By challenging the authority of tribal reservation governments, AIM risked alienating traditional Native Americans and the most powerful of Native Americans relative to all reservation residents. One of the most famous examples of such a challenge comes from the Pine Ridge Reservation in the midseventies when

Guardians of the Oglala Nation (GOONs), a private police force hired by the Lakota tribal government, were accused of overstepping their authority and killing reservation residents unjustifiably. AIM members began to patrol GOONs activity. After several altercations between AIM and GOONs, the FBI was brought in to control the situation. Although no one agrees on the details, the outcome was the arrest and conviction of AIM member Leonard Peltier for the murder of two FBI agents. Peltier remains incarcerated to this day for what many believe is a crime he did not commit.

As access to economic, educational, and political institutions increased, pan-Indianism took on a less militant approach. Today, many pan-Indian organizations represent groups of professional Native Americans in the private sector, in U.S. government, and on university campuses throughout the U.S. Some examples include the Native American Journalists Association, the American Indian Science and Engineering Society, the Association of American Indian Physicians, the Native American Law Students Association, and the American Political Science Association's Indigenous Studies network.

Also expanding in the university is the pan-Indian discipline of American Indian (or Native American) studies. Emerging in the late seventies, bachelor's, master's, and doctoral programs have proliferated. Several philosophies of education, community building, and integration with mainstream U.S. institutions have developed. The diversity of approaches to Native American issues has led to the appearance that the discipline lacks focus as a whole. One example of this inconsistency may be the very name for the discipline. Academic programs founded in the 1980s use the name American Indian studies, newer programs use the phrase Native American studies, Canadian programs call themselves First Nations' studies, and programs being formed today are tentatively called applied indigenous studies programs. Despite the label changes, all these programs share a common concern for the future of Native American people in terms of economic development, access to education, cultural sensitivity in research, and cultural revitalization.

Today, academics of political philosophy are emerging and promoting theories of pan-Indianism as an explanation of world power structures. Based on the premise that the world is composed of developed and developing nations, indigenous studies scholars argue that developing nations can never truly become developed nations. Rather, developed nations are developed only because of their relationship with First Nations' resources. Members of the First Nations' culture generally saw themselves as part of their environment, whereas developed nations saw themselves as masters of their environment. Colonialism allowed developing nations from Europe to become developed at the expense of First Nations' resources. Only those capable of functioning in their environment in nonexploitative ways will emerge from the inevitable resource depletion. Academics in indigenous studies believe only a pan-Indian movement will be capable of leading the world once developed nations consume resources beyond the point of sustainability.

Often taken as a double-edged sword, pan-Indianism is interpreted in terms of positive and negative impacts. The danger of pan-Indianism is that it threatens the purity of tribal cultures that have survived into the modern era. Pan-Indianism contains no language and adheres to a "powwow culture" potentially in conflict with individual tribal cultures. On the other hand, without a pan-Indian movement, many Native Americans throughout the world who have lost their former tribal affiliations would be left without a connection to Native identity. The youth of many tribal and urban Native communities are often brought together in university environments and seek support from other Native youth in pan-Indian student organizations. This is a continuation of the phenomena once experienced by Native individuals subjected to relocation into urban Indian centers. Pan-Indian centers still exist in urban areas in many states, including California, Arizona, Minnesota, Illinois, and Ohio.

Michael Lerma

See also American Indian Movement; National Congress of American Indians; National Indian Youth Council; Native American Church of North America; Society of American Indians; Wovoka.

References and Further Reading

Wilkins, David E. 2002. *American Indian Politics and the American Political System.* Lanham, MD: Rowman & Littlefield.

Deloria, Vine. 1999. *Tribes, Treaties, and Constitutional Tribulations.* Austin: University of Texas Press.

Deloria, Vine, and Raymond DeMallie. 1999. *Documents of American Indian Diplomacy: Treaties, Agreements, and Conventions, 1775–1979.* Norman: University of Oklahoma Press.

Grande, Sandy. 2004. *Red Pedagogy: Native American Social and Political Thought.* Lanham, MD: Rowman & Littlefield.

Smith, Linda Tuhiwai. 1999. *Decolonizing Methodologies: Research and Indigenous Peoples.* London: Zed Books.

Reservation Economic and Social Conditions

On some Indian reservations, small businesses were booming in the early twenty-first century, and there were indications that the typically poor reservation infrastructure was improving. Economic improvement is notable, especially on reservations where gambling has incubated other business activities. Reservations close to urban areas with large gambling clienteles have benefited the most, while those in rural areas, for the most part, have experienced little improvement. Even in rural areas, however, business activity has improved where activities such as Native-owned banks have been initiated. An example is provided by the Montana Blackfeet, in and near Browning, with banking activity founded by Eloise Cobell (who also initiated a class action lawsuit seeking an accounting for the federal government's mishandling of Indian royalty accounts). In general, however, Native Americans living on reservations, especially in the Great Plains, continue to be among the poorest people in the United States.

Poverty on the Plains

In the 2000 Census, Buffalo County, South Dakota, home of the Lower Brule Indian Reservation, had the lowest per capita income in the United States. The second-lowest ranking was Shannon County, South Dakota, home of the Pine Ridge Reservation. In Buffalo County, 61.8 percent of the children lived in poverty, the highest rate in the United States, followed by Zieback County (61.2 percent) and Shannon County (61 percent). These rates were much higher than those in any urban area.

The 2000 Census also indicated that South Dakota as a whole had the largest percentage increase in the United States for household median income between 1990 and 2000. At the same time, Buffalo County, home of the 3,500-member Crow Creek Sioux, and Shannon County remained as the two poorest counties in the United States. In Buffalo County, the largest and most successful business during the 1990s was the Lode Star

Casino. Shannon County has benefited somewhat from federal empowerment zone status that brought the county millions in federal dollars for economic development and a visit from President Bill Clinton.

Crime Rates Rise

According to Jeffrey Wollock, writing in *Native Americas*, crime rates on reservations have been rising. Indians twelve to twenty years old are 58 percent more likely to be crime victims than whites and blacks. Indians under age fifteen are murdered at twice the rate of whites. Census figures for 2000 support this trend.

The contemporary murder rate on Indian reservations is five times the average in the United States as a whole: twenty-nine per 100,000 people, compared to 5.6. The average in U.S. urban areas is seven per 100,000 (Crime Rate, 2003, 11). An Indian Country Crime Report, compiled from 1,072 cases prosecuted in U.S. district courts, did not include felonies committed by non-Indians on reservations. Some small reservations have very high murder rates, according to this report. The Salt River Pima Maricopa community in Arizona, for example, had six murders among 6,405 people, a murder rate seventeen times the national average. The Gila River reservation, with 11,257 enrolled members, suffered eleven murders, for a similar rate (Crime Rate, 2003, 11). According to Mac Rominger, an FBI agent on the Hopi and Navajo reservations, chronic problems such as alcoholism and poverty were compounded by isolation. "Ninety-five per cent of the violent crime out there is directed towards family and friends," he said (Crime Rate, 2003, 11).

Youth suicide among Native Americans is twice the rate of non-Indians. The American Medical Association reports that one in five Indian girls attempt suicide before leaving high school. The alcoholism death rate is four times the national average (Wollock, 2003, 30). Additionally, about 40 percent of Native Americans in the United States live in substandard housing, compared with an average of 6 percent for the rest of the population. The crisis for Native American young people is closely tied to the loss of culture, with youth "stuck between two worlds" (Wollock, 2003, 30). Many more Native youth than in earlier times cannot speak their own languages and have little grasp of their traditional culture and history.

Pikangikum's Continuing Desolation

Statistics can assume a terrifying profile when they are described in the context of one small village. Take, for example, the Ojibwa-Cree village of Pikangikum, about 200 miles northeast of Winnipeg. Pikangikum has the highest documented suicide rate in the world. It is a place where the main recreational pastime for young people is glue sniffing. The reserve's only school was closed for more than a year because of a fuel leak. Pikangikum's water treatment plant closed nearly as long, also because of an accidental fuel leak.

Eighty to 90 percent of the adults in Pikangikum were unemployed in 2003. The village is so overcrowded (with 400 homes for 2,100 people) that some people sleep in shifts to make beds available for others. All food is flown in, so prices are about five times the average for the rest of Canada.

Forty young people killed themselves in Pikangikum during the ten years ending in 2004. The same rate would have yielded 70,500 suicides in a city of 3 million people. Most of the suicides involved women who hung themselves (Elliott, 2001a, A-15). In 2000 alone, nine Ojibwa girls, aged five to thirteen, killed themselves in Pikangikum. Those suicides sent the year's suicide rate up to 470 deaths per 100,000, thirty-six times the Canadian national average. Three more young women killed themselves between mid-May and mid-June 2001. "When young women who are the bearers of life start to kill themselves, it's a real reflection on the health of the community," said Arnold Devlin of Dilico Child and Family Services in Thunder Bay (Elliott, 2000).

Since 1995, the Pikangikum Youth Patrol, a team of young volunteers, has scoured Pikangikum almost every night looking for huddles of gas sniffers, whose spine-chilling howls permeate the community at night, but the young addicts often scatter

President Bill Clinton holds a prayer pipe, the one used to formalize an 1868 treaty between the Native Americans and the U.S. government on the Pine Ridge Sioux Indian Reservation, presented to him by Millie Horn Cloud. Clinton visited the poorest county in the United States on July 7, 1999. (Reuters/Kevin Lamarque/Archive Photos)

into the darkness before patrollers can reach them. At peak suicide times like summer and fall, there's an attempt or two every night (Elliott, 2000).

Alcoholism: The Continuing Toll

Second only to the ravages of smallpox and other diseases, alcoholism has been the major cause of early death and other forms of misery for Native Americans since the "discovery" of the Americas by Columbus. Scarrooyady, an Iroquois sachem, told Pennsylvania treaty commissioners in 1750: "Your traders now bring us scarce anything but rum and flour. The rum ruins us. Those wicked whiskey sellers, when they have got the Indians in liquor, make them sell the very clothes from their backs!" (Johansen, 1982, 68). In 1832, the sale of alcoholic beverages to Indians was made illegal, an act that was not repealed until the early 1950s, when it became evident that prohibition produced a bootlegging industry little different from that which flourished nationwide during the 1920s and early 1930s.

Alcoholism continues to be a major problem today. The disease of alcoholism is the single leading cause of death in many Native American communities. Today, the sharpest increases in alcoholism exist in remote places such as Alaska and the Canadian North, where Native peoples have only recently been deprived of their traditional ways of life. In Manitoba, for example, several hundred Native people whose lands were flooded have been moved to settlements where they are no longer allowed (or able) to wrest a living from the land. Alcoholism and other forms of social disorientation have followed suit.

Even today, among Plains Indians, a large majority of Native American men drink alcohol, as does a smaller majority of Native women. By age seventeen, a majority of Indian boys and a large minority of Indian girls are steady drinkers. Drinking among Indian young people has been related directly to the highest suicide rate in the United States for any age group. Alcohol abuse also correlates to low educational achievement, poor health, and high rates of unemployment and crime among Indian youth.

Nationwide, American Indians have, for several years, averaged twelve times the number of arrests, per capita, as the general population. Three-quarters of these arrests are alcohol-related, almost twice the national average. About half of the Indian Health Service's caseload has been directly or indirectly attributed to alcohol use. Cirrhosis of the liver was a frequent cause of hospitalization and eventually death. According to the Indian Health Service (IHS), cirrhosis of the liver occurs in American Indians at five times the rate of the general population. The IHS also reports that many child-battering cases are alcohol related.

For a number of reasons, most of them cultural, traditional non-Indian treatments, from hospitalization to non-Indian chapters of Alcoholics Anonymous, have had very little success dealing with Indian alcoholism. Indian self-determination has prompted Native treatment programs with mixed results. Although the idea of Indians treating Indians was hailed as revolutionary in some quarters, it is not really new. Since at least the days of the Iroquois spiritual leader Handsome Lake in the early nineteenth century, Indian religious figures have opposed the use of alcohol and achieved moderate success.

Gambling: The New Buffalo?

In the late twentieth century, commercial gambling became a major source of income on some Indian reservations across the United States. While many Native American cultures traditionally practiced forms of gambling as a form of sport (such as the Iroquois Peachstone game), no Native American historical precedent exists for large-scale experience with gambling as a commercial enterprise. The arrival of gaming has brought dividends to some Native American peoples and controversy culminating in firefights and death for others.

The history of reservation-based commercial gambling began in 1979, when the Seminoles became the first Native nation to enter the bingo industry. By early 1985, seventy-five to eighty of the 300 recognized Indian tribes in the United States were conducting some sort of commercial game of chance. By the fall of 1988, the Congressional Research Service estimated that about 100 Indian nations and tribes participated in some form of gambling, which grossed about $255 million a year. By 1991, 150 of 278 Native reservations recognized by non-Indian governmental bodies had some form of gambling. According to the Interior Department, gross revenue from such operations passed $1 billion that year.

American Indian gaming revenue grew to $10.6 billion in 2000, representing 16 percent of the $64.9 billion generated by gaming in the United States as a

whole (Wanamaker, 2002). By 2002, Indian gaming revenue had grown to $14.5 billion, but, according to the National Indian Gaming Commission, 65 percent of the cash was flowing into only 7 percent of the gaming tribes (Fialka, 2004, A-4). Also according to the National Indian Gaming Association, Indian gaming by 2002 contributed approximately $120 million in state and local tax receipts annually, and gaming patrons spent an estimated $237 million in local communities around Indian casinos (Marquez, 2002). Of the 562 federally recognized Native American governmental entities in the United States at that time, 201 participated in Class II or Class III gaming. Class II makes such games as bingo, pull tabs, lotto, punchboards, and certain card games permissible under individual state laws. Class III includes everything else, such as casino-style table games, like roulette and craps, and card games such as poker and blackjack. Indian casinos operated in twenty-nine states under a total of 249 separate gaming compacts (Wanamaker, April 5, 2002).

Individual prizes in some reservation bingo games were reported to be as high as $100,000, while bingo stakes in surrounding areas under state jurisdiction were sometimes limited to $100. The reasons for growth in gambling on Indian land were readily apparent. Native governments sensed an opportunity for income that could make a substantial improvement in their economic conditions. A lack of state or federal regulation provided them with a competitive advantage over off-reservation gambling. These advantages included a lack of state-imposed limits on the size of pots or prizes, no restrictions by the states on days or hours of operations, no costs for licenses or compliance with state regulations, and (unless they were negotiated) no state taxes on gambling operations.

Gambling now provides a small galaxy of material benefits for some formerly impoverished Native peoples. A half hour's drive from the Twin Cities, for example, blackjack players crowd forty-one tables, while 450 other players stare into video slot machines inside the teepee-shaped Little Six Casino, operated by the 103 members of the Shakopee Mdewakanton Sioux tribe. Each member of the tribe receives a monthly dividend check that can amount to several thousand dollars as a shareholder in the casino. In addition to dividends, members became eligible for homes (if they lacked them), guaranteed jobs (if they were unemployed), and full college scholarships. The tribal government took out health insurance policies for everyone on the reservation

and established day care for the children of working parents.

Gambling, Politics, and the New York Oneidas

In 1970, the New York Oneidas' landholdings were down to thirty-two acres east of Syracuse. The tribe had almost no economic infrastructure. Three and a half decades later, the New York Oneidas own a large casino, the Turning Stone, which has incubated a number of other business ventures, making them one of the largest employers in the Syracuse area. Many of the roughly 1,000 Oneidas who reside in the area receive substantial material benefits.

By 2005, the Turning Stone was earning an estimated net profit of at least $70 million a year on about $250 million in gross income. Roughly 5 million visitors pass through the casino's doors per year (many of them repeat visitors). The casino's influence on the tax base of nearby small towns is enormous. James Chapell, mayor of the town of Oneida, for example, said that the Oneidas had taken so much land off the tax rolls that the town's tax revenues fell from $700,000 to $139,000 in one year (Randolph, 2003). The town of Oneida has resisted requesting financial help from the Oneida Indian Nation, but nearby Verona, which faced similar declines in tax revenue, negotiated funding for a water project as well as $800,000 for local services (Randolph, 2003).

Meanwhile, a substantial dissident movement has grown among Oneidas who assert that Raymond Halbritter, the "nation representative" of the New York Oneidas, was never voted into such an office. This group is centered in the Shenandoah family, which includes the notable singer Joanne Shenandoah and her husband, activist Doug George-Kanentiio. They believe that the New York Oneidas under Halbritter established a business, called it a nation, and acquired the requisite approvals from New York State and the United States federal government to use this status to open the Turning Stone. The dissidents' benefits as Oneidas were discontinued after they took part, during 1995, in a march for democracy to make these points (Johansen, 2002, 25–43).

The New York Oneidas under Halbritter's aegis appointed a men's council (a body unheard of in traditional matrilineal Iroquois law or tradition), which issued a zoning code to beautify the Oneida Indian Nation. This code enabled Halbritter's fifty-four-

member police force (patrolling a thirty-two-acre reservation) to "legally" evict from their homes Oneidas who opposed his role as tribal leader. Halbritter's control also was buttressed by the acquisition of a number of other businesses, a phalanx of public relations spin doctors, several lawyers, and ownership of *Indian Country Today,* a national Native American newspaper.

The story of the New York Oneidas is a particularly raw example of conflicts that beset many Native American nations that have attempted to address problems of persistent poverty and economic marginalization by opening casinos. Supporters of the casinos see them as the new buffalo, while opponents look at them as a form of internal colonization, an imposition of European-descended economic institutions and values on Native American peoples.

The recent experience of the Oneidas of New York raised several significant questions for Indian Country as a whole. Is the Oneida model of an economic powerhouse key to defining the future of Native American sovereignty in the opening years of the twenty-first century, as many of its supporters believe? Materially, the New York Oneidas have gained a great deal in a quarter century, including the repurchase of 14,000 acres of land. Have these gains been offset by an atmosphere of stifling totalitarianism and a devastating loss of traditional bearings, as many Oneida dissidents attest?

The Foxwoods Money Machine

Mashantucket means "the much-wooded land." The word "Foxwoods" is a combination of the notion of forest and the Pequots' reputation as "the fox people." Foxwoods started as a very small bingo parlor after roughly forty banks refused to loan money to the Pequots. The bingo parlor began operating in 1986 and became wildly successful, drawing its clientele mainly from the urban corridor that stretches from Boston to New York City. Having obtained backing from outside the United States, the Pequots opened their full-scale casino in 1992. At the time, Foxwoods was the only gaming establishment on the East Coast offering poker, which was banned at the time in Atlantic City.

The first day Foxwoods opened, February 14, 1992, its 1,700-car parking lot was full by 10:30 a.m. Roughly 75,000 people passed through the casino's doors there during that first day, and 2,000 of them were still present at the casino's 4 a.m. closing

time. During the ensuing decade, Foxwoods expanded, and became one of the most notable examples anywhere of Native American economic development.

By 2005, the Foxwoods complex was drawing an average of about 55,000 people most days. The Foxwoods Resort Casino complex includes five casinos housing 300,000 square feet of gaming space, 5,842 slot machines, 370 gaming tables, a 3,000-seat high-stakes bingo parlor with $1 million jackpots, a 200-seat Sportsbook, and a keno lounge. Table games included baccarat, mini-baccarat, big six wheels, blackjack, Caribbean stud poker, craps, Pai Gow, Pai Gow tiles, red dog, roulette, and a number of other games. The Foxwoods complex also includes four hotels ranging in size from 280 to 800 rooms each. In addition to gaming space and its four hotels, Foxwoods also offered twenty-three shopping areas, twenty-four food and beverage outlets, and a movie theater complex, as well as the Mashantucket Pequot Museum and Research Center and a Fox Grand Theater featuring Las Vegas-style entertainment.

Foxwoods quickly became a very large financial success for its sponsors, as well as for the government of Connecticut, to which the casino's management pledged a quarter of its profits. Foxwoods' gross revenues on its slot and video machines alone total about $9 billion a year. By 2004, the Foxwoods casino complex was paying the state of Connecticut $220 million a year in taxes. Foxwoods and a second casino, Mohegan Sun, paid the state of Connecticut $300 million to $350 million most years after 2000. The Mashantucket Pequots have become the state of Connecticut's largest single taxpayer and, with about 13,000 jobs, one of its larger employers. Foxwoods today is an integral pillar of Connecticut's economy and a multimillion-dollar contributor to the state's charities. The Pequots' casino even put up cash one year to help the state balance its budget. The casino complex employs a staff of lawyers and maintains its own permanent lobbying office in Washington, DC.

At the same time, the Pequots also became a significant contributor ($10 million) to the Smithsonian's new National Museum of the American Indian. That amount was soon matched by the New York Oneidas, drawing from its own casino profits. The Mashantucket Pequots also gave $2 million to the Special Olympics and $500,000 to the Hartford Ballet, as well as $5 million to the aquarium at Mystic, Connecticut. In June of 2001, the Mohegans, owners

of the neighboring Mohegan Sun Casino, made an equal pledge.

Death at Akwesasne

While gambling has brought benefits to some Native American communities, it brought violence to the Akwesasne Mohawks of St. Regis in upstate New York. The violence erupted in part over the issue of gambling. After as many as seven casinos opened illegally along the reservation's main highway in the late 1900s, the area became a crossroads for the illicit smuggling of drugs, including cocaine, and tax-free liquor and cigarettes. Tensions escalated after early protests of gambling included the trashing of one casino and the burning of another and after gambling supporters attempted to repress this resistance with brutal force. When in April 1990 residents blockaded the reservation to keep the casino's customers out, gambling supporters responded by destroying the blockades. By then, violence had spiraled into brutal beatings of antigambling activists, drive-by shootings, and firefights. On May 1, 1990, two Mohawks were killed in related violence. The intervention of several police agencies from the United States and Canada followed the two deaths; outside police presence continued for years afterward (Johansen, 1993).

Everyone who is familiar with the Akwesasne Mohawk territory knows it has been the scene of considerable smuggling between the United States and Canada, but no one knew the extent of the traffic until its volume drew the attention of prosecutors and police in both countries. By 2000, with several convicted smugglers awaiting sentencing, the size of the smuggling industry outlined in court records astounded even veteran observers. The evidence presented by prosecutors outlined the largest smuggling operation since the U.S.–Canada border was established.

Akwesasne is the only Native American reservation that straddles the U.S.–Canadian border and, as such, has long provided a smuggling route for anything illegal that may be in demand across either border. This cargo has included cigarettes and hard liquor (which are taxed much more heavily in Canada than in the United States), several varieties of illegal narcotics, automatic weapons, and even human beings. Immigration authorities at one point broke a smuggling ring that was ferrying people (most of them illegal immigrants from Asia) across the border at a cost of $45,000 to $50,000 each. The cigarette smuggling trade is called "buttlegging," wordplay on bootlegging.

The right of Mohawks to cross the border unimpeded is recognized by the Jay Treaty (1794), which Canadian authorities have occasionally contested. Various enterprising Akwesasne residents have become adept at selling their connections as border middlemen, the central link in the smuggling chain. A few years ago, a story floated around the reservation that a local kingpin was negotiating to buy a small island in the Saint Lawrence River for about $225,000 for use as a smuggling base. After the two parties agreed on the price, the new owner walked to a closet in his home, which was stacked floor to ceiling with cash in large denominations. He peeled an inch or two off the top of the stack to pay for the island.

The Canadian federal government has asserted that taxing authorities in that country lost $750 million in potential revenue because of smuggling through Akwesasne between 1991 and 1997, when the big smuggling ring was busted. Nearly as much money was laundered through an armored-car business in Massena, New York. Prosecutors requested that U.S. District Court Judge Thomas McAvoy sentence John "Chick" Fountain of Massena to seven years in prison and forfeiture of an unspecified amount worth of personal property for his role in laundering $557 million through his armored car and currency exchange business. Before starting this business, Fountain had previously lived much more modestly as a New York State trooper.

Fountain, convicted on November 3, 1998, was one of twenty-seven people who prosecutors alleged had important roles in a smuggling ring that at its height operated large warehouses and squads of motorboats, which were used to ferry goods and people across the Saint Lawrence River. When the river was frozen, smuggling often took place in automobiles. The smuggling ring drew some well-known names at Akwesasne into its ambit, including longtime gambling developer Tony Laughing and former St. Regis Tribal Chief Leo David Jacobs, who was convicted of taking $32,000 in kickbacks paid to link Miller with a number of Akwesasne businessmen. One of these businessmen was Loran Thompson, owner of a marina, a restaurant, and what New York radio reporter Neil Drew of Malone, New York, called a very busy cigarette warehouse along the Saint Lawrence River, where millions of cartons were purchased for smuggling into Canada (Drew, 2001).

The alleged kingpin of the smuggling cartel was Larry Miller of Massena, who traveled the world in a Lear Jet and owned five houses in Las Vegas, as well as an estate not far from the source of his income: the porous international border through Akwesasne. According to court records, Miller made as much as $35 million a year at the height of the operation. Prosecutors suggested that Judge McAvoy fine Miller $160 million in cash and personal assets and sentence him to to seventeen to twenty-two years in prison. He was sentenced to 17.5 years in prison.

Small Businesses Boom at Akwesasne

While the smuggling at Akwesasne continues, today the main cross-reservation arterial (State Highway 37) is lined with businesses that did not exist two decades ago—not just the usual cheap gas and cigarettes, but the everyday goods that sustain people who live there. Mohawk-owned businesses secured government-backed loans and grants, resulting in the building of a small strip mall and enterprises ranging from lacrosse stick manufacturing to large-scale construction companies.

The local newspaper, *Indian Time,* in 2005 was flush with advertising from Akwesasne businesses, including A First Americans Food Store, The Village Currency Exchange, EScentULee (manicures, pedicures, facials, and the like), Little Bear Design (embroidery and design), Burning Sky Office Products, Four Seasons Lawn Care & Snow Removal, Grace & Allan's Discount Tobacco Products, St. Regis Mohawk Senior Center, CKON Radio, Broken Arrow Truck Stop/Gift Shop, Physical Limits Fitness Club, Clyde N Performance Plus (boats and motors), Akwesasne Mohawk Casino, Trade Zone Gasoline Station, Oakes Heating and Cooling, and Bear's Den Restaurant and Motel.

Bruce E. Johansen

See also Alcoholism and Substance Abuse; Economic Development; Gambling.

References and Further Reading

Cornell, Stephen, and Joseph P. Kalt. 1990. "Pathways from Poverty: Economic Development and Institution-Building on American Indian Reservations." *American Indian Culture & Research Journal* 14, no. 1: 89–125.

Cornell, Stephen, and Joseph P. Kalt. 1991. "Where's the Glue? Institutional Bases of American Indian Economic Development." Malcolm Wiener Center for Social Policy Working Paper Series, H-91–2. March. John F. Kennedy School of Government, Harvard University.

"Crime Rate on Indian Reservations Much Higher Than U.S." 2003. *Indian Time* (Akwesasne Mohawk Reservation, New York) (October 9): 11.

"Crisis at Akwesasne." 1990. Transcript of hearings of the New York Assembly, July–August. Albany and Fort Covington, NY: State of New York.

Drew, Neil. 2001. Personal communication (July 1).

Elliott, Louise. 2000. "Ontario Native Suicide Rate One of Highest in World, Expert Says." *Vancouver Sun,* November 30. Available at: http://www.vancouversun.com. Accessed December 13, 2000.

Elliott, Louise. 2001a. "Hunger and Suicide Stalk Reserve after Feds Cut Funds." *Montreal Gazette,* June 7: A-15.

Elliott, Louise. 2001b. "Band Talking to Media May Perpetuate Suicide Crisis, Says Nault." Canadian Press. June 22.

Federal Bureau of Investigation. 1989. *Crime in the United States.* Washington, DC: Government Printing Office.

"Federal Paternalism Angers Pikangikum." No date. *Canadian Aboriginal.* canadianaboriginal.com Accessed November 22, 2002. Ganter, Granville. 2004. "Sovereign Municipalities? Twenty Years After the Maine Indian Claims Settlement Act of 1980." *Enduring Legacies: Native American Treaties and Contemporary Controversies.* Edited by Bruce E. Johansen, 25–43. Westport, CT: Praeger.

Giago, Tim. 1997. "Gambling Helps Few Indian Tribes." *Omaha World-Herald,* June 6: 24.

Goulais, Bob. 2000. "Water Crisis Latest Plague to Visit Pikangikum." *Anishinabek News,* November. Available at: http://www.anishinabek.ca

Hornung, Rick. 1991. *One Nation Under the Gun: Inside the Mohawk Civil War.* New York: Pantheon.

Johansen, Bruce E. 1993. *Life and Death in Mohawk Country.* Golden, CO: North American Press/Fulcrum.

Johansen, Bruce E. 2002. "The New York Oneidas: A Case Study in the Mismatch of Cultural Tradition and Economic Development." *American Indian Culture & Research Journal* 26, no. 3: 25–46.

Meriam, Lewis. 1928. *The Problem of Indian Administration.* Baltimore, MD: Johns Hopkins University Press.

Mohawk, John. Spring-summer, 1989. "Economic Motivations: An Iroquoian Perspective." In *Indian Corn of the Americas: Gift to the World.* Edited by Jos. Barreiro. *Northeast Indian Quarterly* 6, nos. 1–2: 56–63.

Mohawk, John C. Summer, 1992. "Indian Economic Development: The U.S. Experience in Evolving Indian Sovereignty." *Akwe:kon Journal* 9, no. 2: 42–49.

Ortiz, Roxanne D., ed. 1979. *Economic Development in American Indian Reservations.* Albuquerque: University of New Mexico Indian Studies.

Pasquaretta, Paul. 1994. "On the 'Indianness' of Bingo: Gambling and the Native American Community." *Critical Inquiry* 20: 694–719.

Randolph, Eleanor. 2003. "New York's Native American Casino Contributes, But Not to Tax Rolls." *New York Times,* October 18.

Smith, Dean Howard. 2000. *Modern Tribal Development: Paths to Self-Sufficiency and Cultural Integrity in Indian Country.* Lanham, MD: AltaMira Press.

U.S. Department of Health and Human Services. 1991. *Trends in Indian Health.* Washington, DC: Government Printing Office.

Walke, Roger. 1988. "Gambling on Indian Reservations." Congressional Research Service, Library of Congress. October 17.

Wanamaker, Tom. 2002. "Indian Gaming Column." *Indian Country Today,* April 5.

Wollock, Jeffrey. 2003. "On the Wings of History: American Indians in the 20th Century." *Native Americas* 20, no. 1 (Spring): 14–31.

Squaw, Debates over Place Names

Controversy swirls around the use of the word "squaw" to name places in the United States. Many Americans defend the practice as means of acknowledging, if not honoring, indigenous peoples. In recent years, American Indians, energized by a cultural and political renaissance, have challenged these interpretations, asserting that "squaw" is a derogatory term and that its use as a place name harms Native peoples and communities.

Language and Power

"Squaw" entered European languages by the middle of the sixteenth century. Two competing theories describe the origins of the word. The first explanation, preferred by many linguists, anthropologists, and etymologists, traces the term to an abbreviation of the Narraganset word, *eskwa,* meaning woman. It was not initially a derogatory or offensive term. In fact, several Native languages contain related words. A second interpretation, favored by activists and political leaders, asserts that "squaw" actually has more vulgar roots and consequently always has carried negative connotations. This account has proposed that French trappers borrowed the Mohawk word for female genitals, *ge-squaw,* to refer to Native women and their sexuality.

Whatever its origins, a constellation of largely pejorative meanings has clustered around "squaw" in English. It has crystallized as a trope of extraordinary power and influence in American culture. The "squaw" of songs, stories, jokes, literature, and film, according to Rayna Green (1990), has been "the darker twin" of the Indian princess: "Squaws share the same vices attributed to Indian men—drunkenness, stupidity, thievery, venality of every kind." They have been sexualized, doing "what White men want for money and lust," not love. And at the same time, expressive culture has often portrayed the squaw as a drudge, an ugly, fat, overburdened, and dependent creature, passively completing chores while her "buck" idles. In popular usage the term has come to be used for a woman or, more generally, a wife. One might hear a man say, "This is my squaw . . ." or "How's the squaw?" Even more generally, it has been employed to describe an effeminate object or action as well as a weak person. More troubling, squaw has long carried sexual connotations. The term not only has often sexualized Native American women, glossing them as prostitutes, it has also described female sexuality more generally, as in World War II, when American soldiers used "squaw" to refer to an ugly prostitute. Today, according to Bea Medicine (quoted in King, 2003), squaw remains "a very derogatory term for Indian women. It equates them with sexuality and perpetuates the stereotype that Indian women are loose and promiscuous."

"Squaw" is not just a hurtful term; it has encouraged violence against American Indian women as well. The most disturbing instances include racist epithets shouted at indigenous women ("dirty squaw") or displayed on placards opposing the exercise of treaty rights ("Save a walleye, spear a pregnant squaw!"), sexual jokes told among friends about the supposed proclivities of indigenous women, and the use of the term in sexual and physical assaults.

Naming and Claiming Places

Euro-American observers have long read landscape and nature more generally in gendered terms, interpreting the virginal, uncultivated, and supposedly

unoccupied land as feminine. Frequently, the accounts of Euro-American explorers, soldiers, administrators, settlers, and tourists extend this tradition to indigenous femininity through which they secured a unique metaphorical hold over, or purchase of, the land. The use of "squaw" in place names conforms to this pattern. And yet "squaw" inscribes more than femininity onto the landscape, projecting the inferiority read into the indigenous cultures as well as the presumed rights of the Euro-American colonizers. In naming the landscape, they set about claiming it, simultaneously foregrounding an element of American Indian life even as they erased indigenous histories and removed Native nations.

In this context, it is perhaps not surprising how popular "squaw" has proven to be as a place name. Nine hundred thirty-eight geographic features in thirty-eight states bear the name "squaw." In contrast, only a handful of places bear the less exotic gender markers: only 179 features bear the name "lady" and sixteen the name "woman."

Importantly, the pervasive presence of the place name veils significant variation. Despite its origins in the Native languages spoken in the northeastern United States, it is much more common in the American West. And while bays, buttes, canyons, flats, hills, hollows, lakes, ledges, passes, and peaks have been paired with squaw, to fashion place from space, more creeks are so named than any other geographic

A Maine Department of Transportation worker places a Big Squaw Township sign into storage in Greenville, Maine, in 2001 after enactment of a state law in Maine to remove the word "squaw" in public places. The word "squaw" has long been considered offensive by American Indians. (AP Photo/Robert F. Bukaty)

feature. In addition to these seemingly innocent names, more overtly disturbing place names include Squaw Humper Creek (South Dakota), Squaw Teats (Montana and Wyoming), and Squaw Tit (Arizona, California, Idaho, Montana, New Mexico, and Nevada).

The Controversy

The contemporary movement to change place names bearing "squaw" began in Minnesota in 1994. After learning of the historical origins of the word, two Ojibwa adolescents, Angela Losh and Dawn Litzau, sought to remove the word from geographic features in the state. They recognized the word as an embarrassing and painful insult, best replaced in official inscriptions with words from local indigenous languages like Ojibwa. After much public debate and legislative hearings, Losh and Litzau succeeded in passing a law banning the word.

Building on this momentum, in 1996, a grassroots movement began in Arizona to change place names in the state. To achieve this end, a group of adolescent indigenous women, led by Delena Waddle (then a sophomore at Mesa High School), founded the American Indian Movement Youth Organization. As in Minnesota, pain, humiliation, and terror inspired Waddle. Although the young women encouraged a local church to change its name and provoked intense public debate, they did not achieve their objectives.

An unwillingness or inability to recognize the equality, autonomy, and dignity of indigenous peoples frustrated their efforts as they have those of state representative Jack Jackson, a Navajo (Dine), who has labored for the better part of a decade to change place names in Arizona. More recently, both Montana and Maine have passed legislation to remove "squaw" from places and features. Whereas in Montana, House Bill 412 passed with little debate or opposition, greater controversy accompanied the ultimately successful efforts of Passamaquoddy Representative Donald Soctomah in Maine.

Not all American Indians have supported efforts to erase "squaw" from the map. In fact, some see in "squaw" a strong validation of themselves as indigenous peoples. On reservations across the country, one can find cars bearing bumper stickers proclaiming "Squaw Power." More central to the controversy over the place name, some American Indians, especially in recent debates in Maine, have suggested that "squaw" or some variation of it is an

element of many Native languages. Moreover, the presence of "squaw" on the map reflects indigenous occupation of an area, while preserving the prominence of Native nations within local histories. To remove it is to remove American Indians once more, enacting a kind of symbolic violence against them and their heritage. A better strategy, they contend, is to keep "squaw" as a place name and to educate Americans about what it really means, challenging their stereotypes about indigenous women and their communities. In some areas, "squaw" has been replaced with Native names in indigenous languages for places that once bore the name "squaw."

For their part, most Americans do not understand how seemingly innocent symbols have become controversial. They balk at the idea of changing names, because too often they fail to grasp the offensiveness of the term or appreciate its history. When American Indians object to the continued use of "squaw," many Euro-Americans have reacted negatively, even hostilely. They are likely to see it as trivial or even pointless. Consequently, "squaw" has provoked a charged backlash that simultaneously questions indigenous critics and their motives, while strongly defending traditional American values and identity.

The controversy over the use of "squaw" to name places is emblematic of the political and cultural resurgence of Native America. It is a forceful reminder of a long history of mistreatment of American Indians, particularly indigenous women, in the United States. It gives powerful testimony to a refusal to be named in the language of the colonizer and an insistence to have Native nations recognized as important participants in American society. Despite much progress over the past half century, as long as Euro-Americans continue to misappropriate and misunderstand indigenous peoples, place names and other symbols will be contentious.

C. Richard King

See also Language and Language Renewal; Mascots.
References and Further Reading
Bright, William. 2000. "The Sociolinguistics of the 'S-Word': Squaw in American Placenames." *Names* 48: 207–216.
Cutler, Charles L. 1994. "Renaming a Continent." In *O Brave New Words! Native American Loan Words in Current English*, 67–78. Norman: University of Oklahoma Press.
Goddard, Ives. 1997. "Since the Word Squaw Continues to Be of Interest." *News from Indian Country*, Mid-April: 19A.

Green, Rayna. 1990. "The Pocahontas Perplex: The Image of Indian Women in American Culture." In *Unequal Sisters: A Multicultural Reader in U.S. Women's History.* Edited by Ellen Carol DuBois and Vicki L. Ruiz, 15–21. New York: Routledge.

King, C. Richard. 2003. "De/Scribing Squ*w: Indigenous Women and Imperial Idioms in the United States." *American Indian Culture and Research Journal,* 27, no. 2: 1–16.

Trade

Before European colonization, Native American peoples carried on extensive trading relationships across North America. Unusual items, such as turquoise from New Mexico, found their way to the East Coast via trade routes that covered the continent (and often presaged the routes of modern interstate highways). Copper from Lake Superior and pipestone from Minnesota were carried, in some cases, many hundreds of miles from their sources. Aztec artifacts have been found along the U.S. Gulf of Mexico coast.

Trade patterns in North America seem to have been well formed as early as 2,300 years ago. The Adena and Hopewell cultures in what is now the U.S. Midwest traded for Lake Superior copper, Gulf of Mexico shells, and North Dakota flint. They used obsidian that originated in Wyoming's Yellowstone region, quartz from Arkansas, and silver from Canada. The following words by Bruce G. Trigger describing eastern North America, were true of the entire continent.

> Eastern North America was . . . crisscrossed by exchange networks, many of which were of considerable antiquity. Trade across ecological boundaries sometimes involved staples, such as the surplus corn that the Hurons [Wyandots] traded with the Nipissings, and possibly with other Northern Algonquian peoples, in return for pelts and dried fish. Most trade, however, was in luxury items, including marine shells, copper, and fancy furs. Exotic cherts continued to be passed from one band to another throughout the boreal forests (1996, 329).

Following European contact, trade took on a more sinister cast, as vectors of disease often followed trade routes. The traders transported pathogens to their families along with trade goods. In a spiraling effect, Native people who had been afflicted by disease often experienced a loss of income (for example, the fur trade in the Northeast, the deerskin trade in the Southeast), inhibiting their ability to purchase arms and ammunition and thus opening them to attack from others who had not suffered similarly. This dynamic, as well as the sheer population decline caused by trade-hastened disease, hugely impacted Native societies in North America.

As the European trade frontiers expanded, Native Americans in different regions both maintained precontact trade specializations and assumed new ones. Many groups in the Northeast specialized in guns and furs. Groups in what would later be called the U.S. Southwest specialized in the horse trade. Horses diffused northward mainly after Spanish settlement began in New Mexico after 1600, but some Native peoples, including the Pawnee, may have had access to them earlier than that. As early as the 1500s, some horses escaped Spanish

Native Americans trade with the Dutch in New Netherland. Dutch colonial governor Peter Stuyvesant attempted to eliminate the unscrupulous trading practices of the Dutch colonists with the Native Americans. (Library of Congress)

herds and bred wild in New Mexico and Texas. These were the "Indian ponies," averaging less than 1,000 pounds in weight and smaller than modern-day riding horses. These agile, fast horses were interbred with larger animals acquired from Spanish (and later Anglo-American) herds. The Pawnees especially became known as horse traders on the Plains.

At times, Native people who shared neighboring territories evolved symbiotic trade relationships. The Crows, for example, routinely produced a surplus of meat and other buffalo products that they traded to the Hidatsas for their surplus of agricultural products. Different segments of the same tribe or nation might also evolve symbiotic trade relationships. Certain bands of Cheyennes, for instance, specialized in various modes of economic production. For example, southern bands specialized in horse raiding, while central bands specialized in the making of buffalo robes. The northern bands usually had a surplus of trade goods, such as knives and kettles, from trade along the upper Missouri River. Whenever people from two different Cheyenne bands were married, ceremonies included substantial gift giving, which performed an economic function of redistributing goods for mutual benefit. (This was true for many North American Indian groups.)

While trade among Native peoples served the same material purposes as similar forms of exchange among non-Indians, trade was viewed by most Native Americans as something more than an economic exchange. Trade also cemented political alliances. In some Plains Native American cultures (the Hidasta, for example), non-Indian traders were adopted ceremonially. Other links were created by traders' marriages to Native women. In trading relationships, bargaining often was not carried on directly in trade between Native people, who considered an argument over price as a breach of friendship. The consideration of a profit motive also was deemed uncouth in public. Trade was generally meant to be a mutually advantageous exchange of gifts.

Many Native peoples associated trade with the formation of a kinship bond. Among the Cheyennes, trade was accompanied by the "making of relatives." Influence accrued to the person with the largest network of "relatives" or "relations." Marriage was regarded as only one way of many that such a network could be built. European traders quickly learned Native customs of trade and

adapted them to their purposes. Because Indians valued reciprocity, Europeans found that generosity on their part often would be returned. The commercial traffic in furs often was carried on according to Native trading customs, just as early diplomacy in America often took place according to Native American protocols.

From a Native American point of view, much of the trade of the Plains was perceived to be reciprocal gift-giving in association with the calumet, or peace pipe. The calumet had been used for hundreds of years in rituals that enabled otherwise hostile peoples to meet and trade in peace. Lewis and Clark's journal explains the ritual: "The party delivering generally Confess their Errors and request a peace[;] the party receiving exult in their Suckcesses [sic] and receive the Sacred Stem" (Wishart, 1994, 32). Bows and arrows, skins, food, guns, and other "gifts" might then be exchanged.

The two most important European trade items during the first years of contact were probably guns (initially banned in most trading areas), horses, and manufactured goods that aided agriculture and hunting, such as metal hoes and knives. All of these items comprised the advance guard of the European-American cash economy. To purchase guns, ammunition, horses, and riding tack (among the many other trade items that came with time), Native American peoples needed a commodity to exchange, usually the skins of fur-bearing animals, such as beaver in the Northeast, deer in the South, and a variety of skins in the Southwest. Everywhere, food was an important commodity, largely because the colonists often were unwilling or unable to raise or hunt enough of it to sustain themselves.

Trade also brought metal kettles, linen shirts, blankets, spinning wheels, Italian glass beads, shoes, drills, and many other items to Native people. The fact that the Industrial Revolution began in England provided that country with the most extensive inventory of trade goods and had a major influence on swinging the balance of North American military power toward England, and away from France and Spain, by the mideighteenth century.

Native American people adopted European trade goods because they made life easier. Still, some treaty records indicate that many Native American leaders questioned whether trade goods should be accepted. For one thing, they made their people dependent on the immigrants and their cultures for manufactured goods that Native peoples

could not provide for themselves. As Indians adopted European manufactured goods, their own inventory of cultural and economic skills tended to decline. Another reason for the suspicion of non-Native trade goods was their association with misery. Not only did disease tend to follow trade routes, especially in the early years of contact and immediate precontact, but some of the imports, such as firearms, increased the level of violence in Native societies.

Nevertheless, because of trade, by the time of the American Revolution many Mohawks (in present-day upstate New York) had material living standards comparable to those of nearby European-Americans. Some of the Mohawks' Oneida neighbors, according to historian Colin Calloway, "lived in frame houses with chimneys and painted windows, ate with spoons from pewter plates, drank from teacups and punch bowls, combed their hair with ivory combs, used silk handkerchiefs, and wore white breeches" (1997, 46). The Cherokees, in a material sense, were living much like their non-Indian neighbors before they were expelled from their homelands on the Trail of Tears in the late 1830s, largely due to the influences of trade.

Human beings were an important trading commodity among Europeans and some Native peoples. Early Spanish explorers traveled in America planning to take slaves. When De Soto's expedition arrived in Florida, they brought leg irons and metal collars linked with chains for the express purpose of conveying Indian slaves along their line of march. After the Pequot War in 1675, Massachusetts colonists sold their prisoners into slavery in the West Indies. The Spanish at about the same time were shipping their prisoners of war to Cuba as slaves. The Apaches greatly enhanced their diets by raiding Spanish settlements and missions for cattle, mules, and horses. The Spanish retaliated by capturing Apaches and selling them as slaves, most of whom were compelled to work in Spanish mines. Any Apache was game for enslavement, even those who had come to trade or who had converted to Christianity.

In 1704, South Carolinians under Colonel James Moore united with Indian allies and invaded northern Florida, which was under Spanish control, razing fourteen missions and capturing about 1,000 people who were taken home as slaves. In 1708, about 1,400 slaves of Native American descent—a quarter of total slaves in the colony—were listed in a South Carolina census. In 1726,

French Louisiana listed 229 Indian slaves and 1,540 black slaves. Pawnees were captured so often that the word "Panis" became a synonym for "slave" in the language of the French colonies. Virtually all of those known as Panis were captured first by other Indians and then traded to the English or French.

The slave trade sometimes became entwined with trade in horses. Having acquired horses in the early nineteenth century, the Klamaths raided Shasta and Pit River Indian villages in northern California, acquiring slaves who were traded at The Dalles, in present-day Oregon, for more horses and trade goods. With the advent of the fur trade in that area, non-Indians also became involved in the regional slave trade, typically using Native people for barter along with other "commodities." Russians colonizing present-day Alaska were occasionally taken as slaves, as were a few Japanese fishermen whose boats drifted too near the coast.

The trading markets of The Dalles were part of a commercial system maintained by the Chinooks along the lower Columbia River. Native people from as far away as Hawaii sometimes changed hands at The Dalles slave markets, where canoes and blankets, as well as horses, were the favored items of exchange. Some of the treaties signed by Isaac Stevens in Washington territory contained legal prohibitions of slavery, an indication that the practice was economically significant at the time. The clauses in question specifically referenced Native American slavery. After the Civil War, agents of the U.S. government actively tried to suppress the Native American slave trade, causing slave prices to rise. In 1830, the going rate for a young, healthy, male slave in The Dalles market was about ten blankets. Within a few decades, the Haida were paying up to 200 blankets per slave.

Into the 1860s, Native Americans who had been picked up by the Los Angeles police were "sold" to local farmers and ranchers as day labor. In 1850 and 1860, the newly established state of California enacted laws that allowed for Indian "apprenticeship," a state-approved form of near-slavery by which property owners could obtain the labor of as many Native young people as they wished, on stipulation that they feed and clothe them, and treat them "humanely." The measure was promoted as a means of teaching the Indians "civilized" habits. A debate rose over the terms of the laws, which in effect made several thousand Indian young people indentured servants at the same time that California had been admitted to the United States as a "free"

state. In the 1850s, the "standard price for the Red-skin" was said to be about $50. The indenture law was repealed in 1863 (as part of the nationwide Civil War debate over slavery), but illegal kidnappings and sales of Indians continued through at least the 1870s, although at a reduced rate. Travel literature sometimes drew the attention of potential immigrants to the advantages of free Indian labor, which was not available in other states.

While some Indian groups traded in slaves, most Native American nations traditionally did not hold slaves as part of their societies. An exception was the peoples of the Northwest Coast culture area, whose nobility held slaves. Slave labor became so important in Tlingit society that women did little or no work. At puberty, an upper-class Tlingit woman was sent into seclusion lasting from four months to a year. The longer the period of seclusion, the higher the person's rank and the greater the necessity of having slaves to attend to one's everyday needs. A woman in seclusion was not allowed to engage in any economically productive activity.

Slaves were important commodities in the social economy of the Tlingit. Slaves might be killed or freed to give family and clan "crests" ceremonial value. Slaves were more often freed than killed, however; freed slaves (often captives from other villages) could then assume important positions in Tlingit society, sometimes because of their talents as carvers, dancers, or sorcerers. A skilled slave had some leverage in Tlingit society, and several families might vie for his or her services. In the richest villages, slaves were said to make up a third of the population; the richest of chiefs might own fifty slaves of both sexes. Slaves had no rights and owned nothing except their ability to work.

Some male slaves among the Makah were initiated into the Klukwali (or Wolf) society; during its ceremonies, they participated as equals with nobles and commoners. Members of this secret society also could lodge complaints against each other and discuss grievances regardless of social rank or class, thus allowing some degree of accountability and equality in what was otherwise a very rigid class system.

Indians living around Puget Sound were prime targets of their slave-raiding neighbors to the north, with the Makahs (some of whom held slaves themselves) notable as middlemen in the coastal slave trade. Occasionally, the Puget Sound tribes struck back. In 1810, Chief Sea'th'l (Seattle) gained influence among his people, the Duwamish (who lived on the site of the present-day city of Seattle), by leading warriors against tribes in the foothills of the Cascades who had taken some of his people as slaves.

Bruce E. Johansen

See also Fur Trade; Hudson's Bay Company; Paleo-Indians; Seattle; Slavery and Native Americans; Trade and Intercourse Acts.

References and Further Reading

Albers, Patricia. 1993. "Synthesis, Merger, and War," Contrasting Forms of Intertribal Relationship Among Historic Plains Indians." In *The Political Economy of North American Indians*. Edited by John H. Moore. Norman: University of Oklahoma Press.

Anderson, Terry L., and Fred S. McChesney. 1994. "Raid or Trade: An Economic Model of Indian-White Relations." *Journal of Law and Economics* 37 (April): 39–74.

Baily, L. R. 1973. *Indian Slave Trade in the Southwest*. Los Angeles, CA: Westernlore Press.

Calloway, Colin. 1997. *New Worlds for All: Indians, Europeans, and the Remaking of Early America*. Baltimore, MD: Johns Hopkins University Press.

Fixico, Donald L. 1984."As Long as the Grass Grows: The Cultural Conflicts and Political Strategies of United States–Indian Treaties." In *Ethnicity and War*. Edited by Winston A. Van Horne and Thomas V. Tonnesen. Madison: University of Wisconsin Press.

Moore, John H. 1997. *The Cheyennes*. Oxford, UK: Blackwell Publishing.

Oberg, Kalervo. 1973. *The Social Economy of the Tlinget Indians*. Seattle: University of Washington Press.

Olexer, Barbara. 1982. *The Enslavement of the American Indian*. Monroe, NY: Library Research Associates.

Ruby, Robert H., and John A. Brown. 1993. *Indian Slavery in the Pacific Northwest*. Spokane, WA: Arthur H. Clark Co.

Snell, William Robert. 1972. "Indian Slavery in Colonial South Carolina, 1671–1795." Ph.D. dissertation, University of Alabama.

Trigger, Bruce G. 1996. "Entertaining Strangers: North America in the Sixteenth Century." In *The Cambridge History of the Native Peoples of the Americas*. Edited by Bruce G. Trigger and Wilcomb E. Washburn, 325–398. Cambridge, UK: Cambridge University Press.

Wishart, David J.1994. *An Unspeakable Sadness: The Dispossession of the Nebraska Indians*. Lincoln: University of Nebraska Press.

Treaty Diplomacy, with Summary of Selected Treaties

According to Francisco de Vitoria's 1532 opinion that defined a doctrine of discovery for European nations, one of two ways in which European nations could legally gain title to land from Native American nations was by treaty, a consensual agreement of willing parties. The other was through "just" war. Native nations often signed treaties as an alternative to wars of attrition that could prove even more devastating than the cession of their land.

Provisions in the treaties negotiated between Indian bands and nations and the United States varied widely, but most of them contained similar elements: a guarantee that both sides would keep the peace, a marking of boundaries between Indian and non-Indian lands, a statement that the signatory Indians were placing themselves under the "protection" of the United States, and a definition of Indian fishing and hunting rights (often applied to ceded land). Many treaties also regulated travel by non-Indians on Indian land and contained provisions to punish non-Indians who committed crimes on Indian land and Indians who committed offenses against non-Indians.

The U.S. Supreme Court, in *Washington v. Washington State Commercial Passenger Fishing Vessel Association* (1979), characterized a treaty between the federal government and a Native American government as "essentially a contract between two sovereign nations." The treaties have been generally held to reserve to Native American governments powers not relinquished to the United States, just as the Tenth Amendment reserves to the states powers not delegated to the U.S. government by the Constitution. According to legal scholars Russel Barsh and James Henderson, these agreements between Native American governments and the federal government are "something more than 'treaties' as they are understood in international law. They are political compacts irrevocably annexing tribes to the federal system in a status parallel to, but not identical with, that of the states" (1980, 270–271). This is an Anglo-American point of view. A Native view probably would accentuate the value of treaties as alliances.

The U.S. Constitution (art. VI, cl. 2) holds that "all Treaties made . . . shall be the Supreme Law of the Land." On that basis, the United States, individual states, or corporations entered into more than 800 treaties with Native Americans between 1778

(with the Delawares) and 1871, when Congress halted any future formal treaty making. Only 371 of these treaties were ratified by the Senate. Even after 1871, executive branch commissions continued to sign treaties with Indian governments until 1914, when the last agreement of this type was signed with the Ute Mountain Utes. These instruments were called "agreements," not "treaties" when presented to Congress.

Treaties have been the most frequent sources of litigation in Indian law. According to legal scholar Charles F. Wilkinson, "These laws are unique in our jurisprudence, for they set aside territory within the United States for self-government, subject to federal supervision, by sovereigns that are both pre-constitutional and extra-constitutional."

Although the term "treaty" carries connotations of diplomatic solemnity and equality, many of the treaties were negotiated under less than agreeable conditions, especially after 1800, when, in the opinion of Vine Deloria, Jr., "The treaty process was allowed to deteriorate from a sacred pledge of faith between nations to a series of quasi-fraudulent real-estate transactions" (1985, 110). Before 1800, the balance of power between immigrant Europeans and Native Americans sometimes partially restrained abuses, although even during the early years of the British colonies and the United States, treaty records indicate that negotiations were liberally lubricated with liquor. Treaties were always written in English and presented to Indian people who did not understand that written language, much less Euro-American concepts of land ownership and centralized governmental regulation, even after the (often questionable) intercession of translators.

Even when Native Americans did have a fair understanding of what they were signing, the Senate sometimes unilaterally changed treaty provisions before ratification. Moreover, treaties were often concluded with Native "leaders" who had been recruited by treaty commissioners who failed to realize that the leaders and the treaties had little or no support among the people of the nation being represented as the contracting party. During negotiations for the 1851 Fort Laramie Treaty (sometimes called the Horse Creek Treaty), for instance, the U.S. representatives insisted that the Sioux designate one leader to speak for all of them. This not being their custom, the Sioux refused, after which the U.S. negotiators designated Conquering Bear as the Sioux leader without the consent of the people he was sup-

U.S. peace commissioners meet with Kiowa and Comanche at Medicine Lodge, Kansas, in 1867. The Indian Peace Commission Act of 1867 had established a delegation of peace commissioners to confer with Native Americans who were waging war against the United States. (Library of Congress)

posed to be leading. The problem was compounded three years later when Conquering Bear was killed by U.S. Army troops during the Grattan fight near Fort Laramie. The Sioux had a great deal of trouble comprehending why the United States had killed the chief whom it had earlier handpicked as the supposed "leader."

In some cases, errors of large magnitude were made during treaty negotiations. In 1868, for example, the Treaty of Fort Laramie granted the Sioux land in northern present-day Nebraska that had long been occupied by the Poncas. The Sioux, traditional enemies of the Poncas, fully approved of the U.S. Army's intervention to force the Poncas off their land and into exile in Indian Territory, later called Oklahoma. This mistake in treaty negotiation gave rise to a long march homeward by Standing Bear and other Poncas, which in turn created the conditions that caused a landmark case to be brought in Omaha during 1879 under which Stand-

ing Bear and his party were held to be "human beings" under U.S. law, able to legally return to their homeland. After several decades of bureaucratic battling, the Poncas finally reacquired some of the land taken from them by the error in the Treaty of Fort Laramie.

Judge George Boldt, in *U.S. v. Washington* (1974), pointed out that treaty negotiations in the Pacific Northwest often were carried out in three languages—English, Chinook (a trade jargon with limited vocabulary), and a Native language. The use of Chinook severely limited both parties' ability to communicate complex concepts. Because of the disadvantages at which treaty making often placed Indians, the Supreme Court has held that treaties should be construed as the Indians would have understood them (*Tulee v. Washington,* 315 U.S. 681, 684–85 [1942]). Treaties, according to Supreme Court rules of construction, are also to be interpreted to accomplish their protective purposes, according to

legal scholar William S. Canby, Jr., with ambiguities to be resolved in favor of the Indians (*Carpenter v. Shaw*, 280 U.S. 363 [1930]).

The Iroquois Influence on Treaty Diplomacy

Between the midseventeenth century and the end of the nineteenth century, the Haudenosaunee negotiated more than 100 treaties with English (later United States) representatives. Until about 1800, most of these treaties were negotiated according to Haudenosaunee protocol. By the mideighteenth century, this protocol was well established as the *lingua franca* of diplomacy in Northeastern North America. As such, an alliance was adopted and maintained using certain rituals.

Initial contacts between negotiating parties usually were made "at the edge of the forest," on neutral ground, where an agenda and a meeting place and time could be agreed on. Following the "approach to the council fire" (the place of negotiation), a Condolence Ceremony was recited to remember those who had died on both sides since the last meeting. A designated party kindled the council fire at the beginning of negotiations and extinguished it at the end. A council was called for a specific purpose (such as the making of peace) that could not be changed once the council was convened. Representatives from both sides spoke in a specified order. No important actions were taken until at least one night had elapsed since the matter's introduction before the council. The passage of time was said to allow the various members of the council to attain unanimity—"one mind"—necessary for the consensual solution of a problem.

Wampum belts or strings were exchanged when an important point was made or an agreement reached. Acceptance of a belt was taken to mean agreement on an issue. A belt also might be refused or thrown aside to indicate rejection of a proposal. Another metaphor that was used throughout many of the councils was that of the Covenant Chain, a symbol of alliance. If proceedings were going well and consensus was being reached on major issues, the chain (which was often characterized as being made of silver) was described as being "polished" or "shined." If agreement was not being reached, the chain was said to be "rusting."

During treaty negotiations, a speaker was generally allowed to complete a statement without interruption, according to Haudenosaunee protocol, which differs markedly with the cacophony of debate in European forums such as the British House of Commons. Often European representatives expressed consternation when carefully planned schedules were cast aside so that everyone (warriors as well as their leaders) could express an opinion on an important issue. Many treaties were attended by large parties of Iroquois, each of whom could, in theory, claim a right to speak.

The host of a treaty council was expected to supply tobacco for the common pipe, as well as refreshments (usually alcoholic in nature) to extinguish the sour taste of tobacco smoking. Gifts often were exchanged and great feasts held during the proceedings, which sometimes were attended by entire Haudenosaunee families. A treaty council could last several days even under the most agreeable of circumstances. If major obstacles were encountered in negotiations, a council could extend for two weeks or longer, sometimes for as long as a month. A main treaty council was often accompanied by several smaller ones, during which delegates with common interests met to discuss problems that concerned them. Usually, historical accounts record only the proceedings of the main body, leaving out the many important side conferences, which, in the diplomatic language of the time, were often said to have been held "in the bushes."

Treaty councils were conducted in a ritualistic manner to provide common points of understanding between representatives who otherwise were separated by barriers of language and cultural interpretation. The abilities of a good interpreter who was trusted by both sides (an example was Conrad Weiser in the mideighteenth century) could greatly influence the course of negotiations. Whether they knew the Iroquois and Algonquian languages or not, Ango-American negotiators had to be on speaking terms with the metaphors of Iroquois protocol, such as the council fire, condolence, the tree of peace, and many others.

Haudenosaunee treaty relations, including trading relationships, were characterized in terms of kinship, hospitality, and reciprocity, over and above commercial or diplomatic interests. Non-Natives could find this protocol irksome. The Dutch, in particular, seemed easily annoyed when they were forced to deal with trade relationships based on anything other than commerce. They, as well as other Europeans, seemed not to understand that, to the Iroquois, trade was conceived as part of a broader social relationship. The Mohawks in their turn seemed to resent the attitude of the Dutch negotia-

tors. In September 1659, a party of Mohawks complained that "The Dutch, indeed, say we are brothers and are joined together with chains, but that lasts only as long as we have beavers. After that, we are no longer thought of, but much will depend on it [the alliance] when we shall need each other" (Dennis, 1993, 171).

From the first sustained contact with Europeans, shortly after 1600, until the end of the French and Indian War (1763), the Haudenosaunee Confederacy utilized diplomacy to maintain a balance of power in Northeastern North America between the colonizing British and French. This use of diplomacy and alliances to play one side off against the other reached its height shortly after 1700, during the period that Richard Aquila called the Iroquois Restoration (Aquila, 1983, 16–17). This period was followed by an "alliance" of most Haudenosaunee with the British and the eventual defeat of the French. (However, the word "alliance" is only the non-Native term. The Onondaga fire was covered in 1777, an act that allowed each individual to make a decision independent of national intent. Thus the traditionals maintain that the confederacy's nations remained out of the war.)

By this time, alcohol was playing an increasingly devastating role in Iroquois society, a fact emphasized by the many requests for restrictions on the liquor trade by Haudenosaunee leaders at treaty councils and other meetings. Aquila wrote: "Sachems complained that alcohol deprived the Iroquois people of their senses, was ruining their lives, and was used by traders to cheat them out of their furs and lands. The Iroquois were not exaggerating. The French priest Lafitau reported in 1718 that when the Iroquois and other Indians became intoxicated they went completely berserk, screaming like madmen and smashing everything in their homes" (Aquila, 1983, 115). After 1763, the Haudenosaunee were no longer able to play the French and the English against each other. Instead, the Iroquois faced pressure to ally with Native peoples to their west against the English. Many Senecas sided with Pontiac against the English in 1763 and 1764.

Today, some members of the Iroquois (Haudenosaunee) Grand Council travel the world on their own national passports. The passport states that it has been issued by the Grand Council of the League of the Haudenosaunee and that the Haudenosaunee continue as a sovereign people on the soil they have occu-

pied on Turtle Island since time immemorial and extend friendship to all who recognize their constitutional government and who desire peaceful relations. The passports were first issued in 1977 to Haudenosaunee delegates who attended a meeting of the United Nations in Switzerland. Since then, the United States, Holland, Canada, Switzerland, Holland, France, Belgium, Germany, Denmark, Italy, Libya, Turkey, Australia, Great Britain, New Zealand, Iran, and Colombia have been among the nations that have recognized the Haudenosaunee documents. Even so, it takes a talented travel agent to get a visa on an Iroquois passport, because formal diplomatic relations often do not exist between the country recognizing the document and the Haudenosaunee Grand Council.

Treaties, Specific Agreements and Provisions

The following is a brief, annotated tour of some of the major Indian–American treaties. Each treaty is a story in and of itself.

Lancaster (Pennsylvania) Treaty (1744)

This important treaty attempted to set boundaries between Indian and non-Indian settlements, and required permission for non-Indians to visit Indian Country or vice versa. Both parties were granted the right to punish intruders under their own laws. The Iroquois negotiated this treaty with Pennsylvania, Maryland, and Virginia; it concerned lands within the present-day boundaries of West Virginia. At the Lancaster Treaty, Canassatego, the tadadaho (speaker) of the Iroquois Confederacy, advised the colonists to unite on a federal model resembling the Iroquois system.

Treaty with the Delaware Tribe (1778) (7 Stat. 13–15)

The first treaty signed by the United States as a national entity guaranteed the territory of the Delaware Nation, and opened the possibility that it might join the Union as a state.

Article IV of this treaty directed that neither party may punish citizens of the other party until "a fair and impartial trial can be had by judges and juries of both parties, as near as can be to the laws, customs, and usages of the contracting parties and natural justice." This idea of joint justice was terminated early in the nineteenth century by the Major Crimes Act.

Treaty with the Wyandots, et al. (1785) (7 Stat. 16–18)

This treaty contained a clause that forbade illegal non-Indian settlement on reserved lands and said that any person establishing such settlement "shall forfeit the protection of the United States, and the Indians may punish him as they please." The treaty also contained a clause saying that any Indian who "shall commit a robbery or murder on any citizen of the United States" would be delivered to the nearest U.S. Army post and dealt with under U.S. law.

Treaty of Hopewell (1785) (7 Stat. 18–21)

After the Cherokees sided with the British during the Revolutionary War, that nation demanded a separate treaty with the United States. The Cherokees refused to recognize the British surrender at Yorktown or the Treaty of Paris. Mutual demobilization was included in the Treaty of Hopewell (1785).

The Hopewell treaty also provided that illegal non-Indian squatters on Cherokee lands must move out within six months or "such person will forfeit the protection of the United States and the Indians may punish him or not as they please." A year later, however, the Shawnee Treaty of 1786 (7 Stat. 26) required that Indians accused of crimes against non-Indians be delivered to the nearest Army post. The same rule was applied to European-Americans accused of wronging Indians.

The Cherokee treaty, like the one negotiated with the Delawares seven years earlier, opened the possibility of their admission to the United States: "That the Indians may have full confidence in the justice of the United States, respecting their interests, they shall have the right to send a deputy of their choice, whenever they think fit, to Congress.

Treaty of Holston (1791) (7 Stat. 39–42)

Negotiated with the Cherokees after the Treaty of Hopewell (1785) was violated, the terms of the Holston Treaty forced them to relinquish much of the subsequently formed states of Kentucky and Tennessee, in exchange for $1,500 worth of goods per year, or a fraction of a penny per acre.

Jay Treaty (1794) (7 Stat. 47–48[?])

Among other provisions, this treaty allowed for the free passage by Iroquois across the United States–Canadian border. This was not an agreement between Indians and whites, but between the United States and Great Britain. In 1968, Mohawks at Akwesasne, which straddles the border, protested the denial of free passage by Canadian officials. Mohawks blockaded the Cornwall International Bridge, and several were arrested, after which they pressed their treaty claims in Canadian courts until charges were dropped.

Treaty of Canandaigua: See Canandaigua (Pickering) Treaty.

Treaty of Greenville (Ohio, 1795) (7 Stat. 49–54)

The Greenville Treaty involved the Miami Confederacy, Delawares, Shawnees, Wyandots, Chippewas, Potawatomis, and Ottawas, and ceded much of present-day Ohio to the United States following the Indians' defeat by "Mad Anthony" Wayne at the Battle of Fallen Timbers. Prior to that defeat, the Indian alliance had inflicted more than 800 fatalities on Army units commanded by Major General Anthony St. Clair, the largest battlefield defeat (in terms of deaths) in the history of westward expansion.

Treaty of Mount Dexter (1805) (7 Stat. 98–100)

This treaty, negotiated with the Choctaws, was notable for the penny-pinching amounts paid by the United States for 4.1 million acres of land in southern Mississippi and southwestern Alabama. The Choctaws were paid $3,000 for the land, or less than a penny an acre.

Treaty Between the Cherokee Nation and the United States (1817) (7 Stat. 156–160)

Provisions for the "removal"—the relocation of entire Indian nations from areas about to be settled by non-Indians—were first laid down in this 1817 treaty between the United States and the Cherokee Nation. By 1830, the federal government had passed general removal legislation.

Treaty of Indian Springs (1825) (7 Stat. 237–40)

The Creeks had become concerned about non-Indian usurpation of their lands by 1818, when the Muscogee (Creek) nation passed a law against the sale of any Creek land without council approval, under penalty of death. In 1825, federal treaty commissioners bribed William McIntosh, leader of the Creek Lower Towns, along with a few of his close associates, to sign a land cession treaty, the Treaty of Indian Springs. The Creek National Council

declared McIntosh to be a traitor and on May 1, 1825, sent a delegation to torch his house. When McIntosh appeared at the door of his burning home, his body was riddled with bullets. The fraudulent treaty was annulled by the United States, but the Creeks were coerced into signing two other treaties (both commonly referred to as the Treaty of Washington), by which they were forced, in the 1830s, to cede their homelands and move, under the provisions of the Removal Act of 1830, to Indian Territory, later called Oklahoma.

Treaty at Prairie du Chien (1825) (7 Stat. 272–277)

This treaty was negotiated between the United States and the Menominees, Sioux, Sac and Fox, Ottawas, and Chippewas, as well as the Ioways and Winnebagos. A major object of the treaty was cease of intertribal warfare.

Treaty with the Choctaws (1830) (7 Stat. 333–342)

This treaty, negotiated at Dancing Rabbit Creek, was the first negotiated under the Removal Act of 1830. As in most of the removal treaties, the government assured the Indians that they would have wide-ranging control over territory and resources in their new homes. For example, the treaty pledged that: " . . . jurisdiction and government of all persons and property that may be within their limits west, so that no Territory or State shall ever have the right to pass laws for the government of the Choctaw nation . . . and that no part of the land granted to them shall ever be embraced in any Territory or State."

Treaty of New Echota (1835) (7 Stat. 478–488)

This treaty implemented the Removal Act of 1830 for the Cherokees.

Treaty of Guadalupe Hidalgo (1848) (9 Stat. 922–930)

This is not an Indian treaty per se, but it did affect many people who were either Indian or of Indian descent.

The Treaty of Guadalupe Hidalgo ended a three-month war between the United States and Mexico in 1846, after which Mexico was forced to cede almost half its land area, including all or part of the subsequently established states of California, New Mexico, Arizona, Nevada, Utah, Colorado, and Wyoming. Under this treaty, the United States acquired 334.4 million acres, or 552,568 square miles of land area.

Article XIII of this treaty extended American citizenship to all residents of the area, including American Indians, a provision that conflicted with U.S. policy in the rest of the country at the time, as well as with court cases such as *Elk v. Wilkins*, which denied Indians citizenship, including voting rights.

Treaty of Fort Laramie (1851) (11 Stat. 749n)

More than 10,000 Plains Indians—among them Lakotas, Araphahos, Crows, Cheyennes, Arikaras, Assiniboines, Hidastas, and Mandans—took part in the largest treaty-related gathering in American history near Fort Laramie, Wyoming. In a conference lasting eighteen days, U.S. treaty commissioners and Native leaders agreed to exchange $50,000 ($1 per year per person represented by the treaty) for fifty years to allow the United States to construct military posts and roads through the upper Midwest. When the Senate ratified the treaty, it unilaterally reduced the payment to $15,000 a year. The peace wrought by this treaty was short-lived; by 1854 friction between Indians and European-American immigrants sparked the Plains Indian wars.

Treaty of Fort Atkinson (1853) (10 Stat. 1013–17)

The Yamparika band of Comanches, the Kiowas, and the Kiowa-Apaches signed the Treaty of Fort Atkinson, which allowed the United States to build roads through their hunting grounds. The United States also was permitted under this treaty to build forts along the Santa Fe Trail and to protect non-Indians traveling the route. The Indians agreed to make restitution for injuries to U.S. citizens. The United States also promised to compensate injuries by its citizens to Indians who were party to the treaty.

Treaty with the Oto and Missouri Indians (1854) (10 Stat. 1130–31; 11 Stat. 605–6)

This was one of several treaties negotiated with Native peoples in the Kansas and Nebraska territories by Commissioner of Indian Affairs George W. Manypenny. These treaties were probably the first to contain clauses for the allotment of land to individual Indians, a measure that was enacted nationwide in the General Allotment Act of 1887.

Treaty of Medicine Creek (1854) (10 Stat. 1132–37)

This treaty ceded large parts of present-day western Washington. In exchange for relinquishing the land, Native people in the area retained "the right of taking fish, at all usual and accustomed grounds and stations . . . in common with all citizens of the Territory. . . ." This treaty was the basis of Judge George Boldt's opinion in *United States v. Washington* (1974) that Indians of the area were entitled to a fair share of the catch, an amount later defined judicially as up to 50 percent.

The Treaty of Medicine Creek was one of many negotiated by territorial governor Isaac Stevens by which the United States acquired most of the Pacific Northwest. Most of the negotiations were exceptionally heavy-handed and hurried. On one occasion, in a treaty signed June 11, 1855, Stevens promised Indian signatories that lands guaranteed to them would not be invaded by non-Indians and then announced them open for settlement only twelve days later. Stevens's diplomatic indiscretions sparked the Yakima War, which reached across the Cascades westward to Seattle.

The Treaty of Hell Gate (1855) (12 Stat. 975–79)

This treaty reserved 1.25 million acres in northwestern Montana for the Salish and Kootenai. Over the years, the reservation drew considerable numbers of non-Indians because of its rich farmland and scenic mountains. The reservation was allotted in the late nineteenth century. By the time the land claim case was adjudicated, non-Natives owned more than half the land and later comprised 81 percent of the area's residents.

The Treaty with the Creeks and Seminoles (1856) (11 Stat. 699–707)

The 1856 Treaty with the Creeks and Seminoles pledged "secure and unrestricted self-government and full jurisdiction over persons and property, within their respective limits."

Treaty of Little Arkansas (1865) (14 Stat. 699–711)

Signed by the United States with the southern Cheyennes and Arapahos, this treaty contained an apology for the Sand Creek Massacre against the two Indian nations on November 29, 1864: "The United States, being desirous to express its condemnation of, and as far as may be, repudiate the gross and wanton outrages perpetuated against certain bands of Cheyenne and Arapahoe Indians . . . while the said Indians were at peace by lawful authority. . . ."

Treaty with the Creeks (1866) (14 Stat. 785–92)

Following the onset of the Civil War in 1861, the Creeks signed a treaty with the Confederate States of America. In 1866, following the end of that war, this treaty was negotiated with the Creeks by the Seneca Ely S. Parker, who had been General U. S. Grant's secretary and who wrote the articles of surrender ending the Civil War. The treaty of 1866 reestablished relations between the Creeks and the United States.

Treaty of Medicine Lodge (1867) (15 Stat. 581–87)

This treaty with the Cheyennes and Arapahos contained among its provisions a pledge of compensation for victims of the Sand Creek massacre. The payments were never made because the Department of the Army considered the attack a battle (e.g., an act of war by the Cheyennes). At the same time, a House of Representatives investigating committee called the killings at Sand Creek a massacre.

Fort Laramie Treaty (1868) (15 Stat., 619–27; 635–47)

The Fort Laramie Treaty of 1868 ended the Powder River War, during which Red Cloud and other Sioux leaders forced the United States to abandon its forts along the Bozeman Trail. In this treaty, the United States recognized the Great Sioux Nation as including most of the western half of present-day South Dakota. The treaty guaranteed that no unauthorized person "shall ever be permitted to pass over, settle upon, or reside in [this] country."

The Black Hills, called *paha sapa* ("hills that are black") by the Sioux, were included as reservation land under the Fort Laramie Treaty of 1868. An expedition led by George Armstrong Custer found rich deposits of gold and other minerals in the Black Hills during 1874, and the discovery sparked a rush of non-Indian settlement there.

The Treaty of Fort Laramie validated land transfers only if approved by three-fourths of the adult men of the Sioux nation. U.S. treaty commissioners attempting to acquire the Black Hills were able to get only 10 percent of the Sioux men to agree. Nonetheless, Congress seized the Black Hills unilaterally in 1877.

In 1920, the Sioux brought a complaint before the U.S. Court of Claims, which upheld the 1877 seizure. After the Indian Claims Commission was founded in 1946, the Sioux sought to reintroduce the claim, but it was barred because of the earlier review as a matter of *res judicata*. In 1978, the Sioux obtained the passage of a special act of Congress that allowed them to bring the case to the Court of Claims again, to be argued on its merits despite the earlier judgment of *res judicata*. In this case, the Supreme Court held that the United States had acted in bad faith in the matter, vindicating the Sioux's decades of legal perseverance.

The Fort Laramie Treaty of 1868 also mistakenly awarded the Sioux land that was occupied by the Poncas, their traditional enemies. To enforce the treaty, the U.S. Army forced the Poncas to march to Oklahoma from their homelands along the Niobrara River in northern Nebraska during 1877. Following the death of his son, Ponca Chief Standing Bear decided to march back to his homeland for the burial; a number of Poncas joined him. This march gave rise to a suit heard in Omaha during 1879 in which District Court Judge Elmer S. Dundy held that Indians were subject to the English common law practice of *habeas corpus*. Therefore, the Army could not compel their return to Oklahoma.

Treaty with the Nez Percé (1871) *(15 Stat. 693–95)*

This was the last Indian treaty ratified by the Senate.

Bruce E. Johansen

> *See also* Canandaigua (Pickering) Treaty; *Cherokee Nation v. Georgia;* Fishing Rights; Fort Laramie Treaty (of 1868); Haudenosauneee Confederacy, Political System; Lancaster, Pennsylvania, Treaty Councils; *Standing Bear v. Crook;* Trade; Trade and Intercourse Acts; *Worcester v. Georgia.*

References and Further Information

Aquila, Richard. 1983. *The Iroquois Restoration: Iroquois Diplomacy on the Colonial Frontier, 1701–1754.* Detroit, MI: Wayne State University Press.

Barsh, Russel, and James Henderson. 1980. *The Road: Indian Tribes and Political Liberty.* Berkeley: University of California Press.

Canby, William C., Jr. 1981. *American Indian Law.* St. Paul, MN: West.

Deloria, Vine, Jr. [1974] 1985. *Behind the Trail of Broken Treaties: An Indian Declaration of Independence.* Austin: University of Texas Press.

Dennis, Matthew. 1993. *Cultivating a Landscape of Peace.* Ithaca, NY: Cornell University Press.

Hosen, Frederick E., compiler. 1985. *Rifle, Blanket, and Kettle: Selected Indian Treaties and Laws.* Jefferson, NC: McFarland.

Prucha, Francis Paul. 1994. *American Indian Treaties: The History of a Political Anomaly.* Berkeley: University of California Press.

Wilkinson, Charles F. 1987. *American Indians, Time, and the Law: Native Societies in a Modern Constitutional Democracy.* New Haven, CT: Yale University Press.

Tribal Sovereignty

To understand the concept of tribal sovereignty, one needs to couple a basic understanding of sovereignty with a recognition that tribal sovereignty is not a static concept, but one that varies over time at the whim of Congress and the Supreme Court. Basically, sovereignty is the authority under which any group of people is ruled. Throughout history, sovereignty has ranged from vast empires with sovereignty vested in the emperor, monarch, or religious leader, to republics with sovereignty vested in the people and to independent tribal groups with sovereignty vested in unique social organizations. Although the traditional Euro-American legal concept of sovereignty is rooted in Western philosophy emerging from the Middle Ages, the very concept of sovereignty is universally associated with the human need to organize social groups, including governments.

Upon arrival in the Americas, Europeans encountered a wide variety of social groups organized into self-governing sovereign states and empires. The scale of social and political organization rivaled that of Europe, as did the population. However, within 200 years of European arrival, disease and war would eliminate approximately 95 percent of the Native population in North and South America. Such massive destruction severely strained the social and political fabric of cultural groups throughout both continents. In North America, the remnants of many different peoples coalesced into the modern tribes that we know today—peoples exercising the basic human drive to reform sovereign governments under which to rule themselves.

Native American sovereignty derives from the legal concepts applied by European colonizing powers to the Native peoples who were thousands of years old when Europeans first arrived in the Americas. Rooted deep in canon law, the concepts sought

to justify the extension of Christian authority over non-Christian peoples during the Crusades. Under these original concepts, only a ruler who received his power directly from the "true Christian God" through the sovereignty of the Pope possessed a legitimate claim to rule. European rulers therefore sought papal authorization for the conquest of "discovered" peoples under the premise that conquest would bring those "discovered" under the legitimate authority of a government recognized and sanctioned by the Roman Catholic Church. Thus, tribal sovereignty was inherently viewed by Europeans as something less than European sovereignty and subject to the doctrine of discovery.

In 1433, the king of Portugal gained exclusive rights to colonize the Canary Islands and all of Africa. The papal edict, binding on the other Christian monarchs of the time, justified the European expansion in the name of bringing salvation to non-believers. With a Portuguese monopoly in Africa,

Spain looked westward for a shorter route to the Indies. In contracting with Christopher Columbus, the Spanish crown empowered Columbus with royal authority to discover and conquer non-Christian lands. Upon word of the "discovery" of the lands now known as the Americas occupied by non-Christian peoples, the pope issued a series of edicts investing Spain with title to the "discovered" lands. Until the Reformation, few Christian European monarchs would risk excommunication by interfering with such title.

Under original Spanish legal theory, Native peoples were provided the opportunity to accept the power of the Church through the pope and the legitimacy of the Spanish crown or face conquest. However, within forty years of Spanish arrival in the Americas, Spanish legal theorist Franciscus de Victoria developed the basic legal principles for the treatment of indigenous populations that serve even today as the foundations of modern international

After the first transatlantic crossing, Christopher Columbus lands in the Caribbean. In contracting with Christopher Columbus, the Spanish crown authorized Columbus with royal authority to discover and conquer non-Christian lands. (National Archives)

law. Victoria espoused three important concepts: (1) Native Americans were rational creatures and therefore possessed the same rights as Christians; (2) Spanish title under a papal grant was illegitimate and therefore could not terminate Native American land rights; and (3) Christian nations could justify conquest based on transgressions against the Law of Nations.

Under Victoria's theories, Native peoples possessed the title to their lands. This title was subject, however, to certain duties such as safe passage for the Spanish through their lands under the concept of "natural society and fellowship." Victoria also advanced that, since Native Americans might not fully comprehend the requirements of the European Law of Nations, that they be placed under the guardianship of a "civilized nation." Further, the interference by Native American sovereigns with the spread of Christianity could justify the conquest of new territory.

Early British legal theory in North America closely followed that of Spain, citing religion as a justification for the European colonization. In fact, Puritan theory even cited divine intervention as the reason that Native American populations plummeted, leaving large areas open for European occupancy. Regardless of this theory of religious rights to Native American lands, the European colonizers found purchases of land through treaties with Native Americans more efficient than conquest in terms of money, effort, and human lives. Such purchases were based on three underlying assumptions: (1) Both parties possessed the sovereign authority to enter into the treaty; (2) the Native American sovereign possessed legal title transferable to the European sovereign; and (3) land acquisition was solely a sovereign-to-sovereign matter—individuals could not enter into such arrangements.

Land acquisition for European powers, and later for the newly formed United States, played a major role in the development and acknowledgment of tribal sovereignty. In fact, land acquisition restrictions on Indian land by the British crown even played a role in the creation of the new American sovereign. Upon securing independence, Indian land issues helped shape the powers of the centralized federal government and resulted in the Indian Commerce Clause of the United States Constitution.

Indian land issues formed the underlying question that first formalized the concept of tribal sovereignty in American legal thought. The U.S. Supreme Court first addressed tribal sovereignty in the 1823 case of *Johnson v. M'Intosh*. Chief Justice John Marshall confronted the task of determining the validity of tribal land sales to individuals rather than to the U.S. government or its sovereign predecessor, Britain. Further complicating this issue, the sale by the tribal government occurred before passage of the Trade and Non-Intercourse Act of 1790, which statutorily confined any land transfer by an Indian tribe to only the federal government. The creation of the entire national public domain and consistency in land titles depended on the analysis in this case.

To establish such title consistency, Chief Justice Marshall needed to establish both the legitimacy of Indian land title and the centralized federal power to negotiate and accomplish the transfer of title. Marshall used the medieval doctrine of discovery to justify both concepts. Marshall reasoned that "discovery" by European powers diminished the full tribal sovereignty present before the arrival of European powers. As full sovereigns, the "discovering" European nations held ultimate land ownership while the tribes with their diminished sovereignty held only a "right of occupancy" that could be extinguished by purchase or conquest. Finally, Marshall established that Great Britain's rights as a "discovering" European sovereign transferred to the United States as its successor in sovereignty upon American independence.

Johnson v. M'Intosh represents the first analysis of the status of the sovereignty of the new republic's neighboring nations. The case reduces the extent of tribal sovereignty through judicial action. Although eroding tribal sovereignty, it did recognize that sovereignty existed for the Indian tribes and that those tribal sovereigns remained in control of its land resources.

By 1828, federal policy called for the forced removal of all tribes to lands west of the Mississippi River. Encouraged by this federal policy, the state of Georgia extended its laws over Cherokee territory and claimed to nullify Cherokee law in that territory. In 1831, Chief Justice Marshall carefully avoided the issue of the validity of the Georgian laws by defining the status of Indian tribes within the U.S. constitutional scheme. In *Cherokee Nation v. Georgia*, Marshall analyzed whether the tribes were classified as "foreign nations" and as such would possess standing before the Supreme Court. Marshall clearly recognized the tribal sovereignty embodied in the Cherokee Nation because the Cherokee met the Anglo-American definition of a distinct government

in control of its own internal affairs. Although a "nation," Marshall decided that the Cherokee Nation was not a "foreign nation," but instead Marshall created the new concept of "domestic dependent nations" in an effort to comport the reality of tribal government with the U.S. Constitution and yet avoid the question of the validity of Georgia's laws over Cherokee territory.

With Georgia still asserting the invalidity of Cherokee law, the state arrested two U.S. citizens living as missionaries in the Cherokee Nation for violating Georgia laws designed to control interaction with the Cherokee. As American citizens, these two men possessed the standing lacked by the Cherokee Nation a year earlier to bring the issue of Georgia versus Cherokee sovereignty back to the U.S. Supreme Court in *Worcester v. Georgia.*

Marshall reviewed the limited references made to Indian tribes in the U.S. Constitution to analyze Cherokee sovereignty. He identified three specific references to tribes in the constitution: (1) war powers, (2) treaty powers, and (3) the regulation of commerce with foreign nations, among the states, and with the Indian tribes. In recognizing the Indian tribes as "nations," Marshall reasoned that, since before European arrival, these groups exercised exclusive sovereign authority within their territories.

The *Worcester* decision established important aspects of tribal sovereignty and excluded state interference with that sovereignty. In recognizing tribal sovereignty, Marshall diminished such sovereignty by placing it under the exclusive control of the federal government and by terminating the tribes' ability to deal with foreign (specifically European) powers as inconsistent with their status under the doctrine of discovery.

Although the Marshall trilogy recognized and established the concept of tribal sovereignty in American legal thought, the Supreme Court in other decisions also established Congress's absolute (or plenary) power to determine the survival of all or a portion of a tribe's sovereignty. Thus, tribes' sovereignty was subjected to the political whims of a body in which Indians had no representation.

By the late 1800s, with organized military resistance in Indian Country ended, the tribes retained little leverage in dealing with the federal government. In this situation, Congress began to extract a toll on tribal sovereignty. In 1871, Congress passed an act ending the practice of negotiating treaties with the Indian tribes. By the 1880s, federal policy embraced forced assimilation designed to suppress

and destroy tribal culture, language, and history. Over time, the program was to result in the final disintegration of the tribes as sovereign entities. In 1885, Congress passed the Major Crimes Act, creating federal jurisdiction for certain crimes and thus impinging on tribal sovereignty. Beginning with the General Allotment Act of 1887, Congress exercised its plenary power over the next twenty years to break up the large tribal communal landholdings by allotting acreage to tribal members and selling "surplus" lands to non-Indians.

During this grim time for Native American sovereignty, the Supreme Court continued to protect the principles of sovereignty while recognizing Congress's complete control of Indian affairs. The Court in *Talton v. Mayes* reaffirmed that tribal sovereignty was independent of the U.S. Constitution and did not emanate from federal powers. Within two years of the *Talton* decision, Congress used its plenary power to abolish the very tribal court systems recognized in the case.

By the late 1920s, the U.S. government recognized that assimilation programs had resulted in an extreme human rights disaster. At the urging of New Deal reformers led by John Collier, Congress passed the Indian Reorganization Act (IRA). Collier and his associates designed the IRA to assist tribes in organizing their governments and developing their economies. The Act completely shifted federal policy toward the tribes. It focused on reviving traditional tribal institutions, rehabilitating tribal economies and securing the remnants of tribal land bases by immediately repealing the allotment laws and restoring "surplus" reservation lands to tribal ownership.

In an effort to solidify tribal governmental structures, the IRA funded the organization of governments and tribal corporations for select tribes. Successive acts brought the same benefits to many Oklahoma tribes and Alaskan Native groups that were originally excluded from the Act. During a short eleven years beginning in 1934, IRA-era reformers made great efforts to respect and reinforce tribal sovereignty.

By 1940, however, critics of the IRA gained control of Congress. Further exacerbating the problem, American entry into World War II drained talent, attention, and resources from IRA programs as well as the tribes. By 1953, congressional policy radically shifted once again to one of termination of tribal sovereignty. In that year, Congress passed Public Law 83-280, which required certain states to assume crim-

inal and civil jurisdiction over Indian lands and granted the option to other states, thus diminishing tribal sovereignty. In June of the next year, Congress began the termination of over one hundred sovereign bands and tribes, starting with the Menominee tribe.

Ironically, the termination policy helped galvanize the various Indian interests and tribes that had begun organizing during the reforms of the 1940s. Indian and non-Indian protests over the next ten years, combined with the states' reluctance to bear the costs associated with assuming authority over Indian Country, killed the momentum of the termination policy. By the mid-1960s, federal policy concerning Indian Country had begun to shift again. In the midst of the Civil Rights Movement, Congress passed bills addressing economic and civil rights issues in Indian Country. By the early 1970s, congressional reports indicated that termination had resulted in yet another example of economic and cultural disaster in Indian Country.

The executive branch announced the beginning of modern executive policy in 1968 when President Lyndon B. Johnson delivered a special address to Congress entitled the "Forgotten Americans." This was the first time a president had devoted a special address to Congress exclusively on Indian affairs. Two years later, President Richard M. Nixon announced a policy of "self-determination" for tribes. Basically, Nixon's recommendations to Congress were to (1) reject termination, (2) grant the right to control and operate federal programs to the tribes, (3) restore specific sacred lands, (4) grant the right to control federal education funds and Indian schools to the tribes, and (5) pass legislation to encourage economic development. In a series of acts passed in the 1970s, Congress began reversing the termination process and instituting the policy of self-determination. Each act reinvigorated a battered tribal sovereignty. The trend has continued with Congress passing legislation that aids tribes in rebuilding their land bases and exercising greater control of natural resources, recognizes inherent sovereign powers, and amends the major environmental statutes to recognize "tribes as states."

At a time when the legislative and executive branches (the traditional enemies of tribal sovereignty) embraced tribal self-determination and sovereignty, the U.S. Supreme Court began expanding judicially imposed limitations. In 1978, two U.S. Supreme Court cases signaled the modern trend of the judicial termination of tribal sovereign powers in

Oliphant v. Suquamish Indian Tribe and *United States v. Wheeler*. The Court reinforced an idea that, although the ultimate source of tribal sovereign power resides outside the U.S. Constitution, Congress's plenary power may completely prescribe the extent of tribal sovereign powers.

The Court also found that Indian tribes lacked criminal jurisdiction over non-Indians within tribal territory unless granted the power by Congress. Most importantly, the Court's analysis relied heavily on the concept that tribes have lost those sovereign powers inconsistent with their status as domestic dependent nations. The Court then provided a list of implicit divestitures imposed by the Court to date: (1) Tribes are no longer free to alienate land to non-Indians; (2) tribes can no longer enter into direct commercial or governmental relations with foreign nations; and (3) tribes can no longer try nonmembers for offenses in tribal courts.

Three years later, in *Montana v. United States*, the U.S. Supreme Court expanded judicial limitations on tribal sovereignty by limiting tribal sovereign power to only that required for protecting tribal self-government or controlling internal relations. Any sovereign powers beyond these require express congressional delegation to survive. In application, the case meant that the tribe could not apply its sovereign powers to nonmembers of the tribe on fee lands. The Court provided two exceptions to this general rule. A tribe might retain inherent power to exercise civil authority over the conduct of non-Indians (1) when a consensual relationship between the nonmember and the tribe or a tribal member exists and/or (2) when the conduct of non-Indians on fee lands within its reservation "threatens or has some direct effect on the political integrity, the economic security, or the health or welfare of the tribe."

The most recent Court decisions have continued to erode inherent tribal sovereignty. In 1997, the Court limited the second *Montana* exception to only what is necessary to protect tribal self-government or to control internal relations. However, the Court did recognize that the "tribes retain considerable control over nonmember conduct on tribal land." In 2001, this concept was undermined in *Nevada v. Hicks*.

In a splintered decision with four opinions, but with all justices concurring, the *Hicks* Court explicitly applied the *Oliphant* and *Montana* restrictions on tribal sovereignty to Indian lands, but with differing approaches. Considering there was no true majority of opinion, all provide an idea of the potential

direction of the Supreme Court in terms of tribal sovereignty.

Justices Antonin Gregory Scalia and William Rehnquist held that tribal land ownership does not alone support regulatory jurisdiction by the tribe over nonmembers. Justice Scalia also continued to limit explicitly that part of the Marshall trilogy prohibiting the application of state laws within Indian Country by concluding the presence of Indian Country only reduces a state's regulatory authority. Therefore, Justices Scalia and Rehnquist determined that it was appropriate to balance the federal and tribal interests with the interest of the state.

Justice David Souter (with Justices Anthony M. Kennedy and Clarence Thomas) articulated the opinion that a tribe's civil jurisdiction does not include nonmember defendants. Justice Ruth Bader Ginsburg carefully limited her concurrence to not allowing tribal jurisdiction over state officials engaged in enforcing a state law. Justice Sandra Day O'Connor (with Justices John Paul Stevens and Stephen Breyer concurring in part) concluded that tribal sovereign powers did not extend tribal civil jurisdiction over nonmembers regardless of whether or not the tribe owned the land. However, Justice O'Connor continued to explain that land ownership should now be considered in the application of the *Montana* exceptions.

Although the Supreme Court appears fragmented in its analysis of tribal sovereignty, these diverse opinions all indicate a trend to continue the erosion of tribal sovereign powers announced in *Oliphant*. In *United States v. Lara,* the Supreme Court's latest decision concerning tribal sovereign powers, the majority preserved its past analysis and restrictions on tribal authority. The Court did, however, recognize Congress's authority to relax those restrictions, though it noted that such Congressional authority may face constitutional challenges if relaxing the restriction interferes with a state's authority or creates due process or equal protection issues.

Since the self-determination era was initiated by President Nixon in 1970, Congressional plenary power has attempted to recognize and restore the inherent sovereignty of the tribes in many areas. A series of congressional acts recognized and stressed tribal sovereignty. Using terms such as "government-to-government relationships," "inherent tribal sovereignty," and "tribes as states," Congress has made more clear than ever its intent that tribes should be treated as sovereign entities. In fact, Congress has expressly declared that the United States

has an obligation to guard and preserve the sovereignty of Indian tribes in order to foster strong tribal governments.

Congress clearly supports tribal sovereignty in the realm of economic development. By the early 1980s, Congress committed to fund the development of tribal energy resource laws and regulations. In the 1990s, Congress approved legislation to assist in the development of tribal judicial systems, thus reinvigorating the judicial aspect of tribal sovereignty. A more recent example is the Native American Business Development, Trade Promotion, and Tourism Act of 2000, which explicitly stated congressional findings that "consistent with the principles of *inherent tribal sovereignty* and the special relationship between Indian tribes and the United States, Indian tribes retain the right to enter into contracts and agreements to trade freely, and seek enforcement of treaty and trade rights. . . ."

The most explicit example of Congress's intent to protect, promote, and restore tribal sovereignty rests in Congress's "Duro fix" to the U.S. Supreme Court decision in *Duro v. Reina*. The Court, in the *Duro* case, found that the tribes had implicitly lost the power to criminally prosecute an Indian nonmember of the tribe. To address the real world practicalities of law enforcement in Indian Country, Congress addressed the Court's finding by amending the Indian Civil Rights Act to recognize that tribes possess the sovereign power to exercise criminal jurisdiction over all Indians within their territory.

The tribal sovereign power associated with the self-rule of tribal members appears to be respected by the federal judiciary, executive, and legislative branches. However, beyond those sovereign powers, tribal sovereignty becomes a confusing world of implicit judicial divestiture of tribal sovereign rights and congressional reinstatement. This situation means that tribal sovereignty must be discerned more and more from Supreme Court cases that implicitly limit tribal sovereignty, coupled with federal statutes that recognize and/or restore tribal sovereign powers. Without a blanket recognition of all inherent rights, the tribes still face the practicalities of trying to restore their sovereign authority in a piecemeal fashion.

John L. Williams

See also *Cherokee Nation v. Georgia;* Indian Civil
    Rights Act (1968); Indian Reorganization Act;
    Oliphant v. Suquamish Indian Tribe; Ross, John;
    Termination; Trail of Tears; *Worcester v. Georgia.*

References and Further Reading

Axtell, James. 1985. *The Invasion Within: The Contest of Cultures in Colonial North America.* New York: Oxford University Press.

Calloway, Colin. 1997. *New Worlds for All: Indians, Europeans and the Remaking of Early America.* Baltimore, MD: Johns Hopkins University Press.

Cherokee Nation v. Georgia 30 U.S. 1 (1831).

Cornell, Stephen, and Joseph Kalt. 1992. "Reloading the Dice: Imposing the Chances for Economic Development on American Indian Reservations." In *What Can Tribes Do? Strategies and Institutions in American Indian Economic Development.* Edited by Cornell and Kalt. Los Angeles: American Indian Studies Center, University of California, Los Angeles.

Debo, Angie. 1989. *A History of the Indians of the United States,* 11th ed. Norman: University of Oklahoma Press.

Getches, David, Charles Wilkinson, and Robert Williams, Jr. 1998. *Federal Indian Law.*

Hecht, Robert. 1980. *Continents in Collision: The Impact of Europe on the North American Indian Societies.* Lanham, MD: University Press of America.

Johnson, Tadd, and James Hamilton. 1995. "Self-Governance for Indian Tribes: From Paternalism to Empowerment." *Connecticut. Law Review* 27: 1251.

Johnson v. M'Intosh 21 U.S. 543 (1923).

Maxfield, Peter. 1993. "*Oliphant v. Suquamish Indian Tribe:* The Whole Is Greater Than The Sum Of The Parts." *Contemporary Law* 19: 391.

Richter, Daniel. 2001. *Facing East from Indian Country: A Native American Early History.* Cambridge, MA: Harvard University Press.

Robertson, L. 1997. "John Marshall as Colonial Historian: Reconsidering the Origins of the Discovery Doctrine." *Law & Politics* 13: 759.

Williams, R., Jr. 1983. "The Medieval and Renaissance Origins of the Status of the American Indian in Western Legal Thought." *Southern California Law Review* 57: 1.

Worcester v. Georgia 31 U.S. 515 (1832).

Uranium Mining

When Native Americans in the western United States were assigned reservations in the late nineteenth century, many were sent to land thought nearly worthless for mining or agriculture. The year 1871, when treaty making stopped, was a time before sophisticated irrigation and before dryland farming techniques had been developed. Industrialization was only beginning to transform the cities of the eastern seaboard, and the demand for oil, gas, and even coal was trivial by present-day standards. In 1871, Madame Curie had not yet isolated radium. Before 1900, there was little interest in locating or mining uranium, which later became the driving energy force of the nuclear age.

In a century and a quarter, the circumstances of industrialization and technological change have made a good deal of these treaty-guaranteed lands very valuable, not least because under their often barren surface lies a significant share of North America's remaining fossil fuel and uranium resources. Nationwide, the Indians' greatest mineral wealth is probably in uranium. According to a Federal Trade Commission (FTC) Report of October 1975, approximately the time when the government and private industry became especially interested in such things, an estimated 16 percent of the U.S. uranium reserves that were recoverable at market prices were on reservation lands; this was about two-thirds of the uranium on land under the legal jurisdiction of the U.S. government. There were almost four hundred uranium leases on these lands by the mid-1970s, according to the FTC, and between 1 million and 2 million tons of uranium ore a year—about 20 percent of the national total—was being mined on reservation land.

Moreover, if the uranium reserves on reservation land are added to those estimated on land guaranteed to Indian nations by treaty, the Indians' share of uranium reserves within the United States rises to nearly 60 percent; the Council of Energy Resource Tribes (CERT) places the figure at 75 percent to 80 percent. About two-thirds of the 150 million acres guaranteed to Indians by treaty have been alienated from them—by allotment, by other means of sale, or by seizure without compensation. Some of these areas, notably the Black Hills of South Dakota, underwent a uranium mining boom during the 1970s, even though legal title to the land is still clouded. Sioux leaders have refused to settle with the United States for the land, despite a price tag that currently exceeds $600 million, including principal and interest.

Uranium Mining in Navajoland

About half the recoverable uranium in the United States lies within New Mexico—and about half of that is beneath the Navajo Nation. As in South Dakota, many Navajos have come to oppose the mining, joining forces with non-Indians who regard

Marvin Sarracino stands at the edge of a reclaimed uranium mine holding pots made by Laguna Pueblos from clay taken from the mine. Many Native Americans worked in or lived near uranium mines in New Mexico but were kept ignorant of the dangers. (Bob Krist/Corbis)

nuclear power plants and arms proliferation as a twofold menace.

Uranium has been mined on Navajo land since the late 1940s; the Indians dug the ore that started the U.S. stockpile of nuclear weapons. For thirty years after the first atomic explosions in New Mexico, uranium was mined much like any other mineral. More than 99 percent of the product of the mines was waste, cast aside as tailings near mine sites after the uranium had been extracted. One of the mesa-like waste piles grew to be a mile long and seventy feet high. On windy days, dust from the tailings blew into local communities, filling the air and settling on the water supplies. The Atomic Energy Commission assured worried local residents that the dust was harmless.

In February 1978, however, the Department of Energy released a Nuclear Waste Management Task Force report stating that people living near the tailings ran twice the risk of lung cancer as the general population. The *Navajo Times* carried reports of a Public Health Service study asserting that one in six

uranium miners had died, or would die prematurely, of lung cancer. For some, the news came too late. Esther Keeswood, from Shiprock, New Mexico, a reservation city near tailings piles, and a member of the Coalition for Navajo Liberation (CNL), said in 1978 that the CNL had documented the deaths of at least fifty residents (including uranium miners) from lung cancer and related diseases.

The Kerr-McGee Company, the first corporation to mine uranium on Navajo Nation lands (beginning in 1948), found the reservation location extremely lucrative. There were no taxes at the time, no health, safety, or pollution regulations, and few other jobs for the many Navajos recently home from service in World War II. Labor was cheap. The first uranium miners in the area, almost all of them Navajos, remember being sent into shallow tunnels within minutes after blasting. They loaded the radioactive ore into wheelbarrows and emerged from the mines spitting black mucus from the dust and coughing so hard it gave many of them headaches, according to Tom Barry, energy writer

for the *Navajo Times*, who interviewed the miners. Such mining practices exposed the Navajos who worked for Kerr-McGee to between 100 and 1,000 times the limit later considered safe for exposure to radon gas. Officials for the Public Health Service have estimated these levels of exposure; no one was monitoring the Navajo miners' health in the late 1940s.

Thirty years after mining began, an increasing number of deaths from lung cancer made evident the fact that Kerr-McGee had held miners' lives as cheaply as their labor. As Navajo miners continued to die, children who played in water that had flowed over or through abandoned mines and tailings piles came home with burning sores.

Even if the tailings were to be buried—a staggering task—radioactive pollution could leak into the surrounding water table. A 1976 Environmental Protection Agency (EPA) report found radioactive contamination of the drinking water on the Navajo reservation in the Grants, New Mexico, area, near a uranium mining and milling facility. Doris Bunting of Citizens Against Nuclear Threats, a predominantly white group that joined with CNL and the National Indian Youth Council (NIYC) to oppose uranium mining, supplied data indicating that radium-bearing sediments had spread into the Colorado River basin, from which water is drawn for much of the Southwest. Through the opposition to uranium mining in the area, among Indians and non-Indians alike, runs a deep concern for the long-term poisoning of land, air, and water by low-level radiation. It has produced demands from Indian and non-Native groups for a moratorium on all uranium mining, exploration, and milling until the issues of untreated radioactive tailings and other waste disposal problems are faced and solved.

By late 1978, more than 700,000 acres of Indian land were under lease for uranium exploration and development in an area centering on Shiprock and Crownpoint, both on the Navajo Nation. Atlantic Richfield, Continental Oil, Exxon, Humble Oil, Homestake, Kerr-McGee, Mobil Oil, Pioneer Nuclear, and United Nuclear were among the companies exploring for, planning to mine, or already extracting ore. During the 1980s the mining frenzy subsided somewhat, as recession and a slowing of the nuclear arms race reduced demand. Some ore was still being mined, but most of it lay in the ground, waiting for the next upward spike in the market.

Since 1950, when a Navajo sheepherder named Paddy Martinez brought a strange-looking yellow rock into Grants, New Mexico, from nearby Haystack Butte, the area boomed with uranium mining. Grants styled itself the "Uranium Capital of the World," as new pickup trucks appeared on the streets and mobile-home parks grew around town, filling with non-Indian workers. For several years before the boom abruptly ended in the early 1980s, many workers in the uranium industry made $60,000 or more a year.

As a result of mining for uranium and other materials, however, the U.S. Geological Survey predicted that the water table at Crownpoint would drop 1,000 feet and that it would return to present levels thirty to fifty years after the mining ceased. Much of what water remained could be polluted by uranium residue, the report indicated. Local residents rose in anger, only to find that they owned only the surface rights; the mineral rights in the area are owned by private companies.

The Largest Nuclear Accident in the United States

The biggest expulsion of radioactive material in the United States occurred July 16, 1979, at 5 a.m. on the Navajo Nation, less than twelve hours after President Jimmy Carter had proposed plans to use more nuclear power and fossil fuels. On that morning, more than 1,100 tons of uranium mining wastes—tailings—gushed through a packed-mud dam near Church Rock, New Mexico. With the tailings, 100 million gallons of radioactive water gushed through the dam before the crack was repaired.

By 8 a.m., radioactivity was monitored in Gallup, New Mexico, nearly fifty miles away. The contaminated river, the Rio Puerco, showed 7,000 times the allowable standard of radioactivity for drinking water below the broken dam shortly after the breach was repaired, according to the Nuclear Regulatory Commission. The few newspaper stories about the spill outside of the immediate area noted that the area was sparsely populated and that the spill posed no immediate health hazard.

The area is high desert, however, and the Rio Puerco is a major source of water. Workers used pails and shovels to clear the contaminated ground because heavy machinery could not negotiate the steep terrain around the river. The cleanup was limited and frustrating. Where were cleanup crews going to put 1,100 tons of radioactive mud, when the

next substantial rain would leach it back into the river course?

More problems began to appear. A waste pile at the United Nuclear mill that had produced the wastes that gushed down the Rio Puerco in 1979 detected leaking radioactive thorium into local groundwater. On May 23, 1983, the state of New Mexico issued a cease-and-desist order to United Nuclear to halt the radioactive leakage. The company refused to act, stating that its leak did not violate state regulations. Allendale and Appalachian, two insurance companies that were liable for about $35 million in payment to United Nuclear because of losses related to the accident, sued the company on the belief that it knew the dam that burst was defective before the spill. The dam was only two years old at the time of the accident.

Death in the Mines

For thirty years after the first atomic explosions in New Mexico, uranium was mined much like any other mineral. "We used to play in [the mining dust]," said Terry Yazzie of an enormous tailings pile behind his house. "We would dig holes and bury ourselves in it" (Eichstaedt, 1995, 140). The neighbors of this particular tailings pile were not told it was dangerous until 1990, twenty-two years after the mill that produced the tailings pile closed, and twelve years after Congress authorized the cleanup of uranium mill tailings in Navajo country. Abandoned mines also were used as shelter by livestock, which inhaled radon and drank contaminated water. Local people milked the animals and ate their contaminated meat.

During the late 1940s and 1950s, Navajo uranium miners hauled radioactive ore out of the earth as if it were coal. Some of the miners ate their lunches in the mine and slaked their thirst with radioactive water. Some of their hogans were built of radioactive earth. Many sheep watered in small ponds that formed at the mouths of abandoned uranium mines that were called "dog holes" because of their small size. On dry, windy days, the gritty dust from uranium waste tailings piles covered everything in sight. The Navajo language has no word for "radioactivity," and no one told the miners that, within a few decades, many of them would die.

In their rush to profit from uranium mining, very few companies provided ventilation in the early years. Some miners worked as many as twenty hours a day, entering their "dog holes" just after blasting of local sandstone had filled the mines with silica dust. The dust produced silicosis in the miners' lungs, in addition to lung cancer and other problems associated with exposure to radioactivity. As early as 1950, government workers were monitoring radiation levels in the mines that were as much as 750 times the limits deemed acceptable at that time, according to Peter Eichstaedt's account in *If You Poison Us: Uranium and American Indians* (1995). By 1970, nearly 200 of the miners had already died of uranium-related causes. Roughly one in four of the miners had died, most of them from lung cancer, in an area where the disease had been nearly unknown before uranium mining began.

Some miners were put to work packing thousand-pound barrels of "yellowcake," ore rich in uranium. These workers carried radioactive dust home on their clothes. Some of the miners ingested so much of the dust that it was "making the workers radioactive from the inside out" (Eichstaedt, 1995, 62). Downwind of uranium processing mills, the dust from yellowcake sometimes was so thick that it stained the landscape a half-mile away.

Bruce E. Johansen

See also Economic Development; Mining and Contemporary Environmental Problems; Radiation Exposure Compensation Act.

References and Further Reading

Eichstaedt, Peter. 1995. *If You Poison Us: Uranium and American Indians.* Santa Fe, NM: Red Crane Books.
Grinde, Donald A., Jr., and Bruce E. Johansen. 1994. *Ecocide of Native America: Environmental Destruction of Indian Lands and Peoples.* Santa Fe, NM: Clear Light Publishers.

Water Rights

With the passage and implementation of the General Allotment (or Dawes) Act in 1887, federal Indian land policy became the main point of contention and conflict between American Indians and the federal government during the late nineteenth century. However, the even more confusing and ambiguous area of federal Indian water policy was the main point of contention during much of the twentieth century, and it continues to be a vital area of conflict.

In the eastern United States, the states have regulated the use of water by a system of riparian rights, which came down from English law, in which

ever remains after the first claimant's use of the water is the property of the second claimant and so on down the line. This worked well in the nineteenth-century West, because the institutions necessary to govern and determine rights in a riparian system were lacking. In a system of prior appropriation, the users themselves were able to determine the first in right, at least initially. The Supreme Court, however, has long recognized that both federal and Indian water rights exist outside the state-regulated water rights systems and must be satisfied as well, creating a competing system of water allotment.

Water policy, for the majority of American Indians in the West, has been determined by the implementation of two apparently contradictory methods of water allocation: (1) the prior appropriation system and (2) the "reserved rights" (or "Winters") doctrine. Put succinctly, in signing treaties with the federal government that resulted in the creation of their reservations, Indians agreed to vast land cessions in return for guarantees that their reservation lands would be permanently reserved for Indian use and occupation. The Supreme Court ruled that, when the Indians did this, they reserved to themselves every right not specified in the treaty. Ownership of the land and implicitly its resources and all sovereignty not expressly relinquished to the federal government were rights "reserved" to the Indian nation. The downside to this system, in terms of prior appropriation, is that the "priority date" assigned to the Indians was the date of the congressional act that created the reservation, rather than a date of "time immemorial," which would seem more appropriate given the lengthy tenure of Indians on their lands.

This system of reserving rights based on reservation status has created anomalies in Indian Country. Land ownership has been the key to New Mexico Pueblo Indian water rights. The Pueblo nations have early priority dates derived from Spanish land grants and the U.S. Treaty of Guadalupe Hidalgo with Mexico (1848). Because of this, the Pueblos have "aboriginal" water rights. Unlike many other nations, the Pueblos reside on lands that they have never left or been forced off of by the United States. While the United States, in the Treaty of Guadalupe Hidalgo, recognized those prior holdings, thereby giving Pueblo rights to federal protection of their land and water, these rights do not depend on any federal action for their existence.

However, most Indian nations during the twentieth century have had to base their hopes for justice in water rights on federal court decisions

A water technician bores a hole to monitor moisture depths for the Navajo Irrigation Project in 1978. The 1950 Navajo-Hopi Rehabilitation Act reinstated federal services to the Navajo and Hopi tribes and provided funds for improvements on the reservations, including irrigation projects. (Ted Spiegel/Corbis)

all who own land along a water source have the right to the use of the water of that source. However, this system has worked well only in places with average to heavy rainfall, where the utilization of water by upstream users does not have a detrimental effect on downstream users.

In the arid lands of the American West, where most American Indians reside, water rights are governed by state laws founded on the principle of prior appropriation. Prior appropriation can be best summed up in the phrase "first in time, first in right." In practical terms, this means that the oldest water right is satisfied in full before later users can have any access to the water supply. In other words, the first to make beneficial use of the water has the right to all of the water they originally used. What-

because Congress had not passed any definitive, all-encompassing water rights bills supporting or even defining their rights. The court decision that formed the most generous basis for Indian water rights, the reserved rights doctrine and thus the most contention with non-Indian water claimants, is the Supreme Court opinion in the case of *Winters v. United States*, in which the Supreme Court held that, when Indian reservations were established, the Indian nations and the United States implicitly reserved, along with the land, sufficient water to fulfill the purposes of the reservations, which in most cases was farming.

Therefore, according to the so-called Winters doctrine that was derived from the decision, Indian water rights are defined and governed by a body of federal law recognizing that Indian nations have sovereignty over the water on their reservations. The Supreme Court held that Indian governments have jurisdiction over both their members and activities on the Indian reservations, and this has affected the ways that Indians can use the water that flows through or adjacent to their reservations. However, by handing down a decision while not providing any way of reconciling it with the prior appropriation system already in use, the court's shortsightedness did more to provoke further conflicts over water between Indian and non-Indian populations than it did to settle them. *Winters* did nothing at all to determine either the scope of its application or the parameters for determining the amount of water Indian nations could claim. Almost from the time the decision was handed down in 1908, and especially during the 1980s and 1990s, many nations have gone to the courts in an effort to quantify their federal water rights, even though it has often meant possibly a serious diminution of the extent of those rights.

Involvement of the federal government in protecting Indian water rights, as well as other Indian-held natural resources, raises two issues. First, the ownership of land and water rights is antithetical to many American Indian cultural and religious systems. The fact that these questions are being discussed at all illustrates the fact that Indian views on these topics have undergone some accommodation to Euro-American culture. Secondly, federal involvement raises the issue as to what the difference is between the dependency of Indian nations on the federal government and self-determination with government protection. This has long been a difficult distinction to draw. Speaking in purely economic terms, by not promoting and protecting the right of

Indian nations to develop their resources, the government perpetuates dependency and poverty. On the other hand, if it protects Indian interests and their rights to develop their resources, the federal government may be guilty of affecting Indian culture, but it can certainly not be said to be perpetuating dependency. Rather, the federal government would be acting to promote the health of Indian economies necessary for true self-determination.

The main reason for the continued difficulty in securing water rights under the Winters doctrine is that it has constantly come up against the prevailing method of allocating water claims in the western United States: prior appropriation. When the doctrine of prior appropriation is taken to include Indian use, the courts necessarily enter the picture to allocate the amounts allocated by right to a given Indian nation as determined by its use of a particular water source. Because Indian reservations were established before most water uses began in the west, Indians often hold the oldest and thus most valuable water rights. Many Indian groups have occupied land since time immemorial (from the European perspective) and thus also have strong ancient priority claims to water for Indian uses. State water laws in the West often place a priority on the idea of "beneficial use," which more often than not has to do with agriculture. Although many Southwestern groups, such as the Pueblos, have a long agricultural tradition predating European contact, and others, such as the Jicarilla Apaches, have a mixed subsistence tradition, the factors of modern reservation life do not always mean that the Indian nations will use the water as the state or federal laws would prefer them to.

Because Indian nations are theoretically not held to state laws in these matters, conflicts have continually arisen over which water rights doctrine is applicable to the adjudication of rivers that flow over both Indian and non-Indian lands. The Winters doctrine would seem to support the view that Indians have a right to enough water to irrigate reservation agricultural lands; yet the doctrine of prior appropriation supports the idea that, if the Indians did not historically irrigate their lands, then non-Indian water claimants would be substantiated. The courts then have to examine what water was reserved for use on the Indian reservations, how Indian water rights are quantified and used, and how these water rights are regulated and enforced. Because of the potential extent and great value of the water that could be claimed by Indian nations under

the Winters doctrine, especially in the American West where water has become increasingly scarce, Indian water rights have constantly been under attack both in the federal and state courts and in other political arenas as well.

As clearly contradictory as the two dominant systems of allocation (Winters and prior appropriation) may appear, the actual situation in practice has been both less contradictory and more confusing than the various federal decisions would make it seem. Daniel McCool pointed out that these two contradictory theories of water allotment created a conflict of interest within the Justice Department. The Justice Department was to be the legal representative for all federal interests, so its official position in favor of prior appropriation in the West was in conflict with the reserved rights, or Winters, doctrine that was supposed to determine Indian water rights. The Winters doctrine theoretically makes the prior appropriation doctrine irrelevant. In practice, however, federal irrigation and reclamation programs were rarely undertaken in the interests of Indian peoples, even when they were constructed adjacent to Indian lands.

The Bureau of Reclamation, dedicated to the doctrine of prior appropriation and the promotion of non-Indian irrigated agriculture in the West, exercised great power and acted decisively in the interests of its constituents when allocating the waters made useful by their construction projects. Even though the Winters doctrine might have given the Indians a theoretically large claim to the waters of the West, battles over access to those waters occupied Indian nations, the federal and state courts, the Department of the Interior (as both the promoter of non-Indian development through the Bureau of Reclamation and as the defender of Indian rights through the Bureau of Indian Affairs), and the Congress throughout the twentieth century.

Even when the rights seem plain, the capriciousness of the court system toward Indian nations has meant that they have had to enter into lengthy and expensive litigation with no guarantee of success. Since the 1980s the federal government has promoted negotiated settlements as the best way in which all parties can work to resolve their water claims. Concluded and implemented at both state and federal levels, these settlements have, in many cases, concluded the endless decades of litigation and carry with them the promise of delivering real, "wet" water to the Indian nations. Settlement negotiations have usually been started after an Indian

nation or the United States has already become involved in a case involving water rights claimed by a state and other non-Indian water users. The negotiation necessary to achieve a water settlement involves the process of alternative dispute resolution, which allows for all of the interested parties to participate. This type of resolution is most effective when there are factual disagreements on technical data between the parties; therefore, they sometimes rely on court decisions to decide basic legal questions such as the priority date of the reservation. Rather than seeking final adjudications in the courts, the parties use the court-determined data to achieve a solution that will satisfy some of the desires of all sides rather than all of the desires of one side. Indian water needs are addressed without eliminating non-Indian water uses, although neither side is usually able to achieve all of its goals.

Negotiations in a land of limited water, such as the American West, mean that the Indian nations usually do not receive the full share of water determined by the Winters doctrine, but in return, they often get money to enable them to construct facilities or projects to utilize their alloted water. Such federal funding has not only allowed Indians to secure water rights, but has also delivered water that can be put to beneficial use. At the same time, non-Indians gained the assurance that they will be able to continue using water without the constant threat of an assertion of Winters rights on the part of the Indian nations.

Steven L. Danver

See also Agriculture; General Allotment Act (Dawes Act); Reservation Economic and Social Conditions; *Winters v. United States.*

References and Further Reading

Danver, Steven L. 2002. "Land, Water, and the Right to Remain Indian: The All Indian Pueblo Council and Indian Water Rights." In *Water on the Great Plains: Issues and Policies.* Edited by Peter J. Longo and David W. Yoskowitz. Lubbock: Texas Tech University Press.

Hundley, Norris, Jr. 1978. "The Dark and Bloody Ground of Indian Water Rights: Confusion Elevated to Principle." *Western Historical Quarterly* 9: 477.

Hundley, Norris, Jr. 1982. "The 'Winters' Decision and Indian Water Rights: A Mystery Reexamined." *Western Historical Quarterly* 13: 17.

McCool, Daniel. 1987. *Command of the Waters: Iron Triangles, Federal Water Development, and Indian Water.* Tucson: University of Arizona Press.

McCool, Daniel. 2002. *Native Waters: Contemporary Indian Water Settlements and the Second Treaty Era*. Tucson: University of Arizona Press.

Wilkinson, Charles F. 1992. *Crossing the Next Meridian: Land, Water, and the Future of the American West*. Washington, DC: Island Press.

Worster, Donald. 1985. *Rivers of Empire: Water, Aridity, and the Growth of the American West*. New York: Oxford University Press.

Women in Native Woodlands Societies

Throughout the eastern woodlands, Native American women enjoyed extensive powers and rights through their official roles in the spiritual, political, economic, and social structures of their cultures. Until quite recently, those roles were ignored and even falsified by Western historians whose own male-dominated, hierarchical systems left them ill prepared to view, let alone comprehend, communal systems functioning in a mutually respectful, female–male balance. Because of the deep skew in Western primary sources created by this cultural blind spot, early chronicles must be tested for accuracy rather than simply quoted for content as most scholars now recognize.

To understand any structure of woodlands economics, politics, or society, readers must first grasp Eastern cosmology, for all human infrastructure in the East coalesces around it. Unfortunately, spirituality in the woodlands has been egregiously misrepresented in even recent Western literature and must be clearly untangled before comprehension can set in. The distortions arise from three causes.

First, the core concepts of Eastern spirituality were completely misconstrued by early European chroniclers, who "naturally" imposed their own worldviews on what they were being told. They thereby missed the central motif of the woodlands, the balanced interaction of Sky and Earth, the natural halves of the cosmos. When woodlanders explained the multiple Spirits of Sky to the Europeans, chroniclers would record their presentations in terms of monotheism's own, solitary Sky Spirit, "God." By the same token, when woodlanders explained the Spirits of Earth, Europeans blithely recorded those discussions as relating to their own "Devil" and his presumed minions. As a result, even the most careful Native descriptions of Sky–Earth logic are hodgepodged together nonsensically in the old chronicles.

Second, missionaries, who comprehended a bit more, promptly interpreted Native spirituality as the Devil's work, deliberately misshaping traditions to cooperate with their Christian ideological agenda. This had the devastating effect of importing cosmic conflict into Native thought, whereas true Native ideation is utterly "conflict-phobic" (Allen, 1985, 98). The Christian God and Devil may be locked in mortal, eternal combat over the fate of humanity, but the point of woodlands spirituality is to harmonize Spirits of Sky and Spirits of Earth, *both* of which are good, respected, and necessary. In woodlands thought, creation is ongoing, with human beings no more important than rocks, trees, fish, fowl, or anything else in existence.

Third, modern pan-Indianism—which is unrelated to actual traditional beliefs—typically accepts and perpetuates the old missionary distortions, particularly "Great Spirit" or "Creator" monotheism. Because traditional beliefs are closely held in medicine societies and not freely shared with outsiders, pan-Indianism (which also accepts the Christian eagerness to lay bare one's beliefs) is the system that is most likely to greet any researcher. Whatever its merits in the present, pan-Indianism cannot provide a window into the woodlands' past. As a result, anyone working today, in the wake of these three skews, needs to clear a path around the debris of colonialism to unlock the original woodlands conceptualization of the cosmos, the true key to understanding women's position in ancient societies.

The cosmology of Earth and Sky holds that there cannot be one until there are first two. Those two must be equal, reciprocating, and balanced—Sacred Twins, in the Iroquoian presentation—a matched pair that constantly interacts under ever changing circumstances to maintain the harmony of the whole. Neither half outweighs, controls, or directs the other. Independent yet interdependent, the two halves of Sky and Earth come together to form the perfect cosmos, in an act of spiritual consensus. This structure is replicated in the twinned clan halves, one of which (often turtle) references Earth, and the other of which (often wolf) references Sky. (Numerous lineage clans exist under each clan half.)

This cosmology has far-reaching implications for human culture, expressed in terms of the naturally occurring pairs noted by woodlanders. For example, humanity falls into the matched pairs of

Elders and Youngers and of Women and Men. These pairs are construed as replications of the cosmic principle of the sacred two making one whole. They constitute the basis of all cultural organization.

In specific terms of women, they result in the major institution of Gendering, which is, intrinsically, Earth/Women and Sky/Men. Under this rubric, women are in charge of everything that is culturally construed as female, notably, dwellings and food supplies, family and human relationships, and Earth medicine. Some cultures carried Gendering to the extent of having separate linguistic expressions, mutually intelligible, but particular to the female or the male sex. Gendering had long fingers, which reached into all spheres of human existence.

Spiritually, women are in charge of Earth medicine (as men are in charge of Sky medicine). Western stereotypes of medicine *men* aside, women were fully half of the spiritual workers in earlier times, for the Sky medicine of the men must be balanced by the Earth medicine of the women. Working only in Sky medicine (as often occurs under pan-Indianism) actually unbalances the cosmos.

Earth medicine deals heavily with water, caves, plants, and blood. (Sky medicine deals heavily with fire, heights, feathers, and breath.) Women's particular medicine skills include dream reading (often telling the future), combing out the hair (straightening out tangled thoughts through counseling), and herbal (allopathic) remedies. (Men use breath medicine.) Both genders use sacred tobacco for sacred purposes; women use it in conjunction with water, whereas men burn it. In addition, both genders practice visionary methods; women achieve vision using water, whereas men achieve it using fire. Having been born pure (life-giving), women need not sweat. On the other hand, because they wreak death in the hunt and war, men must sweat.

Sky and Earth organized political entities. On the level of Gendering, it established female and male councils. On the level of age, it defined the councils as belonging to Elders or Youngers. Thus, each council had twinned identities: Female and Elder; Female and Younger; Male and Elder; or Male and Younger. These entities considered matters independently, yet communicated with one another through their Speakers, specially trained individuals who carried exact messages between political bodies. Women's councils sent male Speakers to the men's councils, and men's councils sent female Speakers to the women's councils. Since Gendering (Earth-Sky balance) was the basis for the

political halves, rather than the literal, sexual identity of individuals, women could be "made" men and men could be "made" women. "Made" individuals cross-dressed.

Specific tasks were gendered. Rendering judgments was, for example, an Earth act, so that judging was necessarily a female job. All judges were "women," whether or not they were born physically female. In the instance of the Lenapes, the entire nation was "made" female by the Iroquois League, because, as the "Grandfather," or Eldest nation in the east, the Lenapes were considered so wise as to be trusted to act as the judiciary for all. On the other hand, warfare was considered a male activity. This did not mean that only men could apply to be a Young Man (usually mistranslated as "warrior"). Women trained in woodlands martial arts and went to war as well, but, because of their occupation, they were "Men." (Cross-gendered work is not to be confused with homosexuality, which was considered an intrinsic form of boundary crossing. Gay and lesbian people were revered as natural medicine workers, not political officials.)

In woodland conceptions, women were obviously the first actors in any event, because they gave birth. Nothing existed until women created it (accounting for women as first actors in all traditional creation stories). Consequently, women's councils considered all issues first, passing along their consensus decisions to the men's councils. Men could not consider a matter until the women did, because it did not exist until the women gave birth to it.

All woodlanders had matrilineal clans, but these were not, as is generally supposed in Western literature, simply social institutions. The clans were emphatically political institutions. Clan Mothers owned all the names, which included all titles of office. Various clan lineages fielded candidates for any open offices, with clan candidates vying for them and Clan Mothers deciding who was best qualified. Titles (i.e., political positions) were then bestowed on successful female and male candidates by the women's councils.

By the same token, should officeholders prove unequal to or unworthy of the job, the women's councils could, after issuing three warnings detailing the infraction, take back their names—i.e., impeach incumbents who refused to mend their ways—replacing them with new officials. (Three was the number of disorder and discord.) Public office was held for life, so that, at the death of an incumbent,

the women's councils took back the title to bestow on a successor. The "petticoat government" (Adair, 1930, 232) that resulted was the moaning bane of European officials, who loathed being forced to deal with women as equals.

Women were instrumental in times of war. They had the right (and, before European meddling, the exclusive right) to declare war. Prior to such a declaration, it was their job to make three good faith attempts to negotiate a mutually acceptable resolution. It was only after three attempts had failed that the women could, at their discretion, give the matter over to the men to do with as they pleased, which usually meant to make war. Even then, women had the responsibility to notify the enemy of the intended attack, in time for that enemy to evacuate, mount a defense, or cave in to demands.

Even in warfare, an absolute law governed the woodlands: the Law of Innocents. This dictated that no one was authorized to make war on noncombatants—i.e., women, children, elders, and nonsoldiering men. Part of women's jobs during warfare was to have a representative sitting at the crossroads of literal warpaths, offering food and clothing to the passing war parties of either side. Rape was absolutely forbidden, a war crime punishable by death. Emissaries of Peace on errands among the warring sides were also granted absolute freedom of passage. Killing an Emissary of Peace was also a capital crime.

When prisoners were taken during war, it was the exclusive right of women to decide their fate, normally adoption, i.e., the granting of citizenship. An adoptee was given the identity of someone deceased in the lineage. Thereafter, that adoptee was loved and treated as if she or he were literally that person. Women and children were automatically adopted into any lineage that was short of numbers. Contrary to settler propaganda, most men were also adopted, although adult, combatant men had to "run the gauntlet." This consisted of a course between two lines of women, children, and a few men, who beat the runner with clubs or slashed at him with knives as he passed. Any runner making it through to the end of the line was lauded as strong and immediately adopted. In fact, a dispute might well erupt over which clan had the honor of taking him in.

At times, however, an enemy male might be put on trial for war crimes and sentenced to death. (Many of the Europeans mourned in settler accounts as tortured to death by the "savages" had actually been convicted of the war crimes of rape, murder of innocents, or injury to Emissaries of Peace.) During these trials, the verdict was not a foregone conclusion. The women gave the defendant a Speaker, who might be able to secure his release through clever argument. Even at the point of execution, any woman who disagreed with the verdict might interpose herself on the criminal's behalf, securing his adoption, instead of his death, as may have happened with John Smith and Pocahontas. Should the execution be carried out, the women were largely in charge of starting and supervising the torture that led to death.

Whole nations might be adopted by other entities, as happened in the 1660s, when the women of the Iroquois League adopted the Lenapes. Indeed, League women were famous for incorporating other nations into the confederacy, although no nation was considered a state unless every single person in it agreed to the adoption. Only the Tuscaroras came in as an entire nation, with no dissenters, which is why the Five Nations became the Six Nations in 1722.

Economically, Gendering granted women ownership of the land, for Mother Earth is a women. Under their Corn Women and Plant Chiefs, they kept vast tracts of the woodlands under cultivation, regularly producing crop yields, astonishing to Western settlers. Women's staple crops were corn, beans, and squash, grown intertwined, but women also grew melons, onions, sweet potatoes, and berries. All but berries were sown in mounded hills, envisioned as breasts of Mother Earth, whose corn milk suckled her children. The mounds prevented soil erosion.

Women knew the medicine of seeds and plants, soaking seeds in medicine water, supplying such things as alkaloids or pest repellents prior to planting. In addition, the women knew the exact depth at which to bury each type of seed for best results, as well as the best distance between plants to ensure them the proper sunlight and moisture. In the case of berries, women allowed them to grow wherever Mother Earth had originally sown them, locating and tending them as carefully as their mound farms.

Women also kept close track of the productivity of the land, knowing which areas produced the best crops and making sure to parcel them out on a revolving basis so that each clan had a crack at the best land. Likewise aware of soil depletion, women used fertilizers (often fish heads) and were careful not to overstay their welcome on any set of fields.

Instead of rotating fields, they rotated their towns. Most clans had enough land to support themselves in various locales, so that no plot was used for more than fifteen or twenty years at a stretch, before the town shifted to the next site along its regular rotation schedule. Typically, land was allowed to lie fallow for eighty to a hundred years, before being cultivated anew.

Not only did women own all the land, but they also owned all of its produce, whether garnered from their own fields or from the men's hunt. It was the Clan Mothers' right, alone, to parcel out the fruits of farming, hunting, and fishing, and it was their duty to ensure that the bounty was equally spread. No one feasted while another famished. To help maintain equal access to the goods and services necessary to life, women held frequent festivals featuring food and gift exchanges, supplied out of what amounted to the public treasury, or town surplus. Gifting festivals (which always included Eat-Alls) also worked on the international level to cement alliances with distant groups by sharing the wealth generally.

Socially, women were the heads of their lineages and households, making (and breaking) marriages, retaining custody of all children until puberty, and acting as counselors and judges of the public weal through their right to judge matters. Upon marriage, men moved to their mother-in-laws' residences and remained under the watchful eye of their new Clan Mothers. Husbands hunted for their wives' families. Because matrilineage ruled, the children followed the clan of their mother. The Sister–Brother bond was the strongest Earth-Sky exemplar in society, so that maternal uncles were normally preferred to biological fathers as male role models for clan boys. Brothers supported their sisters at all costs.

At puberty, girls and boys became sexually active and were encouraged to experiment. Most had multiple partners. Homosexuality was as accepted as heterosexuality; the only rule was that partners had to come from the opposite clan half, as in-clan dating amounted to incest, something carefully monitored and disallowed. After hormones began settling down and emotional maturity began settling in, young girls were asked who their favorites were among their partners. When Clan Mothers descried preferences, they arranged marriages by talking to the contraparty Clan Mothers. The young people involved had a say in the matter, but Clan Mothers also carefully considered the titles of office involved, how they would be spread

due to the new alliance, and whether the marriage increased their own clan's status.

Clan Mothers had the special obligation to keep the peace in the home, which, far from translating into whimpering submission to men, entailed the ability to render final judgment in all home matters. Should a husband offend his mother-in-law, she could dissolve the marriage instantly, sending him home in disgrace. Divorce was easily granted and readily sought, by either side, if a domestic relation did not pan out. All children of divorce remained with their mothers.

Sexual continence and/or monogamy was neither desired nor considered part of the marriage contract, although serial marriages were preferred to promiscuity within a marriage. Among some nations, the Seneca, for instance, polyandry was countenanced, but men did not have more than one wife at a time.

The often misinterpreted institution of Hunting Wife was a female, not a male, institution. One obligation of a wife was to aid her husband on a hunt. Among young, recently married people, the wife of record usually went; her labor was not hard, and the trip was usually viewed as an exciting excursion. However, in later years, as a woman aged, acquiring large responsibilities and public office, she was not in a position to abandon her home duties to accompany her husband on a hunting trip, which might last a year. In such instances, she was responsible for rounding up a proxy—the Hunting Wife—to go out with her husband. Hunting Wives came from the ranks of clanswomen who were either unmarried or who had no desire to marry. They reported back to the Clan Mother who sent them out. Whether Hunting Wives had sex with their proxy mates was entirely up to the consenting adults involved, but it was no necessary part of the bargain. Upon her return, the Hunting Wife handed over all proceeds and goods of the hunt to her head Mother.

Women had exclusive control of their own bodies, which meant that they chose with whom they would, or would not, have sex, marry, or reproduce. A woman was not obligated to name the father of her child, fatherhood being a privilege a woman granted the man. Neither did being sexually active necessarily imply motherhood, for women had, and openly used, abortifacents and contraceptives, bearing children only when they chose. No man had any right to interfere with female reproduction, although mothers might urge it on daughters they considered too immature to nurture a child.

Women alone attended childbirth. The birthing hut included a catch basin, for children were birthed from the sitting position. During labor, medicine women provided painkillers, massages, and midwifery. Outside, female guardians kept at bay any predators attracted by the smell of blood. They also kindly warned men off from the area, since female medicine, particularly as it involves blood, is so powerful that it can kill unwary men. This, and not Western notions of "uncleanliness," is why menstruating women live separately during their "moon times." They are not shunned, but revered as powerful at these times. Hence, pan-Indian "cleansing" sweats during "moon times" are entirely untraditional.

Women carefully spaced their children apart, because each child was to be the sole focus of a family until preferably its fourth year. Children were breast-fed, sometimes into the fourth year. In addition, everyone in the matrilineage was grandmother, mother, aunt, uncle, or sibling to the child, so that child care did not devolve on the shoulders of just one, often young, woman. She had relief and help. Having more children than one could support, physically or emotionally, or having them on too slimly spaced a schedule—say, annually—was frowned upon as socially irresponsible. Other women might be appointed by the Clan Mother to take on the extra children, so that those children had their fair share of attention. Orphans were also carefully placed with attentive mothers to ensure their well-being.

One consequence of women's control of their own bodies was that all children were wanted and cherished. Woman-run child rearing included none of the authoritarian rod so dear to European custom; indeed, striking a child was strictly prohibited. Children were allowed to learn through experimentation, under the subtle supervision of their elders. As they approached adolescence, children Gendered into the boys' and girls' collectives that were later copied as the American Boy Scouts and Girl Scouts. In these units, they practiced adult forms of civic interchange, such as decision making and reliance on and respect for elders. (The oldest child of a unit was its "elder.") At puberty, children took on tasks in the grown-up world, under the Eldership of true adults.

Each woodlands culture, from the Abenaki to the Iroquois, and the Algonkin to the Muscogee, featured strong, powerful women in all of these roles. Each worked out the details of its social, economic, political, or spiritual structure somewhat differently, but the basic balance of Earth and Sky required the complementary roles of female and male to exist in balance.

Barbara Alice Mann

See also Haudenosaunee Confederacy, Political System; Missionaries, French Jesuit.

References and Further Reading

Adair, James. [1775] 1930. *History of the American Indians*. Edited by Samuel Cole Williams. Johnson City, TN: Watauga Press.

Alford, Thomas Wildcat. 1935. "Shawnee Story of Creation," *Indians at Work* 2, no. 18: 7–8.

Allen, Paula Gunn. 1985. "Kochinnenako in Academe: Three Approaches to Interpreting a Keres Indian Tale." *North Dakota Quarterly* (Spring): 84–106.

Allen, Paula Gunn. 2003. *Pocahontas: Medicine Woman, Spy, Entrepreneur, Diplomat*. San Francisco: Harper.

Anderson, Karen. 1991. *Chain Her by One Foot: The Subjugation of Women in Seventeenth Century New France*. New York: Routledge.

Awiakta, Marilou. 1993. *Selu: Seeking the Corn-Mother's Wisdom*. Golden, CO: Fulcrum.

Bartram, William. 1955. *Travels of William Bartram*. Edited by Mark Van. New York: Dover Publications.

Bell, Amelia Rector R. 1990. "Separate People: Speaking of Creek Men and Women." *American Anthropologist* 92: 332–345.

Braund, Kathryn E. Holland. 1990. "Guardians of Tradition and Handmaidens to Change: Women's Roles in Creek Economic and Social Life during the Eighteenth Century. *American Indian Quarterly* 14, no. 3: 239–253.

Brinton, Daniel G. [1868] 1969. *The Myths of the New World: A Treatise on the Symbolism and Mythology of the Red Race of America*. New York: Greenwood Press.

Brown, Judith K. 1970. "Economic Organization and the Position of Women Among the Iroquois." *Ethnohistory* 17: 151–167.

Carney, Virginia. 2001. " 'Woman Is the Mother of All': Nanye'hi and Kitteuha: War Women of the Cherokees." In *Native American Speakers of the Eastern Woodlands: Selected Speeches and Critical Analyses*. Edited by Barbara Alice Mann, 123–143. Westport, CT: Greenwood Press.

Cartier, Jacques. 1993. *The Voyages of Jacques Cartier*. Edited by Ramsay Cook. Toronto, ON: University of Toronto Press, 1993.

Carr, Lucien. 1884. "On the Social and Political Position of Women Among the Huron-Iroquois Tribes." *Peabody Museum of American Archaeology and Ethnology Reports*, 16 & 17, 3, no. 3–4: 207–232.

Charlevoix, Pierre de. [1761] 1966. *Journal of a Voyage to North America*. 2 vols. Ann Arbor, MI: University Microfilms.

Colden, Cadwallader. [1747] 1973. *The History of the Five Indian Nations Depending on the Province of New-York in America.* 2 vols. New York: AMS Press.

Cusick, David. "Sketches of Ancient History of the Six Nations." [1825] 1892. In *The Iroquois Trail, or Foot-prints of the Six Nations, in Customs, Traditions, and History.* Edited by Beauchamp, William M. Fayetteville, NY: H. C. Beauchamp.

Dankaerts, Jasper, and Peter Sluyter. 1867. *Journal of a Voyage to New York in 1679–1680.* Brooklyn, NY: Transactions of the Long Island Historical Society.

Edwards, Jonathan, ed. [1749] 1826. *David Brainerd: His Life and Journal.* Edinburgh: H.S. Baynes.

Fabel, Robin F. A., and Robert R. Rea. 1974. "Lieutenant Thomas Campbell's Sojourn Among the Creeks." *Alabama Historical Quarterly* 36 (Summer): 97–111.

Farnham, Christie Anne, ed. *Women of the American South: A Multicultural Reader.* New York: New York University Press, 1997.

Foster, Martha Harroun. 1995. "Lost Women of the Matriarchy: Iroquois Women in the Historical Literature." *American Indian Culture and Research Journal* 19, no. 3: 121–140.

Frink, Lisa, Rita Shepard, and Gregory A. Reinhardt, eds. 2002. *Many Faces of Gender: Roles and Relationships Through Time in Indigenous Northern Communities.* Boulder: University Press of Colorado.

Grinde, Donald A., Jr., and Bruce E. Johansen. 1991. *Exemplar of Liberty: Native America and the Evolution of Democracy.* Los Angeles, CA: UCLA American Indian Studies Center.

Heckewelder, John. [1820, 1876] 1971. *History, Manners, and Customs of the Indian Nations Who Once Inhabited Pennsylvania and the Neighboring States.* The First American Frontier Series. New York: Arno Press and The New York Times, 1971.

Hunter, John D. [1823] 1970. *Memoirs of a Captivity Among the Indians of North America, from Childhood to the Age of Nineteen.* Edited by Joseph J. Kwiat. New York: Johnson Reprint Corporation.

Hvidt, Kristian, ed. 1980. *Von Reck's Voyage: Drawings and Journal of Philip Georg Friedrich Von Reck.* Savannah, GA: Beehive Press.

Jacobs, Renee. 1991. "Iroquois Great Law of Peace and the United States Constitution: How the Founding Fathers Ignored the Clan Mothers." *American Indian Law Review* 16, no. 2: 497–531.

Jacobs, Sue-Ellen, Wesley Thomas, and Sabine Lang. 1997. *Two-Spirit People: Native American Gender, Identity, Sexuality, and Spirituality.* Chicago: University of Illinois Press.

Jemison, Pete. 1988. "Mother of Nations—The Peace Queen, A Neglected Tradition." *Akwe:kon Journal* : 68–70.

Johansen, Bruce Elliott, and Barbara Alice Mann, eds. 2000. *Encyclopedia of the Haudenosaunee (Iroquois Confederacy).* Westport, CT: Greenwood Press.

Lafitau, Joseph François. [1724] 1974. *Customs of the American Indians Compared with the Customs of Primitive Times.* 2 vols. Edited and translated by William N. Fenton and Elizabeth L. Moore. Toronto, ON: Champlain Society.

Lang, Sabine. 1998. *Men as Women and Women as Men: Changing Gender in Native American Cultures.* Austin: University of Texas Press.

Mann, Barbara Alice. 1997. "The Lynx in Time: Haudenosaunee Women's Traditions and History." *American Indian Quarterly* 21, no. 3: 423–429.

Mann, Barbara Alice. 1998. "Haudenosaunee (Iroquois) Women: Legal and Political Status." In *The Encyclopedia of Native American Legal Tradition.* Edited by Bruce Elliott Johansen, 112–131. Westport, CT: Greenwood Press.

Mann, Barbara Alice. 2003. "Kokomthena, Singing in the Flames: Sky-Earth Logic in the Mounds." In *Native Americans, Archaeologists, and the Mounds,* 169–238. New York: Peter Lang.

Mann, Barbara Alice. 2004. *Iroquoian Women: The Gantowisas.* New York: Peter Lang.

Parker, Arthur C. 1916. *The Constitution of the Five Nations, or The Iroquois Book of the Great Law.* Albany: State University of New York Press.

Perdue, Theda. 1998. *Cherokee Women: Gender and Culture Change, 1700–1835.* Lincoln: University of Nebraska Press.

Pope, John A. [1792] 1971. *A Tour Through the Southern and Western Territories of the United States of North America, The Spanish Dominions on the River Mississippi, and the Floridas, the Countries of the Creek Nations and Many Uninhabited Parts.* Edited by John Dixon. New York: Arno Press.

Powell, J. W. 1879–1880. "Wyandot Government: A Short Study of Tribal Society." *Annual Report of the Bureau of Ethnology to the Secretary of the Smithsonian Institution* 1: 57–69.

Richter, Daniel K. 1992. *The Ordeal of the Longhouse: The Peoples of the Iroquois League in the Era of European Colonization.* Chapel Hill: University of North Carolina Press.

Rothenberg, Diane. 1980. "The Mothers of the Nation: Seneca Resistance to Quaker Intervention." In *Women and Colonization.* Edited by M. Etienne and E. Leacock. New York: Praeger.

Sagard, Gabriel. [1632] 1939. *The Long Journey to the Country of the Hurons*. Edited by George M. Wrong, translated by H. H. Langton. Toronto, ON: Champlain Society.

Seaver, James E. [1823] 1990. *A Narrative of the Life of Mrs. Mary Jemison*. Syracuse, NY: Syracuse University Press.

Shoemaker, Nancy, ed. 1995. *Negotiators of Change: Historical Perspectives on Native American Women*. New York: Routledge.

Strachey, William. [1612] 1953. *The Historie of Travell in Virginia Britania*. Edited by Louis B. Wright and Virginia Freund. London: Hakluyt Society.

Swan, Caleb. 1855. "Position and State of Manners in the Creek or Muscogee Nations, 1791." In Henry Rowe Schoolcraft, *Historical and Statistical Information Respecting the History, Condition, and Prospects of the Indian Tribes of the United States*. Vol. 5. Philadelphia, PA: J. B. Lippincott Co..

Swanton, John R. 1928. *Social Organization and Social Usages of the Indians of the Creek Confederacy*. Bureau of American Ethnology. Bulletin No. 42. Washington, DC: Government Printing Office.

Thwaites, Reuben Gold, ed. [1896–1901] 1959. *The Jesuit Relations: Travels and Explorations of the Jesuit Missionaries in New France, 1610–1791*. 73 vols. New York: Pageant Book Company.

Voegelin, Charles F. 1936. "The Shawnee Female Deity," *Yale University Publications in Anthropology* 8, no. 13: 3–21.

Wagner, Sally Roesch. 1996. *The Untold Story of the Iroquois Influence on Early Feminists*. Aberdeen, SD: Sky Carrier Press.

Wagner, Sally Roesch. 2001. *Sisters in Spirit: The Iroquois Influence on Early American Feminists*. Summertown, TN: Native Voices.

Wall, Steve. 1993. *Wisdom's Daughters: Conversations with Women Elders of Native America*. New York: HarperPerennial.

Wallace, Anthony F. C. 1947. "Women, Land, and Society: Three Aspects of Aboriginal Delaware Life." *Pennsylvania Archaeologist* 17, nos. 1–4: 1–36.

Woloch, Nancy, comp. 2002. *Early American Women: A Documentary History, 1600–1900*. Boston: McGraw-Hill.

Events in American Indian History

Bering Strait Theory

Two obvious possibilities existed for the origins of aboriginal peoples in North America. One possible explanation is a passage by boat from somewhere humans had resided before the Americas were peopled. The other possibility is a passage by land. The most obvious location for a land passage is across the Bering Strait between Siberia and Alaska, where scientists know that at one point there was a land bridge (which they call Beringia) between Asia and North America. The notion of a Siberian origin for aboriginal Americans gained credence from a variety of corroborative evidence, such as similarities of blood types and dental structure between American aboriginals and northern Siberians. Linguistic evidence also pointed to a similar pattern. Gradually a theory emerged, which gained strength by its seeming ability to explain all that a host of scientists—chiefly geologists, archaeologists, and climatologists—had discovered and were discovering about both the land and its people.

It is an axiom of science that the simplest explanation fitting the known facts is usually the most accurate one, and this theory was elegant in its relative simplicity, which was one of the greatest arguments in its favor. The theory was that sometime around fifteen thousand years ago, when Beringia provided a land connection between Asia and North America, human sojourners crossed into North America in search of food. The passage was not an easy one, and it probably took a long time for any individual or party to complete. Although the environment of the land bridge was relatively favorable to human life, the glaciers that then covered the northwestern part of the American continent were not. Some of the new arrivals headed north into the Arctic regions. Others straggled southward along a gap between the glacial ice sheets, making their way into the southwestern part of the continent (which was not covered with glaciers), where the earliest evidence of human presence has been detected. As the ice retreated and the climate changed in the northern part of the continent, more and more people were able to move into the southern regions and

began to travel eastward across the continent, following the game animals.

The land bridge theory seemed appropriate for dealing with virtually all of the existing evidence. To explain relatively similar dates for surviving artifacts from one coast to the other, the theory had to postulate an extremely rapid extension of humankind across the continent in the postglacial period. Gradually the theory hardened into conventional wisdom. Although there were many skeptics and people who preferred other explanations, their arguments were hampered by the absence of any hard evidence that contradicted the standard view, particularly by the lack of indisputable evidence of an earlier occupation of the continent or of an alternate time sequence. Most mainstream scientists insisted that all hard evidence of human habitation from this period (as opposed to such "soft" evidence as linguistic theory or literary legends) comes in the form of stone artifacts that cannot be dated earlier than 12,000 years. These scientists refused to entertain alternate theories so long as the "12,000-year barrier" remained intact. The mainstreamers were particularly scathing in their criticism of those who advocated acceptance of one or more of the alternate theories of peopling, whether by refugees from the continent of Atlantis or by ancient space travelers.

Despite its elegance, the Beringian theory has in recent years come under increasing attack. Much of the critique has come from those who find it unlikely that the Americas could have remained free of any human habitation until only 12,000 years ago, especially given the increasingly great antiquity being uncovered for human/humanoid development elsewhere in the world (Stengel, 2000). There are also other arguments against the standard view of human arrival. One is that very few early human remains have been found in the northwestern part of the continent, where the first immigrants supposedly entered from Siberia, while many more remains, which are extremely old, have been uncovered on Canada's east coast, more than 4,000 miles from Beringia. Moreover, the few examples of early humans found in the northwest are not Mongoloid in appearance, as people from Siberia would have been at that time. This was notably the case for Kennewick Man, found in Washington State in 1996. Another problem comes in terms of the development of languages, chiefly an insistence that twelve thousand years is simply not sufficient to produce the levels of linguistic diversity found in the Americas (Greenberg, 1987). (Language complexities do not

necessarily coincide with social complexities and can exist independently of them.) Recent studies of blood types and teeth across the Americas also suggest that a simple explanation of origin in Siberia will not work. The notion has recently gained ground that travel along the coasts by boat makes more sense than inland movement alongside glaciers (Gruhn, 1988).

There have long been alternative stories for the peopling of America (Sorensen and Raish, 1996). Perhaps more importantly, over the past few years there have been a number of archaeological finds that simply do not fit the standard pattern. Some finds in Chile, for example, have produced artifacts that date older than the Clovis find, an obvious conundrum for those who support the Beringia theory (Dillehay, 2001). A recent find in South Carolina has been uncovered that archaeologists say predates the most recent Ice Age, which ended about ten thousand years ago. What are we to make of the mounting evidence of scattered early human activity in the Americas? At this stage, it is unlikely that the Beringia theory will be totally overturned. There is simply too much genetic and linguistic evidence to support the view that America's "Indians" are mainly descended from Asian peoples. But there are clearly anomalies. It may be possible that this main wave of Siberians traveling swiftly across the Americas was entering a place previously settled by people who had reached their habitations from different places via different routes or who had perhaps come from Siberia in a far earlier period than the present model allows. And it is also possible that new discoveries will force a paradigm shift for the archaeologists. Like most academic disciplines, archaeology is riddled with feuds and petty grievances that have been elevated over time into hardened ideologies.

More than academic reputations are at stake in the Beringia controversy. Because of the huge sums of money involved in litigation over compensation for tribal lands taken by European nation-states, the ancient human history of the continent before European arrival is of new interest and takes on a high political significance. A North American continent on which aboriginal groups migrated constantly and took over the lands of neighbors, often by force, or on which the Native inhabitants hunted birds and mammals to extinction, was hardly an Eden-like paradise of peace and respect for the environment. If it could be established that people of European origin had arrived on the continent long before 1492 and were displaced or absorbed by later cultures, this

would add further weight to the notion that the European intrusion after 1500 was simply a continuation of developments occurring in all parts of the world—and certainly in America—since the world's human beginnings. At least one Canadian newspaper has already used recent academic revisionism as a basis to editorialize in opposition to any moral claim of Native groups to "massive transfer payments and expensive government programs" (*National Post*, 2001, A19).

The sources for information about the early history of humans on the northern part of the North American continent (now the Dominion of Canada) are simultaneously extensive and limited. Material evidence consists chiefly of human artifacts—mainly of stone, which survives better than leather or wood—usually dug out of the ground by archaeologists. Dating these materials typically involves associating the artifacts with the geological remains in which they are found, a process that often does a better job of outlining a sequence of events than it does of providing precise dates for them. Scientific analysis such as radiocarbon dating can provide a rough notion of the date of an artifact. Given the absence of written records kept by any of the early inhabitants of northern North America, virtually the only way modern scientists can make human memory contribute to the record is by using the oral traditions and the languages of the various peoples. For many years, these oral traditions and linguistic remains were treated with considerable suspicion. They are now regarded as quite useful, but they extend only so far back in time.

John M. Bumsted

See also Archaeology and the First Americans; Bering Strait Theory.

References and Further Reading

Dillehay, Thomas D. 1989. *Monte Verde: A Late Pleistocene Settlement in Chile*, Vol. II. Washington, DC: Smithsonian Institution.

Dillehay, Thomas D. 2001. *The Settlement of the Americas: New Prehistory*. New York: Basic Books.

Greenberg, Joseph. 1987. *Language in the Americas*. Palo Alto, CA: Stanford University Press.

Gruhn, Ruth. 1988. "Linguistic Evidence in Support of the Coastal Route of Earliest Entry into the New World." *Man* 23: 22–100.

National Post. 2001. June 12: A19.

Sorensen, John, and Martin Raish, eds. 1996. *Pre-Columbian Contact with the Americas across the Oceans*, rev. ed. Provo, UT: Brigham Young University Press.

Stengel, Mark K. 2000. "The Diffusionists Have Landed." *Atlantic Monthly* 285, no. 1 (January): 33–43.

Dalles Trading Area

Among the most important Native trading centers of western North America was a place called The Dalles, situated about 80 miles (129 kilometers) east of Portland, Oregon, within the Columbia River Gorge National Scenic Area and just east of the present city of The Dalles. A series of narrows and rapids on the Columbia River, The Dalles was for millennia a major gathering place for many Indian groups and is recognized as one of the oldest inhabited places on the continent. The name "dalles" (Canadian French for "trough, flume") originates with French Canadian voyagers who ventured along the river in the early nineteenth century.

Archaeological research at The Dalles has determined this area to be one of the longest continuously occupied sites in the American West. The earliest radiocarbon date for human activity is about 7850 BCE (9800 BP). Excavations near The Dalles disclose huge quantities of salmon bones by 7700 BP, suggesting that a major fishing complex characteristic of Chinookan culture had developed by this time (Cressman, 1977; Pettigrew, 1998).

The Wascos, Wishrams, and Teninos were among tribal groups that controlled this section of the river and its bounty of fish. The Wascos on the Oregon side of the Columbia and the closely related Wishrams on the Washington side were the easternmost people of the Upper Chinook speakers. The Shahaptian-speaking Teninos lived immediately upstream. They all lived in permanent villages along the stretch of the Columbia River from the foot of the Long Narrows east to Celilo Falls, known as *Wyam* by the Wishram and called the Great Falls of the Columbia by the early white explorers (Woody, 1999).

Virtually unlimited fish was the key to the trading role of The Dalles. The river between The Dalles and Celilo was the greatest fishery on the entire Columbia, offering chinook and coho salmon, steelhead, sturgeon, and eels. Salmon were caught in dip nets and by gaffing or spearing from wooden platforms erected from the perpendicular rocks along the channel. From April through mid-October, salmon made their upstream journey toward their spawning grounds, providing the main food source

of Native peoples in the area and visitors who came to trade. Pounded salmon flesh (salmon pemmican) was often stored away for winter use; the surplus also formed an important article of trade with neighboring and distant tribes. Perhaps the most advantageous site for salmon fishing was at Celilo Falls, a drop of twenty feet across the Columbia twelve miles upstream from the City of The Dalles. Several thousand people congregated at The Dalles and Celilo during the peak times of salmon and steelhead migration.

An extensive economic network centered on The Dalles (Stern, 1998, 641–652). The Wascos and Wishrams were intermediate between the Northwest Coast and Plateau cultural groups with whom they maintained trading partnerships. From the coast peoples they obtained European fabrics, firearms, beads, metal goods, sea otter pelts, wapato (Indian potatoes), and a wide variety of marine foods and products including whale blubber, sea salt, and dentalium shells. Products from a great distance were funneled into the Chinook territory of the lower Columbia. From the interior tribes they received animal skins, buffalo robes and meat, horses, Plains-style clothing, pipestone, roots and seeds, and native tobacco. The Nez Percé were the main outlet from The Dalles to the northern Plains via their associations with the Crow and the Flathead. Horses spread northward from Mexico and reached The Dalles area around 1730 through trade with the Cayuse. The Paiutes of the high plateau country south of the Columbia River brought game and plant foods, horses, and obsidian to The Dalles. There was also an important trade route from The Dalles north to the Nlakapamux and Secwepemc in British Columbia.

Acting as middlemen, trading goods between the coast and interior tribes, the Wishrams and Wascos also provided their visitors with dried salmon. The chief location for barter was a Wishram village along The Dalles (at Fivemile Rapids) called Nixluidix, meaning "coming-together place" (French and French, 1998, 362). When Lewis and Clark arrived at Nixluidix in October 1805, they discovered twenty large wooden houses, each home to three families. Their expedition had arrived near the end of the busy trading period and fishing season that had started in mid-April; in his journal, Clark recorded seeing a total of 107 stacks of salmon and estimated their total weight at over 10,000 pounds (Lewis and Clark, 1953, 265). The trade fairs were also a venue for intertribal socializing, gambling, and exchange of information. According to Alexander Ross of the

North West Company, "The Long Narrows, therefore, is the great emporium or mart of the Columbia, and the general theatre of gambling and roguery" (Ross, 1969, 128).

During the height of The Dalles as a trade entrepôt, a major slave market developed in the early decades of the nineteenth century among the Wasco-Wishram people. Women and children were obtained from the Klamath of southern Oregon, who in turn raided them from northern California (Ruby and Brown, 1986, 91). The Klamath Trail, along the Cascade foothills, was an important trade route to The Dalles and Celilo Falls (Hunn, 1990, 225–227).

With the arrival to the area of European goods in the late eighteenth century and the first explorers and fur traders in the early nineteenth century, trade at The Dalles reached its apex. European goods actually stimulated trading activities at The Dalles, and dried salmon found its way to the coast decades before any Europeans arrived in the area (French and French, 1998, 369). Following Lewis and Clark's expedition, the Pacific Fur Company (the Astorians), established a post near the mouth of the Columbia and explored and traded upstream. Portages around the falls and rapids were necessary to safeguard their trade goods, batteaux, and canoes. The Dalles, especially a section called the Long Narrows (later called Fivemile Rapids), was one of the most formidable barriers along the Columbia. The early years of the fur trade between 1812 and 1814 saw several skirmishes between the Indians and whites who attempted to obtain passage around the rocky channels.

An important aspect of the trade was the development of the Chinook Jargon, a trade language based originally on Chinook words. Later incorporating an increasing vocabulary of French and English origin, Chinook Jargon became an important *lingua franca* between the fur traders and Native groups in the late eighteenth and early nineteenth centuries. The jargon was especially useful at The Dalles, at the boundary between the Chinook and Shahaptian language groups.

By the midnineteenth century, The Dalles trading center declined as Native populations were drastically reduced by disease and warfare. A trading post and Methodist mission were established in 1838, and, during a period of Indian uprisings in the 1840s and 1850s, Fort Lee and Fort Dalles were built to protect immigrants along the Oregon Trail and to gain control of the Columbia River and its abundant salmon. The construction of a pioneer road over the Cascade Range in 1846 and the Donation Land Act

of 1850 brought increased settlement to the area. Dalles City, seat of Wasco County since 1854, was incorporated in 1857. About fifty miles (eighty kilometers) south of The Dalles is the Warm Springs Indian Reservation, established in 1855, where the Wasco, Walla Walla, and Paiute peoples were removed, now comprising the more than 3,500 members of the Confederated Tribes of Warm Springs.

The construction of dams on the middle Columbia River directly affected the historic fisheries of the Confederated Tribes. The Dalles Dam three miles east of the city, built in 1957 and expanded in 1973, inundated many significant fishing areas, including Celilo Falls, the tribes' most sacred place. Although the U.S. government provided "replacement sites" in lieu of lost fishing stations when the earlier Bonneville Dam was built farther downstream, as well as $4 million compensation in economic development when The Dalles Dam was built, the dams not only destroyed ancient Native cultures but destroyed an ecosystem that supported their traditional livelihoods of fishing and trading (Confederated Tribes of the Umatilla Indian Reservation, 1994).

The persistence of the Confederated Tribes in their efforts to conserve salmon in the Columbia and its tributaries has seen impressive results. Spring chinook returned in record numbers in 2000 and 2001. The Department of the Interior recognized the Confederated Tribes of Warm Springs with an Environmental Achievement Award in 2002 for exceptional achievements in environmental stewardship (Ikenson, 2003).

First Peoples still come together each year at Celilo for religious observances such as the first salmon ceremony each spring. The traditional role of the river, however, and the original landscape that provided sustenance, economic barter, and spiritual meaning at The Dalles and Celilo Falls are forever gone. The Columbia Gorge Discovery Center and Wasco County Historical Museum, located in City of The Dalles, highlight the long trading history of the region. As well, the present-day Native community of Celilo Village reveals the power of culture in this ancient place.

Kenneth C. Favrholdt

See also Dams, Fishing Rights, and Hydroelectric Power; Salmon, Economic and Spiritual Significance of; Trade.

References and Further Reading
Confederated Tribes of the Umatilla Indian Reservation. 1994. "A Study of the Impacts to Significant Resources of the Confederated Tribes of the Umatilla Indian Reservation and Opportunities Lost as a Consequence of the Construction of the Bonneville Dam and The Dalles Dam." Available at: http://www.ccrh.org/comm/camas/primary%20docs/report.htm. Accessed February 3, 2006.

Cressman, L. S. 1977. *Prehistory of the Far West: Homes of Vanished Peoples.* Salt Lake City: University of Utah Press.

French, D., and K. French. 1998. "Wasco, Wishram, and Cascades." In *Handbook of North American Indians.* Vol. 12: Plateau. Edited by Deward W. Walker, Jr., 360–377. Washington, DC: Smithsonian Institution.

Hunn, Eugene S. 1990. *Nch'i-Wana, "the Big River": Mid-Columbia Indians and Their Land.* Seattle and London: University of Washington Press.

Ikenson, Ben. 2003. Environmental News Network, "Tribes Work to Restore Traditional Fisheries." April 4. Available at: http://www.bluefish.org/tribewor.htm. Accessed February 3, 2006.

Lewis, Meriwether, and William Clark. 1953. *The Journals of Lewis and Clark.* Edited by Bernard DeVoto. Boston: Houghton-Mifflin.

Pettigrew, Richard M. 1998. "Lower Columbia River Valley Sequence." In *Archaeology of Prehistoric Native America: An Encyclopedia.* Edited by Guy Gibbon, 474–476. New York and London: Garland Publishing.

Ronda, James P. 1999. In *Great River of the West: Essays on the Columbia River.* Edited by William L. Lang and Robert C. Carriker, 76–88. Seattle: : University of Washington Press.

Ross, Alexander. [1849] 1969. *Adventures of the First Settlers on the Oregon or Columbia River.* New York: Citadel Press.

Ruby, Robert H., and John A. Brown. 1986. *A Guide to the Indian Tribes of the Pacific Northwest.* Norman and London: University of Oklahoma Press.

Stern, Theodore. 1998. "Columbia River Trade Network." In *Handbook of North American Indians.* Vol. 12: Plateau. Edited by Deward W. Walker, Jr., 641–652. Washington, DC: Smithsonian Institution.

Woody, Elizabeth. 1999. "Recalling Celilo." In *Salmon Nation: People and Fish at the Edge.* Edited by Edward C. Wolf Edward and S. Zukerman, 9–15. Portland, OR: Ecotrust.

L'Anse aux Meadows Viking Settlement

The discovery in 1960 of a medieval Norse settlement's ruins on the coast of Newfoundland proved that Vikings had explored America nearly 500 years before Columbus.

Helge Ingstad, born in 1899, a Norwegian lawyer and adventurer, found the ruins. Ingstad practiced law in Norway and worked as a trapper in Canada's Northwest Territories. After returning to Norway from Canada, he published a popular book about his experience. Ingstad lived for years in the Norwegian Arctic, where he served as a local governor, first in Greenland, then on Svalbard Island and became an expert in Norse history and the Viking sagas. The term "Norse" refers to medieval Scandinavians—residents of the areas that constitute modern-day Sweden, Norway, Denmark, and Iceland—whereas the term "Viking" originally was used to refer to early medieval Norse pirates. In this article, the terms "Norse" and "Viking" are used interchangeably.

While Ingstad was living on Svalbard, Anne Stine, a Norwegian archaeologist, began a correspondence with him. The two eventually met, married, and had a daughter. Both Ingstad and his wife were intensely interested in Viking-era Norse history. They studied the sagas, explored the ruins of Norse settlements in Greenland, and acquired medieval maps. Like many saga readers before them, they became fascinated with the mystery of Vinland.

The sagas began as epic oral histories of the adventures and everyday lives of the ancient Norse. Saga tellers recited and passed down the epics for hundreds of years. Thirty major sagas survive today in written form. Two of these tales, *The Greenlanders' Saga* and *Erik's Saga*, tell of the Norse Greenlanders' travels to Vinland, a land with forests of timber, an abundance of wild game, and ample pasturage that lay twelve days' journey to the southwest of Greenland.

For hundreds of years, saga readers have puzzled over Vinland, questioning whether the land described in the sagas was real and, if real, where it might lie. Based on the saga descriptions of the voyage, other historical sources, and his knowledge of Viking techniques of shipbuilding and seamanship, Ingstad believed that Vinland existed and that it probably lay somewhere on the coast of Newfoundland, a large island in southeastern Canada.

Replicas of Norse sod houses stand at L'Anse aux Meadows National Historic Park in Newfoundland. The Viking settlement at L'Anse aux Meadows is the earliest documented European settlement in North America. (Wolfgang Kaehler/Corbis)

Other scholars disagreed, arguing that, because the saga tells of the Vikings finding wild grapes and naming the land Vinland (Wineland) in reference to these grapes, Vinland must lie in an area where wild grapes grow. Because Massachusetts is the northernmost area where grapes grow today, many scholars believed that the Greenlanders must have journeyed at least as far south as Massachusetts. Ingstad, in contrast, thought it unlikely the Vikings would have traveled so far south. He instead theorized that the word "Vinland" was derived from the Old Norse word *vin*, meaning "pasture or meadow," not from a similar word meaning "wine." He further posited that the passages in the saga that refer to the gathering of grapes were not part of the original narrative, but instead were later additions.

In 1960, Ingstad and his daughter Benedicte explored the coasts of Newfoundland and Labrador by air and sea, attempting to match the geographic features they saw with those described in the sagas and the ancient maps. Eventually, Ingstad's calculations led him to L'Anse aux Meadows (pronounced "Lan-see Meadows"), a site that seemed to correlate exactly with Vinland as described in the sagas. When he asked a local fisherman if there were any ruins in the area, the man led Ingstad to an area of grass-covered mounds and depressions in a bay front pasture a short distance from the village.

L'Anse aux Meadows is a tiny coastal fishing village on the northern tip of Newfoundland. Behind the village is the small, shallow Épaves Bay. From the bay rises a gently sloping marine terrace covered with lush meadowland and bisected by a freshwater brook. It is on this terrace that the ruins are located. From Ingstad's first survey of the site, he believed that it was a likely place for a Norse settlement because it was reminiscent of the farm sites he had visited in Greenland.

Greenland, the world's largest island, was first colonized in 986 by Norse adventurers traveling from Iceland. Greenland's climate is harsh, with long, dark winters and short, cool summers. There are only a few wind-stunted trees on the island and more than 80 percent of Greenland's surface is covered with ice year-round. In the winter, the sea ice pack almost completely surrounds the island, making sea travel impossible. Coastal grasslands along the island's fjords constitute the northernmost reaches of arable land. Life in Greenland is difficult. To survive, the medieval Norse had to exploit all possible means of subsistence. These included trapping; gathering wild plants, berries and eggs; fishing and hunting, as well as managing small farms. When wild resources were scarce, agriculture and animal husbandry helped sustain them.

The technology of the medieval Norse was similar to that of their fellow Greenlanders, the Dorset Eskimo—ancestors of the modern Inuit people. Both groups hunted game with snares and spears and used small kayaks made of animal hide to fish and hunt seals and walrus. Unlike the Inuit, however, the Norse farmed and kept animals, forged iron, and spun and wove wool into cloth. Yet Arctic survival was more difficult for the Norse than for the Inuit, who were more mobile and skilled in ice travel and in the use of kayaks and thus better able to hunt and follow migrating animals. Considering the difficult life they led in Greenland, it is easy to understand why the Norse continued to search for more favorable lands to colonize.

Based on historical and archaeological evidence, scholars believe that the Norse Greenland colony endured until around 1500. The exact reason for its disappearance is unknown; scholars have suggested it may have been due to a combination of factors, such as a cooling trend, the southward movement of Greenland Eskimos, disease, and pirate attacks. Some investigators believe that, after a number of years of population decline, the remaining Norse emigrated, perhaps to Iceland.

Initially, it was not clear if the ruins at L'Anse aux Meadows, which lie seven hundred miles southwest of Greenland, had been a Native American or a Norse village. The answer was left to a series of painstaking archaeological excavations that Anne Stine Ingstad would lead at the site.

The ancient house sites the archaeological team uncovered were made of sod, a building material common to both Native Americans in the area and the Norse Greenlanders. Other elements of the houses, however, led Stine Ingstad to believe that they were built by Norse settlers. For example, the houses contained hearths and cinder boxes similar to those found in the Norse Greenland settlements. Further, one of the houses was identified as a smithy, or ironworker's shop, and the forging of iron was a technology not known to Native Americans at the time. Several Norse items were found at the site, include Viking-era bronze and iron artifacts, a stone spindle whorl used for spinning wool into yarn and thread, and fragments of bone from a domestic pig.

The condition of the ruins and the style of the Norse artifacts led Ingstad to conclude that the settlement was occupied off and on for several years around 1000 by perhaps as many as a hundred people. Subsequent radiocarbon tests confirmed this date. Stine Ingstad based her conclusion that the time of occupation was short on the fact that the middens, or trash piles, the settlers left behind are shallow—no more than ten centimeters deep—and the sod houses, which naturally collapse after twenty to thirty years, show no evidence of having been rebuilt.

Since Vinland offered a more favorable climate than Greenland, better pasturage, ample game and fish, and wooded forests, the question arises as to why its occupation was so short. The evidence points to conflict with the Native people. Native artifacts excavated at the site indicate that the Beothuk people, their ancestors, and Dorset Eskimos occupied the L'Anse aux Meadows area between 1000 and 1500.

When the Norse Greenlanders encountered the Dorset people in Greenland, they referred to them with the derogatory term "skraeling," meaning "screamers," and, by connotation, wretched or uncultured. They used the same word to refer to the Natives they found in Vinland. The sagas make clear that the Norse feared the skraelings and believed them to be dangerous, possibly supernatural beings. As a result, there was limited interaction and exchange between the groups and the Norse were known to kill Natives with little provocation. According to the sagas, such behavior resulted in vengeance attacks by the Natives, whose weapons were essentially the same as those used by the Vikings but whose population vastly outnumbered that of the Norse settlers.

The Viking settlement at L'Anse aux Meadows is the earliest documented European settlement in North America. It predates Columbus by roughly 500 years. Yet Columbus and the Greenlanders must have seen their discoveries in a completely different light. Unlike Columbus, the Vikings received neither fame nor lasting wealth from their discovery, and they had no idea that they had discovered a new continent.

Until the Ingstads brought it to the world's attention, the Norse contribution to the settlement of America was lost for nearly a thousand years. In 1978, as a result of the Ingstads' work, the historical importance of the Norse village at L'Anse aux Meadows was officially recognized and the site was declared a UNESCO World Heritage Site.

Amy L. Propps

See also Norse Exploration of North America.
References and Further Reading
Enterline, James Robert. 2002. *Erikson, Eskimos and Columbus.* Baltimore, MD: Johns Hopkins University Press.
Ingstad, Helge. 2001. *The Viking Discovery of America: The Excavation of a Norse Settlement in L'Anse aux Meadows, Newfoundland.* New York: Checkmark Books.
Ingstad, Helge, and Ann Stine Ingstad. 1977. *The Norse Discovery of America.* 2 vols. Oslo: Norwegian University Press.
Johnston, George, trans. 1976. *The Greenlanders' Saga.* Canada: Oberon Press.
Jones, Gwyn, trans. 1961. "Eirik the Red." *Erik the Red and Other Icelandic Sagas.* New York: Oxford University Press.

Norse Exploration of North America

Before Columbus's voyages, sporadic contact between Native people and non-Natives left a residue of myth, transmitted from generation to generation in oral histories. American Indians from Nova Scotia to Mexico told their children about pale-skinned, bearded strangers who had arrived from the direction of the rising sun. Such myths played a large part in Cortes' conquest of the Aztecs, who were expecting the return of men who looked like him. The Natives of Haiti told Columbus they expected the return of white men; some Mayan chants speak of visits by bearded strangers. The Leni Lenape (Delaware) told Moravian missionaries that they had long awaited the return of divine visitors from the East. These currents, among others, suggest that the peoples of the Old and New Worlds communicated with each other sporadically centuries before Columbus.

In the realm of what critic Stephen Williams calls "fantastic archaeology" (Williams, 1991), theories establishing European origins for Native American peoples have long historiographic pedigrees. Evidence that meets the strictest standards of professional archaeology is scant in support of any of them. One exception is the pre-Columbian landfall of the Vikings. Norse sagas (oral histories) and scattered archaeological evidence indicate that, beginning about 1000, Viking explorers who had earlier settled Iceland and Greenland conducted several expeditions along the East Coast of North America. At up to three locations—Newfoundland, and possibly Cape Cod and the James River of Virginia—some evidence exists of small-scale, short-lived

Viking settlements. One Viking (the word is from the Norwegian *viks* for fjord dweller), Thorfinn Karlsefni, explored 3,000 miles of North American coast in the early eleventh century, according to the sagas.

The technical capability of the Vikings to reach North America is not in doubt. They were capable seafarers and built sturdy longships easily capable of reaching Iceland from Norway, a distance much greater than the voyage from Greenland to North America. In 1893, Magnus Andersen, a Norwegian, sailed a reconstructed Viking ship from Norway to Newfoundland.

Vikings may have followed the Saint Lawrence River and Great Lakes as far inland as the vicinity of Kensington, Minnesota, where, in 1898, a large stone was found inscribed with Norse runic writing that described the ambush and killing of ten men. Testing has revealed the runes as weathered (as would be expected) but authentic. The Norse may have been looking for new sources of furs after the German Hanseatic League captured their trade in Russian furs in 1360 (Kehoe, 2002, 217).

Indisputable proof of Viking landings in North America has been found on the northern tip of Newfoundland. These discoveries began with the explorations of Helge Ingstad, at L'Anse aux Meadows, about 1960. The site has since been excavated and part of it turned into a public park. The evidence there is conclusive—right down to such things as a soapstone spindle whorl, nails, and even the remains of an iron smelter, along with hundreds of other artifacts, many of which have been carbon–14 dated to about 1000. Most other supposed Viking visits to North America (one in the unlikely location of Tucson, Arizona) still reside in the realm of archaeological speculation. According to Frederick Pohl, a science fiction novelist who also has written three books on Norse exploration of North America, eighty-nine locations of Norse landfall have been asserted in North America. Some of these locations are as far apart as present-day Minnesota and New Orleans.

According to the Viking sagas, in about 985 the Viking sailor Bjarni Herjulfsson sighted land (probably Cape Cod) after several navigational errors led him astray on a voyage to Greenland. He finally reached his destination by sailing northeastward along the North American coast. In Greenland, his story of three land sightings to the southwest excited the imagination of Leif Erickson, who interviewed Bjarni and purchased his ship.

According to the sagas that were told after his voyages (which have been written and translated into English), Erickson made landfall at three places. He called the first Helluland, probably Baffin Island; the second was Markland, possibly Labrador or Newfoundland. The third landing, where Erickson established a small winter settlement, may have been on Cape Cod, near Follins Pond. The sagas tell of their ship being beached and stored, a house being built, and salmon caught that were larger than any the Vikings had ever seen. While the Viking settlement in Newfoundland lasted several years and left behind many artifacts, the visit to Cape Cod seems to have been more of a temporary stop, leaving little evidence that survived ensuing centuries.

Thorvald Erickson, a brother of Leif, set out on his own voyage of discovery shortly afterward, in 1007. His plan was to explore the coast north and south of Cape Cod. Along the way, Thorvald's thirty-man crew seized and killed eight American Indians (they called them "skraelings," meaning "screamers," after their war whoops, indicating, by connotation, a wretched or uncultured people). Thorvald later was killed in revenge for those murders, and his crew sailed back to Greenland without him.

A few years later, in 1010, Thorfinn Karlsefni sailed from Iceland to Leif's settlement on Cape Cod, after which he probably explored the Atlantic Coast southward to the James River of present-day Virginia. The trip required four summers. The first winter was spent along the Hudson River of New York State, where the Vikings were surprised by the depth of snowfall for a place so far south. The second winter was spent along the James River of Virginia. The sagas tell of a voyage up the river to the rapids, far enough upstream to have seen the peaks of the Blue Ridge Mountains. At one point, according to the sagas, Karlsefni's crew was attacked by Native Americans who used a large hornet's nest as a weapon. In all, the Karlsefni expedition probably logged about 3,000 miles along the coast and adjoining rivers.

Leif Erickson died about 1025, and his Labrador settlement withered, but not before Karlsefni and Gudrid, his wife, had given birth to a son they called Snorri, the first child believed to have been born in America of European parents. After that, voyages continued from time to time through the thirteenth and fourteenth centuries. King Magnus of Norway and Sweden authorized the Paul Knutson expedition, which sailed in 1355 to explore conditions in

Greenland and Vinland. Knowledge of North America was apparently still being recalled in Iceland in 1477, when a young Italian sailor, Cristoforo Colombo, visited and became excited by sailors' gossip of land to the south and west of Greenland.

Bruce E. Johansen

See also L'Anse aux Meadows Viking Settlement.
References and Further Reading
Kehoe, Alice Beck. 2002. *America before the European Invasions.* London: Longman.
Pohl, Frederick Julius. 1972. *The Viking Settlements of North America.* New York: C. N. Potter.
Williams, Stephen. 1991. *Fantastic Archaeology: The Wild Side of North American Prehistory.* Philadelphia: University of Pennsylvania Press.

Doctrine of Discovery

The Doctrine of Discovery references the logic of fifteenth-century Christiandom that endowed European conquerors with self-assumed divine title over all "discovered" land and peoples. During this time Spain and Portugal were in fierce competition over the extent of their empires. As disputes festered, appeals for resolution often were presented to the pope—the recognized official arbiter between nations.

In 1455, King Alfonso V of Portugal made such an appeal, and in response the pope issued the bull *Romanus Pontifex,* confirming Alfonso's right to dominion over vanquished lands while also underscoring his duty to:

> [I]nvade, search out, capture, vanquish, and subdue all Saracens and pagans whatsoever, and other enemies of Christ wheresoever placed, and . . . to reduce their persons to perpetual slavery, and to apply and appropriate to himself and his successors the kingdoms, dukedoms, counties, principalities, dominions, possessions, and goods, and to convert them to his and their use and profit (Davenport, 1917, 23).

The bull *Romanus Pontifex* provides great insight to the world in which Columbus voyaged in 1492. When he sailed, Columbus did so as a servant to the royal crown of Spain *and* as a soldier of Christ, dutifully claiming and possessing "uninhabited" lands not found to be under the dominion of any Christian ruler.

The "discovery" of the "New World" reignited the competition between Spain and Portugal. King Alfonso V argued that previous bulls entitled Portugal to the newly discovered lands, whereas the Spanish crown disputed Alfonso's claims, appealing to the pope to confirm their right to the New World. In response, Pope Alexander VI issued the *Inter Caetera* (1493), confirming Spain's right to conquests in the New World:

> [Y]ou have purposed with the favor of divine clemency to bring under your sway the said mainlands and islands with their residents and inhabitants and to bring them to the Catholic faith . . . and in order that you may enter upon so great an undertaking . . . we, of our own accord . . . and out of the fullness of our apostolic power, by the authority of the Almighty God . . . do by the tenor of these presents . . . give, grant, and assign to you and your heirs and successors . . . forever . . . all rights, jurisdictions, and appurtenances, all islands and mainlands [to be] found . . . (Davenport, 1917).

As the pope took on the heady responsibility of dividing the New World between Spain and Portugal, the notion of occupancy emerged as a precondition for the dispensations of conquest. The irony of this did not go unnoticed by Native peoples, whose rights of occupancy were not only denied but categorically dismissed by the Law of Nations, a deeply racist "law" that proclaimed the world's "heathen" and "infidels" to be in inherent need of subjugation. These rules of engagement, set forth by church and empire in the fifteenth century, formed the corpus of the Old World's "Doctrine of Discovery," entitling the conqueror to all the spoils of conquest.

The Doctrine of Discovery was incorporated into U.S. law several centuries later through Supreme Court Justice John Marshall's majority decision in *Johnson v. M'Intosh* (1823). The question before the court was whether a land title obtained from Indians under British supervision at an open sale was superior to that obtained by the United States through a sale by designated land officers (Deloria, 1992, 299). The Court ruled in favor of the defendant, finding that only the federal government held the right to issue titles for Indian land. In the decision, Justice Marshall invoked the doctrine of discovery as the precedent by which "the discovering European nation" was granted "an exclusive right to extinguish the Indian title of occupancy,

either by purchase or by conquest" (Williams, 1986, 253–254). In effect, Marshall deemed the United States, as successor to Great Britain, the rightful heir to their spoils of conquest.

While Marshall was fully cognizant that his finding signaled a radical departure from modern, more "civilized" rules of engagement, he justified his ruling as follows:

> [H]owever this restriction may be opposed to natural right, and to the usages of civilized nations, yet, if it be indispensable to that system under which the country has been settled, and be adapted to the actual condition of the two people, it may, perhaps, be supported by reason, and certainly not be rejected by courts of justice (*Johnson v. M'Intosh*, 1823, 591–592).

In other words, Marshall argued that the United States' "claim to property titles was valid because to do otherwise would disrupt everything that had previously occurred" (Deloria, 1992, 300).

Grande (2004) notes that perhaps the most remarkable aspect of the Marshall opinion is the relatively uncritical manner in which it was adopted into U.S. law. One would expect, even by the standards of nineteenth-century democracy, that the invocation of a fifteenth-century Christian doctrine by a Supreme Court justice would be viewed as an act of sedition, especially by a nation struggling to retain the "wall of separation" between church and state.

In subsequent years, however, Marshall's decision (and by implication, the doctrine of discovery) has been a popular rhetorical site of interrogation for legions of indigenous and nonindigenous scholars. Most recently, in *Uneven Ground: American Indian Sovereignty and Federal Law,* David E. Wilkins and K. Tsianina Lomawaima provide a thorough analysis of the doctrine of discovery and its impact on U.S. law.

In their comprehensive study of numerous treaties, laws, policies, and congressional directives, the authors identify three operating definitions of the doctrine of discovery in U.S. law and policy: absolute, expansive, and preemptive. The absolute definition equates discovery with complete conquest, not only denying indigenous peoples legal title, but also usage and occupancy rights. The expansive definition is less extreme, recognizing indigenous nations possessory and occupancy rights

but denying any right to legal title. The operating rationale is that Indians are inherently incompetent to manage lands and are therefore in need of "a benevolent guardian" to hold "full legal title" (Wilkins and Lomawaima, 2001, 21). Wilkins and Lomawaima dismiss both of these interpretations as, at best, ill informed and, at worst, racist and ethnocentric. They furthermore argue that, while expansive and absolute interpretations of discovery abound, a competing and legally sound interpretation of the rights of discovery is both plausible and necessary. As a result of their analysis, the authors advocate a preemptive definition of discovery—one that grants "discovering" European nations "an exclusive, preemptive right to be the first purchaser of Indian land, should a tribe agree to sell any of its territory" (2001, 20).

Indeed, their analysis reveals that the preemptive definition of discovery was the original and most prevalent interpretation of discovery in the precolonial era. Wilkins and Lomawaima examine various documents regarding established treaty relations between American Indians and the Spanish, French, and British empires and conclude that, to varying degrees, all nations recognized and respected Indian title. Their examination of similar relations between the United States and American Indians in the early years of nationhood (1776–1800s) reveals a similar reality: that the United States originally acted as "first purchaser" and not as "ultimate proprietor" of Indian lands (2001, 51).

Wilkins and Lomawaima (2001) maintain that a radical departure from the practice of treating Indian tribes and nations as sovereigns did not begin until 1801 when Justice Marshall commenced his service to the Court and came to a head with the *Johnson* decision in 1823. They write:

> As the preceding analyses show, no previous sovereign—including Great Britain—had acted as if it had a superior title to Indian land. . . . Even in Marshall's time, the preponderance of historic evidence supported a recognition of Indian ownership of the soil that rested in the tribes until they chose to sell that soil to a bidding European sovereign (2001, 55).

Wilkins and Lomawaima furthermore maintain that subsequent cases—*Worcester v. Georgia* and *Mitchell v. United States* — indicate the Court's own discomfort with *M'Intosh,* causing them to "back away from the language of conquest" (2001, 61).

Finally, the authors argue that perhaps the final linchpin in the case against absolutist and expansive interpretations of discovery is the fact that Native American nations did not participate in the *M'Intosh* case, calling into question whether the precedent set by the landmark case was ever legally binding (2001, 58). They conclude with the following compelling statement:

> The doctrine of discovery, when defined as an exclusive principle of benevolent paternalism or, as it was in the McIntosh decision, as an assertion of federal ownership of fee-simple title to all the Indian lands in the United States, is a clear legal fiction that needs to be explicitly stricken from the federal government's political and legal vocabulary. . . . Federal abandonment of the demeaning and unjust legal fiction contained in the absolute and expansive definitions of discovery . . . would be a significant first step in reformulating Indian policy so that policy is based on justice, humanity, and the "actual state of things" (63).

Sandy Grande

See also Tribal Sovereignty; *Worcester v. Georgia*.

References and Further Reading

Davenport, Francis Gardener, trans. 1917. "Romanus Pontifex." In *European Treaties Bearing on the History of the United States and Its Dependencies to 1648*. Edited by Francis Gardener Davenport, 20–26. Washington, DC: Carnegie Institution of Washington.

Deloria, Vine, Jr. 1992. "Trouble in High Places: Erosion of American Indian Rights to Religious Freedom in the United States." In *The State of Native America: Genocide, Colonization and Resistance*. Edited by Annete M. James, 267–290. Boston: South End Press.

Deloria, Vine, Jr., and Clifford M. Lytle. 1983. *American Indians, American Justice*. Austin: University of Texas Press.

Grande, Sandy. 2004. *Red Pedagogy: Native American Social and Political Thought*. Lanham, MD: Rowman & Littlefield.

Johnson, Troy R., ed. 1999. *Contemporary Native American Political Issues*. Walnut Creek, CA: AltaMira Press.

Johnson v. M'Intosh (8 Wheaton 543, 1823).

Lyons, Oren, et al. 1992. *Exiled in the Land of the Free: Democracy, Indian Nations, and the U.S. Constitution*. Santa Fe, NM: Clear Light Publishers.

Mitchell v. United States, 34 U.S. (9 Pet.) 711 (1835).

Pevar, Stephen L. 2002. *The Rights of Indians and Tribes: The Authoritative ACLU Guide to Indian and Tribal Rights*, 3rd ed. Carbondale: Southern Illinois University Press.

Wilkins, David E., and K. Tsianina Lomawaima. 2001. *Uneven Ground: American Indian Sovereignty and Federal Law*. Norman: University of Oklahoma Press.

Williams, Robert A. 1986. "The Algebra of Federal Indian Law: The Hard Trail of *Worcester v. Georgia*, 31 U.S. (6 Pet.) 515 (1832).

Missionaries, French Jesuit

The members of the Society of Jesus, a religious order of the Roman Catholic Church, served as missionaries among Native North Americans during the sixteenth, seventeenth, and eighteenth centuries. Though by no means the only missionaries to attempt to convert the indigenous peoples of the continent to Christianity during this period, the French Jesuits tended to be the most organized and energetic. They are remembered in part for their remarkable travel accounts and historic records.

The Society of Jesus was founded in 1540 by Saint Ignatius of Loyola (born Iñigo López de

Jesuit missionaries were met with a range of reactions as they preached among the natives of New England. (Ridpath, John Clark, Ridpath's History of the World, *1901)*

Loyola). The Society's members, who became known as Jesuits, began as a major thrust of the Catholic Counter-Reformation in Europe, challenging the teachings of Martin Luther and other Protestants, but the Jesuits' work soon extended into the western hemisphere. The Jesuits took the three traditional clerical vows of chastity, poverty, and obedience, in addition to a fourth vow of special obedience to the pope. The multifaceted activities of the Society encompassed education, literary and scientific activities, pastoral care, and missionary work. During the second half of the sixteenth century, its mission field was extended throughout post-Reformation Europe, to Asia, and to Latin America. In North America, sixteenth-century Spanish Jesuits briefly and fruitlessly sought to convert the Natives of the Chesapeake, Florida, and Gulf Coast. A handful of English Jesuits also traveled to Maryland and New York in the seventeenth century, only to be hindered by the fierce anti-Catholicism of the Protestant Anglo-American colonists.

Jesuits played a central role in the seventeenth- and eighteenth-century colonization of New France, the vast territory claimed by the French crown in North America. In 1611, two fathers attempted to establish a mission at Port Royal, Acadia, only to be expelled three years later by an English force. A similar fate befell the Jesuits who returned to the colony in 1625. Unfazed, the missionaries returned to New France for the long term in 1632.

During the 1630s and 1640s, French Jesuits followed Native trade routes and established missions among the Algonquians and Iroquoians who inhabited the region of the Saint Lawrence River, Saguenay River, and Great Lakes. Impelled by the desire to carry the teachings of the Catholic Church to the inhabitants of the continent, the missionaries figured prominently among those who continued to extend the religious, commercial, and political influence of New France. Closer to the core of the French colony, along the shores of the Saint Lawrence, Jesuits were instrumental in inducing a number of Hurons, Iroquois, Algonquians, Nipissings, and Abenakis to settle in a series of *reductions* (reserves).

For the Jesuits, the evangelization of Native America meant imposing monogamy, restraining independence (imposing French sovereignty), and suppressing a range of traditional practices as superstition. Not surprisingly, their message was received with considerable scepticism, often hostility, by Native peoples. Although they were certainly aided by French or French-allied Indian military escorts as well as the ability to channel the French trade toward willing converts (nor were they above frightening Indians beset by smallpox into conversion), the missionaries endeavored to Christianize mainly through example and argumentation. To achieve their aims, they became keen students of Amerindian languages and cultures. Following a precedent set by their brethren in other parts of the world, the Jesuits of New France carefully documented their work and the indigenous ways of life, most notably in a collection of published annual reports known as the *Jesuit Relations* (*Relations des Jésuites* or *Relations de la Nouvelle-France*). Sometimes tolerated only because they guaranteed a commercial and military partnership with France, the presence and spiritual services of the French Jesuits came to be appreciated by many Native communities.

The standing of the Society of Jesus was challenged during the second half of the eighteenth century. Canada became a British possession in 1763, thereby losing its connection to France. Having come under fire for interfering with the enterprises of the royal governments in Latin America, the Society was further suppressed in a number of countries, including France, in 1767. A worldwide papal suppression followed in 1773. Staffed by aging men, the Jesuit missions in North America could no longer be sustained; some were abandoned, while others were taken over by secular "priests" and members of other orders.

The period following the Papal Restoration of the Society of Jesus in 1814, however, was marked by tremendous growth. The Jesuits of Maryland began to expand their missionary enterprises westward, while French Jesuits returned to Canada in 1842 to resume their work of ministering to the converted and undermining the structures and beliefs of traditionalists. The Society of Jesus continues, to this day, its work among Native Americans.

Jean-François Lozier

See also Ceremonies, Criminalization of; New France and Natives.

References and Further Reading

Blackburn, Carole. 2000. *Harvest of Souls: The Jesuit Missions and Colonialism in North America, 1632–1650.* Montreal: McGill-Queen's University Press.

Greer, Allan, ed. 2000. *The Jesuit Relations: Natives and Missionaries in Seventeenth-Century North America.* The Bedford Series in History and Culture. Boston: Bedford/St. Martin's.

Greer, Allan. 2005. *Mohawk Saint: Catherine Tekakwitha and the Jesuits.* Oxford and New York: Oxford University Press.

Parkman, Francis. 1865. "Jesuits in North America." *The North American Review* 105, no. 216 (July).

"Decolonizing and Americanizing the White Man's Indian Jurisprudence." 1986. *Wisconsin Law Review* (March/April): 220–284.

New France and Natives

While the term "New France" came to be applied specifically to the region between Montreal and Quebec, in general the territory stretched between present-day Quebec City in the east and Huronia (southern Georgian Bay) in the west. The French also colonized the Louisiana territory and parts of the Caribbean, areas not considered part of New France proper, but generally referred to by historians as the French Atlantic or French America.

The region that came to be generally known as New France was home to tens of thousands of indigenous peoples at the time of the European invasion. It is difficult to arrive at a precise population of precontact North America; in fact, modern estimates place the population of the continent anywhere between 3 million and 12 million. It is likely that the Iroquoian peoples of New France and present-day northern New York numbered a hundred thousand. When Jacques Cartier visited the village of Tiotontakwe (aka Hochelaga, at present-day Montreal), he recorded a population of fifteen hundred people (Delâge, 1993, 1993, 43–45). We can safely say that Europeans stepped foot on a (sometimes densely) populated continent, of which the Northeast was one of the most thickly populated regions. The French encountered the Beothuk (a group that was exterminated, likely by disease, shortly after contact), as well as the Innu (Montagnais) and Mi'kmaqs (Micmacs), both of the Algonquin cultural family, and the Hotninonshonni (Iroquois Confederacy) and other related nations—the Wendat (Hurons, a confederacy of several nations), the Tionontate (Petun), the Neutrals and the Tobacco.

Essentially the region's two cultural-linguistic groups had two different economic and settlement patterns. The semisedentary Algonquin peoples of present-day Quebec were hunter-gatherers, inhabiting village sites during warmer months and migrating over a wider hunting territory during the winter, following a sophisticated cyclical pattern, which was conceptualized as distinct from nations who practiced horticulture. An Innu hunter explained to Jesuit Paul Le Jeune in 1634: "Do you not see that you and the [Hotinonshonni] cultivate the soil and gather its fruits, and not we, and therefore it is not the same?" (Greer, 2000, 27).

The Wendat and Hotinonshonni groups of New France were mostly sedentary, inhabiting village sites for about ten years before moving to a new location. Historians of ecology recognize that this practice helped to place less stress on local environments, because village relocation allowed the forests to grow back and the soil to regain fertility. These groups practiced horticulture, growing the "three sisters" complex of corn, beans, and squash, with diets supplemented by fish and game. These groups had come to inhabit sizable villages and established large populations. It is estimated that, on the eve of European invasion, the population of Huronia had reached as high as 30,000 people (Delâge, 1993, 49). These horticultural societies divided work along gender lines, with women tending crops and doing other tasks such as sewing, cooking, gathering, and the important work of educating children. Meanwhile, men did some secondary horticultural work, including growing tobacco, as well as hunting and fishing (Delâge, 1993, 50–52).

There is a wealth of written material about the indigenous peoples of New France because French colonial records have survived remarkably well. The diaries and reports of explorers such as Jacques Cartier and Samuel de Champlain give us a picture of indigenous life at the very first moments of European arrival. The voluminous *Jesuit Relations*, yearly reports sent by Jesuit missionaries back to France between 1632 and 1673, detail the customs, spiritual beliefs—essentially the everyday life—of the Natives of New France, whom the Jesuits were attempting to convert.

While contact with northeastern North America began with European fishermen off the coast of Canada in the late 1400s, the first sustained contact between the French and indigenous peoples began when Cartier first visited the area in the 1530s. Cartier described thickly populated villages along the Saint Lawrence River. The people whom Cartier encountered, and whom historians refer to as the Saint Lawrence Iroquois, had disappeared by the seventeenth century, and historians debate whether these people had migrated out of the region or had been exterminated by European diseases. Incidentally, Cartier also kidnapped several indigenous peo-

French explorer Jacques Cartier meets Native Americans at Hochelaga, now Montreal, in 1535. (Bettmann/Corbis)

ples, including the chief Donnacona, taking them to France to appear before King François I (Dickason, 1984, 210–211). French contact with Natives increased over the following decades, with Cartier's subsequent voyages, and the travels of Samuel de Champlain in the early 1600s. Champlain established a fortified settlement at Quebec in 1608.

French immigration to New France remained extremely low, due to the colony's isolation, its inhospitable climate, and a lack of silver and gold. By the 1650s, the colony included only 3,200 French inhabitants, many of them clustered around Quebec and other settlements, such as Trois-Rivières (established 1634) and Montreal (1642) (Greer, 1997, 5). Peter Moogk suggests that 10,825 European immigrants made a permanent home in the Saint Lawrence Valley before 1760 (Moogk, 2000, 113). As was the case across the Americas, infectious European diseases had an overwhelmingly destructive impact on indigenous populations.

As Olive Dickason has illustrated, the early modern French worldview classified indigenous peo-

ples as *les sauvages*, a term that denoted people living away from society, without a permanent residence, "by analogy, one who is rude and fierce" (Dickason, 1984, 63). According to Dickason, this was not a neutral categorization; using their moral framework, the French viewed Natives as "wild men" rather than as humans (Dickason, 1984, 63–64). However, as indicated by the initial trading partnerships with indigenous peoples, the attempts at settling and Christianizing Natives, and the high rate of cultural mixing through intermarriage, despite this disparaging term many French colonists did not view their Native hosts solely with contempt. Additionally, the French view of indigenous peoples changed over time, during the Enlightenment, as thinkers exchanged the image of the wild man for the noble savage (*le bon sauvage*), living in a state of nature uncorrupted by "civil society" (Dickason, 1984, 80–81).

A key feature of European interactions with Natives in New France was missionization. Champlain brought four Recollet (Franciscan) priests from France in 1615 to attempt conversions among the

Wendats. The Recollets had relatively little success and sought help from the Society of Jesus (Jesuits), a newly formed order that had been successful with missions in South America and Asia. The Jesuits came to hold a monopoly on mission work in New France from 1632 until the 1660s (Moogk, 2000, 29). Father Paul Le Jeune became the first Jesuit superior in New France and documented his daily life with the Innu in the *Relations*. When it came to conversions, the Jesuits were met mostly with failure, as it became apparent that semisendentary peoples would not yield many converts. With the hopes of converting indigenous peoples into French subjects, the Jesuits set up permanent mission settlements, such as those at Sillery near Quebec and Sainte Marie-aux-Hurons in Huronia. The missions acted as permanent bases for the Jesuit priests and became the home of Christian Natives, with a separate living area for the unconverted. With Europeans living among Native communities, disease spread through the missions with devastating effects on indigenous populations. Often, Native people blamed the Jesuits' "sorcery" for the death that ravaged their societies after the arrival of the French.

In the mission setting, the Jesuits had much more success with conversions. In Huronia, the Jesuits claimed a thousand baptisms in 1639–1640 and 620 in 1642 (Delâge, 1993, 179). The mission at Sainte-Marie lasted only ten years (1639–1649) because increasing attacks made by Hotinonshonni people from the south resulted in the deaths of several Jesuit priests, including Jean de Brébeuf, and the settlement was seen as too dangerous. The remaining Wendat people were dispersed, some to Lorette near Quebec City and others to the midwestern United States via the Great Lakes.

With the beginning of the Seven Years' War, fought between England and France on both sides of the Atlantic, New France and its scattered European population became literally cut off from the empire when the English made the North American theater of war its main priority. The English victory in the war, which saw the transfer of New France to England, marked the end of French colonial rule in North America. However, despite changes brought about by England's policy toward indigenous people, the legacy of French colonialism remains visible in the province of Quebec today.

Daniel Morley Johnson

See also Fur Trade; Haudenosaunee Confederacy, Political System; Missionaries, French Jesuit.

References and Further Reading
Delâge, Denys. 1993. *Bitter Feast: Amerindians and Europeans in Northeastern North America, 1600–64.* Translated by Jane Brierley. Vancouver: University of British Columbia Press.
Dickason, Olive Patricia. 1984. *The Myth of the Savage and the Beginnings of French Colonialism in the Americas.* Edmonton: University of Alberta Press.
Greer, Allan. 1997. *The People of New France.* Toronto, ON, and Buffalo, NY: University of Toronto Press.
Greer, Allan, ed. 2000. *The Jesuit Relations: Natives and Missionaries in Seventeenth-Century North America.* Boston: Bedford/St. Martin's.
Moogk, Peter N. 2000. *La Nouvelle France: The Making of French Canada, A Cultural History.* East Lansing: Michigan State University Press.
Trigger, Bruce, ed. 1986. *Natives and Newcomers: Canada's "Heroic Age" Reconsidered.* Kingston and Montreal: McGill-Queen's University Press.

Spanish Influence

Spain was the first European country to extensively colonize what today is North America. The Spanish approach to the region came from two directions. One was from the Caribbean area, primarily Cuba and Puerto Rico, into Florida. At its height of development, Spanish Florida included the coastal regions of Georgia and southern South Carolina. The second was into central Mexico and then northward to what today is the northern tier of Mexican states and California, Arizona, New Mexico, and Texas in the United States. The Spanish influence on the Native peoples of America went beyond the actual territories that they colonized. The Spanish first introduced modern horses into North America. Native peoples' acquisition of horses transformed their economy and sociopolitical organization, including those of peoples who moved to the Great Plains on a full-time basis. Spaniards did venture onto the Great Plains but never colonized the region.

Several elements framed the Spanish colonization of the north Mexican frontier and Florida. The first was the *reconquista*, the seven-century-long process of the reconquest of much of Iberia from the Muslims, who first invaded the region in 711. The protracted reconquista often proceeded in fits and starts, and the frontier between Muslim and Christian was permeable. However, the conflict had a profound influence on the development of Iberian

Catholicism and Iberian society, which in turn would impact Native America.

Iberian Catholicism became especially chauvinistic, exclusivistic, and militant. The Spanish state of Castile was the first to initiate a national inquisition independent of the papacy. As the reconquista drew to a close in 1492 with the conquest of Granada, the last Muslim state in the southern part of Iberia, the Catholic Queen Isabella ordered the expulsion of Jews who refused to convert to Christianity. About a century later in 1609, the crown ordered the expulsion of the remaining Muslim population in southern Iberia. Iberian Catholicism also had a strong thread of mysticism and Marianism, and championed the acceptance by the Catholic Church of the concept of the Immaculate Conception. Finally, the reform of the church, and particularly of the mendicant and monastic orders, created a pool of missionaries to be sent to the newly conquered lands to convert the Natives.

Following the discovery of the New World after 1492, the papacy theoretically assumed responsibility for the organization of missions to evangelize the newly encountered peoples. However, the papacy in the late fifteenth and early sixteenth centuries was embroiled in convoluted Italian politics, wars, and massive building projects that left the popes with insufficient resources to undertake such a massive enterprise. The 1494 Treaty of Tordesillas between Portugal and Spain ratified the donation and division of the non-Christian world between the two countries by the Spanish-born Pope Alexander VI (1492–1503). The papacy later made a number of concessions to the crown of Castile known as the *real patronato* (royal patronage).

In exchange for organizing and financing the evangelization of the large Native populations in its newly acquired territories, the crown gained considerable authority over the Catholic Church in its American territories. When the Spanish colonized Florida and the north Mexican frontier, the mission evolved as an important institution that combined the attributes of church and government, through the *real patronato.*

The Spanish developed a colonial Indian policy based on some of the sociopolitical structures of the Native peoples they encountered in central Mexico and other areas such as the Andean region (the Aztecs and the Incas). In these areas the Spanish encountered and conquered highly stratified hierarchical polities. The Native residents of these polities had a tradition of paying tribute and of providing labor services to the state, a system that resembled Spain's in some ways.

The Native peoples of central Mexico lived in nucleated communities, which made it easy to organize labor drafts. Moreover, the Spanish created a system of indirect rule, allowing the Native communities autonomy as long as they complied with their obligations to the Spanish, a system that meshed with prior practice in Spain.

Moreover, community leaders were made responsible for the delivery of tribute and could be held personally accountable for arrears, a structure that the Spanish had used long before they encountered Indian nations.

On the northern frontier of Mexico, Spanish policy created communities modeled on those in central Mexico from scratch, whenever they encountered Native peoples who were not sedentary agriculturalists. The Spanish created the mission as a cost-effective institution to transform the sociocultural and political structure of the Native populations and to convert them to Catholicism.

Through the *real patronato,* the crown controlled the Catholic Church in Mexico and used this control to employ missionaries as quasi representatives of the colonial state. The missionaries created new communities from scratch (except in New Mexico), congregated Natives on the missions, and initiated the process of evangelization and sociocultural change. After a period of time, when the Natives living on the missions were deemed to be sufficiently acculturated, the missions were to be transformed into self-supporting communities. Franciscans and Jesuits staffed the vast majority of missions on the north Mexican frontier, and in 1773 Dominicans assumed control over the Baja California establishments.

After 1770 royal officials experimented with a new Indian policy geared more to the challenge of trying to control Native peoples living on the southern Great Plains and other areas beyond the pale of Spanish control. Peoples collectively identified by the Spanish as Apaches and Comanches, for example, rejected life on the missions and saw greater benefit from trade than subjugation.

The new policy entailed greater coordination of the frontier military, the reorganization and relocation of the military garrisons, campaigns to defeat the Native bands known as Apaches, and a military-trade alliance with the Comanches. Moreover, the Spanish created reservations where they resettled and subsidized bands of Apaches. Finally,

the Spanish relaxed their prohibition on providing firearms to Native peoples as a whole. (The Pueblos had been armed before 1770.)

The Spanish also sought to enhance the dependence of the Natives by providing defective weapons that would break down and require repair and by a growing reliance on trade goods supplied by the Spanish. This new policy became practical following the defeat of the French during the French and Indian War (1754–1763) and the acquisition of Louisiana by Spain. Prior to the ouster of the French from North America, they had served as a viable alternative to Native groups who did not want to live on the missions but who wanted to acquire European trade goods. The reservation and trade policy broke down with the beginning of the independence war in Mexico, which forced the royal government to suspend funding of the policy.

What other influences and effects did the Spanish colonization of northern Mexico have on Native peoples? In terms of material culture, the Spanish introduced livestock and horses, metal tools, and new crops such as wheat. There is no question that the resettlement of Natives on the missions modified their culture and social structure, but the extent of change is difficult to measure. Royal officials required the missionaries to report on conditions on the missions, and the missionaries themselves measured conversion by the number of sacraments recorded. At the same time there is extensive evidence of the persistence of traditional culture and particularly religious beliefs, generally in covert forms. In New Mexico, for example, the Katsinas (Katchina) religion survived efforts by the Franciscans in the seventeenth century to extirpate idolatry. Moreover, syncretism occurred in New Mexico. For example, some Pueblos still perform the Matachina Dance based on passion plays introduced by the missionaries. At the same time there are a number of reports written by missionaries that recorded the persistence of *mitotes*, pre-Hispanic dances, and of the continuing influence of shamans. Another important consequence of Spanish colonization was the demographic collapse of the Native populations resulting from the introduction of highly contagious crowd diseases and other factors. Many Native groups completely disappeared or merged with other polities.

Robert H. Jackson

See also Katsinas; Mission System, Spanish; Slavery.
References and Further Reading

Deeds, Susan. 2003. *Defiance and Deference in Mexico's Colonial North: Indians Under Spanish Rule in Nueva Vizcaya.* Austin: University of Texas Press.

Gibson, Charles. 1964. *Aztecs Under Spanish Rule: A History of the Indians of the Valley of Mexico.* Stanford, CA: Stanford University Press.

Jackson, Robert H. 1994. *Indian Demographic Decline: The Missions of Northwestern New Spain, 1687–1840.* Albuquerque: University of New Mexico Press.

Jackson, Robert H., ed. 1998. *New Views of Borderlands History.* Albuquerque: University of New Mexico Press.

Jackson, Robert H. 2005. *Missions and Frontiers of Spanish America: A Comparative Study of the Impact of Environmental, Economic, Political, and Socio-Cultural Variations on the Missions in the Rio de la Plata Region and on the Northern Frontier of New Spain.* Scottsdale, AZ: Pentacle Press.

Jackson, Robert H., and Edward Castillo. 1995. *Indians, Franciscans, and Spanish Colonization: The Impact of the Mission System on California Indians.* Albuquerque: University of New Mexico Press.

Lockhart, James, and Stuart Schwartz. 1983. *Early Latin America: A History of Colonial Spanish America and Brazil.* Cambridge and New York: Cambridge University Press.

Milanich, Jerald. 1999. *Laboring in the Fields of the Lord: Spanish Missions and Southeastern Indians.* Washington, DC: Smithsonian Institution.

Wade, Maria. 2003. *The Native Americans of the Texas Edwards Plateau, 1582–1799.* Austin: University of Texas Press.

Worth, John. 1998. *The Timucuan Chiefdoms of Spanish Florida.* 2 vols. Gainesville: University of Florida Press.

Pequot War

The Pequot War was the first major outbreak of armed hostilities between Native people and the English settlers of New England. Its outcome radically altered the demographic balance in southern New England. Before it, the English colonists were a tiny minority. After it, they were unquestionably dominant. The Pequot and Narragansett, the two principal Native nations between Boston and Providence, were devastated in the war.

In the early 1630s, the Puritans battled the Dutch for control of the lucrative fur trade around the Connecticut Valley. The Pequots considered this area to be their territory. In 1634, the Pequots, or their tributaries the Western Niantics, murdered a Narragansett trading party in the area. This event

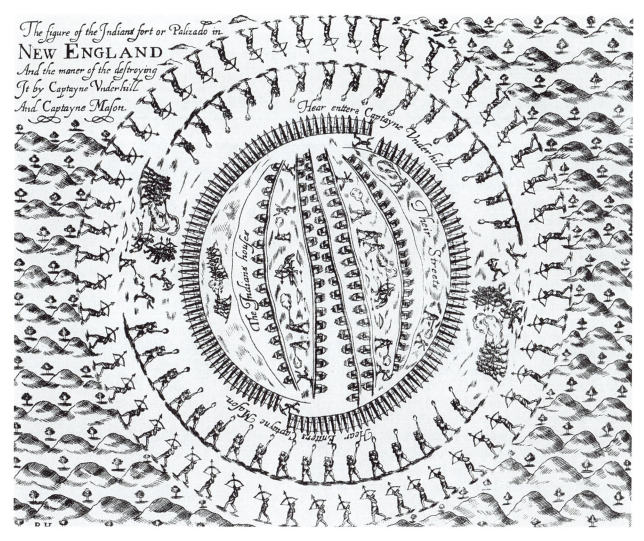

Scenes from the defeat of the Pequot tribe in Connecticut in 1637. The Pequot War was the first conflict between Native Americans and New England colonists rooted in land ownership. (Library of Congress)

triggered a sharp escalation of conflict between the local Indian groups and the Dutch and Puritans.

The papers of Roger Williams, who founded the colony of Providence Plantations (later Rhode Island), provide an insightful window into the English side of the war. When word reached Boston that the Pequots were rallying a Native alliance to drive the Massachusetts Bay settlements into the sea, the Massachusetts Council sent urgent pleas to Williams to use his influence and his "utmost and speediest Endeavors" to keep the Narragansetts out of it. Within hours after the appeal arrived in the hands of an Indian runner, "scarce acquainting my wife," Williams boarded "a poor Canow & . . . cut through a stormie Wind and with great seas, euery [sic] minute in hazard of life to the Sachim's [Canonicus's] howse" (Ernst, 1932, 252). After traveling

thirty miles in the storm, Williams arrived at a Narragansett town larger than most of the English settlements of his day, knowing that the success or failure of the Pequot initiative might rest on whether he could dissuade his friends from joining in the uprising.

Canonicus listened to Williams with his son Mixanno at his side. The younger sachem was assuming the duties of leadership piecemeal as his father aged. The three men decided to seal an alliance, and within a few days officials from Boston were double-timing through the forest to complete the necessary paperwork. Later, Williams also won alliances with the Mohegan and Massachusetts nations, swinging the balance of power against the Pequots and their allies. The Indians welcomed the Puritan deputies with a feast of white chestnuts and

cornmeal with blackberries ("hasty pudding," later a New England tradition), as Williams translated for both sides, sealing the alliance.

The Puritan deputies were awed at the size of the Narragansett town, as well as the size of the hall in which they negotiated the alliance. The structure, about fifty feet wide, was likened to a statehouse by the men from Boston. Canonicus, so old that he had to lie on his side during the proceedings, surprised the Puritans with his direct questions and shrewd answers. The treaty was finally sealed much to the relief of the Puritans, who thought the Narragansetts capable of fielding 30,000 fighting men. Although they had only a sixth that number, the Narragansetts still were capable of swinging the balance of power for or against the immigrants, who had been in America only sixteen years at the time.

Following the murder of the Narragansett trading party, the Dutch held the Pequot sachem, Tabotem, hostage in an effort to punish the Indians. A series of Pequot killings of whites ensued, followed by a Pequot raid on the settlement of Wethersfield in retaliation on April 23, 1637, that left thirty whites dead. The war escalated and reached its climax with the burning of a thatch fort in the Pequot village at Mystic, trapping as many as 600 Indian men, women, and children in a raging inferno. The few who managed to crawl out of this roaring furnace jumped back into it when they faced a wall of Puritan swords. Puritan soldiers and their Indian allies waded through pools of Pequot blood, holding their noses against the stench of burning flesh.

The wind-driven fire consumed the entire structure in half an hour. A few Pequot bowmen stood their ground amid the flames, until their bows singed and they fell backward into the fire, sizzling to death. Bradford recalled: "Those that escaped the fire were slain with the sword, some hewed to pieces, others run through with their rapiers, so that they were quickly dispatched and very few escaped. It was conceived that they thus destroyed about 400 at this time. It was a fearful sight to see them thus frying in the fire, and the streams of blood quenching the same, and horrible was the stink and scent thereof" (Bradford, 1967, 296).

Having described the massacre, Bradford then indicated how little guilt the Puritans felt about it. "The victory seemed a sweet sacrifice, and they gave the praise thereof to God, who had wrought so wonderfully for them, thus to enclose their enemies in their hands and give them so speedy a victory" (Bradford, 1967, 296). While a few Puritans remonstrated, many put the war in the category of God's necessary business, along with all sorts of other things, from smallpox epidemics to late frosts and early freezes.

The Pequot War had the effect of destroying most of the Pequot tribe. Local tribes, vastly reduced by war and disease, were in no position to offer serious resistance to non-Native encroachments and subjugation in southern New England for forty years, until the onset of King Philip's War.

Bruce E. Johansen

See also Canonicus; Massasoit; Pequot War; Williams, Roger.
References and Further Reading
Bradford, William. 1967. *History of Plymouth Plantation.* Edited by Samuel Eliot Morison. New York: Modern Library.
Ernst, James. 1932. *Roger Williams: New England Firebrand.* New York: Macmillan.
Segal, Charles M., and Stineback, David C. 1977. *Puritans, Indians, and Manifest Destiny.* New York: Putnam.
Stannard, David E. 1992. *American Holocaust: Columbus and the Conquest of the New World.* New York: Oxford University Press.
Vaughan, Alden T. *New England Frontier: Puritans and Indians, 1620–1675.* Boston: Little, Brown and Company.

Beaver Wars

The phrase "Beaver Wars" has become an historical shorthand reference for the Haudenosaunee campaign against the Wyandots, western Iroquois, and Algonquin-speaking tribes allied with the French from the 1640s to around 1700. The wars culminated in the defeat of the Wyandots and western Iroquois speakers located in the southern Great Lakes region, and they led to some Haudenosaunee assimilation by 1650. Like most wars, this one had more than one provocation. The most prominent, however, was competition over the diminishing stocks of beaver and other fur-bearing animals. The Haudenosaunee cause during this conflict was aided immeasurably by their relatively recent acquisition of European firearms that the Wyandots and Algonquin nations, for the most part, lacked. The Mohawks, situated near the trading centers at Albany and Montreal, were among the first to acquire a stock of firearms; one French source estimated that they had close to 300 guns by 1643 (Richter, 1992, 62).

French illustration of a "Guerrier Iroquois" or Iroquois warrior. (Library of Congress)

At the beginning of the seventeenth century, the Wyandots (Hurons), who lived near Georgian Bay on Lake Huron, were a prosperous confederacy of 25,000 to 30,000 people, comparable to the Haudenosaunee. The Wyandots had built a confederacy similar in structure to the Haudenosaunee (although more geographically compact). By 1642, the Wyandots had allied with the French and also had entered an alliance with the Susquehannocks, south of the Iroquois.

By 1640, the Wyandot economy was almost completely dependent on trade with the French. At the same time, weakened by disease, the Wyandots found themselves facing waves of raids by the Iroquois (principally Mohawks and Senecas), who were seeking to capture the Wyandots' share of the fur trade. The Wyandots' location at the center of several trade routes also made them an appealing target for attack at a time when the demand for beaver pelts was rising and the available supply of the animals was declining.

For nearly a decade, the Mohawks and Senecas harassed the Wyandots. Fearing Iroquois attacks, the Wyandots curtailed their trade with the French. Between 1647 and 1650, a final Iroquois drive swept over the Wyandots' homeland, causing the dissolution of their confederacy as well as the usurpation by the Senecas and Mohawks of the Wyandots' share of the fur trade.

Iroquois pressure against the Wyandots continued for several years, as Wyandot refugees sought new homes throughout the Great Lakes and Saint Lawrence Valley. Many Wyandot refugees experienced acute hunger, and a sizable number starved. Some Wyandots became so hungry that they ate human excrement; others dug up the bodies of the dead and ate them, a matter of desperation and great shame because cannibalism is directly contrary to Wyandot belief and custom.

Scattered communities of Wyandots gradually revived traditional economies after the hungry years of the 1650s. Many Wyandots settled in or near European communities (including Jesuit missions). Even those who became Christianized, however, continued during these years to live in longhouses, to hunt and trap as much as possible, and to practice slash-and-burn agriculture. At the same time, the Iroquois adopted and socialized some Wyandot prisoners into the various Haudenosaunee families and clans. Iroquois peoples did this to replenish their societies, which had been hard hit by European diseases and the casualties of nearly continual war.

The last half of the seventeenth century saw intermittent warfare and peace, as the Iroquois struggled to gain access to more fur-bearing areas to acquire more beaver, deer, and other furs and skins for trade with the English and Dutch. The Iroquois tried to negotiate commercial treaties with the western Indian nations, but the French worked to keep their political allies distinct from the New York–based English groups. The Algonquin nations—Chippewa, Ottawa, Potawatamie, and others—were forced by the wars to migrate westward. The Chippewa moved into present-day Wisconsin and Minnesota, forcing Native nations in those regions to the south or west. The Lakota, some Dakota, Cheyenne, and Nakota were forced onto the Great Plains in the middle 1700s because the better armed Chippewa came to occupy present-day Minnesota.

By 1700, the Beaver Wars diminished significantly. The Iroquois were nearing exhaustion from the intermittent years of warfare and realized that

the British were starting to occupy the Mohawk Valley in present-day upstate New York. They consequently moved to establish a diplomatic policy of balancing relations between the French in New France and the British colony of New York. The Iroquois also moved to establish diplomatic alliances and commercial agreements with the western Indian nations, promising access to trade at Albany in return for access to hunting and trapping grounds in the Great Lakes region.

Bruce E. Johansen

See also Fur Trade; Trade; Warfare, Intertribal.
References and Further Reading:
Richter, Daniel K. 1992. *The Ordeal of the Longhouse: The Peoples of the Iroquois League in the Era of European Colonization.* Chapel Hill: University of North Carolina Press.
Saum, Lewis. 1965. *The Fur Trader and the Indian.* Seattle: University of Washington Press.

Pueblo Revolt

The 1680 Pueblo Revolt in New Mexico was one of many Native American rebellions against Spanish rule. Unlike the earlier revolts in the region, it coordinated large-scale revolt resulted in temporary independence for many Pueblo villages and a short-term elimination of the Spanish from the region. The Spanish returned in 1692 and reconquered the area.

The Pueblo Revolt was preceded by a generation of starvation and disease that was brought on by warm temperatures, drought-like conditions, and raids by Apaches, Navajos, and other Native groups. As these raids increased in the 1670s, the desperation of the Pueblos increased and they abandoned their communities on the edge of the High Plains. The arrival of refugees furthered the food shortages.

While many Pueblos turned to traditional religious leaders and ceremonies to resolve the crisis, Spanish missionaries used violence and intimidation to enforce and maintain the imposed Catholic orthodoxy. They repressed many Pueblo religious ceremonies, banned liturgical practices, and punished those who continued to practice what the Spanish deemed sorcery. Attempts to resist the new rule were brutally repressed. In 1599, for example, the Spanish burned the pueblo of Acoma to the ground for its resistance to Spanish rule and then cut off the right foot of every adult male Acoman.

Around 1675, the repression increased as Spanish officials vigorously enforced their prohibitions, created new bans on certain dances, began destroying prayer sticks and masks, and seized altars and ceremonial chambers called kivas. The inability of the Spanish to protect the Pueblos from Apache raids created further anger with the Catholic presence.

Across the Southwest, leaders from individual pueblos voiced their anger over these Spanish policies. The Spanish responded swiftly to quiet the discontent. In 1675, for example, Governor Juan Francisco de Trevino had four dozen religious leaders whipped and sentenced to hard labor for continuing to practice banned ceremonies. At least one of these religious leaders, El Popé of San Juan Pueblo, would play an influential role in the Pueblo Revolt.

Repression curtailed localized rebellions in the short term, but it did not quell the frustrations among the Pueblos. Rather than acquiesce to the demands of the Spaniards, in 1680 Pueblo leaders coordinated a unified military response to eliminate the Spaniards from the region north of El Paso. The subsequent revolt united approximately seventeen thousand Indians who spoke at least six languages and various dialects and who lived in more than twenty-four towns across hundreds of miles.

The rebellion emanated from the kiva at Taos, where Pueblo leaders met in secret to orchestrate the rebellion. They sent out knotted cords to various pueblos, with orders to untie the knots daily to count down the days to the attack. Two days before the last knot was to be untied, the Spanish uncovered the plot and captured two Pueblo messengers. As a result, the Indians attacked on August 10, a day ahead of schedule. For the next month, Spaniards fled to Santa Fe and Isleta Pueblo to escape the Pueblo rebels. The Pueblos laid siege to Santa Fe, and, finally on September 21, they allowed the refugees to head south down the Rio Grande to El Paso. Santa Fe was sacked and burned, and the Spanish presence was eliminated from the region.

The rebels killed at least 380 of the 2,500 Spanish colonists, killed twenty-one of the thirty-three Franciscan friars, and rid the region of the Spanish presence. They destroyed churches, stopped using Spanish names, returned to traditional forms of dress, and otherwise renounced their baptisms and conversion to Catholicism.

Andrew K. Frank

See also Spanish Influence.

References and Further Reading

Gutiérrez, Ramón A. 1991. *When Jesus Came, the Corn Mothers Went Away: Marriage, Sexuality, and Power in North America, 1500–1846*. Stanford, CA: Stanford University Press.

Knaut, Andrew L. 1995. *The Pueblo Revolt of 1680: Conquest and Resistance in Seventeenth-Century New Mexico*. Norman: University of Oklahoma Press.

Roberts, David. 2004. *The Pueblo Revolt: The Secret Rebellion That Drove the Spaniards out of the Southwest*. New York: Simon & Schuster.

Weber, David J. 1992. *The Spanish Frontier in North America*. New Haven: Yale University Press.

Russians, in the Arctic/Northwest

The history of Native interactions with Russians in Alaska and the far Northwest is really a history of two institutions that often operated at cross-purposes: the Russian Orthodox Church and the Russian American Company. The church, like so many other religious groups in colonial North America, charged itself with saving the souls of the Natives. The company's self-defined purpose was making a profit from the colony's extensive fur resources. The political interaction between the Russian American Company, the Orthodox Church, and the czar's government back in St. Petersburg would profoundly affect changes both in the short-lived nature of the company's mission and the permanent structure of the church.

Beginning in the seventeenth century, Russia began expanding eastward toward Siberia and China, and the Orthodox faith accompanied Russian colonization efforts from the beginning. Although small, transitory Russian settlements had been built by profit-seeking *promyshlenniki* (fur hunters) throughout the mid-eighteenth century, the first verifiable, permanent settlement was established by Grigorii I. Shelikov, later to head the Russian American Company, on Kodiak Island in 1784. Shelikov was among the first to anticipate the possible profits and benefits of Alaskan colonization. Fifteen years later, the Russian American Company was granted a monopoly on the exploitation of the natural resources and governmental control of Alaska, and the city of Novo-Arkhangel'sk (later named Sitka) was established as the capital of Russian America.

Orthodox missionaries played a major role in the settlement process during this early period of Russian expansion eastward. Native people were baptized by the thousands and given Russian names. Many of these newly Russified Natives were rewarded for their conversion by being released from paying taxes to the Cossack rulers and by promises of employment by the hunters and traders. This conversion of Native people, Russian/Native marriages, baptizing of children, and promises of religiously determined economic gain laid a foundation for the religious conversion policies established in Siberia and the Far East that would be used later in North America.

Between the first Russian American settlement at Three Saints Harbor, near Kodiak, in 1784, and the establishment of the first mission, the explorers themselves were primarily responsible for these rudimentary rituals. The Orthodox mission in Russian America was first authorized by Catherine II in 1793, and then established at Kodiak, the first capital of the colony, on September 24, 1794, by a group of monks sent from the Valaam monastery in St. Petersburg. One of these monks, Archimandrite Ioasaph, was elected to be the first bishop of the new colony.

Ioasaph complained to Shelikov about conditions in Russian America in a letter he wrote in May 1795. Apparently, the company's general manager, Alexander Baranov, was unwilling to assist the priests and even showed outright hostility toward the initial efforts to found a mission church in Kodiak. Ioasaph complained of Baranov's exploits with women, of his encouraging the hostility of the *promyshlenniki* against the priests, and of insufficient resources and food. The company was proving a hindrance to the monks rather than a help. After being consecrated as bishop in April 1798, Ioasaph died in a shipwreck on the way back to America, with all but three of the other monks. For the next two decades only those three surviving monks remained in Russian America, and a state of constant enmity existed between them and Baranov (Starr, 1987, 127). Both religious rituals and missionary activities were almost nonexistent due to the lack of trained clergy in the colony. Finally in 1816, a small church was erected in the new city of Novo-Arkhangel'sk, and Aleksei Sokolov came to serve as its first priest, performing baptisms and other church rituals for people who came from all over Russian America.

Along with the first group of monks sent to America from the Valaam Seminary in St. Petersburg in 1794 was a monk named Herman who was to become the Native populations' most adamant

A Russian Orthodox church on Attu Island in Alaska. Many Native Aleutians were converted by Russian priests before its purchase by the United States and then maintained the religion. (Library of Congress)

defender against the Russian American Company (Rochcau, 1972, 17–18). When Herman arrived in Alaska, relations between the Russians and the Natives were very poor, and, by 1819 (and until 1823), there were only two other monks besides Herman left in Russian America. This period between the first settlements and the reorganization of the Russian American Company in 1821 was a time of great persecution by the profit-seeking *promyshlenniki*, both of the Orthodox Church and the Native populations in Russian America. After the death of Ioasaph, Herman, as the superior among the three remaining monks in Russian America, reported on these incidents in letters back to Russia.

Because the *promyshlenniki* were not adept at the hunting of sea otter furs, and the Aleut and Kodiak populations were, the Russians soon found that they would need to either buy or coerce the assistance of the Native populations to exploit this resource (Starr, 1987, 78). In some cases, the pelts were a form of tribute paid by the Aleuts to the Russians, with hostages being held by the Russians to ensure payment. Later, a quasi-feudal system developed, in which the Aleuts were required to work for the Russian American Company and received the goods they needed to survive in return for sea otter pelts. This system was a reaction to the system in place in Russia. Aleut men were separated from their families for long periods of time and forced to hunt in far-off regions (Starr, 1987, 80). As time passed, many of the Natives began to rebel against this system. In the 1760s, armed Aleuts killed the crews of three (or four, according to some reports) Russian vessels (Starr, 1987, 112).

Incidents such as these made it clear to Shelikov that greater support of the church by the company

would be necessary to control the Native populations, but as of 1820 only one priest and one monk remained in Russian America. However, these factors helped lead to the reorganization of the company in the early 1820s. After this occurred, the relationship between the Orthodox church and the Russian American Company became one of codependence. When the Russian American Company's charter was to be renewed by the czar, Nicholas I stipulated that the company was ordered to provide adequate financial resources from its own profits for the needs of the Orthodox Church and its Russian, Creole, and Native parishioners (Rochcau, 1971, 106). A string of mediocre leaders filled the position of bishop of Alaska from that point until 1840, when Ivan Veniaminov (later named St. Innocent), who had been working as a diocesan priest on Unalaska Island and at Novo-Arkhangel'sk since 1822, became bishop. It would be under his guidance that the Russian Orthodox Church would gain a truly permanent foothold on the North American continent.

Veniaminov reported that, between 1799 and 1828, the Native population had decreased rapidly. This was due in large part to fatalities that occurred during the long hunting expeditions on which the Russian American Company sent parties of Natives. Also, the absence of the Aleut men on these parties caused starvation among the remaining Native peoples in their villages. Veniaminov also noted that the state of the education of the Natives was extremely poor and that Herman was the only monk teaching in a school for Natives. Because he was held in high esteem, Herman's letters back to church and government officials in Russia were effective in that they were one of the causes for the reorganization of the Russian American Company, which eventually led to more ecclesiastical leadership in America. Only because of a new company charter from the czar was there any renewed interest in both education and ecclesiastical leadership. Although the Russian American Company paid the priest's salaries, not many newly ordained clergy were interested in making the hazardous journey into an unknown area where some had already been martyred. To the extent that the ecclesiastical situation had deteriorated, so had the education of Natives, Creoles, and Russians in America.

Veniaminov designed and built the Church of the Holy Ascension, along with his own home and a school in 1826 (Veniaminov, 1993, 47). He and his wife taught in the school, which had about a hundred pupils of both genders, instructing them in scholastic subjects and trades. This education, like all assistance to Native Alaskans, did not come without a price, however. All men educated in company schools were obligated to serve the Russian American Company for ten to fifteen years (Chevigny, 1965, 199–200).

Veniaminov then undertook the task of learning the local language and put it into writing. Although Russian was the primary language taught in the school, after he had gained enough proficiency, he taught a course in the Native language, called Aleutian-Fox. He compiled an Aleutian-Fox dictionary, a grammar, and a primer to teach the children. He then translated into the Native language the Orthodox Catechism, the entire gospel of Matthew, the book of Acts, and part of the gospel of Luke into Aleutian-Fox, along with a sermon he had authored titled "An Indication of the Path to the Heavenly Kingdom" and a brief history of the Orthodox church (Oleska, 1992, 344).

Veniaminov took many trips to the surrounding islands of Akun and Unga, where sizable Native populations lived. While on these islands, he performed and explained the rites of the church, along with the sacraments of baptism and confession, for the Native Aleutians. He also blessed all of the marriages, allowing them to be recognized in the sight of the Orthodox Church. Interestingly, in a demonstration of the overlapping of civil and ecclesiastical authority, Veniaminov also had to administer the oath of allegiance to Czar to all Russians, Creoles, and Natives that he ministered to. Veniaminov even encouraged the older Natives to continue to tell their myths and legends, and he himself was not an apologist for earlier Russian atrocities committed against the Aleut populations. Veniaminov's journals, letters, and edicts verify a view of him as a missionary who did not use forced conversion as a tactic, but who attempted to integrate Russian and Native beliefs.

After the death of his wife, Veniaminov was transferred to Novo-Arkhangel'sk, the new episcopal seat of Russian America, becoming bishop of Alaska in 1840. The Russian American Company was seeking a renewal of its charter at the time, and, because the Russian government was very concerned with the welfare of the church in America, the construction of a new cathedral was a high priority to the company (Nordlander, 1995, 24–25). His growing influence can be seen in the new company charter, in that Russians working in America were forbidden to use force against the Natives, except in

keeping peace, and could not establish any posts without the consent of the local Native population. Governmental and church authority overlapped in this period to prevent Native abuses. This was not always out of sympathy. The fact that the company was better off, in tandem with the appointment of church leaders like Veniaminov, created less pressure to exploit the Native populations for monetary gain. He also became an ambassador to the other colonial powers in the region, as he entertained foreign visitors such as Hudson's Bay Company chief, George Simpson.

From Novo-Arkhangel'sk, Veniaminov directed the expansion of Orthodox mission work in the vast Alaskan interior, whereas before missions had been established only near the coastline. With the establishment of many missions, he would help to create communities of Native Orthodox believers that still exist today. The long-term success of these missions was based on Veniaminov's emphasis on the enculturation of the liturgy and theology of the Orthodox church. Just as he had learned the Aleut language, Veniaminov strove to learn the Tlingit language upon his arrival in Novo-Arkhangel'sk. Other priests were not as willing or able to learn the Native languages as Veniaminov, so a seminary was established in 1845 to train Native clergy, who Veniaminov thought were necessary to the long-term success of the church in America. Most Russians were in America only temporarily, whereas the Native clergy were permanent residents, and they had a stake in the future of the region. The seminary trained priests, deacons, and lay readers. Some of these went on to train further at seminaries in Russia before returning to Alaska. This indigenization of the Orthodox clergy would prove essential to the survival of the faith (and, with it, Russian influence) in Alaska after the sale of the region to the United States in 1867.

Veniaminov's methods may explain the continued strength of the Russian Orthodox Church among Native Alaskans, even a hundred and forty years after the end of Russian rule in the region. During the initial period after the sale of Alaska to the United States, most Russians returned home, and the Aleuts primarily continued the operation of schools, churches, and trading posts (Oleska, 1987, 165). After 1920, nearly all clergy were Native. Veniaminov's vision of an indigenized church is what would allow it to survive both in the changing political climates, and in the lives of Native converts.

Steven L. Danver

See also Fur Trade; Hudson's Bay Company.

References and Further Reading

Chevigny, Hector. 1965. *Russian America: The Great Alaskan Venture, 1741–1867*. New York: Viking.

Nordlander, David. 1995. "Innokentii Veniaminov and the Expansion of Orthodoxy in Russian America." *Pacific Historical Review* 44 (February): 1.

Oleksa, Michael, J., ed. 1987. *Alaskan Missionary Spirituality*. New York: Paulist Press.

Oleksa, Michael, J. 1992. *Orthodox Alaska: A Theology of Mission*. Crestwood, NY: St. Vladimir's Seminary Press.

Rochcau, Vsevolod. 1971. "Innocent Veniaminov and the Russian Mission to Alaska." *St. Vladimir's Theological Quarterly* 15 (March): 1.

Rochcau, Vsevolod. 1972. "St. Herman of Alaska and the Defense of Alaskan Native Peoples." *St. Vladimir's Theological Quarterly* 16 (January): 1.

Starr, S. Frederick, ed. 1987. *Russia's American Colony*. Durham, NC: Duke University Press.

Veniaminov, Ioann. 1993. *Journals of the Priest Ioann Veniaminov in Alaska, 1823 to 1836*. Fairbanks: University of Alaska Press.

French and Indian War

The final intercolonial war between France and Great Britain, the French and Indian War (1754–1763), like the three wars before it, had European roots. Called the Seven Years' War in Europe, the French and Indian War actually began two years earlier than its European counterpart. The three prior French–English conflicts in America were largely centered in the Northeast, but the French and Indian War shifted to the Ohio River Valley, an area that had become increasingly important as European interests began to reach west beyond the Appalachians.

The French, who sought a corridor of trade to connect the Mississippi River and Louisiana with their outposts on the Great Lakes and beyond, built a series of forts in the Ohio Valley, the most important being Fort Duquesne (Pittsburgh). At the same time, the British crown, with a continuing eye toward colonization, had offered large land grants there for settlement. Under the circumstances, it was inevitable that the two powers would collide.

The opening stages of the war saw the advantage go to the French. As early as 1754, a young Virginian named George Washington was involved in an unsuccessful attempt to capture Fort Duquesne. The next year, a second, more determined effort ended ignominiously. A column of British regulars under the command of General Edward Braddock

was ambushed and routed by the French and their Indian allies in July 1755. British casualties were heavy; Braddock himself was mortally wounded. Humiliated and devastated, the British column was forced to withdraw. The Ohio Valley Indians, concerned with the growing threat of European-American invasion, viewed Braddock's defeat as an opportunity to strike a further blow against the English. In the following year, thousands of European-American immigrants from Virginia and Pennsylvania to South Carolina felt the fury of Indian attacks.

The British position continued to deteriorate. Increasingly, Indian nations and tribes, some from as far west as the Great Lakes, threw their support behind the French; they saw an opportunity not only to drive back the hated white settlers but to plunder as well. Despite the efforts of Sir William Johnson, Indian agent, the British, who had seen the powerful

Delaware and Shawnee nations ally with the French, feared that the Iroquois might also join the enemy.

In August 1756, a combined French and Indian force captured Fort Oswego on Lake Ontario and the following year took Fort William Henry, situated at the foot of New York's Lake George. Following the capture of Fort William Henry, immortalized in James Fenimore Cooper's *Last of the Mohicans,* many of the British garrison, including women and children, were massacred by Indian allies of the French as they marched out of the fort, despite the customary assurances of honorable treatment as prisoners of war. The French, mortified at the slaughter, were unable to control their allies.

The 1757 appointment of the controversial William Pitt the Elder as British prime minister was perhaps the turning point in the French and Indian War. One of Pitt's first steps was to strengthen the

Ottawa chief Pontiac and Major Robert Rogers meet in 1763 to agree on peace terms after the siege of Detroit during the French and Indian War. (Library of Congress)

British forces in North America and to appoint able commanders to prosecute the war to a successful conclusion. He also instituted a stronger policy regarding the employment of Indian allies. No less important, particularly in the area of Indian relations, was the work of Sir William Johnson, whose tireless efforts to convince the Iroquois to remain neutral at last bore fruit. The Iroquois, in turn, persuaded the Delawares to cease warfare against the British. The tide was beginning to turn.

During the summer of 1758, a strong British force failed to take Fort Ticonderoga (Fort Carillon to the French), but that failure was offset by the capture of Fort Louisbourg, on Cape Breton Island, and Fort Frontenanc, both located in Ontario. British fortunes were also improving in the south, where General John Forbes cut a new trail through the Pennsylvania wilderness in yet another effort to take Fort Duquesne.

Forbes's strategy produced the Treaty of Easton, in which the British managed to enlist strong Indian support for their effort to take Fort Duquesne, which many of the Indians were anxious to see abandoned—regardless of whom it belonged to. In return for the Indians' support, the British provided certain financial considerations and their promise to withdraw from the Ohio River country. Surrounded and unable to be supplied, the French abandoned Fort Duquesne, which Forbes promptly occupied and renamed Fort Pitt.

A year later, in 1759, a mixed force of British regulars and Iroquois allies took Fort Niagara. Sensing the vulnerability of their position, the French then abandoned Fort Carillon (Ticonderoga) and Crown Point and withdrew to Canada. In September 1759, British General James Wolfe's defeat of the French Army, commanded by Marquis Louis-Joseph de Montcalm, on the Plains of Abraham resulted in the surrender of Quebec. The deaths of the two generals, Wolfe and Montcalm, made the British victory one of the epic stories of history. For all intents and purposes, the British victory at Quebec marked the end of the French and Indian War, although some historians believe France had privately conceded victory to the British.

The Treaty of Paris (1763) officially ended the intercolonial wars between England and France. The conclusion of the French and Indian War was a watershed event that marked the end of French power in North America. As a result of the treaty, England acquired Canada and all of Spanish Florida. For the next two decades, England would be the sole, dominant power in North America.

See also Fur Trade.

References and Further Reading

Hurt, R. Douglas. 1996. *The Ohio Frontier: Crucible of the Old Northwest, 1720–1830.* Bloomington: Indiana University Press.

Leach, Douglas, 1973. *Arms for Empire: A Military History of the British Colonies in North America, 1607–1763,* New York: Macmillan.

Steele, Ian K. 1994. *Warpaths: Invasions of North America.* New York: Oxford University Press.

California Indians, Genocide of

On January 24, 1848, gold was discovered on the South Fork of the American River in California. One hundred and fifty years later, the state of California observed the sesquicentennial of the 1849 gold rush. The anniversary, however, was no cause for celebration among California Indians. The Spanish mission system, the seizure of California from Mexico by the United States, the influx of thousands of American miners and settlers, and California statehood—all had disastrous consequences for the Indian peoples. Sherburne Cook, an expert on California Indian demography, found that between 1770 and 1900 the Native population experienced a fall from 310,000 to approximately 20,000, a decline of over 90 percent.

Genocide

Given the enormity of the population decline and its rapidity following the gold rush, it is appropriate to examine the concept of genocide as defined in international law. The Convention on the Prevention and Punishment of the Crime of Genocide was unanimously adopted by the United Nations General Assembly on December 9, 1948. It became international law following World War II in recognition of the crimes against humanity committed by Nazi Germany that annihilated millions of people because of their religions or ethnic origins. Ninety-seven nations have ratified the Convention, most of them within a few years after its passage, but it was not ratified by the United States Senate until 1985 after almost thirty-six years of delay and contentious debate.

The Genocide Convention outlaws the commission of certain acts with intent to destroy, wholly or in part, a national, ethnic, racial, or religious group. What is less known is that the scope of the Convention is much broader than forbidding the actual killing of such groups. The Convention also includes

Sutter's Creek in Amador County, California, was at the heart of the California gold rush that had a devastating effect on the Native American population. (Library of Congress)

acts of causing serious bodily or mental harm; the deliberate infliction of conditions of life calculated to bring about physical destruction; imposing measures to prevent birth; and forcibly transferring children of one group to another group. Furthermore, the definition includes not only the commission of such acts as punishable, but also the conspiracy to commit genocide, the direct and public incitement, the attempt to commit, and complicity. The Convention specifies that it is genocide whether such acts are committed in a time of peace or in a time of war.

An examination of the California Indian case makes it absolutely clear that the crime of genocide was committed indirectly during the Spanish and Mexican periods of hegemony and directly by the Americans following the 1849 gold rush. The information contained in this essay can provide only a brief outline of the scope of the tragedy.

Spain and the Mission System

The Spanish period of conquest introduced a system of religious missions that began in 1769 and ended in 1821. Spanish policy was to convert the Indians to Christianity and to use Indian labor to further Spanish economic aims. A chain of twenty-one Franciscan missions were established along a narrow section of the California coast from San Diego in the south to San Francisco in the north. The Spaniards also founded

civilian towns (*pueblos*) and military garrisons (*presidios*). In the countryside were *ranchos*, where soldiers and settlers grazed stock using Indian labor.

By 1805 there were twenty thousand neophytes (Indian converts to Christianity) in the Spanish missions. Although Indian persons were recognized as human beings with souls and limited rights, Spanish laws nevertheless permitted armed Spaniards to round up the peaceful coastal Indians and impress them into *de facto* slavery. The Indian lands seized were then held in trust by the Spanish crown under the *encomienda* system, by which the Spanish administered their colonies. California became, in effect, a Spanish military colony. Spanish policy was not to annihilate the Native population directly, as occurred later during the gold rush, but rather to absorb it as a labor force for Spanish ranches and the agriculturally based missions. Mission life was brutal and harsh. Indian neophytes were forced to construct the mission buildings, herd the cattle, work the fields, and wait on the mission priests. Men and women were segregated with the men confined to coffin-like rooms with barely enough space in which to lie down, and the women and girls were housed in bare dormitories called "nunneries." Indian marriage and divorce customs were suppressed, along with all aspects of Native religion. Anglo-borne diseases easily ravaged the concentrated mission populations. A measles epidemic in 1806 killed 1,600, and in some missions children under ten years were almost entirely wiped out. Malnutrition was a persistent problem. Labor was unpaid, and the neophytes were punished by the Franciscans for the smallest infractions. Indians who ran away, or who resisted, were severely punished if not killed. Typical punishments included whipping with a barbed lash, solitary confinement, mutilation, use of stocks and hobbles, branding, and even execution.

Although limited in its geographic scope, the harsh conditions of mission life resulted in the disintegration of most coastal Indian societies and a significant decline in the overall indigenous population of interior California. The total Native population declined by half, from over 300,000 to 150,000 Indians before the end of the mission system.

Missionization often met with Native resistance. Neophytes at times poisoned or murdered the Franciscan fathers. There were also outright revolts. Among the most noteworthy was the 1824 uprising at Missions La Purisima and Santa Barbara. There were also mass escapes, such as the one in 1795 in

The San Xavier Del Bac Mission in Tucson, Arizona, was founded by the Jesuit Eusebio Kino in 1700 as part of the Spanish Mission system in the New World. (Corel)

which over 200 Costanoan Indians fled Mission Dolores. Nonviolent resistance included the practice of abortion and the infanticide of children born out of forced concubinage of Indian women by priests and soldiers.

Mexico and Secularization

After sixty-five years of Spanish rule, the missions were abandoned in 1834 when Mexico achieved its independence from Spain. After the Mexican Revolution, the 1824 Constitution formally secularized the mission system. California's Indians were made citizens of the new republic, and mission property, at least in theory, was turned over to them. Franciscan resistance and the political turmoil of the period, however, forestalled secularization. As late as 1836, the Franciscans continued to mount military campaigns to seize new "recruits" from the interior for labor at the missions. In reality, Mexican policy was essentially the same as that of Spanish rule. Neither Spain nor Mexico acknowledged Indian ownership of the land.

The Mexican period was a time of confusion and disarray for the Indians, and it led to further depopulation. Some of the emancipated neophytes hired themselves out as farm laborers and servants. There were also those who revolted, as in the Santa Ynez Revolt of 1824. Some fled to the interior to join still independent Indian communities. Those employed on the *ranchos* became victims of the hacienda system of peonage bordering on slavery. Yet others were left at the mercy of the *pueblos*, where they were exploited as domestics, plied with alcohol, and left for a life of poverty and debauchery.

These oppressive conditions contributed to the spread of European-introduced diseases that caused most of the deaths during the period of Mexican rule. The Pandemic of 1833 killed an estimated 4,500 Indians, and a smallpox outbreak killed several thousand more. As a result, by the time of the American invasion there were only about 6,000 exmission Indians still residing along the coast, along with 7,000 predominately Indian-Mexicans. There were also about 700 Europeans.

More than a 100,000 Natives remained in interior California.

Americans and the Gold Rush

The American period commenced with the U.S. victory over Mexico and the Bear Flag Revolt by the "Americanos" in between 1846 and1848. The discovery of gold in 1849 and the rush of miners and settlers that followed the discovery completely overwhelmed the Native population. As word of the gold discovery spread, prospectors flocked to the hills to wash the sands and gravels of mother lode streams and rivers. Mining operations destroyed Native fish dams, polluted salmon streams, and frightened away the wild game. A pastoral California, with its Indian population, Spanish missions, and Mexican *ranchos,* was quickly overrun by an invasion of gold seekers from throughout the world, the Forty-Niners. A virulent racism was spawned in the quest for riches, and a holocaust of the California Indians was ensured.

Under the Treaty of Guadalupe Hidalgo, which was signed at the end of the Mexican–American War, the United States was obligated to recognize two kinds of property rights: traditional *rancho* rights of the *Californios* and open land where Indian title was still intact, including Indian villages and the abandoned missions. Yet the American authorities immediately violated the treaty after taking over California.

The discovery of gold at John Sutter's sawmill on the American River in 1848 ushered in a period of extreme abuse of the Indians. To mobilize the dispossessed Indian labor force, the U.S. military government in California decreed that Indians who did not work for ranchers or who did not have an official passport could expect to be tried and punished. Worse, an Indian might be shot on the pretext that he was a horse thief. By the end of that summer, 4,000 miners, half of them Indian, were prospecting for gold. This atmosphere of tolerance toward Indian gold miners lasted no more than a year.

Unlike other Indians in the Far West, Native Californians often lived and worked with non-Indians in the early conquest era. This was especially the case during the Spanish and Mexican periods before 1850. The Gold Rush fundamentally changed this relationship when California became marked by a precipitous Indian population decline, unique in U.S. frontier history. Before the gold discovery, Indians outnumbered whites by nearly ten to one, but by the early 1850s whites had come to outnumber Indians by almost two to one. Gold fever resulted in tens of thousands of immigrants— young single men, flocking to the California gold fields, hoping to strike it rich. Insatiable greed dominated the immigrant population, and unbridled individualism marked the new California society. As a result, the white population steadily rose to more than 200,000 while the Indian population reached its nadir of 23,000 by 1880, about 15 percent of its pre-Gold Rush population.

Most immigrants viewed the Indian people as worthless, and they were appalled by the Mexican custom of sanctioned miscegenation (interracial sexual unions). They were imbued with a frontier mentality that taught them to despise Native peoples as subhuman "diggers." (Many California Indians used digging sticks to harvest roots and other food sources from the soil, hence the name "digger," which became a pejorative.) Before they were driven from the gold fields, some Indian miners were able to enter the trade system by bargaining their gold for trade goods. The traders countered by inventing "the Digger ounce," a lead slug that dishonestly outweighed the legitimate weights used to measure the gold brought in by white miners.

The Massacres

The Forty-Niner Gold Rush initiated a holocaust for California's Native population that scarcely diminished in intensity until the end of the nineteenth century. The Indian people were cheated, debauched by liquor and white demands for sex, starved, rounded up, and herded on brutal forced marches to small reservations (virtual concentration camps), enslaved in debt peonage, brutally murdered and massacred, and denied civil rights and equal justice before California's courts and institutions. The immigrant intruders shot Indians on sight as the Indians were gathering food or fish, or trying to protect their women and daughters from rape and kidnap. Hundreds of Indian homes were burned and the human occupants trapped by surrounding gunfire.

Some Indian peoples, like the Modocs under Kentipoos, also known as Captain Jack, fought back. One hundred and fifty Modoc warriors and their families successfully held off over 3,000 U.S. Army troops for nearly a year. In the end, the resisters were captured and the leaders hanged. After execution, the warriors were decapitated and their heads sent off to Washington for "scientific investigation." Grave robbers later disinterred Kentipoos's body,

embalmed it, and displayed it in a carnival in Eastern cities. His skull was not returned to the Modocs by the government until 1984.

Between 1848 and 1860 there were at least 4,267 Indian deaths attributed to the military, or about 12 percent of the Indian population living at the time. Ironically, it was the gold stolen from Indian lands that paid for the ensuing genocide. Towns offered bounties on Indians ranging from $5 for every severed head in Shasta in 1855, to 25 cents for a scalp in Honey Lake in 1863. Some of the worst massacres occurred in northwestern California. Militia groups such as the Klamath Rifles, the Salmon Guard, the Union Volunteers, and the Pitt River Rangers, armed and paid for by the state government, roamed the countryside with the avowed aim to exterminate "the skulking bands of savages."

Possibly the most notorious massacre occurred at Indian Island near Eureka. On February 26, 1860, the peaceful Wiyot people were holding their annual religious ceremonies when they were attacked during the night as they slept by white "volunteers," who slaughtered them with axes. A Major Raines testified to finding one man, seventeen women, and eleven children among the dead. In addition, eighteen women and an unknown number of children had been carried away by their relatives for burial before his arrival. It was later learned that the Indian Island massacre was part of a premeditated plan by some local farmers and stockmen to exterminate the region's resident Indian population. That same night three other massacres took place simultaneously, two at Humboldt Bay and another at the mouth of the Eel River.

Disease and Starvation

Throughout most of California, the deaths resulting from disease epidemics greatly exceeded those from massacres. In 1853, 500 died in Nevada City of smallpox and typhoid; 800 Maidu died of influenza and tuberculosis in the same year. Venereal disease was contracted mainly from white men who abducted and raped Indian women. Syphilis infected approximately 20 percent of California's Indians, and gonorrhea may have been as high as 100 percent.

Malnutrition paved the way for death from disease. The destruction of Native food sources, either from gold mining or from outright theft, contributed to Indian susceptibility to communicable diseases. Between the years 1848 to 1855, according

to Sherburne Cook, Native population declined from approximately 150,000, or about 66 percent, to about 50,000 (Cook, 1978, 93). "This desolation was accomplished by a ruthless flood of miners and farmers who annihilated the Natives without mercy or compensation. The direct causes of death were disease, the bullet, exposure, and acute starvation," he wrote (Cook, 1978, 93).

The mentality that fueled the nineteenth-century genocide continued into the early twentieth century when Ishi, a Yahi Indian, wandered out of the hills of Tehana County in 1911 as the last surviving member of his tribe. Vigilantes had undertaken raids of extermination against the Yahi and other Indian groups of northern California. Alone and emaciated, Ishi finally allowed himself to be taken by those from whom he had hid for so many years. Ishi's story is recounted by Theodora Kroeber in *Ishi in Two Worlds*.

The "Lost Treaties"

In 1851 and 1852, President Millard Fillmore sent three Indian commissioners to negotiate eighteen treaties with California Indians. Under the treaty terms, the Indians reluctantly agreed to surrender their land claims, and the federal government agreed in turn to provide some 8.5 million acres of good lands, reservations, and goods and services. It was the era of the gold rush, however, and the greed for gold and California's rich lands motivated the state legislature to pressure the U.S. Senate not to ratify the treaties. The treaties were then conveniently "lost" in the Senate archives and not rediscovered until 1905. Because the treaties were never ratified and then "lost," the Indians were forced to give up virtually all of the promised lands and settle instead for small, temporary *rancherias* and farms, a mere fraction of the original 8.5 million acres that were promised them. The 1887 Dawes (Allotment) Act further reduced California Indian landholdings.

A congressional act of 1928 and a 1946 law creating the U.S. Court of Indian Claims permitted California Indians to sue the government for the lost lands. A 1944 award received under the 1928 act was for $17 million, hardly just compensation considering the billions of dollars in gold and resources realized from the stolen lands. Because of the inadequacy of the 1944 award, a new claims case was entered for other lands illegally taken. Yet the 1964

award paid California Indians only 47 cents an acre for approximately 65 million acres illegally seized.

Indenture and Slavery

Until 1867, an estimated 10,000 California Indians, including 4,000 children, were held as chattel. Newspaper accounts of the time noted that while young boys sold for about $60, young women could sell for as much as $200. In some instances, entire tribes were captured, carried into white settlements, and sold. An 1850 state indenture law ordered that any Indian, on the word of a white man, could be declared a legal vagrant, thrown in jail, and have his labor sold at auction for up to four months with no pay.

The indenture law also allowed Indian children to be indentured with the consent of their parents or if they were orphans. The law provided a motive for making Indian children orphans by killing the parents so that the children could then be indentured. Child kidnapping and Indian slavery continued for fifteen years until 1867 when it was finally overturned to comply with the Thirteenth Amendment to the Constitution abolishing slavery and involuntary servitude.

Death Marches and Forced Relocation

The so-called humane alternative to extermination was the policy of "domestication." This involved rounding up Indian survivors of the gold rush, or those occupying lands desired by White settlers, and sending them on forced marches to relocation centers, euphemistically called reservations. Brutal atrocities were committed during these death marches. Many hundreds died as a result of the removal operations by the military, because, if they did not die or were killed along the way, they found no provisions, houses, or other facilities once they reached their destinations and consequently became the victims of disease and starvation. Once on the reservations, the relocated Indians faced exploitation at the hands of crooked Indian agents, some of whom sold government-issue cattle intended to feed the Indians and pocketed the proceeds for themselves.

Summary and Conclusion

Sherburne Cook divides the catastrophic population decline of the California Indians into three stages. The first stage took place from 1769 to 1834 during the Spanish period under the mission system. The major cause of the decline was disease. The second stage extends from the end of the mission system in 1834 to the Mexican war with the United States in 1845. The two demographic processes responsible for the decline during this period were disease and the opening up of land to white settlement. The third and worst stage took place between 1845 and 1855, during the American period of the gold rush. This stage witnessed the decline of the remaining Indian population by two-thirds. The causes for this precipitous population decline clearly fall under the definition of genocide: the committing of acts with intent to destroy, wholly or in part, a national, ethnic, racial, or religious group. In California, especially immediately following the Gold Rush, these acts were deliberate and even institutional in scope.

Steve Talbot

See also Captain Jack; Forced Marches; Genocide; Mining and Contemporary Environmental Problems; Mission System, Spanish; Spanish Influence.

References and Further Reading

Cook, Sherburne F. 1976. *The Conflict Between the California Indian and White Civilization.* Berkeley: University of California Press.

Cook, Sherburne F. 1978. "Historical Demography." *Handbook of North American Indians.* Vol. 8: California. Robert F. Heizer, volume editor, 91–98. Washington: Smithsonian Institution.

Costo, Rupert, and Jeannette Henry Costo, eds. 1987. *The Missions of California: A Legacy of Genocide.* San Francisco: Indian Historian Press.

Heizer, Robert F., and Alan F. Almquist. 1971. *The Other Californians: Prejudice and Discrimination Under Spain, Mexico, and the United States to 1920.* Berkeley: University of California Press.

Kroeber, Theodora. 1976. *Ishi in Two Worlds: A Biography of the Last Wild Indian in North America.* Berkeley: University of California Press.

Moratto, Michael J. 1984. *California Archaeology.* Orlando, Florida: Academic Press.

Norton, Jack. 1979. *Genocide in Northwestern California: When Our Worlds Cried.* San Francisco, CA: The Indian Historian Press.

Mission System, Spanish

Three unprecedented events characterized Spain's epic year of 1492. On January 2, the last Moorish

stronghold in Granada fell. Regaining the country after seven centuries solidified the Spanish ego, sense of identity, and purpose, and it was now time for the married Catholic rulers Fernando and Isabel—he the heir to the throne of Aragon and she the heiress to the throne of Castile—to establish Christian dominance over the country's widespread landholdings. Next, Alexander Borgia, a Spaniard, was elected Pope Alexander VI, providing the king and queen with a strong ally in their Christianizing efforts. Lastly, Columbus's foot, planted on the sandy soil of Hispaniola, introduced the New World to the power, authority, and might of the Spanish empire's imperialism—and to the Spanish Roman Catholic mission system.

Throughout history Christianity has shown great success in propagating itself because it has had a chameleon-like ability to mirror, reflect, and occasionally include stylized aspects of the traditional ways of worship it seeks to replace. This determination has transformed social relations, cultural meanings, and personal experience among indigenes worldwide and has been a cataclysmic event that caused a lasting sea change among thousands of American Indians.

As an example of the progression of the Spanish mission system westward across the United States, active Spanish exploration began with four men: Alvar Nuñez Cabeza de Vaca and three companions who had been shipwrecked off the coast of Texas in the late 1520s. They swam to shore, escaped in 1534 from captivity by hostile Indians, and marched toward the setting sun where they joined a Spanish slave ship anchored off the coast of Guaymas, Mexico (Stockel, 2004, 1). Safely situated in Mexico City, Cabeza de Vaca addressed the viceroy and told of his experience, which led to two subsequent explorations by Fray Marcos de Niza in 1539 and by Francisco Vasquez de Coronado in 1540. The eventual settlement of northernmost Mexico's region followed, including what was to become New Mexico and Arizona.

A set of written guidelines, the Laws of the Indies (Cutter and Engstrand, 1996, 64–65), promulgated in 1573, directed all Spaniards' behavior in the New World, stating, for instance, that the primary purpose of occupation was to convert the Indians to Christianity without injury to them. Twenty years later, in 1595, explorer Juan de Oñate signed a contract for the conquest and settlement of New Mexico but the long march did not begin until

1598. Eighty-three wagons and almost 7,000 head of livestock stretched out along the trail northward from Mexico City for about four miles. Eight Franciscan priests and two lay brothers, eager to work mainly among the Pueblo Indians, participated in the expedition; more than twenty villages containing thousands of Natives awaited.

The area of Spanish religious colonization was in the Rio Grande Valley, reaching from what is now El Paso, Texas, to Taos, New Mexico (Burke, 1974, 84). Along the way the friars might have discussed and planned how to accommodate the Indians' religious beliefs and at the same time instill Christianity. They did not realize that the Puebloans did not represent a unified group, were independent of each other, and had no tribal or political organization or that many did not speak the same language. Shared traditional religious beliefs rested on the fact that their forebears originated near the center of the earth and, after generations of overcoming obstacles through cooperation that helped them climb upward, eventually emerged into the light at the surface of the earth; the most important aspect of pueblo life remained the common good, or the welfare of the group rather than the person. Consequently, Christianity's emphasis on individual salvation was a totally foreign concept and directly at odds with a powerful belief that had been passed down through the generations. Nonetheless, using several methods of persuasion such as introducing agricultural tools and techniques, and teaching construction methods, the friars gradually ingratiated themselves. Another means of convincing skeptical Indians that the Europeans meant no harm was through entertainment. At one village's plaza, colonists staged a mock battle simulating Spain's ancient conflict between Christian kings and invading Moors. Although the pantomime afforded a welcome diversion, it also was meant to convey the impression that the Indians were the current Moors and would be defeated if they resisted (Kessell, 2002, 78).

The plaza was a mission's central site and was usually ringed by the church, missionary's residence, Indians' shelters, carpenter and blacksmith shops, spinning and weaving rooms, stock corrals, fields, and irrigation ditches. The missions were thought to be relatively inexpensive to establish and were expected to continue evangelizing, proselytizing, and indoctrinating Indians for up to ten years, at which time they would become self-supporting, sec-

ular entities responsible to a diocese and would serve as a hub for colonization.

The first part of the seventeenth century has been characterized as a golden age of missions. The friars had established their own rules, answering to the head of missions, a man who was known until 1616 as the "father commissary." He reported to his superiors in the New World, through them to the Franciscan Order in Spain, to the king, and finally to the head of the church, the pope. The priests divided the region into districts, each managed by one Franciscan who was responsible for seeing that a church, a school, and a convent were built. Usually the missionary lived among the Indians while they were creating a large mission complex, but periodically traveled to the smaller villages to serve mass, preach, baptize, and marry or bury the Natives who had become Christians.

New Mexico's Franciscans supervised and Pueblo Indians built approximately fifteen churches in the villages along the Rio Grande. Construction routinely began with the priest marking a church's outline on the ground, after which women and children made and laid adobe bricks and plastered the thick walls. The men cut, hauled, and peeled the logs, called *vigas,* used for roof beams. They next placed branches, called *latillas,* close to one another, often on an angle, across the beams and covered them with loose earth, which became packed down and hardened in time by rainwater and the sun; frequently grass and weeds sprouted from the soil.

Both the New Mexico and Arizona missions were supplied by caravans of thirty-three wagons that left Mexico City every three years. A great deal of space was allotted to articles essential for missionization, especially tools such as metal axes, saws, adzes, augurs, and planes and small materials—nails, latches, and hinges. Religious furnishings for the churches—like sacred vessels, fabrics, bells, a painting or two for the chancel, incense, and missals for the mass—were necessarily included. If any room remained, it was packed tightly with clothing and personal items that had been requested by the priests: Sackcloth for new robes, sandals, and linen were popular requests. Miscellany such as beeswax candles and incense for the censer, as well as sheets of music, could only come northward from Mexico.

The mission system in New Mexico reached its peak around 1640 and stabilized for fifteen years, but it never reached the desired quota of sixty-six

priests throughout the area. Animosities developed between the religious and secular authorities, driving a wedge of competition for free Indian labor. (Surviving Natives had become increasingly disabled and unable to work due to the effect of imported communicable diseases.) But at least two external conditions brought the religious and secular authorities together in the late 1660s and into the next decade: A serious drought affected the amount of food available, and raids by Apaches demanded an alliance of the authorities, particularly since the Puebloans were looking toward the military forces for protection. By 1680 deteriorating trust in Spanish power and prestige motivated a Pueblo revolt that drove the priests, political personnel, and settlers southward, out of New Mexico and into El Paso; thirty-four priests and innumerable Spaniards were killed (Kessell, 2002, 119–124).

Twelve years later, a bloodless reconquest of Santa Fe and the rest of New Mexico brought the Spaniards back. During the intervening years, the Puebloans endured such severe raids from Navajos and Apaches that they welcomed the returning Europeans, including the priests. Missionary and secular work was cautiously resumed. Under the watchful eye of seventeen Franciscans, Indians repaired the churches that had fallen into ruin since the revolt and built new edifices. Once again, however, Indians in some of the pueblos were close to rebellion, and in 1696 another revolt broke out in which five missionary priests and more than twenty Spaniards were killed. Within a few months the military had the situation under control, the mission system became invigorated, and it continued with only a few interruptions.

In spite of continuing Indian threats, the Franciscans stood fast and managed their missionary and exploring activities among the non-Christianized tribes, but success was elusive. Franciscan influence declined over the years and friars either departed or died. Since the supervising Bishop of Durango did not have sufficient diocesan priests to replace them, many churches and chapels in the pueblo villages were vacant by the end of Spanish rule in 1821.

An overlap between Franciscan and Jesuit religious efforts in northern Mexico (present-day Arizona) happened during the early 1600s before the Franciscans were forced, because of a political conflict, to leave the area and concentrate their efforts in New Mexico. Later, in 1636 the first Jesuit stood on

Indian ground in Ures and loudly proclaimed the Word of God; by 1649 the Jesuits had the Sonoran mission field to themselves. Here, the process of mission building began with carefully selecting a site, usually a spot that had been an Indian ceremonial center (Stockel, 2004, 54). The indoctrination of the indigenes into Christianity started by applying a policy of *reducción/congregación*—moving Indian populations out of their villages and resettling them in mission communities where European diseases quickly gained a deadly foothold. (Not incidentally, the policy also left most Indian lands open to appropriation by colonizing Europeans.) Under Spanish supervision in the missions, the disruption of Indian cultures occurred daily as the Natives became ill and were forced to hear about European religion, ideas, customs, and behavior. Importantly, the Jesuits enforced indoctrination into Christianity through supervision, control of labor, and the threat of discipline.

Friendly, sedentary Indian tribes who depended on agriculture for their sustenance were easy targets for the Jesuits, but the nomadic groups, such as the suspicious Apaches, remained elusive. Regardless of the apparent level of cooperation, however, varying degrees of resistance existed among Native peoples while living with the religious Europeans in the missions. Established rules and precepts dictated the type of discipline to be meted out to unruly Indians, ranging from mild punishment such as briefly withholding food and water to the most severe such as flogging or worse.

Before 1687, when the venerable Jesuit Eusebio Francisco Kino arrived and led the Christianization effort in northern Mexico, the Jesuits had already indoctrinated thousands of indigenes into the European ways. Still, Kino's proselytization and evangelization were invaluable examples to the toiling priests; his written description of one village church is testimony to the successes.

> The mission has its church adequately furnished with ornaments, chalices, cups of gold, bells, and choir chapel; likewise a great many livestock fields, a garden with various kinds of garden crops, Castilian fruit trees, grapes, peaches, quinces, figs, pomegranates, pears, and clingstones . . . a forge for blacksmiths, a carpenter shop, a pack train, water mill, many kinds of grain, provisions from . . . harvests of wheat and maize, and . . . horse and mule herds . . . a few gifts and attractions with

which, together with the Word of God, it is customary to contrive to win the minds and souls of the natives (Stockel, 2004, 56).

By the middle to late 1700s, Apache raids on the missions had become uncontrollable and political intervention was necessary to avoid the continuing destruction of the religious complexes. Under the *Instructions of 1786* (Stockel, 2004, 79), which effectively created "peace establishments" out of the missions, all hostile tribes were offered the option of surrendering and living in these facilities under the watchful eye of Spanish military administrators, or of remaining free and risking total annihilation by an increased army presence. Although this policy shift diminished the Franciscans' role by replacing religious authority with military jurisdiction, the priests nonetheless continued proselytizing whenever possible at the peace establishments. Mexico's successful war of independence from Spain ended the Spanish mission system in 1825 when financial support ceased.

By 1683, a short-lived mission had been established at Loreto in Baja California. Two years later, however, Loreto was abandoned due to the lack of water and difficulty in obtaining supplies. It was not until 1697 that a permanent compound, Misión Nuestra Señora de Loreto, was founded by Jesuit Juan Maria de Salvatierra and became home of the mother mission. A positive relationship developed between the Jesuits and many Baja Natives even though the missionaries demanded hard work in the fields and in building the mission complex. Abundantly available stone, rather than adobe, was the choice material in Baja. Friendly, cooperative Indians were taught crafts, trade, preparation of European foods, and they were educated in the Spanish language and Catholic dogma.

The Jesuit era here also ended in 1767 but, during their years at Baja, eighteen *cabceras* (main missions), located from the southernmost tip of the peninsula at Cabo to Santa Maria, 600 miles to the north, were constructed under only sixteen Jesuits' jurisdiction. The tragedy of the Baja effort derived from the European diseases that so overran the missions and decimated the populations that about 25,000 died, leaving only 7,000 souls at the time of the Jesuits' departure.

In 1768 Franciscans Junípero Serra and Fernando Parrón assumed responsibility for the Baja missions, using Loreto as headquarters. With the exception of Serra, the friars stayed in Baja for five

years, until 1773, struggling to gain the same authority and respect enjoyed by the Jesuits, but only one new mission was established, Misión Santa Maria, which became the site of Serra's departure for Alta California in 1769.

The Dominicans followed the Franciscans into Baja and established their first mission in 1774. The following years were filled with struggle and failures. The missions in the south had badly deteriorated and those in the north were always subject to hostile Indian attacks. The Dominican regulations, meant to guide their behavior toward the Natives, called for "swift and sure punishment for all offenses," a striking and—for the Indians—confusing change in policy from the Franciscans' attitude. Remaining constant, however, was the effect of the diseases, so severe that by 1834 the Baja missions were nearly deserted; the last Dominican missionary departed the peninsula in 1855.

In response to the threat of the foreign occupation of Alta California by Russia, the Franciscan Order directed Serra to leave Baja for the northern territory. There, on July 16, 1769, he founded the first Franciscan mission by raising a cross, singing, and calling out the Word of God to curious and unfriendly Indians from under a *ramada* (crude shelter) at San Diego on July 16, 1769; the Monterey mission was next, 650 miles to the north, on June 3, 1770.

Twenty-one Franciscan missions were ultimately founded by Serra and his successors, each begun as a temporary *ramada*, a shelter of stakes with roofs of thatch or reeds, which was eventually replaced by buildings of stone or adobe; each mission was a day's horseback ride or fast march from one another through hospitable terrain mainly of lush grasses and free-flowing water—a landscape often in direct contrast with New Mexico's and Arizona's harsh environmental settings.

When functioning at a high level, the Alta California missions hummed: Men were tanning, blacksmithing, making wine, tending stock, constructing, and working in the fields. Women cooked, sewed, spun, and weaved. However, the education of the Natives in the Spanish language, customs, and religion, the expected by-product of missionization, was difficult to achieve because "the culture of the Indians was so backward." This belief may have fostered the friars' prevalent view of the indigenes as "children who offered little companionship for a highly educated man. Nor could he [the friar] count on his military escort for much personal communion," but

his associate, the second Franciscan [pairs were usually assigned to each mission], kept him from being too lonely in the remote regions of Alta California.

Most mission Indians presented no threat, but still a guard of about half a dozen soldiers at each mission maintained order and returned runaways. Although the military were often in conflict with the priests regarding how best to discipline the recalcitrant Indians, the usual punishment was a day or two in the stocks, quite a contrast with the more severe reprisals in New Mexico and Arizona missions.

Despite this difference, other major procedures, processes, and events occurring among the three missions were similar: The indigenes were congregated in an intense environment controlled by the Europeans, educated when possible in the European culture and religion, forced to erect structures and tend the fields and livestock, punished when necessary, and exposed to diseases against which they had no immunity; in time the survivors were expected to pay taxes to the empire. However, success at indoctrination into Catholicism depended on the individual Indian. While many sincerely adopted the European religion and were converted to Christianity in the Spanish missions, others paid only lip service and hid their ancestral ways in their hearts.

Many descendents of those Indians today practice Christianity openly, but still revere and venerate their rich heritage. Many ancient rituals are still practiced by tribes as they had been long ago. Other ceremonies have been modified in various aspects but still reflect ancestral ways. Even though the Spanish mission system was a powerful force in introducing Christianity to preliterate indigenous peoples of the New World, the Europeans spread illnesses so devastating that the entire religious effort saved only a fraction of the souls initially evangelized and proselytized for what the Spanish in their imperial heyday saw as the greater glory of God and empire.

H. Henrietta Stockel

See also Spanish Influence.

References and Further Reading

Burke, Rev. James T. 1974. *"This Miserable Kingdom:" The Story of the Spanish Presence in New Mexico and the Southwest from the Beginning until the 18th Century.* Santa Fe, NM: Cristo Rey Church.

Cutter, Donald, and Iris Engstrand. 1996. *Quest for Empire: Spanish Settlement in the Southwest.* Golden, CO: Fulcrum Publishing.

Drain, Thomas A., and David Wakely. 1994. *A Sense of Mission: Historic Churches of the Southwest.* San Francisco: Chronicle Books.

Kessell, John L. 2002. *Spain in the Southwest*. Norman: University of Oklahoma Press.

Parsons, Francis B. 1975. *Early 17th Century Missions of the Southwest*. Tucson, AZ: Dale Stuart King.

Polzer, Charles W. 1976. *Rules and Precepts of the Jesuit Missions of Northwestern New Spain*. Tucson: University of Arizona Press.

Stockel, H. Henrietta. 2004. *On the Bloody Road to Jesus: Christianity and the Chiricahua Apaches*. Albuquerque: University of New Mexico Press.

The California Missions: A Pictorial History. Menlo Park, CA: Sunset Magazine.

Vernon, Edward W. 2002. *Las Misiones Antiguas: The Spanish Missions of Baja California 1683–1855*. Santa Barbara, CA: Viejo Press.

Boston Tea Party, Mohawk Images

Few events of the American Revolutionary era have been engraved on popular memory like the Boston Tea Party. Nearly everyone, regardless of sophistication in matters American and Revolutionary, knows that the patriots who dumped tea into Boston Harbor dressed as American Indians—Mohawks, specifically. Regarding *why* the tea dumpers chose this particular form of disguise, we are less knowledgeable.

The Tea Party was a form of symbolic protest—one step beyond random violence, one step short of organized, armed rebellion. The tea dumpers chose their symbols with utmost care. As the imported tea symbolized British tyranny and taxation, so the image of the Indian and the Mohawk disguise represented its antithesis: a "trademark" of an emerging American identity and a voice for liberty in a new land. The image of the Indian was figured into tea dumpers' disguises not only in Boston, but also in cities throughout the Atlantic seaboard. The tea parties were not spur-of-the-moment pranks, but rather the culmination of decades-long colonial frustration with British authority. Likewise, the Mohawk symbol was not picked at random. It was used as a revolutionary symbol, counterpoising the tea tax.

The image of the Indian (particularly the Mohawk) also appears at about the same time, in the same context, in revolutionary songs, slogans, and engravings. Paul Revere, whose midnight ride became legend in the hands of Longfellow, played a crucial role in forging this sense of identity, contributing to the revolutionary cause a set of remarkable engravings that cast as America's first national symbol an American Indian woman, long before Brother Jonathan or Uncle Sam came along.

Paul Revere was one of the earliest Sons of Liberty, a clandestine society that agitated against the British. The Boston Tea Party was only one of its many acts of agitation, propaganda, and creative political mischief. The use of American Indian imagery as a counterpoint to British tyranny ran through the group's activities. Some of the Sons of Liberty's units named themselves after Native peoples before the tea party occurred. Within the Sons of Liberty, John Pulling was called a bully of the Mohawk tribe by an unnamed British satirist.

On Thursday, December 16, 1773, roughly 5,000 patriots gathered at Boston's Old South Church. Suddenly, a war whoop went up from the gallery, then another. A line of "Mohawks" formed in the crowd outside the church and began ambling toward Griffin's Wharf at the foot of Pearl Street. They marched single file ("Indian fashion"), carried axes (which they called "tomahawks"), and shouted slogans: "Boston Harbor a tea-pot tonight" and "The Mohawks are come." As the first group of "Mohawks" boarded the tea ship *Dartmouth* and began to rip open 35,000 pounds of symbolic oppression, others boarded the *Beaver* and *Eleanor*. Several thousand people gathered along the waterfront in the cold, dark, drizzly air, cheering as each tea chest hit the water. During the three hours they took to lighten the three ships of 10,000 pounds sterling worth of tea, the "Mohawks" exchanged words in a secret sign language using Indian hand symbols, and sang:

> Rally Mohawks, and bring your axes
> And tell King George we'll pay no taxes
>   on his foreign tea;
> His threats are vain, and vain to think
> To force our girls and wives to drink
>   his vile Bohea!
> Then rally, boys, and hasten on
> To meet our chiefs at the Green Dragon!
> Our Warren's here, and bold Revere
> With hands to do and words to cheer,
>   for liberty and laws;
> Our country's "braves" and firm defenders
>   shall ne'er be left by true North
>   Enders fighting freedom's cause!
> Then rally, boys, and hasten on
> To meet our chiefs at the Green Dragon
>   (Goss, 1972, 123–124).

Bostonians, dressed as Mohawk Indians, throwing East India Company tea into the harbor in December 1773. (National Archives & Record Administration)

Revere's engravings, which used an Indian woman as a patriotic symbol, often were sharply political. One of them, titled "The Able Doctor, or America Swallowing the Bitter Draught," portrays the Indian woman being held down by British officials, forced to drink "the vile Bohea." Lord Mansfield, in a wig and judicial robe, holds America down as Lord North, with the Port Act in his pocket, and pours the tea down her throat. Lord Sandwich occupies his time peering under "America's" skirt, as Lord Bute stands by with a sword inscribed "Military Law." The bystanders (Spain and France) consider aid for the colonies. In the background, Boston's skyline is labeled "cannonaded"; a petition of grievances lies shredded in the foreground, symbolic of the British government's failure to provide justice for America. This engraving, published in the *Royal American Magazine*'s June 1774 edition, was copied from a similar work in England's *London Magazine* two months earlier.

Bruce E. Johansen

See also American Revolution, Native American Participation.

References and Further Reading

Goss, Eldridge Henry. 1972. *The Life of Colonel Paul Revere.* Boston: G. K. Hall & Co., Gregg Press.
Forbes, Esther. 1969. *Paul Revere and the World He Lived In.* Boston: Houghton-Mifflin.
Johansen, Bruce E. 1985. "Mohawks, Axes & Taxes." *History Today* (April): 18–24.
Labaree, Benjamin W. 1964. *The Boston Tea Party.* New York: Oxford University Press.

American Revolution, Native American Participation

Native Americans, individually and collectively, played a key role in the American Revolution. In particular, Native alliances, especially with the powerful Haudenosaunee (Iroquois or Six Nations) Confederacy, helped shape the outcome of the war. The war also was crucial for the Haudenosaunee Confederacy, which split for the first time in several hundred years over the issue of whether to support Great Britain or the new United States of America. The Oneidas allied

Mohawk chief Joseph Brandt leads a group of Tories and Senecas in a raid on the village of Cherry Valley, New York in 1778. More than forty people were killed in the ensuing massacre. (Library of Congress)

with the Americans and assisted George Washington's army with crucial food supplies during its most difficult winter at Valley Forge. On the other hand, most of the Mohawks and, after initial neutrality, the Senecas sided with the British; the Senecas suffered from brutal raids principally by troops under the command of General John Sullivan. In the words of historian Richard Aquila, "The American revolution became an Iroquois civil war" (1983, 241).

The Seneca Cornplanter advocated neutrality, while Joseph Brant, a Mohawk leader, advocated alliance with the British, as did the Seneca Red Jacket. Indeed, the name "Red Jacket" was a reference to a scarlet coat given to him by the British for fighting with them during the war. Cornplanter insisted that the quarrel was among the whites and that to interfere in something that the Haudenosaunee did not fully understand would be a mistake. Brant contended that neutrality might cause the Senecas to be attacked by one side without allies on the other. Brant had visited England,

acquired a taste for English food and clothes, and had been told that land would be returned to the Mohawks by the British in exchange for alliance.

As one meeting broke up in a furor, Brant called Cornplanter a coward. Brant was influential in recruiting most of the Mohawks, Senecas, Cayugas, and Onondagas to support the British. Brant's ferocity as a warrior was legendary; many settlers who supported the Americans called him Monster Brant. His sister, Molly Brant, had married Sir William Johnson, Britain's chief Indian agent in the Northeast, a lifelong friend of such Mohawk leaders as Hendrick, with whom he had fought side by side in the war with France two decades before his death in 1774.

Although the Oneida Skenandoah asserted his people's official neutrality at the beginning of the American Revolution, he supplied warriors and intelligence to the patriots, as did the Tuscaroras.

As Washington's army shivered in the snow at Valley Forge, Skenandoah's Oneidas carried corn to the starving troops. Washington later named the

Shenandoah Valley of Virginia after the Oneida chief in appreciation of his support. During September of 1778, the Oneidas supplied a key warning to residents of German Flats, near Herkimer, New York, that their settlements were about to be raided by the British and their Iroquois allies under Joseph Brant. The settlers were thus able to get out of the area in time, after which their homes and farms were burned and their livestock captured.

Revolutionary forces often adopted a scorched-earth policy against the Haudenosaunee, who supported the British. George Washington's forces ended the battle for the Mohawk Valley by defeating the British and their Iroquois allies at the Battle of Johnstown. Following the war, the Brant family and many of the other Mohawks who supported the British in the Revolution moved to Canada to escape retribution by the victorious patriots. They founded the town of Brantford, Ontario, and established a new Haudenosaunee council fire there.

The Iroquois figured importantly in the Battle of Oriskany in 1777, the battle at Wyoming Valley in 1778, and the Battle of Newtown in 1779. The war often was very brutal on both sides; Brant's forces torched farms owned by patriots as patriot armies, particularly (but not exclusively) those under Sullivan, systematically ransacked Iroquois villages and fields, meanwhile expressing astonishment at the size of Iroquois (especially Seneca) food stores. The Iroquois often found themselves fighting each other as the confederacy split its allegiance between the British and patriots.

General Charles Cornwallis surrendered at Yorktown in 1781, but war parties continued to clash along the frontier for months after the British defeat became obvious. The Iroquois allies of the British sent out war parties as late as the early summer of 1782. They wanted to continue fighting, but their sponsors had given up. After the war, the efforts of the Iroquois went unrewarded by both sides. The British discarded their Mohawk, Onondaga, Cayuga, and Seneca allies at the earliest convenience.

The Americans did the same to their own allies, the Tuscaroras and Oneidas. At the conclusion of the Revolutionary War, the border between the new United States and Canada (which remained under British control) was drawn through Iroquois country in the Treaty of Paris (1783), without consultation with the Indians. In 1784, during two treaty councils held at Fort Stanwix, New York, many Iroquois realized that the new U.S. government was ignoring most of their land claims. Most of the negotiations

were held at gunpoint, as the Iroquois were forced to give up claims to much of their ancestral territory.

Despite his reluctance to ally with the patriots, Cornplanter became a close friend of George Washington after the war. He was given a strip of land in western New York for his people, whose descendents lived on the land until the midtwentieth century, when it was inundated by floodwaters behind the Kinzua Dam, despite a pledge by President Washington that the land would be protected.

In addition to their role as combatants in the American Revolution, American Indians played a key role in the contest of ideas that spurred the revolt. As early as 1744, the Onondaga sachem Canassatego, Tadadaho (speaker) of the Iroquois Confederacy at the time, urged the British colonists to unite on a federal model similar to the Iroquois political system. Benjamin Franklin printed Canassatego's advice at the 1744 Lancaster Treaty Council and later proposed an early plan for union at the Albany Congress of 1754. This plan, which included elements of both British and Iroquois political structures, was rejected by the colonies but served as a model for Franklin's later Articles of Confederation.

During the early 1770s, before the American Revolution led to armed revolt, colonists adopted Mohawk disguises to dump British tea into Boston Harbor and at several other cities along the eastern seaboard. The American Indian, often portrayed as a woman, was used as a symbol of an emerging American nation long before Uncle Sam was adopted in that role.

Bruce E. Johansen

See also Albany Congress, Native Precedents; Brant, Joseph; Canassatego; Cornplanter; Franklin, Benjamin, Native American Influences; French and Indian War.
References and Further Reading
Aquila, Richard. 1983. *The Iroquois Restoration: Iroquois Diplomacy on the Colonial Frontier, 1701–1754.* Detroit, MI: Wayne State University Press.
Armstrong, Virginia Irving, comp. 1971. *I Have Spoken: American History Through the Voices of the Indians.* Chicago: Swallow Books.
Edmunds, R. David. 1980. *American Indian Leaders: Studies in Diversity.* Lincoln: University of Nebraska Press.
Graymont, Barbara. 1972. *The Iroquois in the American Revolution.* Syracuse, NY: Syracuse University Press.
Grinde, Donald A., Jr. 1977. *The Iroquois and the Founding of the American Nation.* San Francisco: Indian Historian Press.

Kelsay, Isabel Thompson. 1984. *Joseph Brant.* Syracuse, NY: Syracuse University Press.

Mann, Barbara Alice. 2005. *George Washington's War on Native America.* Westport, CT: Praeger.

Stone, William L. 1866. *The Life and Times of Say-go-ye-wat-ha, or Red Jacket.* Albany, NY: Munsell.

Waters, Frank. 1992. *Brave Are My People.* Santa Fe, NM: Clear Light Publishers.

Goschochking (Ohio) Massacre of 1782

The Lenápe and Mahican capital in 1782, Goschochking was located in southeastern Ohio, near the modern-day town of Coschocton. On March 8, 1782, ninety-six Lenápes and Mahicans were brutally murdered on the outskirts of Goschochking by the 160-strong Pennsylvania militia out of Fort Pitt under Colonel David Williamson. On its triumphal way back to Fort Pitt, the militia fell also upon the inhabitants of Killbuck's Island, in the river across from Fort Pitt, killing around thirty more.

Lying along the fringes of the large Lenápe town with its sumptuous fields of corn, beans, and squash, were the three tiny Moravian "praying towns" of Salem, Gnadenhutten, and Welhik Tuppeek (Schonbrunn). These hamlets were suffered to exist, and the Moravian missionaries to be present, because the missionaries claimed political neutrality and had come with converts to Ohio in the wake of the genocidal attacks of the so-called Paxton Boys, a settler death squad trying to eliminate Native land proprietors around Bethlehem, Pennsylvania, under cover of the French and Indian War. In 1763, the 154 Lenápe and eighty-four Mahican converts surviving Paxtonian hits were moved west by Lenápes of the Iroquois League, to the safety of Lenápe land in the Muskingum River Valley in southeastern Ohio.

Although most American histories report that the Revolutionaries were fighting the British alone, the Revolution was, in fact, conducted on two fronts against two foes: the British front along the eastern seaboard, and the Native American front against, especially, the Iroquois League in New York, western Pennsylvania, and Ohio. "Freedom" might have been the battle cry against the British, but land attracted the troops in the Western Department, headquartered at Fort Pitt, Pennsylvania. George Washington was fighting furiously to seize Native American land, particularly in Ohio, for European-American expansion, in defiance of a prohibition by the crown. Washington's armies were held off by the Ohio Union of Iroquois League peoples (including the Wyandots, Lenápes, Mahicans, and Senecas), the Three Fires Confederacy (of the Ottawas, Pottawatamies, and Chippewas), the Miamis, and the Shawnees (in alliance with Ohio Cherokees).

During the American Revolution, Moravian missionaries acted as spies for George Washington, relaying considerable intelligence to him at regular intervals on the movements of the Ohio Union. The League was entirely aware of the spying and put an end to it in 1781, by taking the missionaries prisoner and sending them to the British stronghold of Detroit. At the same time, knowing that settlers and their militias wanted *all* Natives dead, Christian or otherwise, the League spirited 350 Moravian converts to Upper Sandusky, the Wyandot capital, for safety's sake. Although Upper Sandusky was beyond the reach of the settlers, it was not beyond the reach of the massive famine that had been occasioned by Washington's and Congress's total war against the League, which actively destroyed all Native food supplies. (Goschochking and its fields were attacked in 1781.)

At the request of the League Lenápes, who refused to countenance the killing of Innocents—a Native legal category into which the missionaries fell—the missionaries were released by the British. The moment they returned to Upper Sandusky, they immediately resumed sending intelligence to Fort Pitt resulting in their rearrest, this time by League Wyandots, who returned them to Detroit. The harm was already done, however.

As long as they resided at Goschochking as cover for the spying missionaries, the Lenápe and Mahican converts were safe from settler attack, but, once the missionaries' activities had been unequivocally exposed, there was no need on the part of the Western Department to continue sheltering them from harm. Thus, when news arrived at Fort Pitt from the missionaries late in February 1782, that about 130 converts, most of them starving women and children, had gone back to Goschochking to pull up last year's harvest, which had been abandoned before the panicked flight of 1781, the militia decided to seize the opportunity to eliminate them as claimants for southeastern Ohio. The fact that the converts had remained steadfast allies of the United States from the beginning of the Revolution and had

The Goschochking massacre of the Lenápe and Mahican tribes, including women and children, on March 8, 1782. Lenápes and Mahicans were brutally murdered on the outskirts of Goschochking by the 160-strong Pennsylvania militia out of Fort Pitt under Colonel David Williamson, under the authority of General George Washington. (Library of Congress)

even supplied Fort Pitt with food did not faze Williamson or his militia.

Heading into Goschochking, Williamson had a plan. It was to trick the converts by pretending to have come on a mission of mercy, to escort them back to Fort Pitt for their safety. Knowing of the missionaries' communications with and total confidence in military protection from Fort Pitt, the converts believed this until they had conclusive proof otherwise. To organize the "rescue," the militia asked all of the converts to assemble at Gnadenhutten, as a central location. By way of bolstering the scheme, the militiamen discussed theology with the converts as they walked them into Gnadenhutten and accepted the alliance wampum originally granted the converts by Congress. The militia had even brought along older boys to play with the Native children, thus to allay any lingering fears.

The work crews in the fields around Gnadenhutten and Salem were completely deluded by the militia's false message and feigned friendship, bringing in their harvests and unearthing all of the goods they had hidden the year before, handing everything over to the militia. As soon as they were gathered, the militia dropped its pretense and bound everyone with leather thongs. Miffed that the work crews from Welhik Tuppeek had not arrived with the rest, the militia went in search of them, but the people there had been put on their guard by a *moccasin* (messenger) who had made a frantic run from Upper Sandusky, with the news that the missionaries had informed Fort Pitt of their being at Goschochking.

Wary, the Welhik Tuppeek work crew sent a couple of scouts to see what might be afoot. Almost immediately, the scouts found one of their foremost members hacked to pieces and weltering in coagulating blood. Consequently, instead of giving themselves up to the militia, the Welhik Tuppeek people hid in the woods when Williamson's men approached their hamlet. With great trepidation, the strongest adults carrying children and elders on their backs, the work crew made a daring escape, which entailed creeping across a wide plain in full daylight right before crossing the Tuscarawas

River, both acts conducted right under the noses of the militia guards. Successfully making the far shore of the river, the Welhik Tuppeek crew ran all night, bringing the horrifying accounts of what was happening to Upper Sandusky.

Back in Gnadenhutten, on March 7, the captive farmers were not so fortunate. The militia put them on trial as horse thieves (a capital offense) and sentenced them to death. A squabble ensued among the militiamen over the best method of killing so many people at once. Some wanted to confine them in the hamlet's huts and then set the huts on fire, shooting down any who tried to escape the flames. Others pointed out that this would sacrifice their valuable scalps. In light of the lucrative Pennsylvania bounty on Native scalps, the militia decided to club everyone to death first, to scalp them second, and *then* to burn them in the huts. To effect this plan, the men were separated from the women and children, the two groups put in separate "slaughter houses," as the militia dubbed them (*Murder of the Christian Indians*, 1826, 11). The execution was to occur the next morning.

Promptly, on March 8, with some of the militia expressing annoyance that the executions were not begun more expeditiously, the crime spree began. The militia first led out ten longhairs, or nonconverts, among the men for special taunting and abuse before the general massacre. One longhair, despite being bound, attacked his guards, freed himself, and nearly made it to the safety of the woods before he was cut down by several whooping cavalrymen. This was the only direct resistance offered.

Two adolescent boys survived the ensuing massacre, one in the men's and one in the women's hut. Both escaped to Upper Sandusky with their tales of horror. The first boy, a Mahican whom the missionaries had christened Thomas, did not die of his skull fracture or scalping, but woke up amidst a pile of bleeding corpses some time in the afternoon, before the hut was burned. As the militia reentered the hut to double-check their handiwork, Thomas lay as still as death amid the corpses, until the soldiers departed. At dusk, he bravely walked out the door of the hut, directly behind the guards, inching himself around to the back of the hut and locating the Sandusky Trail.

The name of the second boy was unrecorded by the missionaries, because he was not a convert. Ohio oral traditions refer to him as He Runs. He Runs was thrust into the women's hut, which had one advantage: a root cellar. Knowing this, the women had, with their bare hands, started prying up a floorboard, with the intention of stuffing the children into the cellar. He Runs joined their effort and managed to pull up one board, even as the militia headed for the women's hut. Jumping into the cellar, he helped pull down a second child, quite as the militia entered the hut. The boys huddled in the dark, viewing the entire slaughter of their mothers, siblings, aunts, and grandmothers above through the cracks between the floor planking.

In the stillness that followed the last shriek, the smell of smoke wafted down. He Runs looked for a means of escape, locating a small air hole leading to the surface behind the hut. He was able to wiggle through, but the younger boy was trapped in the tunnel, where he suffocated in the ensuing fire. Deeply traumatized, He Runs located the Sandusky Trail behind Gnadenhutten, where he encountered a trembling Thomas. The two watched the militiamen, celebrating their "victory." Then, together, the two boys supported each other all the way home to Upper Sandusky, where they told what they had been through in a graphic detail that reverberates to this day in the oral traditions of Ohio Natives.

The militia stole all of the harvest, horses, goods, and clothes of their victims for sale in Pittsburgh; militia pay consisted mainly of all the auctionable loot militiamen could cart home. Not yet content with its scalp count and loot, however, the militia decided to up its take by attacking Killbuck's Island (no longer extant) on its way home. Again, the roughly forty Lenápes living on Killbuck's Island, across from Pittsburgh, had moved there specifically as allies of the United States, providing many scouts and much intelligence to Fort Pitt. This mattered not a whit to the militia, which fell upon the unsuspecting people. Gelelemund, their chief, was able to hustle a few women and children to safety, but thirty people were never heard from again. Another convert, Anthony, happened to have been in Pittsburgh at the time and watched the massacre from that side of the river. He, too, fled to Upper Sandusky.

The first militia report on the slaughters (most probably composed by Williamson) was published as a "Notice" in the *Philadelphia Gazette*. It characterized the massacres as a great victory (*Philadelphia Gazette,* 1782, 2), and that story might very likely have held as the official version today, had not John Bull, a lay Moravian missionary, who was husband to one and father to another of the people murdered at Gnadenhutten, flatly refused to be still. He prod-

ded the lead missionaries into creating a flap by demanding an investigation. On the defensive, Williamson and Colonel James Marshel, lieutenant of Pennsylvania, were forced to write more truthful reports. Investigators were sent to Fort Pitt and their reports to the president of Pennsylvania were forwarded to the Continental Congress.

After the massacre was exposed, every effort was made to throw the entire blame onto the militia with assertions that it was acting in violation of orders. It is true that Colonel John Gibson at Fort Pitt had little or no control of the excitable militias, but it is also true that George Washington had personally appointed the militias to garrison Fort Pitt. The war was ending; Ohio had not yet been seized, and Washington certainly knew the homicidally racist temper of the militias. On March 8, the very day of the massacre, Washington told General William Irvine, his new commander at Fort Pitt, not to worry about supply issues there, as "measures are actually taking," i.e., steps were in the process of being taken, to provide "provisions, Cloathing [sic] and pay" (Fitzpatrick, 1938, 24, 48).

Although represented to Congress as a matter of extreme importance for the honor of the country (*Pennsylvania Archives*, 9: 552, 553; *Minutes of the Supreme Executive Council of Pennsylvania*, 13: 297), the matter suddenly disappeared from all official records. No final report on the investigation exists, just a couple of obfuscatory, preliminary letters from the lead investigator, who clearly sided with the militia. The Williamson and Marshel reports vanished entirely, never to reappear. The matter was quietly yet promptly dropped.

The official response to the flap was ultimately to order another attack that May, this time on Upper Sandusky. Williamson was again tapped to lead, as second in command to Colonel William Crawford. The militia's announced intention was to "extermenate [sic] the whole Wiantott Tribe [sic]" ("The Haldiman Papers," 1782, 10, 629, 631). This army was conclusively defeated by the Natives, with Colonel Crawford taken prisoner. Crawford was tried for the war crime at Goschochking, found guilty, and executed that June by the Wyandots. Crawford became an instant martyr among the settlers, who centered all future discussions on his fate, which was never thereafter presented in the context of the massacre at Goschochking.

Barbara Alice Mann

See also American Revolution, Native American Participation; Genocide.

References and Further Reading

Butterfield, Consul Wilshire. 1882. *Washington-Irvine Correspondence, the Official Letters.* Madison, WI: David Atwood.

Doddridge, Joseph. [1824] 1912. *Notes on the Settlement and Indian Wars.* Pittsburgh, PA: J. S. Rittenour and W. T. Lindsey.

Fitzpatrick, John C., ed. 1938. *The Writings of George Washington from the Original Manuscript Sources, 1745–1799.* 39 vols. Washington, DC: Government Printing Office.

Heckewelder, John. [1782] 1958. "Murder and Captivity." In *Thirty Thousand Miles with John Heckewelder.* Edited by Paul A. W. Wallace, 170–207. Pittsburgh: University of Pittsburgh Press.

Heckewelder, John. [1818, 1820] 1971. *Narrative of the Mission of the United Brethren Among the Delaware and Mohegan Indians from Its Commencement, in the Year 1740, to the Close of the Year 1808.* New York: Arno Press.

Howells, William Dean. 1884. "Gnadenhütten." In *Three Villages,* 117–198. Boston: James R. Osgood and Company.

Loskiel, George Henry. 1794. *History of the Mission of the United Brethren Among the Indians in North America.* 3 vols. Translated by Christian Ignatius La Trobe. London: Brethren's Society for the Furtherance of the Gospel.

Mann, Barbara Alice. 2005. *George Washington's War on Native America, 1779–1782.* Westport, CT: Praeger.

Minutes of the Supreme Executive Council of Pennsylvania, from Its Organization to the Termination of the Revolution. 1852–1853. 16 vols. Harrisburg, PA: T. Fenn.

Murder of the Christian Indians in North America in the Year 1782: A Narrative of Facts, 2nd ed. 1826. Dublin: Bentham & Hardy.

Muttlery, Charles. 1843. "Colonel David Williamson and the Massacre of the Moravina Indians, 1782." *American Pioneer* 2, no. 9 (September): 425–432.

Pennsylvania Archives. 1853. First Series. Vols. 8–9. Philadelphia: Joseph Severns & Co.

"The Haldiman Papers." *Collections and Researches Made by the Pioneer Society of the State of Michigan,* 2nd ed. Vol. 10, 210–672. Lansing: Wynkoop Hallenbeck Crawford Company, State Printers, 1908.

Zeisberger, David. 1885. *The Diary of David Zeisberger, 1781–1798.* 2 vols. Translated and edited by Eugene F. Bliss. Cincinnati: Eugene F. Bliss.

Fallen Timbers, Battle of

The Battle of Fallen Timbers on August 20, 1794, cleared the way for American settlement into the southeastern corner of the Northwest Territory and nearby enclaves including Detroit and the future site of Chicago. The battle took place a few miles from British-held Fort Miamis (present-day Toledo) in Ohio. A confederation of Native Americans led by Weyapiersenwah (Blue Jacket) planned to trap General Anthony Wayne's army at a fortification made of fallen trees. Uncovering the trap, Wayne's mounted riflemen and infantry attacked, causing a general retreat. The British refused to protect the fleeing Indians in Fort Miamis. The battle, often called the final phase of the American Revolution, led to the British-backed Indians' ceding much land in the 1795 Treaty of Greenville.

The Battle of Fallen Timbers has its roots in the 1783 Treaty of Paris that ended the American Revolution. The new American government declared that Indian lands had been acquired from the British by terms of the peace treaty. Native Americans disagreed with this interpretation, with American demands for Ohio land cessions leading to plainly stated objections on the part of the Indian confederacy. Additionally, British authorities refused to relinquish their military posts on U.S. soil, using them as bases to supply the Indian nations in the Northwest Territory. Angered by American land demands and encouraged by British provisions, arms, ammunition, and moral support, Indians attacked American settlers on the frontier.

The American military responded to the Indian threat. In 1790, President George Washington sent an army under Brigadier General Josiah Harmar against the loose Native American confederacy, but his force was defeated on two separate occasions and forced to retreat. The following year, Washington sent a larger army, this one commanded by Major General Arthur St. Clair, to chastise the Indians who had beaten Harmar. Handicapped by a lack of provisions and equipment, St. Clair's force was ambushed on November 4, 1791 and suffered the most humiliating defeat ever inflicted on an American army. St. Clair lost half of his force in about three hours before his remaining troops ran for their lives from the battlefield near the present Ohio–Indiana border. The victories against Harmar and St. Clair gave the Indian confederacy a large quantity of arms and supplies, as well as the confidence to boldly reject peace proposals from the United States.

General Anthony Wayne's American troops defeat an Indian alliance at the Battle of Fallen Timbers in August 1794. (Library of Congress)

To regain the honor of his young country, President Washington formed a third army, styled the Legion of the United States, and selected Major General "Mad" Anthony Wayne to lead it. A born soldier, Wayne (1745–1796) had a long and distinguished military career that included service in the Revolutionary battles of Ticonderoga, Brandywine, Monmouth, and Yorktown. He was given plenary powers by the administration. With his decisions subject to review only by Washington and Secretary of War Henry Knox, the general would conduct his latest military campaign as he saw fit.

Wayne's primary goals were subjugating the Indians and bringing peace to the frontier, with removal of the British threat an additional interest. These tasks initially seemed overwhelming because of the difficulties with transportation and supplies in the Northwest Territory. There were no reliable maps

of the territory, and even basic information regarding the rivers and streams was nonexistent. Every piece of equipment purchased by the legion—paper, weapons, uniforms, sheet iron, shoes, buttons, needles—had to be purchased in the Atlantic states, carted overland to Pittsburgh, then shipped down the Ohio River to Fort Washington at Cincinnati. From there it had to be hauled overland, generally by packhorse, to forts. Construction projects were often delayed until soldiers could craft the tools they needed.

Further complicating the American situation, Wayne's force was always under strength and many of his soldiers were of poor quality. There was a constant stream of deserters. Yet Wayne was innovative with his troops. In addition to the standard branches of service—infantry, cavalry, and artillery—he employed riflemen, light infantry (armed with muskets of Wayne's own design), and mounted volunteers from Kentucky, who added mobility and firepower to the main body. This arrangement allowed Wayne to locate the enemy, absorb his attacks, and respond with overwhelming force at the critical point. His army was screened by parties of scouts on foot. Other scouts, known as spies, ranged far afield on horseback, occasionally even penetrating into Native American camps in search of intelligence.

Warriors from the Indian confederacy had been waiting for Wayne to advance. The Indian army, estimated at close to 1,500, moved south in two divisions. The first and largest, about 1,000 warriors, was composed of Wyandots (Hurons), Mingos, Shawnees, Ottawas, Chippewas, and Miamis. The second group consisted mostly of Delawares with some Potawatomis and stragglers from other nations.

The Native Americans had moved their women and children out from between the American invading forces and Fort Miamis. The noncombatants were placed in camps along the Maumee River, with settlements stretching from the fort to Swan Creek and to the shores of Lake Erie. This massive influx of refugees brought several thousand dependents to the area, which combined with the arrival of hundreds of Great Lake Indian warriors to place a major strain on available food supplies. British provisions eased the crunch, but the home front situation had mounted pressure on Indian leaders to drive Wayne from their lands. Accepting American peace demands would be equivalent to acknowledging cowardice.

On August 19, 1794, all available warriors arranged a line from the Maumee River bluffs into the timber and waited to ambush Wayne. They were joined by 100 British-Canadian volunteers. The Native American forces now numbered between 1,100 and 1,200 warriors, including about 100 adolescents. About 100 fighters had no guns, armed only with tomahawks. They waited in a jumble of trees blown down years before by a tornado.

Wayne issued an order that troops should be ready to move at 5 a.m. on August 20, modifying the regular order of march by having the formations march two men deep and in closer order than previously. Wayne expected the enemy to strike first, forcing him to fight defensively. A battalion of 150 mounted Kentucky scouts encountered the Indian ambush at 8 a.m. Overwhelmed by heavy fire, the Kentuckians retreated as they were chased by 300 to 400 warriors who had given up their prepared positions in anticipation of a quick victory. A front guard of army regulars was also overwhelmed, but the Indian attack stalled when it encountered a skirmish line of several hundred light infantry and riflemen that were covering the deployment of the main body of the Legion infantry. Once in position, the Legion charged into the fallen timber. The warriors, who had become thinly dispersed across a broad front, were overwhelmed by the infantry and cavalry. Driven back to their original position, the retreating Indians created disorganization and panic among the other warriors. Only on the extreme right of the battlefield was there an organized attempt by 100 Wyandots and the Canadian militia to halt Wayne's charge. Outnumbered and driven from the battlefield, the Indians retreated past Fort Miamis. The Indian dead were then scalped and mutilated by the Americans. None of the Indian or Canadian dead were buried by the Legionnaires, of whom twenty-six had been killed and eighty-seven wounded. Many of the American wounded were still hospitalized five months later.

After Wayne's victory, Indian people faced the reality that they would be compelled to give up the Ohio lands so forcefully demanded by the American government. The territory ceded at the Treaty of Greenville included a large area that had been a homeland for the Delawares, Shawnees, and allied Mingos as well as a hunting ground for the Wyandots. However, all Great Lakes Indians realized that they had a stake in the outcome. Tribes represented at Greenville were the Wyandots, Delawares,

Shawnees, Ottawas, Ojibwas, Potawatomis, Weas, Miamis, Kickapoos, Piankeshaws, and Kaskaskias. For Americans, the Battle of Fallen Timbers demonstrated the need for a standing army to protect American interests on the frontier.

Caryn E. Neumann

See also Northwest Ordinance.
References and Further Reading
Gaff, Alan D. 2004. *Bayonets in the Wilderness: Anthony Wayne's Legion in the Old Northwest.* Norman: University of Oklahoma Press.
Horsman, Reginald. 1970. *The Frontier in the Formative Years: 1783–1815.* New York: Holt, Rinehart, and Winston.
Prucha, Francis P. 1969. *The Sword of the Republic: The United States Army on the Frontier, 1783–1846.* New York: Macmillan.
Sugden, John. 2000. *Blue Jacket: Warrior of the Shawnees.* Lincoln: University of Nebraska Press.
Sword, Wiley. 1985. *President Washington's Indian War: The Struggle for the Old Northwest, 1790–1795.* Norman: University of Oklahoma Press.
Tanner, Helen Hornbeck, ed. 1987. *Atlas of Great Lakes Indian History.* Norman: University of Oklahoma Press.

Creek War

In 1813, a civil war erupted among the Creek Indians in Georgia, Alabama, and Florida. Also known as the Red Stick War, the dispute was largely an internal struggle over the cultural and political direction of Creek society. In this war, which overlapped with the War of 1812, Red Stick Creeks tried to reassert Creek sovereignty in the region and redirect the cultural path of their society. The war resulted in the defeat of the Red Sticks and the further dispossession of Creek lands by the United States.

In the decades prior to the Creek War, the Creek Indians underwent several cultural and economic transformations. After the American Revolution, the Creeks (via the deerskin trade) became increasingly connected to and dependent on the marketplace. Creek men hunted for longer periods, because the value of their skins declined and their dependence on trade goods increased. Unscrupulous traders, who used false weights and the influence of alcohol, outraged many Creek hunters. At the same time, a "civilization" campaign led by U.S. Indian Agent

Benjamin Hawkins helped lead many Creeks to embrace cultural innovations within Indian villages. By 1810, many Creeks herded cattle, owned slaves, spoke and wrote English, grew cotton, wore European clothing, fenced their lands, and intermarried with white Americans. These changes frustrated many Creeks, especially as reliance on Euro-American markets for basic supplies led many Creeks to amass burdensome debts.

While the Creeks became dependent on the marketplace for their survival, they experienced a political transformation that further threatened their independence. The creation of a national council, which Hawkins regularly attended, epitomized the political change. By centralizing authority in Creek society, the council violated Creek norms of localism. By allowing Hawkins to participate, the council further angered many Creeks, who saw his presence and participation as a sign that the Americans controlled the council. To the dismay of many Creeks, the council created a centralized police force, called the law menders, in part to protect individual property rights in Creek society. When the council agreed to allow the United States to build and maintain roads across Creek country, the opposition to the council and Hawkins turned to violence. When the road was completed in 1810, Red Stick Creeks attacked American surveyors, mail carriers, and travelers, and they tried to assassinate Creeks they saw as complicit.

In 1811, when Shawnee religious leader Tecumseh came to the Southeast, many Creeks were already predisposed to his Nativist messages and his calls for pan-Indian resistance. Tecumseh urged Creeks to regain control over their villages, to ally themselves politically with other Indians, and to oppose American expansion. Many Creeks embraced his teachings, especially those in the upper towns who felt most threatened by the recent changes in Creek society. Tecumseh's urging of the Creeks to prevent the further invasion of white settlement similarly resonated, as American squatters, settlers, and surveyors seemed to be constantly invading Creek lands.

When Tecumseh left the southeast, several Creek prophets continued to draw upon and spread Tecumseh's teachings. Religious and political leaders like Menawa, William Weatherford, Peter McQueen, and Josiah Francis called for Creeks to resist Hawkins, eliminate the American presence, and reassert Creek sovereignty. These prophets led war dances, sang spiritual songs, and otherwise demon-

The horseshoe bend of the Tallapoosa River was the setting of the Red Stick village whose leaders executed the uprisings against American settlers in 1813 during the Creek War. (National Park Service)

strated their possession of supernatural powers. They called for a renewal of Creek spiritualism and independence.

Other Creeks, especially those who embraced innovations such as American-style ranching and planting, opposed the Red Sticks. These Creeks were led by William McIntosh, a chief of Coweta, one of the most influential and interconnected towns. Other prominent Creeks, including Big Warrior and Little Prince, also resisted the Red Sticks. The Red Sticks made their attempt to obtain Creek allies rather difficult. Opponents of the Red Sticks were harassed, their property was destroyed, and their lives were threatened. Even before open warfare erupted, many opponents of the Red Sticks were killed and others were physically coerced into supporting the Nativist cause.

After months of intermittent fighting among the Creeks, the civil war slowly became part of the War of 1812. When American frontier settlers were killed by the Red Sticks, Hawkins tried to intervene and obtain justice through the national council. Such actions only exacerbated matters. When the council executed five Creeks for the murder of Thomas Meredith in March 1812, for example, tensions within the Creek nation exploded. Rumors spread that the United States and the Creeks were at war, and within months the rumors became self-fulfilling prophecies.

In this context, the British and the Red Stick Creeks saw an ally in each other. The British provided supplies to the Red Stick majority to help them defeat the United States and its Creek allies. British support of the Red Sticks terrified Americans in the backcountry, who believed that a British–Creek alliance would overrun their settlements. When a party of Red Stick warriors led by Peter McQueen went to Pensacola to obtain supplies from the British in June 1813, militiamen who had formed on the edge of Creek country attacked McQueen and his men. The fighting resulted in the deaths of only a handful of Americans and Indians, but it outraged the Red Sticks, who responded with their own assault.

On August 30, 1813, about 750 Red Stick warriors retaliated by attacking the house of Samuel Mims. Fort Mims, which was located in the Tensaw District in Alabama, housed white traders, their African American slaves, and their Creek allies. Most of the traders at the fort, including Mims, were married to Creek women and were supporters of many economic and cultural innovations within Creek society. The Red Stick warriors completely overran the fort, killing those who resisted and freeing the slaves who were there. The event became known among non-Natives as the Mims Massacre.

After the battle at Fort Mims, the United States took a much more active role in the Creek civil war. Reports of casualties, which were often exaggerated, were met with calls for vengeance. The United States sent forces into Creek country from Tennessee and Georgia, led by General John Cocke, Major General John Floyd, and General Andrew Jackson. In addition, the United States obtained Chickasaw, Choctaw, Cherokee, and Creek allies to help with the invasion. Ordered to attack the Red Sticks they confronted, the armies marched toward the confluence of the Coosa and Tallapoosa Rivers. For about ten months, the American troops burned their way through Creek country. As the campaign progressed, Andrew Jackson emerged as the most successful of the four leaders. During the campaign, Jackson and his 3,000 militiamen from Tennessee razed two Creek villages (Talladega and Tallasahatchee) and helped destroy Red Stick interests in Creek country. Jackson's men killed approximately 1,000 Creek warriors and destroyed many of their supplies.

The Red Stick War culminated in the Battle of Horseshoe Bend on March 27, 1814. At this battle, roughly 2,500 Red Stick warriors faced a force of more than 15,000 soldiers. In addition to the soldiers from all four regiments, the United States was assisted by the so-called "friendly" Creek Indians who were led by Chief McIntosh. Nearly 800 Red Stick Creeks died on the battlefield. After the Battle of Horseshoe Bend, Jackson's army continued to burn and raze Creek villages. By the end of April, the U.S. forces reached Fort Jackson, which had recently been built on the Coosa and Tallapoosa Rivers. From there, Jackson received the surrender of hundreds of Red Sticks.

After the war, the United States coerced the defeated Creeks (Red Sticks and so-called "friendly" Creeks) to sign the Treaty of Fort Jackson. This treaty, which resulted in the cession of 23 million acres and the establishment of roads, trading houses, and military posts in Creek country, officially ended the war. Rather than submit to the terms of the treaty, many Red Sticks moved south into Florida and joined with the Seminole Indians. During the First Seminole War, many Red Stick warriors found a new opportunity to fight the United States.

Andrew K. Frank

See also Jackson, Andrew; Seminole Wars; Tecumseh.

References and Further Reading

Frank, Andrew K. 2005. *Creeks and Southerners: Biculturalism on the Early American Frontier.* Lincoln: University of Nebraska Press.

Martin, Joel. 1991. *Sacred Revolt: The Muskogees' Struggle for a New World.* Boston: Beacon Press.

Owsley, Frank Lawrence, Jr. 1980. *Struggle for the Gulf Borderlands: The Creek War and the Battle of New Orleans, 1812–1815.* Gainesville: University Press of Florida.

Saunt, Claudio. 1999. *A New Order of Things: Property, Power, and the Transformation of the Creek Indians, 1733–1816.* New York: Cambridge University Press.

Seminole Wars

In the first half of the nineteenth century, the Seminole Indians in Florida fought three wars with the United States. The issues that led to the wars varied, but in each conflict the invading American army sought to remove the Seminoles from Florida and fugitive African American slaves from Seminole villages. Although the three campaigns resulted in the removal of almost all the Seminoles from Florida to Indian Territory (now Oklahoma), more than 200 Florida Seminoles never surrendered or relocated.

The use of Florida and Seminole villages as refuges for escaped slaves from the lower South helped to bring about the First Seminole War. After the War of 1812, the United States repeated its demands that Spanish officials do something about the Negro Fort, an outpost on the Apalachicola River in the Florida panhandle that provided refuge for hundreds of runaway slaves. When Spanish officials refused, the United States turned to its military. Led by Major General Edmund P. Gaines, the United States attacked the Negro Fort on July 27, 1816. When a well-placed cannon shot hit the fort's powder magazine, the entire fort was destroyed. Most of the approximately 300 residents of the fort

Seminole chiefs were captured in Florida in 1816 by order of Major General Andrew Jackson. The First Seminole War began in 1816 when U.S. troops, in pursuit of runaway slaves, destroyed a Seminole stronghold in Florida, prompting retaliation by the Indians. (North Wind Picture Archives)

were immediately killed. The United States Army returned to slavery the fugitive slaves who survived.

The destruction of the Negro fort did little to resolve the tensions on the Florida–Georgia border. Slaves continued to find refuge in Florida, and the Seminoles continued to offer them sanctuary. At the same time, Seminoles suffered from the theft of their cattle by Georgians and by others who refused to recognize Seminole property rights. The result was a series of frontier skirmishes that resulted in the deaths of Seminoles and Georgians alike.

After a small party of U.S. soldiers suffered a particularly devastating defeat at the hands of Seminole warriors in Georgia in 1817, the United States authorized its military to track down the offending Indians even if it meant entering Spanish Florida. With orders that forbade attacks on the Spanish, General Andrew Jackson took his campaign across the Apalachicola River and into Florida. Despite his orders, Jackson attacked and captured St. Marks on

April 7, 1818, and Pensacola on May 24, 1818. Seminole villages fared no better, as Jackson's men razed Indian villages and their agricultural fields. Jackson further outraged many Americans and the British when he captured, tried, and executed two British Floridians, Alexander Arbuthnot and Robert Ambrister, for providing aid and comfort to the Seminoles. Jackson declared victory, and almost immediately negotiations began that resulted in Spain's cession of Florida to the United States. This was accomplished by virtue of the Adams–Onís Treaty, signed and ratified by the United States in 1819 and finally taking effect in 1821.

The end of the First Seminole War and the incorporation of Florida as an American territory did little to ease the tensions between Seminoles and the United States. Even with Spain out of the picture, the United States struggled to prevent slaves from finding freedom in Florida. Matters worsened as cotton planters and southern herders began to move

to middle and east Florida. Now, they coveted Seminole lands and brought their African American slaves even closer to them.

In 1823, the United States and the Seminoles signed the Treaty of Moultrie Creek, the first agreement between the two nations. Under the terms of the agreement, which was opposed by many Indians, the Seminoles would be guaranteed protection and reserved lands in central Florida in return for leaving northern Florida, returning fugitive slaves, and allowing the building of roads. In short, the treaty removed the Seminoles and made them active partners in the development of Florida.

Disagreements over the meaning of the Treaty of Moultrie Creek began almost immediately. Seminoles pointed to the signatures of illegitimate leaders and complained that their new lands were ill suited to sustain their herds. Yet by 1826 most Seminoles had moved south and begun to rebuild their lives.

In 1832, the United States once again called upon the Seminoles to move west of the Mississippi. In the resulting Treaty of Paynes Landing, seven chiefs agreed to move within three years. Most Seminoles were outraged and demanded the rights to their land that were earlier outlined in the Treaty of Moultrie Creek. The ensuing dispute resulted in the assassination of Charley Emathla by Osceola for his role in supporting removal. Despite the widespread opposition to the treaty, the United States insisted on enforcing it. When 3,824 Indians went west in according with the treaty, warfare erupted between the resistant Indians under the leadership of Osceola and the U.S. military charged with removing the Seminoles.

The Second Seminole War officially began in December 1835. In a coordinated attack, Osceola and other Seminole warriors killed Wiley Thompson, the U.S. Indian agent to the Seminoles, while other Seminole warriors launched a surprise attack on U.S. Major Francis Dade and his men near Fort King. In the subsequent fighting, the Seminoles took advantage of the shelter provided by the Everglades and used guerilla tactics to keep American troops on the move. The United States, which began the war by fighting in large, heavily armed detachments, made headway in the war's early years. In 1837, as frustrations mounted in American society, the United States arrested Osceola, who had come to Fort Peyton under a flag of truce. The Indian warrior died of malaria in prison soon after.

The war continued after Osceola's death. The circumstances surrounding Osceola's death, as well as the inability to achieve victory, resulted in the replacement of General Thomas S. Jesup by Brigadier General Zachary Taylor in 1838. Under Taylor, the United States pursued a new strategy. Dividing the hostile territory into squares twenty miles wide, Taylor built a series of roads and forts to secure each of the areas. At the same time he ordered Major General Alexander Macomb to pursue an aggressive peace plan that allowed the Seminoles to remain in southwestern Florida. The strategy came to a crashing halt and open warfare returned when Seminoles attacked a trading post on the Caloosahatchee River in July 1839.

In 1840, Brigadier General Walker K. Armistead took command of the U.S. forces in Florida. Armistead sent groups of a hundred soldiers into the swamps of south Florida to track down the resistant Seminoles. While Armistead's men marched south, the Seminoles attacked the plantation settlements in north and middle Florida. Despite the general success of the Seminole people in avoiding capture, many individuals were not so lucky. In June 1841, the United States captured Chief Cooacoochee, shipped him west, and then returned him to Florida in an attempt to convince other Seminoles to move west.

In the end, the Second Seminole War lasted from 1835 to 1842, and it was the longest, costliest, and deadliest of the Florida Indian campaigns. Thousands of Seminoles and nearly 1,500 American soldiers were killed, and the campaign cost the United States more than $30 million. The war resulted in the surrender and removal of approximately 4,400 Seminoles. In 1842, only several hundred Indians remained in Florida.

As white settlers and surveyors began to filter through Florida, the Seminoles remained on the defensive. Although they only numbered in the hundreds, the Seminoles continued to be a nuisance to American settlers. The ongoing tension resulted in the Third Seminole War (1855–1858). This campaign against the Seminoles began when Colonel William Selby Harney, who led a U.S. surveying corps, destroyed Billy Bowlegs' banana crop. This action, which was intentionally designed to outrage Bowlegs, resulted in a renewal of fighting.

The Third Seminole War was marked by few sustained battles. Instead, the Seminoles waged a campaign of guerilla warfare, attacking isolated settlers and small detachments of soldiers. The United States responded with a system of patrols and the use of bloodhounds to track down the enemy. The

Seminoles, using the cover of the Everglades, easily avoided the invading soldiers. In late 1857, the United States turned to using shallow boats to enter the inhospitable Everglades, and in November they found and destroyed Bowlegs's refuge.

On May 7, 1858, Bowlegs and forty warriors finally surrendered to the United States. When Bowlegs and 165 other Seminoles moved to Oklahoma, only about 200 Seminoles remained unconquered in the state. Today, these survivors comprise the Seminole and Miccosukee nations.

Andrew K. Frank

See also Jackson, Andrew; Osceola.

References and Further Reading

Covington, James W. 1982. *The Billy Bowlegs War.* Chuluota, FL: Mickler House Publishers.

Heidler, David, and Jeanne Heidler. 1996. *Old Hickory's War: Andrew Jackson and the Quest for Empire.* Mechanicsburg, PA: Stackpole Books.

Mahon, John K. 1992. *History of the Second Seminole War, 1835–1842.* Gainesville: University Press of Florida.

Miller, Susan A. 2003. *Coacoochee's Bones: A Seminole Saga.* Lawrence: University Press of Kansas.

Missall, John, and Mary Lou Missall. 2004. *The Seminole Wars: America's Longest Indian Conflict.* Gainesville: University Press of Florida.

Twyman, Bruce Edward. 1999. *The Black Seminole Legacy and North American Politics, 1693–1845.* Washington, DC: Howard University Press.

Fleeing bands of Sauk and Fox caught and attacked by American troops, leading to the Battle of Bad Axe, the final conflict of Black Hawk's War. (North Wind Picture Archives)

Black Hawk's War

Black Hawk's War was an outgrowth of the Treaty of 1804, in which the Sauks (Sacs) and Foxes conceded all of their land east of the Mississippi River for a small price. The Sauks were closely allied with the Mesquakie, whom the French erroneously called Fox.

Trouble began to develop after the War of 1812, when southwestern Wisconsin and northeastern Illinois were opened to settlement. As settlers moved into the area, Black Hawk, a Sauk warrior who had fought in the War of 1812, grew increasingly disturbed over the loss of land and attempted to organize Indian opposition to white settlement.

By 1831, settlers had begun to take over Black Hawk's own village near present-day Rock Island, Illinois. Furious, Black Hawk prepared to resist, but U.S. Army troops forced him to move his people to the west bank of the Mississippi. Defying orders, he

returned the following spring and took his people to a Winnebago village, whose leader was sympathetic to Black Hawk's cause.

Upon returning to the eastern side of the Mississippi, Black Hawk was pursued by General Henry Atkinson. Without support from other Indians or from the British, Black Hawk decided to surrender. During negotiations, however, two of his emissaries were killed by unruly militia. Outnumbered, Black Hawk prepared to defend his position. Firing from concealed positions, the Indians struck first and quickly dispersed the militia, who fled back toward their camp. That incident came to be known as the Battle of Stillman's Run.

Black Hawk launched attacks throughout the spring of 1832 and evaded the often incompetent forces sent against him. By the end of June, however, supplies were running low, and, with troops in pursuit, it was becoming riskier to raid settlements. By midsummer, Black Hawk had concluded that it would be safest to cross the Mississippi again. The Sauks moved across southwestern Wisconsin toward the river, still pursued by the Army.

On August 1, Black Hawk reached the confluence of the Bad Axe and Mississippi Rivers, but with no way of crossing and fearing the approach of the troops, Black Hawk decided to move north to find refuge with the Winnebagos. However, most of the

band decided to build rafts to cross the river. Black Hawk and a few followers proceeded upriver.

While rafts were being built, the Army arrived. The Indians tried to surrender, but they were misunderstood, and the troops opened fire, initiating the Battle of Bad Axe. By the battle's end, about one hundred and fifty Indians lay dead; nearly half that number were taken prisoner. Army losses were low. The Indians who did reach the west bank of the Mississippi fared no better; they were attacked by Sioux war parties.

Black Hawk's War lasted only fifteen weeks. However, it was especially costly for the Indians, who suffered four hundred to five hundred casualties. On the other side, some seventy soldiers and civilians were killed. Black Hawk was later captured and imprisoned for a year in Fortress Monroe, Virginia, before being released.

See also Black Hawk.
References and Further Reading
Jackson, Donald, ed. 1964. *Black Hawk: an Autobiography.*
Prucha, Francis P. 1969. *The Sword of the Republic: The United States Army of the Frontier, 1783–1848.*

Trail of Tears

The Trail of Tears was the migration route members of the Cherokee Nation followed in 1838–1839 when the federal government forced their removal from the southeastern United States to Indian Territory in present-day Oklahoma. The relocation resulted from the government's removal policy, which sought to open eastern lands to European-American immigrants and provide a permanent home for Native peoples in the West. The Trail originated in Tennessee and followed an overland route through Kentucky, Illinois, Missouri, and Arkansas.

Most of the Cherokees trudged along this path, although a lesser number navigated a southern water route along the Tennessee, Mississippi, and Arkansas Rivers. Due to the many hardships the Cherokees suffered during removal, they referred to this arduous journey as *Nunna dual Isunyi,* the "Trail Where We Cried." Between 1835 and 1839, approximately 16,000 Cherokees relocated to the West and an estimated 4,000 died. Despite this tragedy, the federal government remained committed to the removal policy.

During the 1820s, as the eastern population expanded, southern states exerted pressure on the federal government to remove Indians from their lands. The government attempted to appease Southerners by negotiating treaties with the tribes that contained provisions for voluntary removal, but few Indians actually moved. Consequently, on May 28, 1830, President Andrew Jackson supported Southern demands and signed the controversial Indian Removal Act. This act authorized the president to exchange Indian lands in any state or territory for lands west of the Mississippi River. Supporters of the removal policy argued that it would open eastern lands to settlement and provide a permanent land base to protect the tribes from encroachment. Although critics blame Jackson for advancing the policy, the removal idea initially was not his own. In fact, Thomas Jefferson thought the lands of the 1803 Louisiana Purchase could provide an outlet for eastern Indians, and Presidents James Monroe and John Quincy Adams believed that removal would solve the so-called Indian problem.

Following passage of the Indian Removal Act, the federal government forced approximately 100,000 Native Americans to move to the West. The Act applied to Indians throughout the states and territories, but it particularly affected the Five Civilized Tribes, who held fertile lands in the South. Between 1830 and 1835, the Choctaw, Creek, Chickasaw, Cherokee, and Seminole tribes all signed removal treaties. The treaties varied slightly, but in each the Five Tribes ceded their eastern lands in exchange for western land, and the government promised to fund the move and provide one year's subsistence.

The Cherokee Nation, which inhabited sections of North Carolina, Georgia, Tennessee, and Alabama, was the last of the Five Tribes to agree to relocate, and ultimately its removal proved to be the most controversial. The impetus for Cherokee removal stemmed from an 1802 compact between Georgia and the federal government in which Georgia ceded its western lands in exchange for the government's promise to extinguish Indian title to lands within the state. Consequently, in 1817 and 1819, the government signed treaties with the Cherokee Nation that encouraged tribal members to relocate to present-day Arkansas. The voluntary nature of the removal provision, however, led most of the Cherokees to reject the idea, and only a few thousand moved west.

By the late 1820s, the Cherokees had demonstrated their willingness to comply with federal policy by assuming a high degree of Anglo-American style civilization. In addition to establishing a bicam-

eral legislature and a Supreme Court, the Cherokees developed a written language, adopted a constitution, and published a newspaper. Indian acculturation, however, was insignificant to Georgians, who were more concerned with states' rights, the discovery of gold on Cherokee lands, and acquiring agricultural lands. At this point, having grown impatient with the federal government's failure to uphold the 1802 agreement, Georgia took matters into its own hands.

In 1828, following the election of President Andrew Jackson, Georgia extended state jurisdiction over Cherokee lands and nullified Cherokee law. It also authorized a lottery to distribute Cherokee lands to Georgia citizens. Jackson, a staunch supporter of the removal policy, refused to obstruct Georgia's sovereign rights by interfering in the matter. Consequently, the Cherokees filed suit in the United States Supreme Court. In two separate cases, *Cherokee Nation v. Georgia* (1831) and *Worcester v. Georgia* (1832), the Court ruled in the Cherokees' favor. In the first case, the Court declared Indian polities, "domestic dependent nations." In the second, it concluded that Georgia could not extend state law over Cherokee territory. Without federal enforcement, however, the victory rang hollow.

Following the Supreme Court decisions, the Cherokee Nation clung to the hope that it could avoid removal. By 1833, however, a rift developed within the Cherokee leadership. A minority group of Cherokees, known as the Treaty Party and led by Major Ridge, his son John, and Elias Boudinot, accepted the inevitability of removal and concluded that it was in the Cherokees' best interest to negotiate a fair removal treaty with the federal government. Consequently, on December 29, 1835, members of the Treaty Party signed the Treaty of New Echota, in which the Cherokee Nation agreed to cede its eastern lands and relocate to Indian Territory. These actions appalled the Cherokee majority, who opposed removal. Led by Principal Chief John Ross, they urged Congress to reject the treaty. Despite their pleas, Congress ratified the treaty on May 23, 1836. In exchange for the land cession, the government agreed to pay the Cherokees $5 million, provide subsistence for one year, and finance the emigration. The treaty stipulated that the Cherokees move within two years of ratification or face forced removal.

For two years following ratification of the treaty, Ross continued his effort to reverse the policy. He appealed to Jackson's successor, Martin Van Buren, and submitted a protest petition containing 15,000 Cherokee signatures. Unmoved, the federal government remained committed to its removal policy.

In the meantime, a minority of the Cherokees journeyed to the West. Between January 1837 and May 1838, approximately 2,000 Cherokees, including members of the Treaty Party, emigrated. The majority of the Cherokees, however, convinced that Ross could reverse their fate, did not prepare for removal. Consequently, at the expiration of the spring 1838 removal deadline, the United States ordered troops into Cherokee Territory to organize a forced removal. Led by General Winfield Scott, the troops seized Cherokees and placed them in stockades to await removal. Although Scott ordered his men to treat the Indians humanely, reports indicate that the treatment was severe. Families were separated during the roundup and their abrupt departure left them little time to gather their belongings.

In June 1838, the first government-led emigrant detachment left Tennessee, traveled by steamboat down the Tennessee and Ohio Rivers to the Mississippi, then entered Indian Territory. The summer heat made the journey difficult, however, and shortly thereafter, Scott postponed removal until the weather cooled. During the hiatus, Ross petitioned for and received permission to allow the Cherokees to remove themselves.

Consequently, in late August, the first of thirteen Cherokee-led detachments left the Southeast for present-day Oklahoma. The group trudged along the northern overland Trail of Tears and arrived in Oklahoma in January 1839. In December 1838, the last Cherokee detachment left the East under the leadership of John Ross. Following the southern water route, the group arrived in Oklahoma in late March 1839. Sadly, Chief Ross's wife succumbed to illness and died during the journey.

The entire removal experience devastated the Cherokee Nation. Between August 1838 and March 1839, 13,000 Cherokees and their slaves followed the Trail of Tears to Oklahoma, and 4,000 died in the stockades, en route, or during the first year in the West. Throughout the ordeal, the Cherokees suffered from disease, malnutrition, starvation, and general exhaustion. The challenges continued in their new homeland. Once in Oklahoma, a struggle ensued in which the Old Settlers, the Treaty Party, and the new arrivals all sought to control the Cherokee government. When the groups failed to reconcile, violence erupted, and in June 1839, Major Ridge, John Ridge, and Elias Boudinot were murdered in retaliation for their roles in the 1835 treaty.

Despite the removal tragedy, the Cherokees remained committed to rebuilding their nation in the West. Soon after arriving in Oklahoma, they reestablished their political institutions and named John Ross principal chief. They also developed an education system that included institutions of higher learning and resumed publication of a newspaper. They endured the American Civil War, the arrival of the railroad, and the loss of their tribal land base when Oklahoma entered the Union. In 1987, more than 150 years after ratification of the Treaty of New Echota, Congress commemorated Cherokee removal by designating the Trail of Tears a national historic trail.

Jennifer L. Bertolet

See also *Cherokee Nation v. Georgia;* Indian Removal Act; Jackson, Andrew; Ross, John; *Worcester v. Georgia.*

References and Further Reading

Anderson, William, ed. 1991. *Cherokee Removal.* Athens: University of Georgia Press.

Kappler, Charles J. 1904. *Indian Affairs: Laws and Treaties.* Vol. II. Washington: Government Printing Office.

Perdue, Theda, and Michael D. Green, eds. 1995. *The Cherokee Removal.* Boston: Bedford/St. Martin's.

Prucha, Francis Paul. 1984. *The Great Father.* Lincoln: University of Nebraska Press.

Rozema, Vicki, ed. 2003. *Voices from the Trail of Tears.* Winston-Salem, MA: John F. Blair.

Oregon Trail

Spanning half a continent and stretching more than 2,000 miles, the Oregon Trail was the key northern overland migration route used by European-American immigrants through the West during the mid-nineteenth century. As well as serving as a route for westbound transit, the Oregon Trail produced Indian–white interactions that transformed Native American lifeways and helped the United States in its cultural goals of Manifest Destiny, including the subjugation of Native peoples.

The trail is marked by a myriad of cutoffs and shortcuts along its route from Missouri to Oregon. The basic route started in Independence/Kansas City, followed the Santa Fe Trail just south of the Kansas River, then angled to Nebraska along the Little Blue River onto the Platte River. It followed the Platte and North Platte Rivers to South Pass through the Wind River Mountians. The trail then followed the Snake River to the Columbia River before arriving at Oregon City (the trail's terminus) or taking the Barlow Road to the Willamette Valley.

Fur traders, trappers, and missionaries during the 1820s and 1830s were the first to use the trail. Their activities altered the economies, marriage patterns, and other lifeways of many indigenous cultures. More significant, however, was the flood of emigrants during the 1840s and 1850s, whose contact with Native Americans fostered a wide range of Indian–white relations.

Myths of the treacherous West and savage Indians plaguing the trail were strong public perceptions during the 1800s. To be sure, some Indian–emigrant violence erupted along the trail, but the great majority of Indian–white exchanges were positive and peaceful, especially during the early years of trail use during the 1840s. Many Indians provided advice to emigrants, guided them, and acted as interpreters or packers. Others helped emigrant groups navigate treacherous western waters. Still others carried mail eastward and cut wood or hay for westbound travelers. Some even operated toll roads and bridges. Much of this Indian–emigrant interaction centered on the exchange and barter of goods, and Indians were shrewd businesspeople and negotiators. Tribes often traded horses, moccasins, robes, lariats, and foods in exchange for trinkets, weapons, ammunition, coffee, sugar, and similar items. The most extensive trading occurred along the more western stretches of the trail between Fort Hall in Idaho and the Oregon country, not on the Great Plains as is the common perception. Both groups viewed each other as strange curiosities with peaceful interaction, trading, and mutual aid prevailing along the trail early on.

Antebellum-era migration quickened along the trail, producing less than friendly confrontations and eventual military conquest of Western tribes. Natives recognized quickly the threats that overlanders posed. Emigrant livestock overgrazed the region, emigrants depleted timber resources, and they also overhunted and drove away buffalo and other game. Waters became contaminated, and epidemic diseases spread. By traveling along major rivers, emigrants monopolized important resource areas as well.

These conditions made the West a contested region between Indians and European-American immigrants. Native peoples responded by demanding compensation or tribute for lost resources, sometimes at the suggestion of government agents. During the 1850s, Manifest Destiny gave rise to a sense

of entitlement and racial superiority and a predisposition toward suspicion and fear that was generated by guidebooks and newspapers, as emigrants became increasingly belligerent toward Native Americans. Some refused to pay compensation and at times violent confrontations erupted. The area of greatest conflict, however, was not the Great Plains region, but westward beyond South Pass where 90 percent of clashes on the trail occurred. One of the biggest problems was the shooting of cattle by Great Basin tribes, who hoped emigrants would leave the wounded animals for the taking.

The result of increased tensions between tribes and emigrants along the trail eventually led to a greater U.S. government presence in the West. Peace commissions and treaty negotiations to open the West and to ensure safe passage for overlanders increased. The Oregon Trail became a major pathway for the U.S. government's colonialization of the region. In 1854, along the trail near Fort Laramie, an incident involving a passing wagon train precipitated what became known as the Grattan Fight, in which an Army officer and his troops were killed. This event altered Lakota–federal government relations from one of peaceful interactions to an inflammatory conflict between the United States and the Plains Indians that would not be resolved until the end of the 1870s. After the transcontinental railroad's completion in 1869, the trail ceased to be used for long-distance travel.

S. Matthew DeSpain

See also Assimilation; Fort Laramie Treaty of 1868.
References and Further Reading
Byers, Roland O. 1984. *The Linchpin: The Oregon Trail in 1843.* Moscow: University Press of Idaho.
Sager, Catherine. 1989. *Across the Plains in 1844.* Fairfield, WA: Ye Galleon Press.

Yakama War

The mid-1800s were a turbulent time in the Pacific Northwest. Oregon and Washington Territories' Native population had been ravaged by disease, resulting in the Whitman Massacre, and news from Indians around the Northwest was keeping racial tensions high.

In 1854–1855, the new territorial governor, Isaac I. Stevens, was on a mission to acquire Native Americans' land in the Pacific Northwest for a proposed transcontinental railroad route from the Mississippi River to Puget Sound (Kent, 1993, 98–99). To do so,

he needed to secure peace in the region and to open the land to European-American immigration. After negotiating several treaties around Puget Sound, Stevens intended to do the same with the Plateau Indians, and then cross over the Rocky Mountains to deal with the Flatheads and the Blackfeet. For the council with the Plateau Indians at Walla Walla, Stevens enlisted the assistance of Oregon Indian Agent, Joel Palmer (Stevens, 1855, 8).

Upon hearing of these plans, Kamiakin, the headman of the Yakamas, called for a meeting of chiefs from several tribes and nations in the region on the Grand Ronde River, during the summer of 1854, to discuss rumors. After meeting for five days, all the men of authority among the Plateau Indians agreed to band together against Stevens and refuse to give up their peoples' lands. Some powerful men, mainly Spokan Garry (Spokane) and Lawyer of the Nez Percé, however, advised the chiefs listen to what the immigrants had to say before entering into an avoidable and costly war (Miller, 2003, 112).

When the Walla Walla council did finally meet in the summer of 1855, the solidarity that had been agreed upon at Grand Ronde quickly broke down and each of the chiefs found themselves scrambling to retain any of his peoples' land at all. In the end, the Yakamas received a relatively small reservation in the Yakima Valley, a loss of nearly 30,000 square miles (Splawn, 1944, 35–36).

This was a devastating loss to the Yakamas and, along with the increased traffic from the Puget Sound settlements to the gold mines in northeastern Washington, Kamiakin's warriors were furious. In September 1855, A. J. Bolon, subagent to the Yakamas, was murdered, sparking open hostilities. Bolon was assumed to have known that some of the white travelers were killed by Qual-chin, son of chief Owhi, who was Kamiakin's half brother, so Qual-chin ambushed Bolon to keep the authorities from punishing him for the murders (Glassley, 1972, 112–113).

Meanwhile, Governor Stevens was meeting with Native peoples in the Rocky Mountains; acting Governor C. H. Mason called on troops from Fort Vancouver and Fort Steilacoom to protect Euro-American immigrants traveling through the area and to escort Governor Stevens on his return to Washington Territory. This duty fell upon Major General Rains, the commander of Fort Vancouver, who ordered Brevet-Major Granville O. Haller from The Dalles, Oregon, and Lieutenant W. A. Slaughter from Fort Steilacoom to join forces (Glassley, 1972, 113).

En route, Haller, with nearly 100 men and a howitzer, encountered approximately 1,500 well armed Indians on Toppenish Creek, on October 6, 1855. The Indians attacked and surrounded the soldiers. Fighting continued for three days, as the soldiers were forced to bury all their extra supplies, including the howitzer, and make a fighting retreat to The Dalles. Along the way, Haller met with a group of forty-five artillerymen on the Klickitat River, under Lieutenant Day. There they built a blockhouse and defended themselves. At the same time, Lieutenant Slaughter had tried to cross the Cascade Mountains through Naches Pass with fifty men, but on the eastern side, he encountered so many hostile Indians that he returned to the west side of the mountains (Glassley, 1972, 113–114).

General Mason then sent Lieutenant Phil Sheridan from Fort Vancouver, along with two companies of volunteers and regulars from The Dalles, plus two government ships from Puget Sound. Governor Curry of Oregon Territory sent four more companies of volunteers against the hostile Indians. Major General Rains, with two companies of Washington volunteers and all the available regulars, combined with four companies of Oregon volunteers under Colonel J. W. Nesmith in the Yakama country on November 7. On the next day, they engaged hostiles near the Yakima River. The soldiers pursued the Indians upstream along the river, but the Indians escaped by climbing the cliffs out of the canyon (Glassley, 1972, 115).

Initially, the Yakima War lasted only a few months, July to November 1855, but, having escaped the pursuing soldiers for the time, the Indians resumed their hostilities against the intruders. By July 1858, war had erupted again, this time with the help of the Palouse, Spokane, and Coeur d' Alene Indians. This war lasted until September 1858, when the Indians were defeated and many of their leaders were hanged. After this, most Plateau Indians resigned themselves to their reservations. Peace was shattered again in another conflict in 1877, when Chief Joseph fled federal troops until his defeat in western Montana.

Daniel R. Gibbs

See also Dalles Trading Area; Disease, Historic and Contemporary.
References and Further Readings

Doty, James. 1978. *Journal of Operations of Governor Isaac Ingalls Stevens of Washington Territory in 1855.* Edited by Edward J. Kowrach. Fairfield, WA: Ye Galleon Press.
Drury, Clifford M. 1979. *Chief Lawyer of the Nez Perce Indians.* Glendale, CA: Arthur H. Clark.
Glassley, Ray. 1972. *Indian Wars of the Pacific Northwest.* Portland, OR: Binfords & Mort.
Josephy, Alvin M. 1965. *The Nez Perce Indians and the Opening of the Northwest.* Lincoln: University of Nebraska.
Josephy, Alvin M. 1976. *The Patriot Chiefs: A Chronicle of American Indian Resistance.* New York: New York Books.
Miller, Christopher. 1993. "Indian Patriotism: Warrior vs. Negotiator." *American Indian Quarterly* 17, no. 3 (Summer): 343–349.
Miller, Christopher. 2003. *Prophetic Worlds: Indians and Whites on the Columbia Plateau.* Seattle: University of Washington Press.
Richards, Kent. 1993. *Isaac I. Stevens: Young Man in a Hurry.* Provo, UT: Brigham Young University Press.
Splawn, A. J. 1944. *Ka-mi-akin: Last Hero of the Yakamas.* Portland: Binfords & Mort (for the Oregon Historical Society).
Stevens, Isaac Ingalls. 1855. *A True Copy of the Record of the Official Proceedings at the Council Walla Walla Valley 1855.* Fairfield, WA: Ye Galleon Press.

Great Sioux Uprising

The Great Sioux Uprising, also known today as the United States–Dakota War of 1862, initiated an era of U.S. military conquest on the northern Plains that continued until the massacre at Wounded Knee in 1890. With the loss of approximately 450 European-American lives, the war resulted in one of the most violent and threatening indigenous attacks on European-American immigrants in United States history. For the Dakotas, the war remains their major point of historical reference because it marks the moment of their physical subjugation and the loss of their Minnesota homeland.

The beginning of the war is usually attributed to the killing of five immigrants on August 17, 1862, in Acton Township by four Dakota warriors from the Rice Creek village. Although this was the act that sparked the full-blown war, it occurred only after decades of conflict that could no longer be contained.

Minisota Makoce, or Land Where the Waters Reflect the Skies, is the ancient homeland of the Dakota people. By the early nineteenth century, the U.S. government was seeking access to those lands and fraudulently achieved its first Dakota land cession in the Treaty of 1805. Despite the fact that only

The siege of New Ulm. The largest Anglo-American settlement near the Sioux encampment, New Ulm was attacked twice during the 1862 Minnesota Sioux Uprising. As punishment for their role in the hostilities, thirty-eight Sioux were executed at Mankato in December 1862. (Library of Congress)

two Dakota signatures were obtained on this treaty to represent the entire Sioux nation, once ratified it allowed the construction in 1819 of Fort Snelling. Protection of the fort allowed an influx of traders, soldiers, missionaries, and other immigrants, resulting in severe threats to the Dakota way of life. Dakota lands became increasingly desirable to immigrants; the U.S. government catered to that desire by securing further land cessions in the treaties of 1837, 1851, and 1858, eventually confining the Dakota to two small reservations (each approximately ten miles wide and seventy miles long), bordering the Minnesota River. The Sisitunwan and Wahpetunwan occupied the tract bordering the upper portion of the river, and the Bdewakantunwan and Wahpekute occupied the lower portion.

Not only were the Dakotas prevented from practicing their seasonal subsistence lifestyle, but, along with European-Americans came unceasing incursions on remaining Dakota lands and the accompanying depletion of game and other food sources. Cultural pressures also ensued from the invasion; missionaries worked incessantly with government agents and traders to eradicate Dakota cultural traditions and replace them with Western notions of civilization. Evidence of the deep factionalism resulting from decades of their colonizing efforts was apparent in the split between the Dakota cut-hair or farmer Indians, who yielded to those pressures, and the blanket Dakotas, who resisted them and attempted to maintain their former way of life.

Regardless of which path the Dakota chose, the winter of 1861–1862 was a time of starvation. The cut-hairs suffered a major crop failure the previous fall and fared no better than the blanket Dakotas attempting to survive on a meager game supply. The treaty payments expected in the summer of 1862 offered the only hope for fending off starvation for the eastern Dakotas and, when the payment of gold did not arrive, desperation set in. The tension was compounded when the Dakotas learned that Agent

Thomas Galbraith held the treaty food supplies in a warehouse while he was awaiting the payment of gold so that he could distribute them together. When 5,000 Dakotas gathered at the Upper Agency on July 14 demanding what was rightfully theirs, Galbraith was forced to issue some provisions under threat of violence, but he kept the bulk of food beyond their reach. At the same time, traders with stores of food also refused to distribute food to the Dakotas. The callousness of white Minnesotans to Dakota starvation was captured in the statement made by trader Andrew Myrick, "If they are hungry, let them eat grass or their own dung!" By mid-August the Dakotas were in a life-and-death struggle and their level of tolerance had been breached. After the Acton killings, driving out the invaders seemed the only remaining solution for the Bdewakantunwan Dakotas.

Realizing that their actions would not go unnoticed or unpunished, the Dakota men responsible for the Acton killings returned to their village leader, Shakpe, and they gathered together a council of Bdewakantunwan warriors, including leaders such as Wabasha, Traveling Hail, Big Eagle, and Little Crow, to determine what course of action should be taken. Although many proclaimed the futility of a military action against an organized military force with tremendous firepower, Little Crow eventually agreed to lead the military struggle against the invading whites, and war was declared.

Their first act of war was waged at the Lower Sioux Agency on August 18, 1862. Myrick was one of the first casualties of the war and when he was found later his mouth was stuffed with grass. Word of the violence quickly spread among the white settlers, and many of them fled to nearby towns for safety or to Fort Ridgley, the only military post in the southwestern region of Minnesota. When news of the war reached Governor Alexander Ramsey in St. Paul the next day, he immediately commissioned Henry Hastings Sibley as a colonel and sent him with 1,400 troops to lead an expedition against the Dakotas. While the Dakotas initially had the element of surprise working in their favor, killing hundreds of immigrants and taking many European-Americans and mixed-bloods as prisoners, their offensive was short-lived. With European-American defenses quickly solidified and the arrival of Sibley's Sixth Minnesota Regiment, the Dakotas quickly shifted to a defensive position. When the Dakotas were unable to take the strongholds of Fort Ridgley and the town

of New Ulm, Minnesota, it was clear that their war effort could not be sustained. The final battle was fought at Wood Lake on September 23, 1862, and the subsequent surrender of the Dakotas and release of the 269 prisoners at Camp Release three days later marked the European-Americans' victory in the United States–Dakota War of 1862. It also marked the beginning of a war of extermination against the Sioux and their forced removal.

In September 1862, Governor Ramsey had declared, "The Sioux Indians of Minnesota must be exterminated or driven forever beyond the borders of the State." Once the war was quashed, Ramsey was free to implement his plan with the support of his angry citizenry, who were well aware that unhindered access to Dakota lands would be their final reward.

When the war ended, the Dakota could either flee or surrender. Those who fled made their way into Dakota Territory or northward into Canada. The 2,000 who eventually surrendered did so believing they would be treated humanely as prisoners of war, but they were wrong. The men were immediately separated from the women and children, shackled, and tried for war crimes. In a makeshift military tribunal, as many as forty-two cases were tried in a single day, some taking as few as five minutes. When the tribunal finished conducting the 392 trials on November 5, 307 Dakota men were sentenced to hanging and sixteen were sentenced to prison. In spite of their rulings, Sibley realized an executive order would be required before the sentences could be carried out and so the trial records were sent to Washington for President Abraham Lincoln's review. At 10 a.m, on December 26, 1862, thirty-eight Dakota men were hanged in the largest mass execution in U.S. history. Those with commuted death sentences were sent the following spring to Davenport, Iowa, where they were imprisoned for three years. By the time they were released in 1886, 120 men, or one-third of their population, had died.

The women and children who surrendered were treated similarly. On November 7, 1862, they were force-marched in a four-mile-long procession over 150 miles to a concentration camp erected at Fort Snelling. An unrecorded number of Dakotas died along the way and hundreds more during the winter of 1862–1863 at Fort Snelling. While roughly 1,600 arrived at the fort on November 13, by the time they left the concentration camp the following spring, only 1,300 were counted. They boarded boats

that were sent down the Mississippi River to St. Louis, then up the Missouri River to the newly created Crow Creek Reservation in South Dakota. In spite of these already harsh actions, to be certain the Dakota population would be eradicated from the state, Governor Ramsey instituted a bounty on Dakota scalps. Beginning at $25 and eventually reaching $200, the bounties offered enough, at the time, for a European-American immigrant to establish a small farm. Within this context, Little Crow, the leader of Dakota resistance in 1862, was killed while picking raspberries with his son in the summer of 1863 near Hutchinson, Minnesota. At the close of the war, Little Crow had fled with other members of his family, but he returned briefly in 1863 and was shot by an immigrant father and his son. The younger Chauncey Lamson received the bounty for Little Crow's scalp, and his father, Nathan Lamson, received a $500 reward for killing the Dakota leader of the war.

Ironically, the delayed gold payment that contributed to the start of the war was sent back to Washington and then redistributed later to European-American immigrants for depredations suffered during the war (totaling $1,370,374 in 1863–1864). After the war, the eastern Dakota treaties were unilaterally abrogated by the U.S. government, the Dakota people were exiled from their homeland, and their lands were opened for immigration. Approximately twenty-five years later, small numbers of Dakota began returning to Minnesota and eventually resettled on four tiny southern Minnesota reservations. The majority of Dakota remain in exile as the devastating consequences of the war have carried into the twenty-first century. While the war remains a painful topic for some non-Natives in Minnesota, they continue to benefit from the Dakota expulsion. On a broader scale, the United States–Dakota War of 1862 epitomizes the process of invasion, conquest, and colonization that characterizes the American government's actions against much of its indigenous population.

Waziyatawin Angela Wilson

See also Battle of the Little Bighorn; Dakota; Wounded Knee, South Dakota, Massacre at.

References and Further Reading

Brown, Dee. 1970. *Bury My Heart at Wounded Knee.* New York: Holt, Rinehartand Winston.
Weeks, Philip. 1990. *Farewell, My Nation: The American Indian and the United States, 1820–1890.* Wheeling, IL: Harlan Davidson.

Long Walk (Navajo)

The Long Walk of the Navajos is the most intensely traumatic experience in Navajo history. An estimated 8,000 Navajos were starved into submission by a prolonged scorched-earth campaign led by Colonel Kit Carson of the New Mexico Volunteers in 1863 and 1864 and then forced to walk several hundred miles to a forty-square-mile reservation on the Texas–New Mexico border that had been established for them and a few hundred Mescalero Apaches. There the Navajos were held captive under starvation conditions until 1868, when they signed a treaty and were allowed to walk back to their homeland, Dinetah.

For centuries, the Navajos were in intermittent conflict with the Spanish in New Mexico as well as with the Pueblos, Utes, and other Indians in the Southwest. In this they were very successful, gaining the title of the Lords of New Mexico. After the United States gained control of New Mexico territory (which then included what is now Arizona) in 1846 from Mexico, sporadic warfare with the Navajo continued, with occasional efforts at maintaining peace. Navajo headmen agreed to make peace, but the Navajos had no unified leadership, and a peace agreed to by one or more groups was not seen as binding by other Navajo-speaking groups. New Mexico colonists found profit by raiding Navajos for livestock and captives to serve as slaves. Navajos retaliated to recover their stolen wives, children, and livestock. Despite laws against slavery, it is estimated that in 1860 there were 5,000 Navajo slaves in New Mexico.

During the Civil War (1861–1865), the U.S. government sought to end the rebellious behavior of the Navajos through a large and prolonged military operation under the direction of General James Carleton. Carleton also hoped that gold and silver might be found on Navajo lands. Luckily for the Navajo, none was found, as it was in the Black Hills in 1874.

As happened elsewhere in the West, troops were initially sent eastward to fight in the Civil War, leading to a resurgence of raiding. Navajos' homes and crops had been destroyed in an all-out war in 1860. Following the withdrawal of troops who had been deployed to enforce the peace, Navajos were beset by raiding Utes, Pueblos, and New Mexicans. As soon as the threat from Texas was ended by John M. Chivington's victory at Glorietta Pass in 1862, the New Mexico Volunteers turned their attention to the Navajos.

Over time, the U.S. military learned from fighting Navajos that only a prolonged campaign against them had any chance of success. Carleton ordered Colonel Kit Carson, an experienced "Indian fighter" who resigned as Ute Indian Agent and enlisted in the New Mexico volunteers in 1861 at the beginning of the Civil War, to lead an army in the field. Carson first fought an invading Confederate army from Texas and then was ordered to move against the Navajos with 261 soldiers, a number that eventually reached 736, the largest military operation ever waged against the Navajos. Carson was a somewhat reluctant commander, having enlisted to fight the Confederacy and wishing to be with his wife in Taos, New Mexico. While known as an Indian fighter, Carson wrote a very critical letter in 1866 regarding Chivington's massacre of Cheyennes at Sand Creek in 1864 that included the killing of many women and children.

Carleton's goal was to end Navajo raiding once and for all. He ordered the building of Fort Sumner at Bosque Redondo on the New Mexico–Texas border, where he idealistically thought that Navajos under the watchful gaze of the Army would become Christians, be civilized, and settle down as peaceful farmers.

Helped by Ute and Pueblo allies, Carson started a scorched-earth campaign in the summer of 1863 to starve the Navajos into submission, using Navajo crops to feed his men and horses. Unlike previous campaigns, Carson kept his troops in the field throughout the winter, harassing the Navajos in their camps. He rebuilt Fort Defiance in Arizona and renamed it Fort Canby in the middle of Dinetah (the Navajo country). He then used it as a staging point for repeated raids that continued throughout the winter and into the following summer and that destroyed Navajo crops and captured, killed, or scattered their sheep, goats, cattle, and horses.

The Navajos were escorted to Fort Sumner in as many as fifty-three groups between 1863 and 1866. Navajos were gathered at Fort Canby, then moved about fifty miles to Fort Wingate (just east of present-day Gallup, New Mexico), After that, they took part in the Long Walk of 250 miles to Bosque Redondo during the spring of 1864.

Navajo oral history tells of the weak and young who could not keep up being taken behind hills and shot. Some drowned crossing the Rio Grande. Hundreds died en route, while several thousand took refuge in the extreme west and northwest of the Navajo homeland (Dinetah) and avoided the Long Walk altogether. One of the leading Navajo headmen, Barboncito, did not surrender till 1864, fled Bosque Redondo in 1865, and surrendered again in 1866. Another prominent leader, Manuelito, remained free even longer, but, harassed by Utes and Hopis and with his followers starving, he surrendered on September 1, 1866.

On the reservation at Bosque Redondo, the Navajos and several hundred Mescalero Apaches were expected to take up farming and thousands of acres were planted, but the alkali soil, insects, and drought-ridden, harsh weather led to repeated crop failures and starvation. The lack of timber in the area also made it difficult to build shelters and keep warm in the winter. Comanche raids became more frequent, averaging one a week, in the spring of 1866, and government corruption in providing rations added to the misery of the Navajos.

Carleton had not realized how many Navajos had been forced to march, and his plans were inadequate to properly care for the thousands his troops captured. The Navajos who had the strength and supplies fled in the summer of 1865, even as those remaining behind were allowed arms to defend themselves from Comanche raids and to hunt. Game was scarce, however. That summer the Doolittle Joint Special Committee of Congress visited and found disease and malnutrition. In September 1866 the Long Walk's architect, General Carleton, was transferred, and the experiment of relocating the Navajos to Bosque Redondo was recognized as a failure. In 1867, authority over Navajos shifted from the War Department to the Indian Bureau.

Many Navajos died of malnutrition and sickness at Bosque Redondo, and in April 1868 Navajo leaders went to Washington, DC, asking President Andrew Johnson to allow them to return to their homeland. Investigators from Washington backed up Navajo complaints, and General William T. Sherman and Colonel S. F. Tappan were sent to negotiate a treaty. Sherman wanted to send the Navajos farther east to Indian Territory (now Oklahoma), but the Navajos were adamantly opposed. Barboncito, a Navajo leader declared at the treaty negotiation, "Our grandfathers had no idea of living in any other country except our own. . . . When the Navajos were first created, four mountains and four rivers were pointed out to us, inside which we should live, that was to be our country, and was given to us by the first woman of the Navajo tribe" (Iverson, 2002, 63).

Treaty negotiations began on May 28, and a treaty was signed on June 1, 1868, allowing the surviving Navajos with their remaining horses, mules, and sheep to walk home in a ten-mile-long column with their children in wagons. The treaty, patterned after other Indian treaties of the time, called for the end of all warfare, the compulsory schooling for Navajo children, and the provision of farm implements to heads of families willing to take 160 acres of land for raising crops. On July 6, 1868, the column of returning Navajos crossed the Rio Grande, and they were again in Dinetah, never to leave again.

The captivity at Bosque Redondo helped unite the Navajos and convinced them of the overwhelming might of the U.S. government, ending the chronic raids that had characterized the previous centuries. The distribution of rations at Fort Defiance until 1879 and the continued presence of troops helped keep the peace.

Jon Reyhner

See also Carson, Christopher "Kit"; Sand Creek
    Massacre.
References and Further Reading
Ackerly, Neal W. 1988. "A Navajo Diaspora: The
    Long Walk to Hwéeldi." Available at:
    *http://Members.tripod.com/bloodhound/longwalk.ht
    m.* Accessed April 25, 2005.
Bailey, Lynn R. 1988. *The Long Walk: A History of the
    Navajo Wars, 1846–68.* Tucson, AZ: Westernlore
    Press.
Bial, Raymond. 2003. *The Long Walk: The Story of
    Navajo Captivity.* New York: Benchmark Books.
Roberts, David. 1997. "The Long Walk to Bosque
    Redondo." *Smithsonian* 28, no. 9: 46–52, 54,
    56–57.
Roessel, Ruth, ed. 1973. *Navajo Stories of the Long
    Walk Period.* Tsaile, AZ: Navajo Community
    College Press.
Thompson, Gerald. 1976. *The Army and the Navajo:
    The Bosque Redondo Reservation Experiment,
    1863–1868.* Tucson, AZ: University of Arizona
    Press.
Trafzer, Clifford E. 1982. *The Kit Carson Campaign:
    The Last Great Navajo War.* Norman: University
    of Oklahoma Press.

Sand Creek Massacre

Located in southeastern Colorado, fifty miles from present-day Lamar, Sand Creek was the site of a deliberate and unprovoked attack on peaceful southern Cheyenne and Arapaho Indians by Col-

orado volunteers. This attack became known as the Sand Creek Massacre. In a little over an hour, 143 Indians lay dead, many of their bodies mutilated for souvenirs.

Included in the land guaranteed to the Cheyennes and the Arapahos in Article V of the Fort Laramie Treaty of 1851 was eastern Colorado from its border with Kansas and Nebraska westward to the Rocky Mountains and south to the Arkansas River. However, the discovery of gold at the confluence of the South Platte River and Cherry Creek drew a multitude of prospective miners into Cheyenne territory during the latter half of the 1850s. New trails transversed Cheyenne hunting grounds, opening the way for immigrants, who constructed settlements and towns on land promised to the Indians. Soon the buffalo and other wildlife grew scarce. Tensions mounted as hunger and disease spread through Indian bands.

The U.S. government sought to relieve the friction by further reducing Indian land. Believing obstinacy and delay would result in a less favorable settlement, Cheyenne leaders Black Kettle and White Antelope, along with an Arapaho delegation led by Little Raven and Left Hand, met with government agents on February 8, 1861, and placed their X on the Treaty of Fort Wise. The document ceded to the United States the vast territory granted to the Indians in the 1851 Fort Laramie agreement in exchange for annuity payments and a small reservation of 600 square miles in southeastern Colorado between the Big Sandy and the Arkansas River. The treaty establishing the so-called Sand Creek Reservation was never approved by Cheyenne and Arapaho leaders, who were not present at the signing.

The Sand Creek Reservation was unable to sustain the Indians who were compelled to live there. Unsuitable for agriculture, the desolate, gameless terrain proved to be a breeding ground for epidemic diseases. With the nearest buffalo herd over 200 miles away, young Cheyenne men left the reservation in search of food. Raids on livestock and passing wagon trains became more and more frequent. Between 1861 and 1864, sporadic violence spread across eastern Colorado and the plains of Kansas and Nebraska, as men from Cheyenne and Arapaho bands clashed with soldiers and volunteer militia units. Fear and panic swept through white homesteaders, who were fully aware of the incidents associated with the Dakota uprising of 1862, which resulted in the largest mass hanging in U.S. history at Mankato, Minnesota.

A telegram to Colonel John M. Chivington, dated July 18, 1864, requesting more troops to combat Native Americans along an overland route in the Colorado Territory. On November 29, 1864, Chivington led the Third Colorado Volunteers to the peaceful camp of Cheyenne Chief Black Kettle along Sand Creek outside Fort Lyon. Despite the American flag and the white flag flown above Black Kettle's teepee, troops charged the village and killed more than 200 men, women, and children. (Corbis)

In June 1864, John Evans, who became the second governor of Colorado Territory two years earlier, issued a proclamation inviting all "friendly Indians" to certain designated forts where they would be fed and allowed to camp under the protection of the military. Those Indians who chose not to comply with this directive would be considered hostile and subject to punitive raids. With most of the territory's regular troops away fighting Confederates, Evans called for civilians to join the Third Colorado Cavalry for 100 days to carry out his plan, stressing that "Any man who kills a hostile Indian is a patriot . . . and no one has been or will be restrained from this" (Hughes, 1977, 59).

The commander of the Colorado volunteers was Colonel John M. Chivington, a forty-three-year old Methodist minister-turned-soldier-turned-politician. In 1862, Chivington replaced his clerical attire with a major's uniform in the Colorado Volunteer Regiment and won acclaim for his role in defeating Confederate troops at the Battle of Glorietta Pass in eastern New Mexico. Now he was to lead an expedition against the Indians, "fully satisfied . . . that to kill them is the only way we will ever have peace and quiet in Colorado."

Black Kettle and six other chiefs decided to accept the governor's invitation and traveled with Major Edward Wynkoop, the commander of Fort Lyon, to Denver to meet with Evans and Chivington. Meeting at Camp Weld on September 28, the Indians were told to submit to military authority as represented by the garrison at Fort Lyon. Black Kettle believed that he had secured peace and safety for his band and others. Unknown to the Indians, Chivington received an order that same day from Major General Samuel R. Curtis, commanding officer of the Department of Kansas, instructing him not to make peace with the Indians. Chivington readily assented to this, with the blessing of Governor Evans.

On November 4, 1864, Major Wynkoop was relieved of command of Fort Lyon, owing to his benevolent dealings with Black Kettle, Left Hand, and Little Raven. His replacement was Major Scott Anthony, who proceeded to disperse the Indians, sending them away from the fort and north to Sand Creek. Chivington, meanwhile, moved his column of nearly 600 men down the Arkansas River toward Fort Lyon, arriving at the post on November 28. The enlistment of his hundred-day volunteers was about to expire, and the men were already disappointed at having never experienced a battle. Chivington, as well, had been ridiculed in the press for his inactivity. Accompanied by 125 men under Major Anthony and four mountain howitzers, the volunteers started out for Black Kettle's camp at 8 p.m. that evening. Having covered the forty miles to the village that night, Chivington's men were in position to attack as dawn broke on November 29.

Black Kettle's camp along Sand Creek was composed of approximately 450 southern Cheyenne and forty Arapaho, split into separate groups of lodges, each headed by a chief. Although a few women were up starting fires for cooking, most of the village was still asleep when the volunteers struck. Major Anthony drove away the herd of ponies and then approached the village from the west. Three companies of the First Colorado crossed the mostly dry creek bed and attacked from the east and north, while the Third Colorado Cavalry under Colonel George L. Shoup charged straight into the center of the encampment. Cheyenne oral history is replete with accounts of confusion and chaos as the Colorado volunteers swept through the village firing indiscriminately into the lodges. The mountain howitzers positioned on the south bank of the creek began to rain grapeshot down on the fleeing Indians. Black Kettle and others were in a state of disbelief over what was happening. The Cheyenne chief tied an American flag that he received in Denver along with a white flag of truce to one of his lodgepoles in an unsuccessful effort to halt the slaughter. Black Kettle, along with Left Hand, was left with no choice but to try and escape with his life. White Antelope chose to remain and face death and was shot in front of his lodge.

The bloodletting continued as Chivington's men chased the remaining Cheyenne and Arapaho for miles up Sand Creek, overtaking and killing as many men, women, and children as they could find. Some of the refugees, including Black Kettle, managed to escape by digging into the sandy soil or hiding under the embankments of the creek. Returning to the village, the Colorado volunteers proceeded to kill all the remaining wounded and mutilate the bodies of the dead—taking scalps, ring fingers, ears, and even genitalia for souvenirs. Chivington did nothing to halt the carnage. On December 1, the remains of the village and its inhabitants were set on fire and the Colorado volunteers left the area bound for Denver. Chivington's casualties at Sand Creek were nine killed and thirty-eight wounded. The Cheyenne and Arapaho dead numbered 148—only sixty were men.

At first, Chivington and his volunteers were wildly praised and rewarded for their actions, as celebrations filled the streets. Soon, however, rumors and testimonials about what really happened at Sand Creek convinced the U.S. Congress to order a formal investigation. Never formally punished for his actions, Chivington nevertheless resigned and withdrew from political life. Black Kettle, having miraculously escaped the carnage, returned to his efforts for peace on the Plains. On October 14, 1865, Cheyenne and Arapaho representatives agreed to a treaty giving up the Sand Creek Reservation in Colorado in exchange for a reservation in southwestern Kansas and Indian Territory.

A 12,000-acre Sand Creek Massacre National Historic Site was dedicated by the National Park Service April 28, 2007.

Alan C. Downs

See also Black Kettle; Fort Laramie Treaty of 1851; Great Sioux Uprising.
References and Further Reading
Hughes, J. Donald. 1977. *American Indians in Colorado*, Boulder, CO: Pruett Publishing.
Josephy, Alvin M. 1991. *The Civil War in the American West*. New York: Alfred A. Knopf.

Alaska, United States Purchase of

Although Europeans had been exploring the coastline of Alaska since the early 1700s, the Russians were the first to establish colonies there. Whereas Russia was the first to colonize Alaska and exploit its vast fur resources, much of the credit for the mapping and naming of places along the extensive coastline goes to the rival countries of Spain and Great Britain. Both countries were busily looking for a fabled Northwest Passage by painstakingly investigating and charting every inlet in southeast and south central Alaska.

The competing powers agreed, at the Nootka Sound Convention in 1790, that colonization had to follow exploration in order for any nation to support a claim of ownership over a new land (Borneman, 2003, 44–45). By that criterion, Russia had beaten its

The Alaska Treaty of Cessation was signed after its negotiation by U.S. Secretary of State William H. Seward, allowing for the U.S. purchase of Alaska from Russia in 1867. (Bettmann/Corbis)

rivals because the Russian American Company had established a fur trading post on Kodiak Island by 1784, the first permanent European settlement in Alaska, as well as others on Yakutat Bay and at Sitka Sound on the Baranof Islands within the ensuing ten years (Borneman, 2003, 61–65).

In 1812, John Jacob Astor of the American Fur Company established a headquarters at the mouth of the Columbia River and proposed that a borderline between Russian America and Oregon Territory be established at 55 degrees north latitude as a boundary for exclusive trade with the Tlingits (Borneman, 2003, 68–69). This boundary was moved in an edict by Czar Alexander I in 1821, to the fifty-first parallel with an offshore boundary of one 100 miles, into which foreign trade or trespass was forbidden. This infuriated the Americans and their British neighbors in Canada, but the czar had made his decision.

In 1823, U.S. President James Monroe stated his position on European powers in the Americas—later called the Monroe Doctrine. The first clause forbade further colonization, and the second, later to become the more famous, forbade European intervention in Latin American independence movements. The first clause was purposely directed at Russia's North American ambitions. In 1824, Alexander found his colonies starving without the trade in food goods from the British and Americans and modified his earlier position by moving the southern boundary of Russian America to 54 degrees 40 minutes north, restoring the three-mile offshore limit, and resuming all trade (Borneman, 2003, 79–80).

When Alexander I renewed the Russian American Company's charter in 1841, he insisted that the company assist in the spread of the Russian Orthodox religion by aiding the works of Bishop Innocent, who had been busy converting Native peoples from the Aleutians all the way to Sitka in the Alaska panhandle. Thus, the Russian Orthodox church became a major influence in Alaska, a position it retains today (Borneman, 2003, 77–78).

Russian fur traders had been steadily depleting the areas in which they operated of the animals on which they depended. Having failed to diversify, the Russians found themselves holding a grand expanse

of territory now devoid of the animal resources they needed to extract profit. In 1854, Russia was at war with Great Britain over the Black Sea. To Russia, the logical, more probable buyer of Alaska was the United States, but the Americans were on the brink of their own civil war, so for the meantime Russia was left nervously holding the bag. The Monroe Doctrine did, however, prevent the British from taking possession of any Russian interests for the time being (Borneman, 2003, 85–86).

Baron Edouard de Stoeckl, the Russian minister to the United States, and U.S. Secretary of State William H. Seward met in March and a deal was negotiated for $7 million (plus $200,000 to finalize the arrangements of the deal). Some technicalities remained, such as the exact boundaries, what to call this land in the treaty documents (Alaska was selected from the name given the Alaskan Peninsula—an Aleut word meaning "great land"), and how to pay for the transaction.

The purchase had been approved as a treaty in the Senate, but it had not passed the House of Representatives as a bill of appropriations. Eventually all of these details were worked out, leaving only one other consideration—how to deal with Alaska's entry into the Union. There was no such assurance of citizenship given Alaska as had been guaranteed in the Louisiana Purchase, the Mexican and Florida Cessions, or the Gadsden Purchase. Neglecting to resolve these problems at the time of the purchase left Alaska and its Native population in a precarious position for most of the next century (Borneman, 2003, 107–109).

The final treaty to buy Alaska was approved on April 9, 1867, with a Senate vote of 37–2. The House finally approved the payment, and the transfer from Russian to American ownership took place on October 18, 1867, in Sitka (Borneman, 2003, 109–111).

Daniel R. Gibbs

See also Russians, in the Arctic/Northwest.

References and Further Readings

Borneman, Walter R. 2003. *Alaska: Saga of a Bold Land.* New York: HarperCollins.

McClanahan, Alexander J., and Hallie L. Bissett. 2002. *Na'eda: Our Friends.* Anchorage, AK: CIRI Foundation.

Baptist Church

Rooted in the formal sacred rites of admitting a person into the Christian Church by way of total immersion in water, the Baptist Church is one of the world's largest Christian fellowships with more than 35 million members worldwide (Livingstone, 1997, 150). The church has made a significant impact on Indian Country, especially in the American South and Southwest. Evolving from the known custom of submerging Jewish converts during the time of John the Baptist and from the words of Jesus Christ, who refers to the practice in Matt. 29:19 and Jn. 3:5, the modern Baptist Church's origins lie with John Smyth, an English minister who separated from the state church of England and emigrated to Holland, where the first Baptist Church began in 1609 with baptism representing a shared faith by the congregation. Subsequently, some of Smyth's congregation began the first Baptist Church after returning to England in 1612 (Livingstone, 1997, 154).

Founded in Providence, Rhode Island, in 1639, the first Baptist congregation in North America preceded significant growth during the Great Awakening throughout the middle Atlantic colonies in the seventeenth and eighteenth centuries (Fahlbusch, 1999, 197). By the nineteenth century, Baptist missionaries began moving into the American South and West, evangelizing to rural Southerners. In 1817, the Baptist General Convention started the process of converting American Indians, turning over the work to the Missionary Union from 1846 to 1865, when the responsibility transferred to the American Baptist Home Mission Society. Peoples impacted by the missions included the Pottawatomis and Miamis (1817), Cherokees (1818), Ottawas (1822), Muscogees (Creek) (1823), Oneidas, Tonawandas and Tuscaroras (1824), Choctaws (1826), Ojibwas (1828), Shawnees (1831), Otoes (1833), Omahas (1833), Delawares and Stockbridges (1833), and Kickapoos (1834) (Armitage, 1890). None of the tribes was more affected than those who were removed from the southeastern United States, such as the Cherokees, Muscogees (Creek), Choctaws, Chickasaws, and Seminoles, to Indian Territory, which eventually became the state of Oklahoma. By 1851, the Muscogee Baptist Association was formed and began its own missions to western Oklahoma peoples, such as the Wichitas and Kiowas. By the beginning of the twentieth century, a Baptist mission existed within the tribal areas of practically every people in Oklahoma, such as the Osages, Pawnees, Comanches, Cheyennes, Arapahos, Caddos, Apaches, and Delawares. Moving west, by the 1950s Baptist missions established themselves in New Mexico among the Mescalero Apache, Navajo

(Dine), and Pueblo peoples such as the Santa Claras, Taos, and Picuris, as well as the Jicarilla Apaches in northern New Mexico (Belvin, 1955, 67–76). Further entrenchment by the Baptists also occurred in the 1950s among the tribes of Arizona, such as the Navajos, Maricopas, White River Apaches, Pimas, and Papagos, as well as in southern Utah (Belvin, 1955, 93–99).

Even though Baptists were making inroads into tribal areas of the southwestern United States, by 1955, 75 percent of American Indians in the Southern Baptist Convention were in Oklahoma (Belvin, 1955, 17). That legacy represents the impact on the Southeastern tribes of the encroaching American society into traditional tribal homelands during the late eighteenth and early nineteenth centuries, and a primary tenet of most of that encroachment was to "civilize," meaning Christianize, the Native peoples of the region. Subsequently, during the removal period of the 1830s when tribal people were rounded up and forced to Indian Territory, Baptist Christianity came with them, then proceeded west under the impetus of missionaries. By the beginning of the twentieth century, Baptist churches operated by and for American Indians could be found from Virginia and Texas to Montana and California.

Hugh W. Foley, Jr.

See also Trail of Tears.

References and Further Reading

Armitage, Thomas. 1890. *A History of the Baptists.* New York: Bryan, Taylor, & Co. Electronic edition available at: http://www.fbinstitute.com/armitage/. Accessed May 25, 2005.

Belvin, B. Frank. 1955. *The Tribes Go Up: A Study of the American Indian.* Atlanta, GA: Home Mission Board.

Fahlbusch, Erwin, ed. 1999. "Baptists." In *The Encyclopedia of Christianity.* English translation. Grand Rapids, MI: Wm. B. Eerdmans Publishing Company and Koninklijke Brill NV.

Livingstone, E. A., ed. 1997. "Baptism." In *The Oxford Dictionary of the Christian Church,* 3rd ed. New York: Oxford University Press.

Washita Massacre

Located in western Oklahoma, two miles from present-day Cheyenne, a tranquil bend in the Washita River was the site of a surprise wintertime attack in 1868 by the U.S. Seventh Cavalry under the command of Lieutenant Colonel George Armstrong Custer on Chief Black Kettle's peaceful band of southern Cheyenne Indians. Black Kettle, a survivor of the Sand Creek Massacre four years earlier, died along with his wife and 101 other men, women, and children.

Custer's attack was the result of the U.S. Army's evolving strategy for imposing the government's reservation policy on noncompliant Indians of the Great Plains. In October 1867, peace commissioners from the United States government met with representatives of the Arapahos, Comanches, Kiowas, Prairie Apaches, and southern Cheyennes in a grove of trees along Medicine Lodge Creek, sixty miles south of Fort Larned, Kansas. There, the principal Native peoples of the southern Plains signed treaties promising to move onto two reservations in western Indian Territory and to take no action to impede the construction of nearby railroads, wagon roads, and government facilities. In exchange for their compliance, signatory tribes were promised agricultural implements, clothing, education for their children, annuity payments, and the prohibition of white settlement on reservation land.

Of the five nations represented at the Medicine Lodge council, the southern Cheyennes were the least united in support of the treaty. Black Kettle was reluctant to sign the document until the militant Cheyenne Dog Soldiers agreed to its terms. Unable to convince War Chief Roman Nose and his band of the merits of peace under the terms of the treaty, Black Kettle nevertheless affixed his mark to the paper. Despite the lack of a unified following, the Cheyenne chief settled peaceably into reservation life below the Arkansas River.

Throughout the winter of 1867–1868, food stores from the autumn buffalo hunts sustained the reservation Cheyennes. As spring approached and supplies dwindled, the promised government support materialized in insufficient quantities. Most disconcerting for the Cheyennes was the absence of the promised guns and ammunition needed for hunting. Notwithstanding the best efforts of Agent Edward W. Wynkoop to reassure the disaffected, some young Cheyenne men, angered by the duplicity of the white peace commissioners, ventured northward away from the reservation to join Roman Nose and the leaders of other resistant factions.

In response to the growing defiance of the government's reservation policy among Native peoples on the southern Plains, Major General Philip Henry Sheridan, commander of the Department of the Missouri (with the support of Lieutenant General

General George A. Custer's Seventh Cavalry raids the Cheyenne encampment along the Washita River. (Library of Congress)

William Tecumseh Sherman), orchestrated a strategy to force submission. Sheridan envisioned a winter operation utilizing converging columns of cavalry and infantry to round up warriors whose limited supplies and grass-fed ponies would make them virtually immobile and susceptible to capture. Accordingly, on November 18, 1868, Major Andrew W. Evans left Fort Bascom, New Mexico, with 563 men and marched eastward down the South Canadian River. Two weeks later, Brevet Major General Eugene Asa Carr and 650 men left Fort Lyon, Colorado, and moved southward (guided by "Buffalo Bill" Cody) toward Antelope Hills in Indian Territory. The third and largest column, comprising the 800 troopers of the Seventh U.S. Cavalry under the command of Lieutenant Colonel George Armstrong Custer, left Camp Supply, a depot on the North Canadian River 100 miles south of Fort Dodge, Kansas, on Novem-

ber 23 and headed south toward the Washita River. Sheridan placed Custer in overall command of his column and instructed the lieutenant colonel to follow a fresh trail in the snow, suspecting its creators to be a Cheyenne raiding party returning from Kansas.

That same autumn, as Sheridan put the finishing touches on his planned winter campaign, Black Kettle and his followers set up an encampment on a bend in the Washita River, forty miles east of the Antelope Hills. Consisting of fifty-one lodges, the village was populated by Cheyenne women, children, and elders as well as recently returned young warriors who were now more willing to accept the peaceful ways of Black Kettle after Roman Nose's death on September 17 at the Battle of Beecher's Island. Downriver, Arapaho, Kiowa, and additional Cheyenne camps dotted the landscape. Learning

that U.S. troops were on the move, Black Kettle and other Cheyenne and Arapaho leaders traveled 100 miles down the Washita River Valley to Fort Cobb to meet with the garrison's commander, General William Babcock Hazen, to seek protection for their people. To their dismay, the heretofore convivial Hazen maintained he lacked the authority to allow the Cheyenne and Arapaho bands to move closer to the fort and instructed Black Kettle to return to his camp.

On November 26, Custer's undetected column drew near the bend in the Washita River occupied by the Cheyenne chief and his band. The trail they had followed led directly to the encampment. Without bothering to determine adequately the size and strength of his foe, the lieutenant colonel ordered an attack for the following day. Just before daybreak on November 27, troopers from the Seventh Cavalry, with the regimental band playing "Garry Owen," charged into Black Kettle's sleeping village from four directions. The shaken and surprised Cheyenne could do nothing except run for safety. A few warriors vainly fought back. Black Kettle and his wife attempted to escape across a ford in the river, only to be gunned down in the mud. Within ten minutes, the Seventh Cavalry controlled the village. Estimates vary, but it is probable that 103 Cheyenne men, women, and children died in the attack, while fifty-three women and children were taken captive. For his part, Custer lost two officers and nineteen enlisted men, most of whom were under the command of Major Joel H. Elliott. Attempting to corral a group of Indians fleeing downriver, Elliot and his men were themselves surrounded and killed by members of the nearby Arapaho and Cheyenne camps who were coming to Black Kettle's aid.

As more and more mounted warriors arrived to overlook the scene, Custer's troopers set up a defensive perimeter and then systematically set fire to the lodges, destroying the winter supply of food and clothing. The cavalry likewise slaughtered more than 800 Cheyenne ponies and mules. To remove his command from an increasingly foreboding environment, Custer abandoned efforts to locate Major Elliott, feigned an attack in the late afternoon against Indian encampments further downriver, then escaped back across the river after dark. The Seventh Cavalry returned triumphantly to Camp Supply on December 2, much to the satisfaction of General Sheridan.

More of a massacre than a battle, Washita proved to be a debilitating blow to the southern Cheyenne. With their winter supplies destroyed

along with their herd of mules and ponies, the majority of the Cheyenne bands found themselves with little choice but to succumb to reservation life. Perhaps of equal consequence, Washita demonstrated to the noncompliant Indians of the Plains that winter no longer provided the element of security it once had.

Alan C. Downs

See also Black Kettle; Sand Creek Massacre: Report of the Joint Committee on the Conduct of the War.

References and Further Reading

Greene, Jerome A. 2004. *Washita: The U.S. Army and the Southern Cheyennes, 1867–1869.* Norman: University of Oklahoma Press.

Utley, Robert M. 1973. *Frontier Regulars: The United States Army and the Indian, 1866–1891.* Lincoln: University of Nebraska Press.

Grant's Peace Policy

At the time Ulysses S. Grant became president of the United States in 1868, approximately 250,000 American Indians all across the nation were under the jurisdiction of a federal Indian policy. Within the Department of the Interior, the Bureau of Indian Affairs was officially responsible for implementing relations with the Native peoples, but the agency had become a dumping ground for the party faithful and "a morass of corruption and inefficiency" (Utley, 1953, 123). Disgusted, reformers and policy makers called for a change that would result in positive accomplishments, such as civilizing American Indians through education, Christianity, and teaching methods of self-support. Not to be overlooked was the immediate need to reform the Indian Bureau. This "new" and untried approach to managing America's Indian peoples actually had another purpose as well: containing Indians for the benefit of non-Indians by removing obstacles to European-American settlements all across former Indian lands.

One year earlier, in response to continuing hostilities with Indians on the Plains, the government had created a Peace Commission, comprised of ten outstanding citizens who were "high minded Christian philanthropists" (Beaver, 1966, Ch. 4) and volunteers serving their country by monitoring, in conjunction with the Secretary of the Interior, congressional appropriations to ensure that (1) Indians would be placed on reservations, keeping them away from contact with the immigrants, teaching them how to be farmers, and exposing them to the

A delegation of Native Americans arrive in Washington, DC, to meet with the commissioner of Indian Affairs and are greeted by members of the Grant administration. Grant's Peace Policy was acclaimed for its defense of Native Americans and its opposition to corruption in the Bureau of Indian Affairs, but it was also designed to isolate Native Americans on reservations, where federal agents and missionaries could work to "civilize" them. (Library of Congress)

aid of Christian organizations; (2) when necessary, Indians would be punished for misdeeds, which should demonstrate the efficacy of following the government's advice rather than continuing their traditional ways; (3) high-quality supplies would be furnished to reservations; (4) through religious organizations, high-quality agents would be recruited, who would fairly distribute goods and aid in uplifting the Indians; and (5) through Christian organizations, churches and schools would be provided, which would lead the Indians to appreciate Christianity and civilization and educate them to assume the duties and responsibilities of citizenship. Along with overseeing these provisions, one of the goals of this appointed body was to formally establish the reservations onto which all of the reluctant Native peoples would agree to be placed, receiving inducements such as education for the children, food, clothing, and instruction in agricultural techniques. Thus, the Peace Commission prepared the foundation of what would become known as Grant's Peace Policy.

A major hallmark of the Peace Policy was a desire to abandon the old treaty system, a patroniz-

ing arrangement that had never worked well and that had caused, at best, innumerable frustrations and disagreements among the Indian nations. At worst, open warfare had resulted with continuing consequences for both the Native peoples and the government. Less than fifty years earlier, similar Mexican policies dealing with that country's Native populations had not succeeded on the colonial frontier, a fact Grant must have known but disregarded, relying instead on several assumptions: Christians would not succumb to temptations resulting in dishonesty; the churches could stop the terrible unscrupulousness; and the righteousness of the handpicked Protestant agents would produce peace among the Indians. Thus, a serious attempt to instill kindness and justice into official U.S. Indian policy was underway and represented an about-face from the failed military policy that emphasized force.

The United States in 1870 was a predominantly Christian nation, mainly Protestant, and many citizens believed that the government should assist religion to improve American society. Appointing churchmen as agents was first proposed to the president in 1869 by a delegation of Quakers. This action, the Friends thought, would raise politics and politicians to a respectable position once again and simultaneously ensure that the nation's indigenes would be well served. Grant favored the idea even though it was not an example of his religious beliefs; the president was only nominally Protestant (Methodist), had never been active in church affairs, and was baptized only on his deathbed.

Grant informed the nation about the change in his first annual message to Congress in December 1869, reporting that "[Quakers] are known for their opposition to all strife, violence, and war, and are generally known for their strict integrity and fair dealings. These considerations induced me to give the management of a few reservations to them and to throw the burden of the selection of agents upon the society itself" (Stockel, 2004, 108). Recalcitrant Indians—those who were not eager to comply—would still be treated as hostiles and disciplined accordingly.

The results of the new policy were initially impressive and in time caused church officials from Protestant sects other than Quakers to speak out and express their desire to participate; the process of selecting religious agents became more expansive. By 1872, "seventy-three agencies had been apportioned among the nation's principal denominations and good religious men set forth to elevate the Indians" (Utley, 1984, 133).

Most churchmen/agents of every belief were extremely dedicated to improving conditions among their Indian charges, but very little progress in relations between the government and Indian nations was noted between 1869 and 1871. Problems quickly appeared. The small salary was insufficient for many agents, and in some cases rapid turnover resulted. Married men brought their wives, many of whom, despite good intentions, learned they could not tolerate the seclusion and demanded a return to "civilization." Congress was not willing to appropriate the monies necessary to sustain the reservations during emergencies, such as the widespread disappearance of game. Political infighting resulted in supplies arriving late on the reservation or not at all. School funds were depleted. Agencies were in debt, and employees unpaid. Worse, incompetent and even corrupt churchmen slipped through the screen of the missionary associations, and the government ultimately became embroiled in religious strife.

Catholics, in charge of 17,856 Indians, felt discriminated against and outnumbered by Protestant agents, a fact that is substantiated by figures: Quakers administered 24,322 Indians; Baptists, 40,800; Presbyterians, 38,069; Methodists, 54,473; Dutch Reformed, 8,118; Congregationalists, 14,476; Episcopalians, 26,929; and other Protestant sects 13,856 (Prucha, 1990, 143). In 1874 the Catholic Church formed a lobbying bureau in Washington, DC, to fight for its fair share.

Conflicts also erupted between the Board of Indian Commissioners and the Department of the Interior over the board's authority, as well as between the churchmen/agents about who should control which reservations. Scandal after scandal ensued, involving the religious stewards in some of the same temptations that had seduced their predecessors: fraud, deception, and infighting for spoils. A movement began that threatened to transfer the Indian Bureau back into the War Department and that called upon the military to administer the reservations. Public confidence fell and the Peace Policy was discredited.

Eight years after it had begun, the policy collapsed. Despite its failure, Grant's Peace Policy had become one of the vehicles by which Indian peoples were pacified. The program also played a major role in redistributing the homelands of many indigenous peoples to Christian Americans who insisted their right to the land must prevail.

H. Henrietta Stockel

See also Bureau of Indian Affairs: Establishing the Existence of an Indian Tribe.
References and Further Reading
Beaver, R. Pierce. 1966. *Church, State, and the American Indians: Two and a Half Centuries of Partnership in Missions between Protestant Churches and Government.* St. Louis, MO: Concordia Publishing.
Prucha, F.P. 1990. *Documents of U.S. Indian Policy.* Lincoln: University of Nebraska Press.
Stockel, H. Henrietta. 2004. *On the Bloody Road to Jesus: Christianity and the Chiricahua Apaches.* Albuquerque: University of New Mexico Press.
Utley, Robert. 1953. "The Celebrated Peace Policy of General Grant." *North Dakota History* 20 (July): 121–142.
Utley, Robert. 1984. *The Indian Frontier of the American West, 1846–1890.* Albuquerque: University of New Mexico Press.

Camp Grant Massacre

On April 30, 1871, a confederacy of Anglo-Americans, Mexican-Americans, and Tohono O'odhams murdered more than 100 western Apaches, mostly unarmed children and women, who had surrendered to the U.S. Army at Camp Grant, just north of Tucson, Arizona. Another thirty or so children were taken captive. Later that winter, a local court charged the assailants with murder, but after a weeklong trial the jury pronounced a verdict of not guilty. Western Apache groups soon left their farms and gathering places near Tucson in fear of subsequent attacks. As pioneer families arrived and settled in the area, Apaches were never able to regain hold of their ancestral lands.

Following the Gadsden Purchase of 1854, American settlers began to enter the San Pedro Valley, the fertile land to the east of modern-day Tucson. However, western Apache groups like the Arivaipa and Pinal bands had control of the valley, as they had since at least the late 1700s. To protect pioneers and subdue Native populations who refused to submit to American authority, the government established military posts to strike directly into Apache communities. On May 8, 1860, the United States erected Fort Aravaypa at the confluence of the San Pedro River and Arivaipa Creek. In 1865 it was renamed Camp Grant in honor of Ulysses S. Grant.

On February 28, 1871, Lieutenant Royal E. Whitman, then in charge of Camp Grant, reported that a small group of elderly Apache women came to the post looking for several stolen children and hoping

to make a lasting peace with the government. Whitman encouraged the Apaches to come in, and soon dozens of Arivaipa and Pinal Apaches were encamped at the fort and receiving rations of corn, flour, beans, coffee, and meat. By late March, more than 400 Apaches had arrived, settling peacefully at a traditional site called *gashdla'á cho o'aa* ("Big Sycamore Stands There"), five miles from Camp Grant, up Arivaipa Creek.

Despite the amiable settlement at Camp Grant, Chiricahua Apaches continued raiding. While Apaches at Camp Grant almost certainly did not commit these depredations, residents in Tucson assumed they did. After the government refused pleas for protection, William Oury conspired with Jesus Maria Elías, two leading Tucsonans, to seek revenge on the Apaches near Camp Grant. The men recruited dozens of local residents and scores of Tohono O'odham warriors. On the afternoon of April 28, 1871, the group met in secrecy and was provided weapons and provisions by the adjutant general of Arizona, Samuel Hughes.

After nearly continuous travel, they arrived at Big Sycamore Stands There in the early morning hours of April 30, they attacked immediately, catching the Apaches off guard. The attack was over in half an hour. The murders were brutal—children were hacked apart, girls were raped. The army at Camp Grant did not hear the screams and gunshots because of the distance from the Apache settlement. When the attackers left, more than 100 Apaches were dead, nearly all women and children, and some thirty children were taken as captives. A half dozen of the children lived for a while with highly regarded Tucsonans, such as Leopoldo Carrillo and Francisco Romero, but were reluctantly returned to Apache relatives in 1872. The rest of the children were sold into slavery in Sonora for $100 each.

The group returned to a jubilant Tucson, while the reaction on the East Coast and even among military personnel was horror and disbelief. When local authorities did not press charges, President Ulysses S. Grant threatened to impose marshal law to prosecute those responsible. On October 23, 1871, a grand jury handed down 111 indictments, 108 for murder and three for misdemeanors, with Sidney R. DeLong as the lead defendant. A weeklong trial was held in December. The jury deliberated for nineteen minutes before announcing a verdict of not guilty.

After the massacre, the Apaches at Camp Grant dispersed throughout southern Arizona. They returned to the post in the spring of 1872 for peace talks and agreed to settle on the San Carlos River to the north. Although this pact did not relinquish Apache territory, Anglo-American and Mexican-American pioneers soon spread roots in the San Pedro Valley and made it their home. When Apaches later tried to return and settle in the San Pedro Valley during the 1880s, they were run off their traditional lands.

Chip Colwell-Chanthaphonh

See also Genocide; Warfare, Intertribal.
References and Further Reading
Arnold, Elliott. 1976. *The Camp Grant Massacre*. New York: Simon & Schuster.
Colwell-Chanthaphonh, Chip. 2003. "Western Apache Oral Histories and Traditions of the Camp Grant Massacre." *American Indian Quarterly* 27, nos. 3–4: 639–666.

Apache Wars

No formal declaration of hostilities signaled the beginning of the bloody Apache wars in the American West. Instead, two separate incidents, one in 1860 and one in 1861, caused a great deal of anguish on the part of the Mimbres and Chiricahua Apaches and sparked a decades-long resistance that came to be known by that name.

History reveals that in 1860 Mangas Coloradas —a tall, muscular, very strong, and well respected chief—lived with his Mimbres Apache followers in southern New Mexico (Sweeney, 1998, 7). The group's vast homelands ranged southward from forested mountains near the head of the Gila River, across deserts and valleys, into Mexico. In May of that year, prospectors discovered gold in the heart of Mimbres territory, causing an influx of more than 700 miners, a sight Mangas and his people never expected. In the spirit of friendship, the chief visited a mining camp and was immediately captured, bound, and whipped. A second offense occurred early in 1863 when Mangas became a prisoner of the military at the recently established Fort McLane. Two army privates, Jonn V. Mead and James Colyer, who were assigned to guard the chained Apache, taunted him by pressing hot bayonets to his feet. When he strenuously objected, they killed him. The Apaches considered both of these events to be intolerable and worthy of revenge.

Apache rancheria with two men holding rifles. Under the leadership of such able warriors as Mangas Coloradas, Cochise, and Geronimo, the Apache struck fear throughout the Southwest during the nineteenth century. (National Archives)

During the same period, Cochise—handsome, kindly, peaceful at heart, a natural leader, an honored chief, and Mangas's son-in-law—was the victim of similar depredations. Cochise ranged with his Chiricahua Apache people across deserts, grasslands, and mountains in the southeastern corner of Arizona (Sweeney, 1991, 4). Known by the Americans as a friendly and cooperative Apache, Cochise had an agreement with the U.S. government to supply wood to the Butterfield Stage Station in the Sulphur Springs Valley. In February 1861, he received word that a contingent of soldiers had arrived, was camped nearby, and wanted to speak with him. Trusting the Americans' word, Cochise complied, only to be mistakenly accused by a young American lieutenant—George N. Bascom—of kidnapping a rancher's son. Although wounded in the fracas, Cochise escaped, but his companions, five male relatives, were held and subsequently killed. According to Apache custom, the event demanded reprisal, so Cochise killed frontiersmen, drovers, stagecoach passengers, mail riders, the military, and everyone else who stepped into his territory. By August of 1861, much of Arizona that had been settled by non-Natives was deserted, with graves all along the roads. The Apaches were convinced for a time that they had driven the Anglos out of the area.

The non-Natives had not disappeared, however, and the Apache wars continued for twenty-five years. All during those battle-scarred decades, the frontier advanced farther westward under the banner of Manifest Destiny, a political slogan legitimizing for many non-Natives American expansion into Indian lands. The eastern populace moved out of cities into the healthier high deserts and mountainous regions of the Southwest. A tide of miners, merchants, businessmen, charlatans, religious men and women, schoolteachers, the military, mercenaries, scalp hunters, and settlers risked their lives when they entered the areas in which Mangas, Cochise, and their followers camped. These people expected protection from the forts that had been established across the Southwest after the Treaty of Guadalupe Hildalgo in 1848 and the Gadsden Purchase in 1853, especially since the military had weapons superior to the Indians' use of rocks, knives, war clubs, lances, and bows and arrows.

Contrary to standard American military practices, the Apaches remained in small bands, each independent of the other, each warrior completely acclimated to the harsh terrain and arid climate and able to travel forty to sixty miles a day on foot with no need for food or water. Each man or woman was supremely confident in his or her abilities, waiting

for orders from no superior, never at a loss to know exactly when to attack or when to retreat, relying solely on guerilla warfare, traveling at night, and hiding during the day in rocky points and high places. Often using the element of surprise or a planned ambush, Apaches attacked, murdered, plundered, burned, scattered, and then regrouped at predetermined sites, carrying with them the rifles, shotguns, pistols, and ammunition taken from their enemies.

Despite the advantages a guerilla force has when protecting its homelands from unwelcome incursion, and in addition to the Apaches' extremely competent leadership, one fight in particular, known as the July 1862 Battle of Apache Pass (Thrapp, 1967, 20), showed how vulnerable the Indians were to American firepower. Apache Pass, located in southeast Arizona, is a narrow defile between the Chiricahua Mountains on the south and the Dos Cabezas range on the north. The area contained a flowing spring, the only reliable water supply for miles around. As Brigadier General J. H. Carleton led a regiment of California volunteers eastward from California to fight the Confederates, he passed through Apache Pass. When the army entered the pass, Apache warriors were on the cliffs high above the spring, ready to do battle. Kicking down rocks and boulders, using traditional weapons as well as American arms, they killed two soldiers and wounded two more, but then the Army's howitzers responded with twelve-pound shells and canisters of shot. Having experienced nothing similar in the past, terrified Apaches fled from their positions, but not before losing an estimated sixty-six warriors. Cochise's warriors half-heartedly resumed the battle the next day, but the troops again fired the howitzers and the Apaches scattered once more. Never again did Mangas Coloradas and Cochise fight together. As a consequence of the Battle of Apache Pass, Carleton recommended that a fort be established in the vicinity; it was built and designated Fort Bowie.

Following Cochise's death in 1874, his son, Naiche, and the warrior Geronimo carried on the Apache Wars (Debo, 1976, 101–102). Never a chief, Geronimo's remarkable abilities as a medicine man and war shaman served the group as it continued to defy the U.S. plan to settle the American West. By 1880, most of the West's Indian nations had capitulated and were put on reservations that encompassed only a small portion of their traditional homelands; the remaining areas were opened for settlement. But the Apaches stayed free and fighting, the warrior group enlarged by the addition of many of Mangas's followers and their descendents.

Frustrated and embarrassed by its seeming inability to subdue the Apaches, the United States sent 5,000 army troops to southeast Arizona to capture the Naiche/Geronimo band of thirty-five people. Simultaneously, the Mexican government placed a price on Geronimo's head. Faced with a Hobson's choice—stay in Mexico and be killed or capitulate to the United States and face imprisonment—on March 29, 1886, Geronimo opted to surrender to General George Crook and the American army at Cañon de los Embudos, Mexico. It appeared that the Apache wars were over, but fate intervened and Geronimo suddenly changed his mind. Under cover of darkness he and the last holdouts left the area and remained at liberty for the next six months. In early September of 1886, however, Geronimo recognized the futility of an ongoing resistance and sent word of his wish to surrender once again. A meeting was arranged with General Nelson Miles in Skeleton Canyon, Arizona. On September 4, 1886, under the watchful eyes of nervous, heavily armed American soldiers, Geronimo placed a large rock under a tree, symbolizing the end of the Apache wars (Thrapp, 1967, 358–360).

H. Henrietta Stockel

See also Cochise; Geronimo: His Own Story; Mangas Coloradas; Manuelito; Victorio.

References and Further Reading

Debo, Angie. 1976. *Geronimo: The Man, His Time, His Place*. Norman: University of Oklahoma Press.

Sweeney, Edwin R. 1991. *Cochise: Chiricahua Apache Chief*. Norman: University of Oklahoma Press.

Sweeney, Edwin R. 1998. *Mangas Coloradas: Chief of the Chiricahua Apaches*. Norman: University of Oklahoma Press.

Thrapp, Dan L. 1967. *The Conquest of Apacheria*. Norman: University of Oklahoma Press.

Battle of the Little Bighorn

The Battle of the Little Bighorn, which took place in southeastern Montana on June 25, 1876, is one the best-known, most studied, and most controversial episodes in American history. The battle, in which a portion of the Seventh Cavalry led by Lieutenant Colonel George Armstrong Custer were all killed, was a crushing defeat for the United States Army at

A depiction of General Custer's defeat at the Battle of the Little Bighorn on June 25, 1876. (Library of Congress)

the hands of Sioux, Cheyenne, and Arapaho warriors. The United States, celebrating its centennial, was caught totally off guard by the defeat of its army. Troops of a western "civilized" nation were not supposed to experience such devastation at the hands of an "uncivilized" foe. What became known as Custer's Last Stand instantly captured the American imagination and continues to do so today. However, following this great victory, the northern Plains tribes soon lost their war against the Americans and were confined to reservations, their equestrian bison-hunting lifestyle shattered.

The Battle of the Little Bighorn was one of the final episodes in the American conquest of the Great Plains, which started with the Lewis and Clark expedition and the Louisiana Purchase. According to the Fort Laramie Treaty of 1868, most of the Black Hills belonged to the Great Sioux Reservation, which contained the area of current South Dakota west of the Missouri River. The treaty also gave the Indians a right to hunt in the Powder River area as long as buffalo and other game were plentiful enough to provide subsistence for them. In the 1870s, however,

rumors of gold in the Black Hills, further confirmed by government expeditions, led to a stampede of white greed that swept away any indigenous rights to the area. Thousands of white prospectors swarmed the area, and, although the government made some efforts to keep them out for a while, it quickly attempted to buy the land from the Indians. The Sioux, considering the place sacred, declared their unwillingness to sell. The federal government responded by issuing threats, including the use of force. In actuality, it declared war through an ultimatum stating that any groups staying outside the reservation boundaries after the last day of January 1876 were to be considered hostile.

The U.S. Army concentrated large numbers of troops in the area. Following a nearly disastrous late winter campaign, the Army opted for a three-pronged summer offensive. Three converging columns were supposed to circle around the Powder River country and close in on the resisting tribes, crushing anyone they met. One of the columns, which had started from Fort Abraham Lincoln and approached the area from the northeast, was led by

General Alfred Terry and included the whole Seventh Cavalry under Custer. From the Yellowstone River, Terry dispatched Custer with approximately 600 soldiers and some indigenous scouts as a strike force to search for the Indians and drive them northward, where Colonel John Gibbon's troops might block their escape. Custer found the Indian trail and followed it into the valley of the Little Bighorn, hoping to strike a decisive blow against the Indians.

Knowing that the Army would come after them, bands of Sioux, northern Cheyennes, and northern Arapahos joined together for an exceptionally large concentration along the stream they called the Greasy Grass. The flood of Indians from the agencies doubled the village size in a few days, from 400 to 1,000 lodges, from 3,000 to 7,000 people, and from 800 to 2,000 warriors. Hunkpapas, Oglalas, Miniconjous, Sans Arcs, Blackfeet, Two Kettles, Brules, and some Yanktonnais and Santees made the five Sioux circles, coexisting with 120 Cheyenne lodges and a handful of Arapahos. This amount of people consumed immense amounts of game, forage, and firewood, and could not remain together for a long period of time. The Indians, angered by the federal government's unscrupulous policies, were ready for a fight. They were strong in number and leadership, extremely confident, and well armed. Just a week earlier, a portion of them had held General George Crook's troops to a stalemate along the nearby Rosebud. Custer was unaware of this battle.

Presuming that the Indians would scatter as soon as they spotted his troops, Custer was eager for a quick charge and divided his command of twelve companies into four groups. One group led by Major Marcus Reno would attack the southern end of the camp, while Captain Frederick Benteen would scout to the south and west and cut off any potential escape routes. Custer himself, with about 200 men, would flank the northern end of the village. In addition, a detachment was left behind to guard the pack train. Custer was clearly more concerned with preventing the Indians from escaping than with their numbers or fighting abilities. This concern was not unusual, because many officers considered that the hardest thing in Indian warfare was to locate the enemy and force them to stand and fight. Thus, Custer had a clear rationale for hurrying.

From the start, the battle was a success for the Indians. Reno's men met heavy opposition and were forced to retreat twice to better positions. Casualties included almost half of his command, and the rest fell under siege. The expected help from Custer never came. Instead, Custer had advanced northward parallel to the river, realizing only then the size of the encampment he had stumbled upon. He sent word for Benteen to join him and rallied his men forward. Warriors charged across the river from the center of the village under Gall, a Hunkpapa leader; more came from the south, leaving the Reno site; and additional force under the leadership of the Oglala Crazy Horse struck from the north. Custer's men were sorely outnumbered, trapped in broken terrain, and fragmented along both sides of the battle ridge. The fight was brutal and short. None of the U.S. troops survived.

The pack train detail and Benteen, whose scout had proven useless, were unable to join Custer but reached Reno's defense position, bringing relief to their distress. Before that, many of the indigenous warriors had fled this battle scene and gone after Custer. Still, shooting at the Reno–Benteen site continued, and on June 26 two assault attempts were driven back by the soldiers. The situation of the troops remained desperate with many wounded, thirsty, and exhausted by the summer heat. Late in the evening the Indians started their retreat, and on the morning of June 27 the soldiers realized they were alone. Now Terry's troops arrived on the scene. All wondered where Custer was. The Reno–Benteen outfit had heard the sounds of fighting on June 25, and some of them had tried to go to Custer's help but were driven back by indigenous fighters. They had not seen Custer's struggles, the smoke and dust having obscured visibility. What they discovered after Terry arrived was total devastation. Custer and all his men lay dead on the slopes above the river. After the soldiers hastily buried the dead, they departed toward the mouth of the Little Bighorn, where a steamer was waiting. Altogether, casualties included half of the Seventh Cavalry; with Custer alone over 200 soldiers had died.

The Battle of the Little Bighorn proved to be, in fact, the last major show of force of the Sioux, Northern Cheyennes, and Northern Arapahos against the invading United States. Stunned and humiliated, the federal government poured men and resources quickly into the northern Plains. Throughout the winter of 1876–1877, regular troops with their Indian allies pursued the free bands continually, striking at their camps and commissary and slowly starving them into submission. The following spring a succession of Indian groups surrendered at various forts and agencies. The war was over. Indians had lost possession of the Black Hills and the Powder River

area, and eventually their large reservation was cut to pieces. Most of the surrendering Cheyennes were transported to the Indian Territory, from which they soon made their escape back north. The followers of Sitting Bull fled into Canada, only to return and surrender in 1881. The Battle of the Little Bighorn had been a major show of indigenous power, demonstrating Indians' courage and tactical skills and resulting in triumphant victory. Nevertheless, self-rule and the equestrian bison-hunting life did not survive its aftermath.

Janne Lahti

See also Black Hills (Paha Sapa); Fort Laramie Treaty of 1868.

References and Further Reading
Gray, John S. 1991. *Custer's Last Campaign: Mitch Boyer and the Little Bighorn Reconstructed.* Lincoln: University of Nebraska Press.
Hutton, Paul Andrew, ed. 1992. *The Custer Reader.* Lincoln: University of Nebraska Press.
Scott, Douglas D., P. Willey, and Melissa A. Connor. 1998. *They Died with Custer: Soldiers' Bones from the Battle of the Little Bighorn.* Norman: University of Oklahoma Press.
Utley, Robert M. 2001. *Cavalier in Buckskin: George Armstrong Custer and the Western Military Frontier.* Norman: University of Oklahoma Press.
Viola, Herman J. 1998. *It is a Good Day to Die: Indian Eyewitnesses Tell the Story of the Battle of the Little Bighorn.* Lincoln: University of Nebraska Press.

Long March (Nez Percé)

The Long March of the Nez Percé, or the flight of the Nez Percé, took place between June and October of 1877. Approximately 600 members of the Nez Percé tribe, seeking to escape the United States Army, traveled 1,600 miles in their attempt to reach Canada and freedom. The Nez Percé involved in the Long March came from the nontreaty factions of the tribe, those who opposed the 1863 treaty that revised the Walla Walla Treaty of 1855 and who did not accept the new reservation boundaries set out in the 1863 treaty. The principal leaders of the nontreaty Nez Percé were Chief Joseph, Whitebird, Looking Glass, Lean Elk, Husis-Kute, and Toohool-hoolzote.

While most versions of the Long March begin with the Battle of Whitebird Canyon, the trek of nontreaty people started in late May as they moved to the Nez Percé Reservation to meet the demands of the U.S. government. On June 13, 1877, a group of young men raided white homes along the Salmon River, creating fear and confusion for Nez Percé and Anglo-Americans alike. Knowing that this action meant war, Chief Joseph and his brother Ollokot led the people to Whitebird Canyon, a more defensible position. As white settlers panicked, the Army moved to confront the nontreaty Nez Percé there. Using their forces effectively, the Nez Percé defeated Army units sent in pursuit, inflicting heavy casualties. After the battle of Whitebird Canyon, Army units attacked the peaceful camp of Looking Glass and his people. Although Looking Glass and his people had not taken part in the earlier conflict, the Army believed that they were aiding the other nontreaty bands and counted them among the nontreaty people. After Whitebird Canyon, several engagements occurred between the Army and Nez Percé warriors as they attempted to retreat to the Weippe Prairie, located in present-day northeastern Idaho.

As soon as the Nez Percé arrived at the Weippe Prairie, they convened to discuss plans and a strategy for eluding the Army. Looking Glass, whose band had joined those fleeing the Army, argued that the best strategy lay in crossing the Bitterroot Mountains over the Lolo Trail. He maintained that crossing the mountains would stop Army pursuit and that the Nez Percé could join with their friends, the Crows. Most of the other leaders agreed with Looking Glass, and Joseph deferred to him since he was a more experienced war leader. It is important to note that no one leader was responsible for all the nontreaty Nez Percé during the Long March. Leaders like Joseph, Looking Glass, Lean Elk, and others shared and conferred in decision making during the trek. For Anglo-Americans, Chief Joseph became the central figure of their historical imagination, thereby condensing and simplifying the narrative of the Long March into one person while negating the role of many different leaders and people among the nontreaty bands.

With Looking Glass leading the way, nontreaty people traversed the Lolo Trail. Near present-day Missoula, Montana, they encountered a small force of volunteers who decided not to engage the Nez Percé. After the encounter, believing that they had eluded the Army, the nontreaty bands traveled south to the Big Hole Valley, where they decided to rest, recuperate, and procure food. This area was familiar to many of the Nez Percé because they trav-

eled here on their way to hunt buffalo on the plains of Wyoming and Montana. Feeling secure and celebrating their escape from the Army, they failed to place guards around the camp. Just before dawn on August 9, 1877, Army troops surprised the Nez Percé at their Big Hole Valley encampment. The troops moved quickly into the camp, firing indiscriminately at men, women, and children. As hand-to-hand combat raged through the camp, women, children, and the elderly escaped; the warriors regrouped and forced the troops out of the camp, eventually surrounding and pinning the soldiers down. Between sixty and ninety Nez Percé lost their lives during the battle (Josephy, 1971, 571). Most of the dead were women and children. Joseph and Ollokot both lost wives, and many in the camp lost their lodges and personal possessions.

On the night of August 10, 1877, while Nez Percé warriors kept the soldiers pinned down, the survivors of the battle escaped from the Big Hole Valley. According to Clifford Trafzer, Looking Glass lost much of his support as principal leader of the nontreaty bands after Big Hole. As the people traveled south and east toward the Yellowstone country, Lean Elk assumed much of the leadership role. Hoping to find refuge with their friends, the Crows, the Nez Percé faced bitter disappointment when their friends rejected their pleas for help because they did not want to anger the U.S. government.

With no friends and little hope of support, the nontreaty bands met in council and decided that the only option left open to them was to attempt an escape to Canada. The Nez Percé knew of the Sioux uprising and the subsequent escape of Sitting Bull and many Lakota to Canada. Lean Elk led the nontreaty bands, but he relinquished leadership to Looking Glass once the Nez Percé turned north toward Canada. As the Nez Percé began their escape, Looking Glass and others, not knowing that units under the command of Colonel Nelson Miles were about to cut off their escape route, encouraged the people to slow down and rest before their final push to Canada. Most of the people agreed, since almost all of them suffered from exhaustion, illness, hunger, or wounds.

Only forty miles from the Canadian border, the Nez Percé decided to camp at Snake Creek, located between the Bearpaw and Little Rocky Mountains. Before they started the last segment of the journey, Colonel Miles's force attacked the camp on September 30, 1877, and caught the Nez Percé by surprise. Once again, hand-to-hand combat occurred within the camp, with women and children fending off soldiers with digging sticks and knives. When the initial attack ended, twenty-two Nez Percé were dead, including Toohoolhoolzote, the leading *tooat* (shaman) of the Nez Percé, and Ollokot, Joseph's brother (Josephy, 1971, 600).

After the initial attack, both sides settled in for a protracted siege. The remaining nontreaty people dug shallow trenches and suffered from the cold and snow. On October 1, Miles proposed a truce and Joseph agreed to talk. At the meeting, Miles demanded that the Nez Percé surrender unconditionally and give up their weapons. As the talks ended, Miles captured and held Joseph prisoner. The Nez Percé retaliated by capturing one of Miles's officers. Joseph and the officer were both eventually released. On October 5, Joseph, the sole surviving leader, prepared to surrender. Joseph based his decision on the plight of the people, who were suffering greatly from the cold, hunger, and injuries sustained in the fight.

Believing that they were offering a conditional surrender, Joseph met Miles and Howard between the two lines. In exchange for their arms, Joseph and the other Nez Percé believed that they would be returned to the Nez Percé reservation in Idaho and that there would be no punishment for warriors who had fought in the war. After the surrender some people, including Whitebird, managed to escape the army and make their way to Sitting Bull's camp in Canada. The remaining 400 Nez Percé survivors were quickly sent to Fort Keogh (Montana), then on to Fort Leavenworth (Kansas). Eventually the Nez Percé were sent to the Indian Territory, where the U.S. government first placed them on the Quapaw Agency and then settled them on a piece of land on the newly created Ponca Agency. During the year and a half after their surrender, many people died from disease, malnutrition, and depression. The survivors of the Long March remained on the Ponca Agency until 1885, when the U.S. government allowed some Nez Percé to return to the Nez Percé Reservation in Idaho. The government forced another group of the exiles, led by Chief Joseph, onto the Colville Reservation in northeastern Washington. Of the 400 survivors after the surrender at Bear Paw, nearly half died during their captivity in the Indian Territory, or, as the Nez Percé called it, *Eekish Pah* ("the hot place").

Robert R. McCoy

See also Joseph, Younger.

References and Further Reading

Joseph, Nez Percé Chief. 1984. *Chief Joseph's Own Story.* Fairfield, WA: Ye Galleon Press.

Josephy, Alvin M., Jr. 1971. *The Nez Perce Indians and the Opening of the Northwest.* Abridged ed. Lincoln: University of Nebraska Press.

McCoy, Robert R. 2004. *Chief Joseph, Yellow Wolf, and the Creation of Nez Perce History in the Pacific Northwest.* New York: Routledge Press.

McWhorter, Lucullus V. 1940. *Yellow Wolf: His Own Story.* Caldwell, ID: Caxton.

Nerburn, Kent. 2005. *Chief Joseph & the Flight of the Nez Perce: The Untold Story of an American Tragedy.* New York: Harper.

Slickpoo, Allen P., Sr. 1973. *Noon Nee-Me-Poo (We, the Nez Perces): Culture and History of the Nez Perces,* Vol. One. Lapwai, ID: Nez Perce Tribe of Idaho.

Trafzer, Clifford E., and Richard Scheuerman. 1986. *Renegade Tribe: The Palouse Indians and the Invasion of the Inland Pacific Northwest.* Pullman: Washington State University Press.

General Allotment Act (Dawes Act)

Passed on February 8, 1887, the General Allotment Act (otherwise called the Dawes Act or the Dawes Severalty Act) was sponsored by Senator Henry Dawes of Massachusetts. It represents one of the most devastating American Indian policies of the nineteenth and early twentieth centuries. It broke up Indian reservation lands into individually owned plots and created a plan for the assimilation of the Indians into the U.S. society.

There really is no one view about this policy. The attitudes and motives for the settlement of the western lands of the United States began eighty years earlier with various military explorations, and with them came hints of the rich natural resources of the west that would undoubtedly lead to disputes with the indigenous peoples who occupied those lands. Beginning with the 1803 Lewis and Clark expedition, President Thomas Jefferson gathered information about the western portions of the United States with an eye to future goals and opportunities for expansion. By the time the political policies of the 1880s came into being, there had been a massive influx of settlers, gold rush enthusiasts, and land entrepreneurs rolling across America. The Indian wars that had begun in the 1850s were coming to an end by the time this Act was passed, and most of the Indian reservations that still exist today

were established during the period from the 1850s to the 1890s. The impact of the Dawes was the final blow to the western lands of the indigenous people and would be the largest land grab in U.S. history.

The fifty years prior to the passage of this bill saw a grand civilization policy that took root and changed the subsistence lifestyle of the American Indian people forever. Some policy makers called it a "civilizing machine" and its methods were ruthless. The first treaties between the United States and the American Indian nations promised friendship and protection of indigenous homelands, and in return the Native peoples promised settlers safe passage through their homelands and allowed for the building of military forts, railways, and roads. Subsequent treaties negotiated for the ceding of Native lands to the United States in return for rations, money, protection, and educational and health benefits. After the treaties were negotiated the "civilizing machine" took American Indian children and placed them in boarding schools hundreds of miles from their homelands. Many died from diseases, fear, and loneliness. They were stripped of their identities and forced to speak only the English language. Families were broken and devastated. An entire generation of Indian children had been removed from their people and that event became part of the racial memories of American Indians forever. That devastation has never healed.

At home on their reserved lands, the parents were robbed of their old ways of securing a livelihood and nothing was offered as a substitute. As a result plans were made without input by American Indians for an allotment policy whose primary aim would be the assimilation of the American Indian.

At the time of the passage of this law, Senator Henry Dawes from Massachusetts was chairman of the Senate Indian Committee and was considered a friend of the Indians. He was convinced that allotting acreage to each Indian person would solve all sorts of economic and racial problems: " . . . at last the restless pioneers could advance unmolested across the Great Plains where once the shaggy buffalo and tawny native had long held sway" (Billington, 1982, 610). Senator Dawes also was a supporter of the Indian Rights Association, which believed that Indian people would be better off living on designated reservation lands. However, white citizens crossing the Great Plains maintained that the Indians should sell unused and unneeded lands and that white people could legitimately settle on the surplus lands. As a way to solve the needs of both groups, he

The General Allotment Act stated that tribal lands would be allotted to individual Native Americans. Many sold their allotments, opening Indian lands to white settlement. On September 16, 1893, over 6 million acres of the Cherokee Outlet in Oklahoma Terrirotry were opened for settlement. (Bettmann/Corbis)

further supported the idea of converting the Indian people to Christianity. The Christian reformers at first accepted the idea of lands held in trust by the federal government and reserved for exclusive use by the Indian people (reservations) and worked within the system. In the end, however, they came to view reservations as an abomination and a divider to Americanization and thus threw their support to dividing up the reservation lands among the many individuals.

President Grover Cleveland signed the bill into law. The profits from the sale of the surplus lands would be held in a trust fund for educational purposes. It has been said: "Land sustains the lifestyle of countless tribes, even when little acreage is in production or has productive value. Land sustains far

more than subsistence, and indeed many Indians recognized decades ago the folly of attempting to sustain their daily needs on acreage that is marginal, both in resources and in per capita size. But land has emotional meaning, a psychological significance for the Indian that is far more intense than our nostalgic longing for family farm and a rural way of life" (Sutton, 1975, 2).

In illustration of the psychological tie to the land, the Dakota Sioux people, one of the greatest tribal groups of the Great Plains, had a strong belief in the Sacred Hoop, or the circle that can be found everywhere in nature. This sacred circle, or hoop, corresponds to all the circles found in nature. The earth is a circle; the sun comes up in the east and sets in the west and comes up again in the east, making a

circle in its journey; birds' nests are circular; animals make circles before they lie down; winds blow in circles; water can swirl in circles; tree trunks are circular; and so on. A circle has no ending and it became the symbol of the endless power of the creator, much like the cross is a sacred symbol among Christians. The Dakota Sioux consider themselves the custodians of Mother Earth and, with their Seven Sacred Ceremonies, they believe they have the right to live on the land. It is unthinkable to buy or sell the land or to give it away. Just as one would not give up a human mother, the Earth Mother cannot be given away. Father Peter Powell has said: "Thus title to the Mother Earth can never be transferred to the United States. All that can be transferred is the temporary use of the land. This is not ownership—only use" (Powell, 1977, 107).

In 1792 Secretary of War Henry Knox delivered a speech to northwestern Indians and in it he hinted that individual ownership of land by the indigenous people would bring them countless blessings of a more civilized life. "The United States," he told them, "should be greatly gratified with the opportunity of imparting to you all the blessings of civilized life, of teaching you to cultivate the earth, and raise corn; to raise oxen, sheep, and other domestic animals; to build comfortable houses, and to educate your children, so as ever to dwell upon the land" (Otis, 1973, ix). This seems absurd in light of the fact that the indigenous people of America had been farming and living on the land for thousands of years prior to European arrival—as if the allotment of Indian lands was part of a grand plan.

The Dawes Committee visited all the Sioux reservations on the Plains and favored dividing up what was negotiated in treaties as the large Sioux Reservation and opening part of it to white settlement. Henry Dawes headed up the committee that would look at that option. He considered much of their lands to be useless and unnecessary, and he proposed the sale of any remaining surplus lands and putting that money into a permanent fund. The annual income from the sale of the surplus lands could be spent on "the civilization, education, and advancement in agriculture and other self-supporting pursuits of the Sioux" (Prucha, 1984, 212). This same idea could then be applied to all the other Indian reservations in the West.

In looking at the aims and motives for the allotment policy, an Indian reservation agent for the Dakota Sioux wrote: "As long as Indians live in villages they will retain many of their old dances, con-

stant visiting—these will continue as long as people live together in close neighborhoods and villages . . . I trust that before another year is ended, they will generally be located upon individual lands for farms. From that date will begin their real and permanent progress" (Otis, 1973, 9). By this time, the westward movement of white civilization had occurred in the form of railroads, gold rushes, and settlers.

Political reformers believed that reservations segregated Indians from whites and prevented violent confrontations, but reformers felt that they could be also seeding grounds for civilization. They further believed reservations to be controlled societies from which Indian tribal ways could be more easily destroyed and Indian children removed. As efforts moved forward, reservations soon developed several political groups: There were the treaty signers and nontreaty signers; "progressives" versus the "nonprogressives" or the traditionalists versus the nontraditionalists; Christian converts and worshippers in the sacred ceremonies that espoused protection of the Earth Mother and all her creatures; liberals versus conservatives; and those who were sent to be educated in the "white man's" schools in the East and those who returned home to take back their traditions. If anything, the federal policies created an unsettled society among the American Indian people with opposing opinions about their own welfare. Those divisions still exist today.

Another author of the bill was Senator Richard Coke from Texas and he was enthusiastically supported by Carl Schurz, who had an outstanding career in American politics. Schurz was the first German-born American in the U.S. Senate. He served as U.S. Senator from Missouri from 1869–1875. In 1876 President Rutherford B. Hayes appointed Schurz Secretary of the Interior. When he retired in 1881, he became editor in chief of the *New York Evening Post*, a post that allowed him a greater voice in American Indian politics. He had this to say about the Dawes Allotment Act: "It will inspire the Indians with a feeling of assurance as to the permanency of their ownership of the lands they occupy and cultivate; it gives them a clear and legal standing as landed proprietors in the courts of law; it will secure to them for the first time fixed homes under the protection of the same law under which the white men own theirs; it will eventually open to settlement by white men the large tracts of land now belonging to the reservations, but not used by the Indians . . . It will also by the sale, with their consent, of reservation lands not used by the Indians, create for the benefit of the Indi-

ans a fund, which will gradually relieve the government of those expenditures which have now to be provided by appropriations. . . ." (Prucha, 1984, 225).

Senator Henry Moore Teller from Colorado criticized the humanitarian ideals that were spoken in support of the allotment policy. He served as Secretary of the Interior from 1882 to 1885. In Teller's view, those who advocated that allotment of Indian lands would make the Indian civilized and Christianized had the whole thing reversed. He advocated that first the Indian people should be civilized and Christianized and then they would respect the value of property.

The Act contained four main provisions. The first was to grant 160 acres of land to each head of household, eighty acres to each single person over the age of eighteen and to each orphan under the age of eighteen, and forty acres to each single person under the age of eighteen. Second, as the land was issued, a fee patent title on the land was to be held in trust by the federal government for twenty-five years, and during this time it could not be sold or alienated in any way. If the federal government held the land in trust, it could not be taxed because the federal government cannot tax itself. Third, the Act allowed four years for individuals to make their own selections of land. After that period of time, if no individual selection had been made, then the federal government, under the authority of the Secretary of the Interior, made the selection for the individuals. Fourth, the right of citizenship was also to be conferred on the allottees and on any other Indians who abandoned their traditional habits of life and who adopted a more civilized life. A ceremony was created to recognize the conferring of citizenship, but that did not mean that states wanted American Indians voting. It would take the passage of the Indian Citizenship Act in 1924 before Indians would be allowed to vote on a regular basis or at least to have some clout to push for their right to vote in many states.

The results of the Dawes Act were many, and one of the first results was the massive decrease in the Indians' land base. The indigenous people of America had given up 90 million acres of land as surplus land, and they had lost their psychological connection to those lands. Another result of the Dawes Act was the destruction of their social order. With the loss of many of their children to schools in the East, many of the tribal leaders became disenchanted. The children who returned to the reservations after their days in the white man's boarding schools wanted their traditions back or came back to attack the traditions of their elders. The transition to assimilation into the white man's society was not an easy one.

A third result was that land once held in total for the common good of all the people was fragmented, and, with individual ownership, different levels of greed and despair developed. A grandfather might have his own 160 acres over twenty miles away from his home and would have to travel many miles by horseback just to improve his lands. The problems with individual ownership became apparent almost overnight. There were people who were invalids, orphans, or unable to work their lands, perhaps because of age or some other infirmary, and who had no way to immediately become self-supporting farmers. Some of the land was not farmable. Many of the individual allotments were desert or mountain land without water. Those who were able to make their lands prosper were not willing to then share the profits.

The issue of the inheritance of land was also not considered. Suppose that a grandfather on the way to his property fell off his horse and was killed. What would happen to his 160 acres? Because the land could not be sold for twenty-five years, his adult sons or daughters would inherit land that was even more distant from their allotments. If the adult son or daughter died, what happened to their allotment and grandfather's inherited land? The problem was enormous. An orphan could inherit his or her grandfather's property and parent's property—and still be too young to work any of it. This is how the checkerboard effect came into existence.

The checkerboarding effect of the Dawes Act was created when the non-Indians who purchased the surplus lands surrounding the reservations utilized their knowledge and expertise in land use laws to take advantage of the new Indian landowners, especially if they were the elderly or orphaned youth. It was the whites who jumped at the opportunity to lease such unencumbered lands and who would then buy the land they leased for years when the twenty-five-year trust period ended. Thus even today there are parcels of land on current Indian reservations with non-Indian ownership alongside parcels of Indian ownership. Looking at a map of an Indian reservation, one can see the checkerboard effect between Indian- and non-Indian–owned lands.

Another problem that remains today is the hundreds of heirs who have ties to original allotments made in the late 1800s. As original land allottees

died, their heirs inherited the land, and sometimes the inheritance might be a tenth of an acre among today's generation of heirs. This means that there are Indian people who are absentee landowners of petty parcels of land. What can people do if they live off the reservation and own twenty parcels of land, but each parcel is no bigger than a postage stamp and the parcels are separated by several miles? Checkerboarding is only one of the administrative nightmares of the allotment policy, and its impact on today's American Indian generation goes on.

As part of the civilization machine's education plan, Commissioner of Indian Affairs J.D.C. Atkins, in his annual report of 1887, argued for the exclusive use of the English language at all Indian schools. He felt that Indian people must acquire the language as rapidly as possible. Issues relating to intermarriage with whites were also topics of federal policy. If a white man married an Indian woman, he could not acquire her property, and if an Indian woman married a white man who was a citizen of the United States, she automatically became a citizen of the United States.

During October 1889, Indian Commissioner Thomas J. Morgan made plans for a national system of Indian schools, using the following justification, among others:

> The work of education should begin with them while they are young and susceptible, and should continue until habits of industry and love of learning have taken the place of indolence and indifference . . . Special pains should be taken to bring together in the large boarding-schools members of as many different tribes as possible, in order to destroy the tribal antagonism and to generate in them a feeling of common brotherhood and mutual respect (Prucha, 1975, 180).

As with most Native American policies, no one thought to ask the Indians what ideas they had for a home, a family, or property. Although American Indian people of the lower forty-eight have endured numerous federal Indian policies, it would be unthinkable today not to ask their opinion on a policy that would have such a devastating impact on their livelihood. Let that be a lesson of history. Federal Indian policies change every twenty years. Some of them are pro-Indian and some of them are anti-Indian. The policy of allotment need not be repeated.

Jeanne Eder

See also Assimilation; Bureau of Indian Affairs: Establishing the Existence of an Indian Tribe; Ceremonies, Criminalization of; Citizenship; Domestic Dependent Nation; Economic Development; Genocide; Land, Identity and Ownership of, Land Rights; Plenary Power; Reservation Economic and Social Conditions; Tribal Sovereignty; Trust, Doctrine of; Wardship Doctrine.

References and Further Reading
Billington, Ray Allen. 1982. *Westward Expansion.* Englewood Cliffs, N.J., Prentice Hall.
"Dawes Act (1887)." Available at: http://www.ourdocuments.gov. Accessed June 23, 2006.
Getches, David H., Daniel M. Rosenfelt, and Charles F. Wilkinson. 1979. *Federal Indian Law: Cases and Materials.* St. Paul, MN: West.
Jackson, Helen 1994. *A Century of Dishonor.* New York: Barnes & Noble.
Oklahoma State University Library. "Indian Affairs: Laws and Treaties." Available at: http://digital.library.okstate.edu/kappler/. Accessed June 23, 2006.
Otis, Delos Sacket. 1973. *The Dawes Act and the Allotment of Indian Land.* Norman: University of Oklahoma Press.
Powell, Father Peter. 1977. "The Sacred Treaty." In *The Great Sioux Nation: Sitting in Judgment on America.* Roxanne Dunbar. Ed. Ortiz. Berkeley, CA: Moon Books.
Prucha, Francis Paul 1975. *Documents of United States Indian Policy.* Lincoln: University of Nebraska Press.
Prucha, Francis Paul. 1984. *The Great Father: The United States Government and the American Indians.* Lincoln: University of Nebraska Press.
Pyne, John, and Gloria Sesso. 1995. "Federal Indian Policy in the Gilded Age." *OAH Magazine of History* (Spring): 46–51.
Sutton, Imre. 1975. *Indian Land Tenure: Bibliographical Essays and a Guide to the Literature.* New York: Clearwater Publishing.
"The Dawes Act February 8, 1887." Available at: http://www.pbs.org/weta/thewest/resources/archives/eight/dawes.htm. Accessed June 23, 2006.

Wounded Knee, South Dakota, Massacre at

Since the bitter cold day it happened in 1890, there has been controversy over whether Wounded Knee was a battle or a massacre. It has also been called the last battle of the Indian wars.

Twenty-two years had passed since the 1868 Treaty at Fort Laramie established the Great Sioux

Reservation. It was a desperate time for the Sioux. Their reservation that had once sprawled across portions of what are now several states now consisted of small islands of land surrounded by white homesteaders. Their rich culture was disappearing and being replaced by something both alien and unsatisfying. Their young children were being educated in special schools that taught them to reject their own culture and to replace it with the values and morals of the dominant white culture.

The Sioux were ripe for the coming of the latest Indian messiah, Wovoka, and his message of a return to the old ways. Wovoka was a Paiute, living in Nevada close to Lake Tahoe. On New Year's Day in 1889 there was a solar eclipse in Nevada. The Paiutes called it "the day the sun died." According to historian Rex Alan Smith, on that same day, Wovoka had a vision that he was taken to heaven. He was told the old world was to be destroyed and replaced by a fresh one. The dead would live again and everyone would be young and happy. The buffalo would return and the white man would disappear. All the Indians had to do was to perform the dance of the souls departed—the Ghost Dance (Smith, 1981, 67).

Wovoka's vision was peaceful, but as it radiated out to other Indians it was imbued with the flavor of individual tribes. The Sioux added a strain of militarism. Adding volatility to the mix was the Sioux leader Sitting Bull, who had returned with his people to the United States from Canada in July 1881. Life on the reservation did not suit him and he longed for the old ways. Among his own people, he became a symbol of resistance and a hindrance to the plans of men such as James McLaughlin, agent at Standing Rock Reservation.

With the spread of the new religion, increasing numbers of Indians professed a belief in a Christian God. In addition, Wovoka told his adherents to farm and send all of their children to school. These were all things that should have been desirable to the white man. In fact, one of the primary duties of an Indian agent was to replace Native religious beliefs with Christian dogma. It would seem that the new Indian religion was doing just that. However, Standing Rock Indian Agent James McLaughlin, called it an "absurd craze" and described the dance as "demoralizing, indecent and disgusting" (Jensen, Paul, and Carter, 1991, 6). He found no reason to change his opinion when he finally witnessed a dance a month after submitting his original assessment.

Shortly before 6 a.m. on December 15, 1890, Lieutenant Bull Head, and forty-three other Indian policemen, arrived at Sitting Bull's cabin to arrest him. According to historian Robert M. Utley, Sitting Bull initially agreed to go peacefully, but as he was leaving his cabin a crowd began to gather. They jostled the policemen and shouted at them to release Sitting Bull, who began to struggle with his captors. Catch the Bear, one of Sitting Bull's followers, shot Lieutenant Bull Head in the leg. As he fell, Bull Head fired a shot into Sitting Bull's chest, and Red Tomahawk, another policeman, fired a shot into the back of the unarmed chief's skull, killing him instantly. A fierce, brutal skirmish erupted, and, when it was all over, Sitting Bull, his young son Crow Foot, and six other tribesmen lay dead. In addition, four Indian policemen were dead and three were wounded, two of them mortally (Utley, 1993, 293).

Frightened that the killing of Sitting Bull might be the first action in an all-out war, a mixed band of Sioux, under the leadership of Minneconjou Chief Big Foot, fled the Cheyenne River reservation. Several fugitives fleeing Sitting Bull's camp joined him en route. Big Foot was headed for the safety of Pine Ridge, hoping that the influential Chief Red Cloud could protect his people. However, some feared he was leading his band into the Badlands to join the hostile Ghost Dancers who were already gathered there. Major Samuel Whitside, with four troops of the Seventh Cavalry, was ordered to intercept and capture him.

Three days after Christmas of 1890, Whitside and the Seventh Calvary caught up with Big Foot and his band of 120 men and 230 women and children. During the night, Whitside's commander, Colonel James W. Forsyth, assumed command. He told Whitside that the Sioux were to be disarmed and shipped to a military prison in Omaha, Nebraska. The Indians were clothed in rags, and the children were hungry and cold. Big Foot had developed pneumonia during the flight across the Badlands in subzero weather. He was so weak he could barely sit up.

A council was called and Forsyth told the assembled warriors they would be asked to give up their guns. With the recent slaughter at Sitting Bull's camp fresh in their minds, the Sioux were fearful of being unarmed and vulnerable. They decided to give up their broken and useless guns and keep their working guns handy. Forsyth soon surrounded the camp. He had 470 soldiers and a platoon of Indian scouts under his command. Four Hotchkiss artillery pieces ringed the encampment.

The body of Sioux Chief Big Foot lies dead in the snow following the Battle of Wounded Knee. (Bettmann/Corbis)

The next day the Indians provided only an assortment of broken and outdated weapons. Forsyth knew there were more guns, so he ordered a search of the camp to gather up all the remaining weapons. Forsyth knew it was a delicate process that could easily lead to a violent reaction. As a precaution, only officers were allowed to enter teepees and search the women.

The tension rapidly increased with the Sioux warriors angrily objecting to the searches of their women. Historian Rex Alan Smith writes that, as the search continued, Yellow Bird, a Minneconjou medicine man, began to dance and chant and throw handfuls of dirt into the air. He called upon the young men to have brave hearts and told them their "ghost shirts" would protect them from the soldier's bullets. One young man leapt to his feet angrily brandishing his gun saying he had paid good money for it and would not give it up. Some said it was a man named Black Coyote while other witnesses claimed it was a man named *Hosi Yanka*, which means "deaf." Two soldiers came behind the young man and tried to seize his weapon. In the ensuing scuffle, it went off. At that point, several young warriors threw off their blankets and fired a brief and ragged volley into the

ranks of the soldiers. Lieutenant James Mann remembered thinking, "The pity of it! What can they be thinking of?" Almost simultaneously the soldiers lines erupted with gunfire. Big Foot was one of the first to die (Smith, 1981, 184–186).

After that initial ragged volley, the Sioux began to flee in all directions. Many fled to a nearby ravine that soon became the target of the Army's Hotchkiss guns on the hills above Wounded Knee. Most who fled to the ravine did not survive. Others were chased down and killed, some more than three miles from the scene of the massacre. In the end, nearly 300 Indians were killed, mostly women and children. Sixty soldiers, many who were victims of "friendly fire," were also killed.

In a story headlined "Horrors of War," the *Omaha World-Herald*'s correspondent told of wounded Indian mothers with their babies and the agonies endured bravely by the injured:

> There was a woman sitting on the floor with a wounded baby on her lap and four or five children around her, all her grandchildren. Their father and mother were killed. There was a young woman shot through both thighs

and her wrist broken. Mr. Tibbles had to get a pair of pliers to get her rings off. There was a little boy with his throat apparently shot to pieces.

They were all hungry and when we fed this little boy we found he could swallow. We gave him some gruel and he grabbed with both his little hands a dipper of water. When I saw him yesterday afternoon, he looked worse than the day before, and when they feed him now, the food and water come out the side of his neck (*Omaha World-Herald*, January 2, 1891, 1).

Colonel Forsyth was court-martialed, accused of mistakenly placing his men so that they fired into their own ranks, but he was found innocent. In a possible attempt to justify the events at Wounded Knee, the Army awarded nineteen Medals of Honor to participants in the engagement. Five additional Medals of Honor were awarded for skirmishes along nearby White Clay Creek. This represented the largest number of Medal of Honor winners for any single engagement in U.S. history.

Hugh J. Reilly

See also Fort Laramie Treaty of 1868; Ghost Dance Religion; Sitting Bull; Wovoka.

References and Further Reading

Jensen, Richard, Eli Paul, and John E. Carter. 1991. *Eyewitness to Wounded Knee*. Lincoln: University of Nebraska Press.

Omaha World-Herald, October 4, 1890–January 4, 1891.

Smith, Rex Allen. 1981. *Moon of the Popping Tree: The Tragedy at Wounded Knee and the End of the Indian Wars*. Lincoln: University of Nebraska Press.

Tibbles, Thomas Henry. *Buckskin and Blanket Days: Memoirs of a Friend of the Indians*. New York: Doubleday.

Utley, Robert M. 1993. *The Lance and the Shield: The Life and Times of Sitting Bull*. New York: Henry Holt.

Relocation

The federal government's Indian relocation program, established in 1952, sought to move Indians from reservations to urban areas, where there were more job opportunities. Closely tied to the termination of Native reservations, the relocation program was rooted in the government's movement to improve Indian education, vocational training, and economic development. It also furthered the government's attempt to relieve itself of responsibility for the oversight of Indian affairs.

The Bureau of Indian Affairs (BIA) patterned the relocation program after a program that it developed in 1948 to assist Navajo and Hopi Indians in New Mexico and Arizona. During the harsh winter of 1947–1948, the federal government airlifted food to the Navajo and Hopi Reservations, and Congress passed Public Law 474 with the expressed purpose of rehabilitating Native peoples by teaching them how to better utilize reservation resources. When the BIA examined the problems, however, it concluded that the available resources could support only a portion of the Indians who resided on the two reservations. Consequently, it implemented an off-reservation job placement program for the two tribes and opened relocation centers in Denver, Salt Lake City, and Los Angeles.

In 1950, Dillon S. Myer, who had directed the War Relocation Authority during World War II, became commissioner of Indian affairs. Upon taking office, Myer proposed that the BIA extend its relocation program to all reservation Indians. Because Native Americans had proven during World War II that they could work effectively with other Americans, Myer recommended that the federal government offer to relocate any reservation Indians who wanted to move to urban areas. He hoped that relocation would improve Native American standards of living, encourage termination, and eventually make Indian reservations unnecessary. Additionally, relocation would ease the strain that returning war veterans placed on reservations that already had high unemployment rates.

Although Commissioner Myer was responsible for implementing the expanded relocation program, the idea of relocating Indians to urban areas was not new. In 1926, Secretary of the Interior Hubert Work requested that a nongovernmental agency conduct a thorough study of Indian affairs. The following year, a team of experts under the direction of Lewis Meriam of the Institute for Government Research initiated a detailed examination of federal Indian policy. In 1928, the team published its findings in a report entitled, *The Problem of Indian Administration*, commonly known as the Meriam Report.

The team concluded that the solution to the government's Indian problem lay in education, and it urged the BIA to teach Indians how to help themselves. One way in which the team thought the BIA

could accomplish this on reservations with severely limited economic conditions was to adopt a policy of encouraging Indians to relocate to cities where they would have better employment opportunities. In fact, by the 1920s, some Indians had already relocated to cities, without encouragement from the federal government.

More than two decades after the publication of the Meriam Report, the federal government implemented an Indian relocation program. At the time, World War II had ended and the tens of thousands of Indians who had either served in the armed forces during the war or worked off-reservation in war industries had returned to their reservations. Because economic resources on most Indian reservations were already inadequate, it was impossible to stretch them far enough to support those who returned after the war effort.

Consequently, in 1952, the BIA expanded the Indian relocation program to include all Indians. Like the Navajo and Hopi Indians before them, participants in the expanded program could choose to relocate to Los Angeles, Denver, Salt Lake City, or Chicago (opened in 1951), where the BIA had established job placement centers. Although relocation was voluntary, BIA officials highly touted the program on reservations and circulated pamphlets highlighting the benefits of urban life.

In the early years of the program, the BIA's primary goal was to make Indians aware of job opportunities that were available outside the reservation and to provide relocation assistance to those who chose to move. Placement workers helped relocatees secure jobs, and they teamed with employment agencies to recruit Indian workers. Most of the jobs were temporary or seasonal, but, as the program grew, the BIA opened more relocation centers and focused on finding permanent jobs for relocatees.

By 1958, the BIA had increased the opportunities available to relocatees by opening relocation offices in Oakland and San Francisco, California; Chicago, Illinois; St. Louis, Missouri; Dallas, Texas; Cincinnati and Cleveland, Ohio; Oklahoma City and Tulsa, Oklahoma; and Waukegan, Wisconsin. Any reservation Indian who was interested in participating in the relocation program could complete an application. The applicant then underwent a physical examination, and the BIA office on the reservation reviewed his job skills and employment records. If accepted into the program, the applicant could select the city to which he wanted to relocate, and the BIA would contact the relocation office there.

After the preliminary details were complete, the applicant traveled by bus or train to the relocation city at the expense of the program.

During its first three years, the relocation program provided participants with limited assistance. After 1955, however, the BIA expanded the services that were available to relocatees. In addition to transportation and job placement, relocation officers briefly schooled program participants in urban life upon their arrival. They helped relocatees find affordable housing, took them to the store to purchase necessities, and gave them money to sustain them until they received their first paychecks. They also provided counseling services, although participants were told that they had to make the transition to urban life by themselves and rely on the relocation office only temporarily.

In 1956, Congress expanded the relocation program with the passage of Public Law 959, which provided vocational training for adult Native Americans. Although this training program was an outgrowth of the relocation program and the problems encountered by unskilled relocatees, participants were not required to leave the reservation for training. Applicants in the program could choose to complete either twenty-four months of on-the-job training or an approved vocational course of study, such as plumbing, carpentry, or cosmetology. The BIA paid for tuition, books, and living expenses, and provided job placement services after students completed their coursework. Program graduates could choose to relocate to urban areas with BIA assistance or remain on the reservation.

By the late 1950s, the BIA had fully developed its relocation program and renamed it the Federal Employment Assistance Program, which helped disassociate the program from the BIA's increasingly controversial termination program. The number and location of relocation centers fluctuated over time, but they remained the centerpiece of the program. In the 1960s, the offices shifted their focus from facilitating the relocation of reservation Indians to helping relocatees adjust to urban life. In addition to the divisions of vocational training, employment, and housing, relocation offices had a community living division, which worked to improve self-sufficiency and family life for program participants.

Despite the BIA's efforts, the Indian relocation program was not an unequivocal success. Critics of the program argued that, instead of improving the situation for Native Americans, it simply moved reservation problems such as poverty, alcoholism,

and limited economic opportunity to an urban setting. To compound this, the outflow of educated Indians created a brain drain on reservations, which affected future leadership.

At its root, the relocation program was too simplistic. Providing job placement services and temporary financial assistance to relocatees was not enough. Neither addressed the cultural shock that program participants experienced in cities. Even the counseling services that the BIA provided were inadequate to help urban Indians overcome language barriers, discrimination, and homesickness. Some relocatees never adjusted to urban life and returned to reservations. Others spent years drifting between reservation and city. The BIA acknowledged a return rate of 30 percent, but other studies indicated that the rate was as high as 60 percent.

Criticisms notwithstanding, the relocation program achieved some success. Between 1952 and 1968, the BIA assisted more than 100,000 Native Americans through its direct employment and adult vocational training programs. Most of the program participants indicated that they relocated for economic reasons, and once in the city they had more opportunities, economic and otherwise, than their reservation counterparts. Additionally, the influx of Native Americans in cities helped increase cultural diversity in urban areas. In the absence of their traditional culture, urban Indians worked together to create a new Indian identity that cut across tribal lines. They strengthened their cultural heritage through the establishment of Indian community centers that offered things the BIA did not, such as legal assistance, social services, and recreational programs. By 1980, half of all Native Americans lived in urban areas.

Jennifer L. Bertolet

See also Bureau of Indian Affairs: Establishing the Existence of an Indian Tribe; Meriam Report; Termination.

References and Further Reading

Fixico, Donald. 1986. *Termination and Relocation.* Albuquerque: University of New Mexico Press.

Fixico, Donald. 2000. *The Urban Indian Experience in America.* Albuquerque: University of New Mexico Press.

Neils, Elaine. 1971. *Reservation to City.* Chicago: University of Chicago.

Waddell, Jack O., and O. Michael Watson, eds. 1971. *The American Indian in Urban Society.* Boston: Little, Brown and Company.

Occupation of Alcatraz Island

On November 9, 1969, Richard Oakes, a Mohawk Indian, and a group of other young Indian college students put into San Francisco Bay in a chartered boat, *The Monte Cristo*. Their aim was to circle Alcatraz Island and claim the island for Indian people. This symbolic claim turned into a full-scale occupation that lasted until June 11, 1971, and that focused the attention of the American people on the government treatment of American Indians. Public sympathy, fanned by an outpouring of newspaper and magazine articles, lay with the Indians. The newly formed supratribal organization, Indians of All Tribes, kept their situation and demands before the public by starting their own radio program, "Radio Free Alcatraz," which was broadcast daily on Berkeley radio station KPFA, in Los Angeles on KPFX, and in New York City on WBAI. As a result, letters and telegrams inundated government officials, including President Richard M. Nixon. The mood of the public could be summed up in a telegram sent to Nixon on November 26, 1969, that read: "For once in this country's history let the Indians have something. Let them have Alcatraz."

Pressure began to build. Legislators entered statements into the *Congressional Record* emphasizing the need for a review of the federal government's Indian policies. Representative Jerome R. Waldie (Democrat–California) identified Alcatraz as a symbol of Indian unity and strength, a rallying point, a place of pride in Indian heritage and ideals. More to the point was the appeal made by California Congressman George E. Brown on December 23, 1969, when he called on President Nixon to negotiate with the Indian people to grant them title to the island to be used as a cultural center and an educational complex. It was in the midst of growing Indian activism and public awareness of the plight of Indian people that President Nixon faced the task of formulating his Indian policy. He stated in his message to Congress:

> It is long past time that the Indian policies of the Federal Government began to recognize and build upon the capacities and insights of the Indian people. Both as a matter of justice and as a matter of enlightened social policy, we must begin to act on the basis of what the Indians themselves have long been telling us. *The time has come to break decisively with the past and to create the conditions for a new era in which*

A teepee is erected on Alcatraz Island to symbolize the claim to native lands during the Native American occupation of the island in November 1969. A group called the Indians of All Tribes occupied the island until 1971. (Bettmann/Corbis)

the Indian future is determined by Indian acts and Indian decisions. [Author's emphasis]

The U.S. policy of termination of the recognition of American Indian tribes, in force roughly from the early 1950s through the 1960s, was the ultimate extension of assimilationist policy under which the Indian future was created by government acts and government decisions. Termination supporters argued for tribes to become subject to state laws in all respects. Since the trust status of tribal lands would end, that land would become taxable and transferable without BIA approval. All federal health, education, and other benefits to individuals would cease. Indian people across the nation began to voice disapproval of the termination policy once it became evident that the end result would be a loss of federal protection and the further loss of Indian lands. During this period, 109 tribal groups, including the Menominees, the Klamaths, the Ottawas, and thirty-six California *rancherias* were terminated. Some groups attempted joint suits to recover lost

lands and rights. Some, such as the Menominees, were partially successful. Others regained nothing at all. Indian people, however, were taking note of the success of national movements such as the black power movement and the La Raza movement, and leaders began to emerge from different tribal backgrounds to assert Indian nationalism. This awareness was coupled with the rapid expansion of Indian education in off-reservation boarding schools.

It was in part a result of the boarding schools' experience, as well as a new common consciousness stemming from experiences such as fighting in World War II and the growing youth/activist movements of the 1950s and 1960s, that the Indian leaders arose who would lead the 1969 occupation of Alcatraz Island, the 1972 march on Washington, DC, and the occupation of Wounded Knee in 1973.

The list of leaders reads like a who's who of Indian leaders: Richard Delaware Dior McKenzie from the Rosebud Reservation; Allen Cottier, president of the American Indian Council, Inc.; Martin Martinez; Garfield Spotted Elk; Walter Means, father

of the well-known Indian activist Russell Means; and Dennis Banks and George Mitchell, founders of the American Indian Movement. Richard Oakes, the founder of Indians of All Tribes, led the main occupation of Alcatraz Island. These young American Indians formed the nucleus of the first Indian supratribal organizations. As Stephen Cornell points out in his book, *The Return of the Native: American Indian Political Resurgence,* "their politics was often confrontational and explicitly supratribal" (Cornell, 1988, 198).

Alcatraz Island soon materialized as a place with which all Indians could identify. In a proclamation presented to T. E. Hannon, director of the California division of the General Services Administration (GSA), the occupiers stated that "it [Alcatraz Island] was isolated from modern facilities and without adequate means of transportation, it had no fresh running water, inadequate sanitation facilities, no oil or mineral rights, no industry, and no health care facilities. The soil was rocky and nonproductive, the land would not support game. There were no educational facilities, the population exceeded the land base, and the population had always been held as prisoners and kept dependent upon others. The Island was therefore equivalent to reservations set aside by the federal government for Indian people." The occupiers' intent was to claim unused Federal land based on the provisions of the Sioux Treaty of 1868 (which allowed the Sioux to occupy any abandoned military base but did not specify where those bases had to be, although later court action found that the treaty applied only to unused federal land adjacent to the Sioux Reservation in South Dakota) and to construct a university for American Indians as well as an Indian cultural center.

After the start of the occupation, Indians began to arrive from all across the United States, Canada, Mexico, and South America. At one point, the number of Indians living on the island grew to approximately 250. In November 1969, some 13,000 Indians visited the island. For the vast majority of Indian visitors, it was the first interaction they had had with Indians from other tribes, the first time they had felt a supratribal unity with other Indians.

The non-Indian private sector responded to calls for assistance from the Indians on the island. Non-Indian citizens, particularly the Asian American community of San Francisco, responded to the needs of the occupiers. They provided clothing, food, water, medical supplies, and school supplies for the children, despite a U.S. Coast Guard blockade of the island. Celebrities such as Jane Fonda, Robert Redford, and Marlon Brando visited the island and encouraged private parties to support the effort not only by donating usable items but by contacting politicians as well.

It was this pressure, coupled with the continuing radio, TV, and press coverage, as well as the art, theater, and other activities of the occupiers themselves, that forced political figures to take a stand on the issue of the future of Alcatraz Island. In addition to California Congressmen George E. Brown, Jr. and Jerome R. Waldie, and Congressman Robert W. Kastenmeier of Wisconsin, others went on record as supporting the Indian occupiers. Congressman Brown's remarks before the House of Representatives calling for a review of the federal government's policy in dealing with Indian people carried the signatures of ten additional congressmen. The comment of President Nixon himself that "the time has come to break decisively with the past and to create the conditions for a new era in which the Indian future is determined by Indian acts and Indian decisions" reflected the changing attitude, both public and private, regarding the need for radical policy change. (This change of attitude eventually led to meaningful, if inconsistent and partial, reform.)

Alcatraz Island had actually been the site of a previous Indian occupation. In 1964, a small group of Sioux Indians made the first attempt to claim the island. The Bay Area Chapter of the American Indian Council sponsored this action. Their attorney, as well as some twenty supporters and newspeople, accompanied the Indians. The *New York Times* gave full coverage of the 1964 occupation and explained the Indian rationale for the occupation. Wearing their tribal regalia, the five men conducted a victory dance and then planted a large American flag. Each then proceeded to physically stake his claim to a portion of the island. Talking with reporters, the Indians then offered to purchase Alcatraz at the price of 47 cents per acre, the price per acre equivalent to that of a settlement being debated for the taking of Indian land from the California Indians. McKenzie and his fellow Sioux Indians claimed homestead rights to the island based on the provisions of the Sioux Treaty of 1868. Reading from a typewritten document, the Indians stated that under the U.S. Code "we as Sioux Indians are settling on Federal land no longer appropriated." Elliott Leighton, San Francisco attorney for the Indians, explained that under the 1868 treaty the Sioux claimants had every

right to stake a claim to federal property "not used for a specific purpose." According to the treaty, said Leighton, "any Sioux male, over eighteen not living on a reservation could claim federal government lands not used for specific purposes." This same right had been granted in the 1887 Allotment Act. Congress revoked the 1887 Allotment Act in 1934 but the Sioux were specifically excluded. The only requirement was that they make improvements worth $200 or more during the first three years of occupancy. This, stated Leighton, "they were prepared to do." The *San Francisco Chronicle* reported that the Bay Area Indian Association wanted a university for American Indians established on the Island. While this "occupation" lasted for only three hours, it received nationwide newspaper coverage and doubtless inspired Indians of All Tribes five years later. After these events, federal authorities made a variety of proposals concerning the disposition of Alcatraz Island. Richard McKenzie and other members from the landing party attended the President's Commission on Alcatraz hearings held in San Francisco on April 24–25, 1964, McKenzie proposed at this meeting that an Indian cultural center and university be built on Alcatraz. The President's Commission met again on May 15, 1964, in executive session in Washington, DC. According to Assistant Attorney General Ramsey Clark, "old treaties aside, Alcatraz does not qualify as available public land and therefore was not open to homesteading or public allotment." It is interesting to note that the findings held not that the Sioux could not homestead under the Treaty of 1868, but rather that Alcatraz did not qualify as available land. McKenzie filed suit on September 13, 1965, in U.S. District Court, seeking to restrain the federal government from disposing of the island. He asked the court to recognize his right to settle upon and improve the island or, in lieu thereof, to be awarded $2.5 million. On June 5, 1968, McKenzie's suit was dismissed for lack of prosecution by McKenzie.

It was in the midst of these various proposals concerning the future of the island that Indians of the Bay Area decided it was time to take action. This second occupation originated as an idea during a discussion at the Native American Studies Program at San Francisco State College in February 1969. Members of the program were discussing the proposals being made for disposition of Alcatraz, and Richard Oakes announced to the students that taking Alcatraz would "be a good thing." Initially received with laughter, the idea remained in the minds of many students. Several months later, at a meeting in the American Indian Center in San Francisco, Oakes found a more receptive audience. Initial plans were made for a symbolic occupation in the summer of 1970. The plan was for the group to dress up in their "television costumes" and just make a pass around the island, to symbolically claim Alcatraz Island for the Indian people.

The symbolic intent of the occupation was overcome by the political and social pressures and frustration felt by the American Indian youth. A growing political and social consciousness on the part of Indians and non-Natives alike was heightened by the publication of books such as N. Scott Momaday's *House Made of Dawn*, Vine Deloria's *Custer Died for Your Sins*, and Harold Cardinal's *The Unjust Society*, not to mention the popular stage show by Arthur Kopit, *Indians*, and the movie, *Little Big Man*. Embodying the activist, politically aware ethos of the time, Richard Oakes and his supporters set out in their chartered boat. Suddenly, Oakes and four others jumped from the boat and swam to the island, claimed it "by right of discovery" in the name of Indians of All Tribes. Prior to jumping, Oakes stated that he "felt a sense of urgency," he "felt he had to do it." Later that same day Oakes and his followers were removed from the island by the U.S. Coast Guard. However, LaNada Boyer, a Shoshone/Bannock woman, urged Oakes and his group to return to the island that night and after nightfall they did so, unopposed.

It was this night, November 9, 1969, that they spent their first night on Alcatraz. The following day, GSA Regional Director T. E. Hannon asked the Indians to leave, which they agreed to do. Prior to leaving, however, they read a proclamation, claiming the island in the name of Indians of All Tribes by "right of discovery," the same authority used by Christopher Columbus for claiming the Americas for the king and queen of Spain. In a prepared statement, Oakes claimed that the Indians had a claim to Alcatraz under an 1868 treaty. Oakes then proceeded to offer to purchase the island for twenty-four dollars in glass beads and red cloth. Oakes and his followers then left the island for the second time. Later the same day in San Francisco, a spokesperson for the group said that the Indians planned to use Alcatraz as an Indian cultural and education center.

After the removal from the Island on November 10, Oakes went to the campus of the University of California, Los Angeles (UCLA) to think, plan, and gather supporters for a more organized occupation.

Oakes appealed for support and as a result recruited eighty supporters from the UCLA campus. Oakes and his supporters then began plans for a November 20th occupation, "this time to stay."

On the night of November 20, the most famous of the Indian occupations of Alcatraz began. Traveling by boat from Sausalito, the Indians were met by a blockade set up by the U.S. Coast Guard. The blockade proved unsuccessful even with the assistance of Coast Guard helicopters, and the landing party put ashore. The Coast Guard continued their blockade for two additional days in an attempt to stop any further occupation of the island and to stop the delivery of supplies to the Indians on Alcatraz. In the words of Oakes "the blockade was completely ineffective . . . we needed food and supplies . . . we couldn't have survived without all the people who ran that blockade."

On the day following the landing, Oakes and an attorney representing Indians of All Tribes presented a list of demands to the regional coordinator of the Department of Interior. Among the demands was the expectation that the federal government would give the Indians full title to the island within two weeks and provide ongoing funds for a major university and cultural center to be built on the island, to be administered by the Indian people. The prevailing national climate of protest against the ongoing war in Viet Nam, combined with the support received from the large number of individual Indians occupying the island, as well as moral and financial support from entire tribes and reservations, soon transformed these proposals into nonnegotiable demands.

On the island, however, the occupation force began to loose cohesiveness as time passed. Jealousy developed as the press identified Oakes as the leader of the occupation and the "mayor of Alcatraz." Oakes's twelve-year-old stepdaughter, Yvonne, was killed accidentally on January 7, 1970, when she fell three stories through an open stairwell in one of the island's apartment buildings. For some, including Oakes, this accident seemed to foretell the end of the occupation. Yvonne's death cast an air of gloom over the whole island. A few days later, having left the island for his daughter's funeral, Oakes announced that he would not return to Alcatraz. Factions had already begun to form among the seven-member elected council on the island.

As the occupation wore on, boredom also increased, and the more militant and vocal Indians began to seize control of the Indian occupation force.

Daily life on Alcatraz began to deteriorate sharply. Hygiene on the island was extremely poor, from sewage disposal to the preparation of food. Reports also began to surface that the sale and use of drugs was very much in evidence. In May 1970, San Francisco newspapers carried reports of Indian plans to begin destroying some of the buildings on the island. On June 1, three building were destroyed by fire. Government spokespeople, while making no direct charges, hinted that Indians had started the fires. On the island, the Indians charged that the fires had been started by a group of non-Indians to increase hostility toward the Indians. In November, some ninety Indians remained on Alcatraz, only three of whom were from the original landing party. Fewer than thirty Indians remained on the island by spring. On June 11, 1971, federal marshals removed the last fifteen Indians from Alcatraz Island without incident.

The occupation of Alcatraz Island produced lasting and important changes on the policy of the U.S. government toward Indian people. In response to President Nixon's call for a thorough evaluation of Indian policy, the historian Alvin M. Josephy, Jr. produced a hard-hitting document that established what many Indian experts already knew: The Bureau of Indian Affairs and indeed Indian policy were in need of a new direction. Although influenced by the Josephy recommendations, the cornerstone of the Nixon Indian policy was taken from the new voice of the Indian people and from the public concern about the treatment of Indian people. With this in mind, President Nixon laid the foundation for a federal policy of Indian self-determination. He acknowledged that the condition of Indian people was the heritage of centuries of injustice, from the time of first contact with European settlers to the ineffective and demeaning termination programs of the 1950s and 1960s. In this spirit, he also moved to honor some treaty provisions that had been ignored over the years. This new respect for treaties and self-determination resulted in part in the return of significant land to various tribes, including 48,000 acres containing the sacred Blue Lake to the Taos people; 40 million acres to the Dene nation; 21,000 acres to the Yakima nation; and 60,000 acres to the Warm Springs nation.

The occupation of Alcatraz Island was only the beginning of collective action by supratribal organizations, most notably the American Indian Movement (AIM). The large increase in such events in the early 1970s marked a shift from specifically tribal

issues, such as land usage or fishing rights, to issues involving Indians generally, and the events were engaged in primarily by urban Indians and Indian nationalist organizations. The occupation of Alcatraz Island was followed by a number of attempted and successful takeovers and occupations by supratribal urban groups: Fort Lewis and Fort Lawton in Washington; Ellis Island in New York; federal land in Santa Rosa and Shasta, California; abandoned missile sites and military installations in Davis and Richmond, California, Minneapolis, Milwaukee, and Chicago; and Mount Rushmore and the Badlands National Monuments. Actions such as the 1972 Trail of Broken Treaties, the occupation of the BIA offices in Washington, D.C., and the 1973 occupation of the village at Wounded Knee, South Dakota, had direct antecedents in the Alcatraz occupation.

Troy R. Johnson

See also American Indian Movement; Banks, Dennis; Land, Identity and Ownership of, Land Rights; Means, Russell; Oakes, Richard; Pan-Indianism; Red Power Movement.

References and Further Reading

Cornell, Stephen. *The Return of the Native: American Indian Political Resurgence.* New York: Oxford University Press, 1988.

Johnson, Troy R. 1994. "Alcatraz Revisited: The 25th Anniversary of The Occupation." Vol, 18, No. 4 (special edition). Berkeley: University of California Press.

Johnson, Troy R. 1996. *The Occupation of Alcatraz Island: Indian Self-Determination & The Rise of Indian Activism.* Urbana: University of Illinois Press.

Johnson, Troy R. 1999. *Alcatraz Is Not An Island.* Documentary. San Francisco: Diamond Island Productions.

Johnson, Troy R. 2001. "The Roots of Contemporary Native American Activism." In *Major Problems in American Indian History.* Edited by Albert Hurtado and Peter Iverson. Boston: Houghton-Mifflin.

Johnson, Troy, et al. 1997. *American Indian Activism: Alcatraz to the Longest Walk.* Urbana: University of Illinois Press.

Josephy, Alvin M., Jr., et al. 1999. *Red Power: The American Indians' Fight for Freedom,* 2nd ed. Lincoln: University of Nebraska Press.

Kemnitzer, Luis. 1994. "Personal Memories of Alcatraz, 1969." *American Indian Culture and Research Journal* 18, no. 4, 103–109.

Smith, Paul Chatt, and Robert Allen Warrior. 1996. *Like a Hurricane: The Indian Movement from Alcatraz to Wounded Knee.* New York: The New Press.

Talbot, Steve. 1978. "Free Alcatraz: The Culture of Native American Liberation."*Journal of Ethnic Studies* 6, no. 3 (Fall), 80–89.

Red Power Movement

"Red Power" was the term given to a generally post-1960 succession of highly visible, often confrontational Native American protest movements and actions that had as their goal the affirmation of American Indian identity and the reclaiming of power—political, social, and economic—over the people's lives. The movement grew out of years—centuries—of Indian poverty and political and cultural repression on reservations and, more recently, in urban environments. Characteristic of the Red Power Movement (RPM) were charismatic leaders, a conscious building on past resistance and social movements, the tactic of property seizure, the assertion of a pan-Indian identity, the formation of national activist organizations such as the American Indian Movement (AIM), and an agenda of self-determination for Indian people and communities.

Early national Indian reform movements, led by organizations such as the Society of American Indians (SAI), were composed of well-educated Indian professionals who favored assimilation as the solution to the poverty and misery of reservation life. These people were involved in the Indian policy debates of the 1920s and 1930s. The SAI and other reform groups laid the groundwork for a modern national Indian policy and an Indian lobbying force in American politics, which came to fruition with the formation of the National Congress of American Indians (NCAI) in 1944.

In the 1950s, in an early representation of Red Power, the people of the Iroquois League used passive resistance and militant protests to block various New York State projects. They demonstrated their opposition to the building of power projects such as the Kinzua Dam in upstate New York that required the displacement of Indians and the flooding of Indian land. Localized activism began to build during this period, as Indian people orchestrated more than twenty major demonstrations or nonviolent protests. These were aimed at ending further reductions of the Indian land base, stopping the termination of Indian tribes, and halting brutality and insensitivity toward Indian people. This rise in Indian activism was largely tribal in nature, how-

ever; very little, if any, pan-Indian or supratribal activity occurred at this time.

The 1960s witnessed a continuation of localized Indian protest actions such as the brief Indian occupation of Alcatraz Island in 1964. Preceding this event, however, were two major events. One was the American Indian Chicago Conference in 1961. Held on the campus of the University of Chicago, this conference was the first major modern pan-Indian event. Roughly 500 people from ninety tribes and bands from across the country met to share information, discuss issues, and formulate a vision for Native America. Dr. Sol Tax, professor of anthropology at the University of Chicago, originated the idea of the conference. Among the conference's major achievements were the publication of a Declaration of Indian Purpose and a dramatic advance in pan-tribal consciousness and activism.

The other major Red Power event in the 1960s consisted of the "fish-ins" along the rivers of Washington state. The fish-in movement began when tribal members and their supporters fished in waters that were protected by federal treaty rights but restricted by state and local law enforcement. In the mid-1950s, Washington authorities tried to control Indian fishing in off-reservation areas on the Puyallup River. The Indians argued that these were "usual and accustomed grounds and stations" within the meaning of the 1854 and 1855 treaties. In 1963, the U.S. Court of Appeals upheld the rights of Indian people to fish in accordance with the guaranteed treaty rights. In 1964, in defiance of the Supreme Court decision, Washington State courts closed the Nisqually River to Indian fishermen in areas off of the Nisqually Reservation. In the same year, the Survival of American Indians Association (SAIA) was formed as a protest organization and achieved success in asserting and preserving off-reservation fishing rights.

By the late 1960s and early 1970s, Native Americans had a rich and long legacy of social movements. Most were tribally centered on treaty or land issues. Others were multitribal, led by groups such as the NCAI, and composed of loose coalitions of tribal groups or members allied temporarily to struggle against a common external threat, such as termination. Most Indian social movements were aimed at issues of injustice, deprivation, or suppression, and the RPM was not unique on this score. It was not unusual for the RPM to rely on a history of past incidents to inform and organize their members and leadership. The RPM drew selectively on many ele-

American Indian Movement members, involved in "The Longest Walk" to protest anti-Indian legislation, walk along the Mall in Washington, DC, going to Capitol Hill to draw attention to their cause. (Wally McNamee/Corbis)

ments of Indian history, especially symbols of resistance. Geronimo, the Apache leader who fought against U.S. control over reservation communities in the 1880s, was a special symbol for the Alcatraz Island occupiers. Custer's defeat in 1876 was used as a symbol of Indian victory and defiance, and the Wounded Knee Massacre in 1890 became a major symbol of Indian repression during the Wounded Knee seizure in 1973.

The RPM was very different from earlier and contemporaneous Indian social movements. The members of the RPM sought change and inclusion in U.S. institutions, while preferring to retain Indian cultural identity. This was a form of nonassimilative inclusion that was not well understood at the time, but which later helped form the contemporary vision of a multicultural society. The defining characteristics of the RPM were its emphasis on

a supratribal identity and the tactic of property seizure, which was used only sparingly by other Indian social movements. Most Indian social movements, while often multitribal, were temporary alliances in opposition to a common threat or issue, and they did not strive to build a nationwide supratribal identity. While there had always been Indian activism, the Red Power Movement broke new ground in terms of tactics, new identity formation, visibility in U.S. society, and bringing attention to Indian issues.

The 1960s and early 1970s were a time of urban unrest across the nation. The Student Non-Violent Coordinating Committee (SNCC) was founded in April 1960, as a nonviolent group consisting of black-led sit-in activists. SNCC provided a powerful paradigm, and, combined with Students for a Democratic Society (SDS), founded in 1962, it formed a new movement that came to be called the The New Left. Young African Americans were hearing an angrier and more militant voice, a voice coming from former members of SNCC and participants in the Civil Rights Movement. Many Indian activists observed the Civil Rights Movement and contemplated how this activity could be brought to bear on Indian issues. At the same time, the United States was deeply involved in an unpopular war in Vietnam. All of these currents, plus the Black Power Movement, the rise of Latino movement La Raza, and the stirring of the new feminism were sweeping the nation, particularly college campuses. Ubiquitous demonstrations raised the level of consciousness of college students. People of all ages were becoming sensitized to the unrest among minority and gender groups, who were staging demonstrations and proclaiming their points of view, many of which were incorporated by student activists. Sit-ins, sleep-ins, teach-ins, lockouts, and boycotts became everyday occurrences on college campuses.

By the late 1960s, more than 50 percent of American Indians lived in cities. This trend toward urbanization of the American Indian population began during World War II as a result of wartime industrial job opportunities, federal Indian urban relocation programs, and the general urbanization of the U.S. population as a whole. In the San Francisco Bay Area, which was one of the largest of more than a dozen relocation sites, newly urban Indians formed their own organizations to provide the support that the government had promised but failed to provide. Eventually, some thirty Bay Area social clubs were formed to meet the needs of the urban Indians and their children—children who would want the opportunity to go to college and better themselves. These people represented a population that was poised on the brink of activism: disillusioned Indian youth from reservations, urban centers, and universities who called for Red Power in their crusade to reform the conditions of their people. These discontented urban Indians were speaking out against the treatment they were receiving from the local, state, and federal governments, both in the cities and on the reservations. The Alcatraz occupation came out of the Bay Area colleges and universities and other California college campuses where young, educated Indian students joined with other minority groups during the 1969 Third World Liberation Front strike and began demanding that colleges offer courses relevant to Indian students. Indian history written and taught by non-Indian instructors was no longer acceptable to these young students, awakened as they were to the possibility of social protest to bring attention to the shameful treatment of Indian people. Despite the failure to achieve their immediate objectives, the Alcatraz occupiers created a watershed moment in Native American protest that resulted in an escalation of Indian activism around the country. The occupation, which caught the attention of the entire country, provided a forum for airing long-standing Indian grievances and for the expression of Indian pride. Indianness would now be judged on whether or not one was present at Alcatraz, Fort Lawson, Mount Rushmore, Detroit, Sheep Mountain, Plymouth Rock, Pitt River, or other protest sites. The RPM controlled the language, the issues, and some of the nation's attention.

The underlying goals of the Indians on Alcatraz were to awaken the American public to the reality of the situation faced daily by Native Americans and to assert the need for Indian self-determination. In this they succeeded. Additionally, the occupation of Alcatraz Island was a springboard for the RPM, inspiring the large number of takeovers and demonstrations that began shortly after the initial landing and that continued into the late 1970s. These included the Trail of Broken Treaties, the BIA headquarters takeover in 1972, and Wounded Knee II in 1973. Many of the approximately seventy-four occupations that followed Alcatraz were either planned by or included people who had been involved in the Alcatraz occupation or who had gained their strength from the new "Indianness" that grew out of that movement.

During and after the occupation of Alcatraz Island, RPM activists spread across the country using the protest tactic of occupying mainly federal property. There were dozens of Alcatraz-type occupations undertaken by Indians from a variety of tribes sharing a common interest in Indian and tribal rights broadly conceived. RPM protest events were sited initially in urban centers and at national monuments and landmarks, but later activism spread to Indian reservations as well. Red Power activists took their early tactical cues from the Alcatraz occupation. An example was the event of November 3, 1970, in Davis, California, in which scores of Indians scaled a barbed wire fence and seized an old Army communications center. Raising a big white tepee on the surplus government property, seventy-five Indians occupied it for use in development of an Indian cultural center.

These RPM occupations represented a tactic designed to draw attention to American Indian historical and contemporary grievances: unsettled land claims, conditions on reservations, recognition of cultural and social rights, tribal self-determination. Most occupations were short-lived, lasting only a few days or weeks, such as those that occurred during 1970–1971 at Fort Lawton and Fort Lewis in Washington, at Ellis Island in New York, at the Twin Cities Naval Air Station in Minneapolis, at former Nike missile sites on Lake Michigan near Chicago and at Argonne, Illinois, and at an abandoned Coast Guard lifeboat station in Milwaukee.

A number of protest camps were also established during the early 1970s, including those at Mount Rushmore and the Badlands National Monuments. During the same years, government buildings, including regional Bureau of Indian Affairs offices in Cleveland and Denver, as well as the main headquarters of the BIA in Washington, DC, also became the sites of protests. Many of these protests and occupations included celebrations of Indian culture and ethnic renewal, while others included efforts to provide educational or social services to urban Indians.

As the 1970s proceeded, American Indian protest occupations lasted longer, and some took on a more serious, sometimes violent tone, revealing the depth of grievances and the difficulty of solutions to the problems confronting Native Americans after nearly five centuries of non-Native contact. An example was the November 1972 weeklong occupation of the Bureau of Indian Affairs in Washington, DC. This unplanned occupation occurred at the end of the Trail of Broken Treaties, a protest event involving caravans that traveled across the United States to convene in Washington at a large camp in order to dramatize and present Indian concerns at the national BIA offices. The breakdown of arrangements resulted in the occupation of BIA offices and the seizure of BIA files by protesters; the protest ended a week later after a series of negotiations with federal officials.

Beginning in 1972, the Alcatraz-style takeovers and occupations ceased as the RPM strategy shifted. The reasons for the clustering of Alcatraz-like events and the reasons for the shift from occupations of federal property to a different form and terrain of contention after 1972 are linked to the organizational underpinning of supratribal collective action, its urban population base, and the major Red Power movement organization, the American Indian Movement (AIM).

The prominence of AIM in Red Power protest after Alcatraz makes inclusion of this important and influential organization important in any discussion of the Red Power Movement. The nineteen-month occupation of Alcatraz demonstrated beyond all doubt that strong actions by Indians could not only result in broad public exposure of the issues and substantial national/international support for Indian rights, but also could potentially force significant concessions from the federal government.

This observation suggests that the Alcatraz occupation marked not only a turning point in American Indian protest and ethnic identity; it also had an important impact on the future course of AIM. Before Alcatraz, AIM was essentially an Indian rights organization, mainly concerned with monitoring law enforcement treatment of Native people in American cities. However, Alcatraz captured the imagination of AIM as well as the rest of the country, and as a result AIM embarked on an historic journey into Indian protest activism.

AIM influenced the direction of the RPM in several ways. First, networks of urban Indian centers, Indian churches, and Indian charitable organizations helped plan and support collective actions by AIM. Also, protest activities and strategies moved through Indian communities via Indian social and kin networks, and through the "powwow circuit," which passed information along to Indian families engaged in travel between the cities and reservations. A third, and perhaps the most important factor contributing to AIM's informal influence on the RPM, was through the news media. AIM leadership

was particularly skillful at encouraging the various news media—newspapers, radio, magazines, and television—to dramatize Indian problems and protests.

AIM's first attempt at a national protest action came on Thanksgiving Day, 1970, when members seized the *Mayflower II* in Plymouth, Massachusetts, to challenge a celebration of colonial expansion into what then was mistakenly considered to be the New World. During this action, AIM leaders acknowledged the occupation of Alcatraz Island as the symbol of a newly awakened desire among Indians for unity and authority in a white world. From this beginning, AIM mounted actions both off the reservations and on them.

The involvement of urban Indian individuals and groups, such as AIM, in protest actions situated on reservations revealed tensions inside Indian communities. These tensions were not only between urban and reservation Indians, or between AIM and tribal governments, or between different age cohorts. They also took place among the political divisions on the reservations themselves. All of these tensions became magnified as the activism of the 1970s progressed. The tone of protest became less celebratory and other-directed and more harsh and inward. No single event of the RPM era more clearly illustrated the combination of Indian grievances and community tensions than the events on the Pine Ridge Reservation in the spring of 1973, a ten-week-long siege that came to be known as Wounded Knee II.

The conflict at Wounded Knee, a small town on the Pine Ridge Reservation in South Dakota, involved a dispute within Pine Ridge's Oglala Lakota (Sioux) tribe over the controversial tribal chairman, Richard Wilson. Wilson was viewed as a corrupt puppet of the BIA by some segments of the tribe, including those associated with AIM. For his part, Wilson viewed AIM as no less than a group of Communist stooges. An effort to impeach Wilson resulted in a division of the tribe into opposing camps that eventually armed themselves and entered into a two-and-one-half-month-long siege that involved tribal police; government, AIM, reservation residents; federal law enforcement officials; the BIA; local citizens; nationally prominent entertainment figures; national philanthropic, religious, and legal organizations; and the national news media.

The siege began with the arrival of a caravan of approximately 250 AIM supporters, led by Dennis Banks and Russell Means, on the evening of February 27, 1973. Although the armed conflict that followed AIM's arrival is generally characterized as a standoff between AIM and its supporters and the Wilson government and its supporters, the siege at Wounded Knee was really only one incident in what had been a long history of political instability and factional conflict on the Pine Ridge Reservation. The ensuing weeks were characterized by shootouts, roadblocks, negotiations, visiting delegations, and the movement of refugees out of various fire zones. When the siege ended on May 9, 1973, two Indians were dead and an unknown number were wounded on both sides. Many of the AIM members involved in the siege spent years in litigation, exile, and prison as a result of the siege and the several armed conflicts that followed in its wake. Although the action at Wounded Knee was inconclusive in terms of determining the balance of power in the Oglala Lakota tribal council, the long siege became an important component of the RPM repertoire of contention.

In the next few years there ensued a number of long- and short-term occupations. Many, but not all, of these occupations were similar to Wounded Knee in that they occurred on reservations and involved tribal factions associated with AIM or urban tribal members. These events included the six-month occupation of a former girls' camp on state-owned land at Moss Lake, New York, in 1974; the five-week armed occupation of a vacant Alexian Brothers noviciary by the Menominee Warrior Society near the Menominee Reservation in Wisconsin in 1975; the eight-day takeover of a tribally owned Fairchild Electronics assembly plant on the Navajo reservation in New Mexico in 1975; an occupation of the Yankton Sioux Industries plant on the reservation near Wagner, South Dakota, in 1975; and the weeklong occupation of a juvenile detention center by members of the Puyallup tribe in Washington in 1976.

As the 1970s proceeded, the RPM protests were increasingly enacted in an atmosphere of heightened confrontation. The last major event of the RPM occurred in July 1978, as several hundred Native Americans marched into Washington, DC, at the end of the Longest Walk, a protest march that had begun five months earlier in San Francisco. The Longest Walk was intended to symbolize the forced removal of Native Americans from their aboriginal homelands and draw attention to the continuing problems of Indian people and communities. The event was also intended to expose and challenge the backlash movement against Indian treaty rights that was

gaining strength around the country and in Congress. This backlash could be seen in a growing number of bills before Congress to abrogate Indian treaties and restrict Indian rights. Unlike the events of the mid-1970s, the Longest Walk was conceived as a peaceful event that included tribal spiritual leaders and elders among its participants; the protest event ended without violence. Thus, Red Power had come full circle, from the festive Alcatraz days, through a cycle of violent confrontation, to the traditional quest for spiritual unity that marked the end of the Longest Walk.

Troy R. Johnson

See also Alcatraz Proclamation: A Proclamation from the Indians of All Tribes; American Indian Movement; Fishing Rights; National Congress of American Indians; Relocation; Society of American Indians; Trail of Broken Treaties.

References and Further Reading

Catalogue of Federal Domestic Assistance, 15.022 Tribal Self-Governance. Available at: http://12.46.245.173/pls/portal30/CATALOG. AGY_PROGRAM_LIST_RPT.show.

Champagne, Duane, ed. 1994. *The Native North American Almanac: A Reference Work on Native North Americans in the United States and Canada.* Detroit, MI: Gale Research.

Cornell, Stephen. 1988. *The Return of the Native; American Indian Political Resurgence.* New York: Oxford University Press.

Deloria, Vine, Jr. 1985. *American Indian Policy in the Twentieth Century.* Norman: University of Oklahoma Press.

Grossman, Mark. 1996. *The ABC-CLIO Companion to the Native American Rights Movement.* Santa Barbara, CA: ABC-CLIO.

Getches, David H., Charles F. Wilkinson, and Robert A. Williams, Jr. 1998. *Cases and Materials on Federal Indian Law,* 4th ed. American Casebook Series. St. Paul, MN: West.

Gordon-McCutchan, R. C. 1991. *The Taos Indians and the Battle for Blue Lake.* Sante Fe, NM: Red Crane Books.

Johnson, Troy. 1996. *The Occupation of Alcatraz Island: Indian Self Determination & The Rise of Indian Activism.* Urbana: University of Illinois Press.

Johnson, Troy, Joane Nagel, and Duane Champagne. 1997. *American Indian Activism: Alcatraz to the Longest Walk.* Urbana: University of Illinois Press.

Matthiessen, Peter. 1992. *In the Spirit of Crazy Horse.* New York: Penguin.

Nagel, Joane. 1996. *American Indian Ethnic Renewal: Red Power and the Resurgence of Identity and Culture.* New York: Oxford University Press.

Ryser, Rudolph C. (principal investigator). 1995. *Indian Self-Government Process Evaluation Project, Preliminary Findings.* Olympia, WA: Center for World Indigenous Studies.

Senese, Guy B. 1991. *Self-Determination and the Social Education of Native Americans.* New York: Praeger.

Smith, Paul C., and Robert Allen Warrior. 1996. *Like a Hurricane: The Indian Movement from Alcatraz to Wounded Knee.* New York: The New Press.

Trail of Broken Treaties

Conceived in South Dakota by members of the nascent American Indian Movement (AIM), the Trail of Broken Treaties strove to unite Indians from reservations all over the country in a protest "march" from the West Coast to Washington, DC. Planned as a peaceful demonstration to confront the government with long-held Indian grievances stemming from broken treaty agreements, the protest is best remembered for its finale—the six-day occupation of the headquarters of the Bureau of Indian Affairs (BIA).

The idea of the march emerged following the annual Sun Dance on the Rosebud Reservation in August 1972 during discussions at the home of AIM's spiritual leader, Leonard Crow Dog, about the future of the movement. Robert Burnette, former two-time chairman of the Rosebud Sioux tribe, articulated the plan and suggested the demonstration be timed to coincide with the upcoming presidential election, thereby compelling presidential candidates to address issues of concern to Indian Country.

Those in attendance at Crow Dog's Paradise decided to hold a formal meeting in Denver the following month to craft a clear strategy and work out logistical details for the event. Accordingly, on September 30, AIM leaders met at the New Albany Hotel in the Colorado capital. In addition to Burnette, those in attendance included Russell Means, Dennis Banks, George Mitchell, Clyde and Vernon Bellecourt, and Reuben Snake.

Outside of AIM, representatives from National Indian Leadership Training, the National Indian Brotherhood from Canada, the National Indian Lutheran Board, the National Indian Youth Council, the Native American Rights Fund, and the National Indian Committee of Alcohol and Drug Abuse, many of whom were already in town for their annual conferences, also attended, along with members from various local activist groups. In three days,

Dennis Banks (left) and preacher Carl McEntire during the 1972 "Trail of Broken Treaties" occupation of the Bureau of Indian Affairs headquarters in Washington, DC. (Bettmann/Corbis)

the gathering organized eleven committees and elected Burnette and Snake as cochairs of the event they chose to dub either the Trail of Broken Treaties Caravan or the less provocative Pan American Native Quest for Justice. Anita Collins and LaVonna Weller served respectively as secretary and treasurer of the group.

As envisaged in Denver, the plan called for three caravans to leave different points on the Pacific coast and travel through Indian communities in the West on their way to an October 23 rendezvous at the Twin Cities in Minnesota. Each caravan would be led by a spiritual leader carrying a sacred pipe. Drums were to be beaten day and night as a reminder to the American people of the broken treaties with Indian nations. Once in St. Paul, leaders of the march planned to craft a document outlining Indian demands of the federal government. The document would then be taken by a single caravan to

Washington, DC, and delivered to the White House. Burnette, emphasizing the need for order, self-discipline, and sobriety on the march, stated, "The Caravan must be our finest hour" (Smith and Warrior, 1996, 143).

In early October, the three caravans set out on the Trail of Broken Treaties. From Seattle, Washington, three cars and a van headed east under the direction of AIM leader Russell Means. Sid Mills, a decorated Vietnam veteran, and Hank Adams, founder and president of the Survival of American Indians Association, also provided leadership for this northernmost column. Both Mills and Adams were active in the struggle for Native American fishing rights in the Pacific Northwest. Traveling through Indian communities in Washington, Idaho, and Montana, the procession stopped often to raise money for gas and food and to attract more participants. On Columbus Day, Means and his

compatriots stopped on the Crow Reservation in Montana at the site of the Battle of Little Bighorn, leaving behind a plaque honoring the warriors who fought there in 1876 against the U.S. Seventh Cavalry.

While Means, Mills, and Adams made their way across the Rockies and onto the northern Great Plains, a second caravan composed of five cars departed San Francisco, California, bound for Nevada and Utah. Led by AIM cofounder Dennis Banks, the cavalcade of vehicles slowly increased in size as it approached Salt Lake City, where Vernon Bellecourt unsuccessfully sought financial assistance from the Mormon Church. The Mormons did, however, provide aid in the form of food and gas. Then heading first toward Denver via the Ute Reservation in southern Utah, Banks ultimately led his group north through Wyoming toward the Pine Ridge Reservation in South Dakota, where he linked up with Russell Means at Wounded Knee.

The third, and last, caravan set forth from Los Angeles, California, under direction of Bill Sargent and Rod Skenandore. After a slow start, the procession traveled through the Southwest before turning north toward Minnesota. In Lawton, Oklahoma, Carter Camp, a member of AIM, made a vain attempt to take over the Fort Sill Indian School. A report of Camp's actions dismayed local and federal BIA officials and provided precisely the kind of publicity Burnette hoped to avoid. As with the other two caravans, this southernmost group depended on local support and hospitality for sustenance and shelter. On October 23, they rendezvoused with the already combined caravans under Means and Banks and merged into one procession as they entered Minneapolis. All told, the three groups visited over thirty-three reservations and garnered nearly 600 participants on their way to Minnesota.

As designed, the caravan paused at the state fairgrounds in St. Paul for four days as the group's leadership, chaired by Reuben Snake, held workshops to develop position papers for collation into a final document outlining Indian demands of the federal government. Owing to his experience in treaty litigation in the Pacific Northwest, the responsibility for drafting the final manuscript fell to Hank Adams. Isolated in a motel room for almost two days, Adams created the Twenty Points—essentially a list of reforms calling for, among other things, the sovereignty of individual Indian nations, the restoration of the authority of existing treaties, the resubmission of unratified treaties to the U.S. Sen-

ate, mandatory federal injunctions against state agencies or non-Indians who contravene treaties, protection of Indian religious freedom and cultural integrity, and the abolishment of the Bureau of Indian Affairs. With the Twenty Points in hand, the assembly prepared to depart for the nation's capital and dispatched Robert Burnette, George Mitchell, and Anita Collins in advance to secure accommodations for the members of the caravan and to make local arrangements for their week of planned events in the District.

With ever-increasing numbers, the Trail of Broken Treaties Caravan left St. Paul bound for Washington via Milwaukee and Indianapolis. Arriving at their destination in the late evening of November 2, five days before the presidential election, the nearly 1,000 participants in the four-mile-long procession soon sought shelter for their stay. Burnette's professed arrangements for food and housing with local churches and civil rights supporters all over the city failed to materialize (there even had been some talk of using RFK Stadium), and the tired travelers wound up in the rat-infested basement of St. Stephen and the Incarnation Church. The following morning, vowing to improve accommodations, AIM leaders took their demand for better housing to what proved to be the final stop on the Trail of Broken Treaties—the Bureau of Indian Affairs.

On November 3, 1972, the caravan of cars, pickup trucks, vans, and buses that had set forth on the West Coast more than four weeks earlier pulled into parking lots and side streets around the intersection of Constitution Avenue and 19th Street in Washington, DC. Ushered into the BIA building's auditorium to await discussion of their grievances with officials, Indian activists found themselves growing steadily frustrated at the lack of a satisfactory resolution to their demands. As the day wore on, AIM leaders sensed duplicity in the government's intentions, and, when U.S. General Services Administration (GSA) police tried to force their eviction at 5 p.m., the activists chose to take control of the building and proclaim it the Native American Embassy. The BIA occupation lasted until November 8, after White House officials agreed to create a task force within sixty days to consider the Twenty Points, to guarantee no prosecution of individuals for the seizure of a federal building, and to provide $66,650 in travel funds to help the participants return home. Before leaving, many of the occupiers (much to the chagrin of some of their leaders) expressed their personal frustration and overall dis-

satisfaction with the government's handling of their grievances by vandalizing the building's interior and confiscating BIA documents and files.

While at its outset a remarkable demonstration of Indian unity, the Trail of Broken Treaties failed to accomplish its goals and broke down in the end. By the beginning of November, the outcome of the presidential election was never in doubt and the caravan's presence in Washington provided no incentive for the incumbent Nixon administration to direct additional attention toward Indian concerns. The administration did, however, respond to the Twenty Points in January 1973, but only in very general terms and by highlighting the president's successful endeavors for Indian peoples during his first term. The petition for treaty reform was denied. Without a doubt, however, the Trail of Broken Treaties helped set the stage for AIM's next major confrontation with the federal government—the occupation and subsequent siege of Wounded Knee in February 1973.

Alan C. Downs

See also American Indian Movement; Banks, Dennis; Bureau of Indian Affairs: Establishing the Existence of an Indian Tribe; Means, Russell; Occupation of Wounded Knee.

References and Further Reading

Banks, Dennis, and Richard Erdoes. 2004. *Ojibwa Warrior: Dennis Banks and the Rise of the American Indian Movement.* Norman: University of Oklahoma Press.

Vine Deloria, Vine, Jr. 1985. *Behind the Trail of Broken Treaties: An Indian Declaration of Independence.* Austin: University of Texas Press.

Means, Russell, and Marvin J. Wolf. 1995. *Where White Men Fear to Tread: The Autobiography of Russell Means.* New York: St. Martin's Griffin.

Smith, Paul Chaat, and Robert Allen Warrior. 1996. *Like a Hurricane: The Indian Movement from Alcatraz to Wounded Knee.* New York: The New Press.

Pine Ridge Political Murders

Following the occupation of Wounded Knee, South Dakota, in 1973, more than sixty American Indian Movement (AIM) members and supporters were killed on and near the Oglala (Lakota) reservation at Pine Ridge for political reasons. Two FBI agents also lost their lives in the tense aftermath of the occupation, deaths for which the Anishinabe activist Leonard Peltier was convicted on what his many defenders around the world contend was falsified

evidence. For three years, the Pine Ridge reservation was essentially devoid of law enforcement or prosecution for the Indian murders, the best known of which involved the Micmac activist, Anna Mae Pictou Aquash.

From the early 1970s until his defeat by Al Trimble in 1976, Pine Ridge tribal chairman Richard Wilson (Oglala Lakota, 1936–1990) outfitted a tribal police force that was often called the GOONs (Guardians of Oglala Nation) squad. This police force, which terrorized the local community, was financed with money from the federal government. The local context of the Wounded Knee occupation included an effort to confront Wilson's policies, which often favored non-Indian ranchers, farmers, and corporations, and to try to end the violence plaguing the community. Wilson answered his detractors by stepping up the terror, examples of which were described in a chronology kept by the Wounded Knee Legal Defense-Offense Committee. One of the GOONs's favorite weapons was the automobile. Officially, such deaths could be reported as traffic accidents. Wilson had a formidable array of supporters on the reservation, many of whom criticized AIM for being urban-based and insensitive to reservation residents' needs.

The struggle between AIM and Wilson also took place within the realm of tribal politics. Russell Means, an Oglala who had helped found AIM, challenged Wilson's bid for reelection in 1974. In the primary, Wilson trailed Means, 667 votes to 511. Wilson won the final election over Means by fewer than 200 votes in balloting that the U.S. Commission on Civil Rights later found to be permeated with fraud. The Civil Rights Commission recommended a new election, which was not held.

Following the occupation of Wounded Knee, AIM cofounders Dennis Banks and Russell Means were charged with three counts of assault on federal officers, one charge each of conspiracy and one each of larceny. Banks and Means, facing five charges each, could have been sentenced to as many as eighty-five years in prison. For several months in 1974, the defense and prosecution presented their cases in a St. Paul, Minnesota federal court. On September 16, Judge Fred J. Nichol dismissed all the charges. The judge said that the FBI's agents had lied repeatedly during the trial while under oath and had often furnished defense attorneys with altered documents. Judge Nichol said that R. D. Hurd, the federal prosecutor, had deliberately deceived the court. "The FBI," said Judge Nichol,

A scene at the Wounded Knee takeover at the Pine Ridge reservation in North Dakota in 1973. (UPI/Bettmann/Corbis)

"has stooped to a new low" (Johansen and Maestas, 1979, 91). To the chagrin of the judge and jurors, the Justice Department responded by presenting Hurd with an award for "superior performance" during the trial.

An activist in the American Indian Movement during the 1973 confrontation at Wounded Knee, Leonard Peltier (born 1944) was caught in a shootout with Federal Bureau of Investigation agents and state police at the Jumping Bull Compound on the Pine Ridge Indian Reservation in June 1975. He was later convicted of killing two FBI agents, Ronald Williams and Jack Coler. The trial, which was held in Fargo, North Dakota; Federal District Court in 1977, has since become the focus of an international protest movement aimed at obtaining a retrial.

Even before Peltier's trial opened, the prosecution's case began to fall apart. Discovery proceedings produced an affidavit, signed by government witness Myrtle Poor Bear dated February 19, 1976, stating that the woman had not been on the scene of the June 25 gun battle in which the two FBI agents had

been shot to death. This information, contained in an affidavit that had not been sent to Canada by the U.S. government during Peltier's extradition hearing, contradicted two other statements attributed to Poor Bear.

More importantly, Poor Bear herself recanted her testimony. On April 13, out of earshot of the jury, Poor Bear told the court (having been called by the defense) that she had never seen Peltier before meeting him at the trial. Furthermore, Poor Bear said that she had not been allowed to read the three affidavits that bore her name and implicated Peltier in the murders and that FBI agents David Price and Bill Wood had threatened her and her children with physical harm if she did not sign them. Despite this and other highly irregular proceedings, Peltier was convicted for the agents' deaths and received two life sentences. He remains in prison today.

Dennis Banks eluded capture during the FBI dragnet that followed the shooting deaths of two agents at Pine Ridge for which Peltier was convicted. Banks went underground before receiving amnesty from California Governor Jerry Brown. Banks went

on to earn an associate of arts degree at the University of California (Davis) and during the late 1970s helped found and direct Deganawidah-Quetzecoatl University, a Native-controlled college. After Jerry Brown's term as California governor ended in 1984, Banks was sheltered by the Onondagas on their reservation near Syracuse, New York.

Anna Mae Pictou Aquash (MicMac, 1945–1976) was one of the most noteworthy of more than sixty people who were killed for political reasons on the Pine Ridge reservation during the three years following the Wounded Knee occupation. Aquash, from Nova Scotia, Canada, became involved in the American Indian Movement during its peak of activity shortly after 1970; she was a close friend of Peltier, Banks, Means, and others who were arrested and charged in connection with the Wounded Knee occupation in 1973 and other events. Following the shooting deaths of FBI agents Coler and Williams in 1975, Aquash was pursued and arrested by the Federal Bureau of Investigation as a possible material witness to the crime. At the height of the violence at the Pine Ridge reservation in 1976, she was found murdered near a Pine Ridge highway.

On February 24, 1976, Roger Amiott, a rancher, found Aquash's body near Wanblee, in the northeastern section of the Pine Ridge Indian Reservation. Dr. W. O. Brown, a pathologist who performed autopsies under contract with the Bureau of Indian Affairs, arrived the following day. After examining the body, Brown announced that the woman, who still had not been officially identified, had died of exposure to the brutal South Dakota winter.

The FBI decided that the only way to identify the woman was to sever her hands and send them to the FBI's crime laboratories in the Washington, DC area. Agents on the scene reasoned that the body was too badly decomposed to take fingerprints at Pine Ridge. Ken Sayres, BIA police chief at Pine Ridge, would say later that no one had been called to the morgue to attempt identification of the body before the hands were severed.

A week after the body was found, Aquash—now missing her hands as well as her identity—was buried at Holy Rosary Catholic Cemetery, Pine Ridge. On March 3 the FBI announced Aquash's identity. Her family was notified of the death March 5. They did not believe that she had died of natural causes. At thirty-two years of age, Aquash had been in good health and was trained to survive in cold weather. She did not drink alcohol or smoke tobacco. Her friends remembered that she had

smuggled food past federal government roadblocks into Wounded Knee during another brutal South Dakota winter, almost three years to the day before her body had been found. A new autopsy was demanded.

In the midst of the controversy, Aquash's body was exhumed. Her family retained an independent pathologist, Dr. Gary Peterson of St. Paul, Minnesota. Dr. Peterson reopened the skull and found a .32-caliber bullet, which he said had been fired from a gun placed at the base of Aquash's neck. The bullet was not difficult to find:; "It should have been discovered the first time," Peterson said (Johansen and Maestas, 1979, 106). Asked about the bullet he had not found, Dr. W. O. Brown, the BIA coroner, replied, according to an account in the *Washington Star* (May 24, 1976), "A little bullet isn't hard to overlook" (Johansen and Maestas, 1979, 106).

Following identification of Aquash's decomposed body, the Canadian government and the U.S. Commission on Civil Rights demanded an investigation. The U.S. Justice Department announced that it would look into the case, but the "investigation" languished in bureaucratic limbo. Aquash's friends refused to let her spirit pass away. On March 14, Aquash's body was wrapped in a traditional star quilt as several women from the Oglala village mourned her passing for two days and two nights.

On April 2, 2003, twenty-seven years after Aquash's murder, federal agents arrested a man and charged him with the death. Arlo Looking Cloud, forty-nine, was arrested in Denver and pleaded innocent to a charge of first-degree murder. Looking Cloud worked as a security guard for AIM, checking people at the gates of events and patrolling the grounds, said Paul DeMain, editor of the bimonthly newspaper, *News From Indian Country*. AIM was beset by internal disputes (and infiltrated by FBI informers) at the time, DeMain said (Walker, 2003). On February 6, 2004, Looking Cloud was convicted of the murder.

Using only documented political deaths, the yearly murder rate on Pine Ridge Reservation between March 1, 1973, and March 1, 1976 was 170 per 100,000. By comparison, Detroit, the reputed "murder capital of the United States," had a rate of 20.2 in 1974. The U.S. average was 9.7 per 100,000, with the range for large cities as follows: Chicago, 15.9; New York City, 16.3; Washington, DC, 13.4; Los Angeles, 12.9; Seattle, 5.6; and Boston, 5.6. An estimated 20,000 persons were murdered in the United States in 1974. In a nation of 200 million persons (the

population of the United States in 1974), a murder rate comparable to that of Pine Ridge between 1973 and 1976 would have left 340,000 persons dead for political reasons in one year and 1.32 million in three years.

Bruce E. Johansen

See also American Indian Movement; Aquash, Anna Mae Pictou; Banks, Dennis; Means, Russell; Peltier, Leonard; Wilson, Richard.

References and Further Reading

Brand, Johanna. 1978. *The Life and Death of Anna Mae Aquash.* Toronto, ON: Lorimer.

Johansen, Bruce E., and Roberto F. Maestas. 1979. *Wasi'chu: The Continuing Indian Wars.* New York: Monthly Review Press.

Matthiessen, Peter. 1991. *In the Spirit of Crazy Horse.* New York: Viking.

Weir, David, and Lowell Bergman. 1977. "The Killing of Anna Mae Aquash." *Rolling Stone,* April 7.

Occupation of Wounded Knee

The 1973 occupation of the Pine Ridge Reservation town of Wounded Knee, South Dakota, took place in the midst of a national backlash against the war in Vietnam and the Black Power and La Raza movements in the United States, and followed the nineteen-month American Indian occupation of Alcatraz Island (December 1969–July 2001). Whereas the occupation of Alcatraz Island had been carried out by a nonconfrontational group, Indians of All Tribes, the occupation of Wounded Knee involved a new group on the national activist scene, the American Indian Movement, better known as AIM.

The American Indian Movement was founded in 1968 by Clyde Bellecourt, Dennis Banks, and Mary Wilson, all Chippewas from Minnesota. AIM arose out of the concerns of Native Americans in Minneapolis, Minnesota, and focused on improving the life of Indians in the urban environment. Members coordinated a neighborhood patrol to circumvent unjust arrests and police mishandling of American Indian residents. They ultimately extended their concerns to include the reform of relations between Indians and the federal government. AIM attracted a new generation of Indian youth to its more activist, confrontational style. The group's initial actions included an occupation of Mount Rushmore, a symbolic Thanksgiving Day occupation of a mock-up of the Mayflower sailing ship at Plymouth Rock, and the Trail of Broken Treaties caravan to Washington,

DC, which ended with the occupation of the BIA building. Most notable, however, was the 1973 occupation of Wounded Knee village in South Dakota that lasted seventy-one days.

In February 1972, Raymond Yellow Thunder, a Lakota Indian, was abducted by two white men in Gordon, Nebraska. After forcing Yellow Thunder to drink alcohol, they stripped him naked from the waist down and threw him in an American Legion Hall where a dance was in progress. He was forced to dance for those in attendance and was then thrown out of the hall and beaten. His body was found two days later stuffed into a car trunk. Such attacks on Indian people by white racists were not uncommon on the Pine Ridge Reservation. The police largely ignored the situation, and white judges refused to try whites for crimes against Indians. Following Yellow Thunder's death, AIM was called on to bring national attention to the cruel nature of the murder, and justice to Indian reservations and for Indian people. AIM answered the call and led a caravan of 200 cars to Gordon, where they forced the authorities to file serious charges against the murderers and urged that the local police chief be dismissed. During the protest, AIM supporters took over the Gordon community hall. Leaders declared a victory after local officials agreed to investigate the circumstances of Yellow Thunder's death.

On January 21, 1973, manslaughter charges were filed in Buffalo Gap, South Dakota, against Harold Schmidt, the murderer of another Indian named Wesley Bad Heart Bull. In Custer, South Dakota, AIM members protested against the relatively light charges. During the protest, the courthouse and chamber of commerce buildings burned to the ground. The FBI now considered AIM to be an armed, subversive militant group, and it increased the number of surveillance teams that were assigned to monitor AIM activities and the movements of its leadership.

Meanwhile, in the spring of 1972, the BIA had backed the questionable election of Richard "Dickey" Wilson as tribal chairman of the Oglala Lakota nation. Wilson, a fierce anti-Communist, saw his election as an affirmation of reform and a defense against groups he viewed as radical and pro-Communist, such as AIM. His election split the nation along the lines of progressives and traditionalists, the latter preferring the old form of Indian tribal leadership. Wilson practiced nepotism in his doling out of jobs and tribal funds. Traditionalists

had no voice in tribal government and were left jobless and even more destitute than most Pine Ridge residents. They turned to AIM for support. In response, Wilson used tribal funds to hire thugs, forming a vigilante police force called GOONs (Guardians of the Oglala Nation) who began a reign of terror against AIM and its supporters. Hundreds of people were threatened, beaten, and killed. The homes of Oglala traditionalists and AIM supporters were burned to the ground. Wilson told AIM leader Dennis Banks that he would cut Banks's hair braids off if he set foot on the Pine Ridge Reservation. By February 1973, a major confrontation was brewing.

On February 27, 1973, AIM leaders and about 200 Indian supporters were en route to Porcupine, South Dakota. Wilson and his GOONs were armed and waiting for their entrance into the town. Rather than entering Porcupine, one of the Indian women suggested that the Indian caravan drive directly to the village of Wounded Knee, the sight of the 1890 massacre of 250 Lakota men, women, and children. Wilson and his GOONs were left armed and waiting while AIM members and supporters occupied the Wounded Knee trading post, museum, gas station, and two churches. Wilson soon requested federal assistance. The occupation marked the beginning of an armed conflict between AIM and the U.S. government that lasted until May 8, 1973.

The goals of the occupation, as outlined by AIM leaders, included reforming tribal government and bringing attention to Native American grievances. Russell Means requested a congressional investigation into conditions on all Indian reservations as well as the corruption Indian people believed was rampant in the BIA. AIM leaders specifically wanted a hearing to take place concerning treaty violations and the reinstitution of treaty making that had formally ended in 1871.

Because the land was Indian Country, the federal government held jurisdiction over the reservation, and therefore state and local forces were not authorized to assist in law enforcement. The Nixon White House, the Department of Defense, and the Department of Justice coordinated efforts throughout the Wounded Knee occupation. Whereas the occupation of Alcatraz Island had been nonviolent, the Wounded Knee occupants were armed and considered dangerous. The government decided that it could not assume a waiting posture as it had at Alcatraz. By March 26, some 340 FBI agents and U.S. forces surrounded Wounded Knee village. (Some Indians in the military were allowed to go on leave

so as not to have to participate in what came to be called Wounded Knee II.) Among the weapons supplied by the Defense Department were seventeen armored personnel carriers, 130,000 rounds of M-16 ammunition, 4,000 of M-1 ammunition, 24,000 flares, twelve M-79 grenade launchers, 600 cases of C-S gas, 100 rounds of M-40 high explosive rounds, as well as helicopters and Phantom jets. This type of equipment was also being used simultaneously by U.S. forces in Vietnam. Government security forces and members of the Oglala GOONs squads manned roadblocks at entrances to Wounded Knee to prevent access to the area. Their primary objective was to isolate the occupiers and to stop food, ammunition, and reinforcements from reaching the occupation force, while preventing injuries or deaths if possible.

Government forces and AIM security exchanged gunfire throughout the occupation. AIM, relying on the experience of American Indian Vietnam veterans, fortified the area by digging trenches, setting up roadblocks, and establishing day and night foot patrols. During the occupation, U.S. Marshal Lloyd Grimm received a wound that paralyzed him from the waist down. Two Indian men were killed during the occupation. During one period of gunfire exchange, a Cherokee man, Frank Clearwater, received a fatal wound while asleep on a cot in an occupied church. Lawrence Lamont, a Lakota resident of the Pine Ridge Reservation, received a fatal gunshot wound on April 26. Following the two deaths, both sides agreed on a tenuous cease-fire. Tensions between the occupiers and the federal authorities grew while the situation worsened. Both groups established, violated, and reinstated cease-fires. AIM security, U.S. forces, and, on occasion, the GOONs squads all were guilty of instigating gunfire exchanges.

Negotiations had begun during the first days of the takeover and continued throughout the seventy-one days that AIM occupied Wounded Knee. The negotiations often stopped due to both sides' interjection of new demands or rejections of proposals. Several factors pressed AIM to end the occupation, including a lack of food, ammunition, and medical supplies, and a complete absence of electricity. Ultimately, the two sides agreed on a disengagement timetable for government forces to enter Wounded Knee, collect all weapons, and transport remaining AIM supporters to a government roadblock, where a team of Defense Committee lawyers would be present to witness the processing procedure. Out of the 129 people processed, 110

were American Indians. Federal forces destroyed AIM security bunkers along with government bunkers and completed the evacuation of Wounded Knee by the end of the day. The occupation had lasted seventy-one days.

South Dakota Senator James Abourezk, under the authority of the U.S. Senate Subcommittee of Indian Affairs, conducted hearings on the events that led to the confrontation and the occupation at Wounded Knee. After hearing evidence by tribal chairman Richard Wilson and AIM leader Russell Means, Abourezk proposed a Senate Joint Resolution to establish an Indian policy review committee. Its purpose included a review of the legal relationship between Native Americans and the U.S. government and to provide support for the development of more effective policies.

The Nixon White House subsequently broke the agreement that had ended the occupation. On May 13, an aide to President Richard M. Nixon read a statement that "treaty making with the Indians ended in 1871, 102 years ago. . . ." AIM demands that the government investigate the FBI's actions never materialized. Tribal chairman Wilson and his GOONs squad members were never prosecuted. Instead, a new reign of terror was carried out against AIM members and their supporters. While the FBI claims that all deaths have been investigated, many residents of the Pine Ridge Indian Reservation still live in fear of government forces.

Troy R. Johnson

See also American Indian Movement; Banks, Dennis; Means, Russell; Peltier, Leonard; Pine Ridge Political Murders; Wilson, Richard.

References and Further Reading

Bahr, Howard M., et al. 1972. "Invisibility." In *Native Americans Today: Sociological Perspectives*. New York: Harper & Row.

Blue Cloud, Peter. 1972. *Alcatraz Is Not an Island*. Berkeley, CA: Wingbow Press.

Castillo, Edward. 1994. "A Reminiscence of the Alcatraz Occupation." *American Indian Culture and Research Journal* 18, no. 4 (Special edition, edited by Troy Johnson and Joane Nagel).

Champagne, Duane, ed. 1994. *Chronology of Native North American History: From Pre-Columbian Times to the Present*. Detroit, MI: Gale Research.

Cohen, Fay G. 1986. *Treaties on Trial: The Continuing Controversy over Northwest Indian Fishing Rights*. Seattle: University of Washington Press.

Cornell, Stephen. 1988. *The Return of the Native: American Indian Political Resurgence*. New York: Oxford University Press.

Costo, Rupert. 1970. "Alcatraz." *The Indian Historian* no. 3, 9.

Deloria, Vine, Jr., 1985. *Behind the Trail of Broken Treaties: An Indian Declaration of Independence*. Austin: University of Texas Press.

Deloria, Vine, Jr., Vine. 1983. *God Is Red*. New York: Laurel, Dell.

DeLuca, Richard. 1983. "We Hold the Rock—The Indian Attempt to Reclaim Alcatraz Island." *California History: The Magazine of the California Historical Society* 62 (Spring), 2–24.

Fixico, Donald. 1986. *Termination and Relocation: Federal Indian Policy, 1945–1960*. Albuquerque: University of Mexico Press.

Forbes, Jack. 1981. "Alcatraz: What Its Seizure Means." In *Alcatraz Is Not An Island*. Edited by Peter Blue Cloud. Berkeley, CA: Wingbow Press.

Forbes, Jack. 1972. *Native Americans and Nixon: Presidential Politics and Minority Self Determination 1969–1972*. Los Angeles: American Indian Studies Center, University of California, Los Angeles.

Forbes, Jack. 1983. "Alcatraz: Symbol & Reality." In *California History* (Spring). Vol. 62, 24–25.

Fortunate Eagle, Adam. 1992. *Alcatraz! Alcatraz! The Indian Occupation of 1969–1971*. Berkeley, CA: Heyday Books.

Gordon-McCutchan, R. C. 1991. *The Taos Indians and the Battle for Blue Lake*. Santa Fe, NM: Red Crane Books.

Harvey, Byron. 1970. *Thoughts from Alcatraz*. Phoenix, AZ: Arequipa Press.

Hertzberg, Hazel W. 1971. *The Search for an American Indian Identity; Modern PanIndian Movements*. Syracuse, NY: Syracuse University Press.

Horse Capture, George P. 1991. "An American Indian Perspective." In *Seeds of Change*. Edited by Herman J. Violaand and Carolyn Margolis, Washington, DC: Smithsonian Institution.

Johnson, Troy. 1996. *The Occupation of Alcatraz Island: Indian Self-Determination & The Rise of Indian Activism*. Urbana: University of Illinois Press.

Johnson, Troy. 1997. *American Indian Activism: Alcatraz to the Longest Walk*. Urbana. University of Illinois Press.

Josephy, Alvin, Jr. 1971. *Red Power: The American Indians' Fight for Freedom*. New York: American Heritage Press.

Josephy, Alvin, Jr. 1978. *The American Indian Fight for Freedom*. New Haven, CT: Yale University Press, 1978.

Josephy, Alvin, et al. 1999. *Red Power: The American Indian's Fight for Freedom*. Lincoln: University of Nebraska Press.

Kemnitzer, Luis. 1994. "Personal Memories of Alcatraz, 1969." *American Indian Culturand Research Journal* 18, no. 4, 103–109.

Mankiller, Wilma, and Michael Wallis. 1993. *Mankiller, A Chief and Her People.* New York: St. Martin's Press.

Senese, Guy. 1991. *Self-Determination and the Social Education of Native Americans.* New York: Praeger.

Steiner, Stan. 1968. *The New Indians.* New York: Harper & Row.

Talbot, Steve. 1978. "Free Alcatraz: The Culture of Native American Liberation."*Journal of Ethnic Studies* 6, no. 3 (Fall), 80–89.

Washburn, Wilcomb E. 1971. *Red Man's Land/White Man's Law: A Study of the Past and Present State of the American Indian.* New York: Scribner's.

Key Web Sites

Alcatraz and American Indian activism: A photographic history of the 1969–1971 occupation of Alcatraz Island by Indians of All Tribes, Inc. Available at: http://www.csulb.edu/~gcampus/libarts/am-indian/alcatraz/index.html. Accessed January 4, 2007.

American Indian Movement: The home pages for AIM, headquartered in the Twin Cities. Available at: http://www.dickshovel.com/AIMIntro.html http://www.aimovement.org/. Accessed January 4, 2007.

CANKPE OPI: The Wounded Knee home page contains important information and links on this historic event. "The contents of this page are approved by traditional elders on the Pine Ridge and Cheyenne River reservations." Available at: http://www.dickshovel.com/WKmasscre.html. Accessed January 4, 2007.

Navajo–Hopi Land Dispute

The Navajo–Hopi land dispute has continued for more than 100 years. In order to understand the dispute, it is important to consider the people involved, the history, and the involvement of the United States.

The Navajo nation (or Dine in the Navajo language) is one of the largest of the indigenous nations living in the United States, in terms of both population and land ownership. Relative latecomers to the Americas, the seminomadic Navajo traditionally made their living by farming and by herding sheep, goats, and horses. Between 1863 and 1868, the U.S. Army forcibly relocated the Navajo to Fort Sumner, New Mexico. When the Navajos signed a peace treaty with the U.S. government in 1868, they began to return to the newly created Navajo reservation. The present-day Navajo reservation extends over 25,000 square miles and is located in an area where the states of Arizona, New Mexico, Utah, and Colorado meet (an area also known as the Four Corners). Between 1868 and 1991, the Navajo reservation increased in size approximately fifteen times (University of Virginia, 1997).

The agricultural Hopis, often viewed as a peaceful people, did not enter into a treaty relationship with the United States. In 1882, however, the United States set aside a 2.5-million-acre rectangle of land for a reservation for the Hopis by way of an executive order. According to the Hopis, this did not include all of their traditional territory (including villages, farmland, and sacred sites), and they have continually complained about Navajo families settling on Hopi lands without obtaining their permission.

The terms of the executive order contain in part the beginning of the land dispute between the Navajo and Hopi nations. The terms provided that the land in question would be " . . . set apart for the use and occupancy of the Moqui [Hopi] and such other Indians as the Secretary of the Interior may see fit to settle thereon (*Healing v. Jones*, p. 48, n1)." This wording did not protect the rights of the Hopis to exclusive use and occupation of the lands being set aside for them, but rather left the question open to interpretation as to which Native American nations might use the lands described in the order.

In the meantime, the population of the Navajos continued to grow. Being a seminomadic people, the Navajos moved around to different areas on a seasonal basis. This movement encroached on lands that the Hopis considered their own. An area of 8 million acres in the town of Moencopi that was the subject of a claim by the Hopis in 1934 had been settled by Navajo families and was eventually added by an Act of Congress to the Navajo reservation. This addition also included all of the traditional lands of the San Juan Band of southern Paiutes (Giese, 1997). There are also several hundred Navajo families living in the Big Mountain area, which is located inside the executive order boundaries of the Hopi Reservation (Giese, 1997).

During the 1930s, the U.S. government divided the Hopi Reservation into eighteen land management grazing districts in an effort to reduce livestock overgrazing. Navajo and Hopi people continued to argue over who had rights to these districts. The Hopis went before the U.S. District Court for the District of Arizona in an attempt to have their land dispute with the Navajos resolved. In 1962, in the case of *Healing v. Jones*, the Court held that all but one of

the eighteen districts were areas of joint use for both the Navajos and the Hopis. The only district reserved for the exclusive use of the Hopis was District 6. The Court explained that since the Department of the Interior had never removed the Navajo, the Navajo had acquired squatters' rights and were entitled to a one-half share of all surface and subsurface resources.

In the interim, the Secretary of the Interior placed a freeze on any construction or development in any area that was being jointly used by the Navajos and Hopis. In 1974, the Navajo–Hopi Land Settlement Act served to partition the joint use lands. In an amendment to this Act, the Navajo were allocated 400,000 acres of replacement lands. A federal Navajo and Hopi Relocation Commission was formed and Navajo families were supposed to be moved off the Hopi Reservation and onto these new lands. Approximately 11,000 Navajos were relocated. However, the families located at Big Mountain refused to move and continue to reside there (Giese, 1997).

Finally, in an attempt to resolve the years of litigation and turmoil over land ownership and land use, Congress passed the Navajo–Hopi Settlement Act of 1996, under which the parties agreed that all ongoing lawsuits would be dropped and the Navajos would either move from the Hopi partitioned lands or enter into a lease with the Hopi nation for a term of seventy-five years, with rent being paid to the Hopi tribe. These leases would set clear definitions of ownership and land use for grazing. Reparation, restoration, and enlargement of existing structures on the land would be permitted, and new construction would be permitted subject to application for a permit from the Hopis. The Hopis reserved the right to terminate a lease for cause.

Despite federal legislation, litigation, and a negotiated settlement, the fact remains that both the Navajos and the Hopis consider the land in question to be theirs. Part of the historic problem must be attributed to federal government policies of relocating American Indian nations in an arbitrary fashion to areas that best suited the government rather than the tribes themselves. Since land is such a vital part of the lives of the American Indian people, the dispute may never be resolved to everyone's satisfaction (Lapahie Jr., 2005).

Lysane Cree

See also Long Walk; Mining and Contemporary Environmental Problems.

References and Further Readings
Benedek, Emily. 1992. *The Wind Won't Know Me: A History of the Navajo-Hopi Land Dispute.* New York: Alfred A. Knopf.
Brugge, David M. 1994. *The Navajo-Hopi Land Dispute: An American Tragedy.* Albuquerque: University of New Mexico Press.
Giese, Paula. 1997. "Navajo-Hopi Long Land Dispute." Available at: http://www.kstrom .net/isk/maps/az/ navhopi.html. Accessed January 4, 2007.
Healing v. Jones 210 F. Supp. 125; 1962 U.S. Dist. LEXIS 3421.
Kammer, Jerry. 1980. *The Second Long Walk.* Albuquerque: University of New Mexico Press.
Kemper, Ellen. 1992. *Navajo-Hopi: Bennett Freeze Area.* Available at: http://www.native-net.org/ archive/nl/9205/0096.html. Accessed January 4, 2007.
Lapahie, Harrison, Jr. 2005. *Navajo-Hopi Land Dispute.* Available at: http://www.lapahie .com/Navajo_Hopi_Land_Dispute.cfm. Accessed January 4, 2004.
University of Virginia. 1997. "Beyond the Four Sacred Mountains: The Effects of the Navajo-Hopi Land Dispute." Available at: http:// xroads.virginia.edu/~MA97/dinetah/dispute2. html. Accessed January 4, 2007.
U.S. Congress. 1996. *Agreement in Principle for Resolving Issues in Connection with the Navajo-Hopi Settlement Act* (Pub. L. 104–301). Available at: http://www.blackmesais.org/ accomodationagree.html.

Ward Valley, Hazardous Waste Controversy

A village of tents and teepees grew in the desert twenty-two miles west of Needles, California, during the last half of February 1998, as several hundred Native American and non-Indian environmentalists put their bodies on the line in an attempt to stop construction of a dump for low-level nuclear waste on land they regard as sacred.

By the third week of February, roughly 250 people were camped at "ground zero" of Ward Valley, eighty acres of federally owned land designated for the waste site. The encampment prevented the soil testing necessary for the planning of the dump, which had been proposed to receive waste from hospitals, nuclear plants, and other industries that cannot dispose of radioactive materials in other landfills.

Iona Dock, right, and other American Indian elders perform a ceremonial dance in 1995, in front of the Federal Building in Los Angeles, during a protest rally to stop Ward Valley, California, from becoming a radioactive dump site. (AP Photo/Rhonda Birndorf)

By February 19, occupants of the encampment had defied two sets of federal orders to leave the site and had blocked roads leading to it. A fifteen-day order that had been issued in late January expired February 14. A new, five-day eviction order issued that day expired February 19, with protesters still eyeball-to-eyeball with a circle of Bureau of Land Management (BLM) vehicles that had surrounded their camp. Protesters said that BLM and other federal agents had been rumbling around the camp in large land rovers and flying over it in small aircraft and helicopters at odd hours of the night in an attempt to intimidate the campers and deprive them of sleep. Religious ceremonies continued in the camp amid the glare of headlamps and the drone of aircraft overhead. Some of the protesters chained themselves together. After complaints (and the arrival of news media reporters), the vehicles were withdrawn from the perimeter of the camp.

Steve Lopez, a Fort Mojave Native spokesperson, said that, in addition to being the habitat of an endangered tortoise species, Ward Valley is central to the creation stories of many Native American peoples in the area. "Taking away the land is taking away part of ourselves. They used to use bullets to kill our people off. Now it's radioactive waste," Lopez said (Johansen, 1998, 7). Ward Valley is sacred to many Native people in the area because of its proximity to Spirit Mountain, the birthplace of their ancestors.

The protesters included a number of elders affiliated with five Colorado River basin tribes: Fort Mojave, Chemehuevi, Cocopah Quechan, and Colorado River Indians. The elders also refused to move. Instead, people in the encampment sent out appeals for supplies and more visitors, asking, according to a Colorado American Indian Movement (AIM) posting on the Internet, "for the physical presence of anyone willing to travel to Ward Valley and participate in the protection of this sacred land and the people defending it" (Johansen, 1998, 7). Donations of food, water, blankets, batteries, and rain gear were requested. Wally Antone of the Colorado River Native Nations Alliance said, "Our ceremonies will

continue here and our elders will not move. You will have to drag us out, and I say those words with honor" (Johansen, 1998, 7).

On February 18, as the BLM's second deadline was set to expire, leaders of the camp invited five BLM officials to their central fire for a religious ceremony, after which the officials were told that the protesters would not move. Andy Mader of Arizona AIM said via the Internet that all the cellular phones in the camp were malfunctioning. Some suspected that the government had shut them down. Meanwhile, supporters of the protest outside the camp had received phone calls indicating that several other AIM chapters were sending people to Ward Valley.

Tom Goldtooth (National Director, Indigenous Environmental Network) reported from the camp via Internet that the protest had become so vigorous not only because the land is regarded as sacred by Native peoples, but because many southern California and Arizona urban areas rely on the Colorado River for water that could be polluted by the proposed waste dump. The same water is used to irrigate crops in both the United States and Mexico.

A position paper circulated by Save Ward Valley, an environmental coalition, stated that the proposed dump lies above a major aquifer, eighteen miles from the Colorado River. Furthermore, the report asserted that all six of the presently active nuclear waste dumps in the United States are leaking. U.S. Ecology, the contractor selected for the Ward Valley site, presently operates four of those six dumps, the position paper said. The coalition also asserted that all the waste buried at such sites is not low-level. As much as 90 percent of the radioactivity proposed for burial would come from nuclear power plants, including cesium, strontium, and plutonium, the statement said.

Speaking on behalf of the coalition, Goldtooth, who coordinated protests by non-Native supporters, evaluated the protest, which eventually caused plans for the dump to be shelved:

Incorporating the importance of your traditional ways and the use of the sacred Fire as the foundation for guidance and resistance as we fight for environmental justice and Native rights has proven successful at Ward Valley. I applaud the many non-Natives from the peace movement to the anti-nuclear movement and the global human family that raised the consciousness of the world that the sacred tortoise and the ecology of a desert environment must not be sacrificed anymore by the whims of the nuclear waste industry. I witnessed the coming together of the non-Native supporters and the Colorado River tribal communities and Tribal Nations in an historical moment where everyone agreed to fight together with one mind and one spirit to defend the sacredness of the Mother Earth and to defend the sovereignty of the Fort Mojave Tribal Nation (Goldtooth, 2001).

Bruce E. Johansen

See also American Indian Movement; Mining and Contemporary Environmental Problems; Uranium Mining.

References and Further Reading:

Goldtooth, Tom. 2001. "Indigenous Environmental Network Statement to Nora Helton, Chairwoman, Fort Mojave Indian Tribe, Other Lower Colorado River Indian Tribal Leaders, Tribal Community Members, Elders and Non-Native Groups and Individuals, in Reference to the Ward Valley Victory Gathering to Celebrate the Defeat of a Proposed Nuclear Waste Dump, Ward Valley, California." Available at: http://www.ienearth.org/ward_valley2.html. Accessed January 4, 2007.

Johansen, Bruce E. 1998. "Ward Valley: A 'Win' for Native Elders." *Native Americas* 15, no. 2 (Summer): 7–8.

Index

Note: Page locators in **boldface** type indicate the location of a main encyclopedia entry.

About the Editors

Bruce E. Johansen is Frederick W. Kayser Research Professor of Communication and Native American Studies at the University of Nebraska at Omaha. He is the author of dozens of books; his publishing efforts are concentrated in Native American studies and in environmental issues. His most recent publication is *The Praeger Handbook on Contemporary Issues in Native America* (Praeger, 2007).

Barry Pritzker is Director of Foundation and Corporate Relations at Skidmore College, where he occasionally teaches courses on contemporary Native America. He has authored books on Ansel Adams, Mathew Brady, and Edward Curtis, as well as *Native Americans: An Encyclopedia of History, Culture and Peoples* (ABC-CLIO, 1998). His most recent publication is *Native America Today* (ABC-CLIO, 1999).